Vocal Traditions in Conflict

Descent from Sweet, Clear, Pure and Affecting Italian Singing To Grand Uproar

Richard Bethell

Peacock Press

Vocal Traditions in Conflict
Copyright © 2019 Richard Bethell

All rights reserved. No part of this publication may be reproduced, stored in a retrieval system, transmitted in any form or by any means electronic, mechanical, including photocopying, recording or otherwise without prior consent of the copyright holders.

ISBN 978-1-912271-49-8

Published by Peacock Press, 2019
Scout Bottom Farm
Mytholmroyd
Hebden Bridge HX7 5JS (UK)

Acknowledgements. I'd like to thank many people for their contributions. Mike Carroll, an excellent system developer and my long-time colleague at Compeer Limited, kindly provided an App for constructing career charts of singers, including the lists of tremoloists and straight toners at the end of Section 4. Peter Bavington [Peter.Bavington@ntlworld.com] invested many hours combing through the 400 page book in completing his copy-edit. Several members of Facebook's *Historical Performance Research Group* have helped by providing answers to particular research related issues which I've discussed in this group. Robert Anderson [robtheillustrator@yahoo.co.uk] provided the paintings for the cover, contrasting the *bocca ridente* (slightly smiling) expressions of 18th century singers with the wide open mouth featuring in the 'grand uproar' production of many vocalists today. Matthew Gale of Maztech [info@maztechuk.co.uk] has been helpful in getting my website up and running; this provides useful definitions, sung examples and playlists. Last but not least, a big thank you to Jeremy Burbidge, managing director of Peacock Press, for pulling out all the stops to achieve the lowest possible price for my full colour book, without sacrificing quality. And of course to Jeremy's team, especially his designer David Miller [dmdesignandprint@gmail.com].

Contents

1.	**General Introduction**	1
1.1	Why This Book? Why Now? Who Is It For?	1
1.2	Gaps in the Research	2
1.3	Structure of this book	3
1.4	Voice Type Definitions and Experiment	5
1.5	Voice Type A	6
1.6	Voice Type B	6
1.7	Voice Type C	7
1.8	Survey Results	7
2	**The Golden Age of Italian Singing (1650 to 1829)**	9
2.1	Introduction	9
2.2	Precepts for achieving good vocal sound	9
2.2.1	Main Treatises Used	9
2.2.2	Vocal Sound: Desired Outcomes	10
2.2.3	Reviewers' Views on Vocal Sound	12
2.2.4	How Critics described Vocal Sounds	15
2.2.5	The Rationale for Bocca Ridente	18
2.3	Reviews of Named Castrati in the Long Eighteenth Century	21
2.3.1	Baldassare Ferri [b. 1610]	22
2.3.2	Giovanni Francesco Grossi (Siface) [b. 1653]	23
2.3.3	Gaetano Orsini [b. 1667]	23
2.3.4	Matteo Matteuccio [b. 1667]	23
2.3.5	Nicolo Grimaldi [Nicolini] [b. 1673]	23
2.3.6	Francesco Barnardi [Senesino] [b. 1680]	23
2.3.7	Antonio Pasi [b. 1697]	24
2.3.8	Giovanni Carestini [b. 1704]	24
2.3.9	Domenico Annibali [b. 1705]	24
2.3.10	Carlo Broschi (Farinelli) [b. 1705]	24
2.3.11	Gaetano Mairorano Caffarelli [b. 1710]	25
2.3.12	Gioachino Gizziello Conti [b. 1714]	25
2.3.13	Giovanni Manzuoli [b. 1720]	26
2.3.14	Gaetano Guadagni [b.1728]	27
2.3.15	Giuseppe Aprile [b. 1732]	27
2.3.16	Ferdinando Tenducci [b. 1736]	28
2.3.17	Giuseppe Millico [b. 1737]	28
2.3.18	Gasparo Pacchierotti [b. 1740]	28
2.3.19	Venanzio Rauzzini [b. 1746]	29
2.3.20	Francesco Roncaglia [b. 1750]	29
2.3.21	Giovanni Rubinelli [b. 1753]	29

2.3.22	Luigi Marchesi [b. 1754]	29
2.3.23	Girolamo Crescentini [b.1762]	30
2.3.24	Giovanni Battista Velluti [b. 1780]	30
2.4	**Reviews of Female Singers in the Long 18th Century**	31
2.4.1	Catherine Tofts [b. 1685]	31
2.4.2	Stella Lotti [b. 1675]	32
2.4.3	Francesca Cuzzoni [b. 1695]	32
2.4.4	Faustina Bordoni [b. 1697]	33
2.4.5	Vittoria Tesi Tramontini [b. 1700]	34
2.4.6	Marie Fel [b. 1712]	34
2.4.7	Susannah Maria Cibber [b. 1714]	34
2.4.8	Giulia Frasi [b. 1724]	35
2.4.9	Caterina Gabrielli [b. 1730]	35
2.4.10	Cecilia Davies [b. 1740]	36
2.4.11	Lucrezia Agujari [b. 1741]	37
2.4.12	Anna de Amicis [b. 1745]	38
2.4.13	Anne Catley [b. 1745]	38
2.4.14	Gertrud Elizabeth Mara, née Schmeling [b. 1749]	39
2.4.15	Elizabeth Linley, later Mrs Sheridan [b. 1754]	40
2.4.16	Maddalena Allegranti [b. 1754]	41
2.4.17	Brigida Georgi Banti [b. 1755]	41
2.4.18	Francesca Le Brun, née Danzi [b. 1756]	42
2.4.19	Aloysia Weber [b. 1760]	42
2.4.20	Anna Maria Crouch [b. 1763]	43
2.4.21	Elizabeth Billington [b. 1765]	43
2.4.22	Amelie Oldmixon, née George [b. 1768]	44
2.4.23	Maria Theresa Bland [b. 1769]	44
2.4.24	Josephina Grassini [b. 1773]	44
2.4.25	Teresa Bertinotti/ Radicati [b. 1776]	45
2.4.26	Maria Poole/ Dickons [b. 1778]	45
2.4.27	Angelica Catalani [b. 1780]	46
2.4.28	Bellochi, Georgia [b. 1784]	48
2.4.29	Violante Camporese [b. 1785]	48
2.4.30	Angela Isabella Colbran, Mrs Rossini [b. 1785]	48
2.4.31	Eliza Salmon [b. 1787]	49
2.4.32	Miss Tennant, later Mrs Vaughan [b. 1788]	50
2.4.33	Ester Mombelli [b. 1792]	50
2.4.34	Miss Carew [b. 1799]	51
2.5	**Reviews of Other Male Singers in the Long Eighteenth Century**	51
2.5.1	John Beard [b. 1716]	51
2.5.2	Charles Bannister [b. 1741]	51

2.5.3	Giovanni Ansani [b. 1744]	52
2.5.4	Johann Ignaz Fischer [b. 1745]	53
2.5.5	Giuseppe Viganoni [b. 1754]	53
2.5.6	John Henry Johnstone [b. 1759]	54
2.5.7	Samuel Harrison [b. 1760]	54
2.5.8	Charles Benjamin Incledon [b. 1763]	55
2.5.9	Charles Dignum [b. 1765]	56
2.5.10	Carlo Angrisani [b. 1765]	57
2.5.11	James Bartleman [b. 1769]	58
2.5.12	John Jeremiah Goss [b. 1770]	58
2.5.13	Felice Pellegrini [b. 1774]	58
2.5.14	Diomiro Tramezzani [b. 1776]	59
2.5.15	William Knyvett [b. 1779]	60
2.5.16	Mathieu Porto [b. 1780]	60
2.5.17	Thomas Vaughan [b. 1782]	61
2.5.18	Pierre Ignace Begrez [b. 1787]	62
2.5.19	Ranieri Remorini [b. 1793]	62
2.6	**Ensemble Singing**	62
2.7	**Straight Voice, Tremolo and Vibrato**	66
2.7.1	Vibrato: Current Critical Attitudes	66
2.7.2	Continuous Vibrato; the Historical Record	68
2.7.3	Vocal Qualities compared to Instrumental Sounds	76
2.7.4	Charles Burney's Testimony	77
2.7.5	Counsel for the Defence of Vocal Vibrato	78
2.7.6	Expressive or Illustrative Vocal Tremolo/Vibrato	81
2.7.7	Vocal Sounds Compared to the Glass Harmonica	86
2.7.8	Some Red Meat for the Vibrato Defenders	89
2.7.9	Conclusions on Straight Tone Singing through the Long 18th Century	91
2.8	**Shake, Performance of**	93
2.9	**Messa di Voce**	97
2.10	**Extended Registers**	101
2.11	**Vocal Volume**	105
2.12	**The French [Dis]Connection**	113
2.13	**Low Larynx Singing**	115
2.13.1	Views Expressed in Treatises	115
2.13.2	Views Expressed in Reviews	117
2.13.3	A Contrarian and Heretical Opinion	121
2.14	**Vocal Timbre: Rich or Thin Voices**	124
2.15	**Articulation**	126
3	**The 19th/20th Century Vocal Revolution (1830 to 1949)**	**133**
3.1	**National Origins**	133

3.2	The Books	134
3.3	The Magazines	135
3.4	The Newspapers	137
3.5	Female Singers Reviewed, before the Recording Era	139
3.5.1	Josephine Fodor-Mainvielle [b. 1793]	139
3.5.2	Benedetta Rosmunda Pisaroni [b. 1793]	140
3.5.3	Catherine Stephens [b. 1794]	141
3.5.4	Lucia Elizabeth Vestris [b. 1797]	142
3.5.5	Giuditta Pasta [b. 1797]	143
3.5.6	Giuseppina Ronzi de Begnis [b. 1800]	144
3.5.7	Maria Caradori-Allan [b. 1800]	145
3.5.8	Deborah Travis, later Mrs William Knyvett [b. 1800]	145
3.5.9	Virginie Blasis [b. 1800]	146
3.5.10	Laure Cinti-Damoreau [b.1801]	147
3.5.11	Mary Ann Paton, later Mrs Wood [b. 1802]	148
3.5.12	Henrietta Nina Sontag [b. 1803]	149
3.5.13	Margaretha Stockhausen [b. 1803]	149
3.5.14	Maria Malibran [b. 1808]	150
3.5.15	Mrs Anna Bishop, née Riviere [b. 1810]	152
3.5.16	Giulia Grisi [b. 1811]	153
3.5.17	Mary Postans, later Mrs Alfred Shaw [b. 1814]	154
3.5.18	Catherine Hayes [b. 1818]	156
3.5.19	Clara Novello [b. 1818]	158
3.5.20	Jenny Lind, Mrs Goldschmidt [b. 1820]	161
3.5.21	Eliza Poole [b. 1820]	163
3.5.22	Charlotte Dolby, Mrs Sainton-Dolby [b. 1821]	165
3.5.23	Marietta Alboni [b. 1826]	166
3.5.24	Louisa Pyne, later Mrs Frank Bodda [b. 1827]	167
3.5.25	Thérèse Tietjens [b. 1831]	169
3.5.26	Melitta Otto Alvsleben [b. 1842]	171
3.6	Male Singers Reviewed, before the Recording Era	171
3.6.1	John Braham [b. 1774].	171
3.6.2	Manuel García 1 [b. 1775]	173
3.6.3	Lewis Bernard Sapio [b. 1784]	174
3.6.4	Alberico Curioni [b. 1785]	174
3.6.5	Charles Edward Horn [b. 1786]	175
3.6.6	Giovanni David [b. 1790]	175
3.6.7	Domenico Donizelli [b. 1790]	176
3.6.8	John Sinclair [b. 1791]	178
3.6.9	Giuseppe de Begnis [b. 1793]	179
3.6.10	Luigi Lablache [b. 1794]	179

3.6.11	Giovanni Battista Rubini [b. 1794]	181
3.6.12	Henry Phillips [b. 1801]	182
3.6.13	Adolphe Nourrit [b. 1802]	183
3.6.14	John Templeton [b. 1802]	184
3.6.15	Gilbert Duprez [b. 1806]	185
3.6.16	Nicola Ivanhoff [b. 1810]	186
3.6.17	Giovanni Matteo Mario [b. 1810]	188
3.6.18	Enrico Tamberlik [b. 1820]	190
3.6.19	Sims Reeves [b. 1821]	192
3.6.20	Antonio Giuglini [b. 1827]	194
3.6.21	Italo Campanini [b. 1845]	196
3.6.22	Joseph Maas [b. 1847]	197
3.6.23	Jean de Reszké [b. 1850]	198
3.7	Recorded Female Singers	199
3.7.1	Adelina Patti [b. 1843]	199
3.7.2	Emma Albani [b. 1847]	201
3.7.3	Dame Nellie Melba [b. 1861]	203
3.7.4	Ellen Beach Yaw [b. 1869]	204
3.7.5	Ada Crossley [b. 1871]	205
3.8	Recorded Male Singers	207
3.8.1	Charles Santley [b. 1834]	207
3.8.2	Victor Capoul [b. 1839]	207
3.8.3	Robert Watkin-Mills [b. 1849]	208
3.8.4	Andrew Black [b. 1859]	209
4	**Descent from Default Straight Voice to Permanent Vibrato**	**221**
4.1	The Introduction of Tremolo and Vibrato	221
4.2	Universal Straight Voice (1800 to 1825)	212
4.3	Innovating Tremoloists (1825 to 1855)	215
4.4	Fierce Resistance to Tremolo Singing Overcome (1855 to 1880)	220
4.5	Tremolo Singing Widely Hated but Dominant (1880 to 1904)	235
4.6	Non-Vibrato Singing in the Nineteenth Century	258
4.7	The Other Side of the Story	262
4.8	Two Case Studies	265
4.9	Recordings show widening vocal vibrato from 1905	268
4.10	Vocal Science Influential—against underground resistance	278
4.11	Conclusions—Implications for Historically Informed Practice	284
4.12	Annex A. Lists of Female Tremoloists and Straight Toners	285
4.13	Annex B. Lists of Male Tremoloists and Straight Toners	289
5	**Descent from Dual Register Emission to Constant Chest Voice**	**293**
5.1	A Top Down View of Male Falsetto	293
5.2	Reviews Endorsing Male Falsetto	294

5.3	Reviews Criticising Male Falsetto	295
5.4	Male Singers Using or Avoiding Falsetto	299
5.5	The Reign of Forcible Tenors	305
5.6	Female Falsetto	308
5.7	Emergence of Dramatic and Forcible Sopranos	310
5.8	Decline in Sweetness and purity	315
5.9	Main Conclusions on Vocal Registration and Volume	316
6	**Descent from Natural Voice to Made Voice**	**319**
6.1	Analysis	319
6.2	New Thinking from Manuel García	320
6.3	Additional Pedagogy on 19th- and 20th-Century Low Larynx Singing	321
6.4	Reviews of Clear [Non throaty] Singing from 1830	323
6.5	Reviews of Throaty Singing in the Century from 1830	326
6.6	Conclusions on Clear versus Throaty Singing	332
7	**Recovery of Historically Informed Singing**	**333**
7.1	A Theory on the Historical Development of Vocal Sound	333
7.2	Differences between Long 18th and 20th C Traditions	333
7.3	Sources of Contemporary Historically Informed Singing	334
7.4	'Vibrato-Free Classical Singing' Playlist	335
7.5	'Vibrato-Free Female Pop' Playlist	338
7.6	'Vibrato-Free Male Pop' Playlist	341
7.7	'Vibrato-Free Folk' Playlist	343
7.8	'Vibrato-Free Ensemble Singing' Playlist	344
7.9	My Conclusions	346
7.10	Amateur Handel Singing Competition	353
7.11	Professional Vocal Training	353
7.12	Unfinished Research Business	355
7.13	Encouraging Informed Critical Attitudes	355
7.14	Unrealized Performance Research Opportunities	357
7.15	Pop to Classical Crossover Opportunities	358
7.16	Campaign for Real Singing	359
Full Text Databases: Service Providers and Sources		361
Primary and Secondary Sources		363
List of Newspapers and Periodicals, with abbreviations if applicable		371
Subject Index		375

Abbreviations

Ath	*Athenaeum*	LMag	*London Magazine*
AF	*Arty Farty*	LR	*London Review*
AuckS	*Auckland Star*	MA	*Morning Advertiser*, London
BCW	*Bang Crash Wallop*	MC	*Morning Chronicle*, London
BDA	*Boston Daily Advertiser*	MCLGA	*Manchester Courier and Lancashire General Advertise*r
BDG	*Boston Daily Globe*		
BDP	*Birmingham Daily Post*	MG	*Manchester Guardian*
BG	*Brighton Gazette*	MM	*Monthly Mirror*
BREMF	*Brighton Early Music Festival*	MP	*Morning Post*, London
Brook	*Brooklyn Daily Eagle*	MusG	*Musical Gazette*
BrookN	*Brooklyn Newsstand*	MusH	*Musical Herald*
Bur	Charles Burney	MusR	*Musical Review*
CE	*Cork Examiner*	MusS	*Musical Standard*
CincDG	*Cincinnati Daily Gazette*	MusT	*Musical Times*
CM	*Caledonian Mercury*	MT	*Manchester Times*
CT	*Chicago Tribune*	MW	*Musical World*
DN	*Daily News*, London	NEMA	National Early Music Association
DT	*Daily Telegraph*	NMM	*New Monthly Magazine*
DubDE	*Dublin Daily Express*	NYHT	*New York Herald Tribune*
EEC	*Edinburgh Evening Courant*	NYT	*New York Times*
EM	*European Magazine*	PMG	*Pall Mall Gazette*
EMP	*Early Music Performer*	QMMR	*Quarterly Musical Magazine and Review*
EMR	*Early Music Review*		
EPNY	*Evening Post*, New York	SatR	*Saturday Review*
Eut	*Euterpeiad*	Scot	*Scotsman*
Ex	*Examiner*, London	SI	Studio Interference
FB	Facebook	SMH	*Sydney Morning Herald*
GH	*Glasgow Herald*	Spring	*Springfield Republican*
Har	*Harmonicon*	ST	*Sunday Times*
HIP	Historically informed performance	Std	*Standard*, London
HP	*Hull Packet*	T	*The Times*, London
ISDN	*Illustrated Sporting and Dramatic News*	TI	*Theatrical Inquisitor*
		YG	*Yorkshire Gazette*
LBA	*La Belle Assemblée*	YP	*Yorkshire Post*
LG	*Literary Gazette*	YPLI	*Yorkshire Post & Leeds Intelligencer*
LM	*Leeds Mercury*		

I dedicate this book to my dear wife Sharon and our family

1. General Introduction

1.1   Why This Book? Why Now? Who Is It For?

Why I've written this book is easier to explain if I outline my own musical background. I came to classical music very late aged 17, when I listened avidly to records of Bach, Handel, Mozart, Schubert and Beethoven.[1] I first got involved in musical performance at that time, joining the Leith Hill Festival Chorus to sing Bach's *Matthew Passion* under Ralph Vaughan Williams. A raw beginner then, unable to read music or play any instrument, I was immediately hooked by Europe's wonderful musical heritage, especially from the Renaissance and Baroque. I also took up the recorder and started to teach myself to play the piano, moving on much later to clavichord and harpsichord.

I was bowled over on first hearing Bach's organ music aged 18. Scraping together my scarce resources, I bought the only recordings available, some 78s by Fernando Germani, on the Westminster Cathedral organ. What a disappointment! The music was played on full organ, in a reverberant space, producing a cacophonous, confused roaring. The counterpoint was unintelligible, and any phrasing undetectable. The organ was a thundering monstrosity. But after the nightmare came the dawn, in the form of a recording of Bach's Toccata & Fugue in D minor, played by Geraint Jones, on the Schnitger organ at Steinkirchen, I think in 1953. I loved the incisive pedal stops, warm clear diapasons, sparkling trebles and lovely flutes. Experts such as Cecil Clutton gave regular talks about historic German organs on the BBC Third Programme, replete with exhaustive detail on low wind pressures and the intricacies of tracker action. I bought recordings by the likes of Helmut Walcha and Lionel Rogg. For me, *Historically Informed Performance* had arrived. I also enjoyed beautiful instrumental music expertly performed on authentic artefacts (strings, woodwind and brass). Virtuosos on harpsichord, lute, guitar and cornetto also emerged through the 1960s and 70s.

My own music making activities developed. By my mid-30s I had achieved a sufficiently good standard on recorders, crumhorns, bass curtal and great bass shawm to play semi-professionally with *Ars Nova* (**Peter Holman**'s first group) and **Michael Morrow**'s *Musica Reservata*. I worked hard on the cornetto for two years, but was unable to master the high Ds then thought essential for Monteverdi's Vespers. I also developed modest skills as an amateur treble viol performer. But I came to realise that I was never going to be expert enough on any instrument to earn a good living as a professional musician. Besides, married and later with two sons, I decided to focus on my business career, which occupied me full time until the age of 72.

I became concerned that, while instrument making and performance has advanced by leaps and bounds in the last 60 years, classical singing has remained stuck in a time warp. I therefore decided to devote all the time I could spare to studying the vocal soundscape of past times. This involved an immense amount of research, which I did part time until around 2006 and full time since then. So the work has been a big retirement project for me, explaining why I'm only going into print aged 85.

---

1   Thanks to Dom Aelred Watkin, my house-master at Downside, who became aware of my interest and lent me a gramophone.

I conclude from my research that, while the best vocalists through the long eighteenth century[2] sang sweetly in default straight, clear tone, their counterparts today deliver often loud, throaty and vibrato-laden sound, the polar opposite to past practices. This was brought home to me when I became aware of the huge chasm separating historically inspired instrumental playing from the vocalism of singers, almost universally trained in the traditional modern opera house style.

This book is primarily for musicologists, musicians and concert/opera goers who love early music but feel strongly that modern vocalism is glaringly inconsistent with the historical record and are keen on reforming both vocal practices and training objectives/methods.

But above all, the book is for singers. In the same way that musicians learning baroque violin might want to consider which model replica to buy (whether Amati, Stainer or Guarneri) and what bow to use, I envisage that vocal students will need to compare their voices from various angles (compass, sound, flexibility, etc.) with historical models.

For example, imagine that my reader is a young baritone. Let him compare his voice with the descriptions of Incledon's voice in Section 2.5.8. Suppose that, when he tries his chest voice, singing in a natural way with neutral larynx and without vibrato, he perceives a beautiful sound, whether sung loud or soft, spanning two octaves from the low A on the bottom line of the bass stave. Then, surmise that he also discovers a rich, sweet, flute-like falsetto, rising from D below the treble stave to a high G, effectively giving him an additional mezzo-soprano register. In such a case, he could make a good living as Charles Incledon reborn. How much better than competing with hundreds of other identical plummy, loud, vibratoey baritones, equipped with generic 'made' chest voices, but without falsetto extensions?

Alternatively, perhaps my reader is training as a young alto, with a range an octave and a sixth up from G below middle C. Suppose that, taking to heart the lessons from Section 2 of this book, and experimenting in a higher range, she finds an unusually wide falsetto extension of at least an additional octave, enabling her to sing soprano parts in early music. If her voice is loud, but sweet and glass-harmonica sounding, could she re-launch her career as a second Angelica Catalani? Or, if her compass is an exceptionally wide 3½ octaves, might she be Lucrezia Agujari reborn? Or, conceivably, a reincarnated diva such as Gertrud Elisabeth Mara or Deborah Travis?

Finally, I'm hoping that my book prompts institutions to diversify their objectives for training singers. This would involve putting in place facilities to train undergraduates to sing in a historically informed way, thereby diverging in part from their (currently exclusive) role as opera singing factories. To achieve this, they would need to recruit singers as vocal coaches who are equipped with the knowledge and skills to achieve this objective.

1.2   Gaps in the Research

Although my research has been extensive, there are some limitations. First, I've relied on English

---

[2]   The period from 1650 to 1830, as discussed further below.

language sources, including translations. Second, I haven't discussed style[3]; this was important, but the treatises agreed that getting the right sound comes first. Also, several sources stress that the quality of vocal sound was crucial in achieving the desired 'affect' on the listener.

Italian opera and Italian-style singing were dominant through most of Europe during the long eighteenth century and later. Italian castrati took the big operatic roles and were influential as stylistic models and in teaching. Handel's and Rossini's operas were set to Italian libretti. Serious opera in the UK was usually described as 'Italian Opera'. Even operas by Meyerbeer, Halévy and Gounod were normally sung in Italian at Covent Garden. Hence, my next section on the golden age of singing is essentially about Italian singing. French vocal practices differed in key respects, with much discussion during the long eighteenth century coming from 'outsiders looking in' on Paris practices and deploring what they found, as is apparent from the *French (Dis)Connection* analysis at Section 2.12. Certainly, there is enough evidence, from **Tosi** and others, suggesting (for example) that tremolo was more common in France. But, as my French is poor, I was unable to investigate French singing from the inside, e.g. by sourcing online descriptions of French vocalists.

The other gap in the book is any reference to singing during the century from 1550 to 1650. As the NEMA/BREMF conference at Brighton in October 2018 made clear, vocal tremolo was certainly practised, but the presenters agreed that it was hard to say what this sounded like, largely due to the dearth of contemporary descriptions of the vocal soundscape. Also, most of the research was on Italian writers such as Zacconi, Bovicelli, and Rognoni, for which knowledge of Italian, besides specialized musicological knowhow, are essential.

1.3 Structure of this book

I stress that, while vocal treatises are important, some 220 pages of this book are devoted to reviews and descriptions of singers' voices. These address perceptions of performance realities, not the treatise writers' views, which could sometimes be theoretical or out of date. But I've tried to cite both source categories, noting where they coincide or disagree.

All my data focuses on the vocal soundscape. For multi-faceted biographical information on nineteenth-century singers, I recommend Kurt Ganzl's 746 page magnum opus, *Victorian Vocalists*. His data on 100 singers is well researched. Each biography contains full particulars of the singer's career, describing in full what he or she sang, where, at what time, with a picture, plus details of family life and personal relationships. Fenner's *Opera in London: Views of the Press 1785-1830* (788 pages) is also valuable.

Section 2 is devoted to the Golden Age of Italian Singing, a stable period from about 1650 to 1830, which I've described as a 'benign hegemony'. The best voices during this period were usually described as sweet, pure, clear and affecting. But it would be wrong to characterise the 'affect' of their singing as ethereal, celestial, or angelic purity, perhaps implying that their vocalism was cold, unromantic or

---

3   Martha Elliott makes clear distinctions between the styles appropriate for different periods of music, viz. the early baroque, the late baroque, the classical era and Italian Bel Canto (Rossini, Bellini, Donizetti). [2006: Elliott]

subtractive. In practice, as the reviews illustrate, singers at this time and later appealed to the heart in a human way, producing real tears.

Section 3 is devoted mainly to descriptions of singers' voices during the revolutionary century after 1830. Vocal paradigms changed rapidly from the mid-nineteenth century, driven in part by the new romanticism of Verdi and Wagner, plus the increasing size of the performance spaces, as well as increased pitch levels in the mid nineteenth century. The vocal descriptions in Section 3 are an essential basis for understanding the huge changes which affected the vocal soundscape, as covered in Sections 4, 5, and 6. Reviews of female and male singers are discussed in turn, both before and during the recording era.

Section 4 tracks the change from default straight voice to universal vibrato, starting around 1830. I've described these radical events and supplied tables identifying which singers were tremoloists and which straight-toners. In my view, the current omnipresence of wide vocal vibrato is the single biggest difference between 18th- and 21st-century singing. As **Frederick Gable** noted: 'The types and uses of vocal and instrumental vibrato, both solo and ensemble, are at once the most controversial and important aspects of sound production in the whole field of early music. The extent to which vibrato is employed and its size and speed can so obscure other elements of a performance that our very perception of a work can change simply on this basis.' [Gable, 1992]

Section 5 relates the change from full registral exploitation by both male and female singers in the early part of the nineteenth century to exclusive focus on the chest voice during the last three decades of the century, besides the associated increase in vocal volume.

Section 6 tracks the gradual change from high or neutral larynx production at around 1830 to low larynx emission over the next 100 years.

After focusing on the distinction between 18th- and 21st-century vocal sound, Section 7 addresses the question: Can the 18th-century vocal sound be found in solo singing today, not only in classical music, but in popular, folk and ensemble singing? I've illustrated this by playlists for each category. Following some conclusions, I suggest some future actions which are desirable if we are to deliver historically informed vocal performance, including: [1] Launching an early music singing competition for amateurs, [2] Reforming professional vocal training, [3] Plugging two research gaps, [4] Encouraging more historically informed criticism of vocalists, [5] Exploiting performance research opportunities, [6] Enabling more pop to classical crossover to happen, and [7] Launching a campaigning organisation CAMREALS [Campaign for Real Singing] .

The concluding sections contain lists of my sources, in two categories, plus a subject index:

- Full text databases utilised in my research over the last 12 years, in order to source reviews in newspapers and magazines

- Primary and secondary sources, containing the sources [mainly books] cited in the text, and other works which have informed my thinking, plus a list of magazines and newspapers accessed

1.4 Voice Type Definitions and Experiment

I define below several different types of vocal sound. The basis for the definitions is a survey I carried out for the 2009 conference on singing run by the National Early Music Association (NEMA) in cooperation with the University of York. The survey's aim was not, How **do** singers sing? Or, How **should** they sing? It was quite simply, What voice type do early music fans prefer to hear in Handel's music? The key question put to respondents was: 'Preferred Vocal Emission. Which single category out of A, B and C below do you prefer for arias in Handel's operas and oratorios?'

A. **Operatic**. Institutionally/ academically trained 'singers' formant' voice, with wide continuous vibrato, low larynx production (generating a dark and plummy sound, especially noticeable from male singers and capable of high volume).

B. **Early Music Mainstream**. A higher larynx position than used by the operatic voice, with narrow but more or less continuous vibrato, producing a sound midway between Categories A and C, with generally lower volume.

C. **Clear Smooth Sweet Chaste**. Fairly soft, straight tone, without vibrato except as an ornament. No low larynx delivery, producing a sound close to the speaking voice.

It was assumed that singing would be in 'chest voice', with none in falsetto, although the latter was common during the long eighteenth century, and from some pop singers today.

NEMA asked **John Potter**, Conference Chair, if he could find a singer able to interpret a Handel song using all three types of vocal emission. **Peyee Chen**, one of Potter's postgraduate students, volunteered. She has a beautiful soprano voice, demonstrating versatility in her vocal contributions at the conference as well as in the experiment. Her eclectic repertoire, with selected sound clips, can be found on her website at http://peyeechen.com/.

First, Peyee Chen recorded an unbroken C, on the third line of the treble clef, in baroque pitch, set at a^1=415 Hz. The note starts in Type A, transitions into Type B, and concludes with Type C. These were used to create the waveform charts[4] illustrated below. Peyee Chen then sang Handel's aria 'Lascia ch'io pianga' in each of the three types.[5]

I define two extra voice types below, neither yet verified by vocal science experiments:

- **Extreme Operatic, Type AA**. This type of voice is sometimes heard in romantic opera and features even wider vibrato of a minor third from peak to trough, pronounced low larynx production, and typically delivered at fortissimo volume.

- **Tears in Voice**,[6] **Type BC**. This hybrid voice type is fundamentally a type C voice, but with the slightest possible vibrato, only barely detectable. I have discussed this in two situations. First, as

---

4 The recordings and waveform charts were kindly supplied by Jude Brereton of the University of York's Vocal Science Unit, now the Department of Electronic Engineering.

5 This is included in the video illustrating my essay 'Vocal Vibrato in Early Music' at www.york.ac.uk/music/conferences/nema/bethell

6 In the emotional sense, of being on the verge of weeping.

a possible explanation for Wolfgang Mozart's famous comment that 'the human voice trembles by itself', and second, for 'tears in voice' singing.

1.5   Voice Type A

The Type A waveform (Illus. 1), typically generated by the standard operatic voice, shows a vibrato of almost a full tone wide (100 cents equals a semitone):

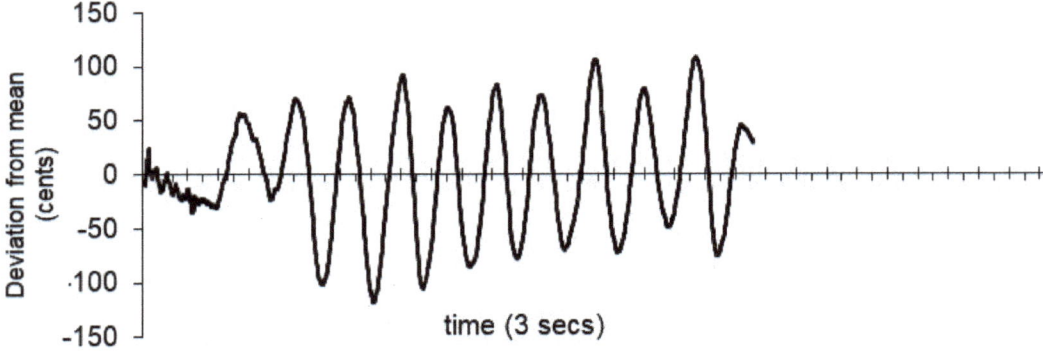

Illus. 1: Voice Type A

1.6   Voice Type B

The Type B waveform (Illus. 2) features a much narrower vibrato of about a semitone from peak to trough, oscillating approximately 6 times per second[7]. In my view, the best Type B exponent in classical music is Dame Emma Kirkby.

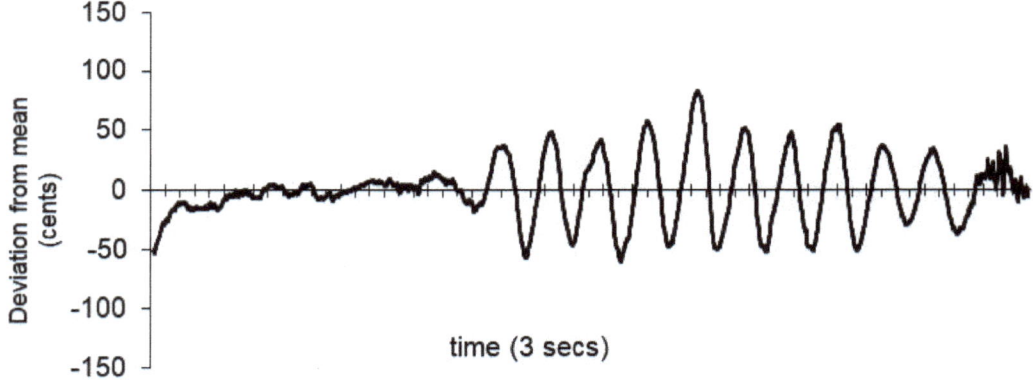

Illus. 2: Voice Type B

---

7   Note that both the Type B vibrato width and oscillation rate produced by Peyee Chen are virtually identical to the measures of vibrato viewed as optimal for singing by Dr. Seashore and his Iowa colleagues in the 1930s [Seashore, *Psychology of Music*, p. 35]. It follows that Type A vibrato would have been viewed by Seashore as unacceptable wobbling.

1.7 Voice Type C

The Type C waveform (Illus. 3) shows Peyee Chen singing straight. It is of interest that the waveform is slightly wavering, although this can't be detected by the human ear. Her version of the da capo repeat in 'Lascia ch'io pianga' includes a few notes with a slight ornamental or expressive vibrato. You can debate whether she's using too much or too little such vibrato, but this is historically informed. For example, Anselm Bayly wrote:

'The manner of *waving* or vibrating on a single tone with the voice, like as with the violin, especially on a semi-breve, minim, and a final note, hath often a good effect; but great care must be taken to do it discreetly and without any trembling.' [Bayly, 1771, passage repeated in 1788 edition]

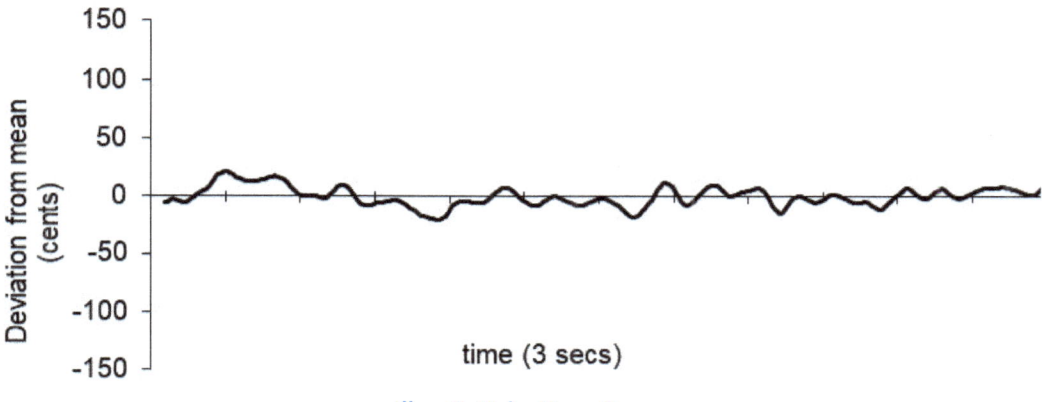

Illus. 3: Voice Type C

1.8 Survey Results

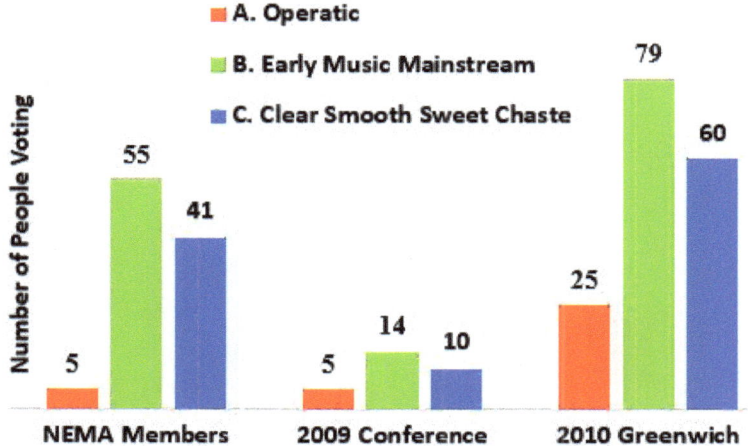

Illus. 4: Survey Preferences for Vocal Sound

Early music lovers' preferences were quantified in three stages: [1] The questions were addressed to NEMA members, [2] The same questions were put to the 2009 conference attendees, and [3] In a follow up survey, 164 visitors to the 2010 Greenwich *Early Musical Festival* were shown the above wave form charts and asked, after listening to Peyee Chen's single note on headphones: 'Which vocal sound do you prefer'. Some correctly noted that the question was out of context, because their preferences would differ depending on what music they were listening to. However, we decided to keep the questions simple.

As Illus. 4 shows, most respondents chose the compromise 'Early Music Mainstream' sound, as developed by singers such as Dame Emma Kirkby. The 'Clear Smooth Sweet Chaste' sound came a close second, which was a surprise because the Type C vocal sound is rare today and is hardly ever heard in professional Handelian performance, even though (as I shall show in Section 2) this style was the norm for at least 180 years through most of Europe, certainly until 1830.

Incidentally, this experiment demolished the widespread notion that, once a singer has formed their style, he or she is stuck with the product, typically the 'one size fits all' operatic voice. Peyee Chen demonstrated to the conference that a good, well-trained singer with a beautiful natural voice can vary their sound and style to suit almost any music, in terms of volume, timbre and a vibrato ranging from wide to zero.

2 The Golden Age of Italian Singing (1650 to 1829)

2.1　Introduction

Note the qualifier in the title. Although the Italian method was unchallenged through most of Europe, there was an important exception (France) which I will look at later.

First, I outline precepts from eighteenth-century treatises on achieving best vocal sound. Second, I present reviewers' views on the singers they heard in order to discover: did vocal sound quality, as evidenced from the reviews, echo the precepts? Third, I address the vexed issue of tremolo and vibrato. Fourth, I examine what we can learn from the historic record about other important features of the vocal soundscape, including the shake, *messa di voce*, extended registers, vocal volume, low larynx emission, timbre and articulation.

2.2　Precepts for achieving good vocal sound

2.2.1　Main Treatises Used

- **Pierfrancesco Tosi**, *Opinioni de' cantori antichi, e moderni o sieno osservazioni sopra il canto figurato*, 1723: translations by Johann Ernst Galliard [1743] and Edward Foreman [1986]

- **Johann Quantz**, *On Playing the Flute*, 1752, trans. Edward D Reilly

- **Johann Friedrich Agricola**, *Introduction to the Art of Singing*, 1757

- **Anselm Bayly**, *Practical Treatise on Singing and Playing*, 1771, and *The Alliance of Musick Poetry and Oratory*, 1789

- **Giambattista Mancini**, *Practical Reflections on Figured Singing*, 1774 & 1777

- **Johann Adam Hiller**, *Treatise on Vocal Performance and Ornamentation*, 1780

- **Giusto Tenducci**, *Instruction of Mr. Tenducci to his scholars*, 1785

- **Giuseppe Aprile**, *The Modern Italian Method of Singing*, 1791

- **Domenico Corri**, *The Singers Preceptor, or Corri's Treatise on Vocal Music*, 1810

- **Jean Jousse**, 1815, *Vocal Primer*

- **Richard Mackenzie Bacon**, *Elements of Vocal Science*, 1824, also serialised in *The Quarterly Musical Magazine and Review* (QMMR), 1818–28

- **Isaac Nathan**, *Musurgia Vocalis*, 1836

- **Manuel Patricio Rodriguez García**, *Ecole de García: traité complet de l'art du chant*, 1840 (Part 1), 1847 (Part 2), translated by Albert García [1924]

The first, and most important, was Pierfrancesco Tosi's *Opinioni de' cantori antichi e moderni*. Other writers, including Quantz, Agricola, Bayly, Mancini, Hiller, Tenducci, Aprile, Corri, Jousse and Bacon, all followed Tosi's precepts, often quoting Tosi extensively. This was well understood then. In his article on Tosi's book for *Rees's Cyclopædia*, Burney accurately commented: 'Though this elementary tract has been written more than fourscore years, no work of the same kind has been produced in Europe since its publication, but upon Tosi's model, and in confirmation of his precepts.' [1814: Bur, Article on Tosi in *Rees's Cyclopædia, V. 36*[8]]

While Tosi only started his vocal career in 1675, I have assumed 1650 to be the starting date of the long-eighteenth-century Italian hegemony, mainly because a few castrati, notably Baldassari Ferri, were becoming important by this time.

Bacon's *Elements of Vocal Science* ranks next after Tosi, in my view. Not only is it content-rich, but Bacon doubled as reviewer, writing (with co-contributors) much valuable material in *The Quarterly Musical Magazine and Review* (QMMR), which he edited between 1818 and 1828. Furthermore, Bacon wrote well, often at considerable length, had an inquiring mind, and was clearly fascinated by the topic of vocal sound, for example, the abilities of different singers to penetrate different sized spaces.

2.2.2 Vocal Sound: Desired Outcomes

Long-eighteenth-century treatises teaching the Italian style all sought the same sound (see Illus. 5). Like the Bible's commandments, these include both MUSTS and DONTS. The first rule, a good *portamento di voce*, is fundamental. Other precepts mostly explored particular attributes, or failings, of this quality. Thus a good portamento, by definition, excludes guttural, throaty or fat tones (known today as low larynx emission or laryngeal development), *and* vibrato, *and* forcing, *and* shrieking on high notes.

But, there was more to *portamento di voce* than simply avoiding faults. An article on the poetry and music of the Italian opera stressed that beauty of sound is the singer's aim, in defining the ***aria di portamento*** as 'a denomination expressive of the carriage (as they thus call it) of the voice. This kind of air is chiefly composed of long notes, such as the singer can dwell on, and have thereby an opportunity of more effectually displaying the beauties and calling forth the powers of his voice; for the beauty of sound itself, and of voice in particular, as being the finest of all sounds, is held by the Italians to be one of the chief sources of the pleasure we derive from music.' [1789: **John Brown**, Letter III].

---

[8] The dates inserted after each source quote are generally *reference dates*, i.e. the date on which the event referred to took place or the comment was first made: this may or may not be the same as the publication date of the source. In the case of newspaper and magazine reports, the dates are always the publication date, to facilitate reference to the original. For dates of publication of other sources, see the List of Primary and Secondary Sources.

The Golden Age of Italian Singing (1650 to 1829)

1. Good Portamento di voce: pure, clear, steady, even, pleasing, sweet, sui generis, NATURAL voice
2. Vocalise clearly and evenly through the whole register, with open and clear vowel sounds, and clear articulation of the words
3. No guttural/throaty/fat tones, or (at the other extreme) nasal tones[9]
4. No involuntary or continuous tremolo/vibrato, although occasional intentional expressive use generally allowed
5. No shrieking or bellowing on high notes, or forcing high in chest voice—instead, develop a well-joined falsetto
6. Sing in time and exactly in tune
7. Develop the flexibility required to negotiate rapid passages
8. Deliver indispensable ornaments well, especially the shake and the *messa di voce*.

Illus. 5: Eight Precepts for Best Vocal Sound

I'll just touch on the other rules. Precept 6 was more difficult then, because musicians did not use equal temperament. They were trained to distinguish between major and minor semitones, with D♯ and E♭, while the same note on a keyboard, being different notes for singers and instrumentalists. The lack of pitch standardisation across different countries and cities added to the difficulties. Agility (number 7) was vital for bravura singing.

Finally, a good shake, and the *messa di voce* (as advised by **Giusto Ferdinando Tenducci**[10] n Illus. 6, and followed by other treatise writers), while strictly speaking classed as ornaments, were always viewed as essential components of good vocal sound.

Illus. 6: Messa di Voce, by Tenducci in 1785

All singers during the period endeavoured to 'appeal to the heart'. And there's no question that they succeeded. As the subject index shows, no fewer than 44 different singers [8 castrati, 28 females and 8 males] were praised for this vital quality. I believe that the reason for these singers' 'heart appeal' can be found in their almost universally perfect *portamento di voce*. Some vocal descriptions support this idea; for example, Elizabeth Linley's 'angelic voice, of so sweet and delightful a tone and quality that it went at once to the heart' [1774: Edgcumbe, p. 148]. On 6 August 2017, I took part in *Throwing*

---

9 Although García parted company with previous authorities in recommending low larynx emission in order to express some emotions.

10 Although Charles Burney stated that the *Instruction of Mr. Tenducci to his scholars* was the work of Aprile: 'When he [Tenducci] quitted the stage, he employed his whole time in teaching to sing; had many scholars, and a good method of instruction; giving to his pupils, in English, a set of axioms or rules of study and practice translated from the Italian, drawn up, as he said, by himself; but which, after his decease, were found in the Solfeggi of Giuseppe Aprile.' [Bur, *Rees's Cyclopaedia*, article on Tenducci].

a Wobbly, a BBC Radio 3 discussion programme on vibrato. To illustrate, Peyee Chen sang Handel's 'I know that my Redeemer liveth' from Handel's *Messiah* in a soft, straight, vibrato-free voice, and followed this by a version in a louder operatic voice, with a wide vibrato. **John Potter** (besides myself) voted for the first, vibrato-free version, because he thought it reflected the human being, unlike the operatic voice, which had a generic, impersonal quality. I illustrate this briefly with a historical example. As is clear from descriptions of her voice included in this book [p. 49], Eliza Salmon's singing, delivered with a perfect *Portamento di voce* and without vibrato, had a powerful emotional appeal. Her voice 'went at once to the soul'; and 'one tone of her clear mellow voice would draw a tear from many a stern eye, or drive him who was too proud to weep to the resource of his snuff-box'.

2.2.3 Reviewers' Views on Vocal Sound

I'll now discuss what reviewers thought of the singers they heard. First, who were the reviewers? Here are three charts listing sources for each of the three time periods.

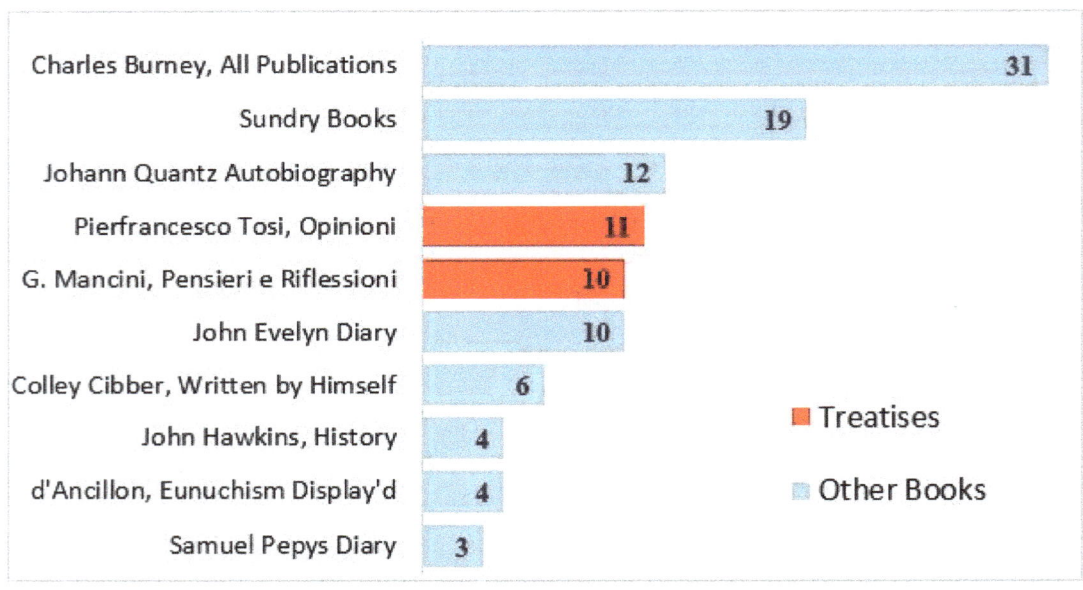

Illus. 7: Number of Review Comments on the Voices of Named Singers, 1650–1749

Illus. 7 covers the period up to 1749 and shows treatises in red and other books in blue. Charles Burney is key in this context, with 31 reviews, some of them second hand from reliable witnesses such as Quantz. Both Tosi and Mancini comment on their favourite singers—one can only conclude that the vocalists praised sang in line with their precepts.

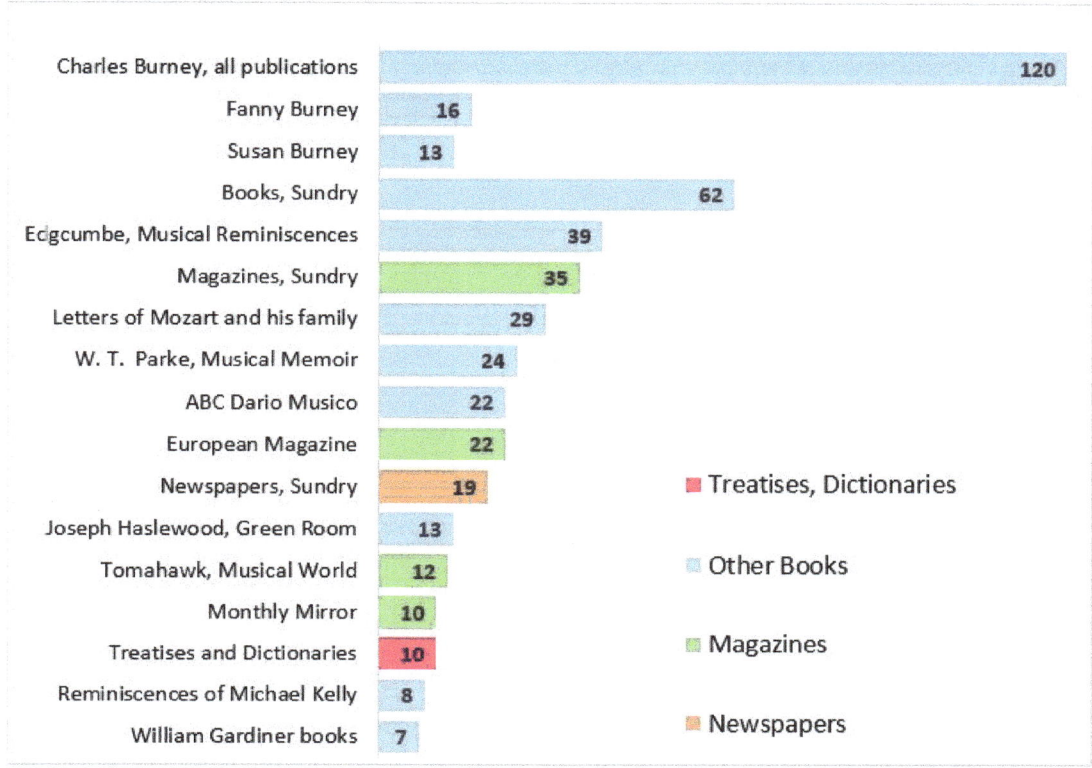

Illus. 8: Number of Review Comments on the Voices of Named Singers, 1750–1799

Charles Burney still leads the table in the second half of the century (Illus. 8). Richard Edgcumbe and the Mozarts (father and son) are also important. By 1800, magazines (green bars) and newspapers (brown) are beginning to make their influence felt.

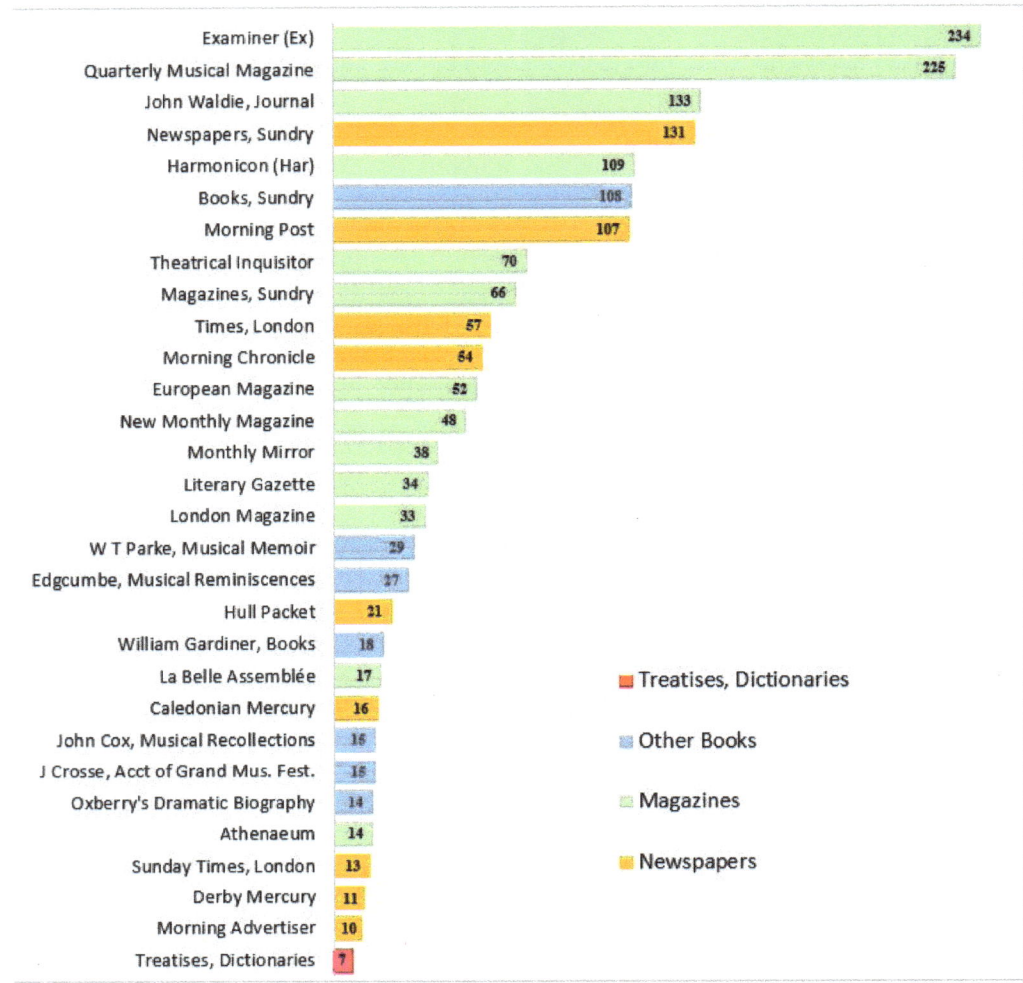

Illus. 9: Number of Review Comments on the Voices of Named Singers 1800–1829

The reviewing profile changed radically during the first 30 years of the nineteenth century (Illus. 9). Magazines and newspapers are now the most important source. While most reviews were London based, provincial newspapers such as the Hull Packet and Caledonian Mercury were growing in importance. The quality of magazine and newspaper reviews improved markedly during this time. Earlier reviews of singers tended to be superficial and perfunctory. Here is a typically uninformative review from the Morning Post: 'It [Peter Von Winter's serious opera *Zaira*] is most happily adapted to the talents of Mad. [Josephina] Grassini, who executed the several airs allotted to her in a very impressive and captivating style, while her interesting action afforded no less pleasure to the admiring circle. She was most universally and deservedly applauded throughout; and all the other performers exerted their respective abilities with great success.' [30 Jan. 1805: MP] Books, treatises and dictionaries are relatively insignificant. The Examiner (Ex) and the Quarterly Musical Magazine (QMMR) together account for over a quarter of the 1,726 vocal reviews, many of high quality. John Waldie, a name which will probably be new to many readers, compiled a journal for 66 years, matching

2.2.4 How Critics described Vocal Sounds

Before discussing a singer's style or musical importance, reviewers invariably commented on what they liked or disliked about his or her voice. Illus. 10 shows the number of reviews in each period, with a top-down view of the descriptions used in generally favourable reviews. Voices were assessed as **sweet** 566 times in 2,296 reviews. The 'sweet' category includes close synonyms, such as exquisite, lovely, delightful and grateful, plus gustatory terms (luscious, delicious, melting, sugary). Critics could sound like today's fastidious judges of fine foods and wines. After praising the natural tone of castrato [Gasparo] Pacchierotti's voice as 'interesting, sweet, and pathetic', Charles Burney savoured its taste as 'superior to the generality of vocal sweetness, as that of the pine apple is, not only to other fruits, but to sugar or treacle. Many voices, though clear and well in tune, are yet insipid and uninteresting, for want of piquancy and flavour.' [1778: Bur, *General History*, Vol. IV, p. 510].

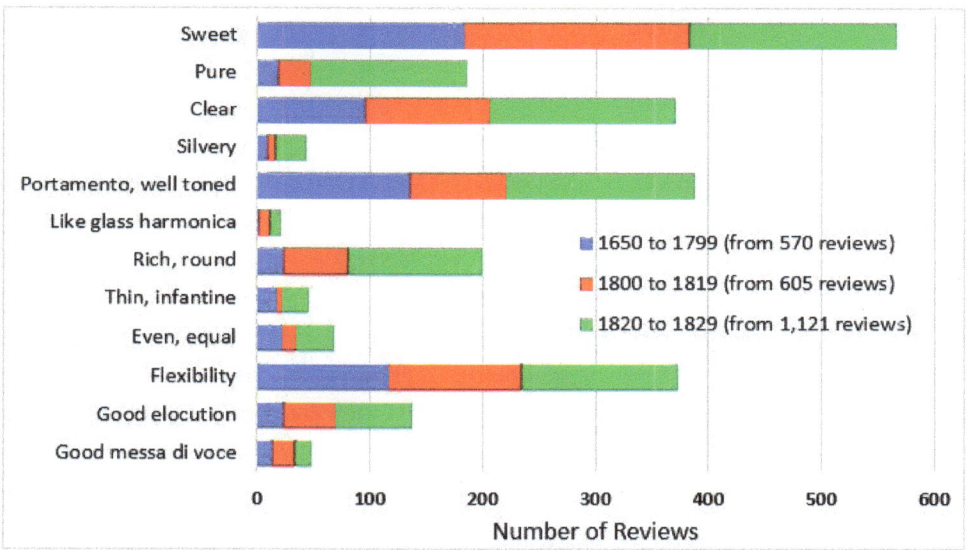

Illus. 10: How Voices were Described during the Long 18th Century

The ubiquity of **sweet** in eighteenth-century vocal descriptions was noted by a speaker at a 2014 conference on *Music in 18th Century Britain*. I asked her: 'What implications do your findings have for historically informed singing?' She ducked it with the response: 'That's a political question!' Obviously, the correct answer is that singers should perform early music sweetly, without shrieking or bellowing, if they aim to be historically informed interpreters.

On **pure**, Bacon enlightens us on the extent to which the properties of the required pure and natural vocal tone are akin to the sound of the glass harmonica and other instruments. The same passage makes clear that richness, sweetness, brilliance and purity are the 'avenues by which sound approaches and invades the dominions of sense and sentiment':

'We can enumerate only five instruments which appear to us severally to enjoy the primary properties of fine tone—these are the musical glasses, the Æolian harp, the bugle, the bassoon, and the flageolet; and it is from hearing and closely attending to the properties of these, that we may be best able to ascertain the genuine effects of mere tone. But it is perhaps to the glasses alone that we can with safety recur as a foundation to reason upon, because the pleasure we derive from them is the least connected with former associations [p.256] … The glasses, if not entirely, are the most exempt from all casual accessions to pleasure. Taking them as our examples, we should say that the finest tone produces for a short time, and but for a short time, an intense delight—that satiety soon comes on and the ear palls. But the first sensations are sufficient to enable us to determine that tone must be rich, sweet, and brilliant, and above all pure, or *sui generis*, distinctly marked by the same continuous quality, whatever the modification in point of quantity, in order to produce the highest order and degree of simple pleasure. To this general rule the finest voices we have ever heard appear to us to conform. Let us not forget to observe, that the tone of the glasses is the most sweet and rich, but it lacks something of the brilliancy of the other instruments. Of these three constituents, as they affect our senses and faculties, we should say that the richness fills, satisfies, and delights the sense—the sweetness partakes in these effects, but adds to them a soothing and more refined gratification—the brilliancy is the *spirit-stirring*, the animating, the enlivening property of tone. These, as it appears to me, are the avenues by which sound approaches and invades the dominions of sense and sentiment. What I mean by pure tone is, that it be free from any obvious taint, such as is derived from the reed or string, by inferior players. There is also a piercing, harsh tone brought from the trumpet when overblown*, that produces the effect to which we allude. By pure tone in singing I mean to describe that which neither partakes too strongly of the lips, the mouth, the nose, the throat, or the head, but which comes freely from the chest, and is delivered justly (without undergoing any perceptible alteration) from that particular place in the passage which we learn by sympathy, and which we perceive to be exactly the same in well-taught singers instructed according to the Italian method. A tone so generated and so emitted is the pure, natural voice. *[Footnote] The effect of Mr. BARTLEMAN's voice is often stringy, and of Mr. BRAHAM's almost always either reedy or overbroke; yet his true tone is more pure and beautiful perhaps than that of any tenor now alive' [Sept 1820: QMMR, *Elements of Vocal Science, Of Tone*, p. 256-258]

Besides **pure**, voices were described as **clear**, as either **rich** or **thin,** and as having a good **portamento**. Singers were praised for their good ***portamento di voce*** in all three periods. I've included some near synonyms under this heading: Well-toned, fine or legitimate method, Italian, best school, good quality, free from defects, polished, refined, firm, steady, *purezza argentina*, *metallo di voce*, granite, crystalline, smooth or suavity, bell-like, flutey, mellifluous, liquid, ductile, angelic. Richard Bacon wrote on **silvery**: 'One of the most constant defects in the formation of the voices of amateurs is the adoption of a thick guttural tone, instead of the "purezza argentina", the brilliant silvery quality of which the Italians speak in such rapturous terms.' [Sep. 1824: QMMR, p. 320]

On **clear**, Bacon quotes Tosi, who wrote: 'Let the Master attend with great Care to the Voice of the Scholar, which, whether it be *di Petto* or *di Testa*, should always come forth neat and clear, without passing thro' the Nose, or being choaked in the Throat, which are two the most horrible Defects in a Singer, and past all Remedy if once grown into a Habit.' [Tosi, trans. Galliard, p. 22]

Bacon defined **portamento**: 'Portamento, by Dr. Burney and the writers before his time, is employed to signify the correct deportment of the voice, that is to say, the production of tone, free from all defects of the throat, the nose, or the mouth.' [Sep. 1822: QMMR, p. 353] Bacon also defined good vocal tone: 'Vocal art presupposes agreable [sic] sounds; and even in the representation of those passions which most convulse the mind, there must always be a reference to this especial postulatum. The finest characteristic of the finest schools has been the preparation and production of the purest and best tone, which is preserved with such uniformity by really well-taught singers, that when loudest or softest, when most sustained or most agitated, there are always the same leading qualities to be perceived. This constitutes in a great degree what the old masters understood by *portamento di voce*, by the deportment of the voice; by that identical bearing that was heard and felt throughout. I therefore maintain, Sir, that this equable beauty, this uniformity of design and execution, technically speaking, is the very first principle of good singing.' [Mar. 1824: QMMR, No. 6, pp. 3/4, 'Present State of Vocal Art in England']

During a Facebook discussion, **Graham O'Reilly** and **Tim Braithwaite** took the view that 'pure', and especially 'sweet', as applied to long-eighteenth-century vocalists, were in essence value judgements, perhaps with a moral dimension. I conceded that, in one sense, both terms might be viewed as 'negative virtues'. Thus, a 'pure' voice was 'natural' without 'made' additions like low larynx emission and continuous tremolo. A pure voice was also 'sweet', without croakiness, roughness or fortissimo screeching/ bellowing in chest voice. I cited some quantitative analysis I had done on how often singers were commended for their sweet singing. Of 21,000 descriptions of voices, nearly all of named singers, just under 2,000 were described as 'sweet'. Many occurred between 1650 and 1829, when compliments on sweet singing accounted for from 24% to 40% of all descriptions. I supply the data below at Section 5.8, plus similar trends on usage of 'pure', noting when and why singing ceased to be described as 'sweet' or 'pure'. For now, the key conclusion I draw is that these descriptions are accounted for not just by the absence of negatives. There is a positive dimension as well, in that voices described as sweet, clear, pure and affecting also had the vital attribute of *portamento di voce*, as already defined. If we just include female singers, the following nineteenth-century artists all possessed these four key qualities:

Teresa Bertinotti/ Radicati [b. 1776]
Angelica Catalani [b. 1780]
Angela I. Colbran, Mrs Rossini [b. 1785]
Eliza Salmon [b. 1787]
Josephine Fodor-Mainvielle [b. 1793]
Benedetta Rosmunda Pisaroni [b. 1793]
Catherine Stephens [b. 1794]
Maria Caradori-Allan [b. 1800]
Deborah Travis, Mrs W. Knyvett [b. 1800]
Laure Cinti-Damoreau [b. 1801]

Mary Ann Paton, Mrs Wood [b. 1802]
Henrietta Nina Sontag [b. 1803]
Maria Malibran [b. 1808]
Giulia Grisi [b. 1811]
Mary Postans, Mrs A. Shaw [b. 1814]
Catherine Hayes [b. 1818]
Clara Novello [b. 1818]
Jenny Lind, Mrs Goldschmidt [b. 1820]
Eliza Poole [b. 1820]
Marietta Alboni [b. 1826]

2.2.5 The Rationale for *Bocca Ridente*

Treatise writers in the long eighteenth century, notably Italian castrati, urged their students to assume the correct *bocca ridente* mouth shape in order to produce the best and clearest vocal tone, as per the following examples. This rule was understood by **Tosi**, **Mancini**, **Corri**, **Jousse**, **Richard Bacon**, **Isaac Nathan** and others, as illustrated below:

> 'Let the vowels be offered to the scholar distinctly, so that he may know them for what they are. Certain singers believe that they are forming the first [a], and let the second [e] be heard; if the error does not lie with the master, it lies with the vocalists, who scarcely out of the lessons study affected singing through shaming themselves by opening the mouth a little too much; some even, perhaps so as not to open too far, confound these two vowels with the fourth [o], and then it is not possible to know whether they have said *Balla* or *Bella*; *Sesso* or *Sasso*; *Mare* or *More*.'[p. 15] ... 'Correct him rigorously if he grimaces with the head, the body and principally with the mouth, which he should compose in the manner (if the sense of the words permits it) more inclined toward the sweetness of a smile [dolcezza d'un sorriso] than to a severe gravity.' [1723: **Tosi**, trans. Foreman, p. 16].

> 'One has seen many youths who, having heard "Open the mouth" repeated endlessly, open it, so that it seems they have opened a small furnace in the mouth, and in this action they look like nothing more nor less than Maskers from Fontana; but if such as these by bad luck encounter an unskilled master, who does not know how to correct them, they will never be able to perceive for themselves their immature judgment, which has reduced them to intemperate opening of the mouth, and thrown the voice back into the throat, and even less will they be able to perceive that the fauces being strained thereby, that natural clarity so necessary for the facile emission of the voice from the organ will in consequence be completely cut off. Hence there remains the poorly conceived placement of the mouth in the uncorrected scholar, and the poor man will sing, but with a voice that is suffocated, crude and heavy.' [1774: **Mancini**, p. 25]

> 'In beginning to sing the first of the key do, the mouth must be put in a smiling but natural form: it will be the means of giving more pureness and perfection to the sound of the voice ...'

[1790: **Borghese**, *A New and General System*]

'I think it [correct pronunciation of "Au" sound, as in "Call" or "All", when singing English poetry] can be assisted by not rounding the mouth too much otherwise it contaminates every good tone.' [1784: **Billington**, *Te Deum*]

'When you are singing, stand erect; hold your head rather high; do not tuck your chin into your cravat—this position of the head obstructs the passage of the voice: this will be the case also if the teeth are not kept open at a sufficient distance. The Italians sing with bocca ridente, a smiling mouth. A person once observed to a professional musician of eminence, a friend of mine, that Signior [Venanzio] Rauzzini always sang as if he were smiling: my friend replied, that he could not execute what he did with his mouth differently formed. The keeping the mouth continually round, with a view to produce a particular kind of tone, makes dreadful havoc with pronunciation.' [Apr. 1810: **Smyth**, *Six Letters*, p. 2/3]

'Here [practice of solfeggi] I may quote my Preceptor, **Porpora**, whose decided opinion it was, that solfeggio were not properly understood; the improvement of the voice he maintained is best acquired by sounding the letter A—the position of the mouth in uttering this letter being most favorable to produce a free and clear tone.' [1810: **Corri**, *Singer's Preceptor*, p. 8]

'What are the principal directions for singing with propriety? … 2. The mouth should be moderately open, and in an oblong form, the lips being drawn so as to shew both rows of teeth. This the Italians term bocca ridente. The tongue must never touch the teeth or the roof of the mouth: its position, after the articulation of any syllable, must remain unchanged. / 3. The position of the mouth must be suited to each syllable, and kept so; for the least change will alter the articulation*. * [footnote] By observing this, the tone becomes equal and steady.' [1815: **Jousse**, *Vocal Primer*, p. 5]

'It must be conceded to them [Italian singers] that their tone is the purest and the best that art has hitherto attained. They appear as far as such an act will admit of being described, to form the tone more at the back of the mouth, keeping the throat moderately open, than either in the chest, the head, or the throat itself. We should say that there is a place at the back of the mouth, where the voice, whether from the head or the chest, must pass, and it seems as if the Italians bring the tone to this spot previous to production, and send it forth in its finished state, from that precise point, untainted either by the nose or the throat, the mouth or the lips. The mouth, which the English singer causes to take a very principal direction, has little, if any, immediate influence in the formation of the Italian tone. The mouth and lips are much more visibly at rest; they assume a gently smiling character; the aperture is lengthened rather than rounded as in English singing.' [Sep. 1820: **Bacon**, QMMR, p. 260]

'The art of singing depends on keeping the voice steady, gradually swelling the Notes, ascending and descending LEGATO and APPOGIATO [sic], taking breath in proper places; in opening the mouth wide enough to produce the sounds free with-out their being impeeded [sic] by the TEETH yet, not so wide, as to be ridiculous, but in smiling form; above all things take particular care to articulate the words distinctly. The Performer who is distinct in his articulation has greatly the advantage over others, who may sing much better, but do not possess it.' [1820: **Rauzzini**, p. 1]

'The voice should come with a pure and steady tone from the chest, divested of all nasal or guttural sound, the mouth to be well opened, a smiling position of it being the most favourable to the production of a good tone.' [1828: **Cooke**, *Singing Exemplified*]

'She [Giuseppina Ronzi de Begnis] always kept her mouth so closely shut, that it was impossible for her voice, which as far as it went, was a very sweet one, to be done justice to. She latterly made it, by her affectation, so mincing and reedy, that it was sometimes even painful to hear her.' [30 Sep. 1828: Har]

'A more slender tone may be produced by contracting the mouth so as to admit but one finger between the teeth, and which will give the sound of the diphthong Ea, as in the word *earth*. / For notes of rapid execution in the upper octave it will be necessary to contract the organs still more, poking out the chin a little, which will produce the still more slender sound of E as in the word *eel*.' [4 Jun. 1832: **Gardiner**, *Music of Nature*, p. 29]

'It is when the mouth is in a smiling form that the sweetest tones are produced, and indeed, were it otherwise, it would be better to forego a little volubility, when we gain a pleasing exterior by the sacrifice.' [1836: **Nathan**, p. 161]

By contrast, some English writers such as 'H R' of the *Examiner* and a *Harmonicon* critic appeared to miss the point. However, their comments on Angelica Catalani, Signor Miartini and Diomiro Tramezzani do at least make clear that some important vocalists did employ the correct 'smiling' mouth shape. The following quotes elucidate this point:

'As an actress, she [Angelica Catalani] has no talent for serious opera. Her mouth is distended in a perpetuity of grin, which is moderated neither by affliction or death.' [1 May 1808: Ex, p. 212]

'It must be painful to himself [Signor Miarteni] to keep his mouth in a perpetual elliptic extension, and it can impart no pleasure to the audience, to whom nature has a thousand times more charms than buffoonery.' [5 Jun. 1808: Ex (H. R.)]

'His performance would be much more satisfactory if he [Diomiro Tramezzani] would divest himself of the appearance of being his own admirer; vanity is perceptible in every simper, and his smiles seem to carry with them the self-conviction, that he is the model of perfection and source of universal admiration.' [21 Jan. 1810: Ex (H. R.)]

In the following 45 pages, I present reviews of singers' voices in four categories: castrati, females, other males and ensemble singing. These descriptions are at the heart of this part of the book, providing the basis for analyses of important aspects of vocal sound, besides some conclusions.

2.3   Reviews of Named Castrati in the Long Eighteenth Century

A pre-condition for guaranteeing the success of an opera was that it should be led by a good 'primo uomo' castrato. The castrati were the 'high priests' of vocal performance. Some, such as Gaetano Guadagni, Giovanni Carestini and Carlo Broschi Farinelli, were admired for their full-toned, strong or powerful voices, which could certainly have filled Milan's La Scala or Naples's San Carlo.

But castrati's voices were often admired for their sweetness and delicacy. Thus, Charles d'Ancillon praised delicate voices of Roman castrati he heard in 1705–6: 'There can be no finer Voices in the World, and more delicate, than of some Eunuchs, such as Pasqualini, Pauluccio, and Jeronimo (or Momo), and were esteemed so when I was in Rome, which was in the Years 1705 and 1706 … for though they were all Excellent in their kind, yet neither of them had the least Semblance with each other … Pasqualini had a Voice much of the same Tone as Niccolini [Nicolo Grimaldi Nicolini], who was lately in England, but then he was infinitely a greater Master, for he was allowed in Rome, even by his Enemies (for Excellency still meets with those) to be the greatest Master of Vocal Musick in the World, and this can be no Disparagement to Niccolini.' He describes Pauluccio as having the finest voice, an Octave, at least, higher than any one else, with 'all the Warblings and Turns of a nightingale, but with only this difference, that it was much finer.' He writes of Jeronimo that 'you are most agreeably charmed a new with the soft Strains of Jeronimo (which I have sometimes almost imagined have been not unlike the gentle Fallings of Water I have somewhere in Italy often heard) lulling the Mind into a perfect Calm and Peace' adding that he had 'a voice so soft, and ravishingly mellow, that nothing can better represent it than the Flute-stops of some Organs.' [1705: d'Ancillon, pp. 30/31]. In a few instances, castrati started as sopranos but at some stage descended to altos. In the case of Gaetano Guadagni, the opposite may have occurred, because Burney noted that, although he began with a compass of only 6 or 7 notes, this had increased to 14 or 15 notes following re-training, probably by exploiting his falsetto register.

Castrati's voices are nearly always described as sweet, even those of powerful singers such as Carlo Broschi (Farinelli) and Giovanni Manzuoli. Powerful voices were certainly welcomed, because they could succeed in large spaces. But soft-voice singers like Venanzio Rauzzini were also valued. Authorities such as **Tosi**, **Mancini**, **Burney** and **Bacon** were very clear that vocal volume must be accepted as a given following training, and that vocalists with naturally soft voices, described as *voce di camera*, should on no account force their voices to be heard in large spaces, as recommended by Mancini: '… when the professor does not find his voice [the scholar's] sufficient for a given vastness, he still should not force it, in order not to ruin the voice, and the chest. It remains only to decide that forcing the voice is one of the great errors which a singer can commit.'[Mancini, p. 32]

Most castrati were also praised for their clear voices. Finally, nearly all them possessed the required *portamento di voce*, with voices praised as pure, firm, granite-like, mellifluous, angelic, silvery, bell-like, well toned, and *bel metallo di voce*. The descriptions are also inconsistent with tremolo or vibrato. Finally, several castrati, including Gaetano Orsini, Gaetano Mairorano Caffarelli and Girolamo Crescentini, preserved their voices into old age, testifying to their excellent training.

Although the castrati were fading by the first three decades of the nineteenth century, they still ruled in some niches such as Rome. QMMR reviewed four castrati in an 1828 article 'On the Actual State of Music in Rome'. The review praised Astolfi's 'delicate purity', Terri's 'delicate, pliant and pure voice', Mariano Patroni's *messa di voce*, and Tarquini's voice as 'incomparable for beauty and purity', claiming that he was superior to Girolamo Crescentini and Luigi Marchesi. I submit that the delicate, pure, delicious voices of these castrati would have been welcomed in the Rome of 1705, and vice versa for the delicate, soft, mellow, organ flute-stop, nightingale-like warblings of Pasqualini, Pauluccio or Jeronimo.

Illus. 11 and 12 show the careers of 23 castrati, together with their voice type, the number of reviews I have on file, plus tessitura if known. Reviews of selected castrati are included after the charts, to give the best idea of their sound. Their singing was often characterised as moving, affecting and appealing to the heart.

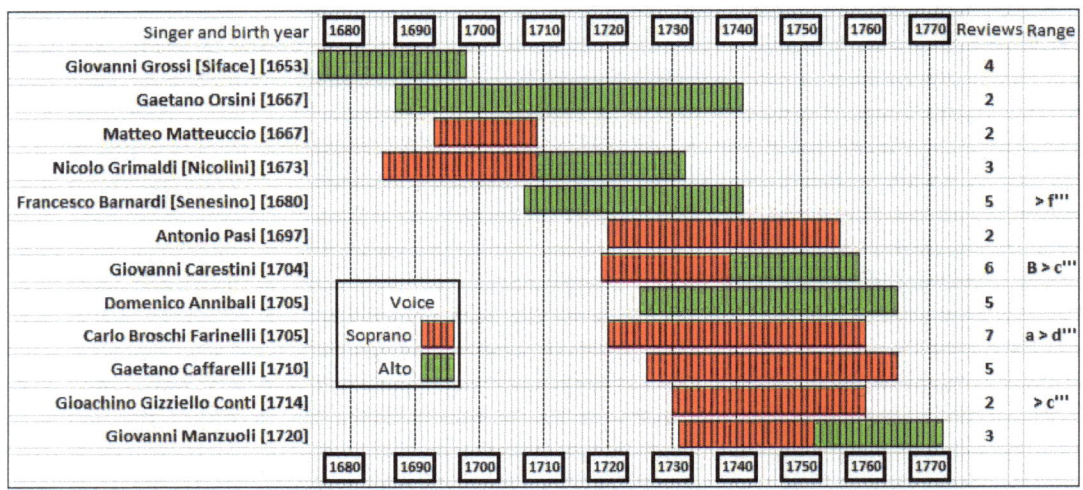

Illus. 11: Careers of the Best Castrati, Part 1

2.3.1 Baldassare Ferri [b. 1610]

'What this noble singer [Baldassare Ferri, excluded from the chart] expressed with his voice is beyond description. There was, to begin with, the purity of his voice and his success with every kind of passage, the impact of the trills and the ease and grace with which he achieved every note. But beyond all that, after a very long, sustained and lovely passage beyond the lung capacity of any other singer, he would, without taking a breath, go into a very long and lovely trill and then into still another passage, more brilliant and beautiful than the first, and all this while remaining still as a statue, without any movement of the brow, the mouth or the body. / To sing a descending chromatic scale, trilling on each note, from the high G and A to the same notes in the lower octave, a feat, if not impossible, certainly very difficult for any other singer, was child's play for Ferri; for again, without taking a breath, he would continue on to other trills, passages and artistic wonders. He often added a soft crescendo to these chromatic scales, building out the trills at the same time, a feat never previously accomplished or heard of.' [1647: Giovanni Bontempi's *Historia Musica*, published in 1695, but referring to around 1647; quoted in Pleasants, p. 55]

2.3.2   Giovanni Francesco Grossi (Siface) [b. 1653]

'I heard the famous Singer the Eunuch *Cifacca*, esteemed the best in *Europe* & indeede his holding out & delicatenesse in extending & loosing a note with that incomparable softnesse, & sweetenesse was admirable: For the rest, I found him a meere wanton, effeminate child; very Coy, & prowdly conceited to my apprehension: He touch'd the Harpsichord to his Voice rarely well, & this was before a select number of some particular persons whom Mr. Pepys (Secretary of the Admiralty & a greate lover of Musick) invited to his house, where the meeting was, & this obtained by peculiar favour & much difficulty of the Singer, who much disdained to shew his talent to any but Princes.' [19 Apr. 1687: Evelyn, p. 771/2]

'*Sifacio*, famous beyond any, for the most singular Beauty of his Voice. His Manner of Singing was remarkably plain, consisting particularly in the *Messa di Voce*, the putting forth his Voice, and the Expression.' [probably c.1687: Tosi, trans. Galliard, p. 102]

2.3.3   Gaetano Orsini [b. 1667]

'Gaetano Orsini, one of the greatest singers who ever lived, had a beautiful, even, and moving contralto voice of considerable range, a pure intonation, a beautiful *trillo*, and an extremely charming manner of execution. In an allegro he articulated, especially the triplets, very well with his chest, and in an adagio he made use of a caressing and touching quality in such a masterful way that he captured the hearts of his listeners. His acting was fair, and his figure not disagreeable. He remained in the Imperial Service for a long time and died only a few years ago at an advanced age, retaining his beautiful voice as much as possible until his death.' [July 1723: Quantz, *Life*, trans. Nettl, p. 296]

2.3.4   Matteo Matteuccio [b. 1667]

'Matteucci, after having served with full satisfaction in the Court of Spain, aggravated by age, returned to his native Naples, where he still lived in 1730, and was in the habit of showing his devotion by singing in church every Sunday morning. This esteemed man, even when he was past the age of eighty years, had a voice so florid and so clear, and sang in every way with such flexibility and agility, that every listener, not seeing him, believed him a youth in the flower of his years.' [1730 Mancini, trans. Foreman, pp. 6/7]

2.3.5   Nicolo Grimaldi [Nicolini] [b. 1673]

'His voice [Nicolini] at this first time [1708] of being among us (for he made us a second visit when it was impaired) had all that strong clear sweetness of tone so lately admired in Senesino. A blind man could scarce have distinguished them: but in volubility of throat, the former had much the superiority.' [1708: Cibber, Vol. 2, p. 53]

2.3.6 Francesco Barnardi [Senesino] [b. 1680]

'Senesino had a well-carrying, clear, even, and pleasantly low soprano voice (mezzo soprano), a pure intonation and a beautiful *trillo*. He rarely sang above the fifth line "f". His way of singing was masterful, and his execution perfect. He did not overload the slow movements with arbitrary ornamentation, but brought out the essential ornaments with the greatest finesse. He sang an allegro with fire, and he knew how to thrust out the running passages with his chest with some speed.' [Apr. 1719: Quantz, *Life*, p. 292]

2.3.7 Antonio Pasi [b. 1697]

'Pasi had a pleasant soprano voice, the range of which was not, however, extremely high. His way of singing an adagio was masterful, and his delivery convincing. The high notes created some difficulty for him, and were not always pleasing, which detracted somewhat from the purity of his intonation. He lacked the vocal ease which is necessary for an allegro movement.' [11 May 1726: Quantz, *Life*, p. 308]

'Antonio Pasi of Bologna, likewise a scholar of [Francesco Antonio] Pistocchi, was celebrated for his skillful singing, and for a completely unusual taste, through the union of a solid portamento with the spinning out of the voice, and he introduced a solidity [*misto di granito*] composed of gracious gruppetti, mordents and tempi rubati, all done to perfection and in their appropriate places, the whole making an individual and arresting style.' [Mancini, trans. Foreman, p. 8]

2.3.8 Giovanni Carestini [b. 1704]

'Carestini also had a strong and well-rounded soprano voice, which by and by changed to one of the most beautiful, strong, and low contraltos. At that time his range extended from approximately the "b" below middle "c" to the "c" above the staff at the most. He showed great fire in *passagien* and like Farinelli, according to the good school of [Antonio] Bernacchi, thrust these out with the chest. He undertook many arbitrary changes, usually successfully, but sometimes to excess. His acting was very good, and his singing fiery. Later he improved very much in the singing of an adagio.' [11 May 1726: Quantz, *Life*, p. 308]

'I have seen this man, who is certainly great in his art, perform in the operas Archidemia, Leucippo, and Demafoonte in Dresden. He sang contralto, ranging from high g" to as low as e♭ and d. His low tones were unusually secure, full, and strong.' [1747: Hiller, p. 44]

2.3.9 Domenico Annibali [b. 1705]

'Domenico had one of the most beautiful soprano voices that I have ever heard. It was full, carried well, and was pure in tone. But otherwise his singing and acting were not lively.' [July 1723: Quantz, *Life*, p. 296]

'To tell you my real opinion of Annibali I found him widely different from the idea I had conceiv'd of him but it was on the right side that I was mistaken for he prodigiously surpass'd my expectations.

His voice it must be confess'd is not so good as some we have had [;] the lower noates of it are very weak and he has not the mellowness of Senesino (nor as far as I can guess) the compass[,] but the middle part of it is clear strong & manly & very tunable.' [18 January 1737: from the fourth Earl of Shaftesbury's letter to James Harris, Salisbury, quoted in Burrows & Dunhill, *Music and Theatre in Handel's World*]

2.3.10 Carlo Broschi (Farinelli) [b. 1705]

'Farinelli had a well-carrying, well-rounded, rich, high, and even soprano voice, the range of which extended from the "a" below middle "c" to the "d" above the staff. Many years later it increased in depth several tones without losing the high ones. For this reason, in many operas, an adagio was usually written for him in contralto range, and the others in soprano range. His intonation was pure, his *trillo* beautiful, his chest unusually strong in the long holding of tones. His throat was very flexible, so that he could produce the largest intervals quickly and with the greatest of ease and certainty. Broken passages, as well as all other runs, provided no difficulty for him, and he was very prolific in his use of the optional ornaments of an adagio.' [11 May 1726: Quantz, *Life*, p. 307]

'His voice was considered surprising because perfect, strong, and sonorous in its quality, and rich in its range from the deepest low notes to the high, the equal of which has not been heard in our times. He was gifted also with a natural creativity which, led by wisdom, made strange things be heard, so individual that they left no room for others to be able to imitate them. The art of knowing how to conserve and take in breath with reserve and neatness, without ever becoming noticeable to anyone, began and ended with him; very perfect intonation, spinning out the voice and swelling the voice, his portamento, the unity, the surprising agility, his singing to the heart and his gracious manner, and a perfect and rare trill, were all equal excellences in him; there was there was no style in the art which he did not execute with perfection and to such a sublime level as to remain inimitable.' [1734: Mancini, p. 39]

2.3.11 Gaetano Mairorano Caffarelli [b. 1710]

'There are, however, innumerable critics, who find his voice strong, but false, screaming, and disobedient; so that he can do nothing considerable without forcing it, and when forced, it becomes harsh and disagreeable. They say that he has no judgment, and by frequently attempting what he is unable to execute, leaves it half finished; that he has an old fashioned and bad taste, and pretend, that they can discover in his graces, the antique and stale flourishes of Niccolini and Mateuccio. They cry out, that no one ever trod the stage worse: that in the recitatives he is an old nun; and in all he sings, there constantly reigns a whimpering tone of lamentation, sufficient to sour the gaiest allegro.' [28 May 1749: Bur, *Metastasio*, Vol. 1, pp. 265–6]

Grimm, who heard him at Versailles in yet another setting of *Didone abbandonata*, this time by Hasse, writes: 'It would be difficult to give any idea of the degree of perfection to which this singer has brought his art. All the charms and love that can make up the idea of an angelic voice, and which form the character of his, added to the finest execution, and to surprising facility and precision, exercise an enchantment over the senses and the heart, which even those least sensible to music would find it hard to resist.' [1753: Heriot, p. 150]

'… to crown ye Whole the first part was sung by ye famous Caffarelli, who tho Old has pleas'd me more than all ye Singers I have yet heard—He touch'd Me, & it was ye first time I had been touch'd since I came to Italy.' [5 Feb. 1764: D. Garrick, letter, quoted in Bur, *Rees's Cyclopædia*, p. 154]

2.3.12   Gioachino Gizziello Conti [b. 1714]

'Handel, never till now, had a first man to write for with so high a soprano voice. Nicolini, Senesino, and Carestini, were all contraltos. There was often dignity and spirit in their style; but Conti had delicacy and tenderness, with the accumulated refinements of near thirty years, from the time of Handel's first tour to Italy. We think it is not difficult to discover, particularly in the first act, that in composing Conti's part in this opera, he modelled his melody to the school of his new singer.' [Bur, *Rees's Cyclopædia*]

'The new singer Conti I have heard twice & will affirm he is all things consider'd the best singer I ever heard & they say in the world[;] he will improve still very much for he is but nineteen years old is very handsome[,] a good actor & very genteel[.] His voice is perfectly clear[,] he swells a noate as full as Farinelli[;] he does not yet go quite so low as he (Farinelli), but his tone of voice is certainly sweeter & he has a greater command of it than Farinelli. Conti's execution is inimitable & his voice goes the musicians tell me thorowly sound & sweet, as far as A in Alte & he can reach B or C though not so truly & distinct. He has sung nothing of Handel's yet but the last duet in Ariodante[;] I really think between him and [Anna Maria] Strada I never was so delighted with any duet I ever heard in my life & it quite charmed the audience.' [8 May 1736: letter by fourth Earl of Shaftesbury to James Harris, quoted in Burrows & Dunhill]

2.3.13   Giovanni Manzuoli [b. 1720]

'Gifted with the finest soprano voice which has been heard on our lyric stage in our memory … Manzoli's voice was the most powerful and voluminous soprano that had been heard on our stage since the time of Farinelli; and his manner of singing was grand and full of taste and dignity… His voice alone was commanding from native strength and sweetness; for it seems as if subsequent singers had possessed more art and feeling; and as to execution, he had none.' [1764: Bur, *Rees's Cyclopædia*]

'A perfect voice or instrument would be that which united force with sweetness. The quality of tone generally determines our idea of its force. The voice of Manzoli, at once extremely powerful and extremely sweet, was miraculous.' [1810: Bur, *Rees's Cyclopædia*, article 'Tymbre']

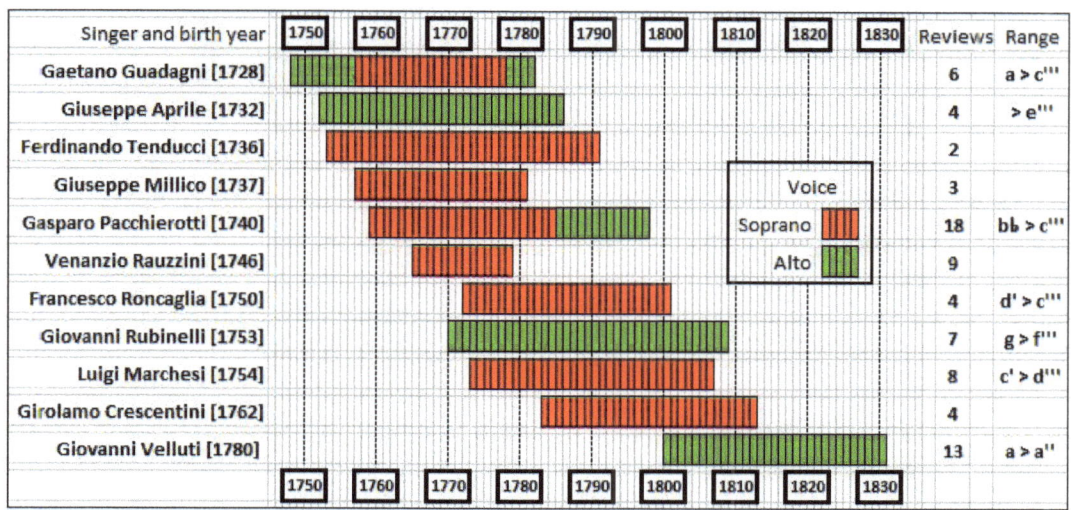

Illus. 12: Careers of the Best Castrati, Part 2

2.3.14 Gaetano Guadagni [b.1728]

'Guadagni, then very young, wild, and idle, with a very fine counter-tenor voice of only six or seven notes compass, performed the serious man's part in these burlettas, and was but little noticed by the public; till Handel, pleased with his clear, sweet, and full voice, engaged him to sing, in Samson and the Messiah, the fine airs which he had composed for Mrs. Cibber's sweet and affecting voice of low pitch: such as, "He shall feed his flock like a shepherd"; "Return O God of Hosts"; and "He was despised and rejected".' [Bur, *Rees's Cyclopædia*]

'… after dinner, even in seeing the gardens and buildings, Guadagni and Rauzzini] sung a great part of the time, particularly in the bath, where there was an excellent room for music; here they went successfully through all Tartini's experiments, in order to produce the third sound[11].' [17 Aug. 1772: Bur, *Present State…Germany*, p. 138]

2.3.15 Giuseppe Aprile [b. 1732]

'Aprile, primo uomo, sings well and has a beautiful even voice. We heard him in a church, when there happened to be a great festival.' [26 Jan. 1770: Wolfgang Mozart to his sister, *Letters*, p. 111]

'Schubart, who had heard him in Württemberg, wrote: "In him the art and nature were marvellously combined … he sang with the purity of a bell up to E above the treble stafe [recte soprano clef], and had a profound knowledge of vocal technique, as well as a warm and sympathetic personality".' [1756: Hiller, p. 158]

---

[11] The Tartini tone, or *terzo suono*, is an auditory illusion. For example, if Guadagni and Rauzzini were to sing an A and C# together as a perfectly tuned (just) interval, i.e. with the C# slightly flatter than in equal temperament, they would both imagine a low A sounding in the bass.

'… has rather a weak and uneven voice, but is constantly steady, as to intonation. He has a good person, a good shake, and much taste and expression.' [Oct. 1770: Bur, *Present State … Italy*, p. 328]

2.3.16   Ferdinando Tenducci [b. 1736]

'An opera-singer in soprano, born at Sienna, whence he at first assumed the name of Senesino, on account of the celebrity of a singer of that city, in the early part of the last century; though neither his voice nor style of singing at all resembled that of the great singer and actor, Francisco Bernardo detto **Senesino**, whose voice was a rich and full contralto, and in whose singing and acting there were more of grandeur and dignity than tenderness and expression, which characterized Tenducci's style; and whose voice was a high soprano of a clear silvery tone, which by great pains he had rendered very flexible … Tenducci had much professional merit; but as to probity, honour, and ideas of right and wrong, they never seem to have extended further than convenience and personal safety.' [1758: Bur, *Rees's Cyclopædia*]

2.3.17   Giuseppe Millico [b. 1737]

'I have no Words to express the delight which his singing gave me. More, far away, than I have ever received—even at the Opera—for his Voice is so sweet, that it wants no Instruments to cover it…For my own part, the mere recollection fills me with rapture—my terms are strong, yet they but weakly express my meaning.' [p. 234] When, a month later, she continued her ecstasies, she was clearly aware of the forbidden fruits she was tasting: 'The Voice of Millico seems continually sounding in my Ear, & harmonizing my Soul. Never have I known pleasure so exquisite, so Heartfelt, so divinely penetrating, as this sweet singer has given me. He is ever present to my imagination, his singing & his songs, are the constant Companions of my recollection … I express myself in very strong terms, but all terms, all words are unequal & inadequate to speak of the extreme Delight which Millico's singing affords me.' [1 Apr. 1773: from Fanny Burney's diary, quoted in Howard, p. 236] .

2.3.18   Gasparo Pacchierotti [b. 1740]

'The natural tone of his voice [Pacchierotti] is so interesting, sweet, and pathetic, that when he had a long note, or messa di voce, I never wished him to change it, or to do any thing but swell, diminish, or prolong it in whatever way he pleased, to the utmost limits of his lungs. A great compass of voice downwards, with an ascent up to B♭ and sometimes to C in alt … [the passage likening Pacchierotti's voice to the pineapple follows, as quoted at p. 15 above] … I have often heard him sing **Ansani**'s and **David**'s tenor songs in their original pitch, in a most perfect and admirable manner, going down sometimes as low as B♭ on the second line in the base.' [1778: Bur, *General History*, Vol. IV, p. 510]

'… but he did So sing!—I never heard him sing so before, much & frequently as he has charmed me—His Voice was so clear, so full, so sweet, & free from every imperfection; he sung with such spirit, such feeling—such animation!—such freedom—such Passion!!—Oh Dear, Oh Dear—How he did sing!' [6 May 1780: Susan Burney, Olleson, p. 156]

'The Italian opera this season again possessed a host of strength in Pacchierotti, who first appeared at the King's Theatre in the year 1778, and, notwithstanding this was his seventh season, his voice (a soprano) was as much admired as ever, and he was still considered a most accomplished singer, though I have frequently heard him hold a note for two or three bars below the pitch, and be enthusiastically applauded for it. This might have proceeded from the Italian system of tuition, which so strictly forbids pupils singing too sharp, that it may perhaps occasion them to fall into the opposite defect of singing too flat. It appears to me, however, to be a hopeless task to attempt teaching persons to sing in tune whose auricular nerves are not perfectly organised.' [1 Jan. 1784: Parke, p. 29]

2.3.19 Venanzio Rauzzini [b. 1746]

'In the execution of these airs, he manifested great and captivating powers: a sweet and extensive voice, a rapid brilliancy of execution, great expression, and an exquisite and judicious taste. I was today even surprised by the strength of his voice, which had before appeared rather too feeble for a great theatre; but it was want of exertion, for now it made its way through all the instruments, when playing fortissimo.' [22 Aug. 1772: Bur, *Present ... Germany*, p. 149]

'His voice was sweet, clear, flexible, and extensive; being in compass more than two octaves. But it was not powerful when I heard it at Munich, two years before; and it was perhaps daily rendered more feeble by his applying closely to composition.' [Nov. 1774: Bur, *General History* Vol. IV, p. 501]

2.3.20 Francesco Roncaglia [b. 1750]

'Roncaglia had a beautiful face, and elegant figure; a sweet-toned voice; a chaste and well-disciplined style of singing; hazarded nothing, and was always in tune. The best part of his voice, which was a soprano, was from D to A; he sometimes went to C, but not easily. Both his voice and shake were feeble; and of the three great requisites of a complete stage singer, pathos, grace, and execution, which the Italians call cantabile, graziosa, and bravura, he was in perfect possession of only the second. As his voice, though of an exquisite quality, was by no means powerful, and little more than a voce di camera (more suited to a room than a spacious theatre), his singing at concerts, when confined to the graziosa style, left nothing for an audience to wish.' [1777: Bur, *Rees's Cyclopædia*]

2.3.21 Giovanni Rubinelli [b. 1753]

'Possessed a contralto voice of fine quality, but limited compass. It was full, round, firm, and steady in slow movements, but had little agility, nor did he attempt to do more than he could execute perfectly. His style was the true cantabile, in which few could excel him: his taste was admirable, and his science great ...' [1786: Edgcumbe, p. 54]

'A most enchanting performer. His voice, without one idle note, or impertinent antick in the play of it, has the compass, the clearness, and variety of tone needful to do all that could be wished ... He has a hold, rather a strong one, upon the heart. We felt it in most of his music' [May 1786: from *Theatrical Cutting*, quoted by Fenner].

2.3.22 Luigi Marchesi [b. 1754]

'His voice is perfectly pure and silvery, and extends from the low C to the D above high C. With the loveliest declamation and deportment, he combines much musical insight. In the execution of passages and the so-called hammer-stroke (*il Martello*) he is commonly reckoned superior to Farinelli.' [1788: Ernst Ludwig Gerber, quoted by Pleasants, p. 88]

'… his vocal powers were very great, his voice of extensive compass, but a little inclined to be thick. His execution was very considerable, and he was rather too fond of displaying it; nor was his cantabile singing equal to his bravura. In recitative, and scenes of energy and passion, he was incomparable, and had he been less lavish of ornaments, which were not always appropriate, and possessed a more pure and simple taste, his performance would have been faultless: it was always striking, animated, and effective.' [April 1788: Edgcumbe, p. 61]

'Marchesi's style of singing is not only elegant and refined to an uncommon degree, but often grand and full of dignity, particularly in his recitatives and occasional low notes. His variety of embellishments and facility of running extempore divisions are truly marvellous. Many of his graces are new, elegant, and of his own invention; and he must have studied with intense application to enable himself to execute the divisions, and running shakes from the bottom of his compass to the top, even in a rapid series of half notes.' [5 Apr. 1788: Bur, *General History* Vol. IV, p. 530]

2.3.23 Girolamo Crescentini [b.1762]

'His supernaturally beautiful voice cannot be compared with that of any woman: there can be no fuller and more beautiful tone, and in its silver purity he yet achieves indescribable power.' [30 May 1797: Heriot, quote from Schopenhauer, p. 168]

'With each scene the interest he [Crescentini, as Zingarelli's Romeo] inspired intensified, until by Act 3 the audience became almost delirious with emotion and delight. In this act, played almost exclusively by Crescentini, the admirable singer caused his audience to suffer the heartbreak of love through a captivating melody, and all the sadness and despair that can be expressed in sublime song.' [c. 1812: Barbier, *Opera in Paris*, quoting the Emperor's valet, p. 22]

'His voice, employed with discreet restraint, is indescribably agreeable, round, pure and flexible; his embellishments rich in noble art and aesthetic propriety, without being overly elaborated. Especially beautiful is the pure, even, ever stronger pulsation of his heavenly voice, with which, in one passage, he makes a crescendo to the high A and then holds the tone at full voice for several measures.' [1805: from *Allgemeine Musikalische Zeitung*, quoted in Pleasants, p. 90]

2.3.24 Giovanni Battista Velluti [b. 1780]

'Among my compatriots, that job [producing the voice] formerly was facilitated; in view of nature's refusal to comply, they made castrati. The method, to be sure, was heroic, but the results were wonderful. In my youth it was my good fortune still to be able to hear some of those fellows. / I have never forgotten them. The purity, the miraculous flexibility of those voice, and, above all, their profoundly penetrating accent—all that moved and fascinated me more than I can tell you. I should add that I myself wrote a role for one of them, one of the last but not of the least—Velluti. That was in my opera Aureliano in Palmira, which was given in Milan in [26 Dec.] 1813.' [1858: Michotte, quoting Rossini]

'Upon a lengthened note he would hold for a considerable time without taking breath, ringing it, so to speak, with increasing and diminishing power, so as to resemble the tone of a bell, which, in all probability, accounted for the term used by the Italians, that he had a bel metallo di voce.' [30 Apr. 1825: Cox, p. 128]

'[Giovanni Velluti's voice] is a soprano in alto, in the highest key. It wants the softness of the female tone, and the gentleness that follows puberty; clear shrill, and penetrating, it thrills in the ear like the prolonged tones of musical glasses; his notes, at times, are sweet, soft, and flexible, but often grate in harsh discords on the ear.' [3 Jul. 1825: ST]

2.4 Reviews of Female Singers in the Long 18th Century

One result of the growth of opera in the seventeenth century was to showcase women's voices to larger audiences. The charts at Illus. 13 and 15 list 33 of the most celebrated female singers completing their careers during the long eighteenth century, with their career span from debut to retirement, plus the number of reviews I have on file, and their tessitura where known. Most were described as sopranos, although a few descended to G, on the 4th line of the bass stave, or even a note lower down to F, normally regarded as alto territory. A wide tessitura was viewed as a valuable vocal accomplishment. Sopranos got better roles than altos and were better paid. Not surprisingly, therefore, females invariably exploited their falsetto register, often ascending as high as e''' or f'''. In each case, I've selected reviews giving the best impression of their sound. It will be apparent that sweet, touching and heart melting female vocal sound often 'went to the soul'.

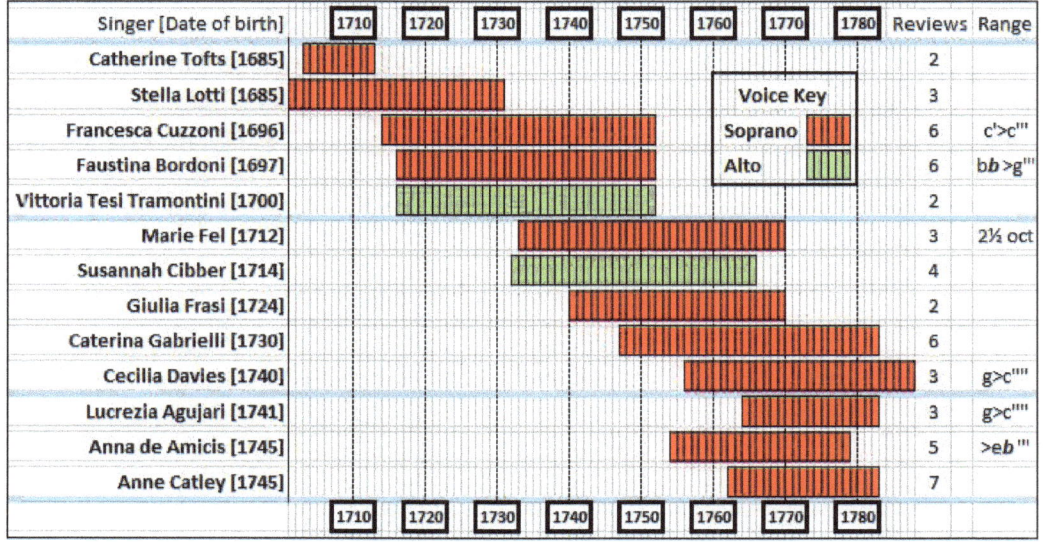

Illus. 13: Careers of the best female singers through the Long Eighteenth Century, Part 1

2.4.1   Catherine Tofts [b. 1685]

'The Beauty of her fine proportion'd Figure, and exquisitely sweet, silver Tone of her Voice, with that peculiar rapid Swiftness of her Throat, were Perfections not to be imitated by Art or Labour.' [1703: Cibber, Vol 2, pp. 54/5]

2.4.2   Stella Lotti [b. 1675]

'Lotti had a very strong soprano voice, good intonation, and a good *trillo*. The high notes were somewhat difficult for her. Her "forte" was the adagio, and I heard the so-called tempo rubato for the first time from her.' [Apr. 1719: Quantz, *Life*, p. 292]

'I will add … that Signora Lotti, accompanied by the same rules [that 'Signora Boschi, to the glory of her sex, has made it heard that ladies who study may teach with the same laws the most rare artifice as men of worth'], and by a penetrating sweetness [soavità penetrante], in singing captured the heart so that one denied it was his own.' [Tosi, trans. Foreman, pp. 65/6]

2.4.3   Francesca Cuzzoni [b. 1695]

'Cuzzoni had a very agreeable and clear soprano voice, a pure intonation and beautiful *trillo*. Her range extended from middle "c" to the "c" above the staff. Her ornamentation did not seem to be artificial due to her nice, pleasant, and light style of delivery, and with its tenderness she won the hearts of her listeners. The *passagien* in the allegros were not done with the greatest facility, but she sang them very fully and pleasantly.' [Apr 1727: Quantz, *Life*, p. 312]

'… she was gifted with a voice angelic in its clarity and sweetness, and because of the excellence of her style. She sang with a smooth legato; she acquired such a perfect portamento of the voice, united to an equality of the registers, that she not only carried away those who heard her, but also captured their esteem and veneration in the same moment / This excellent lady lacked nothing which seems important to us, for she possessed sufficient agility; the art of leading the voice, of sustaining it, clarifying it, and drawing it back, all with such attention to perfection that she was given the valued name of "Mistress". If she sang a cantabile aria, she did not fail in fitting places to vitalize the singing with rubato, mixing proportionately with mordents, gruppetti, volatinas and perfect trills; passes and passages executed in varied styles, now legato, now vibrant with trills and mordents; now staccato, now held back, now filled with redoubled volatinas; now with a few leaps tied from the low to the high; and finally by perfect execution she gave perfect attention to everything she undertook; all was done with surprising finish. All of this together produced admiration and delight. Her voice was so given to exact execution that she never found any obstacle which she did not easily overcome; she used the highest notes with unequaled precision. She was the mistress of perfect intonation; she had the gift of a creative mind, and accurate discernment in making choices; by reason of these her singing was sublime and rare.' [1738: Mancini, trans. Foreman, p. 10 and 81]

'Endowed by nature with a voice that was equally clear, sweet, and flexible. It was difficult for the hearer to determine whether she most excelled in slow or rapid airs. A native warble enabled her to execute divisions with such facility as to conceal every appearance of difficulty; and so grateful and touching was the natural tone of her voice, that she rendered pathetic whatever she sung, in which she had leisure to unfold its whole volume. The art of conducting, sustaining, increasing, and diminishing her tones by minute degrees, acquired her, among professors, the title of complete mistress of her art. In a cantabile air, though the notes she added were few, she never lost a favourable opportunity of enriching the cantilena with all the refinements and embellishments of the time. Her shake was perfect, she had a creative fancy, and the power of occasionally accelerating and retarding the measure in the most artificial and able manner, by what the Italians call *tempo rubato*. Her high notes were unrivalled in clearness and sweetness; and her intonations were so just and fixed, that it seemed as if it was not in her power to sing out of tune.' [Bur, *General History*, Vol. IV, p. 307[12]]

'She [Cuzzoni] came to London a third time, in 1749, just after [Felice] Giardini's arrival, who performed at her benefit, at the little theatre in the Hay-market, the first time he was heard here in public. I was at this concert myself, and found her voice reduced to a mere thread; indeed, her throat was so nearly ossified by age, that all the soft and mellifluous qualities, which had before rendered it so enchanting, were nearly annihilated, in her public performance; though I have been assured by a very good judge, who frequently accompanied her in private, that in a room fine remains of her former grace and sweetness in singing Handel's most celebrated songs, by which she had acquired the greatest reputation, were still discoverable.' [Bur, *General History*, Vol. IV, p. 207–8]

2.4.4 Faustina Bordoni [b. 1697]

'Faustina had a not very clear, but well-carrying mezzo-soprano voice which at the time did not range much more than from the "b flat" below middle "c" to the "g" above the staff, but in time increased several tones in depth. Her way of singing was expressive and brilliant (*un cantar granito*) and she had a light tongue, being able to pronounce words rapidly but plainly in succession. She had a facile throat and a beautiful and very polished *trillo* which she could apply with the greatest of ease wherever and whenever she pleased. The *passagien* could be either running or leaping, or could consist of many fast notes in succession on one tone. She knew how to thrust these out skilfully, with the greatest possible rapidity, as they can only be performed only on an instrument. She is unquestionably the first who has used these *passagien* consisting of many notes on one tone in singing, and with the best possible success.' [April 1727: Quantz, *Life*, p. 312/3]

'This singer, well guided by her master, developed a rare method, consisting of a distinct and purified vocal agility, which she used with incomparable facility, earning applause from the very first years in which she presented herself before the public. Her style of agility was so pleasing because it sounded to the very end, and in a way so new, and above all so difficult, in sustaining a passage with notes in sextolets, or even in triplets, and performing with such exact proportion, without ever slowing down in ascending or descending, giving to each its proportionate coloration, as is exactly necessary for the setting forth of each passage. The perfect and happy execution of this agility is extraordinary, and gives the character of a great professor to anyone who possesses it to perfection. Our Faustina Hasse sang with this rare method, so she could not be imitated. Besides this natural excellence of

---

12   Given that Burney could not have heard Cuzzoni in her prime, he must have sourced this review from someone else, possibly Mancini. However, he did hear her in 1749.

agility she had another kind of agility, accompanying with everything a fast and very solid trill and mordent. She had a perfect intonation, a secure knowledge of spinning forth the tone and sustaining the voice. The refined art of conserving and refreshing the breath, and the excellence of a finished taste. All of these were sublime gifts in her, perfectly mastered, and maintained through assiduous study, by which she attained a facile execution of great perfection, united to the just precepts of the art …' [1743: Mancini, p. 9]

2.4.5   Vittoria Tesi Tramontini [b. 1700]

'Tesi was gifted by nature with a masculinely strong contralto voice. In the year 1719 at Dresden she sang on several occasions the kind of arias which are usually composed for bassos. By now she had acquired, in addition to the magnificent serious tone in her singing, a pleasant softness. The range of her voice was extremely wide, neither high not low notes being difficult for her. A display of virtuosity was not her strong point.' [Apr. 1719: Quantz, *Life*, p. 302]

'… she was born in Florence, where she received her first instruction in the profession of singing from the celebrated maestro di cappella Francesco Redi … An estimable and very complex personality, accompanied by a noble and gracious portamento; a clear and exquisite pronunciation; a sounding of the words according to their true sense; the adaptability to distinguish one character from another as much through a change of facial expression as with appropriate gestures; complete intonation, which did not vacillate in even the most fervent action [e finalmente una perfettissima intonazione, che non vacillò mai anche nel fervore dell' azione più viva], were excellences so singular in her, and so perfectly guided by her art, that she remained the one perfect mistress.' [1743: Mancini, p. 9]

2.4.6   Marie Fel [b. 1712]

'Her sweet, pure, and silver-toned voice delighted the public 20 years, and would have continued in favour twenty years more, if bad health, and a feeble chest, had not obliged her to quit the stage in 1759 [from 1733]. Mad. Fel sung equally well in French and Latin, and was one of the French who had best succeeded in Italian. Her voice was always as young and astonishing as ever, to the small number of friends to whom she devoted the last years of her life, and who cherished her personal qualities as much as they did her vocal talents.' [1759: Bur, *Rees's Cyclopædia*, quoting from Laborde]

2.4.7   Susannah Maria Cibber [b. 1714]

'[Messiah] was admirably performed, with Dubourg for leader, and the late Mrs. Cibber, to sing, "*He was despised and rejected of Men*". This air, the first, perhaps, in our language, has been often sung by Italian singers of the greatest abilities, but never, I believe, in a manner so truly touching to an Englishman, as by Mrs. Cibber, for whom it was originally composed; and whose voice, though a mere thread, and knowledge of Music, inconsiderable; yet, by a natural pathos, and perfect conception of the words, she often penetrated the heart, when others, with infinitely greater voice and skill, could only reach the ear.' [Dec. 1750: Bur, *An Account … Handel*, pp. 26/27]

'Handel himself was extremely partial to her, and took the trouble of teaching her the parts expressly composed for her limited compass of voice, which was a mezzo soprano, almost, indeed, a contralto, of only six or seven notes, with all the drudgery of repetition necessary to undergo, in teaching persons more by the ear than the eye.' [1650: Bur, *Rees's Cyclopædia*]

2.4.8   Giulia Frasi [b. 1724]

'... came to England in 1743 ... At that time was young and interesting in her person, had a clear and sweet voice, free from defects, and a smooth and chaste style of singing; which, though cold and unimpassioned, pleased natural ears, and escaped the censure of critics ... was the principal singer in Handel's oratorios during the last ten years of his life. Having come into this country at an early period of her life, she pronounced our language in singing in a more articulate and intelligible manner than the natives; and her style being plain and simple, with a well-toned voice, a good shake, and perfect intonation, without great taste and refinement, she delighted the ignorant, and never displeased the learned.' [1743: Bur, *Rees's Cyclopædia*]

'Sir Joseph Hankey ... procured me Frasi for a scholar; & Frasi procured me [Gaetano] Guadagni on his first arrival, to accompany him in his studies, and assist him in the pronunciation of the English words in the parts given him in the Oratorios by Handel: and even the acquaintance of Handel himself; who used to bring an Air, or Duet, in his pocket, as soon as composed, hot from the brain, in order to give me the time & style, that I might communicate them to my scholar by repetition; for her knowledge of musical characters was very slight.' [Winter 1749–50: Bur, *Memoirs*, p. 92]

2.4.9   Caterina Gabrielli [b. 1730]

'Her voice, though of an exquisite quality, was not very powerful; and her chief excellence having been the rapidity and neatness of her execution, the surprize of the public must have been diminished, on hearing her after Miss Davies, who sung in the same style many of her songs, with a neatness so nearly equal, that common hearers could distinguish no difference. There were, however, a few fair and discriminating critics, who discovered a superior sweetness in the natural tone of the Gabrielli's voice; an elegance in the finishing her musical periods or passages; and an accent and precision in her divisions, not only superior to Miss Davies, but to every singer of her time.' [1775: Bur, *General History*, Vol. IV, p. 502]

'They expected a Giant in Gabrielli, & behold! A pigmy. I was more pleased than surprised or disappointed. A little, dapper, short-armed, elegant, appetissante figure, was not likely to have the voice of a Stentor. She had a cold, & was put out of humour by the brutality of John [Bull] in the Gallery hissing her Sister [Francesca Gabrielli]. But through all clouds & storms I discovered a voice more like Mrs Sheridan's [Elizabeth Ann Sheridan, nee Linley] in the clear places, than any one I know of: an execution rapid & neat to a very superior degree. After a very long swell in her cadence which I thought had wholly exhausted her air-pump, she set off with such a Volata as arracher'd des louanges [secured praises] from her greatest enemies. Her Cantabile melted me: and I was ready to pronounce her to be two distinct singers: and in the Duet, her & Rauzzini [Venanzio Rauzzini, as Aeneas in Didone] to be only one,—so delightfully did they breath the first part, which was exquisite, together,—& so admirably contend in the 2nd for pre-eminence in rapidity & neatness. And all this while power of voice was wanting to stun the Galleries.' [15 Nov. 1775: Bur, *Letters*, Vol. 1, p. 190]

According to Wolfgang Mozart [see quote at p. 80], Gabrielli had no messa di voce, although such a defect would have been most unusual for a diva at this time.

2.4.10   Cecilia Davies [b. 1740[13]]

'THE bearers of this most reverential address, are two English young persons, travelling under the conduct of their worthy parents, in order to give testimonies at Naples of their several abilities in music; their names are Miss Mary, and Miss Cecilia Davis; the first performs with admirable skill on an instrument of new invention, called the *Armonica*. It is composed of glasses of different sizes, revolving, by means of a pedal, on a spindle. These glasses, forming a regular scale of tones and semi-tones, being delicately touched with wet fingers, during their revolution, produce the most uncommonly sweet, and celestial tones, imaginable; particularly in pathetic strains, for which the instrument is eminently calculated. The other sister, who is possessed of a very pleasing and flexible voice, sings extremely well, with much art and natural expression; and when accompanied by her sister on the *Armonica*, she has the power of uniting her voice with the instrument, and of imitating its tones, so exactly, that it is sometimes impossible to distinguish one from the other. They have been here universally admired, and applauded; and my most august Patroness, who has designed to hear them frequently, has honoured them with munificent testimonies of imperial approbation.' [16 Jan. 1772: Bur, Metastasio, letter to the princess di Belmonte at Naples]

'Miss Davies has the honour of being not only the first Englishwoman who has performed the principal female parts in several great theatres of Italy, but who has ever been thought worthy of singing there at all … Here [in Vienna, staying with the Hasse family] Miss Davies seems to have acquired much of that steady and prudent carriage of her voice, as well as recitative and action, for which she has been so justly admired … Her voice, though not of a great volume, or perhaps sufficiently powerful for a great theatre, yet was clear and perfectly in tune. Her shake excellent, open, distinct, and neither sluggish like the French cadence, nor so quick as to become a flutter. The flexibility of her throat rendered her execution of the most rapid divisions fair and articulate, even beyond those of instruments in the hands of the greatest performers. The critics, however, though unanimous in this particular, did not so readily allow her excellence to be equal in the cantabile style. She took her notes judiciously, they readily granted; sung them perfectly in tune; but was said by some to want that colouring, passion, and variety of expression, which render adagios truly touching.' [30 Nov. 1773: Bur, *General History*, p. 499]

---

13   Her date of birth is sometimes shown as 1756. I have assumed it was 1740 based on a statement by Dr. Rimbault that she was ninety-two in July 1832, quoted in Grove.

2.4.11 Lucrezia Agujari [b. 1741]

Illus. 14: Passage sung by Lucrezia Agujari for Wolfgang Mozart

'In Parma Signora Guari [Lucrezia Agujari, 1743-1783], who is also called Bastardina or Bastardella, invited us to dinner and sang three arias for us. I could not believe that she was able to reach C sopra acuto, but my ears convinced me. The passages which Wolfgang has written down occurred in her aria and these she sang, it is true, more softly than her deeper notes, but as beautifully as an octave stop in an organ. In short, she sang the trills and the passages exactly as Wolfgang has written them down, note for note. Further, she has a good deep alto down to G.' [24 Mar. 1770: Leopold Mozart to his wife, *Letters*, p. 119]

'In Parma we got to know a singer and heard her perform very beautifully in her own house—the famous Bastardella who has (1) a beautiful voice, (2) a marvellous throat, (3) an incredible range. While I was present she sang the following notes and passages [Illus. 14].' [24 Mar. 1770: Wolfgang Mozart to his sister, *Letters*, p. 119]

'Besides its great power, her voice is all sweetness,—and, when she pleases, all softness and delicacy. She sings in the highest style of Taste, and with an *Expression* so pathetic, it is impossible to hear it unmoved. She executes the greatest difficulties that are possible to be given to her, with all the ease and facility that I could say 'my dear Daddy!' / She came before 7—and stayed till 12, and was singing almost all the time! She permitted us to encore almost every song. She sung in 20 different styles. The greatest was son Regina e sono Amante from Didone [composed by her teacher Giuseppe Colla]. Good Heaven! What a song! And how sung! Then she gave us 2 or 3 *Cantabiles*, sung divinely, then she *chaunted* some *Church Music*, in a style so nobly simple and unadorned, that it stole into one's very soul! Then she gave us a Bravura, with difficulties which seemed only possible for an Instrument in the Hands of a great master—Then she spoke some Recitative—so nobly.—/In short—whether she most astonished, or most delighted us, I cannot say—but she is really a *sublime* singer.' [10 June 1775: Fanny Burney, *Journals and Letters*, p. 60]

2.4.12 Anna de Amicis [b. 1745]

'Her voice and manner of singing, exquisitely polished and sweet. She had not a motion that did not charm the eye, or a tone but what delighted the ear … De Amicis was not only the first who introduced staccato divisions in singing on our stage, but the first singer that I had ever heard go up to E flat in altissimo, with true, clear, and powerful real voice.' [18 Nov. 1762: Bur, *General History*, Vol. IV, pp. 479, 481]

'De Amicis is our best friend. She sings and acts like an angel and is extremely pleased because Wolfgang has served her extraordinarily well. Both you and the whole of Salzburg would be amazed if you could hear her.' [26 Dec. 1772: Leopold Mozart to his wife, *Letters*, p. 222]

2.4.13 Anne Catley [b. 1745]

'As an actress, this lady has little pretention to be spoke of; as a singer, she is at present the sweetest warbler on the English stage. Her voice is strong, clear, harmonious, and expressive, notwithstanding these musical requisites, through a careless, inexcusable negligence, she sings with great impropriety, that often renders her vocal performance disgusting; I mention this, as it is in her power (would she take a little more pains) to remedy it. She likewise throws into her parts many indecent, and vulgar attitudes, which is still worse than the former, for as the poet says ['observes' in later edition], / Immodest deeds admit of no defence.' [1 May 1775: William Hawkins, *Miscellanies*]

'Miss Catley, upon the English state, is the only one, I ever heard, who hazards every thing with success, arbitrary changes, embellishments, &c, &c.—I am partial to her wild graces, but cannot help comparing her to a Virginian nightingale in my aviary, whom I could never bring in with the others, to follow the notes of the bird organ.' [1777: de Crui, letter from Mrs. Pierpont to the Duchess [Eliza] de Crui, *Letters*, Vol. 5, p. 17]

'To those who have never heard Miss Catley, I must, as my manner is, try to give some notion of what was peculiar to her.—It was the singing of unequalled animal spirits; it was Mrs. Jordan's comedy carried into music—the something more, that a duller soul cannot conceive, and a feebler nerve dare not venture. Even at the close of her theatrical life, when consumptive, and but the ghost of her former self, gasping even for breath, and wasting her little remaining vitality in her exertion, she would make sometimes a successful attempt at one of her brilliant rushes of musical expression, and mingle a pleasing astonishment along with the pain you were compelled to suffer. No other female singer ever gave the slightest notion of her. She was bold, volatile, audacious; mistress of herself, of her talent, and of her audience.' [Dec. 1826: *Southern Reporter and Cork Commercial Courier*]

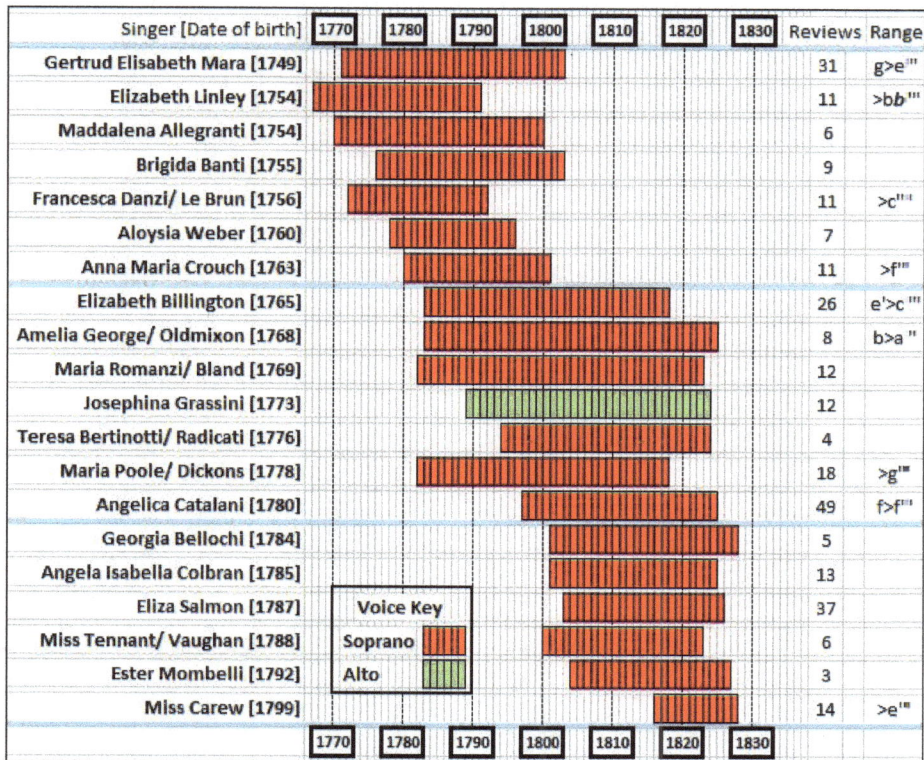

Illus. 15: Careers of the best female singers through the Long Eighteenth Century, Part 2

2.4.14 Gertrud Elizabeth Mara, née Schmeling [b. 1749]

Quote from Burney's contact, a 'very intelligent musical correspondent, in Germany': 'People who have been a long time in Italy, and who have formerly heard Faustina], Cuzzoni], and [Giovanna] Astrua, assure me that she surpasses them all. Indeed, when I heard her at Leipsic, two years ago, I was enraptured. I never knew a voice so powerful and so sweet, at the same time: she could do with it just what she pleased. She sings from G to E in altissimo, with the greatest ease and force, and both her portamento di voce, and her volubility are, in my opinion, unrivalled; but when I heard her, she seemed to like nothing but difficult music.' [30 Sep. 1772: Bur, *Present State…Germany*]

'Mara has not had the good fortune to please me. She has not the art to equal a Bastardella [Lucrezia Agujari] (for this is her peculiar style)—and has too much to touch the heart like a Weber [Aloysia Weber]—or any sensible singer.' [20 Nov. 1780: Leopold Mozart to Wolfgang, *Letters*, p. 663]

'Perhaps the whole of her study [Mademoiselle Schmeling, arriving in spring 1784, in name of Mara] in singing was to imitate the instruments of great performers. In the humble state in which she had travelled with her father, she could have had no opportunities of hearing fine Italian singing by performers of the first order. And it has often been observed by those accustomed to exquisite Italian singing, that her cadences, expression, and execution, however excellent, favoured more of instrumental perfection than vocal.' [1784: Bur, *Rees's Cyclopædia*, 1784]

'Madame Mara's voice and manner of singing in this plain and solemn air, so admirably accompanied on the hautbois by Fisher, had a sudden effect on myself, which I never before experienced, even from her performance of more pathetic Music. I have long admired her voice, and abilities in various styles of singing; but never imagined tenderness the peculiar characteristic of her performance: however, here, though she had but a few simples [sic] notes to deliver, they made me shiver, and I found it extremely difficult to avoid bursting into tears on hearing them. Indeed, she had not only the power of conveying to the remotest corner of this immense building [Westminster Abbey], the softest and most artificial inflexions of her sweet and brilliant voice, but articulated every syllable of the words with such neatness, precision and purity that it was rendered as audible and intelligible, as it could possibly have been, in a small theatre, by meer declamation.' [26 May 1784: Bur, *Account of the Musical Performances*, p. 36]

'Her voice clear, sweet, distinct, was sufficiently powerful, though rather thin, and its agility and flexibility rendered her a most excellent bravura singer, in which style she was unrivalled; but she succeeded equally well in some of Handel's most solemn and pathetic songs, though there appeared to be a want of that feeling in herself, which, nevertheless, she could communicate to her hearers.' [Jan. 1786: Edgcumbe, p. 52]

A very few years ago, an advertisement from Messrs. Knyvett announced for their concerts a most celebrated singer whom they were not yet at liberty to name. This mysterious secret was soon after explained by another announcement, that *Madame Mara's* benefit concert would take place at the King's Theatre on an evening specified, no one being at all aware of her return to England, or even of her existence. She must then have been at least seventy; but it was said her voice had miraculously returned, and was again as fine as ever. But when she displayed these wonderfully revived powers, they proved, as might be expected, lamentably deficient, and the tones she produced were compared to those of a *penny trumpet*. Curiosity was so little excited that the concert was ill attended: but this single exhibition was sufficient to induce Messrs. Knyvett to relinquish her services, and Madame Mara was heard no more. I was not so lucky (or unlucky) as to hear these her last notes, as it was early in the winter, and I was not in town. [1819: Edgcumbe, p. 77]

2.4.15 Elizabeth Linley, later Mrs Sheridan [b. 1754]

'The voice of Mrs S. was as likely to make lasting Friends as anyone wch perhaps has been bestowed by Nature on a Young Female; not from its great Extension, or from its Force, but from a native Sweetness and true Intonation. Its original Quality was good in point of *Tone*, and steady, in *Tune*. Music was become a Language wch she read with as much facility as her Mother Tongue. And she had so long studied the Oratorios of Handel and so frequently sung the best songs in them that she seemed to execute them with more propriety of Expression than anyone had done before. They were the sounds wch she first lisped in her infancy. There was something so pure, chaste & judicious in her manner of Executing them, that joined to her articulate & correct expression of the Words, seraphic looks, and truely natural & Pathetic Expression, it was impossible for the most enthusiastic admirers of more modern music & Italian refinem^{ts} in singing not to be pleased.' [Jan. 1766: Bur, *Memoirs*, p. 191]

'An angelic voice, of so sweet and delightful a tone and quality that it went at once to the heart; and, combined with her touching expression, produced an effect almost heavenly, and moved every hearer.' [1774: Edgcumbe, p. 148].

'Those who get at the force and meaning of the words, and pronounce them as they sing with the same sensibility and expression, as it would require in speaking, possess an accomplishment in singing beyond what all the art in the world cannot convey, and such, even, when they venture upon cantabiles and cadences, will have better because more natural execution than those who fancy they have reached perfection in singing, by stretching and torturing their voices into mere instruments. Mrs. SHERIDAN and Madam [Gertrud Elizabeth] MARA were, according to my idea, the most accomplished singers I ever heard, because they were taught upon this principle ... Mrs. SHERIDAN having had the advantage of sweetly uttering the words with a native pronunciation, and possessing a voice very little indeed inferior to Madame MARA, must be considered, upon this principle, as the best singer I ever heard.' [Dec. 1803: Dibdin, *Professional Life of Mr Dibdin*, p. 114]

2.4.16 Maddalena Allegranti [b. 1754]

'... had a voice which, though thin, was extremely sweet, of extraordinary compass upwards, and so flexible that she executed with ease very rapid divisions, and consequently indulged in a flowery style of singing, which had the merit of considerable novelty.' [1781: Edgcumbe, p. 26]

'Signora Allegranti, who first appeared at the King's Theatre in 1781, possessed a rich, clear, and powerful soprano voice, of extensive compass, blended with exquisite taste and expression. She was a great favourite with the English public, who bestowed on her universal applause. This charming singer, who exhibited no shake, made her closes with so much elegance and effect, that the most fastidious did not regret the absence of that hitherto essential ornament in singing. What then was not the surprise of the frequenters of the Italian Opera when, at her benefit at the latter end of the season, she, for the first time, displayed in her cadences, &c, a shake the most liquid, brilliant, and perfect imaginable!' [Jan. 1781: Parke, p. 19]

2.4.17 Brigida Georgi Banti [b. 1755]

'... we never heard a voice of more grateful tone, or more constant in tune; or an execution (as far as she attempted bravura) more neat, brilliant, and articulate. The low notes of her voice were mellifluous, rich, and full to an uncommon degree.' [1777: Bur, *Rees's Cyclopædia*]

'Her voice was so expressive, and her intonation so perfect, that she reached, not merely the ear, but penetrated to the heart of every attentive hearer.' [Dec. 1795: Burgh]

'But though she had the best masters, she was an idle scholar, and never would apply to the drudgery of her profession: but in her, genius supplied the place of science, and the most correct ear, with the most exquisite taste, enabled her to sing with more effect, more expression, and more apparent knowledge of her art, than many much better professors. Her natural powers were of the finest description: her voice, sweet and beautiful throughout, had not a fault in any part of its unusually extensive compass. Its lower notes, which reached below ordinary sopranos, were rich and mellow;

the middle, full and powerful; and the very high, totally devoid of shrillness: the whole was even and regular, one of those rich voci di petto, which can alone completely please and satisfy the ear. In her youth it extended to the highest pitch, and was capable of such agility, that she practised and excelled most in the bravura style, in which she had no superior; but losing a few of her upper notes, and acquiring a taste for the cantabile, she gave herself up almost entirely to the latter, in which she had no equal.' [10 Jan. 1797: Edgcumbe, p. 79]

2.4.18   Francesca Le Brun, née Danzi [b. 1756]

'She was young, well-looking, had a voice of uncommon clearness and compass, capable of the most astonishing execution, and was an excellent musician. Yet her performance was unsatisfactory, being too much alla Tedescha[14], and more like that of an instrument than of a human voice. She soon after married Monsieur Lebrun, an eminent player on the hautbois, which confirmed her in the bravura style, as she was in the habit of singing songs with an obligato accompaniment for that instrument, in which the difficulties performed by both were quite astonishing, each seeming to vie with the other which could go highest, and execute the most rapid divisions.' [Dec. 1777: Edgcumbe, p. 9]

'… had a voice well in tune, a good shake, great execution, a prodigious compass, and great knowledge of Music … that the natural tone of her voice is not interesting; that she had never been in Italy, and had been constantly imitating the tone and difficulties of instruments; that her chief labour and ambition had been to surprise, concluding perhaps that wonder however excited includes pleasure … forgetting that she is not a bird in a bush or a cage, and that from a human figure, representing a princess or great personage, it is natural for an audience to expect human passions to be expressed in such tones, and with such art and energy, as will not degrade an individual of our own species, into a being of an inferior order.*' '*In the summer of 1778 she went into Italy and sung at Milan with Pacchierotti], Rubinelli], and the Balducci [possibly Giuseppe Balducci's mother Matilde Minutolo]; and during this journey it was imagined that she would have improved her style of singing; but travelling with her husband [Ludwig August Lebrun], an excellent performer on the hautbois, she seems to have listened to nothing else; and at her return to London she copied the tone of his instrument so exactly, that when he accompanied her in divisions of thirds and sixths, it was impossible to discover who was uppermost.' [October 1778: Bur, *General History*, pp. 508/9]

2.4.19   Aloysia Weber [b. 1760]

'She [Aloysia Weber] sings indeed most admirably and has a lovely, pure voice. The only thing she lacks is dramatic action; were it not for that, she might be the prima donna on any stage. She is only sixteen … She sings most excellently my aria written for De Amicis] with those horribly difficult passages.' [17 Jan. 1778: Wolfgang Mozart, letter to Leopold]

Mozart added in the following month: 'Mlle Weber's singing, on the other hand [as opposed to Caterina Gabrielli's], goes to the heart, and she prefers to sing cantabile'. [19 Feb. 1778: Wolfgang Mozart, letter to Leopold]

---

14   Alla Tedescha = German style

'Mme Lange, formerly Mlle Weber, the prima donna, has a very agreeable voice, which is however too weak for the stage.' [Mar. 1781: Deutsch, p. 194]

2.4.20 Anna Maria Crouch [b. 1763]

'The effect of the new Song entitled, Captivity, a serious Air, sung on Wednesday se'nnight by Mrs. Crouch, at Covent Garden Theatre, was such as threw the Audience into a state of the most exquisite Distress. Several Ladies fainted and were thrown into hysterics; not a dry Eye was to be seen in the whole House.' [Sentimental poem follows, with lines like 'Amidst this sad Captivity! / When as my Babes lie hush'd in sleep, / Their couch in briny tears I steep / Hang o'er their lovely forms and weep'] [2 Mar. 1793: *Ipswich Journal*]

'Mrs Crouch, within these last two years, has made rapid advances towards perfection in her profession. Her voice is not only extensive, but extremely plaintive and melodious: better calculated for the delightful songs of simplicity, than the bravura style; yet she has recently been successful in the latter, as those who have heard her in the Siege of Belgrade, &c. will amply attest.' [Dec. 1795: Haslewood]

A most delightful singer, but considerably decreased of late in power, by what means we know not. There is a plaintive, heart-felt tone in this lady's voice, that we never heard from any other singer since the late Mrs. Sheridan. Her face is, or rather has been beautiful, for of late it is puffed up with bloated flesh, and her person possesses the same appearance of unsound increase. [1795: Waldron, quoted in Highfill et.al., *Biographical Dictionary*, Vol.4]

2.4.21 Elizabeth Billington [b. 1765]

'When I first heard her, in 1783, she was very young and pretty, had a delightful fresh voice of very high compass, and sung with great neatness several songs composed for Allegranti, whom she closely imitated ... Her voice, though sweet and flexible, was not of that full nature which formed the charm of Banti's, but was rather a voce di testa, and in its very high tones resembled a flute or flageolet. Its agility was very great, and every thing she sung was executed in the neatest manner, and with the utmost precision.' [1783: Edgcumbe, p. 90]

'I ... went in the evening with my bro'r Hen'y to 2s. gallery at Covent Garden, to see Robin Hood & the Midnight Hour, in the former of w'ch Mrs Billington sung, whose voice, at the distance we were from the stage sounded uncomonly sweet.' [19 Dec. 1787: Marsh, *Journals*, Vol. 1]

'Her voice is naturally sweet, silvery, light, and brilliant. The chords of this happy organ could not be more finely attuned, but it was possible to attain more body, more volume, and compass. All these advantages it now enjoys. From habit, and perhaps the increase of physical strength, it has acquired that firmness and confidence which give to the organ a full tone and commanding expression ... astonished the audience by its variety of combination, its rapidity of movement, its difficulty, and the ease, delicacy, the various beauties and embellishments of the execution ... It emitted all sounds with the same facility, resembling more, in the truth and precision of its vibrations, some fine piece of mechanism, than the uncertain organ of a human being dependent upon the caprice of will and external operations.' [5 Oct. 1801: MP]

'The powers of this exquisite singer, whose last season is now running, seem in no way impaired by age, except that her voice gets a little reedy.' [19 May 1810: TI]

Waldie's review of Billington ticks all Tosi's boxes: 'was heart melting—in sacred music, tho' she does not go beyond the chaste simplicity & elegance of Mara, yet the powerful swell of her voice & softness of her tones have a charming effect: and in the lively & pathetic strains of miscellaneous music she is far before Mara, while in the Bravura style, she is undoubtedly the finest in the world. Such is her affinity with Handel's music, that every impulse seems to be created sympathetically in her utterance of song—the wonderful compass, equality, & sweetness, & power of her voice, and the astonishing taste, feeling, & ease of execution are beyond everything; while the amazing power of running thro' the longest divisions of above two octaves, together with the width of her chest, which enables her to swell, quaver, shake, or hold a note for an immense time, make her completely perfect—if there is a fault, it is in her voice itself—in which, tho' it is altogether the best in the world, the lower tones are some of them not so round & clear as the remainder of her voice … in "From mighty Kings" was beyond every thing—in the quick part of the tune her execution seemed exactly like the finest pianoforte.' [17 Apr. 1803: Waldie]

2.4.22   Amelie Oldmixon, née George [b. 1768]

'Mrs. Oldmixon's voice is of uncommon extent, being from B below the staff, to A in altissimo: that is, A upon the additional keys of the piano forte [a''']. Her tones are remarkably sweet and fluty, if I may use the expression, and her upper notes resemble staccato passages upon the flageolet. Her taste is exquisite—her ornaments are highly polished—and nothing can be more sweet and touching than her cantabiles.' [4 Apr. 1824: Parker, *A Musical Biography*, p. 191]

2.4.23   Maria Theresa Bland [b. 1769]

'Mrs. Bland has a fine voice, which is never, by aukward straining after bravura, thrown out of tune; her taste in music is pure and natural. Her manner is original; she does not conceive so boldly as others, but she *finishes* her work with greater neatness.—She has the grand secret of locking her notes together, which keeps the web of harmony to the end unbroken.' [1795: Haslewood]
'It was sung by Mrs. Bland, with all the refreshing purity of her unsophisticated style, and with that chaste expression and tenderness of feeling which speak at once as it were to the heart.'   [23 Jan. 1813: Kelly]

2.4.24   Josephina Grassini [b. 1773]

'Signora Grassini is unquestionably a singer of the first order … All her natural tones and modulations are excellent, and it is only when she rises into that which she exclusively possesses … a falsetto, that she is least successful. The transitions are too abrupt; they may surprise, but they cannot delight the ear … In several passages she succeeded in touching the heart.' [14 Jan. 1804: T]

'Was the first female singer who appeared on the Italian theatre with a contralto voice, that part having been previously sustained by men. Her tones, though purely feminine, were so new that they were received with distrust; and some time elapsed before the audience were reconciled to a voice which was thought greatly too low for a woman. Her compass did not exceed ten notes, from A in the bass to C in the treble; but such was their rich and mellow quality, that they formed a new species of delight in the vocal art. Her pathos and feeling became the more evident when contrasted with the cold and fluty tones of Billington.' [1806: Gardiner, *Music of Nature*, p. 134]

2.4.25   Teresa Bertinotti/ Radicati [b. 1776]

'She is a very fine singer, but inferior in powers to Catalani.—The tones of her voice are remarkably sweet and clear; and her cantabile is admirable.' [22 Dec 1809, TI]

'As a singer, Madame Radicati holds the same resemblance to Mrs. Billington. Her voice is exquisitely pure and delicate; and some of the tones are of that touching tenderness, which the ear loves to dwell and hang upon, long after the voice has ceased. In her first songs she was evidently under the embarrassments of a first appearance, and her voice was low and fluttering; but when she was a little excited by applause, and began to exert her powers, she exhibited a perfect knowledge of her art, which delighted the audience. There appears nothing in the scale too difficult for her execution, and she ran the most minute divisions, and sprung from note to note, with a truth of articulation, which could have been produced by nothing but the most delicate fidelity of ear and organ.' [24 Dec 1810: T]

'The voice and taste of Madame Bertinotti are her only recommendations, but they are both of a very superior kind; the former is powerful, melodious, and, what we rarely find, perfectly in tune. Her singing is enriched and decorated with a variety of turns and graces, as tastefully conceived as they are correctly executed. Her only defect, and that but a slight one, is a piercing shrillness in her upper notes, which produces rather an unpleasant sensation on the ear.' [30 Dec. 1810: Ex]

2.4.26   Maria Poole/ Dickons [b. 1778]

'During this winter, I was in some measure instrumental in bringing forward that musical prodigy Miss Poole (afterwards Mrs. Dickons), a child of seven or eight years of age, who sung and played some of Mrs. Billington's bravuras with ease, precision, and comparative power.' [20 Jun. 1784: Bernard, *Retrospections*]

'Miss Poole's person [aged 15!] being of a very delicate texture, may perhaps be the reason why her voice is neither full nor round. Her shake is good; and her throat equally flexible to any divisions that can be run in music…Miss Poole would rank amongst our very first female singers, if her articulation of words were but equal to those of her notes; which defect, perhaps, is owing to the want of proper instruction from a regular singing master, before she had contracted those unconquerable habits.' [27 Oct. 1795: MW]

'shews in this piece [Vauxhall song "row dow dow"] that she is not only a very respectable singer, but also a very elegant and judicious actress; but if she could hear the effect of her good and powerful voice at a distance, she would find that she has no occasion to aim at loudness, which sometimes takes away the higher finish of a passage, or overstrains a note—with the most natural flow of her voice she has power enough.' [3 May 1809: Waldie]

'her singing is far superior to any I have ever heard except from Mara, Billington, or Catalani. She has such taste & expression—a thorough knowledge—& so clear a voice—& such astonishing distinctness & precision. Like Mrs. B. [Billington] her lower notes are indifferent, but her cadences rise to f & g in alt with ease.' [3 May 1809: Waldie]

'Mrs. Dickons is the best we have after Braham, and is perhaps as correct a one as any living; she has also considerable power, and may be called upon the whole a very useful and effective singer, a pitch above mediocrity. By many indeed she is thought to possess a good deal of taste; but this we conceive to be one of the impositions arising from the bravura and florid style. To us, besides her unpleasant reediness of voice, there is a coarse, flaunting air in her very best manner; and on no account should she ever undertake to be fascinating.' [12 Feb 1815: Ex]

'Mrs. DICKONS also, who was a good singer before, is much improved in her tones and powers, though the upper part of her voice is still somewhat harsh and reedy ... And even MRS. DICKONS, with all her sweetness and facility, has not got rid of the old error of overloading an air with ornaments.' [18 Oct. 1818: Ex]

2.4.27 Angelica Catalani [b. 1780]

Gardiner faulted her in some respects: 'as a musician she was below mediocrity'. But he acknowledged her achievement: 'The most splendid vocalist of the age, made her appearance in this country, in the year 1806; and such was her extraordinary power of voice, that it was said, 'place her at the top of St. Paul's, and she will be heard at the Opera House'. 'In compass it extended from A in the bass, to C in alt, every note of which was as firm as the tone of a trumpet. Her middle voice, when subdued, possessed a quality of tone that was delightful; the notes g, a, and b, being produced in a way similar to the tone we make in laughing. The force of her execution was extraordinary; she would run through the scale of semitones with the rapidity of lightning, and jump back again over two octaves at once.' [1806: Gardiner, op. cit., p. 136/7]

'We now speak of a talent in its full maturity, of a voice, which is rare only because it is perfect, and the extent of which surpasses the limits hitherto assigned to the organs of the most fortunate; in one word, of the celebrated Catalani, the most wonderful singer of Europe ... Her voice is equally astonishing both in the low and in the high tones; and is no less remarkable for sweetness and flexibility, than for strength and compass ... She is even a very formidable rival to the most able performers either on wind or stringed instruments. Their most brilliant passages cannot be compared with what Madame Catalani easily executes with her natural voice.' [October 1806: MM, Vol. 22, p. 276]

'Of the compass and capability of her voice, of its sweetness, strength, richness, and modulation, it is almost impossible to give an idea. The highest, the most delicate, and thrilling notes of the musical glasses, she combines with the fullness and grandeur of the organ.' [8 Sep. 1807: MC]

'There is indeed a purity, a clearness, a fulness, in Madame Catalani's voice—while, at the same time, she has a sweetness in her more tender passages, and a melancholy sweetness in her pathetic parts which no human being, who has felt the mysterious influence of music over the mind, can for a moment resist. And although she possesses the qualifications of a bravura singer, she is gifted with a flexibility, a complete command of voice, and a clearness in her divisions, which enable her to introduce the ornaments of music, when necessary, with the most perfect facility—and here it is, that, in the ordering of these ornaments—in the beautiful manner in which they are thrown—in the graceful, but chaste, and sparing hand with which she scatters them—and in the taste with which they are blended with the subject of the song, that we think, perhaps, the brightest excellence of Madame Catalani may be discovered.' [19 Jan. 1822: YG]

John Marsh initially praised her: 'With respect to Mad'm Catalani I was much pleased with her as an opera singer, as besides being a good singer, with great powers of voice, & execution, she was an excellent actress, & therefore appeared on that stage to greater advantage than Mrs. B[llington]. She had also another advantage in being the only singer there worth attending to, or to whom the audience seemed to think it worth while to attend, being in fact the only one whose voice made its way through the accomp'ts of the powerful opera band. But at a concert or selection I co'd not help thinking Mrs. Billington wo'd appear to equal advantage from singing in a greater variety of styles, as in Handel's music, glees, &c.- Catalani had however some of Braham's] tricks of running up & down in half notes & skipping from the top of her voice to the bottom, which certainly excited.' [10 May 1807: Marsh, Vol.2, p. 101] But Marsh qualified his views sixteen years later: 'The principal singers at this performance [of Messiah at St. Paul's Church, Southsea] were Catalani (who shouted away as usual).' [30 Aug. 1823: Marsh, Vol.2, p. 352]

'Never did we hear Madame Catalani to better advantage than in the air of Handel's "Angels ever bright and fair". We were at a loss which to admire the most, viz. the volume of tone, or the exquisite taste and feeling with which she executed her part; her close shake was of the first class and order.' [27 Sep. 1828: YG]

'So much had been said of her [Angelica Catalani] falling off, and of the failure of her voice, that I was most agreeably surprised at finding how little change there was in her, and how well she had retained her powers during so long a period, and when arrived to at least middle age. It was, indeed, still beyond any other younger voice. She said herself that she had lost some of its upper notes; but, she added, she had gained in expression what she had lost in compass, and therefore was, on the whole, a gainer. This was, indeed, true … [Singing described. 'God save the King' and 'Rule Britannia' 'electrified and enraptured the audience'.] In myself, it excited feelings with wh ch music had long ceased to inspire me: it was impossible to restrain them. It may seem strange that in her latter years she should please me more than in the most brilliant part of her career. But so it was; and I now found out that, although at that time I liked her less than some of her predecessors, I now liked her better than most of her successors. The last notes I ever heard from her were in my own house, accompanying herself on the pianoforte, in some beautiful little Italian canzonets.' [1 Oct. 1828: Edgcumbe, p. 199]

2.4.28 Bellochi, Georgia [b. 1784]

'… though a good singer and actress in comic operas, was not pleasing from the coarseness of her voice and plainness of her person … She however surprised the public towards the close of her engagement by her excellent performance of the part of Tancredi, for which nothing could be less suited than her figure; but the music was well adapted to her voice, and her singing it was really so good as to make her appearance of no consequence.' [1 Apr. 1817: Edgcumbe, p. 137]

'Madame BELLOCHI's voice possesses a very extensive compass, and the quality of tone is generally very good; in the lower notes it is rich and powerful; in the higher, clear and soft; about the middle it is sometimes rather harsh; nor does it, on the whole, possess that mellifluous sweetness, which, in Fodor, was so irresistibly fascinating.' [26 Jan. 1819: TI]

'Her voice is powerful, sweet, and of great compass; her articulation clear; her divisions of extraordinary ease and flexibility; her expression distinct and to the purpose, though leaning perhaps to the side of force than beauty.' [31 Jan. 1819: Ex]

'Signora Bellochi I recollect once seeing at Florence—she is lively but plain & a coarse voice.' [24 Mar 1821: Waldie]

2.4.29 Violante Camporese [b. 1785]

'The singing pleased us more than the acting; there was throughout a purity of intonation and expression, and a total absence of all meretricious ornament: it is just what singing should be; it makes us forget the mechanism, and think only of the feeling of the passage.' [8 June 1817: Ex]

'Her singing [Madame Camporese], which though always beautiful, used, to our taste, to be occasionally too hard and glassy, seems to have got rid of this fault.' [18 Mar. 1821: Ex]

'She [Camporese] is a capital musician, with a powerful & sweet voice from the breast of a full and rich tone—with no great powers of force, but admirably neat execution. I own I prefer the clear sweet voice and lovely expression of Morandi, tho' Camporese is younger and has more power, and is also very elegant and a charming actress.' [16 Mar. 1822: Waldie]

'Of Camporese's voice, and manner of singing, it may be said of the former, if not of the very finest quality, [it] is extremely agreeable, of sufficient power and compass, and capable of considerable agility: and of the latter, that it is regulated by good taste, and is full of feeling and expression.' [Apr. 1825: Edgcumbe, p. 142]

2.4.30 Angela Isabella Colbran, Mrs Rossini [b. 1785]

'… her voice is exquisite, and her clearness, intonation, and execution are delightful; she has also more feeling than I had supposed.' [31 Jan. 1817: Waldie]

'But we cannot authenticate his [Stendhal's] strictures upon her [Madame Colbran Rossini's] singing by the experiments we have witnessed in England. She exceeds in the delivery of her tone (portamento di voce) any and every female we recollect … There are as few inequalities in her singing as in that of any prima donna we ever heard.' [Mar. 1824: QMMR, p. 56]

'The deportment* of the voice—the purity and uniformity of the tone—the noble simplicity of the declamation--the accurate articulation both of syllables and sounds—the gradual melting and assimilation of tone from the most powerful messa di voce to the softest pianissimo—always in keeping and never violent—the retention of legitimate and the rejection of meretricious ornament—and lastly, the power of bending all these elements to the changeful purposes of expression, declare at once the mind, the training, and the experience of the gifted artist. When we first heard [Benedetta Rosmunda] Pisaroni we felt as when we first heard Colbran. Both were in the decline of their powers—but both in an instant demonstrated that time, the friend of science, the enemy of nature, was alone to blame. *Footnote: We use this term to avoid the double and mixed sense of the word portamento, which, in Burney's time, was always used for the free and pure delivery of the tone.' [June 1828: QMMR, p. 269]

2.4.31   Eliza Salmon [b. 1787]

A personal friend of Eliza Salmon wrote: 'There was something in the musical-glass-like tone of her voice that went at once to the soul; something in the exquisite brilliancy and facility of her passing shake, that not only procured a willing pardon for all faults, but made the hearer doubt whether what would have been musical sins in other less-gifted singers, partook of the nature of sin in Mrs. Salmon. She seldom appeared to be imbued with any deep feeling herself, while one tone of her clear mellow voice would draw a tear from many a stern eye, or drive him who was too proud to weep to the resource of his snuff-box.' [1814: NMM]

'[Eliza Salmon's voice] possesses neither extraordinary compass nor volume; and though it is more inclining to the thin than to the rich class, yet it resembles no other voice that we ever remember to have heard, but comes perhaps the nearest to the tone of the musical glasses, if we can imagine that sound to be somewhat thinned and refined.' [June 1820: QMMR, p. 196]

'Yet we think there is no song [Recit 'Ye Sacred Priests' and Air 'Farewell! Ye limpid springs and floods'] in which, in addition to those exquisite sensations of physical pleasure that her silvery tones awaken, she takes deeper hold of the affections than in this, which is not of a character to require a greater volume of voice than she possesses.' [June 1822: Crosse, *Grand Musical Festival*, p. 262]

'Nature had lavished upon her a voice, extensive, sweet, and powerful, with a warbling flexibility never attained by art. Her tones were not only pure, but rich; and the manner in which she threw them out gave them a liquidity that steeped the ear with delight. Her voice partook more of the powers of an instrument than of a singer, especially when unshackled by words, to which, in fact, she paid but little attention. Her object was tone, with execution, and in this respect she surpassed every other performer. Her voice had all the colour of the rainbow, and her great faculty was that of adapting the colour of her tones to the note she had to perform: naturally warm, her notes had a refulgent glow; yet she could cool them down to the mild ray of a moonbeam. Depending upon these superior gifts, she was careless to a fault in her mode of using her words; in this respect she was more to be censured than admired. Her power of sustaining a note was remarkable; and the neat manner in which she recovered her breath was an example to all singers. Her execution was delicate and felicitous; and her fancy unbounded. That beautiful ornament, the shake, sparkled in her voice with all the lustre of a diamond; and though lavish in the use of it, she never abated the first sensations of delight.' [March 1823: Gardiner, *Music of Nature*, p. 133/4]

'When I hear such a singer as Miss Stephens or Mrs. Salmon, the power of ductility seems carried to its utmost. There are no roughnesses, no breaks—the metal is drawn out exactly, and if we could run it along between the finger and the thumb, or pass the nail over the surface, it would be as even, as smooth, and as polished to the touch as it is brilliant to the ear.' [Mar. 1823: QMMR, p. 193]

2.4.32   Miss Tennant, later Mrs Vaughan [b. 1788]

'I. The qualities of VOICE are Tone and Compass.—Of Tone, the requisites seem clearness, strength, and richness: clearness, as opposed to whatever is thick or husky; strength, to tenuity and tremulousness; richness, to meagreness or harshness. I am far from considering these as all the modifications, good and bad, of which tone is susceptible: there are many others. Nothing, for instance, can be more distinguishable than the ready terseness of [Nancy] Storace's voice, the luscious sweetness of Miss Tennant's, or the smooth flow of Mrs. [Anna Maria] Crouch's.' [Oct. 1802: EM, Vol. 42, p. 283]

'Upon the merits of Mrs Vaughan, as this was her first appearance in the county, we should be willing to descant largely, whether we spoke of the rich mellowness and extreme correctness of her tones, or the pathos with which she executed the various parts allotted for her; but the circumscribed limits of a weekly paper, preclude us from gratifying our wishes; we must be contented therefore with adding, that she was the favorite, nor was her unassuming manner unnoticed by a Cornish audience, an audience which so well knows how to encourage modest merit. Mrs. Vaughan was repeatedly encored, even so as to distress her.' [23 Sep. 1809: *Royal Cornwall Gazette*]

'The air and chorus of "The marvellous work", &c. gave Mrs. Vaughan an opportunity of displaying with scientific effect her chaste and pleasing powers: her voice was sweet and clear, and her execution perfect.' [23 Oct. 1813: *Northampton Mercury*]

2.4.33   Ester Mombelli [b. 1792]

'By comparison, when Ester Mombelli sang the same passage [aria from the finale sung by Cenerentola to Don Magnifico and the Ugly Sisters] in Florence in 1818, it did indeed degenerate into the most shameless *bravura*, dignified only by the rare technical excellence of the performer. I have never heard anything clearer, more crystalline, than this exquisite voice of Signorina Mombelli, trained in all the ingenious graces of the old school; but it was like listening to a display of academic virtuosity; nor did it ever seem to occur to anyone to wonder about the motives which *might* have been stirring in Cinderella's breast, and which were most certainly *not* stirring in the music as rendered.' [Dec. 1818: Stendhal, p. 260]

'Signora Mombelli, the Coquette, is a most charming and natural actress—and sweet singer, very expressive and with much taste and flexibility.' [22 Nov 1819: Waldie]

2.4.34 Miss Carew [b. 1799]

'… the melting, but confined sweetness of whose tones, comes floating upon the listening sense, the essence of all we feel or dream of what is tender and delightful. The applause that constantly attends the singing of Miss Carew, replete with pathos, simplicity, and beauty, has never been more worthily bestowed.' [20 Jul. 1816: TI]

'This lady's voice is a clear, powerful, and sweet soprano, of considerable compass, which has been formed and cultivated in the purest school; her performance is rather remarkable for a fascinating simplicity, a depth of feeling, and a correctness of taste, than for a brilliancy of execution … Her style of singing bears a closer resemblance to that of Miss Stephens], than of any performer we could name; and this naturally arises from that lady having been constantly before her, nor could she have chosen a better model. It is somewhat remarkable, that her voice, too, bears a great resemblance to that of Miss Stephens, and this is as observable in her speaking as in her singing.' [7 Jul. 1818: TI]

'But the powers of her gentle fluty voice are hardly equal to the bravura style.' [16 Apr. 1821: Ex]

'But Miss Carew's voice is deficient (and in that particular comparatively), in volume alone, for it is well toned and well formed. Her ductility is truly admirable; there are no breaks or flaws in the tone.' [December 1823: QMMR, p. 477]

2.5 Reviews of Other Male Singers in the Long Eighteenth Century

Professional tenors and basses were certainly common through the baroque period. But there can be little question that they were overshadowed by the exploits of the castrati, which could explain why ear-witness accounts of tenor and bass vocalists during the high and late baroque periods are relatively rare. However, a good number of male singers earned distinction from around 1780 onwards, at a time when castrato singing was in decline. Like their female counterparts, male voices ranged from naturally loud to soft. Those completing their careers during the long eighteenth century are listed at Illus. 16.

2.5.1 John Beard [b. 1716]

'He [*fl*.1737-67; not included in Illus. 16] knew as much of music as was necessary to sing a single part at sight; and with a voice that was more powerful than sweet, he became the most useful and favourite singer of his time, on the stage, at Ranelagh, at all concerts, and in Handel's oratorios he had always a capital part; because by his knowledge of music the most steady support of the chorusses, not only of Handel, but in the odes of Green and Boyce.' [Bur, *Rees's Cyclopædia*]

2.5.2 Charles Bannister [b. 1741]

'Bannister could take off Tenducci very exactly, and had performed Arionelli both songs and dialogue in falsetto, yet he did not disguise his natural voice either in speaking or singing when he acted Polly; nor, except in holding up his train rather too high when he went off the stage sometimes, did he seem wilfully to burlesque the character—when he sang the songs all was silent attention and the travestie was forgotten; he sang them all in his finest style, and the serious ones in the most pathetic.' [1760: Genest, *Some Account*]

'His voice, uniting, in extraordinary perfection, the extremes of a deep bass and high-toned falsetto, and his ear, which was of great delicacy and perfection, enabled him not only to execute pieces of ordinary description, but to represent, with great humour, and without the grossness of burlesque or caricature, many leading performers of the day, both male and female. These displays first took place at the Haymarket, Foote having given means for introducing them into "The Orators"; they were soon very celebrated; and when Mr. Garrick took Giardini to examine Bannister's imitations of Tenducci and Champneys, the composer declared the likenesses perfect, with only one fault,—that the voice of the mimic was better than that of either of the performers.' [1760: John Adolphus, *Memoirs of John Bannister*]

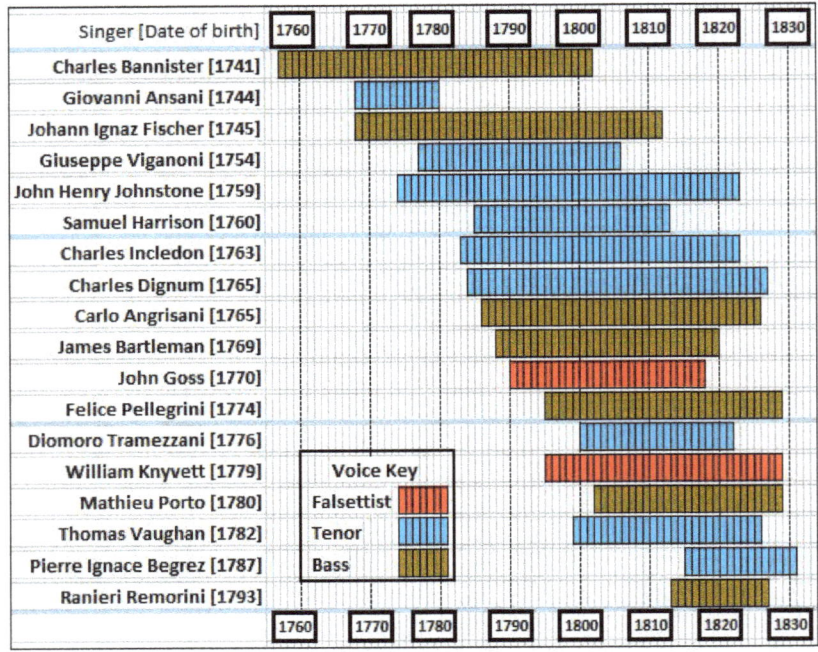

Illus. 16: Careers of the Best Male Singers [non castrati]

2.5.3 Giovanni Ansani [b. 1744]

'He has an excellent tenor voice; is tall, thin, and of a good figure; he accompanied himself on the harpsichord, in several songs, in which he manifested not only great taste and expression, in slow movements, but great neatness in the quick; for he is able to execute, in bravura airs, the most rapid passages. His style is serious, and I never heard a better singer of his sort. He has a great compass of voice, with much strength and sweetness; his shake is a little too close, otherwise I should venture to pronounce him, a perfect tenor singer.' [12 Oct. 1772: Bur, *The Present State ... Germany*, Vol.I, p.

278]

'This performer had a finely toned, full, and commanding voice.' [Dec. 1779: Edgcumbe, p. 18]

2.5.4 Johann Ignaz Fischer [b. 1745]

'Certainly has an excellent bass voice (in spite of the fact that the Archbishop told me that he sang too low for a bass and that I assured him that he would sing higher next time), we must take advantage of it, particularly as he has the whole Viennese public on his side … Osmin's rage is rendered comical by the use of the Turkish music. In working out the aria I have (in spite of our Salzburg Midas) allowed Fischer's beautiful deep notes to glow.' [26 Sep. 1781: Wolfgang Mozart to Leopold, *Letters*, p. 768]

Illus. 17: Passage sung by Johann Ignaz Fischer

'The celebrated German base, Fischer, senior, for whom Mozart wrote the parts of *Sarastro*, in the *Zauberflote*, and *Osmin*, in the *Seraglio*, was in England in 1794, and sang at the Ancient. The extent of Fischer's voice below exceeded that of any base that has been heard in England, or perhaps in any country, either before or since his time; in Winter's *Maria von Montalban* there is a song written for him which contains the above passage [Illus. 17].' [Dec. 1794: Har]

2.5.5 Giuseppe Viganoni [b. 1754]

'On his second arrival in London, he had less voice than when he came here first; but more knowledge of music, a greater variety of embellishments, and more use of the stage. His voice was never powerful, and now he had more falset than real notes in his scale; and such a rage for gracing and changing passages, that he scarcely ever let the audience hear a single passage as it was written by the composer. He certainly knew his business, and was a good musician; but his style of singing was what painters would call *maniera*: for with all his *riffioramenti*, or embellishments, of which he was so lavish, his performance seemed monotonous.' [1796: Bur, *Rees's Cyclopædia*]

'… was most flatteringly received. His voice, though not powerful, is of the sweetest tenor kind, equally flexible to all the tender modulations, as to the most rapid divisions. His "Io parto mio bene!" was given with wonderful expression.' [15 Mar, 1685: from *Theatrical Cutting*, quoted by Fenner]

'From this time [1800] Viganoni took the part of first man, and continued to fill that station, for which he was well qualified, both as singer and actor, during the remainder of Banti's stay, and for some seasons after. His voice was not very strong, nor of a superior tone or quality, but he was an excellent musician, had good taste, and considerable versatility of talent, singing both in the serious and comic opera, and rendering himself generally useful. He must be considered as a performer of great merit.' [1800: Edgcumbe, p. 82]

'… would sing well if he had a voice.' [21 May 1803: Waldie]

'... was a very sweet and polished chamber singer, and was probably heard to more advantage in a concert room than in a theatre.' [Sep. 1826: QMMR, p. 339]

2.5.6   John Henry Johnstone [b. 1759]

'He is much esteemed as a singer, and his falsetto is generally allowed to be pleasingly expressive; but there is a sudden transition from his feigned to his natural voice, that renders it extremely harsh and disagreeable to a fine ear. We mention this as a defect that is easily cured ... Both his natural and feigned voices are excellent, but so totally different, and separated by such a chasm, that when he passes from the one to the other, it is as if an organist leapt at once from the open diapason to the small flute stop. This defect is highly reprehensible, because it is evidently curable. Were he to employ some time every day in sol-fa-ing, the gulf would soon be filled up, and a smooth, connected, and uncommonly extensive voice obtained. / Such practice, too, would improve him in other respects. His volubility and expression would receive that improvement which they want. He would be induced to pay more attention to time. He would learn, in ad libitum passages, to introduce something like a cadence, instead of a protracted scream. He would soon be the most powerful English singer, and enjoy that applause from taste and judgment, which he now receives chiefly from prejudice and ignorance.' [June 1784: Oxberry, Vol. 4, p. 77]

'Before his time [John Braham], the junction had always been very clumsily conducted by English singers. Johnstone, who had a fine falsette, managed it so badly, that he obtained, from the abruptness of his transitions, the cognomen of "Bubble and Squeak".' [31 Jul. 1821: LMag]

'Johnstone had one note (E in alt.) which he took very clearly in his falsetto. It was his delight to dwell on that tone an unconscionable time; so much so, that Suett told Erskine that the Prince once coming into his box whilst Johnstone was at his favourite exercise, turned to his friend, and said, "I verily believe he has held that note ever since we were here last".' [Dec. 1835: NMM]

2.5.7   Samuel Harrison [b. 1760]

'Harrison, the first apostle of this school [the Ecclesiastical and Orchestral School] was very limited in his powers, but his style was the most perfect specimen of the true cantabile an English singer has ever exhibited. Tone is the most indescribable of all attributes, for if we say it is rich, brilliant, and sweet, even to lusciousness, we appeal to other senses which have little analogy with hearing. Such, however, was his tone. Though deficient in power, it filled the ear; it satisfied the sense. Smoothness and exquisite polish, a purity of taste that rejected all but the most chaste and appropriate ornaments, the extremest accuracy of intonation, were his perfections.' [Reference date 1791: NMM, Vol. 2, 1833]

'As a singer, Mr. Harrison may justly be ranked the first tenor performer of the age. His voice is weak, but exquisitely sweet. His ear is perfect, and his intonation just. His shake is delightful, and his cadences masterly. Mr. Harrison's greatest excellence is in pathetic music, in which he stands unrivalled; though he now and then out-steps the bounds of nature, by attempting songs of spirit and hilarity, in which he cannot succeed for want of energy and power.' [19 Nov. 1795: MW]

'The CHEF D'OEVRE of the day, however, was HARRISON's "Total Eclipse". It was rather *spoken* with the most affecting energy than *sung*, and rivetted the attention of all present.' [2 Jun. 1796: *Derby Mercury*]

'the beautiful song of Total Eclipse, which was well suited to the polished smooth tones of his voice, which tho' not very extensive is very equal, round, & sweet, & has great expression, but there is a sameness and sometimes a want of animation in his singing: in some songs, however, he can forcibly move the passions.—The three choruses of the first act, "Oh first created beam"—"Fixed in his everlasting seat"—and "God save the King" from the Coronation anthem were all so grand & affecting that I don't know which to prefer … Harrison's voice is however, I think, the best; it is a sweet medium between the soft tones of Knyvett and the powerful notes of Bartleman.' [17 Apr. 1803: Waldie]

'Though every sound in Harrison's singing was delivered with the most exquisite polish, every note as pure and bright as globes of glass, producing a delicious sensation upon the ear that I have never heard since, still Bartleman was my delight.' [1810: Gardiner, *Music and Friends*, Vol. 2, p. 642]

Bacon described his voice: 'It must yet be admitted to have been pure in the most complete sense of the term … If we may be permitted to compare the human voice to any known instrument, we should certainly say, that Mr. Harrison's in some measure resembled the richest and deepest sounds of the musical glasses, well played, in a good room, and the analogy is brought nearer by the way in which the tone was produced. The performer on the glasses gives birth to his melody by a touch that apportions the gradations from soft to loud and from loud to soft again, in the finest possible manner.' Bacon concluded on a hypnotically soothing note: 'No passion ruffles, no violence disturbs the smooth and delightful flow. It falls upon the ear like the light of a summer's moon upon the eye, soft and soothing, while the balm of the air through which it glides, seems but a part of the sensation itself awakens.' [March 1818: QMMR, p. 81]

2.5.8   Charles Benjamin Incledon [b. 1763]

'On the West India station he changed his ship, and served on board the Raisonable, of sixty-four guns, then commanded by Lord Hervey, where his vocal powers and sprightliness of character endeared him to the officers and men. In this ship he attracted the notice of Admiral Pigot, commander of the fleet, who frequently sent for Incledon, and sang catches and glees with him and Admiral Hughes … Incledon's voice was of extraordinary power, both in the natural and falsetto. The former, from A to G, a compass of about fourteen notes, was full and open, neither partaking of the reed nor the string, and sent forth without the smallest artifice; and such was its ductility, that when he sung *pianissimo*, it retained its original ductility. His falsetto, which he could use from D to E or F, or about ten notes, was rich, sweet, and brilliant, though we certainly are of opinion that music like beauty, "unadorned adorned the most".' [Reference date 1782: *Gentleman's magazine*, Vol.96., Part 1, 1826 Obituary]

'He [Rauzzini] went behind the scenes, took Incledon by the hand, and said, "Sare, I sank you for ze pleasure you af give me; you vas de fus Ingleesh singer I have hear, vat can sing. Sare, you af got a voice—you af got a voice" … The latter [Rauzzini] did not scruple to declare at the Club [the recently formed Bath Catch Club], on the ensuing night, that he had never heard such power, flexibility, sweetness, and fulness, with so rich a falsetto, in any voice, of any country whatever. "Shentleman", said he, "it vas vat I call one natural corioss" (—ity).' [20 Jun. 1784: Bernard, *Retrospections*]

'But Incledon was splendidly gifted by nature; his voice was not only powerful, rich, and *ductile* as gold, but his falsetto was more exquisitely toned than that of any singer we ever heard…His pronunciation was thick, and affected by something like a lisp, which proceeded from a roll of his too large tongue, when he prepared for a forcible passage, or was embarrassed by the word. In this way, too, he used to jump to his falsetto by octaves, for the tone (it was that of a rich flute) was so widely different from his natural voice, there could be no junction. His singing was at once natural and national.' [Reference date 1790: NMM, Vol. 2, 1833, p. 254]

'… had a fine manly voice, with a singular and glib sweetness in the upper tones, and a certain broad strength, not of the most tasteful kind, in the lower…The vulgarity of his style, especially in it's tendency to the extremes of sweetness and strength, was relieved in these characters by an idea of sea hardihood and sincerity, so as to become in it's very prominence subjected to something higher than itself … He would be as nice and delicate as he could manage when he was in a piece of falsetto, but he appeared to seize with triumph the first opportunity of escaping, and if the end in particular of the song gave him the least encouragement, would dash out into a sort of splay-footed uproariousness quite defying.' [30 Mar. 1817: Ex]

2.5.9   Charles Dignum [b. 1765]

'Mr. Dignum made his debut at Drury Lane Theatre in October 1783, in the character of Young Meadows, in the comic opera of Love in a Village. His figure was indeed rather unfavourable for the part he represented; but his voice was clear and full toned, and his manner of singing so judicious and masterly, that he was received with the warmest applause. He then appeared in Cymon, and again experienced the most flattering approbation. This character has since been given to other hands; but those who witnessed Mr. Dignum's performance of it, have reason to lament that he should have relinquished it. On the removal of [Charles] Bannister, sen. [senior] to the Royalty Theatre, Mr. Dignum succeeded to a cast of parts more suited to his person and voice, which is a fine tenor; amongst others, Hawthorn and Giles. The latter character he has performed this season, in a manner superior to any thing since the days of Beard, who was its original representative … Besides his engagement at the Theatre, Mr. Dignum sings during the summer months at Vauxhall Gardens, and contributes much to maintain the reputation of that agreeable place of public recreation. He is also a welcome guest at public dinners, and never fails to augment the harmless stock of pleasure attendant on such meetings. The conviviality of his disposition, and the excellence of his talents, have raised him many friends and admirers, as the crowded benches of Drury Lane, at his benefit, amply testify.' [Dec. 1798: EM]

'Dignum's songs are this year admirably suited to his peculiarly sweet voice.' [31 Jul. 1801: MM, p. 59]

'The elegant Song of Mr. Spenser—The Three Blessings of this World—'Wife, Children and Friends',—was sung by Mr. Dignum to a few simple notes with such charms of intonation, truth and feeling, as to produce a rapturous encore.' [22 Dec 1804: MC]

Reviewers differed on the quality of his falsetto: 'Dignum has a tenor voice, which he has very much injured, by singing in what is called the falsetto, and by which he has not only destroyed the power, but also the compass of his natural voice, the tone of which does not mix well with an orchestra; but in a room, without music, he is often delightful. He has knowledge enough to take a part in a catch, or a glee.' [27 Oct. 1795: MW] 'He possesses a counter-tenor of some power and sweetness.' [20 Jan 1808: TI]

'There was also a difference of opinion as to the quality of his voice. F. G. Waldron, a fellow performer writing anonymously in *Candid and Impartial Strictures on the Performers Belonging to the … Theatres* (1795), was unmerciful but may have had personal motives: "This Gentleman's voice has very little resemblance of those notes which generally come from an English singer. His tones are mostly like those of a cracked reed, but possess occasionally a *fatness* of sound if we may so express ourselves, that are certainly in unison with the *doughy* bulk and flabby appearance of his person, but are not very pleasing to the ear of a British audience. As far as these defects admit, in tender plaintive airs he is heard with some pleasure".' [1795: Highfill, Burnim and, Langhans] However, Joseph Haslewood would have agreed that Dignum's voice suffered from low larynx emission: 'His voice is a soft agreeable tenor, but rendered somewhat unpleasant by being formed too much in his throat' [1795: Haselewood, V1, p. 272] The *Monthly Mirror* was similarly dismissive: 'To this respectful style of acting, Mr. Dignum now adds a sort of singing that is equally laughable. It is said that his vocal powers are agreeable in a room—a dining room of course, and we should suppose before dinner, for after, when he comes to the theatre, he seems so full that his voice can scarcely find utterance, and what we do hear resembles most correctly the tones produced by Punch through the medium cf a comb.' [4 Nov. 1807: MM, p. 349]

2.5.10 Carlo Angrisani [b. 1765]

'[Giuseppe] Naldi has long been in possession of the part of Figaro; and though he imparted an exquisite degree of humor to the character his voice has for this long time, been unequal to the fine music of this opera; he used to play Figaro well, but to slur over the music wretchedly. Angrisani has succeeded him; and the fine, full sostenuto bass of his voice has given full effect to all the fine music of this part. We never heard "Non piu andrai", sung so well; his opening duett "cinque, die ci", was likewise given with peculiar spirit; and in all the concerted pieces, the power and richness of his voice produced a charming effect fine, full sostenuto bass of his voice has given full effect to all the fine music of this part.' [13 Mar. 1819: TI]

'The depth and purity of Angrisani's tones gave a richness to all the music in which he bore a part, and of this quality Placci, a useful performer in his proper sphere, has nothing.' [6 Jan 1823: T]

'The Italian base voices appear to me incomparably finer than those of most English base singers, for example, those of Signors Angrisani and Remorini.' [30 Sep. 1825: QMMR, p. 281]

'His firm and powerful voice arrested, from the very first, the attention of the audience … Angrisani's voice, as far as we can judge from what we have heard, is much more remarkable for its sonorous force and fulness, than for flexibility or rapid execution; but every body knows that these qualities are nearly incompatible, and are not to be found united, to any extent, in any living singer, with the exception, perhaps, of [Filippo] Galli, De Rivis [Nicolas-Prosper Dérivis], and La Blache [Luigi Lablache].' [28 Feb. 1826: *New-York Review*]

2.5.11   James Bartleman [b. 1769]

'His voice was a rich and powerful bass, extending from f below the line to f above it: the upper part was not inferior in quality and evenness of tone to that of Harrison; while the lower was full and reedy. His note upon G was as clear and as well defined as the third string of a violoncello. With a quick and lively imagination, he entered at once into the spirit of every thing he sang. His enunciation was bold and intrepid. In the recitative, '*I rage, I burn, the feeble god hath stabb'd me to the heart*', his manner had all the force of elocution, added to the power of song.'   [Oct. 1788: Gardiner, *Music of Nature*, p. 113]

'… had a compass of more than two octaves, and the tone was as penetrating as that of a violoncello, from which instrument perhaps he caught it, for it bore more resemblance to the clear, vibratory, yet stringy effect of [Robert] Lindley's bass than anything else. Bartleman, too, was himself a violoncello player, which adds force to the opinion.'   [1 Oct. 1788: NMM]

'This remarkable baritone not only possessed the utmost purity and roundness of tone, but manifested an amount of feeling in his interpretation of the older masters which I believe, without desiring to be a laudator temporis acti, has never since been rivalled, not even by Santley.' [1818: Cox, p. 26]

2.5.12   John Jeremiah Goss [b. 1770]

'Mr. Goss has a fine toned Contra alto, which was heard to great advantage, particularly in the song, "Thou shall bring them in", from Israel in Egypt.' [27 Oct. 1810: LM]

'He was much admired as a singer, his voice being, not as is frequently the case, a falsetto, but a genuine countertenor of beautiful quality: his taste in part-singing was both chaste and elegant.' [1827: *Dictionary of Musicians*]

2.5.13   Felice Pellegrini [b. 1774]

'The *cavatina* [from Rossini's *La Gazza ladra*], sung by the Podestà: / *Il mio piano è preparato* / is a brilliant show-piece for a first-rate bass voice…Pellegrini, who sings it in Paris, serves the requirements of the opera as a whole much better by exploiting every facet of the delicacy and miraculous gracefulness of which his delightful voice is capable.' [1824: Stendhal, p. 281]

'His voice is a baritone, not of great strength, but just sufficient for our vast theatre [King's Theatre], sonorous and melodious, including some good tenor-notes, precisely what the part of Figaro requires, and what Remorini's Figaro wanted. Besides these advantages, Signor Pellegrini possesses great flexibility and modulation in his vocal intonation, and a very superior degree of musical knowledge … There is a slight lisp in his articulation, an imperfection occasionally found in bass voices.' [11 Mar. 1826: NMM, p. 151]

'... voice is dull in its tone, and wants that vibratory quality which at once pierces the ear and stirs the fancy ... In point of intonation he is more than equal to Italian singers in general ... We may conclude our notice with a few observations upon the nature of the ornaments Signor Pellegrini introduces, as well as upon the places to which he appends his rifioramenti. With respect to both it appears to us he has somewhat enlarged the range of his department. His graces are certainly more varied, and have less of the rolling and rumbling peculiar to bases (but which it has been the endeavour and the praise of modern composers and singers to lighten and amend) than we are accustomed to hear. They partake more of the nature of tenor passages, which they emulate in lightness of execution.' [Mar. 1826: QMMR, p. 50]

'Signor Pellegrini had too much of European mobility about him; his frame never stood still, and even when the feet were fixed, the body would move or hang on one side or another. In a Turk of quality, gravity is essential to the *bon genre*, and any symptoms of vivacity are held to be *contra bonos mores*. But this is all the fault we can find with Signor Pellegrini's personification of Noradino. His singing was delightful, his voice, although not very powerful, filled the house sufficiently to be heard in every part, and its sonorous sweetness, its fine modulation and uncommon flexibility, charmed every hearer. We never witnessed a better style of bass-singing, or an organ of that description execute divisions and the more delicate vocal figures with such ease, fluency, effect, and correctness.' [1 May 1826: NMM, p. 192]

'Pellegrini, although he begins to grow old, still preserves a pure voice, susceptible of much colouring. We have never met with any singer who possesses in such a high degree of perfection the art of swelling and sustaining the sound ...' [Mar. 1828: QMMR, p. 29]

2.5.14 Diomiro Tramezzani [b. 1776]

'... he [Giuseppe Siboni]was succeeded by Tramezzani, one of the most agreeable tenors I ever remember to have heard...His voice was of the sweetest quality, of that rich, touching, cremona tone peculiar to the Italians, and his singing, if not of the first order, or very scientific, was always pleasing, and full of expression.' [Dec. 1806: Edgcumbe, p. 102]

'a tenor singer of superior talent to any that has appeared on the Opera stage, Braham excepted, since the days of [Giuseppe] Viganoni; indeed there is some resemblance in his style to both these performers, having the force of the former without his execution, and the tenderness of Viganoni without his delicacy. His figure is manly, his action dignified, and his voice possesses a rich mellowness and strength of tone, rarely to be met with, and superior to that of any Italian singer now in the country.' [2 Jul. 1809: Ex]

'Moderately full, but round and voluptuously smooth, mingling tender expostulation (merely sensual) with a melting and passionate intimation of his design.' [Dec. 1821: QMMR, p. 408]

2.5.15 William Knyvett [b. 1779]

'Sprung from a family long eminent in the higher walks of the profession, his father filling the station of organist of the Chapels Royal, Mr. William Knyvett was early initiated into its duties and delights.

From 1788, the first year in which the names of the performers were printed, he appears as one of the treble chorus at the Concerts of Antient Music, occasionally taking the principal parts. In 1795 he was transferred to the ranks of the counter-tenor, and sang in that year "*Jehovah crown'd*", which used to be allotted to Mr. Dyne; yet it was not until 1799, in which year also we have seen him engaged at Gloucester, that his name was classed with those of the principal performers, where it has ever since held a conspicuous place … Small as is the comparative space occupied by the possessor of a counter-tenor voice, Mr. K. has filled it for a quarter of a century, almost exclusively; and though but too deficient in power, like all modern voices of this class, his elegance and polish have given a zest to one species of composition at least, the glee, that is peculiarly English, and which we earnestly hope, will not be suffered by English audiences to be permanently banished from its native soil. Dr. Callcott's exquisite glee, "*With sights, sweet rose*", was written expressly for the range of Mr. K.'s voice, the falsetto of which extends about nine notes from C to D, and does indeed, most beautifully display its sweet and brilliant tones, without requiring more force than he can effectively bestow. In the class of oratorio songs, which, from their more frequent occurrence in the older works, as well as from their character, seem to have been written for performers of a coarser and stronger description than those of later years, the delicacy of Mr. K's voice and his limited physical powers have, perhaps, operated against the production of any very commanding effect in general; yet we were agreeably surprised to hear it so much more distinctly, in the vast area of York Minster, than could possibly have been anticipated' [Sep. 1799: Crosse, Grand Musical Festival, p. 74/75]

'The tone is pure, sweet, and brilliant, but in point of volume it is so limited, that one never hears Mr. K. in a song without lamenting its want of power.' [Sep. 1820: QMMR, p. 473]

'His voice was very pure and sweet, and his style, particularly in glees, most elegant and refined.' [27 Apr. 1825: Phillips]

2.5.16   Mathieu Porto [b. 1780]

'His voice is a bass, and alike remarkable and admirable for quality and quantity. Its compass appears to be quite equal to any compositions which can fall within the province of bass singing; and there is no part of it which is not full, clear, and powerful. The deeper notes possess a richness of the rarest description' [15 Jan. 1823: MP]

'The principal novelty is a Signor PORTO, who has a look of luxurious living and enjoyment that suits well for the corrupt *Podestá*, yet he wants comic humour, and laughs himself instead of communicating the propensity to others. The remembrance of AMBROGETTI in this part is fatal to Signor PORTO as an actor, but in vocal ability he has a decided advantage. His voice is a powerful bass with a most uncommon body of tone, exceedingly rich and firm, but like most of that description has no graces of embellishment or freedom of execution, and is also incapable of that subdued effect essential to expression. Many pieces were injured by its uniform loudness, which seemed to go on like a huge mechanical power regardless of all around it. Altogether he is a singer of no ordinary merit, and a decided acquisition to the company, if he will restrain his voice within reasonable bounds.' [19 Jan. 1823: Ex]

'PORTO'S voice often told with great effect in its deep organic tones, but it wants that facility in subduing or swelling its notes, in which expression so much consists, that it is only in parts requiring great force that he can succeed. He would make an excellent sepulchral ghost for *Don Giovanni*. X' [9 Mar. 1823: Ex]

'Signor Porto's performance of the part of *Eliro*, the father of *Desdemona*, was very effective. This gentleman's style of singing is not distinguished by much delicacy; but it possesses a strength and solidity well suited to those characters which he generally sustains.' [24 Apr 1826: *Evening Mail*]

'Signor PORTO made indeed great efforts in a song "*La figlia, la figlia*", which we suspect to be ROSSINI'S, but, whether from a superabundance of snuff or a cold, sang with a more than customary nasal twang.' [24 Feb. 1828: Ex]

2.5.17 Thomas Vaughan [b. 1782]

'... promises to become one of the most celebrated vocal performers in this country. He possesses a richness, very great power, clearness and melody of voice.' [6 Feb. 1801: MP]

'It [Mr Vaughan's voice] is perhaps neither so rich nor so sweet as Mr. [Samuel] Harrison's, but we should describe it as naturally more pure, if its being less modified may entitle it to such a distinction.' [Mar. 1818: QMMR, p. 96]

'SOSTENUTO is the power of sustaining the voice upon any note, so that the sound is continued to the end without the least wavering. This important qualification is admirably shown in the voices of Knyvett and Vaughan.' [March 1822: Gardiner, *Music of Nature*, p. 117]

'Mr. V's voice is wholly a natural one; a genuine tenor, of a quality rather pure than brilliant or even sweet, and chastened by mature judgment; and without pretending to discuss the comparative merits of living artists, we may say that, if by some he has been thought approaching to tameness, those who were present in York Minster will confess, that *there*, at least, there was no deficiency of vigour. He was heard with the greatest distinctness in that immense space, which is doubtless more attributable to the purity of his tone, and the correctness of his taste, than to mere physical force. There is a sublime simplicity and an unaffected pathos, combined with elegance, in his performance, which, in our opinion, place Mr. V. at the head of English ecclesiastical music, no less than of its legitimate offspring, the English glee; his divisions are clear and articulate, and in the graceful propriety of his ornaments, and the liquid quality of his shake, he assuredly ranks as the first orchestra singer of the day.' [27 Sep. 1823: Crosse, p. 62]

'... was quite as pure as any Italian voice I ever heard. It was brought out nearer the throat, and is therefore not so brilliant nor so facile in execution as Mr. Sapio's or Mr. Braham's.' [30 Sep. 1825: QMMR, p. 280]

'The delightful ballad, "The adieu", called into play Vaughan's silver-toned voice, his pure and polished style of singing.' [26 Sep. 1827: MC]

2.5.18 Pierre Ignace Begrez [b. 1787]

'It was particularly unfavourable to BEGREZ to undertake a character [Narcissus] in which CURIONI had appeared to such advantage. He, however, performed it very satisfactorily, and gave both sweetness and expression to his part. We are glad to find that he is returned to this Theatre; for he is a singer of very pleasing powers, accompanied by prepossessing manners.' [11 Feb. 1822: MP]

His voice is fine, and we prefer his manner of forming, producing, and sustaining his tone, to that of any tenor in London. It is more pure, and at the same time more perfect, which are the legitimate objects of the Italian school. It is scarcely exceeded in brilliancy even by Mr. SAPIO, while in finish and uniformity it outgoes that professor. [30 Jun 1822: QMMR, p. 243]

'He is a good musician, with an indifferent voice well trained and cultivated. He thus always gives satisfaction in his endeavours to please the audience; and he would succeed still better, if he tried less to please himself by a style of ultra-tastiness and sugary douceur, bordering upon effeminacy.' [1 Jun 1824: NMM]

'As Mr. Bregrez [sic] at no time of his life ever gratified us, either as to style or voice, so is he unlikely to do this when both have become inveterate. The air he introduced from Paer's 'Agnese' was, from the beginning to the end, little better than a determined and steady wail.' [2 Feb. 1831: *Tatler*, No. 130, p. 519]

2.5.19 Ranieri Remorini [b. 1793]

'He has an uncommonly fine bass voice, clear, sonorous, and of great extent—his stile of singing of the true school, and ought to be a model for our bass singers.' [3 May 1824: MP]

'The part of *Selim, il Turco*, was filled by Signor Remorini, well known in all parts of Italy as a bass singer of the first rank. For many years he was a great favourite at Milan, Naples, Rome, &c., and has been performing at Lisbon, which city he has just left. His voice is uncommonly powerful, but rather hard; its range is not extensive, and it is defective in the means of expressing that tenderness of passion which becomes a well-bred lover, even though he be a Mussulman. On the other hand, he has plenty of flexibility, and executes his passages with ease and neatness.' [3 May 1824: *Evening Mail*]

'Signor REMORINI has a bass voice of unquestionable power, but less decided sweetness. His style of execution is bold and effective. In the concerted pieces he was sometimes rather too noisy, but on the whole proved himself a valuable acquisition.' [3 May 1824: *London Courier*]

'We have rarely heard a singer, with a voice of equal depth, who could introduce with so much success, so many ornaments as this gentleman does.' [19 Jul 1824: EM, Vol 86, p. 78]

2.6 Ensemble Singing

Ecstatic reviews of beautiful ensemble singing appeared by the end of the period:

> 'Combined with [Samuel] Harrison and [James] Bartleman, was the still more soft and gentle

voice of [William] Knyvett. An alto of great sweetness and beauty, though destitute of those lines of expression, without which the features appear as a blank, his voice is well adapted to the performance of glees, a style of composition then so much admired, that many of the popular songs of the day were harmonized and converted into this species of composition, to meet the public taste. Such attention was paid to the blending and balancing of the voices in these combinations, that the effect was not even exceeded by the equality and truth of the organ' [Mar. 1800: Gardiner, *Music of Nature*, p. 117].

'The Vocal concert, which was last year discontinued, was this season revived, and commenced at Hanover Square on the 6th of March [1818]. The singers were Madame Fodor [Josephine Fodor-Mainvielle], Signora Corri [Either Frances or Rosalie Corri], Mr. [James] Bartleman, &c.; Mr Weichsell led the band, and Mr. Greatorex was the conductor. The Vocal concert was established by Messrs. Harrison and the elder Knyvett, in the year 1792 [11 February], at Willis's Rooms, King Street, St. James's Square, for the performance of vocal music only, viz. canzonets, madrigals, glees, and serious glees; I suppose we shall hereafter have lively dirges. Many new pieces of these descriptions were composed expressly for the undertaking by the admired composers in that line, S. Webbe, Doctor Calcott,—Danby, and R. T. Stevens. This species of music, at the time this concert was instituted, was very fashionable, and was sung there so extremely sotto voce, that it was aptly termed whispering. It was however sung by first-rate singers, [Samuel] Harrison, [William] Knyvett, &c., occasionally assisted by that surprising singer, Mrs. [Elizabeth] Billington, who, instead of taking a part in the old harmonised ballad, "O Nanny, wilt thou gang wi' me", should have gratified the auditors with one of her fascinating "bravuras". To keep a singer of her splendid powers in a situation so subordinate, was like cooping an eagle to prevent its soaring to the skies.' [6 Mar. 1818: Parke, Vol. 2, p. 132].

'Dr. Callcott's glee, for five voices, "Oh snatch me swift from these tempestuous scenes" was sung by Mrs. W. Knyvett; Messrs. W. [William] Knyvett, [Thomas] Vaughan, Skelton and [Richard] Bellamy. It is impossible to describe the rich effect of the combined voices, as they broke upon the ear, in this first glee. The fine harmony of the composition, aided by the full and perfect union of the according tones, and the delicacy with which the lights and shades of the melody were touched by the whole party, as if by one voice or instrument, produced a tout ensemble, truly magical. The same observation will apply to the whole of the glees sung this evening, when their perfection depended on the accurate combination of the powers of the several performers. It was perfection, and the nicest musical ear could not distinguish a blemish!' [18 Dec. 1827: HP]

'Mrs. W. Knyvett (late Miss D Travis) has a voice of the richest quality, combining sweetness with power. Where the sentiment of the words required energy, her bursts of tone were electric; and the perfect accuracy of her ear is most of all valuable and effective in glee-singing, a department of her art in which she is unrivalled. Mr. W[illiam] Knyvett's fine alto voice, and Mr. [Thomas] Vaughan's equally beautiful tenor, are too well known, and too much admired, to require more particular applause from us; and we are compelled to satisfy ourselves with the same brief notice of Mr. [Richard] Bellamy's manly bass: thinking it, however, incumbent on us to express our high opinion of the pure taste with which these three eminent vocalists resist, in the practice of their art, the prevailing tendency towards excessive and ill-placed embellishment.' [2 Feb. 1828: *Lancaster Gazette*]

Starting from the late 1820s, several groups of Alpen singers visited the UK. The first was Les Trois Troubadours early in 1827, followed in the same year by the Tyrolese Minstrels (the Rainer family) and the Bohemian Brothers. The Singers of the Alps came in 1830 and the Hungarian Singers in 1835. Judging from the reviews, the Bohemian Brothers were the most spectacular and probably the best. It's clear that their soprano falsettist, at least, sang in straight voice. Here are some reviews:

'Their voices consist of a soprano, high tenor, tenor, and bass [named elsewhere respectively as Joseph, Robert, Mishel and Martin Wertheimer]. The quality and compass of the first voice are singular and extensive: he reached the D and E flat in alt with apparent ease; and the effect of those high and feminine tones proceeding from a tall, whiskered, and soldier-like man, contrasted with the prodigious growl of the bass, was remarkable. The quality of this latter singer's tone is like that of the serpent, used in military bands. He several times descended below the double C; and if we are not mistaken, more than once to the double double F; a note we never heard from any human diaphragm ...'[15] [23 Nov 1828: *Ex*]

'When they took off their round conical hats, they discovered such swarthy whiskered faces, and such a profusion of dark curls and bushy hair, as betokened, at first sight, certainly more of ferociousness than of melody; but, having formed in rank and file in front of the stage, they struck up the most melodious quartet that ever proceeded from such unpromising, and, apparently, rough looking throats—from whom the audience would rather have expected the war-whoop of savages to issue than any thing harmonious. One sang alto, the next soprano, the third tenor, and the fourth the richest and strongest bass than can be imagined—compared to which Signor Porto's fine bass voice would have been almost like the squeaking of a child's penny trumpet. The audience was in raptures, and though but few could understand the words, (for they sang in German), yet such were the sweetness and harmony of their sounds, their exquisite time keeping, and musical knowledge, that every air was tumultuously applauded and encored, whether slow or quick, solemn or playful.' [29 Nov. 1828: *Exeter and Plymouth Gazette*]

'We had not till Saturday an opportunity of hearing the new Melodies now singing at the Argyll Rooms by the four Bohemians, who are reputed to be brothers, and whom we believe to be so, because although two of the voices, the *soprano* and the *bass,* are very astonishing, the two intermediate singers are more moderate, both in tone and execution, than they would have been had there been any attempt at imposition. The *soprano* shames Velluti without shaming the audience; it is of course a *falsetto*, but clear, harmonious, and almost rich, even to the very

---

15 One has to doubt whether the soprano falsettist actually reached D and E flat in alt (d''' and e♭'''), especially as another reviewer suggested that his top note was an A above the treble stave [a'']. Equally, while the double C (C in Helmholz notation) is just about credible, one has to wonder whether the reviewer really heard the double double F (F₁)

highest note; on which the singer dwells with so much ease to himself, that he gives no pain to his hearers; there is no straining and no distortion, but the sound flows out and swells more like the effect of musical glasses than any thing else, and yet with a vast deal more brilliancy and rapidity of execution than they are capable of ...' [27 Jun. 1829: *Sydney Monitor*]

'... we can compare the counter tenor to nothing so aptly, in quality of tone, as to the rich, full, and bellike sound of a musical glass, capable of all the height and rioting playfulness of the flute in the hands of a perfect master.' [17 Jan. 1831: *The Pilot*]

The music reviewer for *Freeman's Journal* was an enthusiastic fan, unleashing several eulogies and encomiums:

'The "harsh grunting guttural" German has, in their mouths, a softness and flow which we thought belonged only to the Italian. Its rugged clusters of consonants roll out melted in a tide of manly sweetness which pleased without cloying; and for the moment we could fancy German the proper vehicle of song. It is difficult and invidious to particularise any, but two are sure to claim peculiar attention—the bass and the soprano. [18 Jan 1831: *Freeman's Journal*]

'We boldly affirm, that the most vivid notions of the excellence of the singers is conveyed, by describing the effect on the audience. On Monday, for instance, a fair girl sat on the right— gentle, intelligent, thoughtful—whose whole soul was wrapped in ecstasy—sick with delight. Is not that an important fact? We will ground at some future day, a theory on it, which will shame the whole Scotch school[16] of metaphysicians.' [9 Feb 1831: *Freeman's Journal*]

'These Concerts still continue to attract throngs of beauty and fashion, as the newspapers say, and they merit it. Some three or four new songs have been introduced—one, "The Wine Cup", we don't much admire: it has neither Bacchanalian transport, nor languid epicurean enjoyment; we therefore regret and protest against excluding for it the Boat Song, in which we so much luxuriated—it was the very Champagne of music; but among the new is "The Huntsman's Chorus", from Der Freischutz, which alone is worth the money for admission. Nothing, indeed, can be finer; at least our imagination is taxed to conceive one superior. The Soprano, as usual, is the great attraction. What a splendid voice! At one time it has the wild sweetness of "the night song of the breeze"; at another, the precision and facility of an instrument; and again, the clearness of a silver trumpet. In the chorus he gives two imitations of the bugle—the last is to the life, and undoubtedly a very singular thing, but the first affects us with a most intimate delight. His throat is a symphony, a concert in itself. "The man of iron" (we can't omit him) preserves his usual Megatherian roar. You would think that Nimrod himself was pouring a blast upon an antediluvian horn over the carcase of Cuvier's Mastodon; it is positively amusing to hear the unwieldy movements of his voice, and the slow deliberate manner in which it coils itself up like a boa. Those who have not heard the Bohemians may deem our notices overstrained; those who have, think them weak and diluted ... No one but he who has felt it, can conceive the delight with which our mind throws itself on their stream of

---

16 Perhaps the reviewer had in mind Scottish philosophers such as Francis Hutcheson, David Hume, Thomas Reid and Adam Smith.

song, and the dissolved delight with which it surrenders its soul to it.' [1 Mar. 1831: *Freeman's Journal*]

'There can be no more striking proof of the great attraction the Bohemians exert, and the justness of our eulogies, than the houses they still continue to draw—the applause they are heard with, and the much more striking pleasure written on the faces of the audience.' [9 Mar. 1831: *Freeman's Journal*]

'Why, in the Wine-cup, he stands like a hippopotamus, and gulps down wave after wave—a hogshead at every swallow. We wish we could prevail on every one of our fair readers to visit those concerts, and listen to the delightful inflexions of the Soprano's voice, whose curve is the very line of beauty to the elephant-camelo-behemoth roar of the Bass.' [15 Mar. 1831: *Freeman's Journal*]

It's apparent from the historic record that the public couldn't get enough of the Bohemian Brothers, who toured the length and breadth of England, Scotland and Ireland over the next five years. It seems that they had been discovered and trained by composer/ harpist Nicolas-Charles Bochsa, who kept them supplied with arrangements. They made enough money to diversify, or rather, return to their original occupation of cigar making, opening two 'cigar divans', one in Upper George's Street, Kingstown [now Kingston] and the other in Grafton Street, Dublin [later burnt to the ground]. They resumed occasional tours. The last I can find was in 1855 when they were reviewed as follows:

'On Thursday evening the Bohemian Brothers gave a concert in the Shire Hall. There were three vocalists and a pianist; the music was good. One of the vocalists imitated a bassoon extremely well, and another had a splendid alto voice. The mayor and mayoress, B. Young, Esq., and Mrs. Young were present, but the attendance was miserably thin.' [8 Dec. 1855: *Herts Guardian, Agricultural Journal, and General Advertiser*] Reading between the lines, it was a sad occasion, with the badly attended performance by the remaining three middle-aged brothers reduced to a variety act.

2.7   Straight Voice, Tremolo and Vibrato

2.7.1   Vibrato: Current Critical Attitudes

The use of vocal vibrato, or tremolo as it was known during the baroque and early classical periods, is without doubt 'the elephant in the music room', or even 'the mammoth in the opera house' amongst musicians today, some of whom affirm that 'natural vibrato' has always been an integral part of vocalists' normal sound.

Robert Donington wrote: 'the true vocal "vibrato" sounds wonderfully alive, decisive and under control. It is an essential element of voice production, as much so in early music as elsewhere.' [1977: Donington, *Interpretation of Early Music*, p. 522] Frederick Neumann asserted: 'To my knowledge nobody has so far produced genuine evidence that singers before 1800 were expected to sing without vibrato. Sporadic attempts to unearth such evidence have not been convincing.' [1993: Neumann, *Performance Practices*, p. 508] David Montgomery claimed in his polemic *The Vibrato Thing*: 'Singers, as we know, probably always had used continuous vibrato in their natural sound, and not a single historical source presents evidence to the contrary.' [2003: Montgomery]

The views of Donington, Neumann and Montgomery remain the 'party line' of the vocal establishment, recently argued by Beverly Jerold in 'Distinguishing Between Artificial and Natural Vibrato in Premodern Music' [2016: *Music Performance Issues: 1600–1900*]. While conceding that many sources objected to the occasional ornamental vibrato, she asserts that this 'exaggerated, artificial form of vibrato' [*Op cit.*, p. 293] must be distinguished from the 'natural vibrato of the fine singing voice' [*Op cit.*, p. 291]. She concludes: 'Postulating that early singers had very light, nearly vibrato-free voices (because to us it sounds so right for this music), we then equated today's natural vocal vibrato with what has now been shown to be artificially-produced vibrato. In a sense, singing almost continually with a "straight" tone is just as artificial as the exaggerated vibrato they applied as an ornament. Today, large voices with normal vibrato have every reason to perform this repertoire with confidence.' [*Op. cit.*, p. 293] But nowhere does she define exactly what a 'natural' vibrato is, or how and to what extent it differs from the 'artificial' vibrato. Nor does she cite a historical singer who actually used natural vibrato. Her suggestion that today's 'large voices with normal vibrato' are equivalent to historic singers' natural vibrato is equally unsupported by any evidence.

George Newton took a more balanced view: 'According to the early writers on music ... the instruments they created strove to sound like the human voice. Now the situation is reversed and singers are striving to imitate the old instruments. Perhaps that is a little strong. Singers are striving to find an expressive sound that will be compatible with those instruments. Many of them, especially the double reeds, had virtually no vibrato, and so some singers, hoping to be authentic, are cultivating a tone without vibrato. While a vibrato-less tone can give a disembodied, otherworldly quality suitable for the sacred music of the Middle Ages and the early Renaissance, as a cultivated solo instrument it is a mistake. It is too unnatural to the human physiology, which has a natural pulse pervading every part of the body. It also goes too far in completely ignoring the radically different aural expectations of the twentieth-century audience. It is safe to say that most of these experiments enjoy very limited success, but a few have resulted in a revelation of unexpected beauty in the older music, and thus musicians are encouraged to continue searching for the best way to present older music.' [1984: Newton, *Sonority in Singing*, p. 131]

In my view, and I'm not alone, it's clear that today's concert and opera singers, as trained by Western conservatories, produce a wide, **artificial** vibrato which can't conceivably be described as 'natural'. By contrast, vocalists in early music workshops or folk music events, who have not received vocal training, invariably sing in straight voice. What could be more natural than this? Moreover, during the last two decades, a few professionals have sung in a historically informed manner, on a few occasions. I give a few examples in Section 7.

2.7.2 Continuous Vibrato; the Historical Record

If there were eighteenth-century singers with continuous natural vibrato, this should be evident from the historical record. I will start by looking at the pedagogy on the use or absence of tremolo/vibrato.

I then present other evidence, such as comparisons with instrumental sound, and the evidence from ear-witnesses including Charles Burney and the Mozarts (father and son). I couldn't find any evidence for continuous tremolo, whether natural or artificial, by named singers in the eighteenth century. It was almost unheard of, which is why it was normally excoriated on the rare occasions it occurred. I did find reports on ornamental or expressive tremolo, occasional references to vocalists' gritty or reedy singing, and a couple of references to the tremulous voices of ageing vocalists. For example, Daniel Lysons noted that Catherine Galli's 'voice at that time [in 1796, aged 74] was affected by the tremulousness of age, yet she executed some of the passages with much sweetness and firmness of tone, and it was altogether a very extraordinary and interesting performance.' [1796: Lysons, *Origin and Progress*]

> **Greta Haenen** noted: 'A particularly clear early injunction against it [tremolo] was given by Christoph Bernhard (*Von der Singe-Kunst, oder Maniera*, c. 1650): "Fermo, or the maintenance of a steady voice, is required on all notes, except where a trillo or ardire [cadential trill] is applied. It is regarded as a refinement mainly because the tremolo (sic) is a defect ... Elderly singers feature the tremolo, but not as an artifice. Rather it creeps in by itself, as they no longer are able to hold their voices steady. If anyone would demand further evidence of the undesirability of the tremolo, let him listen to such an old man employing it while singing alone. Then he will be able to judge why the tremolo is not used by the most polished singers, except in ardire".' [Sadie and Fortune, *New Grove Dictionary of Music*]

> **Roger North** declared [*Notes of Me*], around 1695: 'It is rarely observed, but let it pass for a truth upon my word, that the greatest elegance of the finest voices is the prolation of a clear pure sound', although he does explain elsewhere that he was happy with ornamental vibrato, e.g. for a 'voice or hand' to 'superinduce [on a plain note] a gentle slow wavering, not into a trill, upon the swelling the note; such as trumpetts use, as if the instrument were a little shaken with the wind of its owne sound, but not so as to vary the tone, which must be religiously held to its place, like a pillar on its base, without the least loss of the accord. This waving of a note is not to be described, but by example.'

I was initially inclined to the view that **Pierfrancesco Tosi** in his Opinioni approved of the ornamental tremolo (narrow pitch vibrato), based on his use of the terms Mezzotrillo and Metrotrillo, which were translated by Galliard in his 1743 translation as 'close shake'. But, after

Illus. 18: Galliard's Mezzotrillo

discussing this with **Lisandro Abadie** on Facebook, I accepted his analysis, viz.: 'Galliard's two mistranslations of 'Mezzotrillo' as 'Close Shake' can hardly be construed to mean 'vibrato'. It is clearly a trill, involving two different pitches, ideal for fast arias and quick movements'. This is apparent from Galliard's illustration of the Mezzotrillo in performance [Illus. 18].

Elsewhere, Tosi appears to disapprove of tremolo in all its manifestations. First, he was clear that the *messa di voce* must be given in straight voice: 'Let them be taught to sustain the notes without letting the voice waver or hesitate [titubi, o vacilli], and if the teaching begins with a note of two measures length, the profit will be greater; otherwise the inclination which beginners have for moving the voice, and the fatigue of steadying it, will accustom them to not being able to sustain, and they will indubitably have the defect of fluttering [svolazzar] which is always in use by those who sing with the worst taste.' [1721: Tosi, trans. Foreman, p. 17] He adds: 'The trill has many defects which must be avoided [Tosi, p. 28] ... the goat-bleat causes laughter, for it is borne in the throat like a laugh [il caprino fa ridere, perchè nasce in bocca come il riso].' [Tosi, p. 29] The pitch oscillating vibrato made Tosi feel sick: 'He will not hear without nausea the invented emetic style of him who sings like the waves of the ocean, provoking the innocent notes with vulgar pushing of the voice; disgusting defect, and rude [incivile], but having been brought from beyond the mountains it passes for a modern rarity.' [Tosi, p. 104] Galliard explained that 'beyond the mountains' meant France.[17] It is hard to understand how Stark, faced with this 'ocean wave' evidence, managed to conclude that 'Pierfrancesco Tosi did not make reference to the vocal vibrato' [Stark, *Bel Canto*, p. 131]. Tosi sarcastically castigates the repeated note form of the tremolo, a kind of trillo, which seems to have gone out of fashion since it was recommended by Caccini and employed by Monteverdi: 'What will he not say of one who has found the prodigious artifice of singing like the crickets? Who should ever have dreamed before the fashion came in, that ten or twelve eighth notes [quavers] in a row could be minced one by one with a certain tremor of the voice, which came in some time ago under the name of *mordente fresco*. [See Illus. 19]/ Perhaps an even stronger impulse will compel him to detest the invention of laughing singing, or singing like hens when they have laid an egg. Will there not be some other small animals worthy of being imitated in order to place the profession in more ridicule?' [Tosi, p. 105]

Illus. 19: Mordente fresco illustration by Galliard

Tosi lavished strong praise on some contemporaries: 'If I should document that which merits imitation, one recognizes those who held it in their souls [tasteful passaggi], among whom the foremost was Signor [Francesco] Pistocchi [1659–1726], musico, the most famous of our (and all) time, whose name remains immortal for being the unique inventor of an inimitable and

---

17   I'd need to consult French sources to find support for Galliard's footnote. However, John Gunn did suggest at the end of the eighteenth century that the 'dumb shake' was going out of fashion: 'There was formerly in use a numerous list of graces, some with and others without characters to represent them, and now for the most part discontinued. Among them was the dumb shake, on stringed instruments, corresponding to what the French call flattement on the flute, and in our language, I think called "sweetenings", made by approaching the finger to the first or second open hole, below the proper note that is sounded, and moving it up and down over the hole, approaching it very near each time, but never entirely upon it; thus occasioning an alternate flattening and sharpening on the note, and like the dumb shake, producing a trembling, palsied expression, inconsistent with just intonation, and not unlike that extravagant trembling of the voice which the French call chevrotter; to make a goat-like noise; for which the singers of the Opera at Paris have been so often ridiculed' [Gunn, *Art of Flute Playing*, 1793].

refined taste, and for having taught to all the beauties of art without offending the measure of tempo. This sole example, which is worth a thousand (O revered Moderns!) ought to be enough to undeceive you, but if you are still incredulous, I will add that Siface [Giovanni Francesco Grossi, 1653–1697], with his divine melliflousness [divino mellifluo], embraced the teaching; that [Giovanni] Buzzoleni [1682-1722] with an incomparable intelligence adored (so to speak) that precept; that Luigino [d. 1707] afterward joined, with his sweet and amorous style, in following the footsteps.' [Tosi, trans. Foreman, p. 65] Tosi admired Signora [Francesca Vanini] Boschi [d. 1744] and Signora [Santa Stella] Lotti, as quoted [in the case of both singers] on page 70. Finally, Tosi paid tribute to his younger contemporaries Faustina Bordoni and Francesca Cuzzoni: 'One [Bordoni] is inimitable through the privileged gift of singing and enchanting the world with a prodigious felicity in execution, and with a sure singular brilliance, is as tasteful as she is inventive (I do not know if from nature or by art), and she pleases to excess. The nobility of the amorous cantabile of the other [Cuzzoni] is united to the sweetness of a most beautiful voice, to a perfect intonation, to strictness of tempo, and to the exotic productions of genius, which are merits as particular as they are difficult to imitate. The pathetic of the latter and the allegro of the former are the most admirable qualities in the one and the other.' [Tosi, trans. Foreman, p. 109] It is inconceivable that any of these singers disregarded Tosi's rules on any type of tremolo.

Giambattista Mancini allowed expressive vibrato in the theatre, although he is clear that this is only one of several varied effects, all to be used at the 'proper time'.

Mancini wrote: 'they [old masters] passed their years in perfecting their intonation, in exercising to insure the firm sustension of the voice [sostenere con femezza la voce], to clarify it [di chiarirla], increase its strength, to learn to produce it, and graduate it, etc.' [1777: Mancini, trans. Foreman, p.101] He explains, in an important passage, that vibrato has its place, as one of several varied effects, for expressive purposes. However, his advice cannot be construed as justifying continuous vibrato. After quoting Manfredini's comment 'How many times have I heard singing to the heart, without hearing a trill' [1777: *op. cit.*, p. 103], Mancini commented that 'this quality of voice and singing shines brilliantly in the place where sinners gather for eight days to hear spiritual exercises' but concludes that 'such a voice will never be suitable for the theatre, because in the scene it will need at the proper time the solidity, the spinning [levelling out, making plain], the sudden decrescendo of the voice … and then these should be united to brio, agility of the voice, vibrato [vibrare], detached notes [distaccare], the drawing back [ritirare], strength, and appropriateness of expression, etc., in sum a perfect complexity of such varied things by which the artist, who assumes the burden of a principal part, is in a position to gain success in any character whatever' [1777: *op. cit.*, p. 103/104]. Clearly, Mancini believed that rapid passaggi, spinning, sudden decrescendos, vibrato and staccato expression, while not required in sacred music, were essential as special effects in opera.

Tosi's insistence on pure, sweet, firm singing was echoed for at least 100 years by subsequent authors, including Giuseppe Riva [1727], John Ernest Galliard [English translation of Tosi, 1743],

Johann Quantz [fl. 1719–1752], Johann Friedrich Agricola [German translation of Tosi, 1757], Anselm Bayly [1771 & 1778], James Nares [1778], Charles Burney [fl. 1745–1814], Johann Adam Hiller [1780], Richard Edgcumbe [1783–1828], William Gardiner [1832–1847], Giuseppe Aprile [1797], Joseph Corfe 1799], Charles Smyth [1810], Jean Jousse [1815], Richard Mackenzie Bacon [fl. 1818–1828], Thomas Cooke [1828], Maria Anfossi [1837], Isaac Nathan [1836] and Manuel García [1840] . Here are a few examples:

Giuseppe Riva wrote: 'An excellent Voice, a fine Taste, the singing perfectly in Tune, which is the Effect of a nice Ear, are Gifts which Nature bestows on very few, and which, if improved by Study, will lead any one to the attainment of all other Qualities which are necessary to make a famous Singer; such are, exact Time, a distinct Expression of the Words, the keeping the Voice firm and steady, the entering into the Design of the Composer: To which I might add the Characterizing, that is, the Embellishing the Composition with proper Graces, and some others of less Account; but if these rare Qualities are not managed with Judgement (by which both Nature and Art must be brought to Perfection,) the Consequence will be, that our best Performances will be but indifferent, our good become bad, and the indifferent, intolerable.' [1727, Riva, p. 13]

Johann Quantz, virtuoso flautist, excellent composer and experienced musical director, but non-singer, felt sufficiently confident to define authoritatively but concisely what good singing involved, in terms indistinguishable from Tosi's treatise: 'The chief requirements of a good singer are that he have a good, clear, and pure voice, of uniform quality from top to bottom, a voice which has none of those defects originating in the nose and throat, and which is neither hoarse nor muffled. Only the voice itself and the use of words give singers preference over instrumentalists. In addition, the singer must know how to join the falsetto to the chest voice in such a way that one does not perceive where the latter ends and the former begins; he must have a good ear and true intonation, so that he can produce all the notes in their correct proportions; he must know how to produce the portamento (*il portamento di voce*) and the holds upon a long note (*le messe di voce*) in an agreeable manner; hence he must have firmness and sureness of voice, so that he does not begin to tremble in a moderately long hold, or transform the agreeable sound of the human voice into the disagreeable shriek of a reed pipe when he wishes to strengthen his tone, as not infrequently happens, particularly among certain singers who are disposed to hastiness. The singer must be able to execute a good shake that does not bleat … He must not express the high notes with a harsh attack or with a vehement exhalation of air from his chest; still less should he scream them out, coarsening the amenity of the voice.' [1752: Quantz, *Versuch*, p. 300] However, he did permit the tremolo as an ornament on the flute, when he wrote: 'If you must hold a long note for either a whole or a half bar, which the Italians call messa di voce, you must first tip it gently with the tongue, scarcely exhaling; then you begin pianissimo, allow the strength of the tone to swell to the middle of the tone, and from there diminish to the end of the note in the same fashion, making a vibrato [*Bebung*] with the finger on the nearest open hole. To keep the tone from becoming higher or lower during the crescendo and diminuendo, however (a defect which could originate in the nature of the flute), the rule given in para 22 of Section IV must be applied here; the tone will then always remain in tune with the accompanying instruments, whether you blow strongly or weakly.' [Quantz, *Versuch*, p. 165]

Dr James Nares advised: 'The first step in Singing should be to endeavour with an easy good Delivery, and steady Voice, to sing slow Notes rising or falling, well in Tune, a good Intonation of the Voice being the first perfection in Singing, and without which all others are useless. The next step is to add the messa di Voce or swelling of the Voice.' [1778: Nares, *Treatise*]

Charles Burney wrote: 'Good singing requires a clear, sweet, even, and flexible voice, equally free from nasal and guttural defects. It is but by the tone of voice and articulation of words that a vocal performer is superior to an instrumental. If in swelling a note the voice trembles or varies its pitch, or the intonations are false, ignorance and science are equally offended; and if a perfect shake, good taste in embellishment, and a touching expression be wanting, the singer's reputation will make no great progress among true judges. If in rapid divisions the passages are not executed with neatness and articulation; or in adagios, if light and shade, pathos, and variety of colouring and expression are wanting, the singer may have merit of certain kinds, but is still distant from perfection.' [1789: Bur, *General History*, Vol. III, p. 8]

Giuseppe Aprile laid down 'Necessary rules for students and dilettanti of vocal music. / I. The first and most necessary rule in singing, is to keep the voice steady. / II. To form the voice in as pleasing a tone, as is in the power of the scholar.' [1795: Aprile, *Modern Italian Method*, quoted by Burney in *Rees's Cyclopædia*]

Joseph Corfe instructed: 'The high notes should be no means be sung *too strong*, but fixed sweetly without any fluttering or tremulous motion. The too frequent *curling* of the notes should also be avoided: the scholar ought first to sing with plainness and simplicity, avoiding all ornaments, or *graces*, till he is sufficiently qualified to use them; and then he should be very cautious that they are not improperly used; for if the composer has taste in what he writes, it will be unnecessary, and indeed not very easy, to add any graces that will make it more beautiful; but too often they may render the piece less perfect [p. 3] … the shake should not too often be heard, and never too long, *nor ever on holding notes*, as here the *Messa di Voce* claims the preference, for "where passion speaks, all shakes and graces ought to be silent; leaving it to the sole source of a beautiful expression" to persuade.' [1799: Corfe, *Treatise*]

Charles Smyth asserted unambiguously that tremulousness was incompatible with a good portamento: 'A good portamento implies also that the notes be properly *sustained*. He who sings *tremulously* and makes that kind of *close shake* which old-fashioned violin and bass-players were so fond of, fails egregiously as to portamento. In order to acquire the *faculty of sustaining notes*, without which your good voice and ear will never conduct you to excellence, practise daily the sustaining about twelve notes of the ascending and descending diatonic major and minor scale, beginning at any pitch which is not *too low* for your voice, or would carry you beyond its natural or artificial compass. / I will now indulge a little playfulness of fancy. / Your notes must resemble in shape a barley corn <>; begin pianissimo, swell gradually till you arrive at fortissimo, and then gradually diminish till you have reduced the sound to pianissimo. The voice must neither be tremulous, or fluctuate as to pitch. If you enquire of the greatest professional singers that ever enraptured the public, they will corroborate my theory, by confessing to you how much time it was necessary for them to bestow on this most essential branch of the vocal art. Be patient. Nothing great is to be atchieved [sic] by idleness.' [1810: Smyth, *Six Letters*]

Jean Jousse favoured a pure *messa di voce* without tremolo: 'The chief object of the student and his master must be to obtain the natural tone of the voice in its purest state. / Q. which is the best mode of forming the voice? / A. To emit a sound, to sustain it without any tremulousness, to swell it by degrees to the full power of the voice, and to diminish it in the same proportion, according to the following *rhomboid* [Illus. 20].' [1815: Jousse, *Vocal Primer*, p. 12]

Jousse added: '*Obs.* 1. [in relation to *messa di voce*] As, in the erection of a building, the greatest care is paid to the foundation, so, in forming the voice, the low notes of the scale should at first be practised until the tone be pure, round, and full; then one or two more notes may be added until the scale be completed. / 2. A smooth, even, and easy delivery of the voice is one of the greatest excellencies in singing, and must be carefully studied./ Above all things, it is important to preserve the power of sustaining an equal tone without the slightest tremulousness.' [1815: Jousse, *Vocal Primer*, p. 14]

Illus. 20: Messa di Voce advised by Jousse

Richard Mackenzie Bacon, in the course of expounding on the need for pure vocal tone on several occasions, explicitly deprecated tremolo. His insistence on pure vocal tone was quoted above [p. 17]. Bacon explained later: 'In the practice of these simple solfeggi, I have in view only the production and sustaining of pure even tone, and the power of swelling and diminishing—in short, the command of the chest and of the organs employed in intoning and articulating notes and passages of the simple structure which is most commonly employed in airs of a declamatory or pathetic cast. Arrived at this point—and certainly not till he has arrived there—I should recommend the pupil to commence the practice of the shake. And if I were asked why I so long postpone this most indispensable attainment [the practice of the shake]—I reply, because I would suffer nothing to interfere with the few but grand and primary elements of the great style, which I have enumerated above. Above all things, it is important to preserve the power of sustaining, without the slightest tremulousness, an equal tone. This must be fixed and confirmed by practice, to such a degree of certainty, that not even the affections of the mind should be able to cause any considerable alteration. It should become a habit, otherwise the diffidence and fear which are always apt to assail the singer will too often paralize his efforts and nullify his powers. The practice of the shake, if begun too early, I consider is more likely to generate the trembling I deprecate than any thing else.—Therefore it should come the last.' [1822: QMMR, p. 271]

Thomas Cooke instructed: 'the voice should come with a pure and steady tone from the chest, divested of all nasal or guttural sound, the mouth to be well opened, a smiling position of it being the most favourable to the production of a good tone ... Let the pupil beware of being flattered into the belief that a strong and powerful voice is to be preferred; many persons are known to sing loudly, but few sweetly. Forcing the voice is allied to bawling, and in using vehemence there is the danger of singing out of tune, as the head and ear may become so confused by this *over-singing* as to counteract the intended effect of the accompaniment, which should be heard with sufficient clearness to keep the voice to the proper pitch.' [1828: Cooke, *Singing Exemplified*]

Isaac Nathan stated: 'Pure tone is the most essential requisite in singing; it is the vehicle of every other beauty in the science; execution, elocution and expression, are all subservient to tone, for without its aid they would be as nothing. Quality more than quantity of tone should be the chief consideration. A judicious singer, with even a weak voice, will frequently, from nice management, excite more pleasure than another whose magnificent volume of tone leads him to loftier flights.' [1836: Nathan, *Musurgia Vocalis*, p. 92] He adds: 'there are so many different toned voices, each arriving at perfection in its own excellencies and qualities, that it would be difficult to bestow the meed of approbation on any one in particular; every tone that is equal without partaking of the nasal or guttural, that is devoid of tremour or harshness, that can gently sink into pathos where required, gradually melt on the ear into silence, like the soft sounds of an Æolian harp, or swell into that majesty of tone which fixes the hearer in astonishment, is alike desirable.' [Nathan, *Musurgia Vocalis*, p. 93]

Maria Anfossi wrote: 'To render the voice firm is to make it capable of dwelling without tremor [senza tremare], and with a perfect intonation on any note. By expanding the voice, is meant modulating it upon long notes. This management of the breath is difficult and fatiguing at first, but amply compensates for the trouble; for a fine and firm *messa di voce* [una bella e ferma spianata di voce], or expansion of the voice, is highly creditable to the singer, and never fails to elicit general applause.' [1837: Anfossi, *Trattato Teorico*, p. 11]

Finally, **Manuel García** approved of the tremolo to express intense grief, but warned it must be used with taste and in moderation: 'When agitation is produced by grief so intensely deep as wholly to overpower the soul, the vocal organ experiences a vacillation called the *"Tremolo"*. This, when properly brought in and executed, never fails to produce a pathetic effect: [example given from Guillaume Tell, Illus. 21]

Illus. 21: Tremolo examples from Guillaume Tell

'The *tremolo* is employed to depict sentiments, which, in real life, are of a poignant character,— such as anguish at seeing the imminent danger of any one dear to us; or tears extorted by certain acts of anger, revenge, &c. Under those circumstances, even, its use should be adopted with great taste, and in moderation; for its expression or duration, if exaggerated, becomes fatiguing and ungraceful. Except in these especial cases just mentioned, care must be taken not in any degree to diminish the firmness of the voice; as a frequent use of the *tremolo* tends to make it prematurely tremulous. An artist who has contracted this intolerable habit, becomes, thereby, incapable of phrasing any kind of sustained song whatever. Many fine voices have been thus lost to art.' [1840: García, p. 65]

Mancini also made crystal clear that recitative should be spoken, not sung, which rules out tremolo/vibrato: 'Now the cantilena of the one and the other of these recitatives [both secco and instrumentato], however intoned, should always be loosened in such a manner that it resembles a perfect and simple spoken declamation. Thus it would be a defect if the actor, instead of speaking the recitative with a free voice, should wish to sing it, tying the voice continuously, and not think of ever distinguishing the periods and the diverse sense of the words by holding back, reinforcing, detaching and sweetening the voice, as a gifted man will do when he speaks or reads.' [1774: Mancini, trans. Foreman, p. 60]

Mancini's views on the performance of recitative were supported by predecessors, contemporaries and successors. Here are four examples.

[1] Charles Burney wrote on the singing of Gabriel Vincent Thévenard], who sang at the Paris opera from 1790 to 1730, quoting Laborde as his source: 'He had a tenor voice, which made the public forget that of [François Beaumavielle; it was sonorous, mellow, and extensive in compass. He sung a little through the throat, but by dint of art, he found the means of rendering this little defect even agreeable. His appearance on the stage was dignified, and his performance wonderful! It was to him that the present manner (1780) of speaking recitative is due.' [Bur, *Rees's Cyclopædia*]

[2] Anselm Bayly: 'We may now define recitative to be an expressive and elegant manner of speaking; which if the composer would set, and the singer execute with sense and gracefulness, let them ask themselves how an orator would pronounce the words, preserving the grammatical construction, touching lightly, without any appogiatura, short syllables and unemphatic words, and giving a due, but not fierce, energy to the emphatic.' [1788: Bayly, *Alliance*, p. 72]

[3] Gesualdo Lanza: 'Q. Is there not a certain style of singing approaching nearer to speaking than songs or airs? A. Yes; it is called recitative or reciting, and is nothing more than recitation, with musical sounds added.' [1813: Lanza, *Elements of Singing*, p. 89]

[4] Richard Edgcumbe: 'The besetting sin of most English singers is, that indistinctness of pronunciation which even in a song is one of the greatest blemishes, and in recitative is still more faulty. The Italians never talk of singing it, but call it reciting, and so it is and ought to be. It is not melody, it is noted declamation; and the first object is, not to warble it into an air, but to deliver the words with distinct articulation, sensible expression, proper emphasis, and with just punctuation, if I may so call the necessary short pauses for taking breath, which are like so many commas. In short, it should be assimilated as nearly as possible to good declamation. To lengthen it out by slow delivery is as wearisome as the dull recitation of a bad actor, orator, or reader.' [24 June 1834: Edgcumbe, p. 248] .

For other examples see **Robert Toft**, *Bel Canto*, pp. 6–9, 11–14, 32–38 and elsewhere.

The views of teachers and treatise writers were supported by reviews of actual singers. Thus, the Spectator commented: 'One defect the singers shared in common—the inability to deal with recitative. They seemed equally and alike to forget that recitative is to be spoken rather than sung, and by common consent drawled out their notes like a dull chant. Recitative is the dialogue, the conversation of the piece; but from Miss **Birch** and Miss **Wyndham** we never caught a word.' [17 Nov. 1838: *Spectator*] The *Athenaeum* commented on **Italo Campanini**: 'Signor Campanini will cause a reaction, if not a revolution, for it will be seen what infinite charm can be conveyed when the voice is produced without strain or effort, when the recitatives are declaimed and not sung, when the sounds are delivered in accordance with the dramatic situation, and when power is put forth at the right moment.' [11 May 1872: Ath]

While Isaac Nathan did not write about recitative directly, he clearly believed that it should often be spoken rather than sung, when he emphasised that certain pieces of music needed to be spoken: 'There are many words in particular situations, when connected with certain sentiments, that require only to be spoken with distinct articulation, to give full force to their meaning—singing them would destroy all delusion. The part of Polypheme, for instance, in the trio of *The Flock shall leave the Mountain*, would lose all effect, if not given in style of recitative. This speaking style of expressing words is not confined to those of anger only; there are various expressions considerably improved in a song, by being smartly spoken, without any apparent attention to melody, such as kiss, bliss, night, light, bright,—tell—think—struck—lip—gush, &c.' [1836: Nathan, p. 208]

2.7.3 Vocal Qualities compared to Instrumental Sounds

Singers' voices were frequently compared to instruments, during a period when default instrumental sound was generally tremolo- and vibrato-free, as it is once again being performed during recent historically informed decades. I've already noted the example of **Jeronimo** in 1705, with his 'Flute-stop' organ sound [p. 21]. I've also quoted sources indicating that the voices (or at least their upper registers) of **Elizabeth Billington**, **Josephine Fodor-Mainvielle**, Miss **Carew**, **Maria Caradori-Allan**,

Mrs. Oldmixon, Maria Malibran, Virginie Blasis and Laure Cinti-Damoreau resembled the flute or flageolet. In addition, Miss Carew was twice praised by The Examiner: '… a very mild yet effective singer, with a pleasing carriage, and fluty kind of voice.' [26 Jul. 1818: Ex] and 'But the powers of her gentle fluty voice are hardly equal to the bravura style.' [16 Apr. 1821: Ex] Mary Paton's duetting was described: 'The song with the flute accompaniment, in the Sultan, obtained more real applause than any throughout the evening; and the reason was obvious; it was a musical-instrument song. When the flute and her voice went together, you sometimes hardly knew which was which.' [24 Sep. 1830: *Tatler*, No. 18, p. 72] The falsetto extensions of Charles Incledon, William Pearman and Domenico Donizelli were also described as flute-like.

Also quoted in this book are descriptions of oboe-like singing by Francesca Le Brun [Section 2.4.18] and Giuseppina de Begnis [3.5.6]. See also quotes on trumpet-like singing from Angelica Catalani [2.4.27], Lewis Bernard Sapio [3.6.3] and Henrietta Nina Sontag [3.5.12]. As I note in section 3.6.1, John Braham produced a clarinet-like sound. It was reported of Mrs. Frederica Weichsell [Elizabeth Billington's mother] that 'her voice was powerful, strictly harmonious, and resembled the tone of a clarinet.' [May 1766: NMM, Vol. 54, p. 345] Henrietta Nina Sontag's was reviewed as 'clear as a bell' [3.5.12].

2.7.4   Charles Burney's Testimony

From his arrival in London (Autumn 1744) until his death in April 1814, Burney always took great interest in the voices and styles of singers. He travelled through much of Europe in the early 1770s with the aim of collecting materials for the accounts of his visits and his *History*, all of which contain full details of performances attended and of the many singers he heard, whether good, bad or indifferent. Descriptions of singers' voices also appear in his letters and articles for *Rees's Cyclopædia*. I've already quoted what Burney expected from vocalists [see p.72 above]. A sarcastic condemnation of tremolo usage can be found in the following *Cyclopædia* article, although he never seems to have asked himself why these instruments were equipped with such stops in the first instance: 'TREMBLANT, in Music, the name of a very disagreeable stop in large church-organs on the continent. Its name describes its effect. In general, a steady tone in a voice or wind-instrument capable of sustaining a note, is the most essential requisite; but in the tremblant stop there is a perpetual quivering, such as we sometimes hear in the streets by the vielle and barrel-organ.' [1810: Bur, *Rees's Cyclopædia*, article on 'Tremblant']

There's no question that, if a frequent or constant vocal tremolo was the norm (sometimes claimed today), Burney would have supplied full details. But both must have been uncommon, because he reports only one clear reference to vibrato or tremolo singing, plus two possible accounts, all derogatory, as below.

> The first was of an unnamed falsettist in an Amsterdam synagogue: 'One of these voices was a falset, more like the upper part of a bad vox humana stop in an organ, than a natural voice. I remember seeing an advertisement in an English newspaper, of a barber, who undertook to dress hair in such a manner as exactly to resemble a peruque; and this singer might equally

boast of having the art, not of singing like a human creature, but of making his voice like a very bad imitation of one. Of much the same kind is the merit of such singers, who, in execution, degrade the voice into a flute or fiddle, forgetting that they should not receive law from instruments, but give instruments law … But though the tone of the falset was very disagreeable, and he forced his voice very frequently in an outrageous manner, yet this man had certainly heard good music and good singing. He had a facility of running divisions, and now and then mixed them with passages of taste, which were far superior to the rest.' [23 Oct. 1772: Bur, *Present State … Germany*, p. 300] The peruque analogy makes clear that this falsettist used a pitch vibrato.

The delivery of high notes 'with a kind of beat', could be a tremolo/vibrato: 'the singing here [in Leipsic] is as vulgar and ordinary as our common singing in England, among those who have neither had the advantage of being taught, nor of hearing good singing. There is just the same pert snap in taking the high notes, which they do with a kind of beat, and very loud, instead of a messa di voce, or swell.' [25 Sep. 1772: Bur, *Present State…Germany*, p. 76]

The following 'trilling' reference might indicate vibrato, as Burney normally described trills as shakes: 'I was more disgusted than ever, at hearing French music, after the exquisite performances to which I had been accustomed in Italy. Eugenie, a pretty comedy, preceded Silvain, an opera by M. Gretry: there were many pretty passages in the music, but so ill sung, with so false an expression, such screaming, forcing, and trilling, as quite made me sick.' [3 Dec. 1770: Bur, *Present State … France*, p. 402]

2.7.5 Counsel for the Defence of Vocal Vibrato

The main citation by defenders of vocal vibrato in baroque and early classical music is Wolfgang Mozart's on Joseph Meissner, quoted in full, in the original and in Emily Anderson's translation:

'Meissner hat wie sie wissen, die üble gewohnheit, daß er oft mit fleiss mir der stime zittert – ganze viertl – ja oft gar achtl in aushalten der Note marquirt – und das habe ich an ihm nie leiden könen. Das ist auch wircklich abscheülich. Das ist völlig ganz wieder die Natur zu singen. die Menschenstime zittert schon selbst – aber so – in einem solchen grade, daß es schön ist – daß ist die Natur der stime. man macht ihrs auch nicht allein auf den blas=instrumenten, sondern auch auf den geigen instrumenten nach – ja so gar auf den Claviern – so bald man aber über die schrancken geht, So ist es nicht mehr schön – weil es wieder die Natur ist. da kömts mir just vor wie auf der orgl, wen der blasbalkstost.'

'Meisner, as you know, has the bad habit of making his voice tremble at times, turning a note that should be sustained into distinct crotchets, or even quavers—and this I never could endure in him. And really it is a detestable habit and one which is quite contrary to nature. The human voice trembles naturally—but in its own way—and only to such a degree that the effect is beautiful. Such is the nature of the voice; and people imitate it not only on wind-instruments, but on stringed instruments too and even on the clavier. But the moment the proper limit is overstepped, it is no longer beautiful—because it is contrary to nature. It reminds me then of the organ when the bellows are puffing.' [12 June 1778: Wolfgang Mozart, letter to Leopold]

I'll take Joseph Meissner's 'zittert' first. I think most people agree that he practised a conscious and deliberate rhythmic pulsation, i.e. a tremolo of amplitude. It must have been very slow, given that Meissner pulsated at crotchet or quaver speeds. It seems not to have been a slow pitch wobble, as some have suggested.

However, Mozart's comment that 'the human voice trembles by itself' is more difficult to interpret. I think it could be read in two possible ways.

1. **Natural Vibrato**. Wolfgang could be saying that the human voice trembles in a natural, involuntary way which is beautiful, but certainly not deliberate, implying that it occurs frequently and possibly continuously. 'But in a way and to a degree that it is beautiful' suggests that he views either excessively frequent use or inartistic delivery (too fast, too slow, or too widely oscillating?) as unbeautiful.

2. **Conscious Vibrato**. The last sentence ['Such is the nature of the voice ... because it is contrary to nature'] could mean that he is equating vocal tremolo with clearly deliberate and expressive (i.e. occasional) tremolo on wind, strings and clavichord, suggesting that, besides imitating vocal sound, instrumentalists also imitated the vocalist's taste in only using tremolo selectively. Again, 'But the moment the proper limit is overstepped' could also mean too frequent use or inartistic delivery.

Most modern commentators support the first interpretation. Frederick Neumann asserted: 'we have the testimonials of Praetorius and Mozart to the effect that the vibrato is a natural component of a desirable voice.' [Neumann, p. 508]. James Stark concluded that 'There can be little doubt that both Leopold and Wolfgang Mozart considered vocal vibrato to be a natural and desirable quality unless it took a faulty form' [Stark, p. 134], although he doesn't cite Leopold's qualification in his *Violinschule* to the effect that 'because the tremolo is not purely on one note but sounds undulating, so would it be an error if every note were played with the tremolo. Performers there are who tremble consistently on each note as if they had the palsy. The tremolo must only be used at places where nature herself would produce it; namely as if the note taken were the striking of an open string. For at the close of a piece, or even at the end of a passage which closes with a long note, that last note would inevitably, if struck for instance on a pianoforte, continue to hum for a considerable time afterwards. Therefore a closing note or any other sustained note may be decorated with a tremolo [tremoleto].' [1756: Leopold Mozart., *Violinschule*] Jerold agrees with Neumann and Stark: 'Nothing in the early sources suggests that singers should suppress their normal vibrato unless it is a defective wobble. In fact, as Mozart has just indicated, the human voice is always the model for the instrumentalist.' [2016: Jerold, *Music Performance Issues: 1600–1900,* p. 290].

One question which commentators never ask is: What singers and instrumentalists did the Mozart family like, and why? Fortunately, nearly 1,000 pages of letters by the Mozarts have come down to us, showing that both Leopold and Wolfgang liked to hear pure vocal and instrumental sounds, all of which tends to support the second 'conscious vibrato' interpretation above:

Wolfgang's approval of Giuseppe Aprile has been noted [p. 27], besides Schubart's comment that 'he sang with the purity of a bell up to E above the treble stave'.

Both Leopold and Wolfgang admired [Lucrezia] Agujari's voice, encompassing 3½ octaves, as already cited at p. 37, with music example.

Anna De Amicis was praised both by Leopold ('sings and acts like an angel') and Burney ('exquisitely polished and sweet') as noted at p. 38.

Wolfgang wrote: 'She [Mlle Kaiser] has a beautiful voice, not powerful but by no means weak, very pure [*rein*] and her intonation is good [*gute intonation*]. Valesi has taught her; and from her singing you can tell that he knows how to sing as well as how to teach. When she sustains her voice for a few bars, I have been astonished at the beauty of her crescendo and decrescendo. As yet she attempts the shake but gently; it will be all the more brilliant when she will force it, for it is certainly more easy in the latter way.' [2 Oct. 1777: Wolfgang to Leopold, *Letters*, p. 290] A month later, Wolfgang added: 'It is true that for a person who had only been studying for three months she sang surprisingly well, and she had, in addition, a very pleasing and pure voice.' [19 Feb. 1778: Wolfgang to Leopold, *Letters*, p. 485]

Wolfgang enjoyed the playing of oboist Friedrich Ramm 'who plays very well and has a delightfully pure tone. I have made him a present of my oboe concerto [identified in footnote as K.314], which is being copied in a room at Cannabich's, and the fellow is quite crazy with delight.' [4 Nov. 1777: Wolfgang to Leopold, *Letters*, p. 355].

Wolfgang admired Aloysia Weber's 'lovely, pure voice' [p. 42]. After critiquing Catterina Gabrielli's coloratura singing, Wolfgang added a month later: 'She [Gabrielli] was not capable of sustaining a breve properly, and, as she had no messa di voce, she could not dwell on her notes; in short, she sang with skill but without understanding. Mlle Weber's singing, on the other hand, goes to the heart, and she prefers to sing cantabile.' [19 Feb. 1778: Wolfgang to Leopold, *Letters*, p. 486]

Leopold wrote: 'What is particularly remarkable is his ability [Carlo Besozzi, oboe] to sustain his notes and his power to increase and decrease their volume, without introducing even the very slightest quiver into his very pure tone. But this messa di voce was too frequent for my taste and has the same melancholy effect on me as the tones of the harmonica, for it produces almost the same kind of sound.' [28 May 1778: Leopold to his wife and son, *Letters*, p. 540]

In contrast to his praise for Friedrich Ramm, Wolfgang wrote scathingly about oboist Johann Christian's intensity tremolo: 'Why, each ritornello lasts a quarter of an hour; and then our hero comes in, lifts up one leaden foot after the other and stamps on the floor with each in turn. His tone is entirely nasal, and his held notes like the tremulant on the organ. Would you ever have thought that his playing is like this? Yet it is nothing but the truth, though a truth which I should only tell to you.' [4 Apr. 1887: Wolfgang to Leopold, *Letters*, p. 907]

On the other hand, the following passage in Wolfgang's letter to his father suggests that expressive tremolo was probably used by Johann Valentin Adamberger as Belmont in the aria 'O wie ängstlich, o wie feurig' in *Die Entführung*: 'Would you like to know how I have expressed it—and even indicated his throbbing heart? By the two violins playing octaves. This is the favourite aria of all those who have heard it, and it is mine also. I wrote it expressly to suit Adamberger's voice. You see the trembling—the faltering—you see how his throbbing breast begins to swell; this I have expressed by a crescendo.' [26 Sep. 1781: Wolfgang to Leopold, *Letters*, p. 769]

2.7.6 Expressive or Illustrative Vocal Tremolo/Vibrato

Many of the accounts of admired voices presented in Sections 2.3 to 2.5 are incompatible with any form of tremolo or vibrato. However, expressive or illustrative tremolo use was usually praised, as per below, although the singers would revert to default straight tone when not tremoloing.

Johann Hiller praised castrato Giovanni Carestini [c. 1747] for his expressive Bebung: 'Now a word about vibrato (*Bebung*), which arises when one does not permit a long sustained tone to sound firmly, but rather allows it to fluctuate without changing the pitch. On string instruments it is done most easily by the rocking back and forth of the finger which is placed on the string. It is more difficult for the singer if he simply wants to bring it out with his throat; some make this easier for themselves by moving their lower jaw. Carestini did this often and always with success' [Hiller, p. 99]. Hiller's string instrument example suggests a slight pitch vibrato. But I have it on the authority of falsettist **Nicholas Clapton** (with whom I discussed the matter on Facebook) that moving the lower jaw could not have induced a pitch vibrato, although 'it might look very odd to anyone not accustomed to it'. Therefore, we should assume that Carestini must have used an expressive amplitude tremolo.

Agricola extensively annotated his translation of Tosi. He favoured selective vibrato, but acknowledged that this was difficult to deliver: 'The vibrato on one note—which is achieved on stringed instruments by rocking the fingertip back and forth on the same note, making the pitch neither higher nor lower, but gently beating it—is also an ornament that in singing is especially effective on long sustained notes, particularly when applied towards the end of such notes. It is quite impossible to express the vibrato in musical notation. It is more easily grasped with the help of oral instruction, but not all throats are capable of this type of execution.' [1757: Agricola, *Introduction*, p. 149] Agricola adds elsewhere: 'When several consecutive notes on the same pitch occur in moderate tempo, above which there is a slur sign and under the slur sign there are dots [See Illus. 22], one must nether separate nor detach the notes, but execute each note instead with a slight pressure from the chest.' [1757: Agricola, ed. Baird, p. 160] Baird observed in an endnote: '* Neumann *Ornamentation*, p. 603, calls this phenomenon "vocal intensity pulsations". Among many examples in the literature in which this phenomenon occurs may be included Handel's cantata for tenor, *Look down harmonious Saint*, and Hasse's cantata *Quel vago Seno* for flute, soprano, and continuo.'

Illus. 22: Example given by Johann Friedrich Agricola

Anselm Bayly's advice is somewhat confused: 'But of the eight shakes mentioned by him [Tosi] only two seem necessary for the church; the moderately quick, proper for grave airs, and the short, close shake, called mezzo trillo, or triletta for brisk and lively. / To continue the close shake, as some do, is exceedingly absurd and offensive; a long shake should be the moderately quick or open, increased into the close shake; which shews the artist and makes an agreeable variety. [p. 52].' However, right at the end of his treatise, Bayly unequivocally approves of selective pitch vibrato, provided it is performed 'discreetly and without any trembling', as quoted on p. 7 above.

I've already quoted [p. 7] **Mancini**'s comments on the use of ornamental vibrato.

Johann Hiller's references to tremolo/vibrato in a passage on trills show that he is referring to their use as ornaments, not continuously: 'The different types which must be taken into consideration are: the whole and half-inverted mordent (*Pralltriller*), the mordent, the turn (*Doppelschlag*), and vibrato (*Bebung*). In general, they merit close attention and much practice on the part of the singer, because without them the melody becomes stiff; and a singer who does not know them at all cuts no better figure than a dancer who has not learned how to move his arms. A trill performed so fast that the second tone can hardly be heard, or cannot be heard at all, is usually called tremolo or *Bockstriller* (goat's trill).' In a footnote Beicken writes: 'Whereas Hiller proceeds to describe the production of the *Bockstriller* without any particular bias, Tosi (*Observations*, trans. and ed. John Ernest Galliard [London: J. Wilcox, 1743], p. 48; Baird, *Introduction*, pp. 120ff.) observes that this shake "like the quivering of a goat makes one laugh", while Quantz (*On Playing the Flute*, trans. and ed. Edward R. Reilly [New York: Macmillan Publishing Co., Inc., 1975] pp. 101–102) altogether consider the *Bockstriller* a "defect".' [1780: Hiller, trans. and ed. Beicken, p. 92]

Thomas Kelly won success as a comic turn in Vienna, showing that tremolo was useful for poking fun at old men: 'There was an old miser of the name of Varesi, living at Vienna, who absolutely denied himself the common necessaries of life, and who made up his meals by pilfering fruits and sweetmeats from the parties to which he was invited; the canzonettas for which Storace asked, he was particularly fond of singing with a tremulous voice, accompanied by extraordinary gestures, and a shake of the head; it was, in fact, this imitation which I was called upon to exhibit, and I did so. During my performance, I perceived Casti particularly attentive, and when I had finished, he turned to Paesiello, and said, "This is the very fellow to act the character of Gafferio, in our opera; this boy shall be our old man! And if he keep old Varesi in his eye when he acts it, I will answer for his success". The opera was brought out, the drama was excellent, and the music was acknowledged the chef-d'oeuvre of Paesiello. Overflowing houses, for three successive seasons, bore testimony to its merits. I played the old man; and although really little more than a boy, never lost sight of the character I was personating for a moment.' [1784: Kelly, *Reminiscences*, p. 238]

William Gardiner noted that tremolo could express either shivering with cold or intense feeling: 'The Tremando, or Tremolo [See Illus. 23], Is a quick reiteration of the same note, to express a trembling sensation. This effect in the early writers was confined to the voice. Purcell introduces it in the Frost Scene of King Arthur, upon the words 'What power art thou?' [James] Bartleman gave this passage with a tremulous motion of the voice, representing the shivering effects of cold. The same thing, as applied by Handel in the oratorio of Joshua, to express the trembling nations, falls miserably short of what the words import, and possesses more the ridiculous than the sublime. In the Chaos of the Creation, it admirably represents a sudden convulsion, or shaking of the earth; and in another part of the same work, when softened into a pianissimo, it reminds us of the buzz and whirl of insects. The voice has nearly surrendered this grace to the instruments, as possessing greater power of expression; yet there are passages of intense feeling, in which the tremolo adds greatly to the effect of the voice. In Purcell's song of Mad Bess, at the words, 'Cold and hungry am I grown', it may be used with great success; and who that has ever heard [John] Braham in Jephtha's Vow, can forget his incomparable delivery of the words "horrid thought?" We need no other instance of the power of the tremolo, when so applied, to depict the workings of the soul.' [Oct. 1788: Gardiner, *Music of Nature*, p. 115]

Illus. 23: William Gardiner's illustration of the 'Tremando'

Bacon reviewed Angelica Catalani thus: '...I shall cite an example of the sublime effect of low and tremulous voicing. It occurred in the recitative—"And lo the Angel of the Lord came upon them, and the Glory of the Lord shone round about them. *And they were sore* afraid." This recitative Madame Catalani performed, with a nobleness of conception and majesty of expression not exceeded even by [Gertrud Elizabeth] Mara herself; for having poured forth the full magnificence of her prodigious volume of voice, supported by the arpeggio accompaniment of the orchestra upon the words, *"The Glory of the Lord shone round about them"*, she suddenly attenuated her astonishingly ductile tone to the least possibly audible sound, and sung slowly, in a voice so slightly as to be scarcely tremulous, *"And they were sore afraid"*.' [June 1821: QMMR, p. 141] There are other examples of expressive tremolo by Catalani.

Giuditta Pasta was praised by *Freeman's Journal*: 'There is one passage which Madame Pasta gives with peculiar effect—When the reviving Juliet breathes the name of her loved Romeo, the tremulous and convulsive interrogatory, "Qui me chiama?" attests of itself the merits of Madame Pasta as a vocalist and an actress.' [20 Aug. 1827: *Freeman's Journal*]

Critics and treatise authors were virtually unanimous in emphasising the supreme importance of the *messa di voce*, well into the nineteenth century. Their language does suggest that most would have agreed with Tosi in forbidding vocal tremolo during a *messa di voce*. For example, Jousse explicitly supported Tosi's view, as per note above [p. 73]. But I did find four exceptions.

> First, Roger North praised the castrato [Nicolo] Nicolini, in terms suggesting that the tremolo occurred in the middle of a *messa di voce*: 'And the swelling and dying of musical notes, with *tremolo* not impeaching the tone, wonderfully represents the waiving of air, and pleasing gales moving, and sinking away.' [1708: *Roger North on Music*, p. 128]

> Second, John Frederick Lampe advised: 'yet by Art we are experimentally taught, that the Duration is made sweeter, more beautiful and delightful, by encreasing of Loudness, which is called swelling of a Sound, and the Decreasing into Softness, which may be called the dying away of a Sound, and if accompanied, with an Undulation or Waving, strike the more.' [1740: Lampe, *Art of Musick*, p. 7]

> Third, nearly a century later, when vocal tremolo was beginning to gain ground, Louis Spohr wrote: 'The singer's voice in passionate passages, or when he forces it to its most powerful pitch, has a trembling which resembles the vibrations of a strongly struck bell. This, the Violinist can imitate very closely, as well as many other peculiarities of the human voice. It consists in the wavering of a stopped tone , which alternately extends a little below or above the perfect intonation, and is produced by a trembling motion of the left hand in the direction from the nut towards the bridge. This motion must however be slight, and the deviation from the perfect intonation of the tone, should hardly be perceptible to the ear. / In old compositions the *tremolo* is indicated by points . . . . or by the word *tremolo*; in new compositions it is generally left to the performer. Avoid however its frequent use, or in improper places. In places where the *tremolo* is used by the singer, it may also advantageously be applied to the violin. This *tremolo* is therefore properly used in passionate passages, and in strongly marking all the **fz** or > tones. Long sustained notes can be animated and strengthened by it: if such a tone swells from P to F, a beautiful effect is produced by beginning the *tremolo* slowly, and in proportion to the increasing power, to give a gradually accelerated vibration. Also by commencing rapidly, and gradually dropping the tone to a sound hardly perceptible, a good effect is produced.' [1833: Spohr, *Grand Violin School*]

> Finally, Isaac Nathan makes clear in defining terms 'Tremolo, Tremente, or Tremolante' that one legitimate use of these effects is as part of the *messa di voce*: 'Tremolo, Tremente, or Tremolante … Swell or draw out the voice with a tremulous motion. This can only be accomplished by strictly practising the crescendo and diminuendo.' [1836: Nathan, *Musurgia Vocalis*, p. 208]

But tremolo was condemned even where it might be justified by the dramatic context, confirming that straight tone was viewed as the norm and tremolo the unwanted exception:

> John Braham was criticised for expressive 'tremulation': 'Braham sang "Deeper and deeper still",

with great pathos; but his performance was, perhaps, rather too theatrical. The tremulation of the voice, while suffering under a strong passion, is natural in ordinary recitation, but it is injudicious in musical declamation; in fact it destroys the music. Mr. BRAHAM is so admirable (we had almost said so perfect) a singer, that we are persuaded he sometimes violates his own judgment in order to please, what he conceives to be the taste of the town. But we assure him that the town will be better pleased if he will lead and improve its taste, a task for which he is well qualified, both by his great popularity and his allowed skill in the art.' [6 March 1813: MC]

In 1826, Mary Anne Paton resigned from a role requiring her to sing tremulously as an old woman, and wrote a letter to the *Morning Chronicle* to explain why: 'I took the part of the White Maid, and did not discover, till the rehearsals convinced me, the difficulties of representing melo-dramatic and pantomimic business, and singing a song (totally unconnected with the part) in a tremulous voice, as an old woman. I then certainly did (word for word, as minutely stated in the paragraph in question) represent to Mr. Fawcett my total inability to render the part effective; nor did I imagine my secession from it of great importance to the Theatre, as no comment was made upon it, nor any anxiety shewn to remove the difficulty of which I complained.' [9 Dec. 1826: MC] I suggest that her objections were artistic and image/reputation related, and certainly not because she was unable to sing tremulously, given that only two years later she was actually praised for ornamental/expressive vibrato: 'She possesses considerable power, with great sweetness, and we were much struck with her very fine close shake.' [27 Sep. 1828: YG]

The Athenaeum took Maria Malibran sternly to task for her portrayal of an old lady: 'Madame Malibran commits an error in judgment when she thinks it necessary to fill out the personification of an elderly lady by palsying and disguising her voice...As for the fault attributed to Madame Malibran, we are disposed to dwell upon it, because it is rather characteristic of her, and because it is in itself dangerous, and might in its consequences do injury to the whole fabric of operatic performances ... And then, even if the performer were as tender, as Madame Malibran is, of the scenic truth, there would be no necessity for the quavering voice and tottering limbs, which, without question, interfere with the due effect of the music. The age of Fidalma is left at the mercy of the performer, and Madame Malibran makes her a sexagenarian to give scope for her own powers of acting such a part. But if she were two hundred years old, we should still object to her being allowed to show any decrepitude of voice, any shrillness or quaintness of intonation, that serves to prop an immaterial illusion, by the sacrifice of almost every thing which makes an opera worth hearing.' [22 Jul. 1829: Ath]

Charlotte Birch was praised in terms which make it clear that she normally sang in straight voice; e.g.: 'In the church, Miss Birch is superior to any foreigner we ever heard for purity and chasteness of expression; and in the concert room she is extremely effective ... Not long since, when singing, "With verdure clad" in St. Michael's church Coventry, the performance of Miss Birch so alternately astonished and charmed, by the silvery and bird-like sweetness and clearness of her voice, that the impression made upon the audience was so complete and overpowering, as to elicit an audible expression of approbation.' [7 Nov. 1838: *Bury & Norwich Post*] But, on one occasion, she was criticised for expressive tremolo: '… her simulated tremulousness of voice at the words "cold and hungry am I grown", is to be counted among those mistakes which many singers are apt to fall into.' [3 Jun. 1838: Ex]

2.7.7 Vocal Sounds Compared to the Glass Harmonica

Towards the end of the eighteenth century, and later, voices were often likened to the sounds produced by Benjamin Franklin's glass harmonica, invariably described as 'musical glasses'. These included some of the most celebrated singers of the time, including Cecilia Davies, Angelica Catalani, William Pearman, Samuel Harrison, Eliza Salmon, Catherine Stephens, Giovanni Velluti (the last important castrato), Giuditta Pasta, Laure Cinti-Damoreau, Miss Povey, the soprano falsettist of the Bohemian Brothers, Clara Novello and Jenny Lind. Some examples are included below.

> We find the first reference in **Samuel Pepys**'s diary: '… we homeward to the Glass-House, and there shewed my cozens the making of glass, and had several things made with great content; and, among others, I had one or two singing-glasses made, which make an echo to the voice, the first that ever I saw; but so thin, that the very breath broke one or two of them.' [23 Feb. 1669: Pepys]

> I've already cited **Burney**'s quotation by **Metastasio**, to the effect that soprano Miss Cecilia Davies could not be distinguished from her sister Mary's playing on the glass harmonica. [p. 36]

> **Leopold Mozart**'s observation on Carlo Besozzi's oboe playing in a letter to his wife and son has been mentioned on p. 80. Burney was also impressed by Besozzi's *messa di voce*: 'Bezozzi's *messa di voce*, or swell, is prodigious; indeed he continues to augment the force of a tone so much, and so long, that it is hardly possible not to fear for his lungs'. [1775: Bur, *The Present State … Germany*, pp. 45–46]

> **Anselm Bayly** wrote: 'Most agreeable united sounds, and nearest to the sweetness of the human voice, are those produced from glasses and the Æolian harp; yet as they are confined, soft only and slow, they deserve no consideration in the study and practice of vocal musick, except perhaps in forming the voice, and in pianos and plaintives … The reed instruments, such as the hautboy and bassoon, are nearest perhaps in sound found to the human voice, and require as great and like care, attention, study and practice, to bring out the tones united beautifully in the piano, forte and swell.' [1788: Bayly, *Alliance of Musick*, p. 16]

> An old *Encyclopædia Britannica* article focused on performance difficulties associated with the Musical Glasses: 'The open shake, or trill, is another unhappy operation upon musical glasses; which can only be performed by the alternate pulsations of two continued sounds, differing from each other only by a note or semitone. But as these pulsations thus managed cannot be distinct, the result is far from being pleasant; nor is there any succedaneum for the close shake, which in the violin is performed by alternatively depressing the string to the finger-board, and suffering it to rise without entirely removing the finger from it, and which, by giving the note

that tremulous sound produced by the human voice affected with grief, is a grace peculiarly adapted to pathetic and plaintive airs.' [1797: *Encyclopædia Britannica*, Vol. VII, p. 316]

A Mrs. Childe's 'voice is not so powerful as that of her predecessor, Mrs. Dickons, but her execution is quite as correct, as far as we have heard it. Her tones are delicate and harmonic, like the vibrations of musical glasses.' [6 Oct. 1811: Ex]

The Examiner characterised William Pearman's voice: 'One of the very few varieties which he displays, consists of that swelling and subsiding, or opening and shutting of the voice, which in Mr. Braham's powerful instrument is like a French-horn, but which in Mr. Pearman's is like a drinking glass rubbed round the edge with a wet finger.' [13 Jul. 1817: Ex]

A British visitor described the sound of the Sistine Chapel choir: 'At stated times the chosen band of choristers, about twenty in number, without any accompanying instruments, poured in their harmony of another world, in strains of profound sadness, at one moment swelling to despair, but soon again softened to mild melancholy,—it seemed the lament of the dead; so deep, so hopeless, yet so calm. The sounds in themselves have been compared to those of the Æolian harp, but they were stronger, and vibrated on the ear more like those of the musical glasses. Fine sounds however are not music, any more than harmonious language is in itself eloquence; and I have heard singing in English cathedrals with still superior or preferable emotions. I thought also that there was something forced and unnatural in the voices of those unfortunate beings, and a sort of unpleasant huskiness frequently observable.' [10 Mar. 1818: Louis Simond, *A Tour in Italy and Sicily*, p. 375]

The *Morning Post* praised Miss Povey's tone and *messa di voce*: 'As a singer she put forth still stronger claims to admiration. Her voice is strong, rich, and clear. She does not possess much science, but some of her tones have the thrilling purity of the musical glasses, and that waving dying fall, which seems to carry the soul into the depths of space.' [7 Oct. 1819: MP]

I've quoted a report by the London correspondent of the *Sydney Monitor* praising the Bohemian Brothers's soprano falsettist for his sound flowing out and swelling 'more like the effect of musical glasses than any thing else, and yet with a vast deal more brilliancy and rapidity of execution than they are capable of.' [27 June 1829: *Sydney Monitor*]

Praise was awarded to a duo: 'The duet singing of the Misses Smith is greatly admired; some passages resemble two well-tuned musical glasses.' [10 Oct. 1836: MP]

In a review of Mori's Concert, it was noted that 'Miss. Birch has a voice of surpassing beauty as well as power, and of that glassy tone which we have not heard since the days of Mrs. [Eliza] Salmon, of whom she strongly reminded us in such songs as "From Mighty Kings" and "Cease your Funning".' [7 Nov. 1838: *Bury & Norwich Post*]

Several violinists and vocalists were compared in a *Musical World* review: 'His chief and matchless excellence [Henri Vieuxtemps] is the magnificent tone he draws from his instrument, so full, rich, and melodious, that the like of it has been only heard in the beautiful concertos of

Jarnovich executed by himself. The tone, however, of this celebrated artist was more subdued, less silvery than velvet, something like the lower notes of [Maria] Malibran]; while that of Vieuxtemps, more powerful, but equally smooth, resembles in its pianos, the delicious pellucid tones of Cinti [Laure Cinti-Damoreau], and in its fortes the voluminous outpouring from the miraculous throat of [Angelica] Catalani, a voice, unmatched even in fable, that made its way to the audience through the thundering crash of five hundred instruments and two hundred chorus singers, yet floated so lightly and gently in the air, that, even when left to itself, it fell like a distant echo upon the nearest ear. To come more closely to the point, the notes of Jarnovich were so many well attuned, clear sounding carillons; while every note of Vieuxtemps is the produce of several musical glasses in perfect unison, touched by the skilful fingers of a Cartwright, and, strange to tell, liable to the same objection—it fatigues the ear.' [30 May 1844: MW]

Euphrosine Parepa Rosa's singing in Balfe's *Bohemian Girl* was praised thus: 'At the close of the second stanza she struck E, leaving untouched the intermediate notes, and gave it with so sustained a power that the audience was carried away with enthusiasm. The tone was clear and sweet, and penetrating, filling so the house that the very air seemed to vibrate—just as water swells and pulsates when a bow is drawn across the edge of a glass. In response to the enthusiastic plaudits, she repeated the stanza, varying the performance by this time rising a half note, and then falling back to the former note. There was no tremulo, no inaccuracy, but such precision and exactness as no other artiste that we know of who is now before the public possesses.' [18 Nov. 1869: CincDG]

Clara Novello was reviewed singing the Agnus Dei in York Minster at a Yorkshire Musical Festival concert: 'Her voice was soft as the tones of musical glasses, yet full of expression; there was deep pathos and prayer in every note; had it not been against the canons, we should have liked to hear it again.' [17 Sep. 1835: CM]

Commenting on my discussion of this review in my 2009 paper *Vocal Vibrato in Early* Music, Sarah Potter wrote: 'This review extract [on Clara Novello's singing in York Minster] is followed by Bethell's assertion that "Benjamin Franklin's Glass Harmonica couldn't produce a vibrato", but this evaluation fails to acknowledge that both the glass harmonica and musical glasses can reverberate audibly on one pitch, producing the effect of a vibrato of intensity.' [2014: Sarah Potter, *Changing Vocal Style*, p. 91] This is certainly the case when you listen to half-filled water glasses standing on a table, probably due to sympathetic vibrations, as in the YouTube example she cites of Robert Tiso playing Bach's Toccata and Fugue in D Minor.[18] However, the intensity vibration from the glass harmonica (more often used in public performance than free standing musical glasses) is much less pronounced. The following account of Angelica Catalani's singing seems to suggest a *messa di voce* rather than a vibration of intensity:

In an 1824 article, 'Reminiscences of the Opera', in *Knight's Quarterly Magazine*, Edward Bruce recalled 'a peculiar vibration on a high note, like the undulating sound produced by

---

18   Can be heard on YouTube at: https://www.youtube.com/watch?v=XKRj-T4l-e8.

running the finger round a water-glass [p. 82] ... I describe her as she was then, yet unspoiled by foreign trickery; when the delicacy of her singing was as remarkable as its power; when every note won its easy way from undistorted lips, graced by a winning smile; when not a look or gesture "o'erstepped the modesty of nature". Never was there such perfect fascination. I waited eagerly for the extraordinary undulating tone, which I mentioned before, so like a musical glass. Catalani made use of it twice, in the course of the evening. The notes on which the vibration is produced, is said to be higher than the highest key on the piano; the Italians call it "la voce di testa" , because the voice is thrown up into the head, instead of being drawn from the chest; and the English amateurs give it the name of "double falsetto". For myself, I never heard any one employ it but Catalani. She appeared to make a sort of preparation previous to its utterance, and never approached it by the regular scale. It began with an inconceivably fine thin tone, which gradually swelled both in volume and power, till it /"Made the ears vibrate and the heart-strings thrill". ' [p. 85] [1824: *Knights Quarterly Magazine*]

2.7.8 Some Red Meat for the Vibrato Defenders

The only eighteenth-century treatise published in England advocating frequent vibrato was issued by **William Tans'ur**, a teacher and composer of hymns and psalmody. He wrote in his editions of 'The Musical Alphabet' and 'The Musical Grammar' [1746 and 1772 respectively]: 'An Accent is a sort of wavering or quavering [in the 1772 edition "quavering" replaced by "Shaking"] of the Voice, or Instrument on certain Notes with a stronger, or weaker Tone than the rest, &c. to express the Passion thereof: which renders Musick, (especial Vocal) so very agreeable to the Ear; it being chiefly intended to move and affect; and on this the very Soul and Spirit of Musick depends; by reason it touches and causes Emotions in the Mind, either of Love, Sorrow, Pitty, or any other Passion whatsoever, &c.'

Tans'ur's views were echoed by subsequent North American composers and arrangers of psalmody:

> **John Arnold**, in *Complete Psalmodist*, 1753, 1761 and 1779: 'Accent, a certain Modulation, or Warbling of the Sounds, to express the Passions, either naturally by the Voice, or artifically by Instruments.'

> **Jacob Kimball**, of Boston, in *Rural Harmony*, 1793. 'ACCENT is a certain modulation or warbling of the sounds, in order to express the passion naturally with the voice.'

> **A. Stevenson**, of Montreal, in *The Vocal Preceptor*, 1811: 'An Accent is a sort of wavering, or shaking of the voice, or instrument, on certain notes, with a stronger or weaker tone than the rest, &c. to express the passion thereof.'

Tans'ur was a marginal figure, ignored by both Charles Burney and Richard Edgcumbe. He was mainly concerned with psalm singing, which was outside the sacred music mainstream. An article 'Musical Education of the People' [Jan. 1839: *London Saturday Journal*] distinguished psalmody from 'proper music': 'Certain it is, that in this country the science of music shrouds itself up in an aristocratic exclusiveness, and is confined to the concert-room, the theatre, or the singing-club. Places of worship are scarcely to be added to the list; for the rude state in which too generally parochial psalmody still remains, can hardly be classed as music.'

As you might expect, some psalmodists didn't share Tans'ur's views. These probably included North America's foremost eighteenth-century composer, **William Billings**.

William Billings, of Boston, in the *Singing Master's Assistant*, 1778: after defining 'A Single Trill' and 'A Double Trill' [Illus. 24], Billings adds: 'B. Many ignorant Singers take great licence from these trills, and without confining themselves to any rule, they shake all notes promiscuously, and they are as apt to tear a note in pieces, which should be struck fair and plump, as any other. Let such persons be informed, that it is impossible to shake a note, without going off of it, which occasions horrid discords; to remedy which evil, they must not shake any note but what is marked with a Trill, and that according to rule, which may be easily learned, under a good master.'

Illus. 24: Billings's trills

Simeon Jocelin and **Amos Doolittle**, of New Haven, in *Chorister's Companion*, 1782: 'Of Tuning and Forming the Voice./... Let the voice be clear and smooth as possible, neither forcing the sound through the nose, nor blowing through the teeth with the mouth shut ... a trembling in the voice is also carefully to be avoided. All high notes should be sounded soft, but not faint ... the low notes full, but not harsh ... let all be done with ease and freedom, endeavouring to cultivate a musical voice; observing for imitation, the sweet sound of the violin, the soft melody of the flute, and the tuneful notes of the nightingale.'

Thomas Billington [*Te deum, etc., with Instructions to the Performers*, 1784, p. 3], an English composer of sacred and secular music, although probably not part of the 'West Gallery' psalmody tradition, would have agreed: 'The performer should also come immediately upon the Note with Firmness, and, as I may say, a kind of Confidence; and not to introduce Trills and Beats, and a kind of Tremulus on every note, which is the bane of all singing, so that before the note in question is well ascertained, he is, through necessity, carried to the next note, which shares the same fate as the former, and so on to the end of the piece.'

2.7.9 Conclusions on Straight Tone Singing through the Long Eighteenth Century

I suggest that the historical record, as recounted above, shows that tremolo, whether natural or assumed, was forbidden as a continuous adjunct to vocal sound by all authorities from Tosi through to Garcia, as well as reviewers. It was certainly allowed as an **intentional** effect. I submit that the sheer weight of evidence, much of it cited in this book for the first time, will compel the objective reader to agree that straight tone singing, with optional selective vibrato, was the norm through the long eighteenth century in operatic, sacred and concert singing genres. I summarise my rationale below:

- The treatise writers, including Tosi, Quantz, Burney and Bacon, all agreed that steady, pure, straight vocal tone was required, without continuous tremolo or what is known today as vibrato. In all four cases, their postures were both supported by and completely in line with their reviews of singers in their time. It is inconceivable, therefore, that the numerous singers praised by these authors employed continuous pitch oscillating vibrato, as suggested by its defenders today, thereby contravening treatise rules.

- The precise enharmonic tuning expected vocally (e.g. distinguishing between D♯ and E♭) would have been unachievable with any amount of vibrato.

- The use of selective vibrato for expressive or illustrative purposes is proof positive that singers would, following ornamental use, have reverted to normal straight tone. For example, when Giovanni Carestini wasn't reciprocating his jaw up and down to produce an emphasis tremolo [see p. 81], listeners would hear his 'unusually secure', and therefore vibrato free, sound by default, given that his voice was highly praised by Burney, Hasse and Hiller.

- A comment by Anselm Bayly suggests that Handel probably disliked tremolo, certainly in 'pathetic' airs: 'Here it were easy to exercise the severe and just scourge of criticism upon performers, some even of the first class, vocal and instrumental, who introduce beats, trills, shakes, turns—into pathetic, lulling airs, and spoil neat simplicity with ill-placed brilliances, so much, that Handel, were he alive to hear, would say one while, Madame, another while, Sir, "That is not my moosick": A hint to the wise is enough.' [Bayly, *Alliance*, p. 54]

- Many reviews cited in this book are couched in terms which rule out tremolo or vibrato. Taking the castrati first, it is unimaginable that these vocalists used anything other than straight tone, given their voices were praised as 'pure' [Ferri], 'a pure intonation' [Orsini, Barnardi and Farinelli], 'purity of a bell' [Aprile], 'vocal sweetness of a pineapple' [Pacchierotti] and "perfectly pure and silvery" [Marchesi]. Much of this praise issued from Tosi, Quantz or Burney, all of whom disliked vocal vibrato.

- Turning to the female soundscape, descriptions are also incompatible with any form of tremolo: 'angelic in its clarity and sweetness' [Cuzzoni]; 'complete intonation, which did not vacillate in even the most fervent action' [Tramontini]; 'good in point of *Tone*, and steady, in *Tune*…so pure, chaste & judicious' [Linley]; '[Her entire compass was] firm as the tone of a trumpet' [Catalani]; 'There are no roughnesses, no breaks' [Stephens and Salmon]; 'Clear, firm, silvery tone in her voice, like the reverberation of a tight-strung instrument' [Fodor-Mainvielle]; 'Her ductility is truly admirable: there are no breaks or flaws in the tone' [Miss Carew].

- Several male singers were praised for their purity, e.g.: Samuel Harrison 'delivered with the most exquisite polish, every note as pure and bright as globes of glass'; James Bartleman 'possessed the utmost purity and roundness of tone'. I've drawn attention to the 'SOSTENUTO' of William Knyvett and Thomas Vaughan who could sustain their voices on any note so the sound is continued to the end 'without the least wavering'. John Sinclair's voice was 'particularly remarkable for its pure and liquid tones' and Giuseppe de Begnis's tone was 'legitimate and pure'.

- Comparisons of singers' voices to instruments suggest that vocalists used straight tone. Thus, Jeronimo's voice was described [see Page 21] as being like 'the Flute-stops of some Organs',

- Similarly, comparisons of many ace singers' voices to the glass harmonica rule out any idea that they used continuous pitch vibrato. I've noted Metastasio's comment [p. 36] that he was unable to distinguish Cecilia Davies's voice from her sister Mary's glass harmonica accompaniment.
- I couldn't find any evidence for continuous tremolo or vibrato, whether natural or assumed, by named singers in the eighteenth century, excepting a few cases attributable to age-related deterioration. If this did exist, then Charles Burney would surely have included full details in his numerous descriptions of singers' voices.
- The vibrato defenders' key argument (Mozart's comment that the 'human voice trembles naturally') is undermined by the fact that both Leopold and Wolfgang liked pure vocal and instrumental sound by default.

These findings confirm the conclusions in my paper for the 2009 singing conference at the University of York (this plus my video can be downloaded from my website or a link on the National Early Music Association website), showing that vibrato was a new nineteenth-century phenomenon. I also cite support from several musicologists:-

Michael Morrow, co-director of *Musica Reservata* during the 1960s and 1970s, abhorred vibrato and tried to get his singers to avoid it, but (on the whole) they refused to co-operate. I once asked Michael why he didn't like it, and he referred me to Tosi's insistence (and other writers after him) on the need to distinguish between major and minor semitones. Tosi wrote: 'A whole tone is divided into nine almost imperceptible intervals which are called commas, five of which constitute the major semitone, and four the minor semitone … An understanding of this matter has become very necessary, for if a soprano, for example, sings D♯ at the same pitch as E♭, a sensitive ear will hear that it is out of tune, since the latter pitch should be somewhat higher than the former.' [Quoted in Duffin, *Baroque Ensemble Tuning Introduction*] Morrow felt strongly that such precise enharmonic tuning would be impossible with any amount of vibrato.

My conclusions are consistent with **Greta Haenen**'s *Das Vibrato in Der Musik des Barock*, published in 1988, where she concludes that reports on the excessive use of vibrato 'are almost without exception related to a frequent ornamental vibrato, and a mostly constant vibrato is nearly always rejected, if it is mentioned at all. Almost all the sources which argue against a conscious, continuous vibrato come from the second half of the eighteenth century; previously the problem did not exist—with a few exceptions which are related directly to singing, all found in Italian sources from around 1600 … Nowhere is a noticeable continuous vibrato approved of. The fact that from time to time warnings are made about it, of course, proves that such a thing existed, but it was at least theoretically not tolerated, and I believe that the better performers tried to avoid it.'

Robert Toft concluded, in relation to the period 1780 to 1830: 'The basic sound of the voice appears to have contained little or no *vibrato*. Singers were expected to be able to sing without any hint of trembling or wavering, and those who could not were subjected to ridicule in the musical press.' [2000: Toft, *Heart to Heart*]

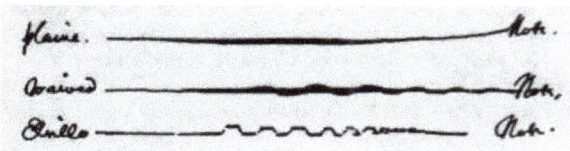

Illus. 25. Roger North's 'plaine, waived & trillo notes'

Toft credits **Frederick Gable** with the best review of scholarly positions on vibrato. Gable, in turn, credits **Greta Haenen** as the first modern scholar delivering some truth on the vibrato issue based on her 'exhaustive and detailed' research. He notes that expressive distinctions between 'plaine, waived and trillo' notes given by Roger North [see Illus. 25] 'cannot be made if the tone continuously contains a wide pitch vibrato, as in modern normal tone production'. After demolishing the arguments of pro-vibratoists **Robert Donington** and **Frederick Neumann**, he concludes: 'It seems clear to me that those writers and performers still trying to justify modern vibrato for the performance of baroque music have had their position fully undermined by these recent investigations [Greta Haenen, cited above, **Will Crutchfield** and **Robert Philip**, cited later in this book]. Of course, vibrato existed in the baroque, but it was not the same as our normal modern vibrato, nor was it employed as often. Why shouldn't earlier music sound somewhat different from more modern music?' [1992: Gable, 'Some Observations']

Richard Wistreich, in his article 'Reconstructing pre-Romantic singing technique', concludes: 'The evidence leads to the conclusion that any extraneous element in the vocal sound, be it simply vibrato or perhaps other acoustical complexes which the modern ear might describe simply as vocal timbre or "grain", would have been regarded as undesirable.' [2000: Potter (ed.), *Cambridge Companion to Singing*, p. 185]

Finally, **Clive Brown** refers, in relation to 'the vast majority of modern performers', to 'the employment of a patently unhistorical continuous vibrato, now almost ubiquitous on many instruments and in singing'. [*Classical & Romantic Performance Practice 1750-1900*, p. 415]

2.8   Shake, Performance of

The shake was always known to be difficult to perform. **Charles Dibdin** wrote: 'There is a thing which as it is generally used I most heartily reprobate, which is a shake. I don't think that in my whole life I ever heard above six singers who had a perfect shake. I have often heard some, under a most comfortable idea that they were perfectly right, shake from the minor third, from a quarter of a tone below it, and so on to almost a tremulous repetition of the tone itself; till at last one might be almost induced to pity them lest they should be under the influence of a fit of the ague.' [1805: Dibdin, *Musical Mentor*]

The value of the shake waxed or waned in public favour, depending on when, where and by whom it was either used or avoided. **Richard Bacon**, regretted the passing of the shake: 'The modern singers of Italy do not set the same value upon the shake, or employ it with any thing like the same frequency that those of the more antient schools, down to the time of FARINELLI, were accustomed to do. The use of this expressive ornament we should say is now very rare, and certainly not so well understood as heretofore.' [1821: QMMR, Vol. III, Article on Madame Camporese, p. 461] A year later, Bacon added: 'The thing which occasions us the most surprise in a singer of his rank [Signor Zucchelli] is, that he is as destitute of a shake as if he had never heard of such a thing—a singular proof how much that ornament is disregarded by the modern Italians. A man cannot get on without it for scarcely a single bar of HANDEL and the old masters.' [1822: QMMR Vol IV, p. 251]

Edgcumbe, in retrospectively eulogising Pacchierotti's shake (around 1834), also testified to the shake's changing fortunes: 'His shake, then considered as an indispensable requisite, without which no one could be esteemed a perfect singer, was the very best that could be heard in every form in which that grace can be executed: whether taken from above or below, between whole or semi-tones, fast or slow, it was always open, equal, and distinct, giving the greatest brilliancy to his cadences, and often introduced into his passages with the happiest effect.*' [reference date c. 1778: Edgcumbe, *Reminiscences*, p. 14] [Footnote]'*This, perhaps the most beautiful of graces, is now entirely lost in Italy: not one singer of that country so much as attempts it. From the English it still is heard, and often in great perfection.'

Edgcumbe's views were corroborated by other reviewers, some being hostile to the shake: 'There is one peculiarity about her style [Miss Bartolozzi, later Madame Vestris] that deserves remark and praise—she did not introduce a single shake from beginning to the end of her performance—a vulgar ornament, to which the best English singers are much too prone, and one which, we may say, is now unknown at the Italian Opera.' [18 June 1828: MC] Others, such as William Parke, made light of the matter: 'It is to be regretted that this excellent singer [Lewis Bernard Sapio] is deficient in that essential requisite, a good shake, as there are few instances in the English style of stage-singing of vocalists making their closes in a finished manner without it. It has been jocosely said that a singer cannot come out of a song, any more than a dog out of the water, without a good shake.' [30 Jan. 1822: Parke, Vol. 1, p. 169]

In taking Sims Reeves to task for leaving out the shake, **Henry F Chorley** is clearly adopting Richard Bacon's and Edgcumbe's position:

> 'From Thursday's performance, we are disposed to credit Mr. Reeves with power to sing the part of *Otello* precisely as written; a supposition which implies him to be possessed of means to take the very highest rank in his profession. On the other hand, the shake (indispensable as a Handelian grace) was missing. It must be forthcoming if Mr. Reeves intends to become our great oratorio singer.' [12 Feb. 1848: Ath]

> 'Mr. Reeves was the *Jephtha*; he seems steadily improving in this ancient music, though almost perverse in denying to it that indispensable Handelian grace, the shake.' [20 May 1848: Ath]

Charles E Pearce, Sims Reeves's biographer, dissented from Chorley's viewpoint: 'Mr. Chorley was quite entitled to his opinion, but considering that for years the strict observance of Handelian traditions had been disregarded, his insistence on the preservation of the shake, which, after all, was as much a fashion as it was a grace, and certainly not peculiar to Handel, suggests straining at a gnat.'

[1924: *Sims Reeves*]

My analysis of the shakes of named singers was restricted to the 100 or so celebrated singers listed in either section 2 or 3. Of the 103 reviews recorded, shakes were praised 82 times, but criticised on the remaining 21 occasions [see Illus. 26]. Most reviews were uninformative, with shakes either praised as beautiful, excellent, good or fine, or criticised as imperfect, not good, weak, or too close. Some of the more interesting positive reviews are supplied below:

Cecilia Davies. 'Her shake excellent, open, distinct, and neither sluggish like the French *cadence*, nor so quick as to become a flutter.' [30 Nov. 1773: Bur, *General History*]

Lucrezia Agujari. 'Then her shake—so plump—so true, so open!—it is as strong and distinct as Mr Burney's upon the Harpsichord.' [10 June 1775: Fanny Burney, p. 60]

Luigi Marchesi. 'He must have studied with intense application to enable himself to execute the divisions, and running shakes from the bottom of his compass to the top, even in a rapid series of half notes.' [5 Apr. 1788: Bur, *History*, Vol. IV]

John Sinclair. 'Mr. Sinclair's shake is quite perfect, whereas Mr. Braham's is a notorious trick.' [6 Oct. 1811: Ex]

'We never perhaps heard Miss Carew to better advantage, particularly her shake, which is as soft yet distinct as a flute.' [22 Aug. 1819: Ex]

William Knyvett: 'The falsetto ... is yet compensated for the shortness of compass, by the delicacy, perfection, and liquidity, with which by such a voice ornaments are performed. This power is particularly exemplified in the shake which is more complete in falsettes.' [Sep. 1820: QMMR, p. 475]

Eliza Salmon. 'That beautiful ornament, the shake, sparkled in her voice with all the lustre of a diamond; and though lavish in the use of it, she never abated the first sensations of delight.' [Mar. 1823: Gardiner, p. 133]

Mary Anne Paton. '... ending with a dulcet, inward, and most delicious shake, fit to be heard in the stillness of midnight, like a nightingale's.' [19 Feb. 1831: Leigh Hunt in *Tatler*, No. 145, p. 579]

Henrietta Nina Sontag. Her beautiful trill was likened to 'the bright jubilation of a soaring lark' [p. 149] . 'One of the most charming characteristics of her singing is her exquisitely clear and open and unerring shake; and of this she gave in the course of the opera some brilliant examples.' [5 Apr. 1850: MC]

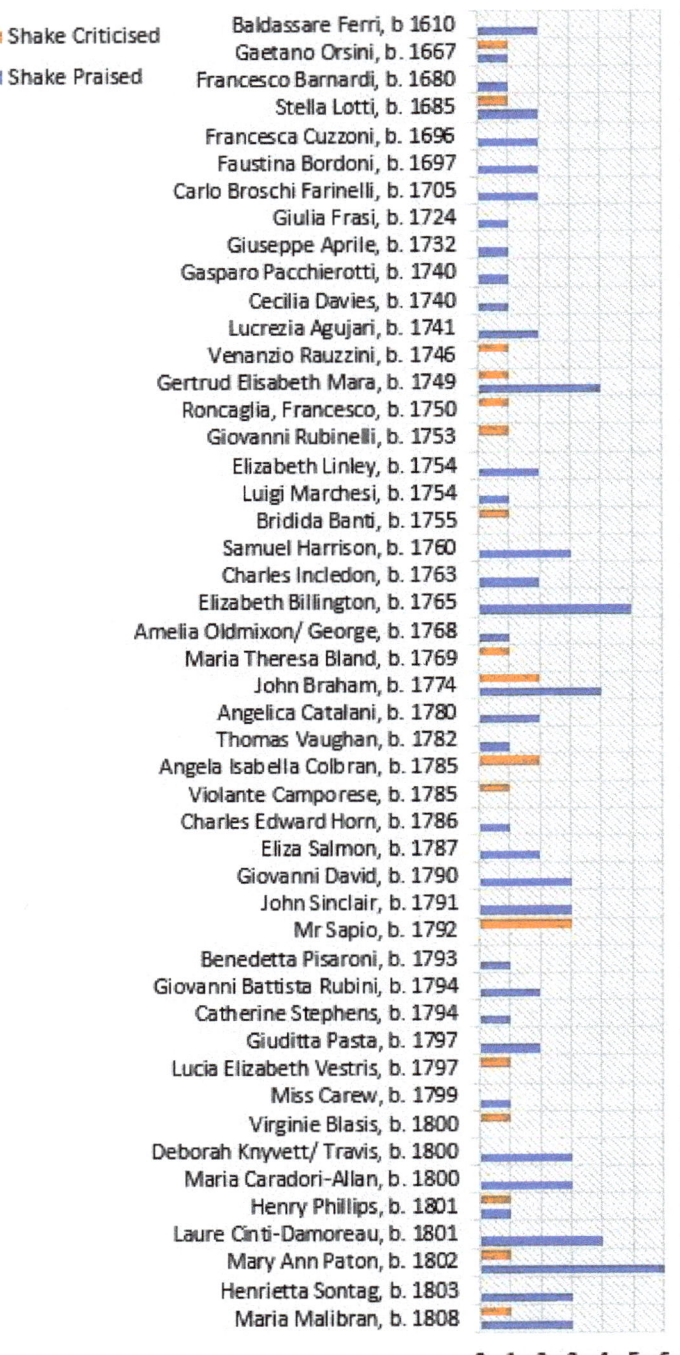

Illus. 26: Views on the Shake

The Golden Age of Italian Singing (1650 to 1829)

Disapproving notices were also aired:

John Braham. 'When he corrects the inelegant shrugging up of his shoulders, and succeeds in making his shake something less like a mere tremble, he will be a more agreeable singer.' [7 Apr. 1807: Tl]

Violante Camporese. 'MADAME CAMPORESE'S shake is not brilliant, but it is not of the rapid forced species that is now erroneously adopted by all except the few.' [Dec. 1821: QMMR, p. 461]

Mary Anne Paton, Mrs Wood. 'Her shake was imperfect, being too close, rapid, and hard, and given out with a jerk rather than with equal enunciation.' This review was inconsistent with the *Tatler* reviewer's quoted above. [9 Sep. 1822: Cox, p. 69]

Maria Malibran. 'Her shake, however, was extremely peculiar, if not defective.' [Jul. 1829: *Lady's Magazine*]

Charlotte Birch. 'was much more successful in the solo, "As from the power", where her clear, strong voice told well; though her shake—at present her evil genius—was both inappropriate and imperfect.' [26 May 1839: Ex]

2.9 Messa di Voce

As noted, the *messa di voce* was crucial to good singing through the long 18th century.

Christoph Bernhard wrote: '10. When on a whole or half tactus one takes care to use the piano at the beginning the forte in the middle and finally the piano again, as in:

Illus. 27: Christoph Bernhard's Messa di Voce

In which case one must pay close attention not to drop suddenly from piano into forte, [or the latter into the former], but rather must allow the voice gradually to grow or decrease, otherwise that which an artistic device is supposed to be would sound quite horrible.' (See Illus. 27) [1650: Bernhard, p. 5]

Pierfrancesco Tosi wrote: '… teach them the art of giving the voice [metter la voce], which consists in letting it come out softly from the least piano, so that it goes little by little to the greatest forte, and then returns by the same artifice from the forte to the piano. A beautiful *messa di voce* in the mouth of a professor who is not stingy with it, and does not use it except on the open vowels, will never fail to make the greatest effect.' [1721: Tosi, trans. Foreman, p. 17] Tosi was followed by every treatise in the period.

Anselm Bayly wrote: 'Let the master teach the art of putting forth the voice, in the manner of a swell, called by the Italians *Messa di voce,* which is formed by giving strength to the voice gradually from *piano* soft to *forte* loud, and returning to *piano*, steadily, without any shaking, quaking, quivering or trembling. / Some have not unaptly likened this progression of the voice to the shape of a barley-corn, or to any spheroidical figure, pointed at the Poles, that is, the ends, and broad at the Equator, that is, the middle. / A beautiful *messa di voce* used sparingly and only on the open vowels, can never fail of having an exquisite effect from the human voice, as well as from the throat of the nightingale. / This is not only ornamental, but useful; for it will prevent a too common and very ill effect, that of pushing the voice and driving it as it were with a kind of start or jerk into a sudden and boisterous loudness, or letting it drop into an extreme softness. / A smooth, easy, and even delivery of the voice, is one great, if not the greatest, excellence in speaking and singing, and must therefore be carefully studied …' [1771: Bayly, *Alliance*, p. 45]

Giambattista Mancini was especially helpful to the modern-day performer, because he suggested exactly where the *messa di voce* should be used: 'Messa di voce describes that action by which the professor gives to each long note a gradation, putting in it at the first a little voice, and then with proportion reinforcing it to the very strongest, finally taking it back with the same gradation as he used in swelling [see Illus. 28].

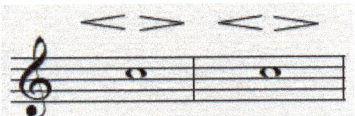

Illus. 28: Mancini's Illustration of the Messa di Voce

Ordinarily this messa di voce should be used at the beginning of an aria, and on notes with hold signs; and similarly it is necessary at the beginning of a cadenza; but a true and worthy professor will use it on every long note, which are found scattered through every musical cantilena. / It is certain that the messa di voce lends great excellence to singing, as it renders it more pleasing to the ear, and if it be executed with perfection, and with the union of a trill, is enough to make a cadenza perfect, and I dare say also make a singer perfect in the sense that it enables him to sustain and graduate without any defect, and with facility, his voice; then he can hope to have come into possession of the secret no less than the art.' [1774: Mancini, p. 37]

Richard Bacon advocated: 'By the same agency, by exercise, the power of swelling and diminishing (*messa di voce*, or *crescendo* and *diminuendo*) upon which so much of expression depends, is gained. All these, which are in truth the grand elements, depend upon a long and steady perseverance in singing the plain notes of the scale—a practice which should *never* be wholly discontinued. / The objects proposed to be thus accomplished by the practice of the scale are the production of the purest and the best tone, uniformity of voicing, and the power of sustaining, swelling and diminishing. These are the very foundations of good singing—the foundations of the great style and of execution, not less than of expression. No attempt should ever be made to go beyond the scale till they are acquired and fixed *as matters of habit*.' [Sep. 1822: Bacon, QMMR]

Messa di voce descriptions for the best singers are included in Section 2 or 3:

Castrati. Giovanni Francesco Grossi [Siface], Nicolo Grimaldi [Nicolini], Carlo Broschi Farinelli,

Gioachino Gizziello Conti, Gasparo Pacchierotti and Girolamo Crescentini were praised for their *messa di voce*.

Female singers were also complimented, including Francesca Cuzzoni, Faustina Bordoni, Elizabeth Billington, Angelica Catalani, Isabella Angela Colbran, Benedetta Rosmunda Pisaroni, Maria Caradori-Allan and Henrietta Sontag. Nathan described two *messa di voce* 'champions' thus: 'As to perfection in the swelling and dying of the voice, of those on our English stage [John] Braham is facile princeps ... but of female singers Miss Shirreff stands unrivalled ... The delicately beautiful and pathetic attenuation of her notes, melting as it were under a magic spell from their more majestic richness, into silvery softness, till they almost seem absorbed into liquid air, alternated with the awfully bursting volume of her swell so full of harmony yet so powerful and so redolent of original talent, marks her decidecly and without prejudice to any one as the gifted queen of song, with whom none may presume to compete. / "Palmam quae meruit, ferat!".' [1836: Nathan, p. 158]

Male singers including Samuel Harrison, John Braham and Domenico Donzelli were similarly approved.

On rare occasions, singers were criticised for the lack of a *messa di voce*, such as Caterina Gabrielli [according to Wolfgang Mozart, as at Page 80 above]. Fanny Wyndham, was taken to task on her debut for the same failing. 'This young lady sang the first part of Handel's air, "Lord! To thee", with considerable feeling; but a stricter attention to the good old rule of swelling every long note would have given more dignity and finish to her style.' [13 May 1837: LG]

On at least one occasion, the *messa di voce* was commended for choral use: 'A few more remarks will be made here concerning choral singing...Piano and forte occur quite frequently in choral works and must be properly observed. The magnificent effect of the increasing of the volume or *messa di voce* for an entire chorus can be experienced in a good performance of the splendid double chorus of our famous Bach [CPE] right in the first entrance of the word *Heilig* in the chorus of the angels.' [1780: Hiller, p. 119]

Isaac Nathan illustrated in his *Musurgia Vocalis* the varying types, volumes and lengths of *messa di voce*, with peak volume occurring earlier or later in the phrase or note, as shown at Illus. 29 below.

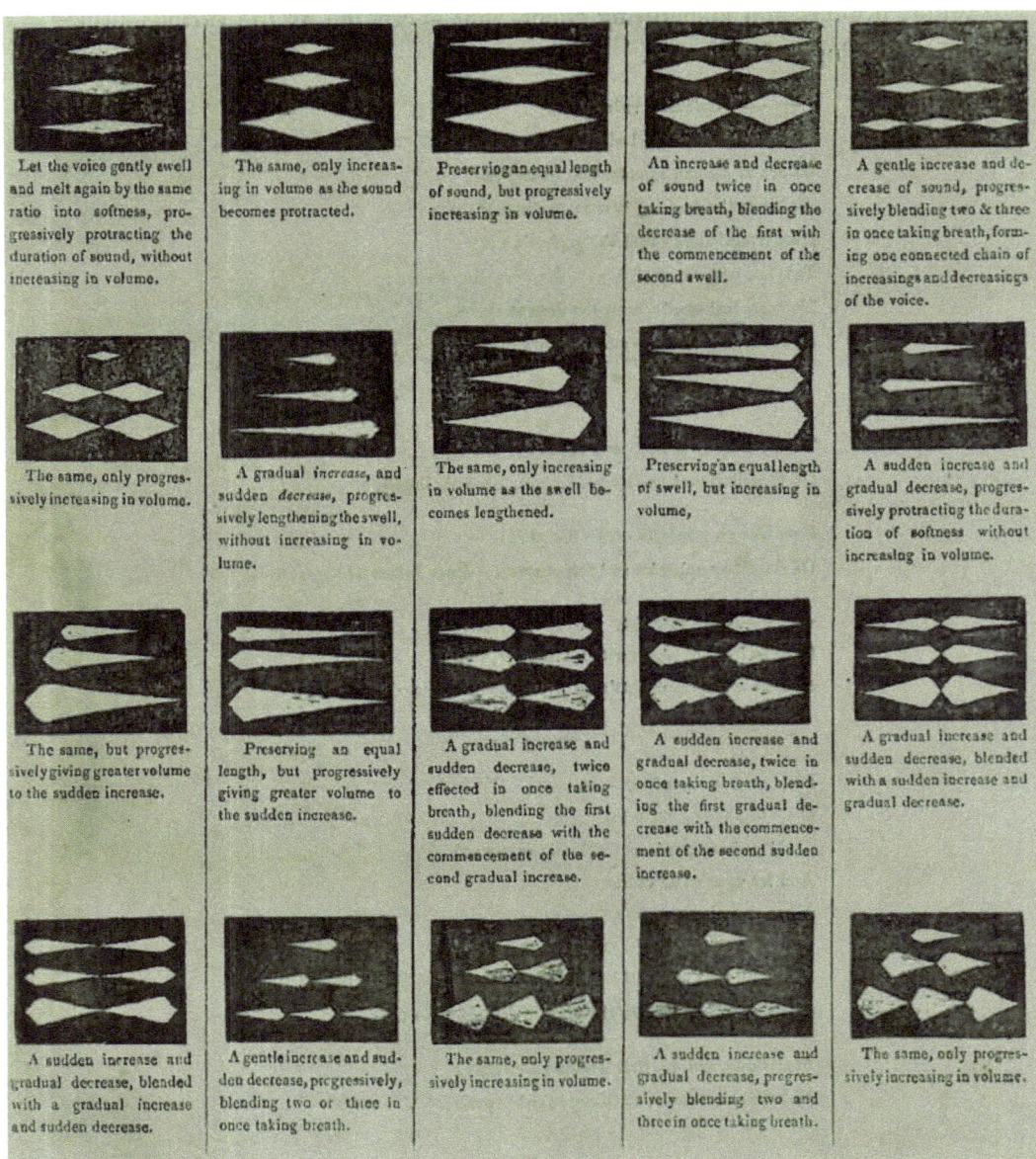

Illus. 29: Isaac Nathan's Messa di Voce Options

Nathan also produced the most eloquent praise for the *messa di voce*: 'This swelling and dying of the voice is the most important to practise, and one of the easiest requisites to acquire, if judiciously treated; on it depends the principal art of singing, for it sweetens, enriches, and gives that delicious roundness and fulness to the tone, so desirable for every branch of vocal science. / It is this swell and dying of the voice, which makes music respond to the various passions, and passes the feeling of one mind to another.' [1836: Nathan, p. 150] His imagery illustrates both the beauty and application of the *messa di voce*: 'Monotonous tones, that are produced with an equal degree of loudness, without any preparation by the *crescendo* and *diminuendo*, by their uniformity tire the ear, as a country, whose sterility admits of no varying scene, wearies the mind; but, as a prospect rich in hill and glade, whereon the eye gazes with delight, the swelling and dying of the voice, by the pleasing versatility of light and shade fascinate the imagination.'

Nathan also recommended an exercise in which the *messa di voce* is sung through a major, then a minor triad, proving that the ornament can be sung during a phrase, not just a single note: 'There is an exercise I particularly recommend, and which for general utility is

Illus. 30: Messa di Voce through a Phrase

preferable to others, as it combines in a very simple process all that will render the voice equable and flexible; I mean the progression by major triads with their relative minors [see Illus. 30]. Let the Tyro commence very softly, and swell gently to the second note, preserving as much as possible the quality of the first—thence let him gradually decline so that the third note be soft, yet still retaining some portion of the colouring of the second; let him return still more softly to the middle note, and conclude pianissimo on the note upon which he begun. The whole should be performed without the slightest break or suddenness, and if perfectly executed, should comprise every intermediate gradation between soft and loud—thus when facility in accomplishing this has been obtained, the phrase may be varied by the addition of a turn, the same character being carefully preserved—and lastly, let the whole passage be doubled, the repetition being an echo of the respective degrees of loudness and softness in the original, to which it should bear the same relation with that of a reflection in a minor [mirror?] to its object.' [Nathan, *op. cit*, pp. 147/8]

2.10   Extended Registers

The important authorities insisted that singers should develop a falsetto extension:

Pierfrancesco Tosi wrote. 'Many masters make their disciples sing contralto because they do not know how to find the falsetto in them, or to evade the fatigue of searching for it./ A diligent instructor, knowing that a soprano without the falsetto must sing within the narrowness of a few notes, should not only attempt to acquire it, but should leave no means untried so that he unites it to the chest voice, in such a way that one cannot distinguish the one from the other, since if the union is not perfect the voice will be of many registers, and consequently will lose its beauty. The jurisdiction of the natural voice, or chest voice, ordinarily ends on the fourth space or the fifth line, and here begins the domain of the falsetto, both in ascending to the high notes and in returning to the natural voice, wherein consists the difficulty of the union; let the master then consider the weight of this correction of that defect which carries with it the ruin of the scholar if it is neglected. In women who sing the soprano one hears occasionally a voice completely of the chest, but in men it is a rarity if they should retain it after they have attained the age of puberty.' [1723: Tosi, trans. Foreman, p. 16]

Anselm Bayly also stressed the importance of joining registers: 'The master should therefore be diligent to discern where the full, natural voice dipetto terminates, generally in a male soprano at d or e, in a contralto at g, a, or b, and from thence upwards help the learner to gain the falsetto, so united with that di petto, as they may not be distinguished, both in going up to the highest artificial notes, and in returning to the real. For if the real and artificial tones do not perfectly unite, the lower covering, like the greater bell, the next above it in equal proportion, through the whole peal, the voice will be of different sounds; or as Tosi says, diverse registers, and consequently cannot be heard with delight. [1771: Bayly, *Practical Treatise*, p. 20]

Giambattista Mancini emphasised the difficulty of joining the registers: 'Have no doubt that of all the difficulties that one encounters in the art of singing, the greatest by far is the union of the two registers: but to overcome this is not impossible to him who will seriously study how it is to be done.' [1774: Mancini, *Practical Reflections on Figured Singing*, p. 17]

Charles John Smyth sternly advised his son: You have, if I mistake not, a power of adding a *falsetto* to your *natural* voice. One direction I would give you. It is this:--Before you have got to the utmost extent of your natural voice, sing somewhat *softer*; by this means, the breach between the two voices will be less perceptible. They will unite better. / I once heard a professional singer of great eminence [probably John Braham], a stage-singer, in a private room. He sung through the compass of two octaves, *chromatically*, that is, by semi-tones, with the utmost rapidity and accuracy of intonation. He afterwards tried experiments upon a musical friend and myself, as to the junction of his two voices; and the result was, that we could not tell where the separation took place. / He afterwards mentioned an unquestionable test of guttural singing. When his portamento was good, and he sang from his chest, if he thumped his chest while he was singing, the tone *fluctuated*. When he sang in his throat, the strokes on his chest did not affect the tone of his voice. The English are lamentably addicted to *guttural* singing; and every real judge wishes they were thumped out of this disgusting habit. [1810: Smyth, *Six Letters*, p. 6/7]

Jean Jousse's advice was similar to Bayly's: 'Obs. The perfect and imperceptible union of the two registers forms an essential part in the art of singing. In passing from one to the other, the student must, by art, strengthen that extremity which happens to be the weakest. To unite the chest voice with the falsetto, practise frequently those notes where the break takes place, so as to be able to pass from one register to the other without any perceptible breach.' [1815: Jousse, *Vocal Primer*, p. 4]

A QMMR contributor was somewhat ambivalent on the desirability of falsetto: 'Where the falsette is occasionally used as by tenors, in a few notes above the compass of the natural voice (*the voce di petto*), the great difficulty is to unite the two without a break, as it is technically termed. It is often successfully combined at the point of junction, particularly if the falsette be taken upon its lowest notes, D or E, by softening the upper tones of the natural voice, in order to assimilate them to the attenuated quality of the falsette—but the change cannot be concealed if the passage rises in the scale*. [*Footnote: MR. BRAHAM is a complete example.] The brilliancy and peculiarity of the falsetto become perceptible, which is always a slight drawback. INCLEDON boldly relied on the superior beauty of his voice, and would very frequently make a skip of a whole octave, ascending from A to A or B to B, as the case might be, and then he would "wanton in the wiles of sound", through passages or cadenzas entirely in the falsette, which, though totally unlike his natural voice, was so superior in brilliancy as well as sweetness and richness, that the anomalous and unscientific effect of the substitution was forgiven for the sake of the mere physical pleasure the tone conferred. There are however great doubts whether a composition (an air) is ever much benefited by running up to such extra-compass as to require the combination of the two voices—I should say where declamatory force or impassionate expression is the object—certainly not—for passages of mere execution allowance must be made. Much of the purity of MR. VAUGHAN's tone and the unity of his style depends, I conceive, upon his never attempting to use the falsetto extensively, if indeed at all. I cannot call to mind an instance in which I ever heard him use it.' [1822: QMMR, from an article 'On the Philosophy of Musical Composition' signed by 'M.' p. 25] The QMMR's views were followed by a number of other commentators from 1830, as covered in Section 5.3 below.

Starting with women, Illus. 31 shows that the voices of some prima donnas often ranged from 2½ to 3 octaves, which is impossible without a falsetto extension. And, of course, Mozart exploited Josepha Hoffer's top F in his famous 'Queen of the Night' aria. Some singers who might today be categorised as mezzo-sopranos, or even altos, cultivated a falsetto so that they could qualify as, and be paid as, sopranos. However, it must be conceded that opera goers didn't always enjoy female falsetto singing. Charles Burney wrote, in relation to 'Madame [Francesca] Le Brun's song of greatest compass, which goes up to B♭ in altissimo': 'But I must own, that such tricks, such *cork-cutting notes*, as they were once well called by a musical lady of high rank, are unworthy of a great singer, and always give me more pain than pleasure.' [Bur, *General History*, pp. 481/2]

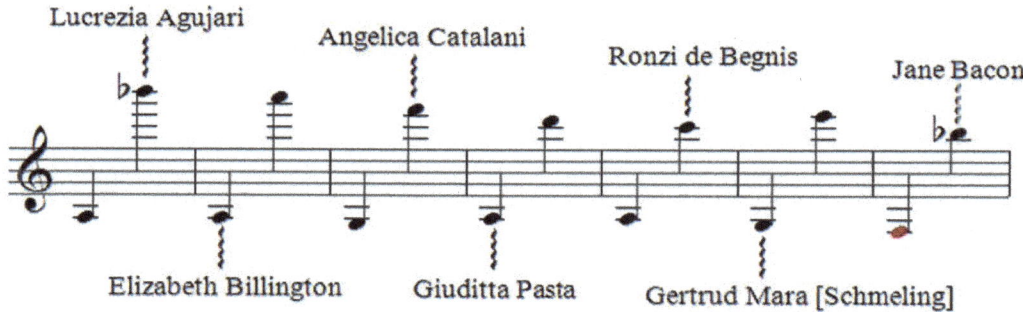

Illus. 31: Vocal Ranges: Women

But stratospheric female singing was generally applauded by audiences, for example: 'Miss [Amelia] George, who performed the part of Lucy, (an uphill singing part), perceiving she had little chance of dividing the applause with the great magnet of the night, had recourse to the following stratagem: when the dialogue duet in the second act, "Why, how now, Madame Flirt", came on, Mrs Billington gave her verse with great sweetness and characteristic expression, and was much applauded. Miss George in reply, availing herself of her extraordinary compass of voice, and setting propriety at defiance, sang the whole of her verse an octave higher, her tones having the effect of the high notes of a sweet and brilliant flute: the audience, taken by surprise, bestowed on her such loud applause as almost shook the walls of the theatre.' [1 Aug. 1789: Parke, Vol. 1, p. 128]

Illus. 32: Vocal Ranges: Castrati

Some castrati had similarly wide compasses, as Illus. 32 shows. Matteo Berselli seems to have possessed the highest falsetto extension: 'Matteo Berselli had a thin, high, soprano voice, the compass of which was so extraordinary, that he could go from the lowest C, in the treble, to F in altissimo, with the greatest ease, by which he surprised the audience more than by his art in singing.' [Dec. 1721: Bur, *The Present State … France and Italy*, p. 175, as recalled by Quantz]. But they certainly had a falsetto register, as Burney makes clear in his description of Giovanni Rubinelli's voice: 'All above C is falset, and so much more feeble and of a different register from the rest, that I was uneasy when he transcended the compass of his natural and real voice.' [1786: Bur, *General History, Vol.* IV, p. 524] But, Berselli apart, they may not have normally ascended higher than D above the treble clef.

With regard to men, for much of the eighteenth century it's not clear how many of them exploited their falsetto register. But, while deep basses like James Bartleman and Johann Fischer kept to the chest voice, some famous tenors and baritones extended into falsetto during the last quarter of the century. See Illus. 33 for male vocal ranges. In the case of Charles Incledon and John Braham, we know their ranges; their wide falsetto compasses are shown in red.

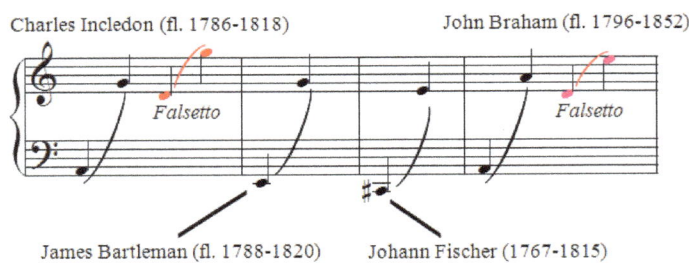

Illus. 33: Vocal Ranges: Men

As noted at p. 56, Charles Incledon had an exquisite falsetto, albeit without a junction to his chest voice. Clearly, he was two singers in one, baritone and mezzo soprano falsettist. By contrast, QMMR noted that [John] Braham's 'junction is so nicely managed, that in an experiment to which this gentleman had the kindness to submit of ascending and descending by semitones, it was impossible to distinguish at what point he substituted the falsette for the natural note.' [March 1818: QMMR, p. 89]

During the first 40 years of the nineteenth century, most tenors and baritones developed a falsetto register, with few exceptions. One critic expressed surprise at the limitations of a Mr. **Knox**. 'His voice is a strong tenor, and much resembles, in its tone, that of Mr. **Incledon**, but its compass is very limited, and he does not seem at all to possess the power of using a falsetto.' [March 1805: TI] Later, singers with a falsetto extension were gradually displaced by the *tenore di forza*, also known as 'forcible' or 'heroic' tenors, as we shall see in Section 5. These sported crowd-pleasing top Cs from the chest, much to Rossini's disgust.

2.11 Vocal Volume

It has been suggested that eighteenth-century singing was softer than today's. It probably was, on average, but the data do suggest that generalisations of this sort are too sweeping.

Edmund Burke believed that aesthetic beauty in music can only be achieved if it is not too loud or changeable: '… I shall add one or two remarks. The first is; that the beautiful in music will not bear that loudness and strength of sounds, which may be used to raise other passions; nor notes which are shrill or harsh or deep; it agrees best with such that a clear, even, smooth, and weak. The second is; that great variety, and quick transitions from one measure or tone to another, are contrary to the genius of the beautiful in musick. Such transitions often excite mirth, or other sudden or tumultuous passions; but not that sinking, that melting, that languor, which is the characteristic effect of the beautiful as it regards every sense. The passion excited by beauty is in fact nearer to a species of melancholy, than to jollity and mirth. I do not here mean to confine musick to any one species of notes, or tones, neither is it an art in which I can say I have any great skill. My sole design in this remark is, to settle a consistent idea of beauty. The infinite variety of the affections of the soul will suggest to a good head, and skilful ear, a variety of such sounds as are fitted to raise them. It can be no prejudice to this, to clear and distinguish some few particulars, that belong to the same class, and are consistent with each other, from the immense crowd of different, and sometimes contradictory, ideas, that rank vulgarly under the standard of beauty. And of these it is my intention to mark such only of the leading points as show the conformity of the sense of Hearing with all the other senses, in the article of their pleasures.' [1756: Burke, *On the Sublime and Beautiful*, p. 58]

On occasion, **Bacon** highlighted the difficulty of using language to describe tone. But he clearly felt that the attempt was worthwhile, because, while 'no two voices are alike', 'it is clear that all expression, purely vocal, depends upon this agent, because tone is the vehicle both of elocution and of execution, and success in all degrees depends upon the manner in which the sense of hearing is affected by its various modifications.' [Sept 1820: QMMR, p. 255] That's why QMMR's articles contain many pages on vocal tone. The treatise authors insisted that a good voice must be a 'natural' voice. As such, it was understood that there was considerable natural variation, so singers could début with a soft but still valued 'voce di camera', or alternatively, they could discover a strong, full and powerful 'theatrical voice', audible even in large spaces.

Clearly, calibration against a decibel scale is impossible, because descriptions of singers' voices as 'loud' or 'soft' can only be relative. But I did some benchmarking, based largely on statements like A was louder than B, C was softer than B, and the like. The table at Illus. 34 below lists some admired female singers, ranked ROUGHLY in order from loud to soft.

I've already noted [p. 46] Gardiner's comment on Catalani that 'such was her extraordinary power of voice, that it was said, 'place her at the top of St. Paul's, and she will be heard at the Opera House.' [Gardiner, *Music of Nature*, p. 135]

QMMR wrote that her compass 'was scarcely less in extent than Billington's, but the quality of voice was essentially different. Billington's was bird-like or flutey, but Catalani's was full, rich, and magnificent beyond any other voice we ever heard. It bore no resemblance to any instrument, except we could imagine the tone of the musical glasses to be magnified in volume to the same gradation of power, then perhaps there might exist some similitude.' [June 1818: QMMR, p. 183].

Voice described as:	Singer:
Loud, Full, Powerful, Rich, Opera-scale ↑ ↓ **Soft, Delicate, Thin, Voce di Camera**	Angelica Catalani Jane Bacon Giuditta Pasta Miss Wilkinson Gertrud Mara Isabella Colbran Brigida Banti Elizabeth Billington Violante Camporese Miss Povey Amelia George Mainvielle Fodor Maria Malibran Miss Carew Catherine Stephens Virginie Blasis Margaretha Stockhausen Eliza Salmon Mary Ann Paton Lucia Vestris Ronzi de Begnis Caradori-Allan Laure Cinti-Damoreau

Illus. 34: Female Singers: Tentative Volume League Table

The approximate ranking of female vocalists by volume is based on reviews written in their early years. However, some singers acquired greater volume later on in their careers:

Rosalbina Caradori-Allan. Aged 22, 'To the distant parts of the theatre her voice, we apprehend, did not tell'. [21 Jan 1822: T] But, at the age of 44, 'her silvery liquid notes, were placed in fine contrast to the trumpet obligato accompaniment, most felicitously played by Mr. Elwood'. [13 Apr. 1844: MT] Four years later, '… in Cimarosa's aria she proved the unfading power and quality of her voice' [25 Mar. 1848: Ex]

Henrietta Nina Sontag. At the age of 24 she had 'a lovely treble voice of immense compass if not great power' [5 Aug. 1827: Waldie] 26 years later, she 'was in fresher, stronger, richer voice than ever in her previous visits'. [17 Dec. 1853: *Dwight's*]

Maria Malibran. As will be apparent from the reviews at Section 3.5.14, while her voice aged 17 suffered from want of power, described as a temporary obstacle to prima donna status, she had acquired a 'clear and powerful voice' some 11 years later at the close of her career.

Catherine Hayes. As I will show in the reviews at Section 3.5.18, while filling La Scala was out of the question for her at age 28, her soprano had matured after 8 years into a 'delicious sweetness, fulness, roundness and power'. [30 Sep. 1854: *Bell's Life in Sydney*]

Clara Novello. A review of her singing aged 17 in York Minster noted her 'deficiency of power, for so extensive an edifice'. [11 Sep. 1835: HP] But, some 20 years later, as I report at section 3.5.19, her voice 'rang out pure and large and trumpet like' in the vast space of the Crystal Palace.

While female singers normally débuted in their teens, male singers typically emerged in their twenties with a fully developed voice. This probably explains why volume expansion by male singers through a career was unusual. Baritone Henry Phillips is perhaps an exception. At the beginning of his career, aged 19, 'His voice was then a mere thread.' [30 Sep. 1830: QMMR] But 16 years later, he 'sang with great power, and a splendid quality of tone.' [2 Dec. 1836: *Hull Packet*]

If you visited a concert at which **Bacon** was present, you might sometimes see him moving around the auditorium at intervals during the music, trying out various locations for quality and strength of sound. He was especially interested in whether distance from the singer affected audibility, besides the hearability of singers in large buildings. He also explained why forcing was counter-productive: 'Mrs. [Eliza] Salmon is remarkable for the peculiar properties of tone which fit it for penetrating to a distance. At the Oratorios in Covent Garden Theatre, she is as clearly audible in the back of the front boxes as near the stage. Yet we apprehend she does not exert herself more than in the Hanover-square Concert Room, where, at the back of the Director's box, the finest attenuations of the executive parts of her "Sweet bird" are as distinct and beautiful as in her own drawing-room. The same principles apply to all voices, and the reasoning upon which CHLADNI[19] builds his division of sound, and his distinction between mere noise and tone, affords probably the true reason why tone, when forced, is not so audible or so agreeable, as when more easily produced. It is founded on mathematical truth.' [Mar. 1822: QMMR, p. 22] He commented later: 'The writer of this article has enjoyed many opportunities of hearing great singers, both in public and private, and of measuring, by singing with them in private, their several capacities and powers, and he has uniformly been surprised at the comparatively small volume of voice they are accustomed to employ. A few months ago he heard Madame [Violante] Camporese] [at around median level in the volume league table at Illus. 34] from the further end of the largest room in London, and she was distinctly heard, even in the most minute turns and embellishments. In a few minutes he stood within a yard of her, in the

---

19 Ernst Chladni [1756–1827] was a German physicist and musician, now labelled as 'the father of acoustics'.

orchestra, when it seemed in that position, as if her voice could not possibly make its way beyond a few feet.' [Dec. 1822: QMMR, p. 62]

Bacon made similar observations on Maria Caradori-Allan's singing. 'Madame Caradori's Deh parlate [Recit. And Song--Madame Caradori--"Deh! parlate" (*Il sacrifizio d'Abram* by Cimarosa), from Part III of First Grand Selection, performed on Tuesday September 13, 1825 in York Minster] was exceedingly delicate, and it was a matter of surprize how her voice made its way through so vast a building, but nothing could be more distinctly heard.' [Sep. 1825: QMMR, p. 435] He added later: 'The circumstance we have noticed in our account of the York meeting corroborates this truth very plainly. No singer was heard so perfectly through the vast space of the Minster as Madame Caradori Allan. Yet Miss Stephens, Miss Wilkinson, and we believe Miss Travis [before marriage to William Knyvett], have much more volume than Madame C.A. The reason then of the tone travelling so far is to be sought in the fact, that it is purer, namely less [presumably the word more was intended?] free from the mouth, the throat, and the lips, than the voices of the other singers named. It is also certainly much thinner.' [Dec. 1825: QMMR, p. 464]

Some spaces were viewed as too large. 'THOUGH my *Regulus* is an opera, of which I am the least ashamed; and though my dear [Anton] *Raaff* is such a performer as cannot be paralleled; I believe that they are not made for each other, and that, joined together, they will both be sacrificed. That is to say, the part of *Regulus* will ruin my poor *Raaff*, and *Raaff* will be the ruin of the part, and of the opera. This drama cannot succeed, unless the principal personage pleases extremely; and our dear *Raaff* is physically unable to support this weight. The reasons are numerous, founded on experience; and I hope that your excellence will believe a man who venerates you, and esteems *Raaff* as much as he merits, that is to say, excessively.—Besides, that immense space in the great theatre of *San Carlo*, will absorb all those inimitable graces, and that wonderful agility, which render this charming singer so admirable in a room: indeed he has split upon this rock elsewhere, in theatres three times less spacious than this; so that I can hardly hope that he will share a better fate in future.' [Nov. 1751: letter from Metastasio to Princess Di Belmonte, quoted in Bur, *Metastasio*, Vol. 1, pp. 405–6]

Some 65 years later, Spohr expressed similar views, as apparent from his sarcastic comments on San Carlo: 'Military movements of infantry and cavalry, battles, and storms at sea can be represented here [San Carlo] without falling into the ludicrous. But for opera, itself, the house is too large. Although the singers, Signora [Isabella Angela] Colbran and the Signori Nozzari, Benedetti, etc., have very strong voices, only their highest and most stentorian tones could be heard. Any kind of tender utterance was lost.' [15 Feb. 1817: Spohr, *Musical Journeys*, p. 176]

Metastasio's and Spohr's comments were echoed elsewhere: 'A very mistaken opinion has been put forth that, though playhouses may be too large, opera-houses cannot. You may, to be sure, increase the strength of the orchestra, but not the voices of the singers; and hence the hard and toneless shouting and screaming, and the rapid destruction of voice. ' [10 June 1835: Von Raumer] However, spaces could also be too small—I've already noted [p. 143] Edgcumbe's comment on Pasta's voice being too forcible and vehement in a small room. By contrast, a correspondent commented from Dresden in a Foreign Musical Report: 'In a theatre of a moderate compass like ours [Dresden Theatre], the talents of the artist are developed in an effective and yet pretensionless manner; none of those violent efforts are necessary, which are not less painful to the singer than to the hearer; this is a blessing which we still enjoy, but which most of the larger cities of Europe have either lost, or are getting rid of as quickly as they can. The great favourite of the season has been a Madlle. Heygendorf, whose voice is said to be of the first-rate quality, and who displays an excellent school. Not only is the lightness and grace with which she gives the ornamental passages excellent, and a proof of the best taste; but the power of her recitative and declamatory song is not less admirable.' [31 Nov. 1825: Har]

John Marsh reports on a visit to Drury Lane Theatre the day after its re-opening on 21 April 1794 following rebuilding. He wrote that he 'was at an imense distance from the stage' while noting that the rebuilding resulted in 'a very great addition to the profits of the house, which was however obtain'd at the expence of the comfort & convenience of the spectators & audience, the house being now on so large a scale that it required great exertion in the actors & much attention from their auditors for the former to be heard all over the house, w'ch they by no means were in the part where I sat.' Brian Robins added a footnote: 'The new Drury Lane theater was the third of that name, replacing the building demolished in 1791. Built by Henry Holland at a cost of £151,000 it was, as Marsh's words suggest, a huge building, seating an audience of 3611. The resulting lack of intimacy in the large new theaters (Covent Garden had recently also been enlarged) caused many of the leading players of the day to modify their acting style.' [21 Apr. 1794: Marsh, Vol. 1, p. 549]

The theatre at the Haymarket (variously called Queen's Theatre, King's Theatre, His Majesty's Theatre and Italian Opera house) was also rebuilt in 1791 and enlarged in 1816-1818 to hold 2,500 people. Several singers over the next few decades discovered that their sweet, soft voices could not be heard in this space. These included Maria Caradori Allan, Virginie Blasis, Laure Cinti-Damoreau, Giuseppina Ronzi de Begnis and Maria Malibran, as indicated by descriptions included later in this book.

Later in the nineteenth century, Friedrich Wieck also complained about large halls: 'That singers, male and female, can make an effect in such a hall [accommodating 2,000-3,000 people] when, instead of singing, they shout in the most modern French, Italian and also, unfortunately, German manner. Thus, instead of helping to reestablish and promote the pure, chaste, art of song, now represented, with few exceptions, only by Jenny Lind and Henriette Sontag, they would, on the contrary, render grievous assistance to the unnatural.' [1852: Wieck, p. 167]

Over the last century or so, both male and female singers in opera or oratorio usually deliver high notes at forte or fortissimo volume, regardless when the music was composed. This approach is certainly inartistic for early music. Treatises through the long eighteenth century consistently urged vocalists to sing high notes softly but low notes loudly, and, above all, not to force the voice.

Pietro Reggio's slim treatise, published in 1677, was devoted exclusively to this precept: 'Here the Bass must have a care, when he is to Sing any Division that runs upon high Notes, to Sing them smooth, and in descending he must increase lowder and lowder, and the lower the Notes the more he must strengthen his Voice, and on the contrary, the higher his Voice ascends, the softer he must sing: this is the most fine way of Singing a Bass.' [Reggio, p. 31]

Tosi's prescription was comparable: 'One should warn, however, that the higher the notes, the more necessary to touch them with sweetness, to avoid screaming.' [1723: Tosi, trans. Foreman, p. 11]

Mancini gave similar emphasis: '… it is natural, that in themselves the lower notes are more vibrant, or sustained by strength according to need, and yet the high notes, however they be used, should always be treated with sweetness, thus there should always be conserved a correspondent proportion between the one and the other. [p. 51] … He who has once tested his voice, and through repeated experience has found it sufficient to be heard in whatever vast place, even though it seemed to him to be somewhat weak and exhausted; for him there is no need to force it, indeed he must ascertain that he is making the usual impression on the auditor. It is true, that the same quantity of voice is not sufficient for every place; and for this reason the great professor uses prior trials, reflections, and practice to know how to proportion his voice to every location: but it is also true, that when the professor does not find his voice sufficient for a given vastness, he still should not force it, in order not to ruin the voice, and the chest. It remains only to decide that forcing the voice is one of the great errors which a singer can commit. [p. 32].' [1774: Mancini].

At the end of the century, **William Jackson** warned: 'There are some things, however, which may be described: such as forcing the Voice in the upper part, where it ought ever to be soft; and singing the lower tones faint, which should always be full.' [1791: Jackson, p. 23]

Giacomo Ferrari agreed: 'By much study and practice the voice may acquire more extent towards its extremities, than it naturally possesses. But great care must be taken never to force it on the acute notes, but to strengthen and exercise it on the grave ones.' [15 May 1818: Ferrari, p. 2]

As late as 1841, **Domenico Francesco Crivelli** instructed: 'RULE 7th. The voice should never be so much strained in the higher notes as to produce a screaming shrill sound; but, on the contrary, it should always be carried to those notes with particular sweetness and softness, unless it be in passages requiring more energy of expression, or a more pointed manner in their performance.' [1841: Crivelli].

Treatise authors sometimes emphasised that one alternative to forcing was to extend into the falsetto register: 'IX. Never to force the Voice, in order to extend its compass in the VOCE DI PETTO upwards; but rather to cultivate the VOCE DI TESTA in what is called FALSETTO, in order to join it well and imperceptibly, to the VOCE DI PETTO for fear of incurring the disagreeable habit of singing in the

Throat, or through the Nose; unpardonable Faults in a Singer.' [1797: Aprile, p. 2]

The similarity of Eliza Salmon's and Catherine Stephens's voices to the glass harmonica has already been noted. Clearly their voices were soft. Incidentally, few of the best singers were accused of shrieking or forcing, which, it is quite clear, audiences were not conditioned to accept, with one huge exception, which I'll come on to shortly. Bacon wrote: 'the most offensive deviations from natural tone, are instigated by a view to singing with greater power, or louder than the habitual structure of the organs seem to admit.' [Sep. 1820: QMMR, p. 262] Soft singing was contrasted favourably with shouting and screaming:

> 'Her voice [Madame Sessi's] would be yet more agreeable, were it not so often on the full stretch, which becomes from long continuance painful, and wants the relief of an undulating softness that might steal upon the ear, with a delicate predominance over the rich harmony that accompanies it. This was the style in which Madame [Josephina] Grassini and the late Mr. [Samuel] Harrison so eminently excelled, and is a thousand times more delightful than the shouting mode which has become such a fatal passion among theatrical singers, from Braham who swells his voice like a news-horn, to [Mr. J] Smith who is as coarse and rough as a nutmeg-grater.' [29 Jan. 1815: Ex]

> 'The honour of her best performance [Catherine Stephens] was shared by [John] Sinclair in a duet, made by harmonizing the air of Roy's Wife to a very slow movement. It held the house in attentive silence, and was like a couple of flutes.' [15 Mar. 1818: Ex]

> 'She [Rosalie Corri] has a considerable power in making her higher notes at once soft and distinct.' [3 Jul. 1820: Ex]

The lightness and grace of Madlle. Heygendorf's singing has already been noted [see p. 109 above].

> 'On Tuesday evening Madame [Adelaida] SALA made her second appearance at this theatre [Covent Garden] as the Countess in the thing insolently called the opera of Figaro…Sala has what we would designate a well-cultivated, motherly voice (if the meaning be comprehensible); and indeed the whole evening we could scarcely divest ourselves of the idea that we were listening to a gentlewoman in her own drawing-room. The quality of her voice is full and round, though not powerful, and she had the good sense not to force it—the vice triumphant of the modern squalling school.' [6 Jan. 1828: Ex]

Mrs William Knyvett's restraint was praised: 'This lady has a purity of taste, a delicacy of expression, and a correctness of intonation which must always render her singing attractive. There is no pretence in what she does, no screaming, no squalling, no striving at great effects.' [17 Sep. 1828: *Derby Mercury*]

However, loud singing was gaining ground, albeit it was invariably deplored:

> Madame Elizabeth Feron was harshly excoriated: 'We hoped, and we even expected, that she would not again sing so injudiciously loud, as to make herself ridiculously conspicuous.

Last night, however, we had the mortification to find we were miserably deceived. Almost all through the play it seemed to be the sole object of her ambition to drown the voices of all who had to sing with her. Instead of that powerful and varied strains of harmony which we had been accustomed to hear, we were frequently almost frightened from our seats by a harsh dissonant scream.' [26 Nov. 1811: MP] .

Miriam Hammersley Buggins was castigated for her unceasing fortissimo: 'Upon natural requisites, we are sorry to alledge, Miss Buggins can, at present, alone depend. Her execution is slovenly and inefficient; her time neither felt or preserved, and her vocal energies wielded at every impulse, without remission or remorse. She drops upon us with incessant uproar, like a Swiss waterfall, and loses the best impressions of power, by forgetting the necessity of contrast.' [3 Jul. 1817: TI]

Charles Incledon fell foul of the critics towards the end of his career: 'Mr. Incledon's attempts at fine singing latterly were mere burlesques; the rugged coarse tones of his voice he endeavoured to correct by falsetto movements executed in the windpipe. The vain endeavour to repair decaying nature always commenced in something resembling a parrot's whistle, and ended by soaring into a squall not more musical than that bird's delectable scream when enraged.' [1818: *New Bon Ton Magazine*]

'Madame [Violante] Camporese] would do well to scream less; her voice sounded unusually harsh and metallic, owing to her strenuous exertion in the arduous performance.' [28 Apr. 1822: Ex]

Miss Hughes was berated: 'The peculiarity of the style we object to—nay, abhor—is that of invariably resorting to the forcing her voice into a loud note, and sinking it immediately into a piano, so as to be scarcely audible; and this not with reference to the sentiment, but for the artificial purpose of producing a violent contrast of light and shade. This was not the style of the inimitable [Josephine] Fodor[-Mainvielle].' [28 Oct. 1827: Ex].

As I will show in Part 5, by the late 1830s audiences were coming under fire from the *Ut de poitrine*.

2.12 The French [Dis]Connection

One country, France, did not sign up to the Italian hegemony. Several authorities agreed that what Italians dubbed the **'urla Francese'**, or French Howl, was objectionable. The evidence, covering a century or so, is presented below.

> **Quantz** recalled his visit to Paris in 1726: 'Though the French style was not unknown to me and I did like their manner of playing very much, I liked neither the warmed-over and worn ideas of their opera composers, nor the small difference between recitative and aria, nor the exaggerated and affected howling of her male singers, and especially her female singers. [Marie] Antier, [Marie] Pélissier, and [Catherine-Nicole] Le Maure were then singing in the theatre. These French singers did not lack beautiful voices, if only they had known how to use them correctly. The male voices, also as received from nature, were not bad.' [15 Aug. 1726: Quantz, *Life*] Quantz explained later on in his *Versuch*: 'The Italians and several other nations unite this falsetto with the chest voice, and make use of it to great advantage in singing: among the French, however, it is not customary, and for that reason their singing in the high register is often transformed into a disagreeable shrieking, the effect of which is exactly the same as that created when you do not cover the mouth hole sufficiently on the flute, and when you try to force out the high notes by blowing more strongly.' [1752: Quantz, *Versuch*, p. 55]

> **Hogarth** wrote: 'It remains to add a few words respecting the French school of singing. Till within a recent period, the badness of French singing has been constantly remarked by all (except the French themselves) who have had occasion to speak of the music of that country ... Rousseau, in his celebrated Lettre sur la Musique Francaise [1753] and, indeed, in all his musical writings, speaks of the French singing with unmeasured ridicule and contempt, characterising the voices as harsh and screaming, the style as vicious, and the expression as affected and unnatural.' [1753: Hogarth, *Memoirs of the Opera*, Vol. 2, p. 272]

> **Burney** recounted: 'The principal counter-tenor had a solo verse [in *Beatus Vir*, a motet] which he bellowed out with as much violence as if he had done it for life, while a knife was at a throat. But though this wholly stunned me, I plainly ***saw***, by the smiles of ineffable satisfaction which were visible in the countenances of ninety-nine out of a hundred of the company, and ***heard***, by the most violent applause that a ravished audience could bestow, that it was quite what their hearts felt, and their souls loved. ***C'est superbe!*** was echoed from one to the other through the whole house.' [14 June 1770: Bur, *The Present State ... France and Italy*, p. 26] Burney seems to have realised that an alternative paradigm prevailed in France, which had nothing in common with the Italian method dominant elsewhere in Europe.

> In letters to his father, **Wolfgang Mozart** took strong exception to French singing: 'What annoys me most of all in this business is that our French gentlemen have only improved their goût to this extent that they can now listen to good stuff as well. But to expect them to realise that their own music is bad or at least to notice the difference—Heaven preserve us! And their singing! Good Lord! Let me never hear a Frenchwoman singing Italian arias. I can forgive her if she screeches out her French trash, but not if she ruins good music! It's simply unbearable.'

[5 Apr. 1778, *Letters*, p. 522] Later, he wrote: 'And then the men and women singers! [at the *Concert Spirituel*] Indeed they hardly deserve the name, for they don't sing—they yell—howl—and that too with all their might, through their noses and throats.' [9 July 1778: *Letters*, p. 564]

Burney commented in Rees: 'French singing at the serious opera of "Iphigenie en Tauride" [Gluck] has been very aptly compared, not to a female in distress, but in labour during the throes of childbirth. The French, always partial to "la musique criarde", have had their taste flattered by Gluck, who knew that though they could not sing, they could scream to some tune. His harsh modulations, and their "éclats de voix", augmented, "à force de l'Orchestre", he was sure would be well heard, and fix his fame.' [18 May 1779: Bur, *Rees's Cyclopædia*]

Edgcumbe reviewed the singing of Madlle [Antoinette] Saint-Huberti: 'She was a fine actress, and in her singing a little less violent and extravagant than the generality of French singers, but still had too much of the national style.' [1 Aug. 1784: Edgcumbe, p. 36]

Michael Kelly noted on his visit to the opera in Paris: '... but the principal singers (God save them) made a shriek louder than I thought any human beings capable of producing.' [1 Apr. 1787: Kelly, *Reminiscences*, p. 284]

John Waldie echoed Quantz's comments: 'The only draw back on the pleasure of this entertainment is the disagreeable style of the music, which tho' faultless in the performance of the Orchestra, and of most admirable harmony in the Choruses,—yet the airs and recitative are very unpleasing, being a continual succession of unmeaning squalls and discords, and a seeming contest between the performers who should exert their lungs most—nothing could be so contrary to any discrimination or delicacy of execution than the continual climax of noise attempted every moment, till the ear is harassed with discords. Gluck himself would be furious if he could hear this painful contest destroy his music. Some of the Singers, especially the two ladies and Lainée, had fine clear and powerful voices, and could they quit that barbarous style, and adopt the delicacy and refinement of the Italians, would become excellent singers, but at present it is no pleasure to hear them.' [8 June 1802: Waldie, *Journal*] Waldie also noted: 'Madame Albert screamed dreadfully.' [2 Feb. 1819, with another reference to her screaming on 10 Feb. 1819] Later the same year, Waldie added: 'Boildieu's music and translated from the French—it was well got up, and the orchestra not much inferior to Madrid—but the singing for screaming out of tune and ugly women exceeded any thing bad I ever heard' [8 Jul. 1819]

Thomas Moore deplored the singing: 'Went to seek for Viotti in order to get permission to attend the rehearsal of Spontini's new opera, "Olympie", this evening ... The rehearsal very singular; the stage lighted up, and all the scenery in form, and the artists in their every day clothes: the music, too, full of notes and overloaded harmonies; and the way it was squalled and mewled out by Madames Branchia and Albert detestable.' [1819: Moore, Vol. 3, p. 90]

QMMR reported on the Royal Academy of Music in Paris: 'It is supposed that the stranger who for the first time enjoys this magnificent spectacle must be overwhelmed with astonishment and delight at all he sees and hears. Alas, no! The first thing that strikes him is, the screaming (criallerie) of the singers and the noise of the orchestra.' [Aug. 1820: QMMR, p. 507]

D. G. Gislason wrote in his 1992 PhD thesis: 'At this theatre, the emphasis on preserving the intelligibility of the text at the expense of the melodic line had produced a heavily accented declamatory style of delivery, known to the Italians since the eighteenth century as the urlo francese or "French Howl". **Castil-Blaze** constantly pointed out in his early articles the absurdity of this singing style, and urged his readers to look instead to the Italian model of musical expression, which he insisted could generate equivalent extremes of emotional intensity, but without resorting to calamitously unmusical shrieks and howls.' [reference to c. 1821: Gislason, *Castil-Blaze, De L'Opéra en France*]

'But the part of Mahomet [in Maometto] was sung by a very handsome man named Derivis [Nicolas-Prosper Dérivis], a French singer, par excellence; that is to say, screaming and howling incessantly.' [30 Jun. 1827: QMMR, p. 180]

However, some French singers came round to the Italian method during the 1820s, encouraged by critics such as Castil-Blaze and Rossini. For example, QMMR noted of Josephine Fodor-Mainvielle: 'Educated in a fine school, her voice has obtained such flexibility that every passage is executed with a lightness and at the same time a tenderness it is impossible to describe.' [2 Mar. 1823: QMMR, p. 418] Edgcumbe suggested that the *urlo francese* era had passed by the early 1830s, which he attributed to Laure Cinti-Damoreau: 'But she would do so only on condition of choosing the operas and parts she should perform; and by her means, a very great change has taken place in the national opera, where good music may now be heard, such as will please other ears besides French; and the former horrible screamings and howlings are nearly exploded.' [Edgcumbe, p. 215]

2.13   Low Larynx Singing

2.13.1   Views Expressed in Treatises

I touched on guttural singing, in defining what was explicitly forbidden in a good ***portamento di voce***. The treatises unanimously condemned low larynx singing, known to today's vocal tutors as 'laryngeal development', but described at that time as throaty, guttural, thick, or fat singing, exemplified as follows:

Tosi warned: 'The greatest diligence of the master should be directed to the voice of the scholar, which, if it be of the chest or of the head, should come out limpid and clear, without passing through the nose nor being suppressed in the throat, which are the two most horrible defects of a singer, and without remedy when they have taken possession.' [1721: Tosi, trans. Foreman, p. 13]

Quantz agreed: 'If you press the tongue against the palate, or clamp the teeth together so that the mouth is not sufficiently open, an obstruction of the tone results which gives rise to the principal defects of singing, that is, the so-called throaty voice and the nasal voice.' [1752: Quantz, *Versuch*]

Mancini explained why singers must avoid low larynx emission: 'That which is known as the defect of the throat, or the defect of the crude and smothered voice, always arises from the failure of the singer to derive and sustain the voice from the natural strength of the chest; he believes he will obtain the best effect solely by stretching the fauces. He is fooling himself, however, and should know for a certainty that this means alone is not sufficient to correct the voice, but is on the contrary absolutely pernicious, for the reason that if the fauces, as demonstrated in the third Article, are a part of the organ of the voice, this cannot come forth naturally and beautifully as long as the fauces are in a forced position, and impeded from working naturally. Every scholar must then tirelessly accustom his chest to give forth the voice with naturalness, and to use simply the light action of the fauces.' [1774: Mancini, p. 27]

Dr James Nares wrote: 'Let the Master attend strictly to the delivery of the Voice, whether di petto or di testa, that it be not checked by contracting the Throat, nor forced thro' the Nose in a disagreeable manner, both which Faults are unpardonable in a Singer.' [1778: Nares]

Thomas Holcroft concurred: '5. To sing from the chest and not from the throat. Cathedral and church singers, with their imitators, offend exceedingly by this fault [singing from the throat], though it requires much pains and practice to acquire it. Allured by a certain roundness and sweetness of tone, its admirers do not perceive that it gives an unvaried monotony and total want of expression. To sing from the chest requires a habit of swelling the chest, retaining the breath, and fetching the sound from the bottom. It is difficult to obtain, but gives great power when obtained.' [1782: Holcroft, *Convivial Songster*].

Anselm Bayly supported Tosi: 'If the sounds are hindered and choked in the throat, or confined within the mouth by the teeth, the tones produced are guttural and disagreeable, after the manner called mouthing and muttering, or mumbling. The throat then, mouth, teeth and lips, moderately opened with steadiness, this it is that gives a proper rotundity to the sounds, and a sweetness superior to that of any instrument whatever.' [1788: Bayly, *Alliance of Musick*, p. 14]

Charles Dibdin commented: 'Fat singing is also a favorite mode, as if a man had eaten too much after dinner; but I know of nothing that so completely destroys the effect of singing, and at the same time is so comical in itself, as swallowing the words.' [1805: Dibdin, *Musical Mentor*]

Charles Smyth sternly warned his son: *Singing in the throat* is occasioned by making a kind of tone which conveys to a hearer the idea that the singer has a *swelling* in his throat; and in addition to this inconvenience has a chord tied tight round his neck. It is very easy to sing the words *Do* and *Sol* in the throat. It is not without effort that a person can sing "La" in the throat. In order to avoid this most disgusting defect, all good singers practise divisions and exercises in solfeggio, to the syllable "La". The Italians, who hold guttural singing in utter abhorrence, always practise to some such word as "La", "Fa", or the word "Amen". I never heard an Italian sing in his throat; but I do remember to have heard a singing-master of great eminence, in the metropolis, who is now no more, form his tone so high in the head, as absolutely to fall into the contrary extreme of *nasality*. [1810: Smyth, *Six Letters*, p. 3/4]

Gesualdo Lanza instructed: 'Each of these voices [voce di testa and voce di petto] may have certain defects, which, if not guarded against, will materially injure the Tone; and as these defects proceed principally from an improper formation of the mouth, the utility of the foregoing rules upon that subject should be strictly enforced. The first of these defects, is, bringing the voice through the throat, thereby causing an unpleasant, thick, and guttural tone! The second, is causing the voice to be emitted through the Teeth, which will always produce a hissing sound, and render singing very difficult: The third is in bringing the voice out through the Nose, this is worse than all, and cannot be too carefully guarded against.' [1813: Lanza, *Elements of Singing*, pp. x and xi]

Jean Jousse wrote in his *Vocal Primer*: 'Q. What are the defects to be guarded against in singing? / A. The first is bringing the voice from the throat, which gives the sound a thick, guttural tone. The second defect is when the sound comes in contact with the teeth, which causes an unpleasant hissing: this defect is easily remedied by keeping the mouth sufficiently open and parting the two rows of teeth from each other. The third defect is forcing the voice through the nose, which renders the tone nasal: this defect is worse than any other, and should be carefully avoided.' [1815: Jousse, p. 5]

I've already noted **Richard Mackenzie Bacon**'s objection to thick guttural tone by amateurs, instead of the brilliant silvery 'purezza argentina'. [p. 16]

2.13.2 Views Expressed in Reviews

On the whole, reviewers agreed with treatise writers in praising clear [non throaty] singing:

Quantz praised **Matteo Berselli**, a soprano castrato: 'Berselli had an agreeable but slightly thin, high soprano, which ranged from middle "c" to high "f" with great ease. He amazed his listeners more through this than through artful singing.' [Apr. 1719: Quantz, *Life*, p. 292]

Burney quoted Quantz's description of castrato **Domenico Annibali**'s voice as 'clear and penetrating, as to make its way through all obstructions', strongly suggesting high/neutral larynx production.

'Her clear, silvery soprano [**Virginie Blasis**], and the purity of her musical articulation, were advantageous features of distinction throughout the part, especially when united to other voices.' [17 Mar. 1829: NMM]

Bacon's comment that **Eliza Salmon**'s 'voice is formed high, but is beyond question exceedingly pure and beautiful' stipulated high larynx emission. [Sep. 1825: QMMR, p. 279]

I quoted [p. 108] Bacon's approval of **Maria Caradori-Allan**'s pure and thin tone, which he felt explained why her voice was heard so well in the vast space of York minster.

Bacon described the voice of **Lewis Bernard Sapio** in similar terms: 'The quality of his tone is full, and it is rendered brilliant by the way in which he brings it forth, namely, very high in the head—perhaps somewhat higher indeed than the Italian method prescribes. While therefore it bestows a superior brightness, if we may so speak, there is at the same time a visible force which we suspect detracts from its sweetness and beauty.' [Sep. 1825: QMMR, p. 280].

Bacon wrote of Filippo Galli: 'His voice is magnificent in volume, and when the tone is not formed so high as to make it nasal, which is sometimes the case, it is round, rich, and smooth.' [Sep. 1826: QMMR, p. 53]

By contrast, as might be expected, reviewers usually deplored throatiness:

Gabriel Vincent Thévenard. 'He had a tenor voice, which made the public forget that of Beaumavielle; it was sonorous, mellow, and extensive in compass. He sung a little through the throat, but by dint of art, he found the means of rendering this little defect even agreeable.' [c. 1690: Bur, *Rees's Cyclopædia*, quoting Laborde]

Mr. Norris 'sang very agreeably, but lately his tones are monastic and guttural. Oxford Christmas brawn has too much fattened his London Lent voice.' [1 May 1780: *ABC Dario Musico*, p. 35]

As I've noted in section 2.3.22, Luigi Marchesi's voice was reported by Edgcumbe as 'a little inclined to be thick'.

Spray family. 'The family of the Sprays were remarkable for their excellent voices; a sort of oily liquidity of tone that I have never since heard ... I once heard the three brothers sing "Wine does wonders every day". It certainly was the most perfect thing of the kind I ever heard. The voices were so much alike, so equal, of that rich quality, and so completely blended together, that I could not distinguish one from the other.' [Dec. 1791: Gardiner, *Music and Friends*, p. 315]

Charles Dignum: 'His voice is a soft agreeable tenor, but rendered somewhat unpleasant by being formed too much in his throat.' [1795: Haslewood]

Josephina Grassini. 'Her voice, though somewhat husky and guttural, was a perfect contralto, and possessed all the soothing and devotional softness which distinguishes that class of voice when breathed from a female organ.' [14 Jan. 1804: Har]

Giuseppe Siboni. 'The male performers with Catalani were for the most part of a very inferior description, and fit only for second singers. The first exception was [Giuseppe] Siboni, who sung well, but with a thick and tremulous voice: he staid however only a short time.' [13 Dec. 1806: Edgcumbe, p. 102]

Miss Poole [Maria Dickons]. 'In the song of "Cease your funning", which, from long custom, is always expected to be sung with flourishes, Mrs. Dickons was justly applauded; but in the gentle airs which stamp the character of the music, and in which embellishments cannot be often introduced, she was by no means so successful. The defect in her tone, which we before mentioned, was here remarkably conspicuous; and the sounds elicited from the throat, instead of the chest, gave a sharpness to that which was always intended to be sweet.' [24 Oct. 1807: MC]

Mr J Smith. 'With much of the little expression of fatness exhibited by Mr. Dignum, his countenance is pleasant, and his figure, of the middle stature, tolerable. He possesses a counter-tenor of some power and sweetness, but it is without any remarkable degree of brilliant or correct execution.' [20 Jan. 1808: MM, Vol. 2.3, p. 50] 'He has considerable power, and occasional melodiousness of voice, but his tones are uncertain and wavering. The ear may detect this deficiency, when he endeavours to hold a high note, for he drops unconsciously through a number of divided tones. His appearance is fat, and, if I may use the expression, his voice is so too; it possesses that sort of inward oiliness, which would induce a blind man to suppose the singer a very jolly personage.' [24 Jan. 1808: Ex]

Mr Doyle: 'Some of Doyle's tones excite better expectations than his execution altogether realizes. I think he would sing better if he did not so studiously and determinedly thrust his chin under his neckcloth—this not only gives him a stiff appearance, but compresses and confines his throat so as sometimes to produce sounds, which, were I in a wood, I should think were uttered by some "tenant of the forest" suffering the pains of strangulation.' [3 Apr. 1808: Ex]

Mr Miller, from Bath 'sings in his throat terribly.' . [26 June 1809: Waldie]

Charles Edward Horn. 'His histrionic powers have all their ancient paucity, and his tones are breathed, as heretofore, with a snuffling thickness, as if the bridge of his nose was compressed by a rigid pair of spectacles.' [3 Jul. 1817: TI]

Violante Camporese. 'From these directions it will be discovered that the point of action in the voice is seated in the throat near where the hair terminates at the back of the neck. This place may be considered as the antechamber to the mouth, in which compartment all the beauties of execution must be prepared, never advancing into the mouth, or sinking into the throat, as the least deviation either one way or the other, will render the tone harsh and hard, thick, throaty, and guttural.' [Footnote: 'Madame Camporese's performance was truly excellent, except that some of her notes partook of the throaty tone, highly sickening and disgusting to the ear.'] [11 Jan. 1817: Gardiner, *Music of Nature*, p. 20]

Mr J Isaacs 'possesses just such a voice as might be poetically supposed to emanate from the Iron Man of Spenser. It grinds into our sensibilities by friction, and makes its way, like a sawing machine, through the stoutest obstacles, without a change of place or posture.' [3 Jul. 1817: TI]

M. Ponchard. 'Ponchard has a very thick poor voice & is vulgar, but animated.' [11 Aug. 1817: Waldie]

Miss Deborah Travis, later Mrs William Knyvett. 'We never heard an Italian singer to our recollection in the slightest degree guttural, we have very rarely indeed heard an English singer, whose voice could in all parts be said to be absolutely free from the throat. There is a thickness even in Miss Travis's tone (though we do not accuse her of singing in the throat) which we are persuaded arises from the tone not coming from quite so high a site in the passage, as the Italians would have taught her to bring it.' [Dec. 1818: QMMR, p. 472]

Madame Cornega. 'Madame Cornega is a most untaking person, with a countenance and figure at once old and young; her voice, like Torri's, is thick and unpleasant, but it has the merit of being well in tune, with an air of knowledge about her that gives precision to her performance, and all the effect her unfortunate tones are capable of.' [12 Feb. 1826: Ex]

Mr Stansbury. 'In his performance as a singer, his powers of execution appear considerable, and his style is tasteful, although a guttural sound is observable in the lower notes of his voice, which is by no means pleasing to the ear.' [13 Aug. 1828: *Evening Mail*]

Miss Hallande. 'It is scarcely pure, for her portamento (we use this word in its legitimate sense for the production of pure tone) has not been originally regulated with sufficient care. The tone therefore partakes a little of the throat—a fault which even now a good and attentive master might correct.' [June 1821: QMMR, p. 384]

John B. Duruset. 'Duruset's voice is like a dismal foggy day in November; but he is still many degrees above Mr Pearman, who ought never to aspire to singing any thing superior to "This bottle's the sun of our table",—and that not before gentlemen.' [11 Jan. 1823: *Scots Magazine*]

I report later on Waldie's critique of Manuel García I's thick voice [p. 174].

Mr Matthews. 'His vocal powers were very great, his voice of extensive compass, but a little inclined to be thick.' [1 Apr 1788: Edgcumbe]

William Pearman. 'Though the tone of his voice is particularly soft and pleasing, it is by no means clear; and it has the common fault of all voices which are formed by the efforts of the student, instead of the hand of nature, i.e. a want of fulness; an effect somewhat resembling that produced by the voice being under some artificial cause of compression this, which most hearers instantly perceive, we find it very difficult to define to our readers, and perhaps the term "smothered sound", will best indicate our meaning.' [Jul. 1825: Oxberry, *Dramatic Biography*]

Mr Plumer. 'His voice is weak, and by over-straining, (which he had better avoid), becomes thick and ruinous to his articulation.' [31 Oct. 1827: *Bury and Norwich Post*]

Miss Cawse: 'We admire neither the voice nor style of this young lady. The first is harsh and violent, it comes upon the ear in a gust, piercing and sharp; her execution is imperfect, and her persecuting love of cadences, and long guttural shakes (those clap-traps of the galleries) render her anything but a fit second in operas. We like a little of the heart in music—with Miss Cawse it is all larynx.' [Dec. 1828: LBA]

'M. Dobler, a bass singer, must be also recorded as possessing a pretty good voice—perhaps a little too fat and quaggy in its depth if rigorously criticised.' [Dec. 1827: QMMR, p. 497]

Elizabeth Inverarity. 'But, at present, it has a grand defect, which practice and study alone can remedy, that is the manner of bringing out the voice. It is too guttural, formed too much in the throat, whereas it should come out freely from the chest, which not only increases the tone, but enables the singer to execute with perfect ease, passages accomplished previously with considerable effort. The articulation of the words is likewise defective; here, again, practice is quite necessary. We know nothing more unmeaning than a song, in listening to which we cannot distinguish a syllable.' [20 Apr. 1829: EEC]

M. Werth. '… too much in his throat and too flat.' [Dec. 1829: Vincent Novello, *A Mozart Pilgrimage*]

2.13.3 A Contrarian and Heretical Opinion

In 1825, a most unusual event occurred. Somebody signing himself off as 'R' penned a long letter under the heading 'English and Italian Tone' to the QMMR's editor. [Sep. 1825: QMMR, Vol. VII, No. XXVII, p. 277] 'R' certainly wasn't Bacon himself, because the writer took what can only be described as a heretical position, suggesting that a degree of throatiness could actually ***improve*** vocal tone, in flat opposition to the prevailing hegemony. At one point, he admits that he is disturbed by attacks of conscience, when he becomes aware of the danger which attends this innovation, viz. his certain knowledge of its 'fatal final effects' that prevents him enjoying the sound. He is also concerned that his attitude 'is breaking the rules'! I supply the whole letter below [including R's original footnotes], as it offers fascinating insights, albeit unorthodox in its time, on attitudes both to rule breaking in general and specifically to low larynx emission at that time:

'Sir, / I am considerably perplexed to determine with absolute certainty concerning the properties of tone, as formed by the Italian and English methods. The Italians, although they contend that they produce the best and most perfect tone of the human voice, unquestionably compass their end by means completely artificial. The English, you will probably say, do no more than imitate the Italian method, and where they differ they fail. For a moment I shall suspend the admission or the contradiction of this universal belief, and merely remark that the English manner is more natural than the Italian.

'It has been laid down that pure tone is "that which neither partakes too strongly of the lips, the mouth, the throat, or the head, but which comes freely from the chest, and is delivered justly (without undergoing any perceptible alteration) from that particular place in its passage which we learn by sympathy, and which we perceive to be exactly the same in well-taught singers, instructed according to the Italian method. A tone so generated and so emitted is the pure voice."[20] I do not dissent from this definition, but the difficulty seems to me to lie in ascertaining the claims of the throat and the head. Any pollution by the lips or mouth is instantly to be detected, and always to be abhorred. But it is not quite so easy to distinguish the limits where the dominions of the throat and the head are to be divided, marked, and assigned. It appears to me that science and nature are at variance upon this point. The throat confers fullness, richness, body—the head, clearness and brilliancy. I would however be considered to speak with due reservation. A voice decidedly throaty or thick, and one decidedly thin and heady, are equally removed from that tinge of either on which I am treating. A singer "with a whole cathedral in his throat", or "with a conventicle in his nose", as the common expression goes, is

---

[20] Bacon's *Elements of Vocal Science*, p. 142.

not the object of my speculation. I allude to such persons as have just predominance enough of the head or throat to enable judges to dispute about the propriety of such a formation of tone.

'Let us proceed to examples; and as the tone of female voices is generally the most easily analysed, I shall draw my first instances from the ladies of the profession.

'The fullest, richest, and sweetest voice I know, is that of Miss [Emma Sarah] Love—but it is as certainly polluted by the throat and the mouth. No Italian would allow this tone to approach even to purity—yet it is very pleasing, not to say more pleasing than that of any other contralto singer.

'The tone of Madame Ronzi de Begnis is as clearly too much from the head. This formation it is which gives that "infantine quality" which has been the subject of remark in her memoir,[21] and which, though she has gotten rid of a great part of this fault of late, is still to be felt as a drawback upon her performance.

'The voice of Miss Wilkinson, the young lady who has appeared this season at the Ancient Concert, is rich, from the fact that it is in a degree throaty—so much so indeed, that I question whether, if this fault were corrected, its quality would remain. Her's is perhaps a case more completely in point than that of Miss Love. The moment Miss Wilkinson breathes a note, a practised ear revolts—an Italian would clap his hand upon his throat, and exclaim "*gola*"! It is nevertheless extremely doubtful whether this doth not confer the chief excellence of her tone. Yet it impedes her facility and lessens the brilliancy. It seems that the Italians have adopted a novel manner of forming the low notes of a contralto—at least I do not recollect to have heard such as are produced by Mad. Pasta before.[22] It is this peculiar formation that gives the three registers—namely, breast voice, to E or F at the bottom of the treble staff—mixt voice to C or D—and falsette, often all above. To unite these well is an immense difficulty, and it is scarcely a less [sic] to use the low notes with effect, except in songs of deep and intense passion.[23]

'The tone of Mrs. Salmon's voice is formed high, but is beyond question exceedingly pure and beautiful.[24] Miss Stephens's is more rich and full (I have heard it called by a very fine professional singer "a lovely voice"), yet perhaps equally pure. Now I conceive the difference between these the best and purest of all our English singers to lie merely in the fact, that Miss Stephens makes greater use of her throat than Mrs. Salmon—the consequence is, Mrs Salmon can execute with more volubility and freedom than Miss Stephens—Miss Stephens can give greater expression in declamation than Mrs. Salmon.

---

21   [Original footnote:] *Musical Review*, Vol. 4, p. 314.
22   [Original footnote:] Madame Pasta's lower notes were what the French critics call *sous voilées*, that is they were not clear, but come forth husky. This is the consequence of the application of too much force, and is overcome by industrious practice. Mad. Pasta's low tones were this season much less husky than before.
23   [Original footnote:] Velluti appears to use his low voice with even more ease than the high.
24   [RIB footnote:] This statement was copied from QMMR.

'The question that puzzles me is as follows.—There are many voices which, by a very slight additional employment of the powers of the throat, would gain sweetness and richness—*but* the instant one hears the least tinge of this guttural tone, science whispers us, it is against the rule, although we can but own the tone to be, so far as pleasing the ear alone is concerned, more agreeable. It seems to me, that a consciousness of the danger which attends this innovation—the certain knowledge of its fatal final effects, which those who have been in the habit of training or attending to the training of the voice apprehend—this consciousness I say instantly abates the pleasure the mere improvement of the tone bestows, and forbids as it were our gratification from an indulgence that we know is not legitimate.

'Of all the voices I have ever heard, that of Madame Catalani I think must be admitted to be the most magnificent both as to tone and volume. It is superior in what the Italians called *metallo di voce*. Is this *metallo* the consequence of the manner of its formation? I have lately heard a voice quite as powerful, but wanting in a degree the round, full, sonorous quality. The effects I have remarked make me very curious to ascertain whether this quality be from the formation or from the mellowing of time? If memory does not deceive me, Catalani's tone twenty years ago was not so full as it now is, but was more rich, more golden, if I may use such a similitude, which I do in reference to the term "*metallo*". At present there appears more volume, but it has lost some of its original lustre. It is like a copper-gilt vessel, from which some of the gilding is worn off—or rather like a piano forte, the hammers of which are grown hard by use.[25] Still however the main question remains to be solved. Is the *metallo*—the quality—in any considerable degree the effect of art, or is it the mere property of nature? That nature has given to Madame Catalani larger and more powerful organs than to others is beyond doubt, but still there may be, and there is I am persuaded, much that is important in the manner of employing these organs, and I potently believe there has been a great addition both of quality and volume from time and use.

'If we extend our enquiry to the phaenomena [sic] among male voices, we shall find similar cases. The same rule appears to hold throughout all classes. Mr. Braham has an organ in point of strength and quality, like that of Catalani, though nothing is more difficult than to apprehend distinctly the real properties of his true tone—so much does he vary from the standard in execution. It is sometimes even a little throaty, often extremely heady and nasal; yet I will venture to affirm, that the true quality was and is superior in respect of volume, power, richness, and brilliancy to any tenor I ever heard. Time has had its effect on his voice: it has gained somewhat in volume, but has lost in brilliancy—it has gained strength and lost flexibility. With an organ naturally less powerful Mr. Sapio has obtained fine quality (when he does not overstrain his voice), by a high Italian formation. The moment he forces it his

---

25 [Original footnote:] That the Italian formation has a tendency to increase the nasality as the singer grows old, I have constantly observed—the English formation tends to augment the throaty quality. Of this the most pregnant instance was to be found in Madame Camporese—to whose style and principles of singing few will object. Just before her retirement her tone was grown exceedingly nasal, so much so, that in singing duets with her in private, I have been perfectly astonished at her formation. I have also observed it in the orchestra. I could quote other instances, but one such is sufficient.

intonation fails. This is not his defect alone—it is common to all voices—but the reason I mention it here is, because I think that voices formed high are liable to fail with less strain upon them than those which come more from the throat—for the same reason, that thin voices go out of tune sooner than thick, as is commonly observed. Mr. Vaughan's voice is of English formation. It is certainly less artificial, and *was* quite as pure as any Italian voice I ever heard. It was brought out nearer the throat, and is therefore not so brilliant nor so facile in execution as Mr. Sapio's or Mr. Braham's.

'The Italian base voices appear to me incomparably finer than those of most English base singers, for example, those of Signors Angrisani and Remorini. Our best English singers, who take the character of base, have been barytones. Messrs. Bartleman and Bellamy were both of this class. Messrs. Lacy and Sale indeed have legitimate base voices, and that of the former is particularly fine and round in quality, as superior in power. Mr. Sale's voice affords a magnificent foundation in a glee. Mr. Lacy was taught by Rauzzini, and I suspect the Italian formation is by far the best for this species of voice.

'Upon reading over all that I have written, the doubts I have suggested and the examples I have cited, I am afraid little more will result from the enquiry than a conviction of the nicety, delicacy, and difficulty of avoiding the dangers incident to the formation by the head or by the throat. For after all there is a tact about teachers which they gather from experience, that sets theory very much at nought. This tact however is liable to errors of habit, and therefore theory may often correct practice. In this hope I have set down my thoughts.'

The comments by 'R' on John Braham are of particular interest, as they anticipate García's view in his 1840 treatise that singers needed to exploit both the *timbre clair* [clear, bright, open] and the *timbre sombre* [dark, closed], depending on the emotion to be expressed. García explained that the *timbre clair* is produced by raising the larynx and the *timbre sombre* by lowering it.

2.14 Vocal Timbre: Rich or Thin Voices

Reviewers characterised singers' vocal timbre either as 'rich', or synonymously as 'round', on 36 occasions. Alternatively, voices were described as 'thin', or rarely, as 'infantine', some 12 times. While 'thin' was generally accepted as a valid descriptive term in the long eighteenth century, it would be viewed as pejorative or insulting by a classical singer today. The charts at Illus. 35 [Males] and 36 [Females] illustrates how vocalists were described. The analysis is restricted to 97 singers described in Sections 2 and 3. Reviews were inconsistent in the case of Gertrud Mara and John Sinclair, which is not surprising given that the notices were penned by different reviewers on various performances on different occasions.

Reviews of male voices (both rich and thin) are quoted below:

Samuel Harrison's voice was quoted as rich and luscious [See p. 54 above]

Mr. Sapio. 'His voice is a rich, low tenor, round in its tones, smooth, very musical, and powerful enough for any legitimate purpose. It has, perhaps, rather a tendency to the guttural, but this inclination may be combatted, and finally overcome; we therefore do not set it down as an established defect.' [Jan. 1825: Har]

Domenico Donzelli. 'The richest tone that can be imagined is poured out from the chest as if the singer's throat were a simple passage for the sound, and sustained in all its purity through every inflection, and from a volume that fills the house to the most delicate articulations which the ear can distinguish. The compass of the voice is no less grand than its power; besides two octaves in the pure chest voice, the head tones are beautifully full and rich.' [2 Feb. 1829: MP]

Luigi Lablache. 'An organ more richly-toned or suave than his voice, was never given to mortal.' [1830: Chorley, *Recollections*, Vol. 1, p. 18]

Burney described the thin voice of **Gaetano Guadagni**: 'Those who remembered it when he was in England before, found it comparatively thin and feeble. For he had now changed it to a soprano, and extended its compass from six or seven notes, to fourteen or fifteen. And let a fluid of six feet in depth be spread over more than double its usual surface, and it will necessarily be shallower, though of greater extent ... I frequently tried to analize the pleasure he communicated to the audience, and found it chiefly arose from his artful manner of diminishing the tones of his voice, like the dying notes of the Æolian harp. Most other singers captivate by a swell or messa di voce; but Guadagni, after beginning a note or passage with all the force he could safely exert, fined it off to a thread, and gave it all the effect of extreme distance.' [1769: Bur, *General History*, p. 494]

Two reports of female voices are of particular interest:

Violante Camporese 'possesses one of the richest voices that we have ever heard; it is full, and penetrates, without any painful effort, every part of the Theatre.' [13 Jan. 1817: MC]

Josephine Fodor-Mainvielle. 'Her tones [**Miss Stephens**'s] wanted the fine, rich, pulpy essence of Madame Fodor's.' [24 Apr. 1817: Hazlitt]

Male Singers	Rich, Round	Thin
Castrati		
Matteo Berselli, b. 1680		Y
Francesco Barnardi, b. 1680	Y	
Carlo Broschi Farinelli, b. 1705	Y	
Gaetano Guadagni, b. 1728		Y
Luigi Marchesi, b. 1754	Y	
Girolamo Crescentini, b. 1762	Y	
Other Male		
Samuel Harrison, b. 1760	Y	
Charles Incledon, b. 1763	Y	
James Bartleman, b. 1769	Y	
John Braham, b. 1774	Y	
Diomoro Tramezzani, b. 1776	Y	
Thomas Vaughan, b. 1782	Y	
Alberico Curioni, b. 1785	Y	
Domenico Donzelli, b. 1790	Y	
John Sinclair, b. 1791	Y	Y
Mr Sapio, b. 1792	Y	
luigi Lablache, b. 1794	Y	
Giovanni Bat. Rubini, b. 1794	Y	
Henry Phillips, b. 1801	Y	
John Templeton, b. 1802		Y

Illus. 35: Rich or Thin Voices, Male

Female Singers	Rich, Round	Thin, Infantine
Francesca Cuzzoni, b. 1696	Y	
Susannah Cibber, b. 1714		Y
Lucrezia Agujari, b. 1741	Y	
Maddalena Allegranti, b. 1754		Y
Gertrud Elisabeth Mara, b. 1749	Y	Y
Brigida Banti, b. 1755	Y	
Francesca Le Brun, b. 1756		Y
Maria Theresa Bland, b. 1769	Y	
Josephina Grassini, b. 1773	Y	
Angelica Catalani, b. 1780	Y	
Violante Camporese, b. 1785	Y	
Eliza Salmon, b. 1787		Y
J. Fodor-Mainvielle, b. 1793	Y	
Benedetta Pisaroni, b. 1793	Y	
Catherine Stephens, b. 1794	Y	
Lucia Elizabeth Vestris, b. 1797	Y	
Giuditta Pasta, b. 1797	Y	
Miss Carew, b. 1799		Y
G. Ronzi de Begnis, b. 1800		Y
Maria Caradori-Allan, b. 1800		Y
Mrs Deborah Knyvett, b. 1800	Y	
Virginie Blasis, b. 1800	Y	
Laure Cinti-Damoreau, b. 1801	Y	
Mary Ann Paton, b. 1802	Y	
Henrietta Sontag, b. 1803	Y	
Nanette Schechner, b 1806	Y	

Illus. 36: Rich or Thin Voices, Female

Three female voices were described as thin, thread-like or infantine:

Susannah Cibber. Burney's noted her 'mere thread' of a voice [p. 34].

Maria Caradori-Allan. 'Thin tone is heard at further distances than that which is thick and rich. Madame Caradori, whose tone is remarkably thin and delicate, was said to be heard as well if not better than any singer in the minster at York.' [Sep. 1826: QMMR, p. 341]

Giuseppina Ronzi de Begnis. For QMMR's description of her 'infantine' voice, 'for it partakes of the querulous plaintiveness of our tenderest age', see page 144.

2.15 Articulation

All treatises insisted on good articulation, especially in recitative. I've noted the emphasis on spoken recitative by Mancini [p. 75], Bayly [p. 75] and Edgcumbe [p. 76].

François Raguenet, in comparing French and Italian music, wrote: 'Besides, the Italian Voices being equally strong as they are soft, we hear all they Sing very distinctly, whereas half of it is lost upon our Theatre unless we sit close to the Stage, or have the Spirit of Divination. Our Upper Parts are usually perform'd by Girls, that have neither Lungs nor Wind; whereas the same Parts in Italy are always perform'd by Men, whose firm piercing Voices are to be heard clearly in the largest Theatres without losing a Syllable, sit where you will.' [Dec. 1709: Raguenet]

John Waldie acknowledged the excellence of Italian enunciation: '… and at least it must be allowed that the extreme distinctness of articulation now in fashion in Italy makes it very easy for a stranger to make out all that passes on the stage.' [27 Oct. 1819: Waldie]

Richard Bacon wrote: 'The elocution of singing admits a pronunciation a little more open, a little rounder than common speaking. If we observe the metropolitan dialect, it differs from that of the provinces most especially in this particular, and hence it derives its peculiarity, richness, and beauty, which no other can be said to partake of or even to approach … It appears that the analogy between the elocution of reading or public speaking of any kind, and singing is very complete. They scarcely differ at all but in degree … In conversation the Italians are rapid and vehement, indulging in great inflexions and transitions—it is the same in Italian singing. The gravity of English discourse has in like manner its operation in the judgment we form of a singer, and what is commonly called chaste singing when it comes to be analysed, will be found to be a freedom from those marked and rapid transitions, those vehement and sudden expressions, those stops and breaks, those vivid and glowing effects of the imagination to be heard in the conversations of the Italians when compared with those of the English Nation.' [March 1821: Bacon, QMMR]

Most of the best singers during the long eighteenth century were praised for their clear and distinct diction, in both recitative and songs/arias:

Francesco Barnardi 'had a powerful, clear, equal, and sweet contralto voice, with a perfect intonation, and an excellent shake; his manner of singing was masterly, and his elocution unrivalled." [1 Apr. 1719: Bur, *The Present State…Germany*, p. 175, quoting Quantz]

'**Senesino** had a very fine even-toned voice, but of rather a narrow compass; some called it a mezzo soprano, others a contralto; it was nevertheless wonderfully flexible; besides this he was a graceful actor, and in the pronunciation of recitative had not his fellow in Europe.' [1719: John Hawkins, *History*, p. 872]

Faustina Bordoni. 'She had … excellent judgment in giving the proper stress to the words which she delivered with great clarity.' [Apr. 1727: Quantz, *Life*, p. 312]

Giulia Frasi. 'Having come into this country at an early period of her life, she pronounced our language in singing in a more articulate and intelligible manner than the natives.' [1748: Bur, *Rees's Cyclopædia*]

John Beard. 'An Organist, now deceased gave me a description of Mr. Beard's singing. His voice was coarse, but his articulation of words was very fine. I suppose he was rather an energetic and declamatory, than a very finished singer.' [Assumed reference date 1751: Smyth, p. 27]

Elizabeth Linley. Burney's description of her voice [p. 40 above] mentions 'her articulate & correct expression of the Words'.

Charles Dibdin. 'Mr. Dibdin had a baritone voice, with enough falsetto to sing any song. He had a remarkably distinct articulation; so that, even after a slight paralytic affection, which he had several years before he took leave of the public, every word he uttered was easily intelligible; for he had that sensible idea about vocal music, that the true intention of it is, to render the words more impressive.' [Apr. 1768: Har]

Amelia George. 'In her singing there is an articulation the most distinct and pointed.' [25 Sep. 1783: EM, Vol. 4, p. 228]

Gertrud Mara. Burney highlighted her ability to project her words into 'the remotest corner' of Westminster Abbey [see p. 40].

Elizabeth Billington. 'In speaking her voice was clear, her emphasis just, and strongly expressive of sensibility.—In singing she articulates, a great quality for a stage singer.' [18 Feb. 1786: T]

Giovanni Rubinelli. 'His articulation is so pure and well accented, in his recitatives, that no one who understands the Italian language can ever want to look at the book of the words, while he is singing.' [5 May 1786: Bur, *General History*, p. 524]

Nancy Storace. 'Though she has passed most of her time on the Continent, yet she is totally free of any foreign accent, and the merit of her singing is much enhanced by her admirable articulation.' [19 Dec. 1789: *British Mercury*]

Miss Arne. '… her articulation clear and distinct, though her voice has more sweetness than power, for, with all the confidence she gained from repeated plaudits, she was unable to exhibit a capacity of tone strong enough to fill the Theatre. Her manner, however, was chaste, and on a smaller stage she may probably afford more satisfaction.' [22 Jan. 1795: EM, Vol. 27, p. 124]

Maria Theresa Bland, née **Romanzini**. 'Though Mrs. Bland was only a singer of the second class, few, if any, English singers who have appeared at the opera sung with such pure Italian taste, or equalled her in recitative and pronunciation of the language. Her maiden name was Romanzini, so she might have been of Italian origin.' [Dec. 1798: Edgcumbe, p. 113]

Miss **Kemble**. 'she articulates the words of songs with uncommon distinctness.' [9 Apr. 1804: MM, Vol. 17, p. 279]

Miss **Greene**. 'Her voice … its articulation is clear, and no singer on the stage combines more distinctness with more volume.' [15 Dec. 1804:]

Signor **Naldi**. 'Naldi's style of pronouncing the Italian language is so perfect, that to every hearer in the least degree acquainted with that tongue, every syllable he uttered was perfectly intelligible.' [1 May 1806: Burgh]

Angelica Catalani. 'Her pronunciation of the English words though tinctured by a foreign accent, was correct.' [8 Sep. 1807: MC]

Charles Incledon. 'In the delivery of dialogue, Mr. Incledon is comparatively good with the generality of singers.' [Dec. 1808: Gilliland, *Dramatic Mirror*]

John Braham. 'Mr Braham is the first singer; and the compass of his voice, the power and sweetness of its tones, the science of its management, the accuracy of its articulation, and, above all, the ardour of his feeling, undoubtedly justify, in the fullest degree, that admiration, which, in spite of his diminutive person, the public so amply bestow on him.' [Dec. 1808: *Edinburgh Annual Register*]

Dorothea Francis, later **Mrs Jordan**. 'Mrs. Jordan's voice was not only sweet, but distinct, she articulated particularly well—tho' she was not a professed singer.' [9 Dec. 1810: Genest, Vol. 8, p. 430]

Madame **Bertinotti Radicati**. 'Her voice was sweet, and so articulate, that when by chance it was not overpowered by the ceaseless eloquence of the surrounding circle of elegance and fashion, it was heard distinctly in the most remote parts of the theatre.' [22 Dec. 1810: Burgh]

Catherine Stephens. 'The elegant prettinesses, and mellifluous distinctnesses of her articulations, reminded us frequently of Bertinotti.' [13 Sep. 1812: Ex] But other reviews of Stephens's articulation are not consistent. Thus the Harmonicon twice found fault with her articulation: 'Miss Stephens would have sung the song from Susanna, "If guiltless blood", better, had she bestowed a little more attention on her articulation',[Apr. 1824: Har] and 'Miss Stephens would warble it ["Heart thou seat", from *Acis and Galatea*] charmingly if she would add words to her silver tones.' [19 May 1824: Har]

Mrs. **Bellchambers**. 'Principal singer, it appears, from the Dublin Theatre. A more vivid sensation has hardly been aroused in the Bristol theatre than the début of this young lady is calculated to create. With unquestionable loveliness she has united a firm contralto voice, rich in volume, delicacy, and elocution; her songs were rapturously applauded.' [22 Oct. 1816: TI]

[Madame] Canonici. 'I was delighted with Canonici from the Fiorentini who played Matilda most excellently. She speaks the words so plain and is so unaffected and feeling, and her voice in such admirable tune that I prefer her style to Colbran, tho' her powers are not so extensive or highly finished.' [25 Feb. 1817: Waldie]

Gaetano Crivelli. 'His tones in singing are full, clear, and so articulate, that any one at all imbued with the Italian language can follow the words with ease.' [19 Jan. 1817: Ex]

Giuseppe Ambrogetti. 'His fine full-bodied voice, joined to the most distinct articulation and to consummate harmonic abilities, gave effect to every piece he had assigned to him singly, or in which he bore a share.' [19 Apr. 1817: LG, p. 199]

Georgia Bellochi. 'Her voice is powerful, sweet, and of great compass; her articulation clear; her divisions of extraordinary ease and flexibility; her expression distinct and to the purpose, though leaning perhaps to the side of force than beauty.' [1 Jan. 1819: Ex]

Mrs Bianchi Lacy. 'It is certain that the organization of some persons appears to be most beautifully adapted to utterance,* while others labour under great natural impediments. *[footnote] This was eminently the case with Mrs. Bianchi Lacy, whose organs appeared more delicately formed, and whose pronunciation both of English, French, and Italian, all of which she thoroughly understood, was the most finished I ever remember to have observed.' [Mar. 1821: QMMR, p. 26]

Miss Kelly. 'Her articulation is as yet faultless, and we take blame to ourselves that in our recent enumeration of those public singers who do justice to the sense of a song, we overlooked Miss Kelly.' [8 Jul. 1821: Ex]

Laure Cinti-Damoreau. See p. 147 for NMM's description of her voice, which mentions 'her articulation precise, neat and delicate'.

Giuseppina Ronzi de Begnis. 'Her correct intonation and uncommon flexibility, joined to the most distinct articulation, never more commanded our admiration than in this opera.' [1 June 1822: NMM]

Miss Deborah Travis, later Mrs Knyvett. 'Every syllable was distinctly heard; every note was distinctly articulated.' [6 Oct. 1823: CM]

Mr Sapio 'whose natural requisites are, perhaps, greater than any contemporary, aided by as much science and taste as go towards the formation of a great singer, unites to these that energetic delivery and clearness of articulation, which have so eminently contributed to the long admitted supremacy of Braham.' [Oct. 1823: Har]

John Sinclair. 'His intonation is remarkably clear and sweet, and his articulation so distinct, that, amidst all the decoration, which he sometimes lavishes with unbounded profusion, the ear can easily follow the words of the air.' [20 Nov. 1823: MC] 'His articulation is remarkably distinct, so much so that his singing, but for the melody, be considered a new mode of speaking.' [7 Aug. 1824: Scot]

Mr Broadhurst. 'We were never more struck and never so much affected with the power of a sweet and clear well-toned voice, fine articulation, and natural expression.' [6 June 1824: QMMR, p. 228]

Miss Graddon. 'She has a proper regard to enunciation, which in her is remarkably distinct.' [14 Nov. 1824: Ex]

Miss Cawse. 'In the way of performance, the principal novelty of the evening was the first appearance of Miss Cawse, a pupil of Sir George Smart, a young lady under fourteen years of age, with a voice particularly sweet and clear, a distinct enunciation.' [16 Apr. 1825: LG]

Maria Caradori-Allan. 'Madame Caradori is not in her place in the vastness of the opera stage, which reduces great, and all but annihilates powers of a second order. Madame Caradori's voice and manner are, however, delightful in their kind. Elegance, precision, and delicacy, reign through all she does; and there is an innocency which sets off and enhances the polish of art. Few singers will give purer pleasure, for whatever she does is perfect in its kind. Her pronunciation of English, when she sings, is better than that of almost any foreigner we remember.' [22 Apr. 1825: LMag]

Mr C. Bland 'is a strong and clear tenor—the middle notes the best: his articulation beyond all comparison the most distinct now on the London boards: in this respect, indeed, he reminds us strongly of that gifted qualification in his mother.' [15 Jan. 1826: Ex]

Signora Centroni. 'A young candidate for musical fame, possessing a soprano voice of great depth and clearness, a pure intonation, and a clearness of accentuation which gives the best hopes.' [Jan. 1826: Har]

Giuditta Pasta. 'Her recitativo parlante was the most perfect I have ever heard, every word being as distinctly enunciated as if it had been actually spoken.' [Jan. 1829: Cox, p. 169]

Mr Atkins. '... has a firm and powerful bass (or, as the scientific more accurately term it, barytone) voice, for the most part of fine quality; his style though not highly finished, is pleasing, and his articulation perfect. His Trumpet shall sound, with Harper's Obligato accompaniment, was very effective; and his Rolling in foaming billows shewed the great sweetness of his voice in the upper notes.' [27 Sep. 1826: Ex]

Rosalie Corri. 'Her voice possesses both sweetness and power. Her style of singing is extremely pure; her articulation perfectly distinct.' [1 Nov. 1826: T].

Domenico Donzelli. 'His recitative particularly impressive, his elocution generally good.' [1827: *Dictionary of Musicians*]

'MISS FANNY AYTON is the only English *soprano* of eminence who has appeared upon the Opera stage since the time of Mrs Billington. Having been educated in Italy, she is perfectly free from that heavy style which our language is apt to produce. Though limited in voice, her vivacity never fails to carry her through the part of a *prima donna* with a lively and dramatic effect. Her execution and enunciation are of the most rapid kind. In the opera of *Cenerentola*, she utters more than twenty syllables in a second of time, with a neatness and precision not easily surpassed.' [1 Nov. 1826: Gardiner, *Music of Nature*, p. 158, 163]

Henry Phillips. I cite praise for his 'talking in tone'. [p. 182]

Nina Sontag. 'Mademoiselle Sontag has a distinct articulation, and deals in all the minutiae of refinement.' [Dec. 1828: Holmes, *Ramble*, p. 226]

Benedetta Pisaroni. '... the magnificence and perfect articulation of her recitative.' [30 Mar. 1829: MC]

Isabella Colbran's 'accurate articulation both of syllables and sound' has been noted at p. 49.

In spite of the numerous encomiums reported above, a perception that enunciation was poor was sometimes expressed, as in a diatribe from the Examiner:

'This repugnance to recitative, as obstinately maintained by the French, but at length triumphantly surmounted—(indeed it forms now among them perhaps the most important article of critical examination)—will never lose its entire force until our singers reform the viciousness of slovenly or affected enunciation. This fault, unpardonable in recitative, which has excited the derision of the best writers, from old TOSI downwards, has never been endured by the Parisians. Clear articulation is with them a sine qua non; without it the finest voice, joined to the purest taste in other respects, would be dismissed with contempt. We wish we could exempt (besides two or three comic singers) our stage-vocalists from this reproach; but rarity enhances merit; we can only instance Mrs. BLAND and BRAHAM. Miss CUBITT and Madame VESTRIS are making that merit their object.' [10 June 1821: Ex]

Nevertheless, the list of singers with poor enunciation is much shorter:

Anna Maria Crouch, née Phillips. 'It is very well worth the attention of those who sing in public, to imitate Romanzini [see praise for Maria Theresa Bland at page 128] in her articulation. We understand every word she sings, but it is impossible to catch a syllable of what falls from Mrs. Crouch.' [28 Oct. 1789: *Prompter*]

Maria Dickons, as Miss Poole. 'Miss Poole would rank amongst our very first female singers, if her articulation of words were but equal to those of her notes; which defect, perhaps, is owing to the want of proper instruction from a regular singing master, before she had contracted those unconquerable habits.' [27 Oct. 1795: *Tomahawk*]

Mrs. Rosemond Mountain '... has ... very fine voice, but she is totally inarticulate in singing, and, of course, does not deserve to be denominated a great singer.' [Dec. 1808: *Edinburgh Annual Register*]

Miss Wilson. 'She has, however, something yet to correct; her shake is still tardy and reluctant; her action rather too exuberant, and her words are generally inaudible.' [18 Jan. 1821: EM, Vol. 79, p. 66]

Miss Carew. 'Miss Carew's singing was of its usual sweetness; but why will she not condescend to pronounce her words?' [10 Oct. 1821: EM, Vol. 80, p. 381]

Eliza Salmon. See quote at Page 49 taking her to task for poor articulation.

Signor Raineri Remorini. 'A fine, clear, sonorous voice, but a bad articulation.' [May 1826: Har]

Miss Hughes. 'Her voice wants richness, is unsteady, her articulation is indistinct, and, what is worse than all, her intonation is distressingly imperfect.' [17 Nov. 1827: Har]

Elizabeth Inverarity. 'The articulation of the words is likewise defective; here, again, practice is quite necessary. We know nothing more unmeaning than a song, in listening to which we cannot distinguish a syllable.' [20 Apr. 1829: EEC]

Reviewers sometimes linked poor articulation with other faults, such as low larynx emission:

There could be a similar link in the case of Elizabeth Inverarity, who was taken to task by the Edinburgh Review in the review just quoted for her guttural timbre. Similarly, a Mr. Plumer [see review on p. 120 commenting on his thick timbre] was also criticised for poor enunciation.

The Literary Gazette expressed dissatisfaction with Mary Anne Paton: 'Nor do we admire the guttural tone she has acquired; it is not only disagreeable in itself, but it destroys all clearness of articulation' [17 Mar. 1832: LG]

3 The 19th/20th Century Vocal Revolution (1830 to 1949)

3.1 National Origins

I've included this intermediate section in order to present much of the data I have collected in support of Parts 4, 5 and 6 of this book. The section is devoted to contemporary nineteenth-century reviews of the most highly regarded singers. Out of some 17,600 reviews, 2% were from books, 15% from magazines and 85% from newspapers.

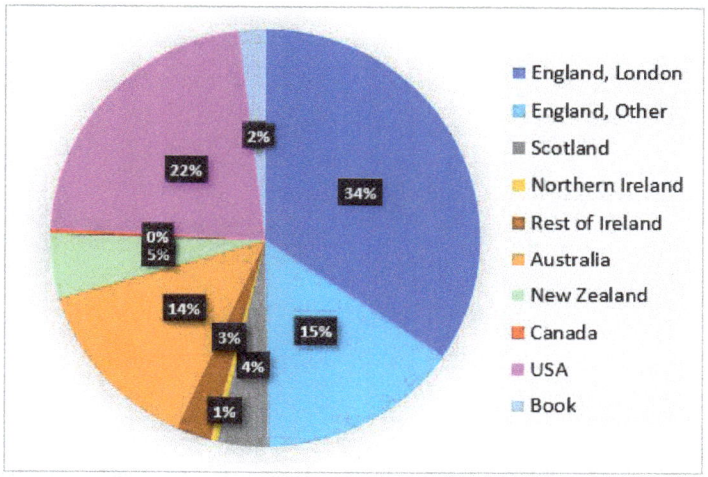

Illus. 37: National Origins of Review Data

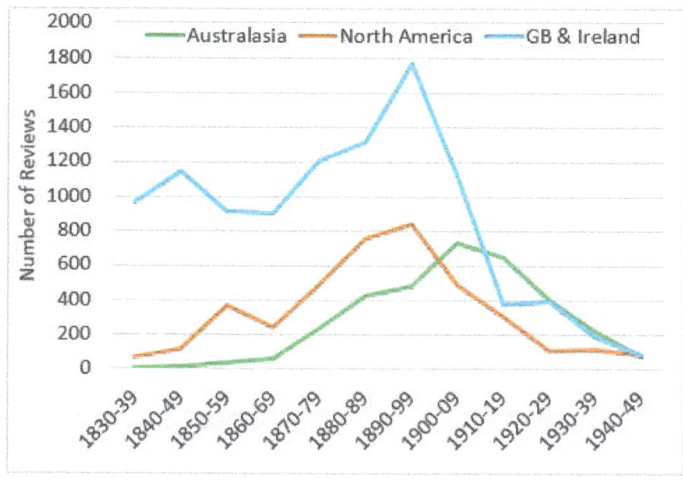

Illus. 38: National Origins over Time

Illus. 37 shows that roughly half the reviews came from England, a quarter from North America and the rest from Australasia, Scotland or Ireland. Books are shown separately.

Illus. 38 shows how these sources varied over time, peaking around 1900, mainly because around three quarters of all reviews related to the occurrence (or absence) of tremolo/ vibrato.

This is a suitable occasion to note that there are discontinuities in some data subsequent to 1900, all relating to English sources. The main sources where sources remain unscanned, or have not at the time of writing[26] been captured in full-text databases, are shown in Illus. 39:

Source	No Data for:
Athenaeum	1901-1931
Leeds Mercury	1901-1912
London Standard	1910-1949
Manchester Guardian	1910-1949
Manchester Times	1901-1922
Morning Post	1910-1937
Musical Times	1910-1949
Sunday Times	1918-1949

Illus. 39: Main Sources Unavailable

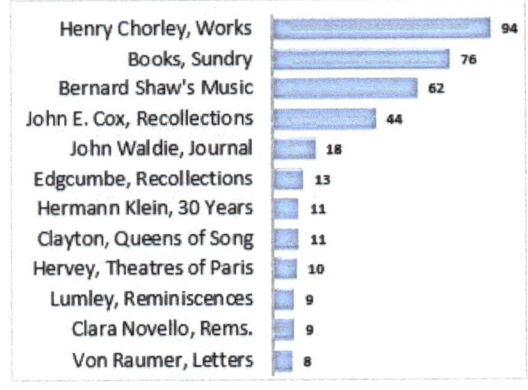

Illus. 40: Number of Reviews from Books

3.2   The Books

The list [Illus. 40] is headed by **Henry Fothergill Chorley**, who as regular opera goer established himself as music critic of the Athenaeum and London Times. This gave him the background to write his important work *Thirty Years' Musical Recollections*, covering the period 1830 to 1859, a revolutionary period for both opera and singing. An eccentric but conservative figure, he was a good critic with a happy turn of phrase. For example, his description of Marietta Alboni's voice was both forensic and poetic: 'Hers was a rich, deep, real contralto, of two octaves from G to G—as sweet as honey—but not intensely expressive; and with that tremulous quality which reminds fanciful speculators of the

---

26   October 2018.

quiver in the air of the calm, blazing, summer's noon.—I recollect no low Italian voice so luscious'. One comment suggests that he was an early advocate of what we understand today as *historically informed practice*: 'Music must, somehow or other, reflect the manners and fancies of its birth-time and birth-place...I believe that thoughtful science, not shrinking from retrospect, not averse to discovery, will increasingly refer to Record, not to Tradition,—will increasingly separate that which is of the hour, from that which does not pass away. The "players" have had their riot:—the orchestra and its combinations have been driven into that prominence and perfection to which extravagance and corruption may be the inevitable sequel. The turn of the singers may be again to come.' [Chorley, *Musical Recollections*, Vol. II, pp. 319, 321]

George Bernard Shaw was a lively music critic for many years. Shaw had studied singing and published many informative reviews of singers between 1877 and 1894. Only occasionally do his reviews lack precision. For example, one would hope for a better definition of what he meant by vibrato here: 'Suane, the tenor à la Gayarré [Julian Gayárre] without which no opera company is now complete, is thoroughly in earnest about his work, and shews much artistic feeling as a singer and actor. Those notes of his which are steady enough to have any recognizable pitch are by no means unmusical. But he is so afflicted with goat-bleat (vibrato is all nonsense—quite a different thing) that the house loses patience with him.' [5 Nov. 1890: Shaw, Vol. II]

John Edmund Cox's recollections are generously claimed to cover half a century, from around 1818 when he heard James Bartleman (aged six!) to the briefest reference on 1866 when they included 'Mdlle. [Maria] Vilda, who could sing but not act, and Mdlle. [Aglaja] Orgeni, who could act but not sing.' [Cox, Vol. 2, p. 369] While most comments on singers are original, chunks of text were occasionally pirated (unacknowledged) from others.

For **John Waldie**, see section 'Unfinished Research Business' on p. 355.

Hermann Klein's memories include descriptions of the voices of most of the great singers from Thérèse Tietjens in 1866 to Sims Reeves in 1900.

Of the remaining authors, Clara Novello is one of the most interesting. She retired in 1860, while still in her prime, and lived till 1908. She wrote scathingly in 1886: 'This substitute for music [Puccini's *Le Villi*] is now the mode and consoles me for being old. When I was young, music was music indeed, and "oiled one's soul"; now, what is imposed on one, instead, turns me into a Barbary hen, ruffling all my feathers up the wrong way! After the "Villi"[27] we had "Traviata", both sung by a Miss J. of Cincinnati; lovely in face and person, but singing in the palsied fashion and from her tonsils, not from her chest. Palsy has invaded all the arts, not only in singing; painting is all bloches and smears, orchestra pieces are written all in tremolo.' [31 Aug. 1886: Clara Novello, *Reminiscences*, p. 200]

3.3 The Magazines

I discuss these magazines [Illus. 41] heading the list: *Examiner* [1808-1880], *Athenaeum* [1828-1921], *Musical World* [1836-1890] and *Dwight's Journal of Music* [1852-1881].

---

27   Probably Puccini's opera-ballet *Le Villi*

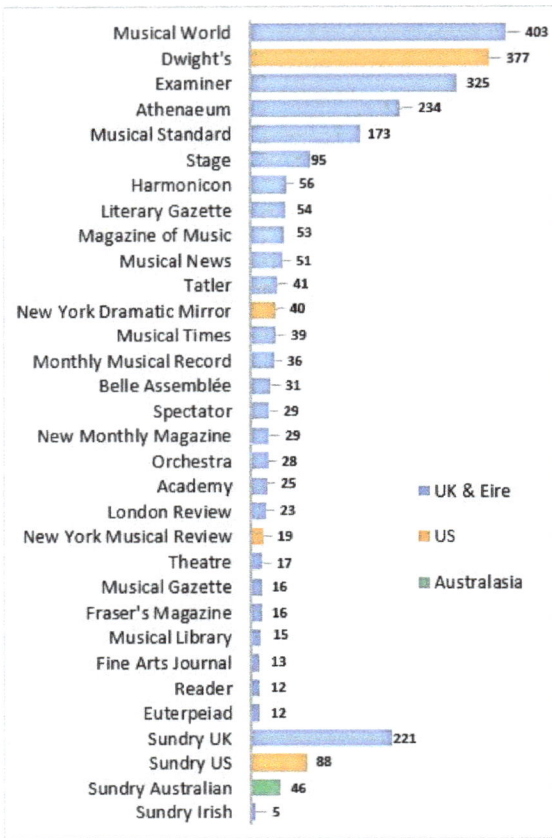

Illus. 41: Number of Reviews from each Magazine

The Examiner was started in 1808 by brothers John and Leigh Hunt. Leigh Hunt is said to have written most of the opera criticism until 1822. Here is a sample: 'Mr. Braham was in all his glory of flourish and demisemiquaver. It is surprising that this beautiful singer exhibits so bad a taste as to scatter his voice into atoms when he might present us with a noble solidity. He has certainly contributed to deprave the musical taste of this country, for he has substituted mere admiration for feeling; he has opened our eyes to shut our hearts. The air of Fair Ellen, that exquisite piece of poetry that ends with so exquisite a bull, was literally lost in his ornament. The Greeks had a phrase, you speak roses, which may be applied to Mr. Braham's style, for he really gives us nothing but flowers. He is like an exhibitor of fire-works, totally employed in sudden shoots, and whirls, and a scatter of brilliant nothings.' [24 Jan. 1808: Ex] The following amusing account of Adelina Patti's singing might be from Henry Fothergill Chorley: 'As a singer this young lady [Adelina Patti] has worked for and obtained considerable volubility, though to the detriment of the quality of her voice, and she has acquired certain volata of the ad captandum kind, which, after twice or thrice hearing, become wearisome; the staccato kind of hopping about upon B, C, and D, with the shaking of the head as if those high notes could only be jerked out, not sung, are tricks, but no such tricks as a Grisi, a Malibran, a Sontag, or a Persiani would have stooped to. Her confidence, too, is unbounded; she dashes continually at the chromatic scale of two octaves, of which the first notes may be chromatic, but the rest a kind of sliding down the bannisters after a diatonic fashion. John Bull, however, is a strange fellow; and, since he is usually kindly and happy in his little enthusiasms, must not be put into the coercion chair for a slight lunacy on the subject of Mlle. Patti.' [9 Aug. 1862: Ex]

The *Athenaeum, Journal of Literature, Science and the Fine Arts*, was initiated by James Silk Buckingham, but passed through various hands. As already noted, Chorley contributed articles on music and opera performances. A witty article on 'scaling the altitudes' might have been contributed by Chorley: 'The other four ladies announced being contralti; their voices stretched, as the humour of the time demands, into mezzo soprani. These were the bénéficiare [Mrs Alfred Shaw], Madame [Emma] Albertazzi, Madame Meerti Blaes, and Madame Frederic Lablache [was Fanny Wyndham]. Some thirty years ago, the extent of occupation to which these ladies could have aspired, must have been the possession of Handel's counter-tenor songs contested with some middle-aged gentleman, whose unctuous warble, in seven notes out of every bar, called for an ear-trumpet as its expositor. To be clearer, basses were driven up into the tenor scale, and compelled to flourish as soprani had not done before them:—tenors required to adopt that vicious French thing, a high treble falsetto—their register becoming substantially identical with the ground of the contralto:—and that voice was compelled, in its turn, to scale the altitudes. Thanks to the sharpened diapason of the orchestra, the highest voice of the quartett could not thus be excruciated: the consequence being, that it has, in some measure, lost its place and occupation, if not its repute.' [3 May 1845: Ath]

The *Musical World; a Weekly record of Musical Science, Literature, and Intelligence*, was founded by J. Alfred Novello. The original editors were Charles Cowden Clarke and Henry John Gauntlett, although James William Davison became the owner and editor of the Journal from 1844 till his death in 1885. The magazine included reviews of published music, concert and opera performances and biographical sketches of singers. Far from being Anglo-centric, content included regular reviews of continental concerts and news, such as 'Chit-Chat from the Continent'.

Dwight's Journal of Music was created by John Sullivan Dwight, and published in Boston, Massachusetts. It was for thirty years the most important and influential music periodical in the US. Reviews of performances and singing by touring operatic troupes and concert parties constituted an important part of the journal, which was published fortnightly. Like *Musical World*, the journal included frequent reports from Europe, often under the heading of 'Foreign Musical Intelligence'.

3.4 The Newspapers

The newspapers at Illus. 42 and 43 are listed either under newspaper name or geographic location. The list is headed by three London based newspapers, the *Morning Post* [reviews from 1830-1909[28]], *Era* [1839-1943] and *The Times* [1830-1949]. While the *Morning Post* and the London *Times* were important national daily newspapers, *Era* was a special case, being a Sunday newspaper with substantial content devoted to theatrical and musical reviews, albeit the general level of *Era's* journalism was workmanlike rather than inspired. Examples from the *Times* and the excellent *Brooklyn Daily Eagle*, the leading US newspaper, are appended:

> 'La Cenerentola was produced last night for the debut of Madame [Emma] Albertazzi, of whom it may be safely pronounced, on this her first essay before a London audience, that fame has not said too much … Her voice is absolutely beautiful—a deep contralto, intensely passionate in its expression, amidst the very repose in which she veils it, and yet with a compass in the higher notes which is very rare in a voice of that description. Between her falsetto, and her natural voice there was none of the break perceptible, which is a defect some of the greatest singers have not been able to overcome. The connexion was always well preserved. The flexibility of her voice is as remarkable as its purity and compass; the divisions steal, as it were, upon the ear—seem to come of themselves, and cost her no effort.' [19 Apr. 1837: T]

---

28 Although *Morning Post* only ceased publication in 1937, issues from 1910 were not available at the time of writing.

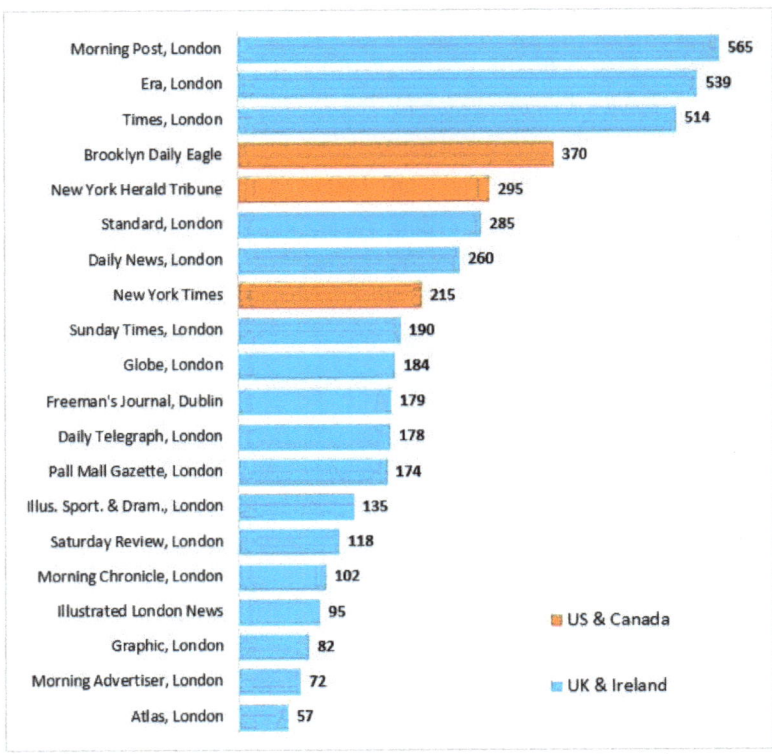

Illus. 42: Named Newspapers by Geographic Location

'Nor is there any occasion whatever for her [Marie Van Zandt] to make her exit with a run after she has sung a high note. Of all the silly practices in Italian opera that of scuttling away after singing a song is the silliest. Yet all the singers in Italian opera do it and have done it. Gerster, at her fattest and heaviest; Kellogg, when she was large and lethargic; Nilsson, when she was cold enough to redden the noses of the chorus; Patti, when she was trying to assume her best dignity—these women and hundreds more would gather up their skirts and skip and waddle for the door as if a basketfull of mice had been loosed from the prompter's hood. Mr. Abbey has never posed as a musical reformer, but for the sake of common sense and order and art, he ought to train his singers to walk off from the stage like sane creatures.' [6 Jan. 1892: Brook]

Looking at the papers grouped by geographic area, readers may be surprised to see that reviews from New Zealand, and the two most populous Australian states (NSW and Victoria) head the list. A probable reason for this is that both countries have built the excellent websites Papers Past (New Zealand) and Trove (Australia);[29] these hold long runs of numerous publications, including some from small towns covering remote rural areas, which have been scanned. By contrast, British and US newspaper and magazine sources are fragmented across different electronic sources besides several regions and areas.

---

29   https://paperspast.natlib.govt.nz/ and https://trove.nla.gov.au/newspaper/

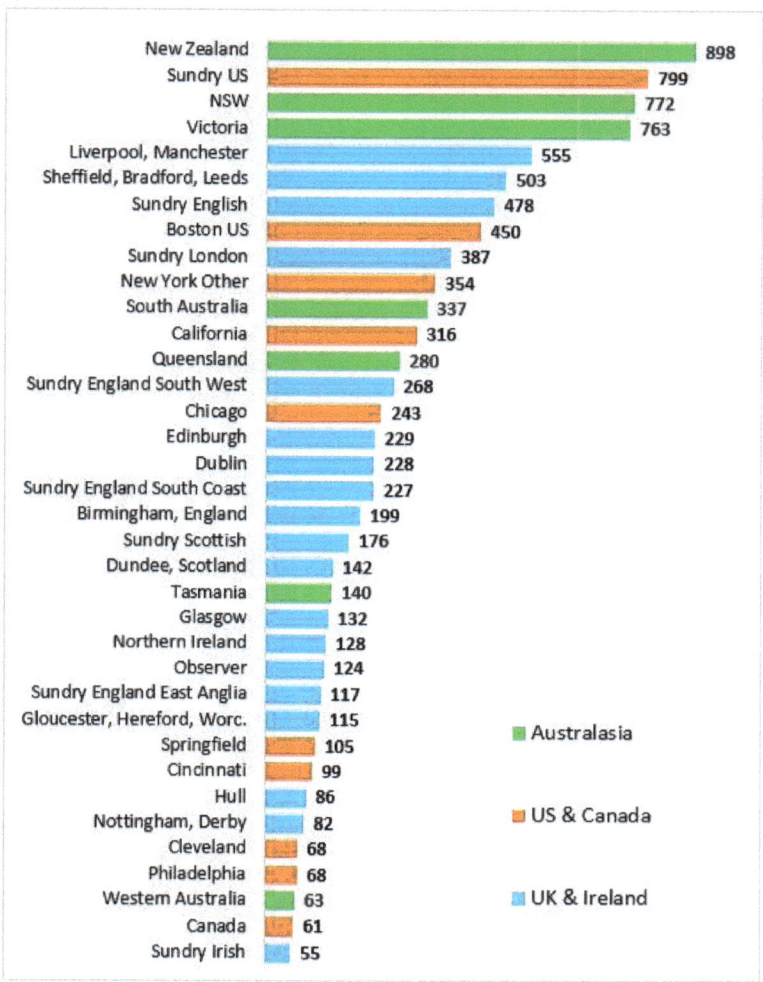

Illus. 43: Other Newspapers by Geographic Location

3.5 Female Singers Reviewed, before the Recording Era

This section quotes vocal descriptions of twenty six highly regarded *prime donne* through the nineteenth century, based on contemporary reviews. Note that, in most cases, certainly when reviewed before 1830, only minor changes in vocal style are evident, when compared with the singers discussed in Section 2. However, differences in volume and timbre continue to be apparent across the field, as already noted at section 2.11. Famous female singers whose voices have been recorded are covered in section 3.7.

3.5.1 Josephine Fodor-Mainvielle [b. 1793]

'Her upper notes are distinguished for a clearness and thrill of tone which we have scarcely heard equalled, except by the flageolet.' [13 Jan. 1816: T].

'Her voice is clear and forcible, and has a kind of deep, internal volume, which seems to be artificially suppressed. Her hard, firm style of execution (something like the dragging of the painter's pencil) gives a greater relief to the occasional sweetness and power of tone which she displays.' [14 Apr. 1816: Ex, (Hazlitt)]

Hazlitt described her voice: 'There is a clear, firm, silvery tone in her voice, like the reverberation of a tight-strung instrument, which by its contrast gives a peculiar effect to the more melting and subdued expression of particular passages, and which accords admirably with the idea of high health and spirits in the rustic character of Zerlina. We are tempted to say of her in this character, what Spenser says of Belphebe, "—And when she spake,/ Sweet words like dropping honey she did shed,/ And 'twixt the pearls and rubies softly brake/ A silver sound, that heav'nly music seem'd to make".' [19 Apr. 1817: Hazlitt, *A View of the English Stage*]

'Such a Zerlina has probably appeared on no other stage; in her acting, there is a freshness, a naiveté, a sprightliness which must be seen to be appreciated; and in her songs, which are animated by the same characteristic features, we are delighted by the utmost chasteness and correctness of execution, aided by a voice, the clear intonation and command of which exceeds the purest tones of a first rate flute ...' [26 Apr. 1817: review by Richard Bacon, LG]

'Educated in a fine school, her voice has obtained such flexibility that every passage is executed with a lightness and at the same time a tenderness it is impossible to describe.' [2 Mar. 1823: QMMR, p. 418]

3.5.2 Benedetta Rosmunda Pisaroni [b. 1793]

'... in the character of Xerxes, makes us forget the dissimilarity that exists between her, and the idea we are led to form of this great king, our attention being exclusively engaged by her song, in which nature and art have combined to subdue the soul by beauty, sweetness, and power. We do but repeat what is already known, when we say, that the highest purity of sound, a flexibility, without effort, an extremely soft modulation, a perfect trill, and a distinctness of pronunciation, all combined in an inimitable mezzotinto, entitles this singer to the praise of being a genuine mistress of her art. If any fault is to be found, it is that she injures her simplicity by too great an endeavour after the curious embellishments of art. This defect was particularly visible in the opening air of Xerxes, which the composer [Pacini] had doubtless written expressly to shew her vocal powers; but when these ornaments are not carried to excess, and the beauty of her voice is allowed its full and natural play, it must be acknowledge that the organ of Pesaroni is enchantment itself.' [May 1825: Har]

'Her tone was pure, rich—particularly in the lower parts of the scale—sweet, and uniform. Her volume was also large although not possessing the power of Catalani, or even of Pasta. With the purity and uniformity of her voice she associated a noble simplicity of declamation, a most accurate articulation, and the power of assimilation from the loudest messa di voce to the softest pianissimo; whilst she utterly rejected everything approaching to meretricious ornament, and contented herself with relying simply upon legitimate vocalization.' [Jan. 1829: Cox, p. 169]

By 1829, the Examiner reported that Pisaroni was past her best: 'Had this lady appeared somewhat earlier in life, she would probably have made a great sensation, for she appears to be an excellent musician, but her voice begins to have the tremulousness of old age, and is besides of a reedy, oboe-like quality, far from agreeable. It is a powerful contralto; best, as is usual with such voices, in its lower tones, but possessing a more than ordinary freedom of execution.' [3 Feb. 1829: Ex]

3.5.3 Catherine Stephens [b. 1794]

'Her round, full, rich, lovely voice, her natural manner, her simple style, deformed by no sort of affectation, immediately won upon the public; and both in the orchestra, the church, and the theatre, she became universally admired. No female singer perhaps ever built so true an English style upon Italian rudiments ... Her purity rendered her performance the very model of what our nation terms "chaste singing".' [23 Sep. 1813: NMM]

'Her voice is powerful, yet, mellifluous; her intonation rich and various, yet, in the highest degree articulate, and pathetic; her conception of character as correct as her expression of that conception is effective. It is the peculiar characteristic of her execution, that it speaks the sentiments of the heart, and awakens the sympathy of the auditor, as much as it gratifies his musical taste, and satisfies all the demands of musical criticism. It is the privilege of other singers, to delight and astonish, Miss Stephens possesses the peculiar prerogative of doing both. The man of science applauds her execution; the lover of novelty is astonished by the compass and the sweetness of her voice; and the man of simple feeling, who is unacquainted with the technical of the musical art, and would rather yield to the impulse of delight, than sit in critical judgment on the means by which that object is accomplished, is melted into tears, aroused to indignation, or enflamed with the enthusiasm of warlike resolve. The music of Miss Stephens penetrates to the heart ... H.' [Dec. 1813: TI, p. 260]

Her singing is of that unique description, which at once astonishes by its extent of power, and delights by its clear articulative melody; for the effect she produced in one of the plaintive airs, by her exquisite style of giving "What was my pride is now my shame", was equally impressive as was the brilliancy of execution she displayed in the "Soldier tired".—On Wednesday Miss Stephens personated Clara, in the Duenna : and, in "Adieu thou dreary pile", introduced a cadence, accompanied by Mr. Loder on the violin, in which she gave full scope to her wonderful extent of voice : her command of the highest note E was produced with the greatest ease, and sustained in a most surprising manner. Her execution is remarkably rapid and distinct, and her songs were all given in a style of excellence never surpassed. [3 Jan. 1814: MP]

'Miss Stephens's voice we think the finer of the two [Catherine Stephens and Anna Maria Tree]. It is even, clear, and sweet; and has an exquisite vein of gentle pathos throughout it, that perpetually seems to appeal to you.' [27 Dec. 1819, Ex]

Her voice had a musical-glass quality: '... the tone of the musical glasses exhibits the best standard of instrumental perfection for the soprano. Miss Stevens's is of this quality, taking a middle part of the scale. Mrs. Salmon's lies higher. The one is therefore richer—the other more brilliant and not less sweet.' [21 Mar. 1822: QMMR, p. 20]

'No female singer has continued so long the favourite of the British public as Miss Stephens. Her beautiful voice and artless manner are often delightful; but it is in the simple ballad, which never rises above general comprehension, that she excels. Though she has acquired an easy execution, she is deficient in that fervour which is requisite to the *bravura*. Her excellencies and defects are closely combined: the pretty mode in which she delivers her words is often disfigured by the offensive slides introduced between her notes, a practice so common with inferior singers. The *portamento*, or slide, when properly introduced, is a grace of passionate expression; but, when used without thought or discretion, is an effect that is nauseous and ridiculous. / The silvery tones of her voice are sometimes cast into shade by the incorrect manner in which she ascends from the *tonic* to the *dominant*, making the fifth too flat, a defect common to the greatest singers; and it happens, unfortunately for Miss Stephens, that in her celebrated song, "*I know that my Redeemer liveth*", this disagreeable skip occurs not less than eight different times; but where the fifth is relieved by the interposition of the third, as in the following passage [Illus. 44], the G sharp forming a stepping-stone for the voice to light upon, in no instance was the same interval incorrectly given. / As songs of execution Miss Stephens chose "*Sweet bird*", and "*Hush, ye pretty warbling choir*", so highly adapted to show the bird-like tones of her voice. As sentimental pieces, "*In sweetest harmony they lived*", "*Pious orgies*", and "*Farewell, ye limpid streams*". These songs called forth her lowest notes, the most impassioned part of her singing; but the well-known ballad of "*Auld Robin Gray*" was the most happy exhibition of her powers. The weeping tone and soft lament she threw over this song gave it a peculiar charm, and though she could neither astonish nor surprise, her simple manner and penetrating sweetness of voice touched every heart.' [estimated date 1823, around 11 years after her début: Gardiner, p. 126]

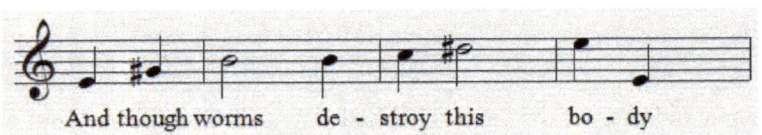

Illus. 44: 'And though worms' from Messiah

3.5.4 Lucia Elizabeth Vestris [b. 1797]

'... of more extended compass than is usual, very sweet and pure, and her style is more that of true expression than of modern agility.' [Sep. 1820: QMMR, p. 377]

'This lady is now so completely identified with the stripling Juans, Narcissuses, and Medoros of the stage, that she would be more disguised by female drapery than by male attire. What with her fine legs and her fine voice, to say nothing of her eyes, which "sound a parley of provocation", there is no such thing as looking in any other direction than the stage till she has capered or sauntered off. Madame Vestris is rather short in stature, but beautifully formed, and her countenance is capable of the most animated expression; she is aware of all this, and plays her all-conquering artillery upon the susceptible hearts of the younkers in the boxes without mercy.' [1826: *Cumberland's British Theatre*, Vol.VIII, p. iv]

'[Vestris] delighted us on Tuesday evening, in Susanna, in the Marriage of Figaro: both with the rich and full tones of her voice; for when at the loudest—and they are always strong enough—they are still tones, and not screams: also with the high polish of her style, judiciously selecting and sprinkling her melodies with uncommon-place ornaments, while these are always suited to the character and sentiment of the music she is singing, and seldom redundant; and finally, with the unerring certainty of her intonation.' [26 Oct. 1828: Ex]

'She [Madame Vestris] does not amaze like Malibran, nor does she equal Paton—alas, that once delightful name!—in rapidity or power of execution; but in sweetness of tone, and grace and humour combined she cannot be surpassed. The songs "where are you going to", and "The light guitar", "Love was once a little boy", and "What can a poor maiden do", were all rapturously *encored*. The repetition of the latter was one of the finest specimens of harmony of sound and expression—of the face we mean—that we ever witnessed. Every look spoke language inexpressible. We heard some body observe that the Vestris was looking thin. If so, who would ever be fat? Her arms—those models of symmetry—appeared to us to be as fair and as round as ever.' [13 Jun. 1831: *Freeman's Journal*]

3.5.5   Giuditta Pasta [b. 1797]

'If we were to express our opinion honestly, we should say that we received most pleasure from Madame PASTA'S Telemachus. There is a natural eloquence about her singing which we feel, and therefore understand. Her dress and figure also answered to the classical idea we have of the youthful Telemachus. Her voice is good, her action is good: she has a handsome face, and very handsome legs. The ladies, we know, think otherwise; this is the only subject on which we think ourselves better judges than they.' [19 Jan. 1817: Ex]

'She now sings from A in the bass, to C or D in alt, about eighteen tones.' [30 Jun. 1824: QMMR, p. 218]

'Madame Pasta's incredible mastery of technique is revealed in the amazing facility with which she alternates head-notes with chest-notes; she possesses to a superlative degree the art of producing an immense variety of charming and thrilling effects from the use of *both* voices. To heighten the tonal colouring of a melodic phrase, or to pass in a flash from one *ambiance* to another infinitely removed from it, she is accustomed to use a *falsetto* technique covering notes right down to the middle of her normal range; or else she may unconcernedly alternate *falsetto* notes with ordinary chest-notes. In all such displays of virtuosity, she apparently finds as little difficulty in securing a smooth transition between the two voices when she is employing notes in the *middle* of her normal chest-range, as she does when she is using the highest notes which she can produce.' [1824: Stendhal, p. 376]

'And Pasta, though she is considered an outstanding singer, did not delight me either. She has an uncommon amount of expression, fire, and life, a wealth of embellishments, sings nicely, and looks pretty, but—her voice is raw and unclear, and her intonation is not clean, and so far I haven't been able to overlook these two faults.'[6 Apr. 1825: Felix Mendelssohn, *Letters*, p. 36]

'In a small room her voice was too loud and sometimes harsh, her manner too forcible and vehement*;

but in the theatre all blemishes disappeared: she is really a first-rate performer both as singer and actress, and that by mere dint of talent without any very pre-eminent natural qualifications: for, though a pretty woman, her figure is short and not graceful; and her voice, though powerful and extensive, is not of the very finest quality, not free from defects. No part could be more calculated to display her powers than that of Medea, which affords opportunities for the deepest pathos, and the most energetic passion. In both she was eminently successful, and her performance both surprized and delighted me. None since Banti's had equalled it, and perhaps she even excelled her great predecessor as an actress, though in quality and sweetness of voice she infinitely falls short of her. *Footnote: It may be remarked that the modern music spoils the singers for concerts, especially in private houses. The constantly singing concerted pieces, adapted only for the theatre, gives them the habit of so forcing their voices that they know not how to moderate them to the small space of an ordinary room. Neither are noisy finales and such like pieces suited to the place, or agreeable, without the orchestra and without action. The ear is often absolutely pained by their loudness.' [June 1826: Edgcumbe, p. 169, quoted in John Potter's *History of Singing*]

Giuditta Pasta 'sung an Aria in her wonted energetic and expressive style, some of her upper notes, resemble the musical glasses, but her lower ones are not calculated to give due effect to plaintive strains, such as a Stephens breathes in her ballads.' [11 Apr. 1828: MP]

3.5.6   Giuseppina Ronzi de Begnis [b. 1800]

'With an arch and beautiful face, and slender voice, she executed every thing with all the neatness and reedy precision of the oboe*. *This instrument she could imitate exactly, by rather closing her mouth.' [1816: Gardiner, *Music of Nature*, p. 143]

'... voice was from A, fifth line of the bass, up to C, second leger line of the treble, or seventeen notes, in tone silvery, but in quality rather thin. Her intonation was the most sure, and her execution the most rapid and polished that had been heard in this country since the retirement of Mrs. Billington, whom she strongly recalled to the memory of those amateurs who recollected their distinguished countrywoman.' [19 May 1821: Har]

'The Lady is remarkable for the delicate tone of her voice, which is of an excellent quality, but hardly powerful enough for so large a Theatre [King's Theatre, Haymarket]. Her execution and science are indisputable. She is extremely valuable, too, as an Actress. Many of her traits remind us of Mademoiselle Fodor.' [21 May 1821: MP]

'Her voice is not remarkable either for sweetness or volume, and the formation of her tone does not appear to have been conducted in the most judicious way. There is a quality, in the upper parts most especially, which we can only characterize by the word infantine, for it partakes of the querulous plaintiveness of our tenderest age, and indeed would scarcely be thought to proceed from an adult, or even from the same person as the lower notes, by any one who should hear and not see the singer.' [Sep. 1822: QMMR, p. 314]

3.5.7 Maria Caradori-Allan [b. 1800]

'Her voice is sweetly delicate; its silvery purity, resembling the mellow intonation of the finest flageolet, enchanted those that were near enough to seize every breath. A first debut may have checked the full force of her tones, but we doubt whether it will ever be of sufficient strength to reach every part of so large a house as the King's Theatre [Haymarket]. In the concerted pieces, her part could not be heard.' [1 Feb. 1822: NMM]

'Signora Caradori sung "Ah si perdo", "La plus Jolie", "Dammi un Segnaio", and "Ca m'est égal", charmingly; in the latter she was encored. Her style of singing is classically chaste and natural; her melodies make their way to the heart; and while she can direct such an effect, success in every effort must be its concomitant. Her voice is powerful [when heard in the *Old Ship*, Brighton], and of great compass; and there is a naiveté in her manner, which imparts delight visually to heighten the enjoyment of the listening faculty.' [7 Oct. 1822: *Brighton Gleaner*]

'There was a clearness and purity in her tones, combined with great feeling, and a power of voice exquisitely appropriated to the dignity of the subject. The effect we could observe upon the auditory was that of enchantment.' [26 Sep. 1834: HP]

'Her voice is very sweet; it has all the delicacy of her frame and countenance; it steals gently over the ear, winning its way tenderly and gradually, and secure in reaching the heart. Madame Caradori Allan possesses a Soprano voice of considerable compass, extending to nearly three octaves, and combining the rare qualities of exquisite sweetness and great flexibility with that of perfect intonation.' [3 Oct. 1838: *Boston Musical Gazette*, p. 91]

'Madame Caradori Allan's "Angels ever bright and fair", with the recitative preceding it, was given in the most delicious, delicate, and affecting manner that can possibly be conceived, and brought tears into the eyes of many of the auditory.' [27 Sep. 1840: *Era*]

Her voice was stronger towards the end of her long career, but without loss of quality: ' "Let the bright seraphim", followed, and again Madame Caradori Allan charmed the company with the brilliancy, sweetness, and fullness of her tones. The ease with which she executed the most intricate passages, her wonderful power of protracting articulation upon one note, until, like a bee-rifled flower, all its sweetness was extracted, and her bird-like shake delighted the audience … And her silvery liquid notes, were placed in fine contrast to the trumpet obligato accompaniment, most felicitously played by Mr. Elwood.' [13 Apr. 1844: MT]

'In the exceedingly pleasing 'Spanish Chant',—a simple air and chorus, in what may be called the modernized Gregorian style—Madame Caradori-Allan was very charming; and in Cimarosa's aria she proved the unfading power and quality of her voice, as well as the unaltered delicacy of her taste.' [25 Mar. 1848: Ex]

3.5.8 Deborah Travis, later Mrs William Knyvett [b. 1800]

'The Tone of Miss Travis's voice is naturally full, rich, and sweet, with a slight exception perhaps against two or three of the notes just above the common point of junction between the chest and the head-voice, which are a little more thin and feeble than the rest of her scale. Her method of forming the voice has little or none of Italian art; the mouth is scarcely elongated, and upon some passages is even rounded; yet we do not hear that the tone is affected in its passage either by the throat, mouth, or nose. Her singing is pure and unadulterated,—without the slightest mixture of constraint, force, or affectation. It is sweet, sensible, natural, and in sound English taste.' [1818: QMMR, p. 471]

'In nothing does Miss Travis more fully show us the value of thought and judgment, as controlling mere liquidity of execution, than in the propriety and character with which she invests that beautiful ornament, the shake, which she possesses in perfection. Her compass of voice is about nineteen notes, from G to D, and in glees it harmonizes more delightfully than that of any other female we ever heard [p.79] ... Miss Travis has been said to be 'all correctness', and, undoubtedly, her taste has been formed in a severe school, but mere correctness only would not have moved all hearts, and drawn forth tears from so many eyes, as her performance [of the song 'What though I trace each herb and flower' from *Solomon*] did this morning: it was not only eminent for distinctness and clear articulation, but for deep feeling; the enunciation of the words "Jehovah's power", was finely energetic, while that of "How vain were all I knew", was no less remarkable for its affecting pathos.' [p. 309] [Sep. 1823: Crosse]

'Her voice is uncommonly clear, sweet, and melodious, and of good compass—her style of singing is simple and affecting, and her whole demeanour pleasing and unaffected.' [28 Oct. 1824: CM]

'Her singing is pure and unadulterated—without the slightest mixture of constraint, force, or affectation. It is sweet, sensible, natural, and in sound English taste. She neither takes by storm nor surprise, but she gradually wins upon the understanding, while the ear, though it never fills the other senses with extacy, drinks in full satisfaction. There is never any thing to condemn, however distant from brilliancy and power, and there is always to be commended a purity and sobriety, a graceful and dignified reserve, which is at all times grateful to the national estimate of character and manners. / We may complete our portrait by saying, that as a whole, Mrs. Knyvett is a correct, sweet, and polished English singer. Simple in her manner, pure in her tone, accurate in her intonation, chaste in her declamation, and with so much of science that her auditor is never distressed by her failure or extravagance.' [29 Jan. 1828: *Cumberland Pacquet*]

'... Mrs. W. KNYVETT sang "*But thou didst not leave*" with a pure and perfect pathos which could not be excelled' [3 Nov. 1828, MP]

'Mrs. Knyvett's solo, "The marvellous work", was sung very chastely in regard to style, and exhibited her remarkably pure-toned voice to great advantage.' [11 Sep 1835: HP]

3.5.9   Virginie Blasis [b. 1800]

The voice of the *débutanté* is a soprano, but not of the first quality. It is thin in the upper notes, and when strained, as of necessity it is, to fill a salon so large as this Theatre [King's Theatre, Haymarket], it loses the richness and sweetness of which in the lower notes it has much; and, though extremely pleasing within its appropriate sphere, it is quite unequal to the arpeggio passages attempted by Mademoiselle BLASIS. Her style is good, subject to the observation that there is an effort at embellishments of a nature rather beyond her powers. [9 Mar. 1829: MC]

'Gifted, as this lady is, with a pure, clear voice, skilled and cultivated in her art, and always eager to do her best, if that best is not quite the best we have heard and seen, she still is sure to give satisfaction.' [6 Feb. 1830: NMM]

'Mademoiselle Blasis may boast of a circumstance, probably unique in the history of the King's Theatre; that of having, in the short space of less than eight weeks, enacted the prima donna in eight different operas, with a perfection of study rarely surpassed, and with universal approbation; although one half of the parts were entirely new to her.' [1 May 1830: NMM]

'Blasis is just the *prima donna* we desire for a small theatre; her voice is as true and flute-like as ever.' [24 Dec. 1836: Ath]

3.5.10 Laure Cinti-Damoreau [b.1801]

'Signora Cinti's voice wants volume and force to fill such a house as the King's Theatre; but in saying this, we have mentioned all that can be stated in the way of objection. Her style of singing is of the most chaste description; she is evidently the pupil of the most perfect vocal school; her intonation is true, distinct, easy, and flexible, and her articulation precise, neat and delicate.' [1 June 1822: NMM]

'Madame Cinti acted and sang well as Donna Elvira. If her voice were a little more powerful, we should have had nothing to wish for; but her soprano in the concerted pieces was often scarcely audible.' [30 Jul. 1822: NMM]

'This night's performance introduced Cinti, who played Rosina, notwithstanding the claims of Camporese and Ronzi de Begnis to the part, which were with no little difficulty got over. Perhaps they were only persuaded by an expectation that Cinti's voice, inferior in power to that of either of their own, would preclude her from being much regarded; an opinion which their experience of Caradori should have repressed.' [1 June 1822: Ebers, *Seven Years of the King's Theatre*, p. 165]

'Occasionally we thought the accompaniments too loud, especially when supporting voices of inferior power, such as those of Signore Cinti and Caradori.' [1 Sep. 1822: NMM, discussion of the orchestra at the King's Theatre]

'Her vocal abilities are of a high order. Her voice is not powerful, but it is clear, rich, and remarkably flexible,—and her intonation is perfect. By nature she appears to be deficient in energy, so that her style is more adapted for the gentler passions.' [31 May 1830: Har]

'It was quite refreshing to hear her in our orchestra; we trust we shall have her on the remaining nights of the season. She sings charmingly in tune, her embellishments are always in good taste, and above all, she possesses feeling,—without which, as we have too frequently had occasion to remark, the most elaborate singing is little better than "sounding brass or a tinkling cymbal".' [26 May 1832: Har]

'I went to the Opéra Comique in search of Cinti-Damoreau's silver voice and flute-like cadences.' [3

Dec. 1836: Ath]

She was praised extravagantly on her New York début*:* 'Her's is a voice that falls upon the ear, like drops of water upon a musical glass—it possesses that liquid sweetness of which we read so much in poetry, but so rarely meet with in reality, and her execution is remarkable for its brilliancy, its neatness and its purity.' [21 Oct. 1843: *Brother Jonathan*]

Her voice grew in strength: 'Mad. Cinti appeared in an Italian scene composed for her by Adam, and never did she in her two previous concerts sing with a voice so pure, clear, fresh, strong and touching.' [11 Nov. 1843: *New World*]

3.5.11   Mary Ann Paton, later Mrs Wood [b. 1802]

'Her compass appears now to extend from A to D or E, or about eighteen or nineteen notes.' [Mar. 1823: QMMR, p. 193]

'She introduced on Monday night the *Soldier Tir'd*, and words cannot convey the effect her singing in this produced: we can scarcely call it singing, it was more like the sound of some instrument expressing at once the combined tones of the flute, hautboy, and the human voice, and played by a master hand, so astonishingly sweet, true, and accurate, was the execution of the triplets as written and in variation. Then the manner in which she gave the passage, "But if the brazen trumpet sound", letting out in measured cadence the full volume of her voice, and beautifully contrasting it with the rapidity of the preceding and following movements. In all this there is no grimace, no effort—the sounds flow forth as smoothly as if the mere parting of her lips produced, or rather set them loose, as so many "imprison'd thoughts", and then her intonation is as clear, and her articulation as perfect, as though she were *reciting* not *singing* poetry.' [31 Dec. 1828: *Dublin Evening Mail*]

'Miss Paton appeared during the third part of the performance, and delivered a recitative from Handel's Opera of Susannah, which was followed by an air from the same work, and beginning "If guiltless blood". The air is pleasing and sweet, but could scarcely be supposed capable of producing the effect which followed Miss Paton's unrivalled performance of it. To the well-known brilliancy and vigour of her execution, and the fulness and decided firmness of her tones, she added a softness and pathos which may not perhaps have been expected from her. The concluding words, "Oh, righteous Heaven, thy will be done", were delivered with an expression of meekness and resignation, and with a softness of tone and manner, which deeply affected the audience, and stamped this performance as the most effective of the day.' [26 Sep. 1828: MA]

Like Catalani, Mary Paton was also praised for her close shake: 'She possesses considerable power, with great sweetness, and we were much struck with her very fine close shake.' [27 Sep. 1828: YG] 'Her execution of "Cease your funning", was in that tasteful yet commanding style, which, combining the due extent of science with pure expression, makes out the union which is at once so desirable and so rare.' [29 Sep. 1822: Ex]

'HAYMARKET.—*Lionel and Clarissa* was revived here last evening. Miss Paton performed *Clarissa*, and gave several introduced airs in most exquisite style. "Willow, willow, willow", was charmingly sung in the most pure manner, and with a melody that was delightful; the more so, as it was divested of those graces and flourishes which spoil natural simple airs, and are rather calculated to surprise than please, and lead us to wish, with Dr. Johnson, that they were impossible.' [8 Oct 1830: *Globe*]

'I particularly remember her rendering of the famous soprano song, "To mighty kings he gave his acts". Her voice was beautiful in quality and of considerable extent. It possessed a liquid and fluent flexibility, quite unlike the curious staccato and tremolo effects so much in favor to-day.' [2 Jan. 1841: *Atlantic Monthly*]

3.5.12 Henrietta Nina Sontag [b. 1803]

'The voice was neither full nor strong, but pure as a bell, clear as a pearl, silver-bright, mellifluous, particularly in the middle, flexible, distinctly articulated and of seductive sweetness. And how beautifully she trilled—like the bright jubilation of a soaring lark. Then again there was the brilliance of her singularly high head tones in the most difficult passages and roulades—as precise as a delicate musical clock. Incomparably enchanting was her *sotto voce*. And it all came so easily, so effortlessly from the charming little mouth that the listener had but to relax and enjoy it, confident that nothing could go wrong.' [3 Aug. 1825: Account by Karoline Bauer of Berlin début in *L'Italiana in Algeri*, Pleasants, p. 194]

'Her voice pleasing, and of considerable compass; her method is that of the Italian school, she sings with great precision and amazing lightness, and employs the mezza di voce, and all the other ornaments of song, with the most winning grace.' [Jul. 1827: Har]

'… is a true soprano, of the full compass, extending, we are told, from A below the clef, to E in alt.' [May 1828: Har]

'As years drew on, emotion and warmth increasingly animated her performances; but when she began she could do little more than look lovely—display her beautiful voice, and careful finish—and be steady as a rock in her execution. [p. 68] … the incomparable steadiness with which she wrought out her composer's intentions.' [Dec. 1849: Chorley. *Recollections*, Vol. 2, p. 78]

'… possesses a voice of the greatest richness, power and flexibility. Her high notes resounded through the hall with the clearness of a trumpet …' [2 Oct. 1852: *Weekly Herald*]

'… was in fresher, stronger, richer voice than ever in her previous visits. In her rendering, the much abused Robert, toi que j'aime was refreshingly lifted up and restored to all the original charm of its musical beauty and dramatic force. Mozart's Vedrai Carino and Schubert's "Serenade" were sung with exquisite purity of tone and feeling.' [17 Dec. 1853: *Dwight's*]

3.5.13 Margaretha Stockhausen [b. 1803]

'Possesses a clear-toned agreeable voice, not very powerful or of any vast compass, but well adapted to concert rooms, and more particularly to private saloons, to which she wishes, we understand, chiefly to confine herself.' [14 May 1827: Har]

'Her voice was a clear high soprano, the upper part of the register being unusually sweet and liquid, qualities which she rarely missed the opportunity of exhibiting, for she almost always terminated her songs on the highest octave.' [14 May 1827: Phillips, *Recollections*]

'It was generally remarked that her style of singing was so chaste and elegant, as to remind the audience more forcibly of Mrs. [Eliza] Salmon than any singer heard since that lady's retirement. It is a general observation amongst the members of the orchestra, that if she made sacred music her study, she would prove an excellent substitute for the lady already mentioned, who was one of the best singers in that style.' [7 Oct. 1828: HP]

'Madame Stockhausen, in an air from a Litany of Mozart, displayed the clearness of execution, the singular purity of voice, and the chaste German style, which are her distinguishing characteristics.' [30 Jun. 1834: MC]

' "Rejoice greatly", sung by Mdme. Stockhausen; her voice has not the grandeur and fullness requisite for Handel's sacred music; but it is pure, sweet, and bears marks of a good school.' [16 Apr. 1835: Von Raumer, p. 95]

'In consequence of the great reputation Madame Stockhausen has so justly acquired, she, by particular request, sang, "With verdure clad", from Haydn's Creation, with the same angelic sweetness and purity of tone, the same finished taste and charming expression, with which she sang twelve years since, and which is so immeasurably superior to any we ever heard, in the same air.' [26 Mar. 1840: MW]

3.5.14 Maria Malibran [b. 1808]

... Every one was enchanted at the first public rehearsal; in the moment of enthusiasm, it was declared that nothing equal to her voice had been heard since the days of Marchesi. And to say the truth, in the beginning, her beautiful, clear, and flexible soprano voice, combined with great distinctness of pronunciation, created a great sensation. / But this excellent voice began soon to get out of tune ... Perhaps the size of our theatre [King's Theatre, Haymarket] might have been the cause why her voice thus suddenly lost its tone; indeed so vast an interior requires lungs of brass, and has proved the wreck of many a promising debutante. [31 May 1825: Har]

'There were a few things of this kind breathing remarkable purity and sweetness, and which shewed that Mademoiselle [née] Garcia had not listened to the exquisite touches of Pasta in vain. But with all this excellence there is a temporary obstacle, necessarily dependent upon her youth, which will prevent her from immediately taking the high range of characters as prima donna. Everybody will perceive that this is the want of power—noise alone can contend with the orchestral and choral thunders of such an establishment [the 'Italian Opera' at the Haymarket], and at the age of seventeen a lady's lungs are seldom qualified for that stentorian task. In her solo singing, or even in the concerted pieces which are not very full, this defect is scarcely remembered; for the voice possesses in an eminent degree that quality which makes the softest intonation distinct wherever the sound penetrates.' [13 June 1825: MP]

'Madame Malibran's voice is of extraordinary power and very considerable compass. In the first of these attributes it is equal to most others, extending probably from F upon the second line of the base staff (she uses G with great power and effect) to C in alt ... In point of tone, Madame Malibran's voice is distinguished by no peculiar beauty. It is formed with great purity, great equality, and singular art, but its natural qualities make no impression proper to itself, and distinct from or superior to other voices of the same class. If it may be likened to any instrument it more resembles the richer tone of the flute than any other, on account of its clearness and brilliancy. The lower notes, however, are strong, smooth, and rich, and by far the finest portion of the voice. We therefore consider that the higher is the praise due to the expressive power of the singer; since unendowed with any natural gift of organ that places her above many, very many others, (except perhaps the larger extension of her compass below) the mind breaks forth and establishes her supremacy, and it is the more curious, since the quality of the tone is that generally least expressive.' [30 Sep. 1828: QMMR, pp. 323/328]. *Penny Cyclopædia*, Vol. XXVI [Illus. 45 below] indicates that her voice ranged from D on the middle line of bass staff to top C in alt.

'Her extraordinary compass of voice is astonishing, and, probably, unparalleled; on the present occasion, she sang down to F sharp, on the fourth tone in the bass clef, and she has sometimes been heard to skip with the most extraordinary exactitude from the E flat of the bass to the E natural upon the third ledger tone above the treble stave,—the surprising, difficult, and uncertain distance of three octaves and a semitone!' [8 Apr. 1829: Ath]

'Her voice much resembles that of PASTA, and is of a most sweet and liquid quality throughout, combined with all the firmness and decision of the finest wind instrument. It is extremely flexible, and capable of every modulation that the most ardent admirer of the ROSSINI school could desire, without perhaps the brilliant coruscations and musical snuff-box passages, to which we attribute the extraordinary sensation made last year by Mademoiselle SONTAG. She may probably be able to do likewise, but she shows her good sense and taste in abstaining from what after all is merely mechanical.' [26 Apr 1829: Ex]

Malibran has the quality of a *contralto*, but her compass is that of a *soprano*. From G below the line to G upon the line, the quality of Malibran's voice is round, rich, and exceedingly sweet. Above G on the line there is a decided break. A, B, and C are pure, but ineffective notes, and it requires all the consummate art she possesses to conceal this defect. The first quoted octave consists of notes evidently produced from the chest; beyond that octave she uses the *voce di testa*. Malibran is not gifted with much natural flexibility—very few voices of mixed character are—but her vocalization is extremely perfect, her certainty in fitting difficult intervals, and beautiful way of progressing from note to note, render her an eminent instance of the power of cultivation combined with tact and genius, and in this, to our humble thinking, consists the charm of her singing. Her defects are those of exaggeration. She is continually seeking to create a sensation of surprise in her audience, and frequently, in this pursuit, the effort becomes *un coup manqué*. What can be more ridiculous than her treatment of the finale to *La Sonnambula*,--delighting us one moment by the exquisite richness of voice she displays in her transition from E on the fourth space to C below the line, in the words "Embrace me", and the next moment attempting a *tour de force* (which is a complete failure) by shaking on D in alt, which shake is accompanied by grimace and an exertion which puzzles her audience exceedingly; their ears tell them that the sound is by no means agreeable; they see that the lady is almost in convulsions in the attempt; but—it is a difficulty, and it is Malibran who is attempting to overcome it, and, *ergo*, it must be very fine and *all right*, so the professors laugh, and the amateurs cry *brava* and applaud. Quere, does not the lady laugh in her sleeve? [29 May 1836: Ex]

3.5.15   Mrs Anna Bishop, née Riviere [b. 1810]

'A Miss Riviere made her *debut,* and sang, with no ordinary taste and judgment, CIMAROSA'S unparalleled scena, *Ah! Parlate*. Her voice is a brilliant *soprano*, and her style is untainted with a superfluous redundancy of embellishment, which young vocalists are apt to introduce. Of the debutantes which have been heard at these Concerts [Concerts of Ancient Music], this young Lady is the most promising.' [22 Apr. 1831: MP]

'Madame Bishop's is one of those voices, rare now-a-days, which in Italy are known as the soprano sfogato. It is of that delicately veiled quality of which Rossini, the composer, has expressed himself so ardent an admirer. Its regular compass is from F on the first space to E flat on the third line above the stave, all good notes, on which she can depend; but, when occasion requires, she can sing both lower and higher than the extremes indicated. It is in all respects a pure and undeniable soprano—such a voice as Handel wrote for in his Messiah, and the Italians, from Cimarosa to Rossini, in most of their noted operas. The most celebrated possessors of the soprano sfogato voice, whose names will now be recognized, are Ronzi, Sontag, Grisi, and Persiani, though, by the way, Grisi is only a pure soprano in the middle voice, the upper and lower notes appertaining to the mezzo soprano, of which there are so many existing specimens among our own English vocalists. For the purposes of dramatic singing the best notes of Madame Bishop's voice are from B flat on the stave to C above the stave. As in the case with every soprano sfogato, the chest-notes are less resonant than the higher ones in passages where great dramatic energy is demanded; but in the ballad style Madame Bishop can sing as low as D beneath the stave with facility and good effect. Before she went on the continent, Madame Bishop's voice was mistaken for a mezzo soprano, and F or G was the highest note she attempted but at Naples, when the popular composer, Mercadante, wrote an air with variations for her, which more than once touched upon E in alt, she found she executed it with ease, and thence the true nature of her voice was declared … In actual power and volume of tone there never was perhaps the equal of Malibran; but in undeviated purity of intonation and unfailing perfection of execution Madame Bishop has certainly the advantage over that greatest of dramatic singers. No instrument could surpass the unerring neatness of her mechanism, and to this is joined natural grace, judicious and elegant use of ornament, propriety of expression, variety of dramatic colouring, and wonderful fervour and depth of passion.' [9 Oct. 1846: T]

'Without intending to institute any invidious comparison between two orders of talent so totally distinct, and equally great in their way, as those of Madame Bishop and Miss Poole, considerations for art induce us to dwell for a moment on the opposite effects produced by their voices on the audiences. Here was Madame Bishop, with a high *soprano* (with little or no lower notes) cultivated to the highest degree of perfection, with correct intonation, and the purest method, but with indistinct articulation, and labouring incessantly for effect from beginning to end, giving often the painful notion that such continuous exertions must come to a stand still. On the other hand was Miss Poole, with a *mezzo soprano* of great purity of tone, singing without effort, without any attempt at a mechanical exhibition of vocalisation, but whose simple and unaffected style goes to the heart, and creates the most pleasurable sensations. It was the triumph, in fact, of nature over art—simplicity versus mechanism. Miss Poole vocalises as if she could not help it; every word she utters is heard; Madame Bishop sings artificially, and declamatory power is absolutely wanting. The audience evidently decided in favour of the ballad over bravura: amazement at the florid divisions in the *Rondo finale*, so brilliantly executed by Madame Bishop, was created; but the genuine rapture of the soul was only excited when Miss Poole was heard in a melody, than which nothing could be more unassuming in form, but deriving an especial charm from the natural style of the vocalist.' [14 Nov. 1846: *Illustrated London News*]

'She appears before the New-York public again, with a voice as fresh and beautiful as when we first heard her in this city a great many years ago. Indeed, we think, that in point of volume and purity, it is now better than it was then. Madame Bishop's style is thoroughly admirable; her school is pure, being free from that nauseating tremolo, which disfigures the manner of too many of our modern singers, and there is nothing in the elaboration of ornament which is beyond her reach.' [30 Aug. 1865: NYHT]

3.5.16 Giulia Grisi [b. 1811]

'Giulietta Grisi, younger sister of the former singer of that name, but very much superior to her in all respects, combining every requisite for the situation; handsome person, sweet yet powerful voice, considerable execution, and still more expression; she is an excellent singer, and excellent actress; in short is described to be as nearly perfect as possible, and is almost a greater favourite than even Pasta or Malibran.' [1833: Edgcumbe, p. 218]

'A voice, a most pure and perfect soprano, sweet, clear, flexible, powerful, unerringly in tune, and responsive to every gradation and change of feeling, however impassioned or however subdued; execution, developing all the resources of science, in conjunction with the truest and most touching expression. This is a "catalogue of perfections"; and, nothing being perfect in this world, it follows that she must have some faults, which it is an important part of critical duty to discover.' [13 Apr. 1834: Ex]

'We have said that Signora Grisi's voice is a genuine Italian soprano. It is all pure from the chest, remarkably equal, brilliant in tone, luxuriant in its flexibility and compass, and combining apparently any extent of power which the singer chooses to exert, with a softness so delicate and exquisite that the ear strains to catch its minutest vibration. This delightful contrast appears to be a peculiar characteristic of her style, and is one of the chief advantages of her fine portamento, giving to her cantabile singing a variety and richness such as we can remember but in few singers that we have ever heard.' [16 Apr. 1834: MP]

'And what a soprano voice was hers!—rich, sweet—equal throughout its compass of two octaves (from C to C) without a break, or a note which had to be managed. Her shake was clear and rapid; her scales were certain; every interval was taken without hesitation by her. Nor has any woman ever more thoroughly commanded every gradation of force than she—in those early days especially;— not using the contrast of loud and soft too violently, but capable of any required violence, of any advisable delicacy. In the singing of certain slow movements *pianissimo* … the clear penetrating beauty of her reduced tones (different in quality from the whispering semi-ventriloquism which was one of Mademoiselle Lind's most favourite effects) was so unique … the sounds that never wavered.' [Dec. 1834: Chorley, *Recollections*, Vol. 1, p.110]

'Mademoiselle Grisi is reported to have sung "Rejoice greatly" with the full power of her magnificent voice! That we dare be sworn she did. The less Mademoiselle Grisi knows any music, with the more unbounded confidence she stands up to it, as if the judgment of the audience were to be taken by storm, and their ears invaded by noise to the total overthrow of reason. It is a manifest absurdity to set Mademoiselle Grisi to sing Handel: her music education fits her for her post at the modern opera, and for light concert-room songs, in which she can exhibit her clear execution; but beyond this she is absolutely useless in classical performances.' [20 Sep. 1835: Atlas]

'… but by some magic or other Grisi has restored herself to such a glorious state that the *habitués* of the house are perfectly astonished. Several uneasy doubts were expressed in the course of last year. Her execution was observed to be less fresh, and she sometimes had to strain her voice to such a degree, that not only did it pain the ear but even the eye, so obviously were the efforts marked by the flushed countenance, and the swelling veins. But now *elle a changé tout cela.* She is as she was in her very best days; and we even find recorded several opinions that she never sang so well in her life as during the past week.' [13 Apr. 1844: Ex]

'With Grisi, a severe artist can find more fault [than with Mario]; for among other things her trill is quite imperfect; she trills with the wrong note and cannot, I presume, trill with a whole tone; for she never trills but half a one. The perfect artist always gives a whole-tone trill:—but after all, there are not many people who care for these things. And when an artiste, like Grisi, offers us so much that is exquisite, and in some things where we have no right at all to claim superior excellence, why should we be captious?' [30 Sep. 1854: MW]

'She is not the Norma of former days. Her acting and grace are as fine as ever, but her voice is now thin and lacks power. This was very palpable last night. There was no enthusiasm produced in the audience, except the conventional enthusiasm which must of course attend upon the "Casta Diva", and the trio between Norma, Adalgisa, and Pollio. Throughout the performance—the vocal performance—Madame Grisi seemed to us just to get up to a certain level, which created anticipations of something great to come, which never came. Some of her cadences were shrill and wiry, and in no part did she display anything like a rich full sonorous tone.' [28 Oct. 1858: MC]

3.5.17 Mary Postans, later Mrs Alfred Shaw [b. 1814]

'She has been three years in Italy under the tuition of Madame Catalini [Catalani], and is but about two months returned to England. She possesses a peculiar voice for a female—that which in music technicality is designated contralto—being that which Handel in some of his pieces had set male parts to, but which it is found there exists great difficulty to find males equal to the execution. Miss Postan's voice, while it possesses all the masculine character of strength and firmness, has all the characteristic excellence of feminine melodious sweetness; and her execution is strongly marked of the school in which she has studied.' [24 Oct. 1834: MA]

'... the noble contralto-singer, whose voice subdued all hearts by its silvery and bell-like purity.' [26 Sep. 1839: MW]

'In her (Mrs. Alfred Shaw's) duet with Assur, as well as in her solo passages, her contralto register shone in its rather extensive compass, pure, clear, sweet and mellow, reaching its highest notes with ease and suavity, whilst her musical cultivation sported in a profusion of the most chaste and graceful ornaments.' [3 Oct. 1842: MP]

'The first few bars of her recitative she gave with such truth and firmness, with such perfect tranquillity, and so simple and touching was her reading, that the audience, even at this early stage of her performance, began to give spontaneous demonstrations of their delight. And here it may be observed, that Mrs. A. Shaw seems to be the only English singer who thoroughly understands the use to be made of recitative, which is so often little more than mere speaking. She grasped it thoroughly, made it musical, avoiding without an effort coarseness on the one hand and feebleness on the other, and giving every sentiment its proper force. Her voice is a contralto cultivated to the highest degree, her intonation as true as possible, her execution perfect, every passage being turned in the most delicate and finished manner, and given with the most beautiful variety of light and shade.' [3 Oct. 1842: Std]

'In common with many contralti voices, Mrs. Shaw possesses a slight want of that creamy liquidity which is so delicious in the female organ. But as a singer this is the only objection that could be urged by the most hypercritical of censors ... In tone, she marvellously reminds us of that most exquisite of our musical memories—poor Malibran, with a comparative paucity of expression in that dramatic fervour, which it will not disgrace this accomplished singer, should we express a disbelief in her capacity of ever rivalling. Her enunciation is the sharpest and cleanest we have ever heard, unaccompanied by that pedantic ostentation of syllable, which must destroy its beauty.' [5 Oct. 1842: MP]

'It is allowed by the musical profession generally that Mrs. Alfred Shaw is the best contralto singer this country ever produced. She does not pump out her notes when descending the scale as too many contralti do, in imitation of bass voices, but all is equal and smooth, perfectly in tune, throughout a range of 17 notes [Compass agrees with Illus. 45 below]. The ornaments she introduces are in the best possible taste, and, what is of great importance, always appropriate.' [10 Oct. 1842: MP]

'... but a good voice is a glorious thing, and as the ripe yet bell-like notes of that exquisite contralto fell among the audience, the muse of melody asserted her supremacy. The fine recitative of "Delightful hour of rapture" was delivered as Mrs. Shaw, of English singers, can alone deliver recitative. Nothing could surpass its firm, yet exquisitely finished articulation.' [23 Oct. 1843: MP]

'Her voice was indeed lovely, rich, equal—delivered with a graceful serenity, distinct from coldness, which was most attractive.—Her pronunciation of English was the best and most refined in my recollection.—Every word told—yet not a word was theatrical. Her expression, I have heard it said, was derived from her singing-master; but this was not to be detected.—It was grievous that a career, which might have lasted so long, and have been so rich in success to herself and pleasure to others, was shortened by mistaken ambition.—After her voice was settled, and her place as a concert-singer was assured, beyond all precedent, she would return to Italy, try the stage, and, most fatal of all, add a few upper notes to her voice.—This is never to be done with impunity. In Mrs. Shaw's case, when she appeared with Miss Kemble in the English versions of "Semiramide" and "Il Matrimonio", (a more drily comical Fidalma was never seen), it was evident that the quality of her notes was impaired—that they had lost some of that equal richness, which had made a quaint speaker say that her voice reminded him of *black velvet*. The intonation, of course, very soon gave way—and there was no choice for the artist, save retirement.' [1862: Chorley, *Recollections*, Vol. 1, p. 221]

3.5.18   Catherine Hayes [b. 1818]

'Hayes is the prima donna. Her voice is good, and she is a first-rate musician; but as to filling the Scala, it is entirely out of the question.' [23 Sep. 1846: *Freeman's Journal*]

'The voice of Miss Hayes is, as we had been led to expect, a pure and liquid *soprano* of great compass (about three octaves) but limited volume. We cannot say that we detected many "evidences of fatigue" in the notes in alt; and those of the *mezzo* register are remarkably satisfactory. To our taste, the finest part of the organ lies in the octave between B flat and G or A flat in alt; but her D flat is touched with ease, and taken with decision. Of the lower notes we, as yet, hesitate to speak positively. The intonation of Miss Hayes is, generally speaking, unerringly exact; and her tone, although deficient in richness, is by no means thin, though occasionally rather hard. The *fioriture* are introduced with taste and discretion, the chromatic scale is under excellent discipline, and the shake, if not perfect, is indubitably good.' [15 Apr. 1849: Era]

'Miss Hayes is more the conventional Lucia of the Italian stage than (like Jenny Lind) the Lucy Ashton of Scott; and her whole performance was akin to that of Persiani, whom she resembled in the thin but pure quality of her voice, in its flexibility, and in the facility and grace of her embellishments.' [2 May 1849: MCLGA]

'The audience were at once stilled in wrapt silence [at the start of 'Kathleen Mavourneen'], and the fair vocalist broke forth in a tone of wild and plaintive melody, rendering the sweet and heart-breaking music of this exquisite ballad with a degree of pathos, feeling, and taste, that kept the audience as if spell-bound. These, together with the recitative and cavatina, "O luce di quest' anima", from the *Linda*, formed her crowning triumphs.—Mddle Hayes, in person, is exceedingly prepossessing. She is somewhat thin, but eminently graceful and symmetrical in figure. Her eyes are large and lustrous, and the expression of her features, which are regular, is full of intellectuality.—Combined with that nameless charm which continental habitude produces, Miss Hayes' manner seems racy [sic] of that artless, yet inimitable grace, so peculiarly distinctive of the Irish girl. The fine enthusiasm, in voice and manner, that marked her rendering of the Irish ballad, seemed to win every heart and cause every hand to applaud her.' [6 Nov. 1849: *Freeman's Journal*]

'We confess we were at first more struck by the quality of her voice, which is a deliciously pure and flexible one, than by any special aptitude for the work which was the occasion of its exhibition; but this feeling was afterwards considerably changed by the greater amount of warmth and fusion which she threw into her treatment of the work in hand. At a first hearing, however, this same quality of voice will always be matter of curious interest; and it certainly could not be otherwise in relation to such an organ as that of Miss Hayes, the intense purity of which is almost startling.' [24 Nov. 1849: MT]

'We would describe Miss Hayes's voice as a pure and true *soprano*, reaching as high, if we mistake not, as D above the line, and richest and fullest in the uppermost octave. We detected none of the fatigue or *wornness* attributed to it on her arrival from Italy; on the contrary, we thought her voice, if not remarkable for volume or richness of quality, distinguished for purity, clearness, and freedom from all harshness, even in the highest notes of the scale. Her execution is good, and her taste highly cultivated and chaste; she throws off rapid divisions and florid *fioriture* with liquid sweetness and great ease; and without ease a singer, though she might mount to G in alto, could never give pleasure to a listener. No one, we presume, could find fault with Miss Hayes's intonation; but we think her articulation, especially in some of her English songs, might be amended, as not unnaturally, considering circumstances, she appears to have a propensity to gloss over the consonants and dwell upon the Italianised vowels. There was something very impressive and grand in the manner in which she gave "*Casta Diva*", though we have heard "readings" of that air which we like as well as her's; her embellishments at the *finale* were of the most ornate description, and executed in a style which bespoke great previous labour and cultivation. This *cavatina* was *encored,* as was, also, the *polacca*, "*O luce di quest' anima*", which she gave with great lightness and grace; indeed, we would say that, in those songs best suited to her, grace does as much for them as power. "My last thoughts are of thee", a ballad composed expressly for Miss Hayes, is simple, pretty, and unpretending, but not sufficiently effective for a concert-room, although all that taste and elegance could do for it, were done for it last night, by Miss Hayes. The duet between her and Miss Poole—"Meet again"—is a beautiful one in itself, and was beautifully sung by both ladies, whose voices blended together in most exquisite harmony; and, sung before a Belfast audience, it is almost unnecessary to add that it was *encored*. They kindly responded to the call, by giving the celebrated duet between Norma and Adelgiza. The gem of the evening, however, was the "Non giunge", which, we freely confess, was sung with a luxuriancy, a brilliancy, and dashing fearlessness of difficulty which completely took us by surprise: we refer particularly to the *finale*, where Miss Hayes's voice rose sweet and clear to an altitude seldom *attempted* by even good *sopranos*, and where she executed a shake of such evenness, length, and clearness, terminating in an elaborate *roulade*, as drew down a thunder of applause, many persons rising from their seats in their enthusiasm, and waving their hats. Miss Hayes's voice seems, at first, to have been an *unwilling* one, as have been originally the voices of many of our greatest singers, but this description of organ is the one above all others which is capable of the greatest brilliancy of execution when its natural difficulties have been overcome by labour and sound training. Nothing can present a more decided proof of this assertion than the feats performed by Miss Hayes in every species of embellishment, shake, *roulade*, or *cadenza*, whilst her pathos and feeling must speak to the heart of even the least cultivated. Though we are far from saying of Miss Hayes "that her face is her fortune" (her voice alone would make one), it certainly can offer no impediment to it. Her countenance is at once handsome, pleasing, and intelligent, her figure light and graceful, and her carriage and air are strikingly elegant and lady-like. We are not astonished, that, excelling in their favourite art, and gifted as she is with such personal attractions, she should have created such a sensation among the Italians, to whose sunny daughters she must have formed so *piquante* contrast. [19 Feb. 1850: *Northern Whig*]

'Her voice has gained greatly in power, and there is more decision in her tones. The peculiar sweetness and plaintiveness, so remarkable before, are as conspicuous, and her intonation as faultless, as ever.' [14 May 1851: MW, 'Memoir of Catherine Hayes', p. 37]

'Catherine Hayes, in her voice, leaves nothing to be desired. Her upper notes are as clear and ringing as a bell; the middle voice round, full, and sweet; and the lower voice, without losing the distinctive character of the other two registers, possesses the depth, strength, and sonority of the true contralto. These three divisions are blended together with singular art, and constitute a perfect organ of nearly three octaves in extent. We may conscientiously affirm, we never heard a pure soprano with such a middle and low voice. Herein Catherine Hayes possesses an enviable advantage over Jenny Lind, whose voice is circumscribed in the lower division; and herein may also be said to lay the power of the singer in varying the expression which renders Catherine Hayes's ballad singing so irresistibly touching … By-the-bye, Catherine Hayes has one of the most perfect and beautiful shakes we ever heard.' [1 Sep. 1851: *Freeman's Journal*]

'… is a Soprano of delicious sweetness, fulness, roundness, and power; and also possessing a contralto quality. Its compass extends from G below the treble clef to D above the staff, which is in reality equal (within three notes) to the most surprising Soprano the world every produced, that of Madame Catalani, that lady commanding for her compass three octaves from F below the treble clef to F above the staff … Miss Catherine Hayes has not only the great advantage of compass, but is perfectly mistress of the art of commanding her tones at will and pleasure, by the crescendo and diminuendo, that is by swelling into rich volume, and gradually melting into softness, until the memory of sound only remains on the ear.' [30 Sep. 1854: *Bell's Life in Sydney*]

3.5.19   Clara Novello [b. 1818]

Clara Novello was a famous concert and oratorio artist, active on and off from 1833 until her retirement in 1860. 'At the early age of eleven she became a pupil at the "Institution Royale de Musique classique et religieuse" in Paris … on the trial day, the French examiners found that the English child was a very exceptional student, and abnormally gifted with a silvery, bell-like, clear and ringing voice, which, after studious cultivation, became a fixture and a lifelong possession.' [Jun. 1832: Clara Novello, *Reminiscences*, p. 1]

'A more solid tribute to her rare musicianship was the fact that on Christmas Eve, in the year 1832, she sang the principal soprano part in the first performance in England of Beethoven's Mass in D [Missa Solemnis]. She was then only fourteen years of age, and it should be remembered that Sontag, in her girlhood, had in vain implored Beethoven himself to make the soprano part less difficult.' [24 Dec. 1832: Novello, *Reminiscences*, p. 1]

'She had a charming soft and flute-like-soprano, and had been well drilled in the ancient school of music by her father, my esteemed friend. Her voice was not flexible, but she sustained her notes with exquisite pathos.' [1 Jun. 1834: Phillips]

I've already noted the *Caledonian Mercury's* praise for her voice in York Minster as 'soft as the tones of musical glasses' [p. 88].

'The Agnus Dei was sung by Miss Novello with her usual chasteness of style and purity of tone, but she is deficient in the energy required on such an occasion as this.' [18 Sep. 1835: HP]

'Miss Novello's sostenuto, too, stands in need of regulation. We know not better how to illustrate our counsel than by stating our opinion that even where they possess, as she does, the fullest sustaining power, the utmost certainty of intonation, our native singers, for the most part, appear to have an almost traditional objection to that delicious level singing which gives such unity to cantabile performance; they are too fond of passing swells and diminutions of tone, and their performances, as a whole, become broken and unsatisfactory.' [29 Apr. 1837: Ath]

'Miss Clara Novello agreeably surprised even those best acquainted with her voice, by the apparent ease with which she accomplished the extensive compass of the fine song of Mozart's, "Non piu di fiori", the two extremes of which are, from the lower G below the line, to C in alt.' [NB. The *Penny Cyclopædia* table at Illus. 45 below agrees with this] [12 May 1837: MW]

'... we have heard Miss Clara Novello, with that loveliest and freshest of young voices—and a style, sound and excellent as far as it goes—failing, however, wholly in the great essential of articulation, and showing as yet few symptoms of the warmth and passion which future years may supply.' [Jul. 1837: LG]

Felix Mendelssohn commented in a letter on Clara's singing: 'Since that moment she was the declared favourite of them [the Leipzig public], they are equally delighted with her clear and youthful voice and with the purity and good taste with which she sings everything ... she possesses just those two qualities of which the public is particularly fond here, purity of intonation and a thoroughbred musical feeling ... I must also add that I never heard to greater advantage than at these two concerts, and that I liked her singing infinitely better than I ever did before; whether it might be that the smaller room suits her better, or perhaps the foreign air.' [2 Nov. 1837: quoted in Novello, *Reminiscences*, p. 65]

'Her voice is so melodious, clear, and silver-toned, so well proportioned in all its parts, possesses so charming a portamento, combines with majestic strength such melting tenderness, that the audience, overpowered by the feelings she excited, burst out, even in the midst of her song, into the loudest applause; and on her second appearance greeted her with rapturous acclamations.' [26 Jan.

1838: MW]

'Her voice is amazingly rich and round in quality, and its power is marvellous, but the very fullness of the organ is a drawback on its flexibility. Thus, whilst her vocalization was exquisitely true and touching in level passages, her fioriture was not so remarkable for precision. Her prolonged shakes are not perfect, and her intervals not distinctly marked. She possesses, however, a chaste and classical style, and this makes up for brilliancy.' [3 Apr. 1843: MP]

'The Americans, and therein travellers most harmoniously concur, describe the ne plus ultra of gustatory pleasure to be derivable from the imbibing of a mint julep; and if we were to compare things divine with things human, we should be inclined to assimilate Clara Novello's voice to a mint julep of the real Virginian manufacture; sweetness, spirit, fragrance, coolness, each in so happy proportion, and so nicely combined, as to enhance the value of all the other elements. There is not, in her entire compass, a faulty semitone. We never heard anything that, for equality, came near it. Low, middle, high, highest, there is no roughness, no thickening, no attenuation. With this the notes drop from her mouth like the pearls from the good princess in the fairy tale, with so little apparent effort, that she seems almost unconscious of their presence. There she stands—the full and fervent flow of sound pouring forth, without stint or stay, like the bright and sparkling waters of a perennial fountain, and not a muscle strains, not a breath is fetched more than ordinary, not a distortion of the features, not a motion of the body is perceptible.' [24 Jun. 1843: MP]

'Costa was punctual, and we had not been five minutes in the building [Crystal Palace] before we went over to the other end of the great transept, far beyond where the Queen's dais is to be, and stood on the spot where the orchestra will be stationed. The experiment answered triumphantly. [Clara Novello's] voice rang out pure and large and trumpet-like … When she arrived she telegraphed to us by waving her parasol, a white one, and I answered by waving mine in reply. Then she sang the verse, and the effect was one of the most curious I ever heard in my life, and almost supernaturally beautiful; it was like an angel—clear, sweet and exquisitely distinct, but remote. "God save our gracious Queen." It came trilling and vibrant, but singularly distinct…We always knew that Clara's voice was extraordinarily powerful, in combination with its delicious sweetness; but we never could have believed the extent of its power had we not actually made this curious experiment.' [1 Jul. 1854: *Dwight's*]

'She certainly put in one unhappy little appoggiatura, which caused the voice-part to make consecutive fifths with the bass; but singers do not mind such trifles, and audiences never find them out. With this exception, Madame Novello sang the song irreproachably; and merits our warmest praise.' [18 Jun. 1857: MP]

'Madame Clara Novello was in the fullest possession of her extraordinary powers, and sang (as she can do when so disposed) with great spirit and expression. As to her voice, it is, as we have often said, incomparable. There is an abstract beauty in it which, apart from all precise meaning—independently of all emotional, sentimental, or objective expression—fascinates and delights us. It is an "affectionate", caressing, angelic voice, and rings purely as virgin gold. It can be very gentle without weakness—extremely powerful without coarseness. Try it where you may, you will find it of one quality, and that the best.' [27 Aug. 1857: MP]

'The next principal feature of the composition [*Engedi*, an English oratorio based on Beethoven's *Christ on the Mount of Olives*] consisted of a recitative, "What sorrow", and an air, "Praise ye Jehovah's goodness", which were allotted to Madame Clara Novello. Her incomparably clear and sweet soprano voice rang through the building [Gloucester cathedral] with an exquisite tone, between a flute and a trumpet, and her articulation in the difficult variations of "The proud he brings to shame", excited subdued applause. The music is exquisite up to this point.' [17 Sep. 1859: *Gloucester Journal*]

Further descriptions of Clara Novello's voice are included in Section 4 [p. 258].

3.5.20   Jenny Lind, Mrs Goldschmidt [b. 1820]

'With a voice remarkably sympathetic in the chest tones, she has, by industry, acquired great facility in the management of her upper register. Her shakes are well prepared, articulated, and terminated. The few notes above the lines up to B natural are brilliant, and by far the best part of her vocal organ… in timbre of voice, beauty of method, genius in pathetic delivery of cantabile, she does not approach Alboni … Her Alice is engaging but not overwhelming. Hear her in the upper octave and her notes are pure, limpid, and resonant; below, husky, veiled, and ineffective. Her shake is perfect, in the pianissimo it is delicious, her chromatic scale is admirably articulated.' [1 May 1847: MC]

'Her voice, a true soprano, is rich, full, and mellifluous—clear, distinct, and voluptuously bell-like—while there is a charming evenness of texture throughout. It extends to D in alt, a point she reaches without loss of power of tone. Her capacity to execute volant passages seems to be similar to that of Sontag, every note being accurately and separately articulated with the nicety and finish of an instrument.' [5 May 1847: Std]

'… has a quality of delicious roundness, softness, and evenness, to which our knowledge of the Italian, French, or German stage, presents no parallel. In execution it is perfect. With a range that is astonishing, and no diminution in any part of it from the rich and bell-like beauty of its fullest tones, its effect in the swell and fall of the notes is inexpressibly charming. We despair to do it justice. It is impossible to speak of it without the language of exaggeration. At the close of the prayer to the Virgin in the second act, the voice rose upward in one exquisite note, prolonged and softened into silence with such gradual and ravishing effect, that it seemed not so much to have absolutely ceased, as to have passed the confines of mortal hearing. We do not desire to limit others' experiences by our own, or to speak for critics more learned in music than we can pretend to be, but we never heard any thing in music to compare with this. Of such may be angels' singing, but on earth it appeared quite new.' [8 May 1847: Ex]

'The sensation the fair Swede excites is no wise extraordinary when we reflect that she has all the sweetness of Sontag, with far more vocal power, and all the dramatic energy of the great Malibran, with the advantages over the latter that she never exaggerates feeling, and that her voice, instead of being a beautiful contralto forced into an unequal soprano, is throughout even, round, clear, and bell-toned.' [9 May 1847: MP]

'Bristol.—(From a Correspondent).—The fact that Jenny Lind's appearances at Bath and Bristol would be her last in England added no small impetus to the excitement which her engagements originated...I, for one, felt quite charmed, and though I would not rank her with such vocalists as Grisi, or Alboni, I must say she is a very superior artiste. The quality of her voice is I think over-rated. There is an unpleasant guttural sound in her singing, which I have never heard in the Italians. I take it her ART is her all in all ... In the final aria from Sonnambula, she was also excellent, and vocalised with great precision. The throatiness of her voice, just mentioned, injured, occasionally, the effect of this very brilliant display.' [15 May 1847: MW]

'... Mdlle. Lind's voice was a *soprano*, two octaves in compass—from D to D—having a possible higher note or two, available on rare occasions; and that the lower half of the register and the upper one were of two distinct qualities.—The former was not strong,—veiled, if not husky; and apt to be out of tune. The latter was rich, brilliant, and powerful—finest in its highest portions.—It can be told, that the power of respiration was possessed by Mdlle. Lind in the highest perfection; that she could turn her "very long breath" to account, in every gradation of tone; and thus, by subduing her upper notes, and giving out her lower ones with great care, could conceal the disproportions of her organ ... Her execution was great;—and, as is always the case with voices originally reluctant, seemed greater than it really was. Her shake (a grace ridiculously despised of late) was true and brilliant—her taste in ornament was altogether original.' [1847: Chorley, *Recollections*, Vol. 1, 1847, pp. 305, 306]

'Jenny Lind was found at once last night superior to herself last year. At first the auditors marvelled at the increase of volume of her voice; the quality of tone at the same time being such that, however poor the comparison, we can only compare it to the sound elicited from musical glasses, but the vibration dwelling on the ear long afterwards, with a peculiar penetrating power of extraordinary fascination. The next circumstance that struck the audience with amazement was the character of the sustained notes, and the trilli introduced by this marvellous singer—now loud, now whispered, they appeared capable of being prolonged at will for any given time, without effort of iteration—the sound pure and argentine, beyond every instrument and every other voice. The embellishments introduced resembled nothing we have heard before; not only so bright and playful, but so involved and chromatic, and at the same time so germane to the musical subject and the dramatic position, whilst in appearance natural, and the offsprings of passing inspiration.' [5 May 1848: MP]

'If it were possible, we would describe the quality of that voice, so pure, so sweet, so fine, so whole and all-pervading, in its lowest breathings and minutest fioriture as well as in its strongest volume. We never heard tones which in their sweetness went so far. They brought the most distant and ill-seated auditor close to her ... Of those who have been before her we were most frequently reminded of Madame Bishop's quality (not quantity) of voice. Their voices are of metal somewhat akin. Jenny Lind's had incomparably more power and more at all times in reserve; but it had a shade of that same veiled quality in its lowest tones, consistently with the same (but much more) ripeness and sweetness, and perfect freedom from the crudeness often called clearness, as they rise ... Her's is a genuine soprano, reaching the extra high notes with that ease and certainty which make each highest one a triumph of expression purely, and not a physical marvel. The gradual growth and sostenuto of her tones; the light and shade, the rhythmic undulation and balance of her passages; the bird-like ecstacy of her trill ... But do not talk of her flute-like voice; the flute tone is not one a real voice need cultivate; except where it silvers the edges of a dark mass of orchestral harmony, the flute's unmitigated sweetness must and should contrast with the more clarionet and reed-like quality of a voice as rich and human as that of JENNY LIND'. [12 Sep. 1850: NYDT]

'*Timbres, Clear and Sombre.*—The distinction between the various timbres had become nearly undistinguishable with Mme. Sontag; and the clear voice predominated entirely. She sometimes attempted the sombre, but seldom with advantage ... *clear and Sombre Timbre.*—The two timbres are very well defined. Jenny Lind attains very fine effect in the use of the sombre voice. By C. Bassini.' [29 Jul. 1854: *Dwight's*]

'... And we may here observe that she gives to recitatives effects which it never occurred to any one to suppose they were capable of having infused into them. They are not with Madame Goldschmidt spiritless chants, often most slovenly performed—a few bars of musical speaking in a kind of monotone, to precede or connect something more important—but carefully-studied and effectively rendered pieces of execution, given with as much earnestness as she displays when singing airs of the most matchless beauty. We may particularly mention the startling effect given to the words "and they were *sore afraid*" in her first recitative, by means of an exquisitely modulated *tremulo* on the words italicised. Then again, when she exclaimed "unto you is born this day *a Saviour which is Christ the Lord*", her voice literally thrilled throughout the Hall.' [9 Feb. 1856: *Norfolk Chronicle*]

'Those clear, bell-like notes, liquid in tone as a flute, yet penetrating as a trumpet; that intense, heart-felt devotional earnestness which made her singing of sacred music resemble rather the spontaneous offering of religious worship than a public exhibition of artistic skill—much of these high qualities still remains, if with some loss of executive force, with no diminution of those greater intellectual powers that are far more valuable than material excellence. Some of her upper, if not the highest, notes still retain the purity and resonance of past years, while in intensity of expression and depth of feeling Madame Goldschmidt's singing to-day will bear comparison with any of her previous performances.' [22 Aug. 1867: DN]

3.5.21   Eliza Poole [b. 1820]

'To those whose fears and apprehensions of the prevailing disorder have yielded to the love of the Drama, the performances of MISS POOLE at our theatre, during the week, have proved a source of pleasure, as rarely enjoyed as it is agreeable and surprising. This young fairy, who is not more than 11 years of age, has the power of interesting and attracting the continued attention of a whole audience, during a long evening ... Her singing is also sweet and expressive. She possesses a voice of considerable compass, and its modulations are managed with much taste and effect. Its peculiar charm is the innocence and purity of its tones, while coming from a breast as yet unacquainted with guile, is deeply touching to the reflective mind.' [28 Jul. 1832: *Royal Devonport Telegraph, and Plymouth Chronicle*]

'Is there nobody that will write for MISS POOLE? Here is talent lying dead which might be turned to excellent account. She has one of the sweetest ballad voices in the world, is a pretty actress, and a pretty person too, and would be eminently attractive if she had but the opportunity. Her song of *The Roses of Provence*, in the pleasant farce of *Gemini*, is one of the most delightful things we ever heard.' [15 Jul. 1838, *Bell's New Weekly Messenger*]

'We say this [criticism of costume] because Miss Poole's singing [as Pippo] reflects the highest credit upon her vocal talents. Always in time, with a pure quality of voice, the music was given chastely and correctly. With a little more assumption of feeling in the duet in the prison scene, and a little more energy, the part could hardly be more effectively performed. Miss Poole should also, in parting from Ninetta in the prison, and until the recovery of the lost silver, curtail the smiles on her countenance, and infuse a little less gaiety into her manner.' [21 Oct. 1838: Ex]

'Miss Poole is fortunate in possessing a voice of most splendid quality of tone and great compass. We scarcely know which to admire most, her contralto or soprano tones, both are so rich and even. Of the two, perhaps we prefer the former, and we think the reason is, that, as is usually the case with voices that possess so full a quality of tone, there is less facility of attaining that execution which we look for in the soprano; not that we would have it inferred from this, that we consider Miss Poole deficient in this respect, but there is a natural pathos in the voice itself which sinks at once into the hearts of her hearers, and affects them in a much greater degree than the most florid execution possibly could.' [9 Jan. 1841: *New York Mirror*]

'Miss Poole, though not an absolute Swedish nightingale, warbles as sweetly as any singing bird in the entire range of ornithology; and we must bear in mind that the songstress is an English singing bird—and very proud are we of her fresh young voice, and distinct enunciation, and modest manner, and pure style; and then she beats the drum [in *Daughter of the Regiment*, Surrey Theatre] with a grace and distinctness of roll sufficient even to awaken the military ardour of a member of the Lumber Troop! Very piquant, also, is her costume—with the close-fitting vest and coquettish petticoat. Altogether, her cheerful chirruping and rich roulades form a very appetising combination.' [Feb. 1848: *Mirror Monthly Magazine*]

'The round flute-like sweetness of her voice improves every time we listen to her strains.' [13 May 1849: *Lloyd's Weekly*]

'The duet between her [Catherine Hayes] and Miss Poole—"Meet again"—is a beautiful one in itself, and was beautifully sung by both ladies, whose voices blended together in most exquisite harmony; and, sung before a Belfast audience, it is almost unnecessary to add that it was *encored* … Miss Poole, whose reputation stands well in the *Sacred* and *Philharmonic Concerts*, has one of those pure *contralto* voices which penetrate the heart, as well as engage the ear of the hearer. Her organ is rich, strong, solid, and extensive, retaining the true *contralto* quality of its uppermost register. She has no need, and, therefore, never attempts, to eke it out by the addition of a *falsetto*; nor does she seek to astound us by those *double bass* tones, which so many female singers now think it meritorious to groan out by way of concluding the phrase with effect. She was *encored* in the ballad, "She shines before me like a star", as well as in "Come hither, pretty fairy". Her pleasant looks, her true intonation and distinct articulation, combined with the rich roundness of her voice, would carry her far upon the operatic stage, should she ever think proper to grace it.' [19 Feb. 1850: *Northern Whig*]

'Pity it is that the pure voice of this cultivated and tasteful singer is not more frequently heard than it is. We have few artists so undeniably able, whether as regards execution or style, while the vocal organ is of bell-like beauty, and its intonation faultless.' [25 May 1856: MP]

'The concert opened well with Shield's delicious trio, "Oh, happy fair!" sung by Miss Poole, with a voice still silvery and clear as we first remember to have heard it twenty years ago.' [28 Aug. 1858: MC]

'Did you ever hear Miss Poole sing "Wapping Old Stairs" in that pure mellow voice of hers, and marvellously distinct enunciation, in which every word has its place, and is precious as every gem in a necklace of orient pearls.' [Dec. 1860: Brough, *The Wellcome Guest*, Vol. 1, p. 285]

3.5.22 Charlotte Dolby, Mrs Sainton-Dolby [b. 1821]

'Miss Dolby exhibited a wonderful improvement of manner, voice, style, and execution. She has a beautiful contralto voice, and, whilst her higher notes are perfect in tone and exquisitely sweet, she is enabled to descend lower [see Illus. 45 for her compass, extending from F below middle C to G on top line of treble clef] and with a fuller and more powerful enunciation than any English female vocalist we ever heard.' [14 Jan. 1841: Era]

'Miss Dolby made a sensible impression by her expressive and tranquil delivery of the charming air, "The Lord is mindful of his own", on account of which, three years ago, she received a high compliment from Mendelssohn himself.' [8 Jun. 1845: Era]

'If we except only a tendency to a tremolo on the voice, which some imagine is effective,—we differ, altogether, and think this sort of style should not be resorted to.' [Jul. 1846: *Connoisseur*]

'Miss Dolby, a veritable bird of silver throat and golden plumage … the exquisite pathos and angelic purity of Miss Dolby.' [5 Jan. 1849: MW]

'Her execution is marked by considerable firmness and finish, and her tremolo, though but little tested in the pieces she had to sing, gave token of much flexibility.' [24 Feb. 1855: *Leeds Times*]

'The recitative commanding Elijah to go to Horeb, ushered in the delicious "O rest in the Lord", which Miss Dolby sang with delightful purity and sweetness; it, too, was repeated.' [25 Aug. 1855: *Hereford Times*]

'With a pure contralto voice of immense compass—able to sweep aloft like an eagle, or float lightly as thistledown—simple, tender, pathetic, she is, on the whole, as good an artist for the work she does as any I have ever heard. She also has the capital merit of equality; she never fails. It was curious to remark how little response there was when Mlle. Titiens sang "Come unto Him"—from the text of which she departed—as compared with the same air in the adjacent "He shall feed his flock", as sung by Madame Sainton-Dolby. It was the difference between a beam of magnesium light and a sunbeam.' [15 Jun. 1868: *Harper's*]

3.5.23 Marietta Alboni [b. 1826]

'A physiognomy like that of Alboni has but to be seen to command admiration—and a voice such as she is gifted with has but to be heard to be approved of and applauded. Your recommendation, therefore, was superfluous as far as regarded this artist; but it was most agreeable to me, because now, and ever, I am delighted to be able to give you new proofs of the high esteem—I dare not write "friendship"—which I entertain for you. L'Alboni made her début in the "Linda", and the most certain confirmation of her success is, that in the first and second representation she repeated, amidst the "vivas" of the audience, the duettino with Tadolini.' [from letter by Donizetti to Rossini] [30 Apr. 1843: *Era*]

'The Signor, or Signora, has the features of an angel, and the shoulders of a captain of Cuirassiers, the voice of a seraph, and the fist of a boxer; the voice fascinates and the fist actually kills. When she made her first appearance on the stage, astonished at such sweet beauty crowning such corpulence, at so clear and limpid a voice flowing from so vast a chest, the Germans, who knew the names of all the artists in Europe, at first fancied they had before them the famous Crescentini, of the Neapolitan conservatory. But the Germans discovered their error to fall into great stupefaction. That heavenly and fluted voice, whose notes vibrated like the magic flute which Beethoven has set to music—that celestial voice, we say, had suddenly uttered low notes of a volume, sound, and gravity, such that it was utterly impossible to ascribe them to so historical a throat as Crescentini's ... The Signora's style of dressing is as singular as her voice. If the Signora were not clad like a woman her dress would be quite a natural one; but the female costume does not the less render her eccentric; and such is the reason the Signora has disdained a great coat and trousers. The Signora smokes and takes snuff, and jags about in the cavalier fashion of a drum-major, disguised as a suttler; her only regret is that she has as yet no beard; but it must surely grow some day or other; nature, who has already gifted her in so many ways, cannot deny her such a trifle.' [15 Dec. 1845: *Freeman's Journal*]

'Mdlle. Alboni is a legitimate contralto. Her voice, which extends in compass from G below the stave to B flat in alt., has the honeyed mellowness of quality that appertains to the contralto character to an extraordinary degree. Her tones are ripe, full, and sonorous. A group of notes falling from her throat has upon the ear much the effect that a bunch of heavy, drooping, juicy grapes would have upon the eye. The mouth waters for their very lusciousness. Her execution is marvellous for a contralto, and her command of the upper notes, which have the same effect as the falsetto of a tenor, is really astonishing. Her style is overflowing with passionate expression, which, in the cantabile, sometimes leads her into exaggeration—particularly exemplified by her excessive use of the legato and the glissando (a term we use for the want of a better) method of taking the more distant intervals—but in the cabaletta, where she has no time to hyperbolize, her correct expression, energetic manner, and faultless execution, her chaste and exquisite use of ornament, her finished method of rounding and completing the cadences, are worthy of the highest admiration.' [23 Oct. 1847: MW]

'Since that day the genial contralto has, herself, changed singularly little—save in consequence of attempts made to extend her voice; and these (after its register is settled) *must* impair its tone.' [Reference date 1847: Chorley, *Recollections*, Vol. 2, p. 9]

'... we must enter our protest once more against this lady's imitation of the infirmity of age—against that tremulousness of voice which many of the Italian singers of the present day affect. This is what they call vibrazione di voce—a vice which can only be accounted for by supposing that the constant practice of singing occasionally damages the brain. Madlle Alboni, notwithstanding, was encored in this her performance: we must therefore conclude that the distressing feebleness of the vocal organ, unhappily attendant on very advanced years, may, if simulated by a popular singer, be considered as a graceful, an estimable quality.' [13 May 1848: Ex]

The following review compares Alboni's soprano extension against real sopranos: 'In a different style we must mention the Cavatina "Nacqui ali' affanno", from Rossini's Cenerentola. This was the purest if not the most surprising effort of vocal music of the whole evening. The tones of her voice were meltingly soft, yet round and full, and her sustained notes were maintained with the utmost ease. There no apparent striving—not the slightest tendency to unsteadiness, or loss of pitch ... And when she gave the "Nos piu mesta", the roulades and florid passages, the sudden leaps by octaves, indeed all the intricacies and artistic difficulties of the fine rondo were given with a precision and clearness of articulation which might be looked for in a musical box, but which is seldom achieved by the human organ. The execution was as exact and true to time as though performed by a piece of mechanism, while the intonation was as clear and ringing as a series of chimes ... Although Mademoiselle Alboni may be able to sing as high in the soprano as either of the singers named, she is not so powerful in her upper notes as they [Grisi and Lind] are.' [4 Sep. 1848: GH]

'She eschewed any attempt at ornament, it is true, and so far her version of the air was judicious and good; but the style in which she sang it [Handel's air from *Rodelinda*] appeared to us cold and almost listless; and besides there was an artificial tremolo employed throughout, which struck us as inappropriate. In short we were disappointed with her singing of the air, to say nothing of the extreme impropriety, in such a place, of the original words, which form a love ditty.' [14 Sep. 1848: *Berrow's Worcester Journal*]

'Thanks to her perfect method of singing, her voice even now betrays none of that detestable tremolo which is the pervading defect of the modern school, and the superb tones of her incomparable contralto had the effect of the notes of an organ in the "Agnus Dei", from Rossini's mass, which no artist has ever rendered so well. Mme. Alboni's singing is a lesson to a now bygone school.' [2 Jan. 1887: NYT,]

3.5.24 Louisa Pyne, later Mrs Frank Bodda [b. 1827]

'The ladies [the two Misses Pyne, pupils of Sir George Smart] are very pleasing vocalists, with voices well cultivated though not of great compass.' [23 Apr. 1842: *Cambridge Chronicle and Journal*]

'Miss L. Pyne sang so sweetly and unaffectedly a pretty Scotch ballad, by F. Eames, that it elicited an enthusiastic repetition. This very young lady, for we believe she has not yet reached her sixteenth year, has a soprano voice of rich quality and extensive register; her intonation is singularly correct, and her taste the result of sound musical acquirements.' [26 May 1844: Era]

'Miss L. Pyne unites to exquisite sweetness and considerable power of voice perfect intonation and unwavering certainty in execution. Miss Pyne, whose voice is a delicious mezzo-soprano, sung with great feeling and effect Rossini's "Oh tu ch'io chiamo".' [20 Sep. 1844: *Leicester Journal*]

'… the reports that came here of the skill she displayed were strongly eulogistic. Her voice is clear and melodious, and preserves its intonation faithfully.' [2 Oct. 1849: Std]

'Miss Louisa Pyne is an imitator of Jenny Lind, or, as some aver, a rival. If Mademoiselle Lind's talent consists in music without meaning, then we subscribe to its insurpassable beauty; for Miss Louisa Pyne's was more the laugh of an angel than the song of a human and rational creature—fine but without sense.' [20 Jan. 1853: *Fife Herald*]

'Why Miss Louisa Pyne has never previously been found among the stars of a Manchester theatre, belongs to the mysteries of management. Her voice is pure, round, and silvery in its tones, brilliantly flexible, and its upper range equal to any modern soprano with which we are acquainted.' [4 Dec. 1853: Era]

'In "Sonnambula", the singing of Miss Louisa Pyne was worth travelling on foot ten miles to hear. The plaintive sweetness of her voice it is almost impossible to describe. She sings as if she had a "nest of nightingales in her throat".' [Nov. 1854: *Knickerbocker*]

'Her voice [Louisa Pyne], not very powerful, is musical and sweet and flexible and evenly developed, and she executes the most florid music, like Rode's variations, introduced in the last scene, with an ease and liquid evenness and finish that remind one of Sontag. In all the little playful dialogue music, too, she was felicitous; in recitative, too, and in speaking, her voice was always clearly, pleasantly inflected.' [2 Dec. 1854: *Dwight's*]

'The Editor of the *Battle axe of Freedom and Tomahawk of Liberty*, writing from Philadelphia, after hearing Miss Louisa Pyne sing the song of the "Skylark", says "her voice is delicious—pure as moonlight, and as tender as a three shilling shirt".' [15 Jun. 1855: *Limerick Reporter*]

'Miss Louisa Pyne has recently returned from an extensive tour in the United States, where she met with a most gracious reception. Her silvery voice and brilliant execution seem, from the many glowing accounts we have read in the American journals, to be just the class of music to catch the popular ear … Miss Pyne is an accomplished singer, with a voice that wins upon the ear rather than fatigues it.' [25 Jul. 1857: MT]

'… has three songs, two of which, "Fly nimbly with your work, my fingers" and "At my cottage door", the latter a nightingale song, with flute obbligato, are really beautiful. Miss Pyne here has abundant scope for the display of her exquisite vocalisation, and not even Madame Miolan Carvalho could have surpassed the delicious shake with which she rivals the bird of eve.' [2 Dec. 1860: ST]

'To hear Miss Louisa Pyne—whose voice is as pure, and as round, and as smooth as an opal—is always a treat.' [19 Oct. 1861: *Aris's Birmingham Gazette*]

'… we are constrained to say that the quality of her voice [Adelina Patti] is inferior to that of Miss Louisa Pyne, who may be termed our English *prima donna* … As far as the expression of it went it was beautiful, but we could not help remarking a deficiency in roundness of tone.' [18 Sep. 1862: BG]

'In the recitative, "Oh rank, thou hast thy shackles!" and in the following air, Miss L. Pyne gave what would be full scope to her vocal power were it not judiciously tempered by incomparable sweetness and tenderness. It is, we believe understood that a prima donna is to be allowed to choose her own time and place for the introduction of ornaments and colouring; and as Miss Pyne's thrills, and quavers, and sustained notes always afford delight to the general public, it would be a graceless and, probably, a bootless office even for a composer to make any reference to a severe standard of taste.' [9 Nov. 1862: Era]

'Miss Louisa Pyne's bell-like voice was heard to advantage in an air and variations from Auber's Les Diamans de la Couronne; the successive shakes, pure vocalization, and the rapid flight of notes, a la Cruvelli, were rendered to perfection, but withal, her voice appeared to be fading, whether it was attributable to a slight cold we cannot tell, but there was not that fullness of tone which we have been accustomed to hear at Covent Garden. With respect to her vocalization, it is equal to that of almost any foreign artist of the day.' [21 Apr. 1864: BG]

'In the earlier airs allotted to Mrs Bodda we could not reconcile ourselves, notwithstanding her highly-finished execution, to the want of clearness in her voice. Either there was indisposition, or there was inability to rise and fall with ease,—a sort of huskiness that robbed her notes of mellowed sweetness. But she revindicated her claim to nobly-earned popularity by her charming interpretation of "I know that my Redeemer liveth", eliciting loud and prolonged applause.' [2 Jan. 1869: Ex]

3.5.25 Thérèse Tietjens [b. 1831]

'Mdlle. Titien's [sic] voice is a pure soprano of exquisite quality, in its tone clear and liquid as a silver bell, of extreme brilliancy, and far more than ordinary compass. Her upper notes have an openness of sound which we do not remember to have heard in any other singer. If we add to these qualities unusual fluency and facility, an unerring intonation, an admirable method, and a largeness of style which belonged to Pasta alone of all preceding singers, our readers will entertain some idea of the vocal powers and attainments of Mr. Lumley's new prima donna.' [14 Apr. 1858: Std]

'She has the next best German voice to Madame Jenny Ney:—an organ strong, even, extensive in compass, fairly well produced, and, if not supremely charming, more than usually clear of the national harshness.' [17 Apr. 1858: Ath]

'The voice of Madlle. Titiens is of full and telling quality, of unimpaired freshness, and free from any unpleasant peculiarity, and above all from the tremulousness, involuntary or affected, so common among singers of the day ... It dominates wherever it enters, and by unflinching correctness of intonation gives firmness and precision to the music—a quality which has been pointed out in the voice of Signor Giuglini. We do not know the extreme height which Madlle. Titiens can command, but the high C is produced and sustained with perfect ease, and in certain passages with quite startling effect.' [17 Apr. 1858: SatR]

'Three repetitions of "Les Huguenots" have strengthened our conviction of the excellence of the upper notes of Mdlle. Titiens' voice. Altogether, it may be described as ranging with the voices of Mesdames Jenny Ney and Stöckl Heinefetter—a stout soprano, able to abide "tear" as well as "wear" on its top notes. The lower register holds out less bravely, and the lady on acquaintance proves more remarkable as a voice than as a singer; familiarity with her public having developed certain tricks of style, which do not stand in stead of vocal completeness. Among the latter are the disposition to speak (not to sing) recitative, to which a greater predecessor, Madame Schroeder-Devrient [Wilhelmine Schröder-Devrient], could never reconcile us, and a large amount of make believe execution. The new lady attempts to shake without commanding a shake; and though she executes one scale-passage effectively—the descent from c in alt in her duett with Marcel—elsewhere, in place of real execution, she exhibits the same sort of evasion as vexes us in the singing of Herr Formes and Herr Reichardt, and which (in fact) amounts to the German idea of "how to get through".' [24 Apr. 1858: Ath]

'Her voice is a high soprano, of great power and beauty. Her compass is from C to E, two octaves and a third, though her lower notes have little ring to them.' [5 Nov. 1859: *Dwight's*]

'In noticing the Handel Festival, Mr. [William] Pole, [*Macmillan's Magazine*, Nov. 1862] pays a well-deserved tribute of admiration to the purity of style of Mdlle. Titiens, by far the greatest singer of the present day—"She deserves the greatest praise for one notable feature in her singing—that is, a determined effort to abolish the ridiculous tremolo which has unfortunately so long been in fashion".' [9 Nov. 1862: *Oxford Chronicle*]

'Mdlle. [Mathilde] Enequist had to stand the severe test of being heard in conjunction with her great contemporary [Tietjens], and much similarity in the quality of the two voices made the duet particularly effective; but although that of Mdlle. Enequist is characterised by the most delicious purity of tone, it is brilliant rather than sonorous in quality, and wants much of the depth and richness which characterise that of the great prima donna.' [24 Jan. 1865: *Bury & Norwich Post*]

'When I first heard her, at one of the general rehearsals for the festival of 1866 (some eight years after her début in England), her voice was not only fresh, powerful, and penetrating, but it possessed in a greater degree than then that sympathetic charm—that curiously dramatic "human" quality—which was perhaps its most notable attribute. / Her style was marked by the same rare individuality. Her phrasing offered a curious blending of vigor and grace; and she had a trick of employing the portamento when approaching a high note, which in any other singer might have been thought almost ugly, but in Tietjens seemed both natural and artistic. At the same time, her attack was superb. Never have I heard the opening phrase of the "Inflammatus" in Rossini's "Stabat Mater" delivered with such magnificent energy and such absolute purity of tone. To hear Tietjens in those days sing "Let the bright Seraphim" (especially to the trumpet obbligato of Tom Harper) was a treat never to be forgotten.' [Dec. 1866: Klein, *Thirty Years*]

'Among the vocal soloists, by far the most effective was Madlle Tietjens, whose splendid organ, by its power alone necessarily distances competition in an area like the Crystal Palace, where ordinary voices are so completely swallowed up in the vastness of the locale. Effects of distinctness which the other solo vocalists achieved only occasionally and with evident effort, were in her case the results of her softest utterance, and when she did put forth her lung power, her tones rang through the vaulted space clear, full, and bell-like those of a silver flute.' [16 Jun. 1868: BDP]

'Like her renowned predecessor, Giulia Grisi, Mdlle Tietjens never forces her voice; and this apparent self-denial cannot be too often or too earnestly commended. The "tremolo" on certain notes—an inevitable result of inefficient early training—not, as many suppose, the premeditated means of creating effect by a more than common display of expression—is, and has ever been, a fault unknown to her. Thus, and by other no less praiseworthy means, she has been able not only to cultivate but to preserve the gifts with which nature has so richly endowed her, and to remain the singer whom all amateurs continue to admire and applaud.' [2 May 1874: MW]

3.5.26   Melitta Otto Alvsleben [b. 1842]

'Mme. Otto-Alvsleben, the débutante, possesses all the qualifications to make a really good singer. She has a sweet bell-toned musical voice, fairly trained; she sings correctly [at Crystal Palace Concert], and executes her runs neatly, but wants more expression. Her voice reminded us of the bell-like quality of Clara Novello's.' [15 Mar. 1873: MusS]

'She sang the first air of the "Queen of Night" in the original key, the range being D below the staff to F in alto, and which in this she gave evidence of her clever executancy; in the Cavatina of Weber (at the opening of Act III), a good cantabile style commended itself to notice.' [29 Mar. 1873: MusS]

'Mozart's aria, "Non mi der, bell' idol mio", by Madame Alvsleben, was sung very sweetly [in St. George's Hall Bradford], and with a pure, clear tone, devoid of the objectionable tremolo in which many foreign artists like to indulge.' [17 Mar. 1873: LM]

'New amongst these [pieces by Wagner] were only the quintette from the "Meistersinger" and Elsa's address to Ortrud, or, more correctly, the duet of Elsa and Ortrud with the omission of the contralto part, which consists only of occasional interjections unessential to the flow of a beautiful melody. It was rendered by Mdme Otto-Alvsleben, who also took the leading part in the quintet … The effect of this performance, however, was anything but harmonious, the voices of the other singers not being able to hold their own against the powerful soprano of the accomplished German prima donna.' [23 May 1874: Ex]

3.6   Male Singers Reviewed, before the Recording Era

Contemporary reviews of the most important male singers are supplied below. As with the female group, I've focussed on descriptions reflecting vocalists' tessitura, registral capacity, volume, tone, timbre and emotional appeal.

3.6.1   John Braham [b. 1774].

'… Voice is a tenor, enlarged in compass by a falsetto, and its whole range of really useful and good notes extends from A in the bass to E in alt,—a scale of twenty notes. The tone, when not forced, approached the very best sounds of a clarinet, beautifully played, less reedy, though perhaps always a little lowered by that defect. It was so perfectly even and equal, and he possessed so thorough a command over it, that he could produce any given quantity or quality upon any part of it at pleasure;

while, if he ran through his whole compass by semitones, it was impossible to point out at what precise interval he took, or relinquished, the falsetto, though the peculiar quality of that voice, when he rose high, was sufficiently perceptible.' The review, while it refers to an earlier period around 1794, includes a quote from Quarterly Music Magazine: 'Perhaps he [Braham] is right in the belief he entertains, that he was born about twenty years too soon,—that he preceded his age. The singers of Italy, of the present day, do commonly what he introduced about thirty years ago.' [reference date 1794: NMM, 1833, pp. 254 & 255]

'His intonation is perfectly just; his shake, in particular the upper notes, is beautiful, his tone somewhat resembling a well played bassoon, and his execution far beyond any male singer now before the town.' [27 Oct. 1795: MW]

'Report had extolled, but not magnified, the powers of Braham. He was said to possess the finest tenor voice in Italy, and it must truly be said, that its volume, sweetness, and pathos are most wonderful. His natural compass, though limited, has the most irresistible influence on the heart. His full, clear tone, coming directly from the breast, makes the most heart-felt impression on the auditory; and this is the moral end, as well as the perfection of the science. We speak of his natural tones: but, when he aims at the fashionable art of execution, his ornaments, instead of embellishing, weaken his cadence, and we sigh for his return to simplicity and pathos. He has acquired science in Italy, as well as strength. The exercise of his powers has enlarged them. His sostenuto has a bottom unrivalled; and within his own scale every tone is sound, full, clear, and melodious; but, with the science of Italy, he has acquired also some of their glittering feats which are as distant from true taste as they are from nature.' [10 Dec. 1801: MP]

'... In the even'g went to Salomon's Concert at Willis's Rooms, to w'ch as a stranger, Mr. S. very readily admitted me, telling me he co'd by no means plead *want of room* so to do, there being about 3 fourths of the benches in that large Room empty the whole evening. I was however entertain'd with a very fine concert, in which Mrs **Billington** & Braham sung ... Amongst the *few* auditors was Dr Burney, who I was very glad to find coincided with me in thinking Braham a great deal too profuse in his ad libitums & graces, w'ch he thereby made as we thought, much too cheap.' [10 May 1802: Marsh, Vol. 1, p. 752]

'Not only is the general style of his singing meretricious, but the ornaments with all their exuberance are frequently misplaced, and so far he wants the common taste even of floridness. He wears bells on his toes, as well as rings on his fingers. He will run divisions upon the most insignificant words, and trill, quaver, and roll about at you without remorse. He lights up, as it were, fifty wax candles to exhibit a nut shell; or resembles a fantastic fellow, who instead of approaching you by the ordinary path and in a strait manner, should come up with all sorts of fluttering gestures and meanders, and accompany his concluding bow with a shake of the head and checks of five minutes duration. One of his most disagreeable tricks is that of swelling out and iterating his voice like a mail-coach horn,—which is all very well on proper occasions, but when it comes forth upon a word that does not call for it, is as ridiculous as if he were to ask you, in the same manner, how you did. At the same time, it must not be denied that he can divest himself now and then of all this absurdity, and give you a simple ballad or piece of pathos in it's native beauty; but then the very applause which rewards him for so doing and would encourage him to persist in it, tends to lead him astray again, and off he goes into some ridiculous catching and quavering.' [12 Feb. 1815: Ex]

'Nothing is more difficult than to apprehend distinctly the real properties of his true tone—so much does he vary from the standard in execution. It is sometimes even a little throaty, often extremely heady and nasal.' [Sep. 1825: QMMR, p. 280]

John Braham's expressive tremulousness was praised by QMMR: 'When the prodigious volume of his voice is fully estimated—when the heart-rending pathos, to produce which he sometimes assimilates the shuddering tremulous tones almost to the actual expression of the most natural grief—when the loud, ear-piercing, animating sounds with which he invests a call to glory, are remembered—when the inspired, pure, consoling words of adoration or thanksgiving united in his melody—when the tenderness of his amatory airs and the volant lubricity of his astonishing execution he brought to recollection—our readers will at once acknowledge the superiority of his intonation.' [Mar. 1818: QMMR, p. 87]

Braham's voice was described in similar fashion by the Examiner: 'In omitting Mr. Braham among the singers who shine at Oratorios, we are only comparing him with his effect on the stage; but he shines still in one sense of the word; indeed he flames out every now and then, like a roaring fire; his voice turns into a view-hallo; he opens his throat like a French horn, or rather like a school boy who is resolved to let all the world know that somebody is thumping him; and the house are sure to consider this as an illustrious thing. But the Italian refinement seems to puzzle him; and the feeling and tremulous fervour which occasionally delight us in his voice, are apt to be followed by such a heap of common-place quavers and ornaments, such a scatter of base coin to create a scramble among the galleries, as becomes the more offensive from the true wealth that precedes it.' [12 Mar. 1820: Ex]

3.6.2   Manuel García 1 [b. 1775]

'… is a fine tenor, of considerable compass; but we sometimes thought it rather harsh, and not always very clear. In the upper tones it is peculiarly sweet, but not powerful. His execution is rapid, brilliant, and extremely neat, and the ease with which he produces the effect is very pleasing.' [14 Feb. 1818: Tl]

'His voice, when in its proper order, is a very sweet and perfect tenor, perhaps not inferior to any in Europe … There is a tremulous richness in the higher tones of GARCIA'S voice which is singularly pleasing.' [10 May 1823: *Drama*]

'His voice has extensive compass, considerable power, is round and clear. Its flexibility is remarkable, but betrays him into that which we shall always consider as an error of the first magnitude, namely, a continual departure from the sostenuto style of singing; or in other words, an exuberance of ornament, an almost unbroken succession of roulades, which metamorphose the air into a vocal exercise.' [May 1823: Har]

'We doubt whether, commanding as it was in volume, compass, and facility, he ever enjoyed that quality, which of all the Italian tenors we have ever known, [Giuseppe] Viganoni and [Gaetano] Crivelli alone partook. We conceive this want of liquidity to proceed from forming the tone so high in the head, by which the several parts of the organs suffer more contraction than consists with the production of this liquid sweetness. Hence the hardness which is too often one of the prominent characteristics of Italian tenor tone, particularly when the singer exerts himself to increase the volume or extend the compass in the higher parts of the scale.' [Sep. 1826: QMMR, p. 340]

3.6.3   Lewis Bernard Sapio [b. 1784]

'He is obviously very content in the management of his voice, which is also of the first quality. His notes, indeed, are like those "of a trumpet with a silver sound". He is not anxious to display his powers; and he manifestly detests the idea of owing anything to trickery, or a meretricious use of ornament. His style is chaste and refined. His intonations are accurate in the highest degree; and exquisite as they are true. In "the Serenade", indeed, his tones were magnificent; and through the whole of his performances, there was so much taste and keeping, that no one felt the transitions from his natural voice to the falsetto. All seemed equally easy; and his low, middle, and high notes were all equally fine—equally pleasing.' [1 Aug. 1824: Ex, quotation from Scot]

'… has obtained fine quality (when he does not overstrain his voice), by a high Italian formation. The moment he forces it his intonation fails. This is not his defect alone—it is common to all voices—but the reason I mention it here is, because I think that voices formed high are liable to fail with less strain upon them than those which come more from the throat—for the same reason, that thin voices go out of tune sooner than thick, as is commonly observed.' [30 Sep. 1825: QMMR, p. 280]

'Mistaking basses for baritones, and baritones for tenors, is of common occurrence … To give one among many instances of the fatal effects of mistaking the character of a voice:–Sapio came out as a tenor, whereas his voice is naturally a fine baritone of very high quality. By the aid of a good chest and a great deal of energy, he forced it up beyond its natural compass, and the consequence was that a season or two as a dramatic singer fairly knocked him up. His feeling and impulse only accelerated this result; a huskiness came over his voice, and its intonation was no longer under control.' [30 Apr. 1835: NMM, p. 449]

3.6.4   Alberico Curioni [b. 1785]

'His voice is well formed, rich, sweet, but limited in compass. He uses two or three notes of falsette with effect.' [June 1821: QMMR, p. 381]

'Garcia's voice [Manuel García 1] is got thick—and tho' he has more force, he has too much grimace. I do not like him on the whole so well as Curioni, who has more real feeling & a sweeter tone of voice.' [20 May 1823: Waldie]

'One of the sweetest tenor voices we have ever heard; Curioni unites a style abounding with purity and chasteness, seldom or never sacrificing melody to ornament.' [25 Apr. 1825: MP]

'Hence the hardness [forming the tone so high in the head] which is too often one of the prominent characteristics of Italian tenor tone, particularly when the singer exerts himself to increase the volume or extend the compass in the higher parts of the scale. It follows as a necessary consequence that this hardness appertains more to voices of small or of moderate than of great power. Signor Curioni's is of the middle term; it has considerable but not superlative volume, and has certainly been augmented in its quantity by exercise. It is pure to the most polished degree, and is not without brilliancy; but the defect we describe as appertaining to Italian tenors in general, is always to be regretted, whenever this excellent singer finds it necessary to aim at increasing his power.' [30 Sep. 1826: QMMR, p. 340]

3.6.5 Charles Edward Horn [b. 1786]

'Mr. Horn's voice and style [on début] are delicate and tasteful, though of small Power.' [2 Jul. 1809: Ex]

'Of Mr. Horn we must speak in little—his voice is little, but pretty, and capable of improvement; his acting is incapable of deterioration: if nothing is stationary in this world, we think, he must rise.' [5 Jul. 1809: MM]

'A kind of dramatic resurrection took place this evening, in the return of Mr. Horn to the stage as the Seraskier. Most of our readers probably will recollect this gentleman, who performed here some years since. His voice, at that time, though rather sweet, was extremely feeble, and his acting remarkably tame and insipid; he now, however, seems destined to hold a foremost rank among our vocal performers. His voice, during his retirement, has increased wonderfully in strength and compass, and the various songs allotted to the character were executed in the finest manner.' [1 Jul. 1816: TI]

'The bravura song of "The Soldier tired", was unanimously encored: it surpassed all expectation. Mr. Horn was very cheeringly received, after a few years absence from Drury Lane. He is considerably improved in science, but his voice is scarcely equal to fill so vast an area with effect.' [20 Nov. 1816: EM]

'Mr. Horn is at home in both the simple ballad and the bravura. In the first song he showed the perfect master in gliding from his natural voice into the falsetto.' [30 Oct. 1827: *American and Commercial Daily Advertiser*, Baltimore]

3.6.6 Giovanni David [b. 1790]

'I never heard more perfect harmony by two tenors [Andrea Nozzari and Giovanni David] of such great power, expression, and flexibility. They are the two best men I have heard for many years ... and I think David, yet young, will soon have quite the power of Braham, with more clearness, and equal flexibility.' [28 Jan. 1817: Waldie]

'Davide, in the part of "Otello", created the greatest enthusiasm. The following account of his performance is given by a French critic, M. Edouard Bertin, in a letter from Venice, dated 1823: / "Davide [presumably Giovanni David] excites among the dilettanti of this town an enthusiasm and delight which could scarcely be conceived without having been witnessed. He is a singer of the new school, full of mannerism, affectation, and display, abusing, like Martin, his magnificent voice with its prodigious compass (three octaves comprised between four B flats)".' [1823: Edwards, *History of the Opera*]

'David, the first tenor, may be reckoned old for a singer; his voice is tremulous, his face effeminate, and his person thin and attenuated. In former days there was doubtless some foundation for the praise which has been lavished upon this singer by those who have visited Italy, and at present he discovers little to warrant his great fame, unless we perceive it in a style full of that frippery for which [Gaetano] Crivelli and Garcia have made themselves remarkable. David has the appearance of an antiquated beauty; his throat is whitened, his features look enamelled, and, except when exerting himself in his falsetto to reach [top F shown in notation in treble clef] (at which time they are moulded into a shape something between smiling and weeping) they are immoveable.' [Oct. 1827: QMMR]

Richard Edgcumbe was not happy with David's voice when he heard him eleven years after his début: 'The first tenor that appeared that year was David, son of the excellent singer who was here just forty years before. The younger did not equal his father, but had enjoyed great reputation in Italy. When he came to this country he was passé, and his voice come so unsteady that he was obliged to disguise its defects by superfluity of ornaments and passages; but he had always been too florid a singer.' [10 Nov. 1828: Edgcumbe, p. 207]

'The great David, whom I knew at Tome eight years since, and saw then in the same part, was Otello: and he was indeed most splendid, most exquisitely full of powerful expression, and superb execution and force; and his style is less extravagant, and more full of genuine pathos, and grand effect. His first recitation and air of "Ah si per voi" was such a powerful effort that I was in an ecstasy of delight and really burst into tears. His semitone descent, and his shake, and his falsetto in alto are truly unrivalled.' [10 May 1828: Waldie]

'Signor David, being a stranger in England, was cordially welcomed by the audience; but his singing has not caused me to alter the opinion I formed of him some years since, when I heard him at Vienna. His style is florid in the extreme; indeed his shake being very neat, and his falsetto the best part of his voice, he is almost constantly trembling in alt, like an octave flute in an ague. His natural voice in tone resembles an oboe; and as, whilst singing, his body is considerably distorted and bent, one cannot help pitying the poor man for the internal agony he seems to be enduring, which feeling is enforced by repeated catchings in his breath.' [17 Feb. 1831: *Tatler*, No. 143, p. 571]

3.6.7   Domenico Donizelli [b. 1790]

'SIGNOR DONZELLI has, perhaps, the finest, most sonorous, yet pure voice that ever tenor possessed. His *messa di voce* affects more from its volume and tone than that of any singer we ever remember to have heard. But he sacrifices too much of the lighter and expressive graces of singing to the display of this power.' [29 Sep. 1822: Ex]

'He [as Othello, in Vienna] has a beautiful, mellifluous tenor with which he attacks the high A in full chest-voice, without once resorting to falsetto, while Signor [Giovanni] David [who sang the Roderigo] rejoices in this higher voice and, on this occasion, once ascended to high F [above high C]. Donzelli's action is thoughtfully conceived, his interpretation well ordered, and full of vitality and expression, his declamation exemplary, particularly in recitatives.' [Dec. 1823: from *Allgemeine Musikalische Zeitung*, quoted in Pleasants, p. 160]

'In our own immediate times Signor Donzelli was the Otello of the epoch; and those who heard him in the part can never forget the magnificence and power of his singing, more particularly in the aria d'intrata "Ah, si per voi". Since the time of this grand-voiced singer nearly all "robust" tenors have turned their attention to the music of Verdi, and Rossini has gone out of vogue.' [24 Jun. 1828: MC]

'A tenor voice of extraordinary beauty, compass, and power. It is so sonorous and pure, and he sings with such undeviating accuracy as to tune, that we could be almost content to sit and hear him were he to do nothing more than to practise the scale up and down. Its quality is much the same as that of the elder Crivelli [presumably Domenico Francesco Maria Crivelli, 1793–1856], but exceeds his in strength. He has a falsetto, or *voce di testa*, which reminds us of Incledon, and he is equally prodigal in the use of it. This is its defect; not satisfied with what nature has so bountifully bestowed on him, he has recourse to that which is artificial, useless, and displeasing to the real connoisseur.' [Jan.1829: Har]

'His voice, which is of the richest quality of tenors, reaches to B flat, in its natural compass; and in the above Aria he sang D, in his falsetto, with such strength and purity of tone, and descended to his natural voice with such ease and perfect intonation, as elicited the most enthusiastic applause.' [25 Feb. 1829: MP]

'His voice is full sonorous, and powerful, and he modulates it with infinite skill; at one time vigorously loud, and, when required, delicately tasteful, especially in the falsetto notes, which go to C within the stave (violin cleft) [sic], while his natural tones descend to the C in the bass octave below.' [1 Mar. 1829: NMM]

'His voice had a clearness, a brilliancy, and a power—a metallo or natural vibratory power—that belonged to very few, either before or since his time. His tone was formed high in the head, his compass combining the falsetto to a very large extent; whilst he possessed such complete command over his vast volume of voice, that he could send it forth in all its body, or in its softest attenuation, at pleasure. He managed the junction of the chest and head registers with the utmost skill, so that it was quite impossible to discover upon what note the actual transition took place, although the fluty quality of the upper notes immediately made its use apparent. The ascending notes of his scales were generally given out from his chest voice until he rose very high, and passed into the falsetto, the almost inevitable consequence of which was, that they were sometimes too strong by their comparative volume. His descending divisions and fioriture, on the contrary, when they commenced upon the higher notes of his voice, were taken in falsetto, which he carried very low down before using his mixed or natural voice. From such extreme contrasts the ear was not seldom cheated into a belief of this having been done expressly to convey the notion of an echo or distant sound, the equality was disturbed, and the general effect of the performance diminished.' [21 Mar. 1829: Cox, p. 171]

'One of the most remarkable qualities in this extraordinary singer is, that great as is the power of his voice, he always appears to have a corps de reserve,—that he does not put forth all his might; one can fancy that his clear mountain-tone might be heard from the summit of the Jura: but what is better than the mere possession of this qualification, he knows how and when to subdue it; his piano and crescendo—in common terms, his "swell", is as perfect as we ever heard. And, to crown all, he evidently loves the highest class of music, and sings as he loves it.' [2 Aug. 1829: Ex].

'He had one of the most mellifluous robust low tenor voices ever heard—a voice which had never by practice been made sufficiently flexible to execute Signor Rossini's operas as they are written—but who even in this respect was accomplished and finished, if compared with the violent persons who have succeeded him in Italy—each one louder and less available than his predecessor. The volume of Donzelli's rich and sonorous voice was real, not forced … When he gave out its high notes there was no misgiving as to the peril of his blood-vessels; and hence, his reign on the Italian stage was thrice as long as that of any of the worse-endowed, worse-trained folk, who have since adopted the career of forcible tenors, partly from a wish to split the ears of the groundlings, partly from that innate laziness which, together with the increased facilities in gathering gains during modern time, has so largely corrupted art.' [Dec. 1830: Chorley, *Recollections*, Vol. 1, p. 6]

3.6.8 John Sinclair [b. 1791]

'The character of this gentleman's delightful voice is, that it is always music,—clear, perfect, exquisite music; but it is a stream, not a fall, of waters; a chrystal fountain welling away through summer gardens and soothing the ear with delicious attention; not a torrent, to go headlong over crags and precipices, and deafen and turn us giddy.' [17 Nov. 1811: Ex]

'He [Mr. PEARMAN] is a sweet singer worth hearing, and may become a formidable rival to another of the same class, Mr. SINCLAIR. Who, we must confess, grows very tiresome (to use the phraseology of the ladies) with his miminy-piminy affectations, and his weeths, woines, and diviones (with, wine, and divine) …' [13 Jul. 1817: Ex]

'The time that this gentleman has passed in Italy, appears to have been by no means misspent. His voice, which was always of a very fine quality, is greatly improved in power, and his execution is, perhaps, the most finished we have ever heard. His high notes are so extremely clear, that they resemble a fine-toned instrument much more than any thing we have been accustomed to meet with in the human voice, at least, from a male singer; and the style of his falsetto is no less beautiful and highly cultivated. His lower notes, though not quite equal to his upper, are nevertheless of a very perfect kind; and we think he may be pronounced, without fear of contradiction, the most accomplished singer of the day.' [22 Nov. 1823: LG]

'This gentleman's re-appearance, since his return from Italy, has given rise to much speculation to the improvement that celebrated school must have effected on a voice of almost unprecedented sweetness and power … His voice is full, sonorous, and highly musical in its natural key, which we judge extends to A; yet, by an artificial junction of a singularly sweet falsetto, he is enabled to run passages of amazing difficulty and distance with the utmost ease.' [24 Jan. 1824: *Bath Gazette*]

'Mr Sinclair's voice, it is well known, combines strength and compass, with extreme sweetness—it is particularly remarkable for its pure and liquid tones; and this great natural gift he has duly improved by cultivation and study.' [5 Aug. 1824: CM]

'His voice [Sinclair's] is pleasing, but not perfectly clear; has sufficient compass, but no great power. His falsetto, which he uses profusely, is better than Pearman's, but not to be compared with the magic flute of old Incledon. He seems to desist the art of not joining it to his natural tones that the transition may be as little observable as possible; and starts so suddenly from one to the other that the effect is sometimes almost as ludicrous as the contrast between male and female tones of one Roberts's burlesque monopolylognes.' [21 Oct. 1831: EPNY, quoted from the *Philadelphia Chronicle*]

3.6.9   Giuseppe de Begnis [b. 1793]

'He sang in it an aria buffa, in the style of the old rondos, and in which he imitated with his falsetto the celebrated singer Pacchierotti.' [Jul. 1815: *Dictionary of Musicians*]

'Signor de Begni is a great acquisition to this stage. His voice also is deficient in power but it is one of the most pure and flexible, for a bass, that we have ever heard. As an Actor he is gifted with a rare talent for humour, which is always chaste and effective, and seldom degenerates into buffoonery.' [21 May 1821: MP]

'If we may judge by the finished results, appears to have been trained in a good school. His tone is legitimate and pure, and these we esteem to be its capital distinctions.' [Sep. 1822: QMMR, p. 310]

'The part of "Il Fanatico" demands a bass voice of much power and flexibility, and a falsetto of extraordinary compass and clearness, in addition to a fine perception of all that is ridiculous; always, however, tempered and chastened by a correct judgment. Signor de Begnis is possessed of all these qualities, and therefore he was eminently successful in his performance of the very difficult and arduous character of Don Febco.' [9 Jan. 1825: *New Times*, London]

'In the trial passages, he made a run, in triplets, in the soprano clef, from F below to F in alt, making three full octaves. The whole upper octave was in falsetto. He sustained his voice on the last note, F, the key note of the music, for an extraordinary length of time.' [12 Jun. 1843: *Daily Atlas*, Boston]

3.6.10   Luigi Lablache [b. 1794]

Edgcumbe described him on his London debut as 'a bass of uncommon force and power. His voice was not only of deeper compass than almost any ever heard, but when he chose, absolutely stentorian, and he was also gigantic in his person; yet when he moderated its extraordinary strength, he sung pleasingly and well.' [30 June 1828: Edgcumbe, p. 205]

'His voice was of considerable compass, and its weight exceeded everything that was ever heard from a human chest. When put forth to its full power and extent, it not only overwhelmed every other upon the stage and resounded above the loudest orchestration, but entered into the most successful competition with the most sonorous instruments. This stentorian strength and gigantic power he, however, used with the utmost discretion, only now and then displaying it, and then most justifiably. Its quality was superb. So round, clear, and sympathetic was every note, that if he had only sung his scales—which he could do most perfectly—it would have produced the utmost gratification. It also blended well with other voices. Nothing could exceed the accuracy of his intonation, a quality that can never be too highly valued, whilst his steadiness indicated the superiority of his musical training.' [17 Apr. 1830: Cox, p. 183]

'We will speak first of his voice. This is a high base, reaching up to F; but the lower tones, which now were not often called for, seem deficient, by comparison certainly in strength. The power of this organ exceeds all that we ever heard from a human chest; it not only when put forth overwhelms everything on the stage, but enters into very successful competition with the most sonorous instruments in the orchestra. This Stentorian strength, however, is confined to a few notes—from A, the fifth line, to D, appears to be its limit, and he uses this gigantic power with discretion, only now and then displaying it, and then justifiably. The quality of his voice is excellent; clear, round, and musical, it would please were he to sing but the scale up and down, and it blends well with others. Nothing can exceed the accuracy of his intonation, a virtue which can never be too highly valued; and his steadiness indicates a knowledge of music. But on this point we speak with reserve till we have had a fairer opportunity of forming a correct judgment. His style is plain, but pure, and such as becomes a base voice.' [31 May 1830: Har]

'An organ more richly-toned or suave than his voice, was never given to mortal. Its real compass was about two octaves—from E to E. In the upper portion of the register four or five of his tones had a power which could make itself heard above any orchestral thunders, or in the midst of any chorus, however gigantic either might be. This remarkable force was not, as in the case of many singers, displayed on all occasions; but it was made to tell in right places.' [Dec. 1830: Chorley, *Recollections*, Vol. 1, p. 18]

'The quality was no less admirable than the power was stupendous. Open, clear, and produced directly from the chest, without, we may say, one head note, Lablache's voice differed essentially from all the basses we ever heard. His was, in fact, a purely natural voice, and did not seem to include one made note.' [1 Apr. 1834: *Dwight's*]

'Lablache, in Norma, put forth his splendid cannon-ball tones and artillery voice to the greatest advantage. His lower notes are like an eruption of Vesuvius, while his falsetto dances about with the awful velocity and elasticity of a playful thunderbolt.' [Dec. 1836: *Figaro in London*]

'The compass of Lablache's voice is from G in the bass to E natural, embracing but thirteen notes; but the *timbre*, power, and vibration of his tones are prodigious, taken as they are with unerring precision. Hear him in grand concerted pieces, with all the surrounding voices in full development, and the orchestra putting forth its powers—Lablache surmounts the whole, overpowers both chorus and instruments; and the *éclat* of his bass phrases, streaking the general mass of sound, is never confounded with unisonous accompaniment. It is impossible to describe the effect of his magnificent organ in *morceaux d'ensemble*; it is as cannon amid a rolling fire of musketry; as thunder amid the tempest. Nevertheless he has a perfect control over this immense volume of tone, subduing it at pleasure, and endowing it with grace, delicacy, and occasionally even a spice of coquetry … One evening, during a representation of *La Prova*, Madame Malibran took a fancy to discontent her colleague, by introducing ornaments and caprices of extreme difficulty, which it was the business of Lablache to imitate. But the trap for this vocal Hercules availed only to cause a display of his agility;

note after note, trait after trait, shade after shade, did Lablache reproduce in falsetto the fioriture which Malibran had taken such pains to mature. On meeting behind the scenes, Malibran could not help expressing to Lablache her astonishment at the ease with which he had surmounted such difficult passages, and the latter, with his usual *bonhomie*, replied that he had not been aware of the difficulty.' [14 Nov. 1839: MW]

3.6.11   Giovanni Battista Rubini [b. 1794]

'A most delightful, but not a powerful tenor, with a fine toned, equal natural voice of great compass and flexibility most astonishing.' [28 Feb. 1820: Waldie]

'The hero of the Opera, at this moment at Milan, is Signor Giovanni Battista Rubini, unquestionably a tenor of great volume, flexibility, and sweetness. The falsetto of Rubini is perfect. Naturally he is as highly endowed as Donzelli, while he possesses infinitely more science and cultivation.' [6 Oct. 1829: *Courier*]

'Rubini's voice was of the richest quality, of a compass of eleven or twelve notes, from about E flat or F to B or C. To this was added a falsetto certainly reaching to E or F. His intonation was of the purest, and his delivery free from all impediment; but he may be said to have introduced that system of tremolo, of which there has been so much reason to complain in hosts of modern singers, male and female—a fluctuation of tone, so to speak, which rather excites the idea of age or weakness than as indicative of the effects it resorts to for the purpose of producing passion. His shake was excellent, and he was never weary of introducing it, accompanied with an overwhelming multitude of roulades, latterly adopted to conceal the ravages of wear and tear, which, after a time, was apt to produce weariness amongst his hearers. He had also the habit of suddenly forcing out his voice, as it were, in gusts, and so suddenly withdrawing it, as to be nearly inaudible. This was done upon no fixed principle, or in order to express any particular sentiment or epithet, but merely to produce a succession of contrasts, that were thought by not a few, who, from the experience of the past, preferred a more level method of vocalisation, to be violent and unmeaning.' [26 Apr. 1831: Cox, Vol. 1, p. 266]

'We are accustomed to hear that "singing AND music" are both taught in ladies' schools, and we have been always infinitely puzzled to know how these could separately exist; the aspirant to the cross of the Legion of Honour furnishes an ample solution of the mystery, for exactly at the point where everything that is natural, beautiful, emotional in music leaves off, his singing begins, and rushes on to a perfection that has scarcely been attained by any votary of the classical style we have ever heard. Perhaps this perfection is the greatest evil of Signor RUBINI's performance; for, were his mountebank evolutions to be executed with one atom less mastery over the difficulties he has created for the sake of conquering, the audience must be convulsed with laughter instead of delight, and the bad style he propagates would take its proper place in the contempt of the public. We will endeavour to describe one of Signor RUBINI's most applauded exhibitions: he began with a tottering voice that appeared to be rendered tremulous by incessant exercise, a passage that the author evidently intended for a smooth, clear gush of sound to be poured freely from the chest, or from the heart within it; he then sank into an ultra-pianissimo that made us long for the discovery of a musical microscope that we might be able to ascertain if sound really did or did not exist; while in the abstraction of this curious, this almost painful speculation, we were startled by a kind of shriek on a very high falsetto note, which only gave us time to recover our shocked sense from the effect of its piercing reverberations, when it was followed by a shower of the minutest possible dots of sounds, like the tail of sparks that follows the discharge of a rocket, and these eventually lost themselves in the enthusiastic thunder of the audience.' [1 Aug. 1840: *The Atlas*]

3.6.12 Henry Phillips [b. 1801]

'He is a perfect singer—his time and intonation (the first and most essential requisites for a singer) are of an inexplicable firmness. His voice is beautiful, and a *tenor* in all its extent. He has the most admirable art of uniting the upper and lower notes, and in short he is a perfect master of his art.' [3 Aug. 1822: Eut]

' "When storms the proud" [Handel's *Athalia*] is a fine song, but it is too much for Phillips—when he has to encounter the lower f or even g, he reminds us a little of what is vulgarly called snarling—his upper notes are, on the contrary, clear and mellow, his ear very correct.' [27 Apr. 1825: Har]

'Its volume is considerable, but by no means vast, and we conceive it is alike his interest and his inclination to cultivate finish and sweetness rather than grandeur or power, so far as tone is concerned in the production of these effects. It is in fact a genuine English voice, by which we mean a voice that demonstrates very little of artificial formation.' [31 Dec. 1825: QMMR, p. 465]

'Mr Phillips possesses in a high degree that desirable accomplishment in a singer, and which has not often been heard since the days of Bartleman—of talking in tone. We would instance the above observation by referring to his enunciation in that inimitable first quintet, when, in answer to the triumphant rantings of Ferrando and Guglielmo,—"You see, Sir!"—he says, "Yes, I see, Sir, and I say, Sir, the ides of March are not ended". His intonation, and the correctness with which he each time hit that drop to the seventh, was perfectly satisfactory.' [11 May 1828: Ex]

'Mr HENRY PHILLIPS is in our estimation one of the greatest singers of the present day, and there is every appearance that he will progressively improve, since he is not too conceited to avail himself of his opportunities at the King's Concert of Ancient Music (the finest school in Europe), and has sufficient good taste to refine upon his own excellent style with whatever, in his own estimation, he may find superior. He is an example of the most rapid improvement in a singer within our recollection ... He approaches nearer to Bartleman in excellence every day; and it is no slight praise to Mr Phillips to say, that with the recollection upon us of that singer's perfect performance of the fine air, "Tears such as fathers shed", we were charmed with his singing that tender melody. The fiery movement, "Why do the nations so furiously rage", he threw out with an energy for which we were not prepared to give him credit; tameness, and an absence of that "authentic fire" in his composition being the only drawbacks to his general performance. His high notes were round, full, and of a manly yet sweet quality: indeed, it was altogether one of the most perfect efforts in singing during the four days' entertainment.' [12 Oct 1828: Ex]

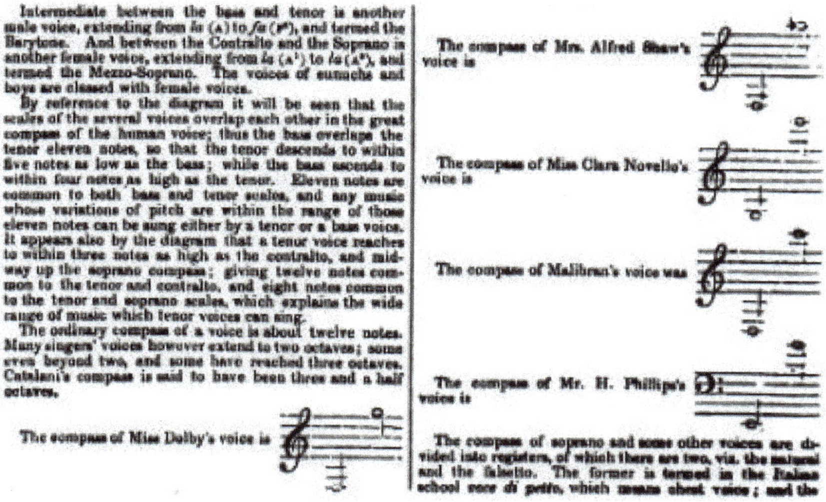

Intermediate between the bass and tenor is another male voice, extending from *la* (A) to *fa* (F#), and termed the Barytone. And between the Contralto and the Soprano is another female voice, extending from *la* (A^1) to *la* (A^2), and termed the Mezzo-Soprano. The voices of eunuchs and boys are classed with female voices.

By reference to the diagram it will be seen that the scales of the several voices overlap each other in the great compass of the human voice; thus the bass overlaps the tenor eleven notes, so that the tenor descends to within five notes as low as the bass; while the bass ascends to within four notes as high as the tenor. Eleven notes are common to both bass and tenor scales, and any music whose variations of pitch are within the range of those eleven notes can be sung either by a tenor or a bass voice. It appears also by the diagram that a tenor voice reaches to within three notes as high as the contralto, and mid-way up the soprano compass; giving twelve notes common to the tenor and contralto, and eight notes common to the tenor and soprano scales, which explains the wide range of music which tenor voices can sing.

The ordinary compass of a voice is about twelve notes. Many singers' voices however extend to two octaves; some even beyond two, and some have reached three octaves. Catalani's compass is said to have been three and a half octaves.

The compass of Miss Dolby's voice is

The compass of Mrs. Alfred Shaw's voice is

The compass of Miss Clara Novello's voice is

The compass of Malibran's voice was

The compass of Mr. H. Phillips's voice is

The compass of soprano and some other voices are divided into registers, of which there are two, viz. the natural and the falsetto. The former is termed in the Italian school *voce di petto*, which means chest voice; and the

Illus. 45: Compasses of Five Famous Singers

'We cannot yet reconcile ourselves to the way in which Mr Phillips's voice is intercepted and made fat by his throat, in its passage from the chest; but we hear him universally admired, and are willing to think we shall become sensible of his merits. Leigh Hunt.' [19 Feb. 1829: Tatler, No. 145, p. 579]

'... there is a pathos in the exquisitely beautiful song from Deborah [Recit. & Song, Mr Phillips, "Tears such as tender"] that never fails to reach the heart of all who are sensible to the effect of musical sounds. The chaste and feeling manner, too, in which Mr Phillips delivers this effusion of paternal happiness—his clear articulation and purity of intonation, give it every advantage that the warmest supporters of the oratorio style can wish.' [9 May 1841: Ex]

'His falsetto is the sweetest we think we have ever heard.' [29 Sep. 1843: HP]

In the same year (1843) Volume 26 of the Penny Cyclopaedia was published, containing a chart (Illus. 45) showing compasses for Henry Phillips plus those of Charlotte Dolby, Mary Postans (as Mrs Alfred Shaw), Clara Novello and Maria Malibran. [Dec. 1843: Penny Cyclopaedia, Vol. 26, p. 418]

'We have never heard Mr Phillips in finer voice. The clear upper notes, so full and yet so sweet, were as fresh as ever; and, in one or two of the songs, his falsetto astonished us by its power and the ease with which it was blended with the natural voice. We still think him, as we have always deemed him, one of the very best of our English singers. Purity of style and distinct articulation are among his distinguishing characteristics. The beauty of his voice charms the multitude; the refinement of his artistic acquirements delights the musician.' [7 Feb. 1850: BG]

3.6.13 Adolphe Nourrit [b. 1802]

'I never heard any thing sweeter than Nourrit's voice and manner. His two opening songs of love for Mathilde, his anguished "Ses jours qu'ils ont osé proscrire" on his father's death, his sorrowful air "Asile héreditaire", and then his rousing "Amis, amis, secondez ma vengeance", brilliant and soaring, gave grand display to the power and passion of this tenor. His voice and appearance remind me much of Rubini.' [26 Aug. 1829: Waldie]

'Throughout the opera he sung in the sweetest and most finished style; even when he was obliged to have recourse to falsetto, it was with a skill which rendered the break hardly perceptible.' [13 Jun. 1832: MC]

'It is to be regretted, however, that the modern fashion of pushing the tenor voice to an extravagant height, only to be reached by the assistance of falsetto, influenced Rossini in writing "Guillaume Tell",—that he should have worked for Nourrit, instead of the whole company of after singers. This peculiarity is the one opposing chance to his music retaining its popularity in years to come.' [8 Dec. 1838: Ath]

3.6.14 John Templeton [b. 1802]

'His voice is exceedingly powerful, more so perhaps than that of any singer of the present day; but though it is loud, it has not what is termed a great volume. The tone is thoroughly in tune, but piercing and brassy; and some of his notes (those about F sharp), are evidently produced with difficulty, being on the ridge of his voice. His falsetto is very good, sweet and mellow, nor is his shift generally bad; but he has a sad habit of rising at once a full octave, without any preparation. Indeed, he is altogether very deficient as a singer; he has a good instrument but has not learned how to use it.' [11 Sep. 1828: BG]

'To each verse he gave such characteristic expression, such light and shade, as to present to the imagination all the frightful realities of the subject of the ballad. The long shake and undulation of the voice at the end of the line, "We hail her with three cheers", is quite a new feature, and produced a startling effect' [19 Nov. 1838: CM].

'Templeton's chest voice has a range of two octaves, and though not remarkable for fullness of tone in the lower notes, is highly so in the middle and upper ones, being capable of sustaining the A and B flat in alt, with much ease and power. His mezza voce, a rare combination of the falsetto and chest voice, also gives him great advantages in those tender and subdued passages, which cannot be effectively sung with the upper notes of the chest voice, or the lower ones of the falsetto … It would be superfluous to dilate on the pure and liquid quality of his falsetto, as that is the subject of universal admiration. It appears unlimited in compass, and even in the very highest notes possesses a power and roundness of tone, which is rarely to be met with in a vocalist of this or any other country.' [16 Sep. 1844: CM]

'It is one of the excellent properties of Mr Templeton's singing, that he knows when to give the exuberance of ornament, and when to forbear. Take two songs—"I love her, how I love her", and "A man's a man for a' that". In the first, Mr Templeton shows the excellent union of the different registers of his voice, blending the chest voice and falsetto, by the bridge voice, so gracefully as to hide the change. Then he makes the song a series of beautiful ornaments. The second is a contrast, sung with perfect simplicity, but with the excellent bearing of a round full note, that satisfies the ear.' [13 Nov. 1845: *Daily Atlas*, Boston]

'It would be difficult to describe the character of Templeton's voice. It is more like some curious instrument than a human voice—the sweetness of his upper notes lead to the belief that it is a *falsetto*; but this illusion vanishes when we hear him, without moving a muscle, or taking breath, swell from the breathing of the flute to the blast of the trumpet. Perhaps we can best account for the effects he produces by saying that they emanate from that, which neither the finest organisation, nor the result of the most careful discipline, could of themselves accomplish.' [6 Nov. 1847: MW]

3.6.15   Gilbert Duprez [b. 1806]

'His voice [Duprez] is not so richly sweet as Donzelli's, but it is far more masculine than Rubini's; and if not so exquisitely flexible and under management, is totally free from that tremulousness which throws a sameness—a certain languor over all the performances of the Italian artist, whether passionate or pathetic. Neither has it any of Nourrit's nasality; and his style is prodigiously animated and expressive, without any approach to extravagance.' [28 Nov. 1837: Ath]

'But Duprez [as Albert] must be heard to have a notion of his thrilling tones—of that utter *abandon*—that *eclat de voix*—that tremulous *falsetto*, of that impassioned style, which all penetrate to the heart's core.' [4 Apr. 1839: MP]

'The chest voice of Duprez extends from E to C above the lines, and he reaches E in falsetto. Since his arrival in Paris, he has given birth to a remarkable mania. An impression was prevalent, that Duprez had created for himself a voice refused by nature. The climate of Italy must have worked the wonder. Whole crusades of singers accordingly set out on an expedition to the land of promise, there to make conquests of voices such as none ever had before. These enthusiasts little dreamed that neither the earth, air, or sky of Italy had given anything to Duprez. Previously to quitting France, he had done little but cultivate his head voice, which was naturally very beautiful, and was barely conscious of the possession of a fine chest register. Nature had been bounteous, and Italian training did the rest./ We have to signalize another mania of equal absurdity. The C note, as given from the chest by Duprez, caused a furore of imitation. Every owner of a voice was fired with the ambition of doing likewise. The *ut de poitrine* was like the golden fleece, to the pursuit of which these Argonauts devoted themselves, sacrificing thereto whatever limited powers they may have originally possessed. Nothing was heard but parodies of Duprez—*Uts de poitrine* resounded through every saloon, delivered in every possible variety of tone—shrieks and yells became the order of the day, and true taste was banished from our circles. Nor has this folly even yet entirely passed away.' [30 Jan. 1840: MW, p. 67]

'The tone of M. Duprez is less elastic, perhaps, but less tremulous than that of Rubini. One prodigious advantage, however, must not be overlooked; namely, the ability of the French artist, when in full force, to dispense with *falsetto*—that musical monstrosity, which, be it treated with ever so consummate a mastery, has, nevertheless, a semi-comic effect, as giving a *patchiness* to the music, which no good composition—say by Mozart or Rossini—will bear … That the wear and tear of the *Académie* have told upon the voice of M. Duprez, may be true; he has now more frequent recourse to *falsetto* than when we first heard him, and manages his energies, whereas, of old, he lavished them.' [9 Mar. 1844: Ath]

'We must not look for an Italian voice: for those even mellifluous sounds, which flow from the lips of a Mario; on the contrary, the organ is naturally of a thick quality, and severe cultivation has alone enabled him to bend it to his will. His range of pure tenor notes, proceeding from the chest, is immense: he is enabled to reach the C above the treble stave. This range cannot, however, be exhibited without considerable effort, and when the exertion is very great, the intonation of the higher notes is not invariably perfect. His tender passages are exquisite; to these he can subdue his organ in the most delicate manner, and the breathings of love cannot be conveyed in tones more soft and insinuating. / To all his other qualifications must be added the great one, that he is essentially a dramatic singer. His voice can wail with grief; can swell with indignation; can burst upon the ear with energy: and the whole man appears under the effect of an inspiration.' [9 Mar. 1844: Ex]

'Within the last few years, the voice of this celebrated tenor has lost much of its original power and sweetness: he still sings with the energy of former days, and can still astonish the house with an occasional ut de poitrine, but the exertion is too painful to be often repeated. It would, indeed, be marvellous if his voice retained its pristine freshness and melody after so long and fatiguing a career. Not only has Duprez had for nine years to bear up against the overpowering loudness of M. Habeneck's orchestra, but he has also sustained a part in almost every opera produced in that interval.' [Dec. 1847: Hervey, *Theatres of Paris*]

3.6.16 Nicola Ivanhoff [b. 1810]

'... a new tenor named Ivanhoff, a Russian by birth, who has studied in Italy, has a very beautiful voice, and chaste simple style of singing, but little execution.' [Dec. 1832: Edgcumbe, p. 218]

'From the lower C natural, to the double-octave C sharp, which he gives firmly with his natural voice, every note is of the most faultless purity—his falsetto is not less good.' [5 Oct. 1833: *Albion and The Star*,]

'The *Messager* of Monday's date, received this morning, in speaking of him, says:—"Sa voix est limpide, bien timbrée, et penetrante…Ivanhoff chante généralement avec la voix de poitrine et n'a que rarement recours à la voix de tête".' [9 Oct. 1833: *London Courier*]

'Ivanhoff's voice although placed in the category of tenors, was, from its high compass, more strictly an alto; and when not too much exerted was flexible and of good quality. In the upper part of his scale he had greater force than Rubini possessed, and in the union of the chest and head voices he was somewhat more equal, whilst he also firmly sustained his notes; but he most certainly had to yield to the Italian in intensity of feeling and facility of execution. He was, however, deficient in power, which was easily enough discovered when he sang anywhere else than at the King's Theatre; so that whenever he put forth any effort—which was, it must be confessed, but seldom—the result was almost always injurious.' [4 Apr. 1834: Cox, Vol. 1, p. 294]

'The young Russian is a good singer, of fine taste, and with a delicate voice, but that is all, as far as we can yet form a judgment from his performance of *Percy* in BELLINI's *Anna Bollena*. He is indisputably many degrees inferior to RUBINI in facility of execution; he is inferior to him also in the volume of his voice, but he has the advantage in steadiness of tone, and continuity of sound. Both are called tenors, but they are in fact contraltos, and the compass of each may be considered pretty equal. IVANHOFF sings comparatively little from the chest, but his falsetto is very sweet, and if he do not introduce so much ornament as RUBINI, he introduces enough, and that, as we have already said, in the best taste of the school to which he belongs.' [16 Apr. 1834: MC]

'We are sure, therefore, that the full capabilities of his powers and talents were not heard. But enough was heard to convince the audience of the King's Theatre that he is a singer possessing an organ of delicious sweetness, and feeling to direct its use to the greatest advantage. Its extent upwards is great, and in the higher parts, where the voce di testa is resorted to, there is a more than ordinary degree of power which makes the point of union with the chest voice almost imperceptible. The cause to which we have before alluded, a slight hoarseness, gave an appearance of effort to passages where energy was required, which we have no doubt will be removed. M. Ivanoff must not believe the common libel upon our national taste, that we prefer noise to every thing else. We are quite sure that the pure quality of his tone will make him heard without its being forced, and that the chaste and expressive style which he has chosen will find its way to the favour of the English public.' [16 Apr. 1834: MP]

'His voice is that of Haitzinger, but is sweeter in quality. It is a high tenor of a peculiarly agreeable character, and his voce di testa is delightfully clear. He manages it too with such excellent effect that no difference is perceivable in his head and chest voice. We hear him now under some disadvantages; for he is evidently suffering from the climate of the country. The only thing he is deficient in is power.' [24 Jun. 1834: LBA]

'Ivanoff had no reason to complain of his reception; he has acquired more power, and he retains the intensity of expression, which, coupled with a voice of the sweetest quality, was so much admired on his former visit.' [10 Apr. 1835: *London Courier*]

'A duo from Guillaume Tell, by Madame Stockhausen and M. Ivanhoff, produced a beautiful effect. We never heard anything more perfectly melodious than the blending of the voices of the two singers.' [13 Jun. 1835: *Court Journal*, p. 376]

'In the second act, Ivanhoff sang an air from Rossini's 'Otello'. A beautiful voice, but the unnatural and impure style of the modern Italian school pushed to the utmost: violent shouting, alternated in the same bar, with an effeminate and almost inaudible whisper: light and shade blotched on in hard and unartistlike contrast; no sustained style, but a superficial striving after effect. But this is what the musical multitude like.' [16 Apr. 1835: Von Raumer, p. 96]

'Ivanoff, in the prison scene, produced an electrical effect by his singing of the "Bel raggio di luna", in which his voice was as clear, as serene, and as calm as moonlight itself. The harp obligato to this delicious melody is in excellent accordance with the subject. It was as if an Æolian lyre was recalling the happy scenes of by-gone days, and the silvery tones of Ivanhoff were never heard to more advantage.' [21 Jul. 1838: CM]

3.6.17   Giovanni Matteo Mario [b. 1810]

'The compass of his voice is very extensive, it rises from the chest (we repeat the words of a celebrated professor) to si natural, and even to do; his notes from the throat are pure, and he passes with ease from one key to another. The principal quality of his voice is the tone, which is clear and vibrating, a little tremulous in sustained notes. In short, he possesses the best qualities that heaven can bestow upon a tenor. The only defect is, perhaps, an occasional want of roundness in the tones; his voice is not yet quite fixed; there is something guttural occasionally, especially when he wishes to obtain forced effect upon the higher chest notes. But these are defects which study and age (Signor Mario is very young) will necessarily remove.' [31 Jul. 1839: *Court and Lady's Magazine*]

'Sig. Mario's voice is a high tenor, of sweet quality in the upper part of his compass; not very flexible: for this, however, we care little, for the rage for flexibility has sacrificed all just and grand expression. It is rather "plummy" in the middle and lower divisions, but is correctly in tune when not over-exerted.' [28 Feb. 1840: Ath]

'His person is handsome, his action is replete with grace and decision, his voice has a firm and manly quality, and he sings with a style too charming to suggest any wish for something better, except when a misplaced anxiety to imitate the fashionable tenor of the day induces him to impart a tremulousness to his tones, which, in Rubini's case, is the result of decaying energy.' [21 Aug. 1841: Atlas]

'Mario took the audience's stronghold of approbation by storm. His *voce vibrata* he certainly strains most injudiciously for his own sake, and without regard to the future consequences, but the public can only feel unqualified delight at the present enjoyment. He has not the *voce di testa* notes of Rubini, but then he sings fairly and roundly from his chest, and, unlike the sly *Bergamasco*, he is not contented to mouth, and to "pocket his voice", during the concerted pieces, but he joins heart and soul in the business of the stage, heralding the way for his minor companions to tread with more certainty and effect.' [26 Apr. 1843: MP]

'If he has not the endless fioriture of the voce di testa notes of Rubini, he sings without the mechanical trick and florid artifice of the great Bergamasco tenor—while his voce di petto notes are as lusciously sweet, they are more firm, chaste, and masculine; and he sings them fairly and roundly from his chest … Though we and the public can only feel unqualified delight at the performance, he, to our ear, occasionally *strains* his *voce vibrata* with too hazardous a disregard of consequences.' [27 May 1843: *Court Gazette*]

'Now Mario delights all—his exquisitely clear and firm organ—the beauty of his style—his touching simplicity, are universally acknowledged. "Feathery" notes, lavish ornaments, perpetual tremulousness, are not asked for. The song is evenly, steadily sung,—every note is firm,—the flow of melody is liquid and unimpeded,—and the effect is charming.' [7 Sep. 1843: MW]

'He has been engaged successfully in the task of smoothing and strengthening and sweetening his falsetto, and by his gradual ascent to a high treble note made the stalls scream with delight, just as they were used to scream for Rubini. We are, on principle, opposed to this method of eking out the voice, deeming it calculated to produce musical confusion rather than musical effect; but (to say nothing of our being just now somewhat seduced by Herr Pischek's high notes) we hardly see how the singer is to make his way without some such artifice through the extravagant modern music.' [3 May 1845: Ath]

'Whilst he has preserved the depth of his lower notes, he has both the vocal vibration (the *voce vibrata*), the pathetic veiled sounds (the *voce pannata*), as well as the purest and most fluted notes in the head voice.' [12 May 1845: MP]

'He afforded, on this occasion, another proof that his voice, which is naturally graceful and tender, is utterly deficient in force, and becomes even ludicrous when striving to give utterance to the wild vibrations of revenge which are agitating the noble but savage heart of the Moor. Indeed, whenever the situation urges the amateur tenor to extraordinary exertions, his notes take a guttural sound, which entirely destroys the limpidity and sweetness which we have said are their proper character.' [29 Mar. 1846: Era]

'The most extraordinary improvement is, however, that which Mario displays. He is no longer the same tenor—the huskiness—the semi-baritone voice have vanished, and he now possesses a pure tenor, to whom no flight appears too daring. Softness, grace, and ease, now characterize his style; there is no hurry in his executions; every shade is delicately displayed, and at the opportune moment he uses the voce vibrata or the flebile[30] so as to awaken every thrilling chord of sympathy. The "Credea di Misera" was the test; the most trying passage, "Ella e spirante, Ella e tramente", he gave in the softest flute-like tone, without apparent effort.' [15 Apr. 1846: MP]

'The peculiar quality of Mario's voice originated the above remarks [difficulty of comparing voices]. In all our acquaintance with public singers, we cannot say we ever heard a voice to which it could be compared. It is not bell-toned and sonorous like [Domenico] Donzelli's; it lacks the supreme delicacy of tone and expressiveness of Rubini's; nor does it possess the richness and fullness we have heard in other tenors; but it is an organ, notwithstanding, of surpassing beauty and sweetness; pure and mellifluous ... and capable of being modulated to every variety of feeling. No tenor, perhaps, was ever more richly endowed by Nature than Mario ... The first cavatina, "Ecco ridente il cielo", [*Barber of Seville*] is one of the most beautiful tenor songs ever written—Ah! How different from the screaming, cat-call tenor *melodies* of the Italian school!—beautiful, not merely as a composition, but as exhibiting all the natural and best qualifications of a voice of this character. Donzelli's singing the first part of this *cavatina*, was, perhaps, the most luscious and exquisite display of vocalization we ever heard from any tenor. But he had not sufficient flexibility for the florid passages in the second part, and failed, in consequence, to give the song its true effect. It was here that Mario's superiority was felt. With a voice hardly inferior to Donzelli's in sweetness, roundness and volume of tone, his marvellous flexibility made Rossini's most difficult *fioriture* a matter of the greatest possible ease, and this flexibility was absolutely necessary to render the music of Count Almaviva entirely effective.' [8 Jan. 1848: MW, *Operatic Stars. No. v.—Mario*]

'His voice—of the decline of which we had heard and read so much—is as beautiful and touchingly

---

30 Tearful voice.

sympathetic as when he quitted us five years ago. A pure and perfect tenor, every note of which, so admirable is his intonation, strikes the ear with the clearness and precision of the finest-toned bell. Instead of declining, as has been stated, his organ appears to us to have manifestly improved since he was last in Paris. The same commendation thoroughly applies to his method, which, always of an excellent school, is now that of a perfect master in his art. M. Mario's *falsetto*, although sweet, we do not so much admire, and observed with pleasure that he uses it very sparingly; with such abundance of power and beauty in his chest notes, we are quite content to dispense with it altogether.' [28 Nov. 1853: MP]

'Those who remember Mario twenty—fifteen—ten years ago, marking now some rustiness in that fine falsetto which fascinated all who heard it, may perhaps be led to reflect how many leaves have been added to the history of the world since those silvery tones were first heard; but we shall content ourselves with wishing that the day may be far distant when the "voice of the charmer" may no longer be listened to. The ring of the metal may not be so pure and unbroken as of yore, but the metal is the genuine metal nevertheless.' [2 Dec. 1864: *Carlisle Journal*]

'Having played the "Knight of the Swan" to the Elsa of Mdlle Albani, at New York, Signor Carpi is quite familiar with it. He not only possesses a tenor voice of sterling quality, but knows how to use it, and can sustain high notes without recourse, voluntary or otherwise, to that "tremolo" which is the crying sin of recent times, and of which, it is worth remarking, the greatest of modern tenors—Mario and Sims Reeves, for example—never showed a trace.' [3 Jul. 1875: MW]

3.6.18   Enrico Tamberlik [b. 1820]

'On first presenting himself it was evident that he was exceedingly frightened and nervous; his face was pallid, and his voice so tremulous, that, when singing the barcarole, we were apprehensive he would break down. We understand that Signor Tamberlik only arrived from Spain on Wednesday, and had the disadvantage of appearing after one rehearsal only, and whilst suffering from the effects of a hurried journey. Hence his voice must, independent of the nervousness of a first appearance, have been considerably affected; but even under these disadvantages he displayed a voice of a rich, broad, and powerful quality—of extensive compass—and a falsetto that can scarcely be distinguished from the chest voice.' [6 Apr. 1850: *Atlas*]

'Signor Tamberlik's voice is a *tenore robusto*, or pure chest voice, of a fine, ringing, sonorous quality, capable of the most varied expression. The upper notes are powerful and clear, the middle round and sweet, possessing a remarkable evenness throughout. The voice is very extensive, reaching as high as the C in alt, which the singer gave out with tremendous power on Thursday evening. Signor Tamberlik makes no use of his *falsetto,* at least uses it very rarely. He thus presents a strong contrast to Rubini and Mario, some of whose best effects were and are produced by this means. Signor Tamberlik's *sotto voce*, however, is admirable, and serves him instead of a falsetto. The new tenor belongs decidedly to the Donzelli school; but he is a better artist than the great head of that school. His style is simple, pure, and unaffected, and his best effects are produced by legitimate means. He never exaggerates … He commenced the barcarole well in tune, and took the first A *sotto voce* beautifully;

but in the repeat, taking it in the chest voice *forte*, the note was so tremulous as to sound any thing but agreeable to the ears.' [6 Apr. 1850: MW]

'His style is evidently of the sentimental order, his singing is more characterised by display of intense feeling than by efforts of vocalisation, for, in regard to mere singing, though his tone is generally tuneful and sweet and his method good, yet we have heard many more complete performers. His voice possesses the rare quality called by the Italians simpatico, and in the middle and lower parts of his register this is exceedingly pleasing, but as he passes into the voce di testa the tone is apt to become altered in timbre, and, to our ear, seemed sharp, frequently in consequence of the extraordinary force employed in uttering, and an excessive use of the voce vibrato; this latter is a fine quality in a singer, but it is possible to abuse it to a pitch of unpleasantness to the listener. At his entrée Sig. Tamberlik was excessively nervous, and the additional tremulousness and sharpness which this gave to his voice made it almost painful to the ear, but the audience kindly encored his barcarole, and this gave him confidence and improved his singing much; subsequently he continued to improve, and, in the aria andante, at the opening of the fourth act, "Sweet Sleep", was heartily applauded ... more evenness, and less of the vibrato, would render him a great singer.' [31 Apr. 1850: LG]

'Here the tremor which has been remarked on certain notes of his voice gave additional intensity to the passages of vehement grief, and produced a thrilling effect. Whether this tremor be a natural peculiarity, or an artifice of the singer, is, we think, if small consequence. Those who remember Rubini will not have forgotten that he had it too; and it was with that great singer, as with Signor Tamberlik, a frequent and happy agent in the expression of pungent and overpowering emotion, while at the same time it must not be denied that it is occasionally monotonous and tiresome, more especially in plain recitative, and passages of level singing.' [8 Jul. 1850: T]

'I read in your [Heugel] Ménéstral [sic] that at the performance of Otello the audience seemed transported...transported, I suppose, by that excruciating shout, to an operating session in the maternity hospital. Oh, the ninnies! ...' [p. 97] 'Now comes Tamberlick. That jokester, wanting ardently to demolish Duprez's C, has invented the chest-tone C-sharp and loaded it onto me. In the finale of my Otello there is, in fact, an A that I emphasized. I thought that it, by itself, launched with full lungs, would be ferocious enough to satisfy the amour-propre of tenors for all time. But look at Tamberlick, who has transformed it into a C-sharp, and all the snobs are delirious! Last week, he asked to come to see me. I received him. But, fearing a second, aggravated edition of the Duprez adventure, I cautioned Tamberlick please, when he came to see me, to deposit his C-sharp on the hall tree and pick it up again, guaranteed intact, when he left.'[p. 99] [10 Apr. 1858: Rossini, quoted by Edmond Michotte in *An Evening at Rossini's*]

'The peculiarities of Signor Tamberlik's voice are well known. It is powerful rather than sweet, but of a fine, even quality through the extensive range of two octaves, brilliant and voluble, but affected to a considerable degree with that tremulous rattle which we can never look upon as anything else than a defect, though in certain passages of emotion it may seem appropriate.' [3 Jul. 1858: SatR]

'It was hardly possible to believe that he who sang, last night, with such delicacy of expression, steadiness of voice and purity of tone, was the same artist to whom we had listened the previous night. There was scarcely a break in his voice from the rise to the fall of the curtain; it was full and clear, and also deliciously sweet, at times.' [31 Oct. 1873: BDG]

'In order to represent the operatic Othello respectably, a voice and some faculty for acting are indispensable. Signor Tamberlik possesses neither of these qualifications. He sings in a doubtful falsetto and his movements are unmeaning, and frequently absurd. For the C sharp in the celebrated duet L'ira d'avverso fato, he substituted a strange description of shriek at about that pitch. The audience, ever appreciative of vocal curiosities, eagerly redemanded it.' [20 Jun. 1877: Shaw, Vol. 1, p. 136]

3.6.19 Sims Reeves [b. 1821]

'But much care and study will be necessary [by Mr Reeves, on debut as Lupin] to get rid of a certain throaty effect, which too faithfully reminded us of that unpleasant quality of Templeton's.' [20 Mar. 1842: Era]

'We think we are correct in saying that it reaches B in alt, without falsetto.' [13 Oct. 1843: MG]

'Mr Reeve has a fine tenor voice, which he manages skillfully. The lower tones are somewhat harsh, but the upper ones are exceedingly sweet. He joins his falsetto to his natural voice very beautifully; the change is scarcely perceptible. He is the best English tenor we have heard.' [12 Nov. 1847: *Daily Atlas*, Boston]

'The following flattering notice of this gentleman's first appearance on the metropolitan boards appears in the Daily News. The other London papers are equally complimentary in their observations on his debut … "His voice [as Edgar Ravenswood in *The Master of Ravenswood*] is a pure tenor; he brings it from the chest throughout its whole compass, according to the modern method, hardly, if ever, using the falsetto. It is clear, sweet, and flexible; capable of the softest expression, and sufficiently powerful for the most intense and violent passion".' [13 Dec. 1847: CE; 'Mr Reeves' Debut on the London Stage']

'He had not sang a dozen bars till the house recognized a novel organ and a novel use of it; and before he was ten minutes on the boards he had impressed every listener with the consciousness that the days of the vocal humming-tops of the Harrison school were numbered, and a first tenor, fit to be so called, was at last restored to the English stage. The first characteristic of his voice that struck the hearer was the volume and sweetness of its middle register; next its power in that and the lower range; then, the extent of the chest run upwards, and the flute-like tone of the falsetto, then, its flexibility; then its extraordinary purity throughout its whole compass; and, lastly, the ease wherewith all those attributes were associated in one rare aggregate for the attainment of the highest purposes of the vocal art … with the exception of Mario's, there was the inestimable charm of freshness in Reeves' voice nowhere to be traced in the worn voices of the others [Moriani's, Salvi's].' [15 Dec. 1847: CE]

'Mr Reeve is the best English tenor we ever heard. His voice is clear, round, sweet and expressive. He sounds his upper notes with the least exertion of any man we ever heard sing, and he is entirely free from the national faults of English singers. His manner is free, easy and unaffected, and he sings with taste and expression. He has not enough vigor, and lacks abandon, but his voice is one of those which we love to hear for itself alone; we are always delighted to listen to its clear, bell-like tones, without caring for the rest.' [1 Jan. 1848: *Daily Atlas*, Boston]

'His voice is a pure tenor, of great power and compass, and is most exquisitely managed. It is truly an Italian voice, and reminds us at times of Mario's, only it is not so lavish of the falsetto.' [18 Mar. 1848: MW]

'He has an alternate crescendo and diminuendo too, which on first hearing produces a great effect, as he does it very well, but which he uses much too often. For these reasons, wonderful as Mr. Reeves's high ringing metallic quality of voice is, and great as is the control he has over it, we cannot give our adhesion to the London opinions of him as a tenor singer. He is not a Mario, a Donzelli, or a Braham; he has not the *chest* voice of any of the three; and although his *head* voice enables him to do without the aid of falsetto, he must sing with greater and more distinct expression to be a truly great English tenor.' [15 Apr. 1848: MW]

'But the mere enunciation of the opening passage, "Linda, Linda", in the softened tone of the highest range of Reeves's voice, so peculiar to himself, and to define which our musical nomenclature supplies no adequate phrase, instantly stamped him as a new singer of the rarest class on the minds of those who had not heard him before, and assured all who had that he was the very man for the great sphere he now filled … Much as Reeves excels in bravuras and every species of declamatory vocalism, it is in tender and pathetic compositions of this nature that he excels himself; for in these it is that the extraordinary liquidity of his chest tones is most apparent, and here he makes chiefly manifest that singular gift of taking up the most prolonged sostenuto passages in the softened voice already spoken of, as if a fresh organ altogether, with fresh breath, were called into play, ventriloquizing, as it were, or echoing the original voice, and this without at all trenching on the falsetto register. The faculty alluded to is, we believe, called voce reverberator, or voce sympatheteca, by the Italians, and its constant use is one of the chief and most charming traits in Jenny Lind … Correspondent of Liverpool Albion.' [24 May 1848: CE]

'We have, not long since, heard Mario on the same boards warble in his beautiful tones "Ah perchè non posso odiarti", and Gardoni, at her Majesty's Theatre, declaring his wretchedness to Jenny Lind's Amina with "All is lost"; but Sims Reeves will bear comparison with either. He surpasses both very far in acting, and if he has not the delicious evenness and purity of Mario, he has greater animation and power; while, in regard to Gardoni, he is in tone, compass, falsetto, management, power—indeed in every respect—his superior. We confess we have been at a loss to know how Mr. Lumley failed to appreciate his services, for Sims Reeves would have been an invaluable acquisition to the Haymarket establishment … We would, however, caution him against straining his voice, which at times sounds harsh from being over-taxed.' [25 Oct. 1848: MG]

'M. Reeves was here somewhat at fault, his forte being occasionally too loud, and his diminuendi on the other hand too piano; so much so that his sotto voce passages, delightful to those seated in the orchestra, were almost unheard in the more remote parts of the theatre.' [21 Mar. 1851: MP]

'I first heard him sing at the Norwich Festival of 1866, when he took part in Costa's oratorio "Naaman". His voice was then still in its prime. A more exquisite illustration of what is termed the true Italian tenor quality it would be impossible to imagine; and this delicious sweetness, this rare combination of "velvety" richness with ringing timbre, he retained in diminishing volume almost to the last.' [Dec. 1866: Klein, *Thirty Years*, p. 460]

'Sims Reeves has been the model singer, and deservedly so; and with such a model before them the host of young aspirants could not but follow. See what the English style is—straight-forward, honest, manly vocalisation. Pure and firm in tone, it has neither the hateful tremolo of the French school or the effusiveness of the Italian.' [8 Jul. 1877: ST]

'Santley and Sims Reeves together, and in good voice too. I declare I would rather hear them, in the autumn and winter of their powers, than most of the modern singers—no vibrato, no tricks of any kind, but pure vocalisation.' [30 Jun. 1893: *Magazine of Music*]

3.6.20   Antonio Giuglini [b. 1827]

'The principal tenor was Antonio Giuglini, this being his first season in Milan, I believe. He had created a perfect furore. Wherever music happened to be the subject of conversation, Giuglini was the hero, a curious fact, considering that powerful lungs are supposed to carry the day. Giuglini was a proof that physical force does not always win; his voice was not powerful, but it was of sympathetic quality, although slightly throaty, and his phrasing was perfect; any ornament he introduced he invariably executed with precision and elegance. He was not a clumsy man, but as an actor he was ungraceful, and lacked intelligence. In the part of Raoul, the part in which I first saw him, he sang charmingly, but manly bearing and fire were entirely wanting, with the result that his performance was dull and insipid. In "I Puritani" he was quite at home, his rendering of Arturo's music, than which more delicious love-strains have never been written, riveted the attention so completely, that the actor was lost sight of [p. 76] ... I never could understand why Gardoni should be comparatively forgotten, and Giuglini quoted as one of the great artists who have lived. Gardoni was the superior in every way; his voice was pure, Giuglini's was throaty. He was a handsome man, and in parts which suited him an excellent actor. Giuglini was an awkward, ungainly man, and no actor at all; Gardoni could sing any style of music, *cantabile* or florid; Giuglini could not execute a rapid passage of four notes. What I conceive established him as a great favourite was a lackadaisical sentimentality which the public, especially the British public, accepts for poetic sentiment. Withal, Giuglini was the last of his race; there has been no tenor on the Italian stage since who has been able to fill the place he left vacant. [p. 232]' [Reference Date Oct. 1855: Santley, *Student and singer*]

'The only singer of any merit from whose lips it [hymn in the monastery, from Donizetti's *La Favorita*] has failed to move our audiences, has been Signor Giuglini, whose delight in his clear and finished tones often seduces him into a languor devoid of proportion and measure, which, in music like that of the movement alluded to, becomes fatiguing and fatal.' [Estimated reference date Dec. 1855: Chorley, *Recollections*, Vol. 1, p. 160]

'His voice was a pure Italian tenor, with considerable flexibility, and a most happy blending of the head voice and chest notes, but it was rather light than robust in quality.' [Estimated reference date Dec. 1855: Cox, Vol. 2, p. 308]

'His voice is a pure tenor, bearing some physical affinity to that of Tamberlik, though lighter and mellower in its texture, and more sympathetic in its influence upon the hearer. His chest notes are remarkably good throughout, and ascend high in the scale; while his falsetto, as far as we have yet discovered, is sure, clear and resonant.' [15 Apr. 1857: Std]

'Giuglini was more successful than ever. He is just the singer to give the greatest effect to Bellini's smooth, flowing, somewhat luscious and monotonous music. His beautifully-sustained sounds— the roundness and delicate finish of all his phrases—his intonation as perfect as the finest violin— combine to charm the ear; while the sameness of the composer's narrow range of vocal passages is relieved by the rich variety of the singer's colouring and expression.' [2 May 1857: *Spectator*]

'His voice, approaches most nearly in point of sweetness to Mario's of any of our present tenors, while it possesses the stamina necessary for the most arduous parts.' [6 May 1857: MC]

'The next was a solo by Signor Giuglini. This artist has gained much admiration since his arrival; his voice, uniting great power and delicacy to a mellifluous, almost excessive sweetness, and governed with the talent of a musician, at once attracts attention. Nothing could have been more delicate and exquisite than his rendering of particular passages. If his voice wants anything it is a certain masculine tone, which is essential to a tenor voice as a certain development of muscle is to the beauty of a manly figure.' [17 Oct. 1857: *Saunders's News-Letter*]

'With a voice of peculiar lusciousness, which could only be reproached with its over-honied sweetness, and possibly the singer's tendency to prolong its notes even to the danger of cloying the ear; with a command of power, as well as delicacy of feeling; with a faultless intonation, and a chest voice which scorned the use of falsetto; no wonder that Signor Giuglini quickly penetrated the hearts of his audience.' [Dec. 1857: Lumley, p. 405]

'... although Giuglini has slightly scratched the pearly coating of his voice, he is still the prince of the light tenors, as Tamberlik is of the heavy ones.' [19 Oct. 1861: *Aris's Birmingham Gazette*]

'Whatever may be our opinion of Signor Giuglini as a private citizen [criticised for travelling with Mrs. Wyndham], we cannot but admit that, as a public singer, he is incomparably the first tenor of the Italian stage in England. His lower tones have a mellow richness which reminds us of Mario in his best days, while his higher notes are as pure and clear as the tinkling of a silver bell. In the plaintive Romanza "Colli Nativi", these qualities were displayed to the greatest advantage, while in the rendering of "La Donna Mobile", which he gave on being recalled after singing "Ah si ben mio", the great flexibility of his voice was shown.' [8 Dec. 1862: *Dundee Courier*]

'Signor Giuglini here drew out a note to the most delicate piano, and at the same time sustained it without a break or vibrato being anywhere apparent, with the most delicious effect. Certainly many singers might do well to study Signor Giuglini in his method of producing and sustaining a pure tone in his notes.' [7 May 1864: SatR]

3.6.21   Italo Campanini [b. 1845]

'His voice is remarkable for purity as well as strength, and, what does not always happen in the case of operatic singers gifted with good voices, his knowledge of his art is as perfect as the most exacting person could desire. Signor Campanini has studied in a good school, and his vocalisation is entirely free from vices which have crept into the system of operatic singing of late years, to the utter destruction of the pure Italian method upon which the greatest artists have built their reputation, and which we must still regard as the model school. Signor Campanini takes all the high notes well from the chest, and without any apparent difficulty. His voice is not only of somewhat exceptional strength, but is sweet in tone, and flexible in an equal degree. Now-a-days it is a positive treat to meet with a tenor, or, indeed, a vocalist of any kind, who disdains the use, or rather the abuse, of the vibrato. Signor Campanini is not in the faintest degree addicted to this vice. On the contrary, his tone is produced steadily, and sustained properly.' [5 May 1872: Era]

'There is no vestige of harshness in the tone, and, what is by no means common, the voice is even throughout its whole compass. The upper tones are strong, full, and resonant, and the lower register is of corresponding quality. / Signor Campanini's method is admirable; in fact he sings in the pure Italian school. He places no trust in the detestable vibrato and other wretched tricks of vocalisation which operatic artists so often affect; in fact, his style of singing is as pure as his voice, and that is saying much.' [6 May 1872: MA]

I've already quoted [p. 76] the *Athenaeum's* report on Italo Campanini, to the effect that his voice 'will cause a reaction, if not a revolution', because his singing was without vibrato or tremolo, even in recitative.

'What he lacks, so far as we are competent to judge, is flexibility. He has little or none of what Italian professors suggestively call "agilità"—of which Mario was so incomparable a master. Thus his florid singing generally, and his execution of grupetti in particular, is seldom satisfying. He declaims, however, with genuine expression; never tortures his phrases by spinning them out indefinitely; is free from exaggeration and affected sentiment; free also from the so-called "tremolo", a prevalent vice with the actual race of singers; a complete adept in mezza voce singing; and, last not least, his intonation is rarely at fault.' [29 Jun. 1872: SatR]

'His voice is wonderfully sweet, far sweeter and more touching than ever Brignoli's was,—and yet is possessed of great power and compass. He is a true artist, does not overwork his voice, or indulge in any show-passages, and is cautious about too many holds in the very highest notes. If he has a fault, it is the occasional use of the falsetto, and a tendency to rather too much pianissimo singing, to which he is tempted by the extraordinary softness and sweetness of his voice.' [28 Jul. 1872: CT]

'Last evening it was evident that the "Ah, Matilda", which had been transposed at least three semitones lower, was an effort; and the famous trio in which he made himself prominent only by a violent effort, left him with a vibrato that was anything but effective.' [30 Mar. 1882: EPNY]

'… has reached a point where, out of respect for his well-earned fame, he should retire from the concert room. In lyric opera, stage experience and dramatic attainment can do more to offset the waning voice; in concert singing there is greater temptation to cover defects by mere tricks of style and by resorting to exaggerated, sensational effects.' [17 Mar. 1889: *Pittsburgh Dispatch*]

'Thanks to the beautiful quality of his voice and his freedom from the tremolo, he at once made his mark, and, indeed, in one night he stepped from a comparative obscurity into fame. His chief vocal defect was a certain throatiness, which he did his best to overcome, although never quite successfully.' [24 Nov. 1896: GH (from obituary)]

3.6.22   Joseph Maas [b. 1847]

'Mr. Maas as Thaddeus did finely; his voice is of very pleasing quality, light and flexible, though of hardly sufficient volume; but under excellent cultivation and good control. "Then you'll remember me", and "When the fair land of Poland" were admirably rendered, displaying the same purity so noticeable in Kellogg's singing.' [4 Mar. 1874: *Worcester Palladium*]

'His singing was admirable. His voice is of the purest tenor quality, sweet, rich, and velvety. He always sings in tune, never uses the falsetto, avoids exaggerating and forcing, and is consequently free from "tremolo", phrases well, and articulates clearly. The charming quality of his mezzo voce singing was manifested in the music of the "garden scene", and its power and brilliancy were striking displayed in the delivery of high chest notes in the "combat trio". In the air, "Hail, thou dwelling pure and lowly!" ("Salve dimora"), the good quality of his lower notes was no less observable than the resonance and clearness of his higher notes, and throughout the opera he displayed vocal and artistic qualities which could not easily be surpassed by any vocalist on the modern Italian or English stage.' [16 Mar. 1878: ISDN]

'Mr. Maas has entirely conquered the tendency to sing "throatily" which four years back interfered with his success. His production of voice is excellent; free from tremolo, bright and resonant, without any forcing. His phrasing and intonation are equally good, and there are few tenor vocalists whose singing is more delightful. Without resorting to falsetto, he attains high notes with ease, and his mezzo-voce strongly recalls that of [Antonio] Giuglini.' [6 Apr. 1878: ISDN]

'The Manrico of Mr Maas was really admirable. His voice is of that rare description that combines the sweetness of the tenorino with the power of the tenore robusto.' [26 Nov. 1878: YP]

'In the final cadence he wisely omitted the D flat in alt, which would have necessitated the employment of the falsetto voice.' [22 Sep. 1880: BDP]

'We have no hesitation in saying that Mr. Maas sang Balfe's melody as not even Sims Reeves could now sing it. The performance was as near perfection as could be—voice clear and pure as a bell, style delicate, method most pleasingly artistic.' [25 Feb. 1881: *Nottinghamshire Guardian*]

'Mr. Maas scorns, as emphatically as Mr. Reeves himself, the vicious defects of the modern operatic school—the vibrato, and the rest of the tricks which have served to ruin many promising aspirants to fame—and has done a great deal to preserve the simple beauty of the cantabile method amongst English singers. Indeed, we make no hesitation in saying that he is, far and away, the most richly-endowed vocalist at present before the public.' [22 Dec. 1881: *Derby Daily Telegraph*]

'Mr. Maas's style is no longer heavily ecclesiastical, as it was some years ago, when he played Rienzi at Her Majesty's, and when Miss Georgina Burns made her first striking success in London as the Messenger of Peace. His voice is soft, rich, and unforced; and the delight of the public in it seems to be boundless. On the other hand, his gifts are not various. In passages where promptitude, force, and incisive declamation are required, Mr Maas is a trifle sleepy.' [11 Apr. 1885: Shaw, Vol. 1, p. 226]

3.6.23   Jean de Reszké [b. 1850]

'Alike in a vocal and a histrionic sense, it was supremely great. His "velvety" tones, fresh, clear, and mellow as a bell, were emitted with an unsparing freedom that would thrill the listener not once, but twenty times, in the course of a single scene. There was no "saving up" for the last act then; it was "laissez aller" throughout, with plenty to spare at the finish. And what tenderness, withal, in that famous grand duet of the fourth act!' [Jun. 1881: Klein, *Thirty Years*, p. 224]

'... is nearly free from the vibrato which is the besetting sin of French vocalists.' [16 Jan. 1886: MW]

'I had heard so much that my expectations were of the highest kind; nor was I disappointed. This truly great artist once sang as a baritone, but whatever his voice may have been like then it is now unmistakably a tenore robusto. His high notes, produced with ease and always in perfect tune, are of magnificent quality and resonant as a bell. He sings without a suspicion of the tremolo, uses the messa voce with moderation, declaims with splendid vigour, and phrases with a purity and nobility of expression that never fails to impress. What a treat to hear this superb organ and frank, dignified delivery, after some of the "bleating", shouting tenors to whom we have had to listen of late years!' [19 Jun. 1887: ST]

'A slight tendency to the tremolo on occasions is his one trifling drawback, but the tendency is so slight that it is scarcely worth mention.' [5 Jun. 1889: Std]

'We do not know whether Mr. De Reszké ever heard of what the Germans call the "bebung", but he has it very badly. It is not a tremolo, however, and that is to his credit. Except in the case of his high notes this tenor produces his voice with the same care and tenderness as that with which Russell Sage[31] produces a $5 bill; but all notes above the staff Mr. de Reszké carries by assault, not unmingled with battery. His delivery is as full of explosions as a dynamite factory, yet he sings with a good deal of feeling and often startles his audience.' [16 Dec. 1891: *Musical Courier*]

'Is "Hood" not confusing the cultivated tremolo with the natural vibrant fulness of a big voice? Most certainly our best and most artistic singers do not use it. If "Hood" will go to Covent Garden in the season, and listen, say, to M. Jean de Reszke, Mr. Bispham, M. Plançon, and Madame Eames, who have no cultivated tremolo, and then to Mr. B. and Madame A., who have, he will soon see the distinction I mean, and will probably cease to take any further interest in the tremolo".' [1 Sep. 1897: MusH]

---

31   Russell Sage (1816-1906), an American financier, railroad executive and Whig politician, amassed a fortune on Wall Street

3.7 Recorded Female Singers

3.7.1 Adelina Patti [b. 1843]

'Her voice is a pure, delicious soprano, of great evenness and purity of tone, amply powerful in the upper and medium parts, and promising greater strength in the lower. It is a fresh, unspoiled voice, with no tremble in it, and none of the cracks that exposure to the Verdi fire always makes in that delicate article, the female voice. It is as flexible as Sontag's, with a good natural shake.' [17 Dec. 1859: *Dwight's*]

'Although the young vocalist ascended as high as E flat, on Tuesday night, and in one instance, we believe, even reached F, her organ cannot be considered as by any means developed at present, and, with increasing study and experience, it will doubtless assume a volume of tone which … Madlle. Patti's powers of vocalisation are extraordinary, when the age of the artist is taken into consideration. She has great command over both the staccato and legato styles of singing, her shake, even on extreme notes of her compass, is perfect, and she possesses the rare quality of repose, which enables her to give the utmost effect to phrases that depend more upon expressive rendering than dazzling execution…In one respect may we at once administer a caution to the debutante. The frequent attack of high notes in the "pique" style, which seems to be getting popular, and of which instances are furnished in the final cadenza of "Ombre Légère", and in "My long hair is braided" (Wallace's Amber Witch), is at variance with the good old rules of vocalisation, and is not favourable to the preservation of the voice. Not alone in the cadenzas does Madlle. Patti indulge in this sharp method of producing tone, but the commencing notes of some cantabile phrases are thus squarely commenced, and the sympathetic quality of the voice is for the moment destroyed. With the flexibility she commands there is no necessity for hard vocalisation, and such a variety should be but sparingly introduced.' [19 May 1861: ST]

'Her renderings of the cabaletta, "Perchè non ho", and the florid part of the scena (the "mad scene" beginning "Il dolce suono"), were characterised by refined taste and extraordinary brilliancy. Madlle. Patti's almost exclusive cultivation of what is termed the "bright tone" has won for her a quite exceptional power in a certain style of vocalisation, and if this were not accompanied by unsteadiness in the middle register (too frequently the result of devotion to this manner of singing), and were not so constantly expressed by the "pichettata staccato" and "martellata" style of execution, we should have nothing but admiration for it. In the pieces demanding fullness of tone, broad phrasing, declamation, and dramatic accent, Madlle. Patti was less excellent.' [27 May 1861: MP]

'The natural quality of her voice, especially in the upper register, enables her to surmount those difficulties which others, to whom nature has not been quite so bountiful in that respect, could not accomplish. She has gone through the ordeal of the London press, and, although the various critics differ in many respects as to her ability, we believe they all agree that she has wonderful facility of execution. She has been compared to Jenny Lind, but, as we heard her last night, her voice is of not nearly so good a quality as the "Nightingale's" voice, when first Made. Goldschmidt was heard in England. It is not so silvery, neither do we think that Madlle. Patti will ever be so good a singer. She appears to be the star of the Gassier and Piccolomini school of singing, but she is not a Jenny Lind … She rendered the popular air, "Ah non giunge", with powerful effect. The artistic manner in which she ran the chromatic scale, and the extraordinary close shake on A and B in alt, and the powerful note she threw out at the finish of the song, was another triumph for her.' [19 Sep. 1861: BG]

'Equally commendable is the manner in which she delivers more tranquil passages. It is really refreshing now-a-days to meet with a singer who will condescend to favour us with firm, clear, steady notes, without the incessant *tremolo* which is really becoming a vocal nuisance. Mdlle. Patti knows when to use this, and does so with excellent effect, but she also knows when to abstain from it, which is a much rarer qualification.' [Dec. 1861: *National Magazine*]

'The more we hear the charming little songstress, the more are we struck with her genius. What else is it that electrifies the audience, in spite of defects of voice and style? Some say that Mdlle. Patti's voice is thin, others find fault with a slight tremulousness of delivery. Her constant use of staccato passages is blamed, and the over-elaboration of her cadences considered objectionable. There may be some truth in this, but all agree that a more fascinating, more gifted, and more sympathetic singer, has not appeared for years.' [10 May 1862: LR]

'[Marietta] Piccolomini had a thin voice, but not worn so much as that of Madlle. Patti, which is also thin, and not of the best quality, although shrill and telling. This young lady also rejoices in having unsettled the stability of her voice by practising the aguish tremolando which the Italians have lately introduced, and dignify by the term vibrato. If she had sung the first act and part of the second without that objectionable tremor, and had given the audience the benefit of well-sustained notes held, swelled, and diminished, how much more effective would the impassioned scenes of the dying patient have been rendered by the use of the tremolando, when trembling and unsteadiness were perfectly in place … Sig. [Italo] Gardoni was the Alfredo, and sung unaccountably flat in the first act, but recovered his usual good intonation in the second and third acts. The way in which this correct singer indulges in the trembling mania, and the way in which he and Patti occasionally vibrated one against the other, absolutely was absurd. Neri Baraldo [Pietro Neri-Baraldi], with certainly as good, if not a better, voice than Gardoni, and with clear, well-sustained notes coming out boldly from the chest, is in every way preferable.' [7 Jun. 1862: Ex]

'Mme. Patti's singing is simply faultless; and the reedy quality of her voice renders it still more susceptible of expression than of [Angiolina] Bosio. Compared to hers, it is as an oboe to a flute. It is, moreover, full of warmth, and it faithfully translates every shade of feeling suggested by the singer's fervid nature.' [14 Oct. 1869: *Dwight's*, quote from *Athenaeum*]

'This quality [bird-like] seems entirely to have disappeared, though it is still wonderfully smooth and even throughout its whole range, rich and warm in quality, without even a trace of the metallic quality that so often comes with a singer's maturity. The slight tremolo noticeable, far from becoming objectionable, is so skilfully handled and controlled as to constitute an additional charm, heightening its power of passionate expression. Her technical facility is certainly marvellous, for no difficulty of execution seems to have any existence for her. Yet it is not the vocal agility which charms, but the wonderful smoothness throughout its entire compass, which permits the most extended embellishments to be executed with a scarcely perceptible change of register. While all this is true, it is at the same time true that it seems lacking in point of magnitude.' [5 Jan. 1882: CT]

'Her voice too is unique. We have been so often disgusted with the abuse of the vibrato that we sometimes forget how effectively it may be used as an occasional ornament. Madame Patti illustrates this by frequent, but never tedious, employment, and she has never permitted it so to affect the perfect control of her voice as to deprive her of the power of sustaining sounds with a steadiness and purity such as we too seldom listen to.' [5 Oct. 1883: MG]

'Madame Patti has much variety of tone, great power, great skill in passage singing, and, what is very rare in female singers, she can pass unperceived by the hearer from the smallest fluty falsetto tone to the full power of an organ of noble full timbre.' [13 May 1884: DubDE]

'The performance fell far below her old standard as regards evenness and purity. The flute-like tones of her earlier years are gone beyond hope of recall, and although all the music is transposed for her benefit, she often sings more or less false, especially when she pushes her voice for the attainment of dramatic power in the delivery of her tones. False intonation was more frequent and more noticeable last evening than it has been at any time this season.' [12 Mar. 1890: CT]

'Another critic writes of him [Ysaye] in a San Francisco journal: "... But it is not in what is capable of being described that the subtle difference between Ysaye and the others who stand nearest him in remembered performances consists. It is in an indescribable but vivid individuality in his tone, as impossible to be caught in words as the color in the few great voices the world possesses. Like them, it has the mysterious vibrant quality as far away from vibrato as the tones of Adelina Patti's voice at its best, and yet with a throb and a thrill which occasionally seem startlingly like the vox humana stop in a fine organ." ' [18 May 1895: *Sacramento Daily Record*]

3.7.2 Emma Albani [b. 1847]

'Mdlle. Albani is one of those singers whom it is a pleasure to see and hear, but who excite no very deep emotion, and certainly cause nothing so vulgar as a "sensation". She exercises upon the audience the charm inseparable from youth, beauty, and an agreeable voice; she sings naturally but with sufficient care, expressively but without the least exaggeration ... To Mdlle. Albani's singing in the mad scene no exception whatever need be taken. It was very brilliant, and at the same time very correct. As with many other light sopranos, the upper part of the débutante's voice is the best, the notes of the higher region being unusually clear and resonant.' [15 Apr. 1872: PMG]

'Her youthful and interesting appearance, combined with the freshness and purity of her sympathetic voice, could not fail to attract the sympathies of her audience, and she was applauded to the echo ... and if a fault must be found it must be with the too frequent use of the tremolo, which she employed to such an extent in the "Ah, non credea" that the notes sometimes sounded like a succession of shakes. It is to be hoped that Mdlle. Albani will abandon at once this defective mode of giving expression. She is quite capable of displaying abundant pathos, without resorting to meretricious means.' [27 Apr. 1873: Obs]

'Mdlle. Albani has added another to the list of her previous successes, by her first performance of the character of Elvira in I Puritani on Saturday ... The exquisite quality of her voice—so fresh and pure; so delicate and yet so full and resonant—the silvery beauty of the extreme upper notes (extending to D in alt), the refined grace of her style and her brilliant execution—were all triumphantly displayed.' [5 May 1874: DN]

'It is worthy of remark that she makes use of the much decried tremolo with singular effect. In most cases the tremulous production of a note—a very different thing from the shake proper—is a symptom of weakness or defective method; with Mdlle Albani it is a beautiful embellishment, used sparingly and at the proper time.' [11 Oct. 1875: *Irish Times*]

'Mdlle. Albani's vocalisation was in most respects delightful, and would have been entirely satisfactory but for her occasional tendency to relapse into two faults of which she is not yet quite cured. These are, the employment of an artificial tremolo in pathetic passages, and a slackening of the time in movements already slow. Mechanical voice-tremblings are miserably poor substitutes for the natural vibration which accompanies real emotional power, and Mdlle. Albani, who often has "genuine tears in her voice", is heard to disadvantage when she endeavours to simulate pathos by means of a tremolo which resembles a defective shake and is obviously artificial.' [29 May 1877: *Theatre*]

'Mlle Albani's artistic abilities, though not of the rarest, are still of a very estimable order. She has to thank nature for a faculty for hard work, and a voice of the most beautifully clear quality in its highest register. Everything else she owes to her own unspared exertions. It is to be regretted that these exertions seem to be always directed to the attainment of new and often visionary excellences, and never to the remedying of defects which are painfully obvious, and which mar, more or less, her most admired performances. Her intonation is frequently false; and the fatal tremolo is already perceptible even in her clearest notes. No amount of talent could neutralize these two faults, which seem to gain ground every season.' [4 Jul. 1877: Shaw, Vol. 1, p. 149]

'The passionate dramatic style required for the stage is utterly unsuited to the pure, noble simplicity of sacred music; and I noticed that all these opera singers, from continually declaiming in the strained accents of love or despair, have acquired a tremulous quaver in the voice. This was especially remarkable in Albani's rendering of "Angels ever bright and fair", where not one of the sweet long-drawn notes was held steadily for two seconds.' [25 Aug. 1880: London correspondent of the *Sydney Morning Herald*, 'Odds & Ends from the Old Country']

'Besides the vast amount of license which Madame Albani allowed herself, completely regardless of the composer's expressed intentions, she indulged far too much in that vile mannerism, the vibrato, which she seems to have cultivated so assiduously that at times the hearer is in doubt whether the effect she is producing is an imperfectly produced shake or a too well developed wobble. Truly it is lamentable to see such marvellous gifts turned to such base uses.' [22 Dec. 1887: YP]

'For, all that Mme. Albani knew was taught to her by Francesco Lamperti. It has since occurred to Mme. Albani that her old master was short-sighted and that after all she is a dramatic soprano. She has encouraged the idea and has, indeed, indulged it. And it has had its revenge. But it is not responsible for everything. Whatever class of music she may choose, there is no shadow of reason why she should shriek, why she should not sing in tune, why she should sing frontale, why she should encourage a vibrato, why she should slur up and down to every other note, or, for that matter, even why, after having delivered some particularly bathetic passage—if I may use the expression—she should wildly clutch at the signboard of the pianoforte next which she happens to be standing, and cast her eyes up at the peculiarly dispiriting ceiling of the Queen's Hall. I say there is no reason why should do any of these things, and she does them all.' [19 May 1895: CT]

'Her pianissimo, or sotto-voce, singing, is perfection, and the full beauty of her voice is revealed in the upper register. Here the quality of her notes is exceptionally beautiful—rich, round, mellifluous, and sweetly penetrating. Her mastery of the art of vocalisation is superb, her light and shade, her modulation, and her phrasing, perfect. Albani makes free use of the vocal shake (as distinct from the tremolo), and very effective it proves. She does not altogether discard the tremolo either, this being noticeable from time to time in sustained notes.' [21 Sep. 1907: *New Zealand Herald*]

3.7.3 Dame Nellie Melba [b. 1861]

'Possessed of a graceful figure, pleasing features, an easy carriage, a voice of two octaves in compass, the timbre of whose upper notes are sonorous and clear as a bell, and a certain dramatic power in her acting, it is not surprising that the fortunately endowed lady achieved a most satisfactory success, and promises to do yet better things, from an histrionic point of view, when she shall appear in a less conventional work than Donizetti's well worn, though ever melodious, "Lucia di Lammermoor".' [27 May 1888: *Reynolds's Newspaper*]

'"Although Madame Melba", writes the Standard, "does not come to us in the first blush of her youth, her voice is fresh and resonant, her figure juvenile and pleasing, and her capacity as an actress quite sufficient to render all possible justice to the unhappy bride of Lammermoor. Her school, unfortunately, is not of the best, and the use of the vibrato is excessive; but, on the other hand, the lady possesses abundance of natural means, remarkable executive facility, and enters life and soul into the task set before her. Under such conditions no wonder that she pleased all hearers, and was complimented with the usual amount of honors which fall to a new comer. Madame Melba is a really clever vocalist, and good, if not absolutely great, things are to be expected of her in the future." ' [18 Jul. 1888: *Northern Argus*, Rockhampton, quoting from *The Australian*]

'A voice of bell-like purity, of the most extended compass, flexible yet brilliant, and with the true Patti "production"; fluent, smooth vocalisation, a real shake—not the close vibrato so often made to do duty for it.' [15 Feb. 1893: BDP]

'Her trills, chromatics, and scale passages are veritable gems of execution, every note being round, pure, and distinct, even in the most rapid passages, which were sung with marvellous ease and fluency. As all the world knows, the cantatrice's voice is a pure soprano, rather of the light order than the dramatic, but still not of the lightest class, and it possesses quite a distinctive timbre, that in the lower register may almost be likened to the delicate reediness of the famous Cremona violins. The middle and upper register are alike remarkable for their pure bell-like character, and there is a perfect evenness of tone throughout. Another feature that strikes one on a first hearing is the soprano's infallible intonation, which was never even a beat off the true pitch.' [13 Nov. 1902: *Evening Journal*, Adelaide]

'The continual "vibrato" is the outcome of the farewell visit of [Nellie] Melba to this country when she was at an advanced age and in ill health, and when she was urged to sing against her better judgment, and the wavering voice of the old woman, always a favorite for her sweet spirit, inspired some of the toadying ones to try to imitate her, and it was at the first called the "Melbino". The foregoing is from no less an authority than Madam Marchesi [presumably Blanche, who was herself widely criticised for her tremolo!], one of the best authorities on vocal work in the world. She further says: "The vibrato is the worst defect in the world of singing, and is a certain sign that a voice has been forced, or is worn out or affected, and in any event, it is spoiled".' [28 Jul. 1913: *Ann Arbor News*]

'The part of Violetta was in the hands of an obviously inexperienced performer, whose name was given on the programme as "Madame Melba". Who Madame Melba is we do not pretend to know, but plainly she is not an operatic artist. Her intonation was frequently faulty, and her singing at all times betrayed a deplorable vibrato. At a time when the country is suffering from a shortage of domestic help it seems a pity that a person who possibly possesses a real aptitude for the domestic arts should devote herself to a calling in which her chances of success are so meagre.' [16 Jul. 1916: *Herald*, Melbourne]

'Dame Nellie [Melba] reappeared, and sang Liza Lehmann's "Magdalen at Michael's Gate", an unusual type of song exacting constantly changing expression. The general tenor had intermingled with it a tone of levity, but the climax of the last verse was deeply devotional. Sustained notes heralded by an awkward approach were immaculately rendered, and enriched by a gentle vibrato.' [11 Mar. 1927: *Examiner*, Launceston]

'Melba's voice is a great gift of nature. It has no registers—from top to bottom the voice is all one perfectly equalised whole. She is a great stylist, by reason of her finished cantilena, her polished legato, her perfect messo di voce [sic], her freedom from vibrato, her perfect mastery of breath (and tone) emission, and her complete mental and emotional poise ... However that may be, it is all very wonderful, and the fact that Melba can sing, in her seventieth year, with purer tone quality than most young sopranos of the day, is confirmation, strong as holy writ, of the perfection of her production.' [12 Aug. 1928: *Sunday Times*, Sydney]

3.7.4   Ellen Beach Yaw [b. 1869]

'The possessor of the most phenomenal voice on record is stated by the New York Herald to have been discovered in the person of a young lady, Miss Ellen Beach Yaw—not a musical name, but that is easily rectified. "The highest vocal range of a singer recorded by history", the correspondent who has found the phenomenon has discovered, "was that of Lucrezia Agujari. Mozart says that in 1770 he heard this soprano range from G below the middle C to C above the high C, a range of twenty-five notes. This is noted by the 'Encyclopaedia Britannica' as the only known instance of the kind; but Miss Yaw can sing as low as Agujari and one note higher in the upper register", and can without an effort sustain the note. The lady is twenty-two years of age, has golden hair, blue eyes, features of pink delicacy, and a slim neck "as graceful as a swan's"—so the writer who has interviewed her declares, though the familiar comparison never strikes me as complimentary. Because a voice is high it is by no means necessarily agreeable, it may be remarked, and I gather from the statements made that Miss Yaw's intonation is far from as accurate as it might be; but she is said to be in the hands of competent teachers, and is believed to have a future.' [17 Jun. 1893: *Illustrated Sport*]

'Even the highest of our soprano singers, whose top note you listen for with breathless attention, is content if she can reach the high E. Patti herself can go no higher than this "E in alt", and it is a note for any prima donna to be proud of. But Miss [Ellen Beach] Yaw, the Californian soprano now singing at the London Promenade Concert, sings the E in altissimo, an octave above the famous diva's highest note … Even with an octave knocked off Miss Yaw would have a voice of more than average range, for at present she can sing three octaves and a sixth, from G below the middle C to this E. She even confessed, in an unguarded moment, that she could go higher, but declined to give details. / Mozart once wrote with astonishment of a voice which was a third lower than Miss Yaw's, saying he could not have believed a voice could go so high had he not heard it.' [8 Dec. 1898: *North Otago Times*]

'The young California vocalist is an artiste. She has her limitations, because she has devoted herself to those bright birdlike vocal examples through the accident of possessing a particularly high clear voice. I cannot say that all her work was strictly founded on legitimate lines, but this I can assert[:] her general production was excellent. In the first place there is not the slightest trace of the vibrato in her voice. Her tone is clear, fresh, and infallibly sustained. This is mainly due to the excellent employment of the breath and definite methods as to facial influences. So perfectly does she use her breath, her command of tone becomes absolute. The most perfect of all her renderings, however, I was sorry to find, did not receive the recognition due, whereas little staccato runs founded upon something approaching tricky expedients passed muster for the true art. I have not heard for a long time a vocalist with the natural methods which so closely approximate to real art. W. H. BREARE.' [3 Sep. 1904: *Pateley Bridge & Nidderdale Herald*]

3.7.5 Ada Crossley [b. 1871]

'Miss Ada Crossley offered a pleasing contrast [to a preceding singer's indistinct delivery of the words] by her clear and simple rendering of Sainton Dolby's "Out on the Rocks". Miss Crossley possesses a contralto voice of good quality and moderate power, with distinct articulation.' [8 Apr. 1889: *Argus*, Melbourne]

'Australia was well represented, not only by Mrs. Palmer's pupils but by Miss Ada Crossley, a sweet contralto singer whom Gippsland has given to the world of music. Miss Crossley is still in her early twenties, and has a rich voice, full of organ-like notes. She is perhaps the best contralto Victoria has yet produced.' [29 Oct. 1892: *Sydney Mail*]

'Miss Ada Crossley, who has no rival amongst Australian contralti, was very happy in her version of Gounod's fine song, "The Worker". The absence of all apparent efforts in the production of her voice, and the full mellow richness of its quality are exceptionally attractive. There is no trace of the guttural hardness which is heard in the low notes of some very eminent contralto singers, but, instead, a calm ease and grace in their delivery which fascinate the hearer.' [1 Apr. 1893: *Sydney Mail*]

'Certainly the importations [English contraltos] have come to us in their decadence, yet none of them give evidence of ever having possessed a finer voice than our Australian songstress. The "Australian Patey", as she has been admiringly described, is very anxious to get to London.' [15 Jul. 1893: *Tasmanian*]

'Speaking of a concert recently given at the Erard Salle, a Paris correspondent says: "Among the 17 ladies who did credit to the Ecole Marchesi there was one star so conspicuous that special mention must be made of her. It was Miss Ada Crossley, the already famous Australian contralto. Her magnificent voice, faultless intonation, and deep-felt expression, won the admiration of everybody in the hall. The long sustained notes in 'In questa tomba', and her marvellous decrescendo, kept the audience spellbound".' [18 May 1895: MCLGA]

'Miss Ada Crossley, an Australian contralto, who was heard in Nottingham for the first time, created a notable impression. Her voice is round and firm in quality, and eminently powerful, and she evinces rare taste and refinement in her work.' [13 Dec. 1895: *Nottingham Evening Post*]

'… who may be congratulated on possessing one of the most exquisite voices ever heard. It is a pure contralto, not a loud, hard mezzo-soprano, forced downward, and in the present dearth of genuine contralto voices that of Miss Crossley ought to bring her fame and fortune.' [7 Nov. 1896: *Era*]

'Miss Ada Crossley made a deep impression by her singing of the chief contralto music, and has thereby, no doubt, won a deserved place among vocalists of the first rank in our country. Her voice is strong, resonant, and of excellent quality; her pronunciation is clear, and she sings with ease and much expression, but occasionally lapses slightly into the objectionable tremolo.' [14 Sep. 1897: *Bristol Times and Mirror*]

'Then there is the tall and stately Ada Crossley. The last time I heard her was in the choir of the Australian Church in Melbourne, but she became known also in Adelaide. She now has a full, strong, yet mellow voice, which filled better than any other during the evening that vast hall [Albert Hall, London]—by far the largest concert room in the world … Her contralto voice filled the hall finely; it was exquisitely sweet, though with a little excess of tremolo; but the song [piece by Gluck from *Orfeo* 'a little too severely classical'] fell flat.' [7 Dec. 1898: *South Australian Register*, London correspondent]

'Miss Ada Crossley, of London, who is making her first visit to this country, and sang here for the first time last evening. This was by far the best singing of the whole festival … Miss Crossley has one of those contraltos of the grand order, few of which are given to a single generation, and sings with a nobility, simplicity, and dignity befitting her magnificent organ. Rich, smooth, and ample in volume, unblemished by tremolo, yet not wanting in warmth, her voice might have been created especially to fit this grave and tender air of Handel's. No such oratorio contralto has been heard in this country in recent years.' [19 Apr. 1903: Spring]

'It is a voice of full and pure quality, round and velvety in timbre, and even throughout; not a "big" voice, perhaps, but assuredly not a small one. It is under perfect control, and is equally at home in cantabile and declamatory phrases, while it is used with consummate art, and, when occasion serves, vibrates with sympathy. The intonation is perfect, and—lest haply the last sentence may be misconstrued—there is no trace or hint of a tremolo from one end of the gamut to the other. High notes—from the contralto point of view—and low are equally beyond reproof, nor is there any suspicion of a "break". Moreover, the frequent failing of your "heavy" contralto—that of singing monotonously and relying for effect mainly or entirely on the beauty of the voice—is notably absent here. Miss Crossley feels what she sings, and makes others feel it too, and she can be lightsome and sprightly when the song calls for such treatment.' [5 Oct. 1903: *Punch*, Melbourne]

'Ada Crossley's contralto voice still retains its sympathetic and full timbre, entirely free from vibrato; indeed, time has dealt leniently with her, and there is no apparent defect of her powers observable.' [3 Feb. 1914: BDP]

3.8 Recorded Male Singers

3.8.1 Charles Santley [b. 1834]

'But in passages of execution Mr. Santley is deficient. His method of producing the voice, moreover, is not invariably legitimate; his power of sustaining notes of duration, without wavering in pitch, is at the best variable; and he should labour assiduously to get the better of a certain tremulousness which deteriorates from the quality of tone without bringing (as in the case of some of the best Italian singers) any equivalent advantage.' [9 Jan. 1858: T]

'His beautiful voice falls delightfully on the ear in the numerous passages in which they are called into requisition, whether alone or in concert with other voices. Had we any control over this admirable "organ", we should exercise it in drawing the "tremolo" stop a little less often. The best efforts are apt to become wearisome on frequent repetition.' [4 Jun. 1869: *Globe*]

'If the sentimental baritone with the "tremolo" increases amongst us at the present alarming rate we will soon have few singers who will be able to attempt in public this fine solo ['O! Ruddier than the cherry']. As it is, one seldom hears it performed with the perfection of phrasing and absence of strain that marked Mr Santley's interpretation.' [12 Nov. 1899: GH]

3.8.2 Victor Capoul [b. 1839]

'… and Capoul, of the Opéra Comique, is a veritable Apollo, the very beau ideal of a stage lover, and possesses a voice whose exquisite sweetness and purity are simply as indescribable as they are unsurpassable … A fat basso is well enough, and a certain amount of embonpoint in a baritone is pardonable, but alas for the tenor whose sweet tones proceed from the figure fashioned after the model of a beer-barrel!' [Feb. 1871: Lucy H Hooper, *Souvenirs of Song*, p. 162–3]

'To the average range of a high tenor voice, he adds a third register of "falsetto" notes of unusually agreeable quality. These he last night only called into requisition once or twice; but then with great effect. The quality of his first and second registers is a little metallic, as the quality of French voice is apt to be; but it is bright and penetrating, and, to all appearance, thoroughly under his control. His style is, if a trifle over-elaborated, thoroughly refined; and barring the frequent use of the *vibrato*, not unmanly.' [6 Jun. 1871: *Globe*]

'The operas of Meyerbeer, Halevy, and Verdi are for the most part so fatiguing for tenors, and the shouting and screaming style of singing has in late years so completely supplanted the refined vocalisation of the earlier Italian school, that the majority of our operatic tenors have rapidly injured their voices by overforcing, and have become unable to abstain from the tremolo which sapient advisers have recommended them to discontinue. There are some, however—and M. Capoul is one of these—who voluntarily introduce an artificial trembling of the voice, as an artistic embellishment. It must be admitted that in strongly pathetic situations it is quite natural that the voice of the singer should lose its firmness.' [28 Apr. 1877: ISDN]

'All the men quivered and wavered, so that at times it was impossible to tell what note they were singing. The only man we ever heard who could "seeth" and quiver continuously without being intolerable was Capoul, whose delicious voice alone saved him. One would really think, to hear these tremulous gentlemen night after night, that there was no one still alive who could remember [Antonio] Giuglini. That incomparable tenor sang with the firmness and smoothness of a clarinet, and always with the same striking effect.' [19 Jul. 1884: PMG]

3.8.3   Robert Watkin-Mills [b. 1849]

'Mills is an honest, hearty, straightforward, manly, Handelian bass of the good old sort … last, but not least, his complete freedom from the abominable tremolo.' [2 Feb. 1895: *North Wales Chronicle*]

'Mr Watkin Mills, the English basso, who visits us this month, evidently does not affect the tremolo. Speaking to an interviewer, he said: "I hate the wobble. It is a sign of a weak voice—a voice that has been strained beyond its powers. It is not tolerated in England, where the introduction of a tremolo stop into the voice means a slating. The colleges all preach against it, and to practise it means ruin. The voice that can't sing sustained notes won't last, not to mention the irritating effect it has on the ear. Vibrato is all right enough in its place, but a voice that's perpetually vibrating like a sail in the wind—oh, I've no use for the wobble at all! Neither has any singer or teacher of repute at Home. You don't hear singers like Melba, Ada Crossley, and [Antonia] Dolores wobble, do you? It's a peculiar thing that it's the national style of America—if a singer doesn't wobble, he or she is blamed for want of soul—the more you wobble the more soul you've got! It is a style cultivated to a painful extent by the German, French, and Italian schools, but it's not English. The cause of it? — generally speaking, I think it's due to straining the voice beyond its capacity to produce big tones, or it may be caused by taking too much breath into the lungs—it's mainly the former. Yes, I hate the wobble, for it's inartistic—not merely bad art, but no art at all. They don't get any wobble from me, you may be sure!".' [6 Aug. 1904: *Evening Post*, Auckland]

'His voice extends from low D to baritone F, and he can, if occasion demands it, reach low A, and although clear and telling, it is a pure bass in timbre. There is not a suspicion of vibrato, every word is enunciated with great distinctness.' [6 Oct. 1904: *Southland Times*, NZ]

3.8.4 Andrew Black [b. 1859]

'His voice was full, rich, and resonant as ever, and only in the Handelian aria ['Honour and Arms', *Samson*] was there any sign that the singer required to manage it with more than ordinary caution.' [6 Jan. 1890: GH]

'The principals are so well known that it is only necessary to say that Mr Andrew Black—heard here in oratorios for the first time—made a deep impression by his refined expressive singing and the purity of his intonation.' [23 Oct. 1890: LM]

'Mr Andrew Black, on the other hand, sang the part of "Elijah" not only with artistic fire and expression, but with an earnestness and high intelligence which place him now on a level with some of the best and most experienced singers of the day. His voice has gained in sweetness and expressive power, the method of production is natural and unstrained, and the singer gains steadily not only in artistic insight, but also in control over the means he has at his disposal. It is a very long time since in Glasgow the part of "Elijah" has been rendered with such fervour and refinement.' [17 Dec. 1890: GH]

'A very fine position of the part of the prophet was that of Mr. Andrew Black to-day. His voice, so rich in tone, sympathetic in quality, and so remarkably flexible, enabled him to do every justice to the vocal requirements of the part; whilst the fire and passion he infuses into the dramatic scenes lifts the whole conception to the highest artistic level. Moving, almost to tears, was his singing of "It is enough", and his declamation in the Baal scene was grand. Mr. Black, in the most exciting and dramatic situation, never forgets that Mendelssohn's music requires singing, and his whole performance was a great artistic triumph.' [11 Sep. 1895: BDP]

'It is indeed pleasurable to note conviction and sincerity in his every tone; imagination, fire, spontaneity, tenderness, versatility, instinct with atmosphere and temperament; beauty of vocal tone, ease and mastery with details, and an exquisite sense of finish and polish about every phrase— dramatic or lyrical as it demands—these are some of the qualities of Andrew Black's art, and go to make a charming and interesting man one of the finest baritones of the day.' [26 Jan. 1903: *Belfast Telegraph*]

'The last-named gave a fine all-round performance of the titular part. His voice is not less bright than it is flexible and sympathetic, and he was able to pourtray and emphasise each aspect of the character of the stern prophet, yet tender-hearted man, as they were presented in the progress of the work. The scene where the widow's son is restored to life was sustained with pathos as well as dignity, and fine dramatic power was evidenced in the Baal scene, the noble scorn with which the Baal priests were invited to commence their invocations, and the change in demeanour when Elijah says, "Draw near all ye people, come to me!" being striking incidents of a great performance. "Is not his Word" lacked something in effect, owing to the lower range of the singer's voice being less powerful than the upper. "It is enough" was touching in the extreme. There was the "tear" in the note without weak sentimentality. "For the mountains shall depart" was an equally fine performance, and Mr. Black deserves commendation for adhering to the proper scanning of the words.' [13 Oct. 1903: BDP]

'His voice is of exceptional quality, round, and flexible, and of extensive compass, reaching as high as

G in the upper notes and as low as D in the chest series, while he has that rarest of vocal attainments, a pure and well-balanced legato, not the slightest suspicion of vibrato, and last, but not least, every word is enunciated with delightful clearness. In the scale passages his voice moves evenly and distinctly, and the sustained intervals are given with breadth and dignity, never breathless, never heavy; to hear his legato alone is a study in finished vocalisation.' [29 May 1906: AuckS]

[quotation from the London *Times*, date unspecified] 'Mr. Black produces a pure even tone, and has a perfect control over his voice. His compass is from the low D in the upper G from our own testing, but Mr Black prefers it from low F to upper G—the true baritone range, and we admire him for it, although we could find no fault with the lower tones...One never notices his breathing, he has that most desirable and valuable power of using the "mezza voce" with undiminished breadth; he can always call up a little bit extra without showing the end of his resources. He keeps a fine, firm hold of his notes, and, like a true British artist, despises the tremolo.' [9 Oct. 1906: *Camperdown Chronicle*, Victoria]

4 Descent from Default Straight Voice to Permanent Vibrato

4.1 The Introduction of Tremolo and Vibrato

As I've shown in Section 2, although vocal tremolo/vibrato was admired during the long eighteenth century as an intentional or expressive effect, it was unknown as a permanent feature of vocal sound. So, the key question is this: When did it first come in? I've addressed this issue before, in an article prepared for the proceedings of the 2009 singing conference run by NEMA with the University of York.[32]

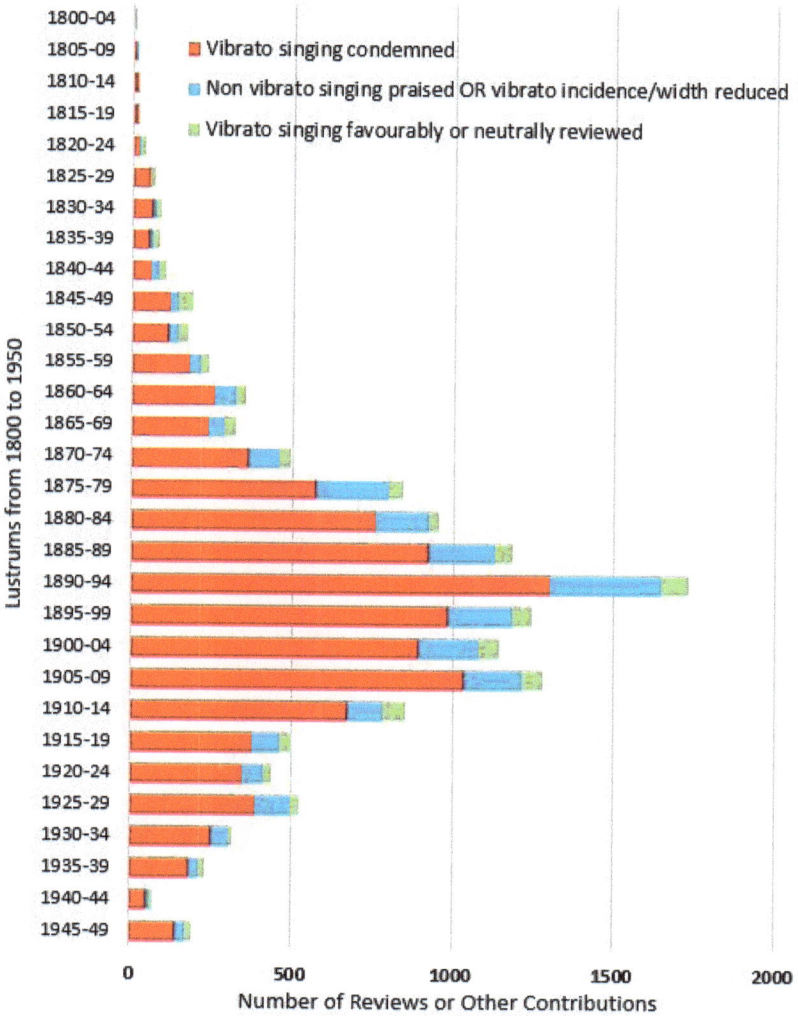

Illus. 46: Views of 19th/20th-Century Reviewers on Tremolo/Vibrato

---

32   *Singing* music from 1500 to 1900: style, technique, knowledge, assertion, experiment, 7–10 July 2007.

I have since re-scoped my research by: (1) including more sources, (2) adding data on the identities, careers and vocal characteristics of the singers, both 'tremoloists' and 'straight toners', (3) extending the period covered to 1949, and (4) reviewing what critics thought about vibrato and why they hated it so much. To start, I looked top-down at 13,670 reviews, mostly of named singers. Illus. 46 shows the number of sources identified in each lustrum (5-year period), broken down into 3 categories. Note the preponderance of uncomplimentary notices (red bars), which account for 76% of the total over the whole 150-year period. 17% of notices (blue bars) praise non- or reduced vibrato singing. Only 7% (green bars) report on vibrato in favourable or neutral terms.

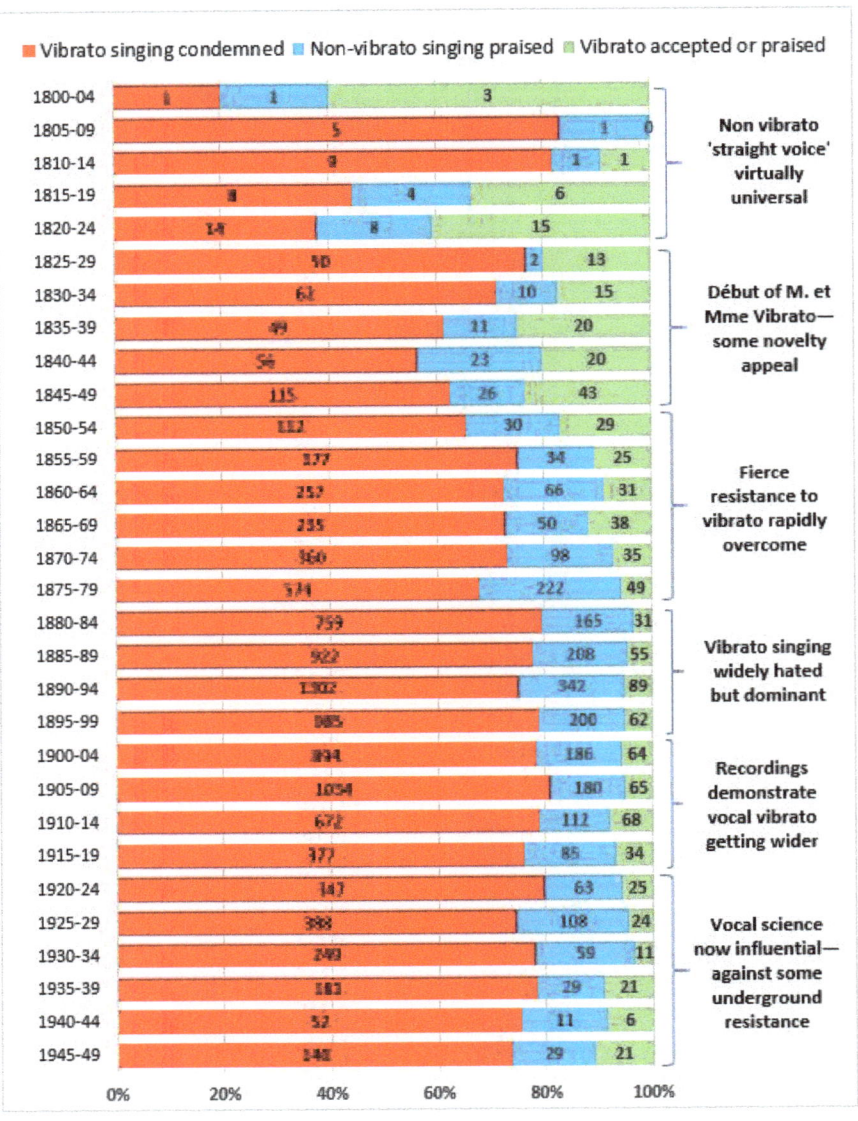

Illus. 47: Stages of Tremolo/Vibrato Introduction

I then look at the same numbers in percentage terms [Illus. 47], over six periods., with analysis and examples similarly grouped. The division into periods is not hard and fast, given that tremolo/vibrato only grew gradually from 1825 onwards.

4.2   Universal Straight Voice (1800 to 1825)

As Illus. 47 shows, only two or three notices on tremolo appeared in each year during the first 20 years of the century. Clearly, any tremolo singing which occurred, produced by just a few singers, wasn't registering with the musical public as a trend. I've already included in Section 2 examples of tremolo used as an expressive effect. There are very few descriptions of unintentional tremolo or vibrato; some are listed below:

> 'Some of her lower notes [Elizabeth Billington] were rather tremulous at the commencement of the Opera; but this circumstance must be attributed to her emotions on again coming forward as a candidate for public favour after so long an interval.' [5 Oct. 1801: T]

I've already quoted Edgcumbe's reference to Giuseppe Siboni's 'thick and tremulous voice [p. 118]

> 'A new Singer, named Smith, from the Liverpool Theatre, appeared on Wednesday as Lorenzo, in the miserable puppet-shew of the Cabinet. He has considerable power, and occasional melodiousness of voice, but his tones are uncertain and wavering. The ear may detect this deficiency, when he endeavours to hold a high note, for he drops unconsciously through a number of divided tones. His appearance is fat, and, if I may use the expression, his voice is so too; it possesses that sort of inward oiliness, which would induce a blind man to suppose the singer a very jolly personage. He is at a great distance from [Charles] Incledon and from [James] Hill, but he met with great encouragement, and may become a good subordinate singer.' [24 Jan. 1808: Ex]

> 'His voice [Signor Miarteni] is a base, possessing great firmness and power, and peculiarly well adapted for taking a part in the compositions for many voices, with which the Italian Operas abound. In songs it is harsh, and has an unpleasant nasal sound, and a rattling effect, which would almost make me imagine that he in some degree imitated Demosthenes, and sung with pebbles in his throat.' [5 June 1808: Ex]

> 'The powers of this exquisite singer [Elizabeth Billington], whose last season is now running, seem in no way impaired by age, except that her voice gets a little reedy.' [19 May 1810: Tl]

I've referred [p. 46] to the reediness of Maria Dickons's voice.

> 'In 1815 a Signor GENI made his debut in Adelasia. His voice was somewhat too weak for the King's, "but this singer has obvious qualities which give the best compensation for power—his taste is delicate, his execution finished, and that general spirit of the Italian School thrown over his talent, without which vigour of organ is violence and weariness". The Chronicle thought him "a very fine tenor". But five months later, "the tremulous tones of Geni were but indifferent vehicles of the rage of the headstrong and silly Emperor".' [Fenner, *Opera in London*, p. 321]

'On her entrance was greeted with the enthusiastic applause of the house, but whether from the emotion excited by this zealous welcome, or that she had not yet possessed herself of that confidence she [Miss Byrne] is so well entitled to feel in her powers, the first song, "Virgins are like the Fair Flower in its Lustre", was executed in a tremulous tone, which, though appropriate enough to the sentiments expressed in the poetry, was evidently not the result of intention.' [5 Jul. 1817: MP]

Charles Lamb's description in one of his *Essays of Elia* suggests that Mrs Blacket's voice, as well as being a novel oddity, featured a wide pitch vibrato: 'The shake, which most fine singers reserve for the close or cadence, by some unaccountable flexibility, or tremulousness of pipe, she carrieth quite through the composition; so that her time, to a common air or ballad, keeps double motion, like the earth—running the primary circuit of the tune, and still revolving upon its own axis. The effect, as I said before, when you are used to it, is as agreeable as it is altogether new and surprising.' [1822: LMag]

'In Handel's "Holy Lord" that far surpassed any of her former exertions; her intonation was generally in this song perfect; and her enunciation clear and distinct: several times she brought to my mind the dulcet notes of Mrs. Salmon, the Syren of the English Orchestra—Mrs. Holman also sang "Comfort ye my people", the opening recitative and air of the Messiah—This, however, is not adapted to her voice—and though pleasingly sung, yet it naturally produced a reediness in many notes that was disagreeable.' [28 Feb. 1823: Eut]

'His notes [John Sinclair] are often wiry, vibrating, and tremulous; resembling rather the chords of a musical instrument than the full and animated sounds of a human voice.' [30 Nov. 1823: *Lancet*]

A Mr Benson's singing was dismissed: 'He has evidently musical knowledge, but neither his voice nor his style are likely to secure to him much success as a theatrical singer: The former has a ceaseless tremor, and the latter is marked by a mouthing delivery.' [3 Sep. 1828: MP]

I suggested in my earlier paper that Anna Maria Tree was the first professional tremoloist. She arrived on the London scene in 1819, concluding on marriage after a short professional career. Here are some of her reviews:

'Her voice is not at all powerful; but it is perfectly clear and sweet in the upper notes, and some of the lower ones have a fine, rich glowing tone— like the musical murmur of the honey-bee … Her execution is laboured and difficult to herself—and therefore it gives neither pleasure nor surprise. But when she trusts to simplicity and nature, which she really appears to do as much as the present state of musical taste will permit her, there is a purity and sweetness of expression about her singing that is quite delightful.' [30 Oct. 1819: *Blackwood's Edinburgh Magazine*]

'Miss Greene's voice [as Polly], which is not always the case, is very good in speaking as well as in singing. It is of excellent quality, round without fatness, powerful without being harsh, clear, flowing and equable throughout. If it may not be able to go so low as Miss Tree's, it falls into the lower tones without such a marked difference of body between those and the upper. If not so fine as Miss Stephens's, it is richer. Miss Tree's voice is like a bottle of cordial with a long neck to it; Miss Stephens's like one fine-drawn pipe of chrystal; Miss Greene's is cast like the latter, but more weighty. We make these comparisons however, not invidiously or ungratefully, but for the sake of what the reader expects in the way of explanation. The three vessels have all their own merits, and pour wine and oil upon our hearts.' [24 Sep. 1820: Ex]

'The tone of her voice [Anna Maria Tree] is delicious. There is a peculiar reediness in its low notes, (one is really obliged to coin words in describing such indescribable things), which would enable my ear to distinguish it among a thousand others.' [Dec. 1823: *Knight's Quarterly Magazine*]

'This effect, moreover is greatly heightened by the fascinating quality (timbre) of her voice [Bonini], in which there are some beautiful notes of the sweetest tremulousness that vibrate to the heart of the hearer. It was a similar quality of tone which proved irresistibly sweet in Miss Tree's voice, and rendered her singing more effective than that of a rival of greater professional skill.' [31 May 1826: NMM]

'She [Anna Maria Tree] did not improve on our good opinion. She is very much like Mr. Thorne, of the English Opera House. Similar face, especially as far as its more prominent feature is concerned; a similarly unfinished and rather repulsive style of singing; and certainly not much more melodious notes. They are indeed rather harsh and wiry.' [27 Sep. 1826: *Morning Advertiser*]

'Her voice is powerful, but in its middle tones thin and wiry.' [1 Oct 1826: Ex]

'Miss A. Tree sung Tenero aggetto—her voice is like a knife scraping a plate.' [2 Jun. 1827: Waldie]

Taking all the reports together, her voice was reedy (1 report), tremulous (1 report), wiry (2 reports), but also like the murmur of a honey bee or a knife scraping a plate. These reviews suggest that Tree emitted a rapid tremolo, probably with little if any pitch fluctuation, occurring frequently but not continuously in her lower notes. Sarah Potter cited Martyn Stewart ['Honey Bee', *The Sound of Critters: Bird and Animal Sounds Across the Planet*] in support of her idea that 'Although the honeybee can change the pitch of its sound, its general effect is not of pitch oscillation, but rather undulation of intensity upon the same pitch.' [2014: Sarah Potter, *Changing Vocal Style*, p. 76]

4.3   Innovating Tremoloists (1825 to 1855)

A rival claim as the first tremoloist could be made in respect of Signora Bonini. While most of her reviews were pejorative, she was praised by New Monthly Magazine:

'The King's Theatre opened for the season on the 7th of January, with Meyerbeer's "Il Crociato in Egitto", in which Signora Bonini appeared for the first time in England, in the character of Palemida. Her voice would have been full, clear, and well regulated, if it did not possess a tremulousness, the effect of weakness, and it had not great compass or flexibility.' [Jan. 1826:

Parke, *Musical Memoir*]

> 'Madame Bonini [as Palmide] is the venerable remains of a very excellent singer; but her voice has begun to lose its firmness, and to quiver with the symptoms of age.' [15 Jan. 1826: Ex]

> 'It is half piteous, half ludicrous to see (we don't mention hearing) her sing. The severe struggle with which she draws a thin and wiry note ab imo pectore[33], and the awkward pain with which she delivers herself of it, can only be likened to one operation in nature. She obviously labours under a vocal constipation.' [Mar. 1826: LMag]

> 'Her voice is sufficiently powerful in point of volume, and is extensive in compass, but when she uses it to its full extent there is a tremulousness which indicates a want of strength in the organ, and which is the great drawback from the excellence of her performance.' [30 Apr. 1826: QMMR]

> 'This [intensity of feeling] is the case with Mademoiselle Bonini: there is an internal enthusiasm which animates her vocal performance; it is only through the medium of sounds she seems to feel deeply, and affects our feelings powerfully. This effect, moreover is greatly heightened by the fascinating quality (timbre) of her voice, in which there are some beautiful notes of the sweetest tremulousness that vibrate to the heart of the hearer …' [May 1826: NMM]

Histories invariably cite tenor Giovanni Battista Rubini as the singer who invented vibrato, in the mid 1830s. But it seems that wiggle-voiced[34] ladies were there first, by a decade or so. Bonini and Tree were succeeded by Mesdames Feron, Schutz, Henriette Méric-Lalande, and Katharina Sigl-Vespermann, as suggested by the following reviews:

> 'Her voice [Madame Feron, Mrs Glossop], however, but too clearly manifests the injurious tendency of over-exertion: the tone lacks quality—that fullness and that brilliancy, which the Italians denominate metallo, or perhaps, more definitely, purezza argentina. Madame Feron can sing soft, or she can pour fourth a swelling body of tone; but the intermediate quantity upon which the artist must rely for general use, is not at her command. Her mezzo forte is infirm and tremulous; reminding us of the defect of Signora Bonini, and conveying the notion of the coming on of age.' [Jul. 1827: QMMR]

> 'The great drawback upon her singing [Madame Schutz] was an occasional infirmity in the sustaining power, not unlike, though not to the same extent, as the trembling of voice observed in Mademoiselle Bonini.' [Jan. 1828: QMMR, p. 72]

> 'Her voice [Madame Schutz] is very pleasing and powerful, not, as has been asserted, a contr'alto, but a soprano, and of good quality, excepting an occasional tremor like that in Mrs Feron's; though we should be sorry for a moment to confound the fine feeling and judgment of one with the vulgar, common-place trumpery of the other, who seems to have no sense of anything in music higher than noise and perpetual motion.' [9 Mar. 1828: Ex]

---

33 From the bottom of my heart
34 'Wiggle-voiced' was a favourite term used by the Diarist contributing to *Dwight's Journal of Music*.

'In the lower notes of her voice and also in her tremula, she [Madame Schutz] not unfrequently reminds us of Catalani.' [16 Apr. 1828: MP]

'The fair débutante's appearance [Henriette Méric-Lalande], though somewhat passé, is tolerable; but, with considerable facility of execution, her voice is deficient in strength and firmness; in fact, it has a tremulousness, either natural or brought on by over exertion, which greatly impairs its general effect. In declamation, too—for recitative is declamation—she is rather defective.' [17 Apr. 1830: LBA]

'Her voice [Katharina Sigl-Vespermann] has a shrillness, and also a tremulous quality in its lower notes, which counteract in a great degree the charm that its high cultivation and her good taste would otherwise impart to her singing.' [28 Feb. 1831: T]

Henriette Méric-Lalande also received a scathing review from Maria Malibran, daughter of Manuel García, a famous but rather jealous rival. The opera was probably performed in May 1830. As a drama queen herself, Maria brings the scene to life.

'I went to the opera with Lady Flint, her husband, and her daughter; and having taken my seat and adjusted my *lorgnette*, I impatiently awaited the entrance of the Pirato, who was represented by Donzelli. / The overture commenced. Humph! very so so. It is not effective. The curtain rose. The opening scene was pretty, and was loudly applauded. Dramatic authors and composers know how much they owe to the scene-painter. / Enter Il Pirato. He blustered, and strutted about, sang loudly, enchanted the audience, and was clapped. In acknowledgement of the applause, Donzelli bowed at least thirty times, and continued bowing until he was actually behind the side-scenes. / The first air was tolerable. / Change of scene. / Venga la belle Itáliana, said I to my little self. I was all impatience, and as she appeared I stretched over the box to catch a glimpse of her. Alas! what a disappointment! Picture to yourself a woman of about forty, with light hair and a vulgar broad face, with an unfavourable expression, a bad figure, as clumsy a foot as my own, and most unbecomingly dressed. / The recitative commenced. Her voice trembled so, that none could find out whether it was sweet or harsh. I therefore waited patiently for the cavatina. It commenced, and the prima donna opened her mouth with a long tremulous note. / Concluding that this arose from timidity, I could not help pitying her. But, alas! the undulating tones of her voice continued throughout, and utterly spoiled the pretty cavatina. At its conclusion she was vociferously applauded, and made a thousand curtsies, which is the custom in London. Next came the beautiful duet. In this she was just as cold and tremulous as before. In a word, not to weary you with a long account of each morçeau, she finished her part in the same bad style in which she began it. / [She concludes:] I have discovered that this tremulous style is Madame Lalande's constant habit of singing. It is her fashion—immovable, fixed, eternal! You may therefore guess how well our voices are likely to blend together—two and two, like *three* goats. Her middle notes are wiry, and have a harsh and shrill effect.' [May 1830: *Monthly Review*, 'Memoirs of Madame Malibran, by the Countess de Merlin and Other Intimate Friends']

Awareness of tremolo singing grew steadily amongst the musical public during this period, with favourable or neutral reviews relatively high, at around 20%. The sheer novelty of tremolo/vibrato singing had some appeal, which was occasionally recognised at the time. It was obviously new to the music critic of *The Caledonian Mercury*:

> 'The long shake and undulation of the voice [John Templeton] at the end of the line, "We hail her with three cheers", is quite a new feature, and produced a startling effect.' [19 Nov. 1838: CM]

However, tremolo singers were as yet too few to be a threat to the established order. This is apparent from the charts at Annex A listing female singers, both straight vocalists and the new breed of tremoloists. The equivalent data for male singers are at Annex B. Note that a few start as straight toners but finish as tremoloists; I have made this assumption based on the year in which mention is first made of the singer's tremor, reediness, wiriness, tremulousness or tremolo.

The term 'vibrato' was rare at this time, receiving only occasional mentions starting from around 1835. The terms 'tremulous', 'tremolo', 'tremulando' and 'vibrato' were synonymous until the end of the century, when reviewers started to distinguish between the terms used. Except in a few cases, it is impossible to be certain whether a singer's tremolo was a pitch waver or an emphasis fluctuation; I return to this point later.

Note also that the term 'vibrato', also described as 'vibrazione', 'voce vibrato', or 'voce vibrata', can mean something different at this time, viz. a type of sforzando on individual notes. I won't expand on this type of use, given that this is more an aspect of style than vocal sound. **Robert Toft** covers it in his *Bel Canto* [2013]. However, I've included three examples of Mario's 'voce vibrata' in Section 3.6.17 above.

Focussing on innovating male tremoloists, a couple of early notices on Giovanni Battista Rubini were both uncomplimentary:

> 'The great blow struck by Rubini was on the hearts of the ladies, by the introduction of a tremor on his voice; and when *"La Sonnambula"* was in its zenith, I had the pleasure of hearing him sing the great *tenor scene* on the Italian stage, which I think Mr. Wood first sang in America. Nothing could be more heart-broken and touching than the *tremor* so used; and I admired him with the most fervent of the *Rubinists*. The next performance heard was *"Anna Boleyna"*; he there used the *tremor*, beautifully, but I thought a little *de trop*. I could not understand, in his moments of indignant feeling, why his voice should be tremulous, when the sentiment called for firmness. Shortly after, an opportunity occurred of hearing him sing the Trumpet duet from *Tancredi*, with Malibran, on the occasion of some benefit; and to my complete disgust, he did not hold one firm note from beginning to end. The opera of *"La Gazza Ladra"* gave us his first joyous song with a tremulous voice; and, in short, all his various *morceaux*, in all his parts, were executed in that manner. Where strong passion does not exist, the effect is that of an elderly gentleman with a touch of the palsy, warbling a war-song, or amorous ditty. That which was originally a great beauty, and, in his best days, was used occasionally by Braham, has become now a serious defect in Rubini; for, by constant use of this *tremor*, he cannot hold one firm

note.' [29 Sep. 1838: MusR]

'His vocal organ, indeed, bears marks of the wear and tear of thirty years' unremitting labour. Its fulness and firmness of tone are impaired; and a long-drawn, simple note, finely swelled and sustained, cannot be enumerated in the list of his beauties of execution; but nothing can exceed the skill with which he covers this defect. The very tremulousness which he cannot help is converted by him into a means of expression; while his prolonged notes are decorated with such a graceful and delicate embroidery, that we cease to regret the absence of still more graceful simplicity.' [26 Aug. 1841: MC]

The baritone Antonio Tamburini is an example of a singer who débuted with a straight voice but morphed into a tremoloist with age:

'His voice is a fine baritone, well defined, extending from A to F, occasionally reaching G♯, and sometimes descending to G♭. I might have allotted to him the two full octaves without reserve, but I prefer to retrench the semitone, above and below, that I may give to his voice and tone the full praise it merits. It is round, rich, and clear, of wonderful flexibility, and such astonishing firmness, that it is impossible to suspect any note is passed over unperceived. He has the neatness and precision of execution that Ber and Barizel have acquired on the clarionet or bassoon. The tone is equal in its whole extent, taking and holding F♯ with as much ease as a tenor voice would do, or running over the notes with a vivacity unheard of till now.' [May 1833: Har, quoted from Castil-Blaze]

'That Tamburini is damaged by time is proved by the increased tremulousness of his voice, and here and there an uncertainty. But the qualities which formerly gave him the appellative of the "Rubini of bass singers", are still in existence, and he still displays that flexibility and adroit portamento, the polish, freedom, and variety which have given him such large credit not only here, but everywhere else.' [7 Apr. 1847: Std]

Here are reviews on Signor Pantaleoni [a student and protegé of Rubini] and the bass Luciano Fornasari:

'Imitation [by Pantaleoni] of his maestro, although servile—for he favours us with the vibrato—is not unpleasing.' [10 Aug. 1836: MP]

'He [Luciano Fornasari] possessed a very handsome face, a sufficient voice, though its quality was not pleasant … The tremulous quality of his voice (that vice of young Italy, bad schooling, and false notions of effect), became more monotonous and tiresome than the coldest placidity could have been.' [Dec. 1843: Chorley, *Recollections*, Vol. 1, p. 221]

Enrico Tamberlik was one of the most famous early vibratoists. Reviews of his voice have been included at section 3.6.18. Critics generally approved of his singing, although they often had reservations about his voice:

'But Tamberlik—the glorious Tamberlik! … I don't like the constant tremulousness of his voice; it is a defect in him as in Rubini; but what singers they are in spite of their defects! Tamberlik is not perfection—he is not equal to Mario—but, all deductions made, he is the second tenor in Europe, and one who really does transport his audience.' [12 Apr. 1851: *Leader*]

'The richness of his tones, accompanied by that peculiar "vibrato", which, after some discussion, has been accepted not merely as a peculiarity, but (when under entire control, as now) a beauty, gave additional effect to his large and finished style of phrasing.' [29 Mar. 1852: T]

4.4   Fierce Resistance to Tremolo Singing Overcome (1855 to 1880)

In this phase the innovators were followed by numerous imitators. From the late 1840s, and increasingly through and following the 1850s, reviewers reported that continuous tremolo was becoming common, as per examples below. The number of favourable or neutral reviews on vibrato singing fell sharply, and critical notices on vibratoists came thick and fast.

I'll now discuss the voices of two singers of interest from the definitional angle, Anna de La Grange and Maria Spezia-Aldighieri. Here are some reviews of Anna's voice:

'Her low notes are rich and reedy.' [12 May 1855: *Dwight's*]

'A troublesome tremolo, almost amounting to a shake, marred the effects of all the slow and sustained passages, indicating, it would seem, that Mme. Lagrange's voice is not exerted with impunity.' [22 May 1855: NYT]

'But it is more than a merely sweet and flexible organ; if it resemble an instrument, it is not the flute, for it has a certain rich and reedy quality, an expressive coloring varying throughout its compass like a clarinet, or even like the most expressive of instruments, the violin.' [16 Jun 1855: *Dwight's*]

'… but it is in the pure sunshine of the upper octave, in exquisitely finished birdlike ornaments, in soft staccato passages, where each note shines with the soft pure lustre of a pearl, that she [Anna de La Grange] delights to revel with a wondrous freedom and perfection of grace … One fault she has, however, in her singing, in common with too many singers of the day, and in so remarkable a degree, that only all her excellencies and various fascinations make it tolerable; and that is the trick of an incessant tremolo,—what our "Diarist" has quaintly called the "wiggle" of the voice.' [8 Nov. 1856: *Dwight's*]

'… shows more signs of decay in this kind of music than any other. The pulsation in the voice, when the tone is to be sustained, is painful. Some call it a tremolo, but that is not the right name for it. It is not rapid enough for the tremolo, but is a quick pulsation, the result of an effort to produce a steady, prolonged sound with vocal organs that are worn out.' [2 Jan. 1858: *Dwight's*]

I'll turn now to Maria Spezia-Aldigieri's voice:

'A perpetual vibrato—that besetting sin of a large proportion of singers of every clime—disguises the real quality of her organ …' [18 Apr. 1857: MusG].

'One drawback, however, appeared obvious—the uniform tremulousness of voice in which she indulged, as much, it appeared to us, from affectation as from any natural defect in the firmness of her vocal organ.' [22 Aug 1857: *Leeds Times*]

'That Spezia is an accomplished and artistic vocalist, cannot be denied, but nature has not gifted her with a good voice. Instead of being either round, rich or full, it is of a reedy sharp and grating quality (which is more perceptible in her forte notes, both in the mezza soprano and soprano, than in the piano), although it possesses sufficient flexibility. In the performance of operas the harsh quality of the voice may in all probability be less perceptible, but it is a voice far from pleasing in such a room as the Music Room of the Pavilion. She gave the celebrated cavatina, "Una voce", in a manner that displayed her artistic skill, and in some of the subdued passages of her singing there was considerable sweetness of tone, but in all her outbursts that harshness of voice was unmistakeable.' [8 Apr 1858: BG]

'Madlle. Spezia's upper tones are hopelessly worn, while she can hardly sustain a note, high or low, for any lengthened period, without degenerating into that "tremolo" (St. Verdi's dance?) which is the Nemesis of so many fine voices and promising singers.' [10 Jul. 1858: LG]

Anna de La Grange was criticised on 13 occasions for tremolo, tremulousness or wiggle, twice for reediness and once for her 'quick pulsation'. Maria Spezia-Aldigieri was faulted twice for vibrato, five times for tremulousness, and twice for reediness. I conclude that all these descriptions amount to the same thing. Interestingly, there are very few reports of reediness after 1858, but a huge number of comments on vibrato or tremolo.

I append further reviews of tremoloing females, including instances of expressive use.

'Of these, two only are analogous in quality of voice—[Balbina] Steffanone and [Teresa] Truffi … The same imperfection is revealed by one and the other, which is an inequality more or less sensible in her finer notes, and a slight tremulousness (tremolo) of the larynx, which a though very effective in certain impassioned movements, becomes a defect when involuntarily produced in a recitative; which should be given in a round and full volume of sound.' [28 Mar. 1849: *Times-Picayune*]

'Her higher notes [Anna Zerr] tremulous and a little uncertain.' [5 Jan. 1853: MG]

'Madame Doria made much too frequent use of the tremolo, which appears at present to be so fearfully in fashion.' [27 Jul. 1853: MG]

'… although it is to be regretted that she [Giuseppina Medori] makes such a constant (and, we fear, involuntary) use of the tremolo, which would be effective in so rich and powerful a voice as hers were it only heard occasionally.' [4 Apr. 1863: *Dwight's*]

'… and her voice [Lucy Escott], a high soprano, is remarkably clear and flexible, with that vibrating quality which conduces greatly to expression. Her intonation is beautifully true, and her execution and style are those of a highly accomplished artist.' [3 Jul. 1855: DN]

'But for that modern nuisance in vocalism—the constant tremolo—which Miss [Elise] Hensler was forced to learn when in Italy, her rendering of the song would have been nearly faultless.' [19 Dec. 1855: *Dwight's*]

'We ... express the hope that this distinguished singer [Constance Nantier-Didiée], will not fall into the error, becoming too common now, as a *genre*, of indulging in the *tremolo*. Admirable as this is in passages requiring pathetic and intense expression, it is a decided defect when it is so often used as to become permanently characteristic of a voice.' [20 Apr. 1857: *Evening Star*]

'Her voice [Angiolina Ortolani-Tiberini] is somewhat hard and unsympathetic in quality, besides being affected by a constant tremulousness, the reverse of agreeable. Her method is not of the best, and in the expression of impassioned passages she betrayed a tendency to scream, which made us wince a little.' [29 Apr. 1857: MP]

'In the pathetic portion of her rôle, commencing with the second act, she depends too much upon the vibrato style of singing for awaking the sympathies of her audience; Madame [Angiolina] Bosio's voice is not unsympathetic, and she might, at least occasionally, dispense with this very redundant and tiresome proceeding, without risk of diminishing effect. Putting a "tremulant" on the voice would appear to be quite a fashion, for we have had to complain of it seriously this season in two other vocalists of consideration—Madame Spezia and Mdlle. [Angiolina] Ortolani-Tiberini.' [23 May 1857: MusG]

'Her chief faults are, shaking her voice (tremolo), and occasionally screaming a bit; she [Frau Róza Csillag] has the very common habit of letting her voice loose to bring down the house, just as almost all the Italian singers do.' [10 Dec. 1859: *Dwight's*]

'Her voice [Adelaide Borghi-Mamo] is impaired; mostly tremulous: —often out of tune. Her execution is thoroughly defective. She comes as a singer at a long interval after Mesdames [Pauline] Viardot, [Marietta] Alboni, and Nantier-Didiée, and such pleasure as she gave seemed to us merely because her performance was a shade less frantic than that of Mdlle. [Thérèse] Tietjens or Signor [Antonio] Giuglini, who seemed to be in due which could out-shout the other.' [21 Apr. 1860: Ath]

'... has a fresh clear voice of considerable compass and flexibility, and she [Euphrosine Parepa Rosa] displays in her style the result of good tuition and considerable study. There is at times a tendency towards the excessive use of "tremolo".' [2 May 1860: *Liverpool Daily Post*]

'[Rosina] Penco with a delicious organ, is wiggle-voiced, so that she afforded me but very little pleasure; but oh! [Giovanni Matteo] Mario and Alboni! Those pure, flowing, grand tones—when Verdi gave any opportunity for them to employ them! 'Tis wonderful. The Alboni sort of voice is of all the most charming to me. The deep full tones are so full of feeling— so passionate—they flow down in the heart so luxuriantly.../I never heard Mario before and whether he was in good or bad voice, I do not know,—but [Joseph] Tichatschek at Dresden is the only tenor I have heard, who approaches him.' [2 Feb. 1861: *Dwight's*]

'Throughout the opera this lady's acting [Marie Caroline Miolan-Carvalho] was so chaste, so easy and natural, that audience and actors were alike fascinated. Her intonation was, as heretofore, faultless, and her delivery fluent and without any traces of art. "Caro nome" was warbled with a grace impossible to describe, and the duet afterwards with [Giorgio] Ronconi appealed unmistakeably to the finest feelings of the house. The effect of her upper notes seems as great as ever, but the use of the tremolo is a defect which, on this occasion, seemed a little too apparent.' [14 Apr. 1861: *Bell's Life in Sydney*]

'I think the young lady [Pauline Lucca] must be warned against using a capricious "vibrato".' [27 Apr. 1861: MW]

'Some of her contralto notes [Hermine Rudersdorff] were worthy of Alboni, her upper register was equally good, and the close shake at the end of the song was really a marvellous piece of execution.' [19 Sep. 1861: BG]

'Her singing [Antoinetta Fricci], always earnest, if occasionally exaggerated in style and faulty in execution, would be still most expressive if she could divest herself of that fatal "vibrato", which is the Nemesis of so many dramatic vocalists of the present era.' [4 Jun. 1862: *Brighton Guardian*]

'She [Josefa Gassier] indulges, and indeed always did, in a perpetual tremolo style of singing which is not agreeable, while her articulation is so indistinct that it is wellnigh impossible to tell in what language she may be singing. One faculty she possesses in a rare degree, that of a rapid and brilliant shake.' [22 Nov. 1862: EEC]

'[Ilma de Murska] in the course of training, has picked up a decided leaning to the fashionable vibrato that afflicts so many of our opera singers, and against which the Examiner has protested again and again for some years past.' [3 Jun. 1865: Ex]

'... her voice [Ida Gillies] is a clear soprano, of good compass, ranging from about the lower to the upper C, and of sweet tone, except in the highest notes (which sound rather hollow and screamy); that she is fluent in the execution of florid music, doing better in that than in the cantabile style; and that she possesses the vibrato in all the perfection of its ugliness. If she could subdue this fault—which is perhaps more than can be expected of a singer who has evidently taken special pains to cultivate the nuisance—she would be a really pleasant singer of music of the Opera Comique school.' [18 Nov. 1865: *Reader*]

'Madame [Janet Monach] Patey[-Whytock] gave the contralto music with ruthful expression, making much of the air "O thou that tellest", which few singers ever make effective. There was something too much of the tremolo in "He was despised".' [26 Dec. 1868: MCLGA]

'She [Anna Régan] made too free a use of the "tremolo", which is effective only when sparingly employed, and as a rule is much better avoided.' [29 Mar. 1869: MP]

'... performance [by Clara Louise Kellogg] was vocally thin, weak in expression, and marred by a frequent indulgence in tremolo which is among the more glaring and annoying proofs of the singer's decadence.' [28 Feb. 1870: Brook]

'[Christine] Nilsson appeared in other selections, of an operatic nature, and demonstrated the fact that she is a good—but not great—artist. Her upper notes from E flat to B flat are clear and bell-like in their purity, while her lower notes are not remarkable, some of them being somewhat nasal. She makes excessive use of the tremolo.' [5 Jan. 1871: *Independent Democrat*]

'Mrs. Cordner's singing is too well known to need comment, further than to point out that the artificial tremolo which she uses at all times decidedly impairs the effect of a really fine voice. Some few singers possessed this quality naturally, as, for instance, Madame Malibran, Madame Bosio, and Catherine Hayes; they used it without effort, and in passages of deep feeling it was undoubtedly effective.' [15 Apr. 1871: *Sydney Mail*]

'Mdlle. [Pauline] Rita has a voice nearly always in tune, but of a shrill and unsympathetic quality, and she indulges from time to time in that fatal vibrato to which we have so often objected.' [23 Oct. 1872: GH]

'… in many respects very satisfactory, and would have been completely so but for the unfortunate, and at times absolutely distressing, tremolo which disfigures her singing [Anna D'Angeri].' [13 May 1873: *Academy*]

'As Gilda and Lady Henrietta she [Alwina Valleria] did not show herself worthy of a place among the great prime donne. Her execution is marred by the constant vibrato, and is jerky and unfinished, nor is her voice always to be depended upon.' [31 Jul. 1873: *Illustrated Review*]

'Her voice [Marie Roze] is a singularly pure and bright soprano though she is not quite free from the vice of the vibrato.' [29 Nov. 1873: MG]

'… though her high notes [Sofia Scalchi] are not free from vibrato.' [13 Apr. 1875: Std]

'Signor Verdi himself conducted[35], and was warmly welcomed by the English audiences with which, for the first time, he was personally brought into contact. The soloists were Madame [Teresa] Stoltz (soprano), Mdlle. [Maria] Waldmann (mezzo-soprano), Signor Masini (tenor), and Signor Medini (bass). The only exception that could be taken to the singing was the adoption of the tremolo style, now so fashionable, and, at the same time, so effeminate, and destructive of musical effect.' [23 May 1875: *Lloyd's Weekly*]

'And we would suggest to another contralto singer of a splendid voice, who shows a little tendency to this poor business, to think how Miss [Anne Louise] Cary's glorious voice would be degraded if she were to take on the tremolo. This tremolo does not express feeling. It does not give the voice a sympathetic, but a mechanical quality. In many cases it is apparent that the singer is giving her mind to this affectation. It also makes a shakiness which gives an impression of feebleness and uncertainty. And it shows a bad taste which is a bar to any high attainments. If the he or she who invented this detestable tremolo had died just before, or been hanged just after, the world would be better for it.' [17 Jun. 1878: CincDG]

---

35 The singers were chosen by Verdi himself to sing the premiere of his *Requiem* in the Albert Hall.

Some reviews of tremoloing males are appended below:

'In the aria of Cherubini [Recit. And Aria, M. Staudigl, "Ardo d'un cieco amore", Faniska, Cherubini], the trembling of his voice [Joseph Staudigl] was most distressing. If this is a natural infirmity, it is to be pitied; if an infirmity of taste, it should either be corrected or must encounter censure.' [19 Apr. 1845: Ex]

'By the way, this gentleman [Roger Gustave-Hippolyte] deserves more notice than a mere passing remark, on his first appearance before a Manchester audience. His singing and acting on this occasion possessed much merit, though very far from being perfect; he has a sweet tenor voice, though not powerful; he uses too much the tremando, and frequently, in the excess of his anxiety to give effect to his acting indicates a musical idea by a kind of slur (approaching very nearly to the travestie) rather than sings; nevertheless, he frequently gave great pleasure, particularly in the tender pathetic parts.' [13 Sep. 1848: MCLGA]

'… he [Italo Gardoni] has taken rather inordinately to that complaint too fashionable at present among singers in general—sopranos and tenors in particular—that excessive tremolo of the voice, which is neither more nor less than a misuse and absurd perversion of a means for occasional beautiful effect. Thus, his version of "Una furtiva lagrima" (which was encored) would have been admirable, if one could but have made sure that any one of his upper notes was in reality what it was intended for. When either a singer or an instrumentalist will persist, without any express reason, in the use of such an amount of vibrato as confounds all distinction between two neighbouring semitones, he cannot wonder if the ears of his audience be occasionally a little puzzled, not to say distressed.' [16 May 1855: ST]

The Times urged Charles Santley [p. 207] 'to get the better of a certain tremulousness'.

'… considerably marred by an excessive use of the vibrato [George Perren].' [28 Jan. 1860: Cheltenham Looker-On]

'M. [Jean-Baptiste] Faure would, however, do well to correct that constant tremulousness which, although very effective when reserved for occasional display, becomes a positive defect when unceasingly indulged in.' [6 Jun. 1860: DT]

I've noted [p. 200] the reviewer's comment on the absurdity of Italo Gardoni indulging in the trembling mania, as well as the way in which Adelina Patti and Gardoni occasionally vibrated one against the other. [7 Jun. 1862: Ex]

'We must enter a protest against the vile habit in which he [Emilio Naudin] is apparently inclined to indulge of applying the tremulando to every note. Judiciously used the tremolo is capable of producing a great impression—constantly employed it becomes a positive nuisance.' [16 May 1863: MCLGA]

'If tremulous at times [Karl Johann Formes], and not getting a firm grasp on those emphatic high tones in his first great solo: Triompf! &c.' [29 Oct. 1864: Dwight's]

'It was a perfect relief to a musician to hear [Hermine] Rudersdorff's firm sustained singing after Mademoiselle [Marie] Battu's thin voice, its defects in that respect brought out by the quavering vice called by Italians the vibrato; by the way, [Lodovico] Graziani might take a hint and imitate the firmer singing of his rival, Santley, in respect of that odious practice.' [23 Apr. 1864: Ex]

'The remarks, however, which we have made regarding the frequent employment of the tremolo, are even more strongly applicable to Signor [Roberto] Stagno than to Mdme [de Meric] Lablache.' [23 Feb. 1866: Scot]

'He [Ernesto Nicolini] is extremely partial to that excessive amount of tremolo now too common among foreign singers.' [26 May 1866: *Anglo American Times*]

'Mdlle. [Carlotta] Grossi gave that of the page Urbano with considerable effect, notwithstanding an excessive use of the vibrato, which is now becoming a prevalent vice among Italian singers; another instance of this defect being furnished by the Marcel of Signor [Filippo] Colini. Of this gentleman's début, as Bertram in "Roberto", we spoke in the London Review of April 25. His more recent performance can scarcely be considered an advance on his first effort. The excessive tremolo in which he indulged on this occasion is especially unsuited to the music of Marcel, the characteristic of which throughout is of stern, rugged determination and inflexible energy. To sing the Lutheran chorale, therefore, as Signor Colini did, conveyed an effect of tremulous fear rather than the intended impression of almost fierce and defiant trust. This gentleman has many good qualities of voice and style, which would be heard to better advantage in some other parts. M. Petit, too, although in some respects an excellent Saint Bris (especially in the conspiracy scene), was occasionally led into the prevalent vice already alluded to, and which bids fair to make its way from the Italian to the French school.' [6 Jun. 1868: LR]

'Setting aside a disagreeable tremulousness, a style too common amongst vocalists, which Signor [Alan James] Foli affects too much.' [2 Feb. 1869: MG]

'… sacrifices more than half the effect of the music by making a liberal use of the tremolo, which is very telling when sparingly used, but becomes tiresome when generally employed, and lays the singer under the reproach of labouring to conceal defects by a poor trick; and Signor [Antonio] Cotogni may not be aware that the voice under the influence of the tremolo rarely sounds in tune.' [26 Apr. 1869: MP]

'Voice [Victor Maurel] is a high baritone, neither very rich nor very robust, and marred a little by the vibrato which seems to be ineradicable from French voices.' [4 Oct. 1873: NYHT]

'His voice [William Shakespeare] is exceedingly pleasant in quality, round and sympathetic, although apparently not very powerful … the chief fault of his singing is a tendency to the "tremolo", a prevailing fault of the Italian school of the present day, and one so irritating to English ears that Mr. Shakespeare will do well to endeavour to overcome it.' [27 May 1875: Std]

However, it is possible that the reviewers might have been exaggerating the size of what they saw as a problem, given that my analysis of the best singers circa 1855 (Females at Annex A, and Males at Annex B) shows that tremoloists or vibratoists still accounted for well under half the total. However, if the reader considers all the charts for both females and males, it will be evident that 85% of singers were vibratoists by 1880.

Reviewers often assumed a nationalistic viewpoint in censuring tremolo singing, viewing it as a 'French vice' to which French trained vocalists were addicted, although blame was occasionally attached to Italian singers. Here are some typical comments. While most were written starting from 1850, I've included an earlier review from the *Examiner*.

> 'Of all the singers in the world, those we least like are the French; not that they are always deficient in taste and expression, but that they are given to a boisterous and blustering manner, which is at variance with good sense. They are always on the top of their compass, bellowing or screaming with all their might, as if strength of feeling were allied to strength of lungs. There is nothing placid or soothing, but all is tragedy or stilts; and as in older times they were hooped and fur-belowed, or stiffened with buckram and covered with periwig, so they are now always in extremes, and equally removed from grace or propriety. In saying this, we express our opinion of Madame MERIC LALANDE, who lately made her first appearance at the Italian opera, and in conformity to the French school, she selected a character incessantly in a whirl of distress and agitation, screaming with a quivering voice, that seems to have been shattered with over-exertion.' [25 May 1830: Ex]

> 'A want of refinement as distinct from accuracy or finish ran through all her performances [Delphine Ugalde-Baucé] ... her voice ... had been trained in the French school, and was, in its best days, not agreeable, because of a certain harpsichord tone—something of the quill and something of the wire—which ran through its compass.' [1851: Chorley, *Reminiscences*, Vol. 2, p. 138] Two other reviews comment on this singer's reedy tone. Another review indisputedly charged her with tremulousness, albeit slight: 'The merit of command over arpeggi, roulades, &c., allowed for and admired to the uttermost, there can be small question that the voice of Madame Ugalde-Baucé is fourth-rate in volume—third-rate as to quality. Even here it is not always audible in the concerted pieces which demand a penetrating sostenuto; while in the finales and coarsely instrumented morceaux d'ensemble of modern Italian opera it must be null. Nor have its tones the charm of any remarkable sweetness. They are, throughout the register, slightly tremulous; and the tremor has more of the comb than of the cremona or the chalumeau in its quality,—which the least over-emphasis or exaggeration renders unpleasing.' [14 Apr. 1849: Ath]

> 'Madame Marie Cabel—a Parisian artiste of considerable fame, with a thoroughly French voice, of thin and wiry quality and considerable florid execution ...' [24 Apr. 1860: Cox, *Recollections*, p. 350]

> 'It is refreshing to hear music with no tremolo [sung by Madame Harriers Wippern], that curse of modern singing, and for which we are indebted to the French school, which turns out singers possessing great facility and neatness of execution, but utterly unable to sustain for a couple of

bars any note with steadiness or pureness of tone.' [18 Jun 1864: SatR]

'Of Madlle [Ida] Gillies I will say but this much, that her singing abounds with that to be abhorred tremolo, the inevitable evidence of a French musical education.' [18 Nov. 1865: *Sporting Times*]

'M. Petit, the successor to M Faure in the part of Mephistophiles, has a good barytone voice, which, despite the use of the customary French vibrato style, he knows how to exhibit to advantage.' [13 Apr 1867: *Bell's Life in London and Sporting Chronicle*]

'... her excessive use [by Madlle Reboux] of the vicious French tremolo, which generally in the end ruins both voice and style.' [26 Jun. 1870: *Era*]

Victor Capoul was similarly taken to task: 'In quality of voice and style of delivery M. Capoul is essentially French; while the besetting sin of French tenors—the vibrato—often mars his efforts.' [10 Jun. 1871: *Illustrated Times*]

'... but for the French vibrato, which makes a proper delivery of cantabile music impossible, his singing [Ernesto Nicolini] would give entire satisfaction.' [27 Apr. 1872: *Graphic*]

'Mdlle. [Carlotta] Grossi is a German, and the vibrato—the vice of the French school of singing—is fortunately absent. This is worthy of record nowadays.' [17 Jun. 1872: *Morning Advertiser*]

'It is to be regretted that she indulged in the unpleasant "vibrato" of the French school. Miss Cole is one of our most promising artistes. If she used the "vibrato" from choice we counsel her to abandon it; if its use be involuntary, it is to be hoped she will seek the cause, which seems likely to be the undue forcing of her voice.' [22 Dec. 1872: Obs]

'... Though we must confess that we should admire the lady's style more if she [Madame Stella Bonheur] would be less lavish of the tremolo which obtains with some Italian masters, but which English critics abhor. If, at times, it enhances the effect of the voice, it will be more generally found to destroy the general purity of the notes.' [13 Feb. 1875: *Preston Herald*]

'Every note she [Mdlle Albert] sang was formerly marred by a strong vibrato, but it would seem that she has discovered that this characteristic of French vocalists is not acceptable with English audiences, and has accordingly done her best to master it, for it is now but slightly perceptible.' [5 Jul. 1875: MP]

'The part of Fra Diavolo was sustained by M. Tournié, who both in singing and acting left nothing to desire except a little less of the vibrato which seems inseparable from the French style of singing. There is hardly a member of this company who is not afflicted with it to a greater or less extent; and the only thing to do is to accept the inevitable ... EBENEZER PROUT.' [10 Jul. 1875: *Mackay Mercury,* Qld]

I quoted on p. 194 a review [8 Jul 1877] on Sims Reeves noting his pure and firm tone, free from the 'hateful tremolo of the French school'.

The final question I now address is this. When reviewers described a singer as 'tremulous', did they mean a pitch waver or emphasis fluctuation? The following notices, including those of singers using a 'close shake' or 'wiggle', suggest the former interpretation:

I've noted Lampe's support in 1740 for 'an Undulation or Waving' during a *messa di voce* [p. 84].

Burney's reference to a falsettist he heard in 1772, with a voice like 'the upper part of a bad vox humana stop in an organ', which reminded him of hair dressed by a barber to resemble a peruque [p. 77].

Smyth's comment in 1810 [p. 72] to the effect that a singer using the close shake like old-fashioned violin and bass performers 'fails egregiously as to portamento'.

'A most rapturous encore followed the performance of the last duet, "O take this nosegay", by the Demoiselles De Lihu, the preparation for the grace at its close, was an admirable effort of genius, and the close shake which followed, discovered the acme of perfection in its execution.' [13 Aug. 1818: *Cheltenham Chronicle*]

I've referred [p. 214] to Lamb's account of Mrs Blacket's 'tremulousness of pipe'.

'Voice he [Giuseppe Ambrogetti] had little, but he had articulation and rapidity that are seldom found together—his close shake before returning upon the subject, and seeming ease, though so exhausted as he must have been.' [Dec. 1826: *New Times*]

Angelica Catalani and Mary Anne Paton were both praised for their close shakes. [p. 47 and p. 148 respectively].

'She [Madame Panorma] gives a very clear reason for so many excellent singers not having that beautiful ornament, a perfect or close shake; this ornament to a falling cadence she executes herself with great perfection.' [14 Oct. 1837: *Hampshire Advertiser*]

'Her voice [Mdlle. Adelaide Tosi, on debut] is extensive and strong but unequally pleasant. The inferior extremity of its compass is forcibly, but scarcely agreeably, produced, after the custom of the modern soprani, and its highest portion, from about F on the fifth line, appears to be modelled on the huskiness of Pasta. Her execution is passably neat—except a detestable shake, or shiver, or rather whinney, very much in the manner of the trillified vileness which [Giulia] Grisi, thanks to her good sense, has at length abandoned—her enunciation is clear and impassioned, and her style replete with the fervour of her country.' [9 Apr. 1840: MW]

'The Misses Williams, whose duet singing is considered the most perfect of its kind; their extreme neatness of execution, close shakes, and correct intonation, place them foremost in the ranks of our native vocalists.' [12 Nov. 1845: *Derby Mercury*]

'The constant and indiscriminate employment of the shake is unmeaning, and amounts to nothing less than absurdity. We fain would admonish her upon this point, and recommend her [Mrs Sunderland] to use the tremolo sparingly and judiciously.' [18 Mar. 1846: MCLGA]

'She [Fortunata Tedesco] has a prominent fault, a something that may be compared to the flickering of a candle or the rippling of water as heard in the little falls of some quiet brooklet. It is not like the tremolo of [Signora] Borghese, for that, like Hamlet's madness, had method in it, and was sometimes a beauty. This quality that we are trying to describe in Tedesco's sounds, we consider a sheer deformity—a total blur—the very opposite to the perfection of tone, which is firmness. As if to prove the justice of our strictures, there is connected with this fault a varying of the pitch after taking the note; a sharping of the worst kind. That this very ripple of the voice may be considered by some, as a beauty, we have no doubt; for it is the most striking characteristic of Tedesco's voice.' [11 Aug. 1847: *Boston Evening Transcript*]

'In this piece Mr. [Frank] Bodda appeared to great advantage; his fine bold style of singing, ornamented now and again with a prolonged close shake, solicited repeated plaudits from the gratified audience.' [11 May 1850: *Staffordshire Advertiser*]

'... there was less tremulousness than usual observable. A large share of the applause which he obtained we attribute to an abatement of this vitiated habit; it is very rare to find a singer possessing so much dramatic expression in the recitative, and such attainment as an actor; and it is therefore lamentable that he [Enrico Tamberlik] should damage his fine voice by the excess of an exaggerated effect, which oftentimes renders it doubtful which of two notes is meant to be given.' [25 May 1850: *Atlas*]

'On her first appearance she [Cicely Nott] manifested a slight nervous agitation, which rendered her voice somewhat tremulous, and perhaps this detracted from the correctness of her intonation.' [5 Feb. 1853: MW]

'Her voice had acquired the habit of vibration to so terrible an extent, that on a long note, it seemed, sometimes first too sharp, and then too flat, or vice versâ, ere it settled itself—and Madame [Giuseppina] Medori had a propensity for long notes.' [1853: Chorley, *Recollections*, Vol. 2, p. 206]

'The close shake in the upper part of her voice [Clara Novello] was beautifully executed, and the sustained note, C in alt, displayed the power and quality of her upper notes,—so finely a sustained note it has rarely fallen to our lot to hear.' [30 Nov. 1854: BG]

'The Zerlina was [Leopoldine] Tuczek-Herrenberg ... excellent except at times oppressed with "wiggle".' [22 Apr. 1855: *Dwight's*]

Italo Gardoni's excessive tremolo left the reviewer uncertain as to what note he was singing, as quoted at p. 225 above.

'Mrs. Sunderland sang Bellini's "Qui la voce", introducing a beautiful close shake.' [4 Dec. 1858: *Northern Whig*]

'A couple of young women from Vienna sang; Frauleins Sofia and Krauss, wiggle-voiced women to the most shocking degree; neither gave a smooth, sustained note from beginning to end.' [Mar. 1859: *Dwight's*]

'There is only too much of the tremble, the fashionable "wiggle" in her voice [Colson]; and so it was with Mme. [Josefa] Gassier.' [22 Oct. 1859: Dwight's]

'The close sustained shake in sotto voce at the end of the melody, displayed a skilful management [by Hermine Rudersdorff] of a naturally clear and flexible voice.' [18 Apr. 1861: BG]

'We preferred hearing this [variations on Rode's air] to the same singer's *sostenuto*, in which she [Marietta Alboni] is, perhaps, too much devoted to a frequent use of the *tremolo*—a device always the most effective when seldom employed, but which most of our *contralto-soprani* seem to think they can never use too often. It is not at all times easy to mark the boundary dividing the simple shake from this *tremolo*.' [23 Apr. 1861: DubDE]

I referred to Adelina Patti's close shake on A and B in alt [p. 200]

'The habit of straining the voice [Signor Ferri] beyond its natural limits, has weakened it to such a degree, that it is no longer under control. What is the result? Every note becomes a shake through the incessant "vibrato", which is either a defect or a weakness. Owing to this the intonation suffers materially, as instead of one note two or three are distinctly audible.' [26 Oct. 1861: SatR]

'She [Marie Battu] has that unfortunate modern defect of singing every note with a tremolo, to such an extent that every chord in which she sustains a part sounds out of tune by reason of her singing two notes while the other singers are content to sing one, as set down for them by the composer.' [16 Aug. 1862: SatR]

'It is, however, our disagreeable duty vehemently to protest against this celebrated singer's abuse of the tremolo, which Madame [Josefa] Gassier employs so frequently that the most careful listener can scarcely distinguish it from the shake,—the every-day, regular, time-honoured trill with which the vocal phrases are terminated. This is the more pity since the lady in question possesses much to admire, both in compass, quality, and the execution of vocal difficulties.' [29 Nov. 1862: DubDE]

'Like too many other singers, she [Madame Lemaire] indulges in so continuous a use of the tremolo that it frequently mars her intonation and renders her incapable of holding a sustained note. When judiciously employed it is an ornament, but when indiscriminately used it becomes a blemish.' [6 Dec. 1862: Scot]

'With Madame Demeric-Lablache we were somewhat disappointed. There is a throaty quality in the lower notes of her register, and a general tremulousness throughout which renders her intonation uncertain.' [29 Jan. 1866: Scot]

'An unwonted superfluity of undulation or tremulo detracted from the distinctness of her intonation [Madame Demeric Lablache], and this was prominent even in passages which would have been more properly staccatoed.' [27 Feb. 1866: CM]

'... but, alas! He [Signor Amodio] has got hold of the horrid tremolo—that stage device which we read that Mozart disliked so greatly, as well he might, and which all those singers that the world accepts as great artistes wisely avoid. At times last night it was by no means easy to distinguish between the quivering of this new Valentine and that common every-day shake which precedes a cadence, cut and dry. Now, we would not for the world be straightlaced, nor would we object to a tremolo when passionate situations may be supposed to call for such an artifice; still an earnest protest should be made against the delivery of every vocal phrase in chronic shiver.' [13 Mar. 1866: DubDE]

'She gave G. B. Allen's ballad, "Little bird so sweetly singing", in which she [Mdlle Liebhart] carolled like a bird, most musically … the lengthened close shake at the end of the ballad displayed her artistic skill in a marvellous manner.' [18 Nov. 1867: BG]

'The first air of Madame [Jenny] Baur, '"Twas night and all around was still", again showed the great extent of her register, singing up to a rich, full C in alt, making a splendid close shake on the penultimate note.' [16 Apr. 1868: BG]

'Miss Rose Hersee has a pleasing voice and manner, which would make her attractive on the platform if she had not acquired the offensive use of a perpetual vibrato, which makes it impossible to say with certainty what note is being sung at any particular moment. Her taste is good, and she would be a most welcome vocalist if she would be content to sing simply and naturally.' [12 Feb. 1869: MG]

'Then signor Bottero was again unsatisfactory. His intonation was painful, uncertain, and the vibrato he indulges in made every sustained note sound like a would-be shake.' [14 Jun. 1869: DT]

'M. Petit and Signor [Antonio] Cotogni, whom we may group together, sang in an uncertain style because of the inordinate use of the tremolo so that it was easy to see that their desire was to accommodate their voices to the variable pitch, for any note sung in tremolo may be anywhere near the exact note without truly touching it.' [4 Apr. 1870: MP]

'Madame Anna Bishop's pure, sweet and fully-sustained notes in "Casta Diva" displayed the finished singer, and the steady, unquavering tones she uttered were in delightful contrast to the shaky tremolo style which is the one prevailing fault of too many of our lady singers. Miss Norton, a lady with a fine voice and cultivated taste, entirely spoiled her rendering of "Kathleen Mavourneen" with one continued shake of her voice in the tremolo from the first note to the last.' [29 Apr. 1871: Brook]

'The good effect of his delicacy of execution and pleasant upper notes [Signor Villani] was impaired too often by uncertain or erroneous intonation, and is expressed by a tremolo so violent that it often passed all bounds of legitimate artifice. The thrill which is so impressive in a sympathetic delivery during moments of intense passion or deep feeling, becomes annoying when it degenerates into the "wobble".' [12 May 1871: NYHT]

'That tremor in the voice called *vibrato* is an undulatory sound produced by a forced rapidity of exhalation. To acquire this is not easy. As a preparatory exercise use the scales, repeat an emphasis upon the same note four, six, or eight times, as much in the form of waves as possible. *Vibrato* should be used very sparingly and only in passages appropriate to the employment. There is no sign to indicate the *vibrato*, but when it is required, I have used a waved line [Illus. 48].' [1872: John D'Esté, *Vocalists Vade Mecum*, p. 62]

Illus. 48: Vibrato

'... No criterion to distinguish when she [Mdlle Natali-Testa] is trilling and when she is not: she keeps the tremolo stop out all the time.' [19 Mar. 1874: *Cincinnati Daily Enquirer*]

'Miss Alice May claims our next attention. "Angels ever bright and fair", from Handel's "Theodora", so familiar to us all, is capable of much variety of expression, according to the temperament of the cantatrice. We do not recollect any two having precisely the same conception of it since many years ago we heard it sung by Clara Novello with severe simplicity. Last evening, Miss May gave a very beautiful version of it, not the less pleasing because of its originality. Perhaps here and there the close shake was slightly overdone; a fault that the author of "Musical Recollections" pronounces a "mischievous and miserable system of tremulousness"; but for pathos and sweetness we have seldom heard the song better sung.' [4 Apr. 1874: *Evening Star*]

'Mlle. [Marie] Heilbron, although evidently an earnest artiste, and well drilled in all the conventional forms of stage-business, lacks the one first essential of a singer—voice. Yet, a small voice may be trained to execute well, but in training, also, Mlle. Heilbron is deficient, and her want of power of sustaining causes a tremolo, which at times makes it very difficult to determine whether she means to sing a G, a G sharp or a G flat.' [16 Dec. 1874: BDG]

'Of his singing [Signor Ernesto Nicolini] we cannot speak so highly, for the simple reason that the vibrato which so often spoils the effect of this tenor's best efforts was distressingly conspicuous. Considering how much of the vibrato we have to endure now-a-days, it should not be a little that makes me complain, but a line must be drawn somewhere, and we cannot endure with entire equanimity singing which leaves in doubt which note the vocalist wishes us to hear.' [21 Jun. 1875: DT]

'Moreover, he [Julian Gayárre] employs the vicious vibrato to such an extent that the ear is never satisfied as to the exact pitch of the note he is supposed to be singing.' [9 Apr. 1877: MP]

'S. Gambetti's voice is pure, his intonation perfect, and his acting is the acting of an educated gentleman, why will he injure the effect of all by the perpetual trembling of his voice, called, we believe, by his countrymen, the "voce vibrata". A vibrated note introduced occasionally is effective, but when used constantly the habit becomes wearisome, purity of tone disappears, and the deeper the note the greater is the mischief. Signor Gambetti's voice is in the highest degree musical when the notes are delivered true and pure, yet we cannot say that it gives us any pleasure to hear it when uttering a tone so violently trembling that one cannot tell what the note is.' [8 Feb. 1878: AuckS]

'Her terrible indulgence [Miss De Fonblanque] in the heinous modern sin of the vibrato—the great fault which neutralises so many excellences—militates fatally against her success. When will vocalists abstain from the perpetual use of what is only very occasionally permissible as a grace, and relegate to exceptional exigencies the hateful tremolo which is destructive of correct intonation and an offence to good taste?' [17 Jan. 1879: *Manchester Evening News*]

'Mdlle [Louise] Redeker is afflicted with the great curse of modern vocalisation—the tremolo. This unhappy mannerism detracts from the charm of her beautiful voice and excellent style, and more than imperils the accuracy of her intonation.' [13 Feb. 1879: Obs]

'… the listener's enjoyment was marred by the evidence of voice straining. Further than this, it must be observed that Signor Sylva has lost the command of sostenuto, and cannot sing a semibreve without a tremolo so strongly marked as almost to resemble a shake.' [10 May 1879: ISDN]

Several reviews seem to describe either a form of trillo or emphasis fluctuation. The number of these diminished as the nineteenth century progressed. It is apparent that by the first decade of the twentieth century virtually all the vocalists were recorded emitting a pitch vibrato. Some reports quoted earlier suggest that an intensity type tremolo was used:

- Faustina Bordoni had a 'very polished *trillo*' delivering 'many fast notes in succession on one tone [p. 33]'.
- Giovanni Carestini often produced an emphasis tremolo by moving his lower jaw, as I've noted on p. 81.
- The slow trembling [p. 78] of Joseph Meissner, as commented on by Mozart.
- The trembling of James Bartleman and John Braham in Purcell [p. 83].
- The rattling [pebbles in throat] effect delivered by Signor Miarteni [p. 213].
- Angelica Catalani's undulating sound like running a finger round a water-glass [p. 89].

The following reviews may also suggest an intensity tremolo:

'M. [Jean-Baptiste] Faure delivered in that throaty French-academical style which suggests now barking, now the operation of gargling, the baritone air from 'Le Siège de Corinthe'.' [15 Jun. 1870: PMG]

'His style of production [Signor Mendioroz] is influenced by the modern mania among singers for the free indulgence of the tremolo, so that in more than one instance the bleating tone produced by him marred the effect of his singing. The tremolo, if natural or acquired, but judiciously used, is most telling at times; but to have it indulged in on every note, in season and out of season, becomes wearisome and annoying.' [5 Jul. 1871: MP]

'The earliest singer I remember in that line [comic opera] was [Giovanna] Sestini, who at her first coming over was handsome, sprightly, and a good actress, if great exuberance of gesticulation, activity of motion, and affected Italian *smorfie* could make her one; but her voice was gritty and sharp (something like singing through a comb), and she was nothing of a singer, except for lively comic airs. Yet she was much liked at first, and long a favourite with the mass of the public, though not with the *connoisseurs*' [1775:Edgcumbe, p. 33]

'Any one of us in Cologne hearing the name of Anna Regan thinks at once of Schubert's "Haideröslein", with which the lady once transported us at the Ullmann Concerts, and immediately we heard the first note of the present Mdme [Anna] Regan-Schimon, we immediately recognised her who was once simply Anna Regan. Still the same voice, small, and, in its thinness, almost sylph-like, but clear, crystaline, and pure as a bell— only with a tendency, formerly not characteristic of it, towards a warmer vibrato, a fact which does not strike us as a step in the wrong direction. There is something especially naïve and almost childlike in the quality of Mdme Schimon's organ, and when she sings German songs as she does sing them, with a slight tremor in her voice, we feel under the influence of a particular spell.' [9 Dec. 1876: MW]

4.5   Tremolo Singing Widely Hated but Dominant (1880 to 1904)

Firm statistics have not been available in the past, although a claim by the famous tenor Sims Reeves carries some weight:

'According to Mr Sims Reeves, writing in *The Idler*, it is scarcely necessary to describe the tremolo. He might have added that, if one is to be polite, it is also impossible to describe it. The veteran tenor goes on to point out that five out of every six modern singers are afflicted with this wobble, "and consequently there is a great deal of make-believe that the tremolo is a splendid vehicle for the expression of sentiment and passion. But experience soon proves that an audience never mistakes affectation—and tremolo is nothing else in effect—for sincerity; and the singer finds, when it is too late, that the tremolo has literally got him by the throat and he cannot get rid of it".' [1900: 'Musicus', writing in *Weekly Standard and Express*]

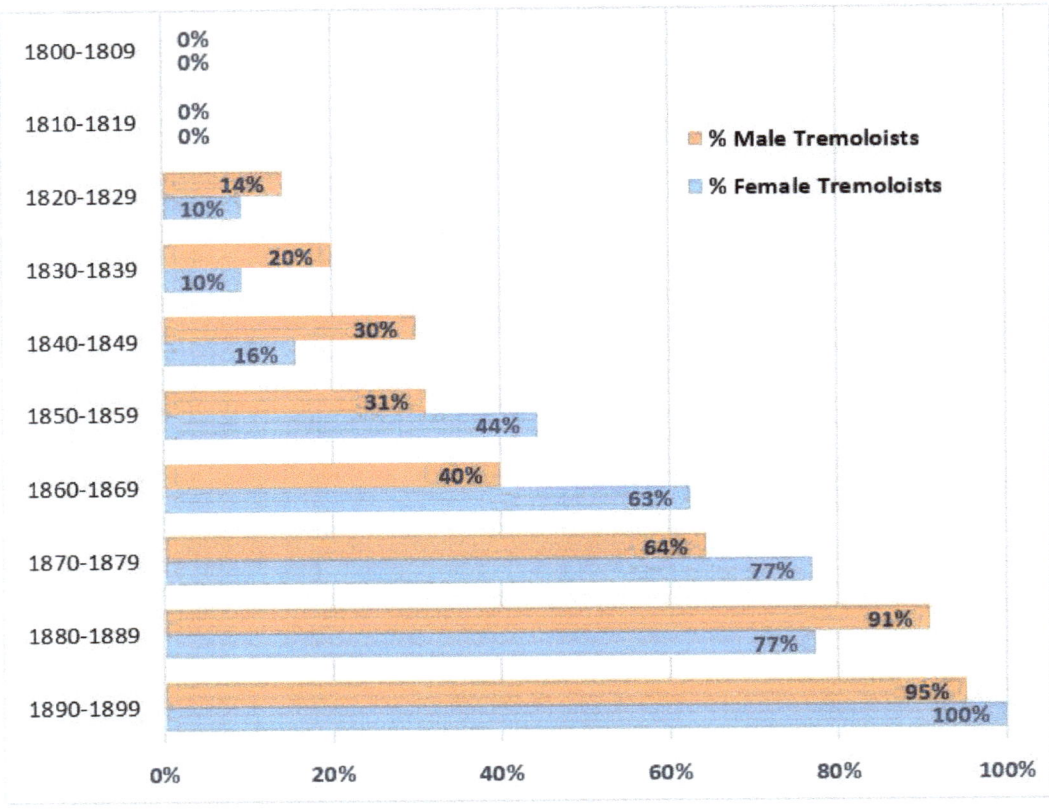

Illus. 49: % Tremolo Singers at Mid-Career Point

It is clear from Annexes A and B that, by the end of the century, nearly all opera vocalists, if not concert singers, were using tremolo continuously. The chart at Illus. 49 above shows, for both male and female singers, the estimated percentage of tremoloists in each decade through the nineteenth century. This is based on how each singer is classified in mid career between debut and retirement. It would appear that Sims Reeves's estimate of five out of six singers being wobble afflicted [83%] could be a slight underestimate.

As in the previous period to 1880, pejorative references to the French, and sometimes Italian, tremolo continued through till the end of the nineteenth century, and even later:

> 'What a delightful contrast her method offers to that of nine in ten of the prima donnas on the stage … Nearly all students of French and Italian schools sing with a vibrato that speedily shakes their voices off the key, one should not sing, but Mme. [Pauline] L'Allemand's method is simple and natural. Except that her voice has the pliancy and sustaining power that come alone from practice[,] her singing suggests that of a child. Her accuracy, too, is wonderful, and after the first half dozen bars the ear gives assurance that there shall be no flatting or sharping, no jar, no screaming. Her voice is light but sweet, and its use most judicious.' [30 Oct. 1886: Brook]

'The *débutant*, Signor Lorrain, from Rome, proved to be an intelligent though somewhat conventional Mephistopheles and a promising young singer—somewhat, however, addicted to the tremolo, that bane of the French and modern Italian vocal Schools.' [4 Jun. 1887: *Graphic*]

'Hers [Alice Gomez's] is like a voice from another planet. Her phrasing is admirable, and there is, at present, not a trace of that vocal palsy known as the "vibrato", which has ruined the French and blighted the Italian school of the period.' [5 Jun. 1890: *Royal Cornwall Gazette*]

Manuel Garcia's views were still respected in 1900: 'I cannot sing any more. You see how the voice trembles. That, you must not imitate. The tremolo is an abomination—it is execrable. Never allow it to appear, even for a moment, in your voice. It blurs the tone and gives a false effect. Many French singers cultivate it, and I will tell you why.' [Tells the story of Giovanni Battista Rubini whose voice shook with increasing age]. [Apr. 1900: *Mackinlay*, p. 281]

Roberto Hazon, distinguished conductor and music teacher, worked in Australia between 1889 and 1907. J. C. Williamson interviewed him, writing: 'I drew on my recollections of famous singers of four years ago, and recalled that none of the big singers of the 1897 season had tremolo—such great sopranos, for instance, as Melba, Marie Engel, Emma Eames, Frau [Milka] Ternina, Miss [Margaret] Macintyre, Calvé, and the greatest of all, Madame Patti. So I ventured to ask—/ "Is the tremolo taught in Italy?"/ It seemed a sore point. The Maestro [Roberto Hazon] blew a cloud of smoke from his pipe, and replied evasively, "No! it is not taught but it is not avoided!" and hurried on to another theme. / "It was no picnic, this search for talent", he said. "It was a case of 'first catch your hare, and then cook him".' [21 Sep. 1901: *Freeman's Journal, Sydney*]

'"Lancelot" in the Referee renews the fight: "My recent remarks on voice production have elicited an interesting letter from a Paris Refereader concerning the vibrato which prevents the acceptance in England of so many French singers. He says 'Most French voices have a light natural or beating ring, or resonance, which is a national characteristic. Although it may not please, it cannot be called a defect in the technical sense so long as it does not mar purity or steadiness of tone. It attracts attention, adds dramatic effect, and produces singing which can never be called dull, whereas that adjective is applicable to the average German and English performance' I quote this passage because it goes to the root of the whole question. My correspondent, judging by his or her signature, is French, manifestly knows a good deal about vocalization, consequently the above opinion may be taken as representative of the taste of cultured French music-lovers. To them the beating ring adds charm to the voice; to us it detracts from its beauty. To them it is not a defect; to us, it is. The apparent admiration for the beating ring, it may be noted, causes the writer to impart a relative meaning to the term steadiness of tone. To us any beating or pulsation is contradictory to steadiness".' [21 Sep. 1902: *Boston Journal,* from long article by Philip Hale *Mr. Henry W. Savage and English Opera*]

'Mme. [Jean] Jouve has one of those enviable contralto voices whose rolling tide need not always be represented at the full. A deeper swell on which to draw is there when the singer chooses. A too-insular critic might object that this is precisely the kind of voice which needs training according to British notions rather than French, so that all tendency to vibrato and to inequality of tone in the scale shall be sternly fought against; he might say that Mme. Jouve's style is better suited to a foreign than a British audience.' [13 Mar. 1917: T]

But, rather surprisingly, there are several reports from this time, and a few both earlier or later, claiming that the vibratoists were on the retreat, in the UK, Ireland, the US and Australasia, as I show below. Most of the comments appear to be wishful thinking rather than observation of actual practice, given the certainty that more and more singers were using vibrato as the millennium drew closer. Also, as I shall show, vibrato oscillation was getting wider as time went by. Looking at these events in retrospect, one senses the historical inevitability of these trends—an inevitability which contemporary reviewers obviously couldn't perceive.

'I find one source of congratulation, that is, we are getting rid of the disgusting tremolo that many singers indulged in. It was a French importation, though freely bestowed upon us by some of the Italians, some of whom have so addicted themselves to this voce de capra [goat voice] that they cannot sing a pure note.' [26 May 1860: MW]

'Her shake is good, she [Emilie Ambré] avoids the unpleasing tremolo which until quite recently was in fashion, and her intonation is almost invariably correct.' [17 Nov. 1878: Obs]

'A day surely will come when the vibrato craze, like steel petticoats and other Gallic ultra fashions, will become a thing of the past, and people will wonder how it was ever tolerated by intelligent artists.' [27 Apr. 1883: DubDE]

'The characteristic feature of the Italian style is the tremolo, and that is no longer popular. Instead of it, the round, full, clear tone is demanded.' [11 Feb. 1886: BDG, 'How to Sing Without Hurting the Mucous Membrane of the Throat']

Following a notice on a Signor Lorrain who was 'not altogether free from the tremolo', the reviewer concludes: 'The day is possibly not far distant when the vexed question of the tremolo must be settled one way or the other. It is no longer held to be mere evidence of fatigue, and it is now generally admitted that this most vicious of all vocal mannerisms is actually cultivated as a grace in some of the Continental singing schools. Thirty years ago or more a similar craze was in full force, particularly in Italy, but English audiences have always refused to tolerate it, and, with one or two notable exceptions, the great vocalists of our own time have all escaped the taint.' [30 May 1887: DN, Review of *Faust*]

'She ... has either been ill-advised or unadvised, or she would not impair her natural gifts by such a profuse use of the *vibrato*, which happily seems to be dying out; not, however, before it has buried the reputation of some who would otherwise have been fine singers.' [21 Dec. 1888: *Sheffield & Rotherham Independent*, 'Miss Effie Thomas in St John the Baptist']

'Her one failing on Saturday, with which evident nervousness had possibly something to do, was the continuous vibrato which for several seasons, not so long ago, was, apparently, with operatic singers a sine qua non. Fortunately a healthy public opinion has now, for the most part, debarred it, and as Signora [Emilia] Guidotti becomes acclimatised here, she will, no doubt, become aware of that fact.' [15 Aug. 1891: *Australasian*]

'This style of singing [vibrato] came into vogue about 40 years ago, but, happily, it is now beginning to disappear.' [1 Mar. 1892: MusH, 'Questions and Answers: Vibrato and Tremolo']

'Madame [Lilian June] Henschel [née Bailey] did not shine to such advantage as on her last visit, her solos being marred by too frequent use of the now antiquated tremolo, which seems to settle on some singers and violin players like a disease.' [7 Feb. 1895: *Dundee Evening Telegraph*]

'... with a little touch of that tremolo [by Mrs John B Wright], which is fast losing caste as a vocal embellishment.' [27 Jun. 1895: *Evening News*, Lincoln]

'... the tremolo or voice vibrata become fashionable. However, this phase of public sentiment did not last, fortunately, and the production of a pure tone is now required by good musical taste.' [8 Jul. 1896: AuckS]

'My conclusion is that whilst the old Italian school of vocalisation—of tremolo, vibrato and meaningless roulades—is discredited and almost departed, another and a far better school has taken its place, a school of grand production and high dramatic expressiveness.' [28 Jul. 1896: *West Australian*, Perth]

'He [Mr Scaramberg] has a light, tenor voice, which the selection did not suit in the best conceivable manner, but even when forced it was agreeably free from the vibrato. What has become of that once almost universal aid to expression? We ask without the smallest intention of searching for it, if it be lost; desirous only to be assured that a vicious affectation has had its day.' [10 May 1897: DT]

'Exception may again be taken to the perpetual tremolo and vibrato [by Nini Mazzi], a relic of the old Italian school' [16 Oct. 1897: *Los Angeles Herald*]

'... while except when he [Allesandro Bonci] grows excited he seems almost free from the tremolo, a vocal vice which a few years ago under the influence of certain great artists and teachers, was cultivated in Italy as a vocal ornament.' [2 Jun. 1900: EPNY]

'Happily the vice of incessant tremolo in singing is now going out of fashion, and that which constitutes a valuable artistic aid in its proper place is much less abused than it used to be.' [1 Nov. 1900: MusH]

[Continuous tremolo] 'has gone out of fashion in the cultivated musical world for a long time, and those singers who imagine they are up-to-date in continuing it, really show that they are among the has-beens.' [7 May 1906: *Deseret Evening News*, 'The "Gargling" Style']

'Despite a slight tremolo which is now rapidly being swept away from the voices of operatic singers, she [Mlle. Frances Alda as Gilda] sang exceedingly well.' [14 Jun. 1906: PMG]

'Miss [Gertrude] Hunt's soprano was heard to advantage, and an encore resulted. In the more recent teaching the tremolo methods of the Italian school are discarded, and the clear, sustained notes almost exclusively cultivated. Miss Hunt has evidently a leaning towards the older school, and it must be admitted that the effect was not displeasing.' [14 Nov. 1914: *Kadina and Wallaroo Times*]

'Her vocalisation [Carmen Torbari] was not altogether free from that vibrato which is supposed to be a thing of the past.' [1 Apr. 1924: SMH]

'The new school of Italian singing and acting, as revealed by the young artists who form the present opera company, marks a great advance in art in every way. The vibrato and the forcing of the voice which was accepted as characteristically Italian is quite abandoned.' [10 Apr. 1924: *Table Talk*, Melbourne]

'Any singer who suffered from the "wobbles" (he would not dignify it by terming it vibrato) stood no chance of being taken any notice of by adjudicators to-day; it was old-fashioned before the war.' [20 Jun. 1924: *Leamington Spa Courier*]

'The most glaring and distasteful defect of those mentioned above, false tremolo or wavering on sustained notes was the more noticeable. Some years ago this was not considered a technical fault, but was purposely acquired as a fashionable frill in the make up of every vocalist. It was a product of a noted French singing master. Fortunately the craze soon met with a sudden death by becoming very unpopular amongst European music critics and first-class vocalists. To-day it is anathema, and only noticed in quasi-professional and badly trained amateur vocalists. It is both unwarranted and unnatural.' [19 Mar. 1931: *Examiner*, Launceston]

A counter-reformation of sorts was certainly taking place. There are reports of singers being sacked for their vibrato, or even run out of town. Critical hostility had certainly intensified as the nineteenth century passed. Sources throughout the English speaking world are sprinkled with impassioned anti-vibrato diatribes, anti-tremolo jokes, reports of vocal sketches caricaturing vibrato singing, satirical poems and letters to the editor from disgusted music lovers. Some selections follow, illustrating both the widespread extent of reviewers' antipathy to the practice and the reasons for their distaste.

One of the first was in 1844: 'In her [Signora Borghese] was first remarked here, among vocalists of distinction, that trembling of the voice when it is pressed in a crescendo which has since become so common as greatly to mar our enjoyment of vocal music. This great fault, unknown before the appearance of Verdi, is attributed by some musical critics to the influence of his vociferous and strident style. It may be so; but that which follows is not always a consequence of that after which it comes. Certain it is, however, that from this time forward very few of the principal singers who have been heard in New York—only the very greatest and those whose style was formed before Verdi domineered the Italian lyric stage—were without this tremble. Grisi, Mario, Sontag, Jenny Lind, Alboni, and Salvi were entirely without it; their voices came from the chest pure, free, and firm.' [28 Feb. 1844: *Century*]

'For some time past it has been my fate to hear no sopranos but those third rate singers, who endeavour to conceal their incapacity to utter a full, clear tone, by a constant tremolo, like a whistle with a pea in it. This as an ornament, or rather as expressive of deep emotion, is at times very effective; constantly heard however it becomes unbearable.' [11 Nov. 1854: *Dwight's*]

'What a glory there is in a pure, sustained tone, swelling and dying away without the slightest perceivable waver or variation of pitch. How such a tone will fill one with music! Oh ye wiggle-voiced men and women, will ye never learn that one such tone touches the heart more than a whole evening of tremolo, and that it is only she who is capable of the pure tone, who can touch your heart of hearts, when in the depths of feeling the voice begins to waver and tremble with emotion.' [15 Apr. 1855: *Dwight's*, comments by Alexander Wheelock Thayer]

A diatribe from *The Examiner* featured a rich variety of disparaging terms: continual ague, shivering, eternal quaver, unsteadiness, tremor and tremble: 'The *Matilda* of Madame [Marie Caroline Miolan-]Carvalho we have already spoken of; her voice is thin, but the conception of her music is good; we cannot, however, consider her entirely equal to illustrate Rossini, nor can we admit that school of tuition to be correct which puts the voice into a continual ague, and takes away from the vocalist the power of sustaining notes; Madame Carvalho has this most objectionable quality,—and although we give her every credit for her conception of the beautiful Romanza "*Selva opaca*", yet we painfully felt this shivering of the voice in the almost unequalled descent from A flat above the line to E flat on the line, accompanied as the passage is by an unrivalled sequence of diminished sevenths. / The whole beauty of the passage is lost unless the singer gives every note with firmness and precision. Madame [Hermine] Rudersdorff acted *Jemmy*. How Guglielmo Tell happened to have a son called Jemmy we do not know. We doubt if there be a Jemmy at present to be found in any of the Swiss cantons, but Madame Rudersdorff acted Tell's son to perfection. She had not any music of consequence. We advisedly say that Madame Rudersdorff is one of the best singers on the stage, and far superior to Madame Carvalho in every point. From the style and *method* of the ladies and gentlemen arriving within the last few years from Italy, we should say that the science of teaching music was at a low ebb, or that musical taste had degenerated. Firm connected *mezza voce* singing and smooth progression are not to be had, but eternal quaver and unsteadiness of the voice, or else shouting, seems the order of the day with soprano, tenori, and bassi. The admirers of this mode of singing tell us that it is intended to denote feeling. We must borrow the American word *bunkum*, and apply it to such a ridiculous notion. Granted that there may be a tremor introduced with effect in passages where the singer is supposed to be agitated; but for the whole of the *dramatis personae* of an opera to tremble from end to end of the drama in joy and in sorrow according to the present fashion is simply ridiculous. Signor [Enrico] Tamberlik has contracted this vice to a fearful extent. [Domenico] Donzelli had it not. Signor [Giovanni Matteo] Mario has it not, nor Madame [Giulia] Grisi, nor had [Maria] Malibran or [Henrietta] Sontag. Madame [Marie Caroline Miolan-]Carvalho and Madlle Didiée, and Madame Gordosa, a *debutante* of English origin, are fearful specimens of this musical ague. / Well, we expected to hear Mr [Charles] Santley do honour to his country as a native vocalist, and uphold her musical reputation on the Italian boards as *Il Conte di Luna* in

Verdi's *Trovatore*, nor were we deceived. We found Mr Santley a little nervous at first, we felt a shade pass over his voice, which however went off. It was a perfect relief to hear Mr Santley's sustained singing; he has had too good a master to adopt a custom which makes a voice old before it is in its prime, and therefore he used the tremor sparingly and with judgment. We trust that Mr Santley will not be carried away by bad example, but maintain this superiority over most of his contemporaries. True talent requires no fictitious aid,—frequently it meets with difficulty in taking its place at first,—but talent will overcome the ways of the world. Mr Santley has had the good taste to follow the example of Mr Sims Reeves, and to consider that his name did not require to be re-cooked in Italy; and Mr Gye deserves the thanks of the profession for giving us a singer with an English name and an English voice, perfected by the best Italian instruction.' [19 Apr. 1862: Ex]

' "TREMOLO". —The following capital verses "from a Musical Sufferer" we find in the Boston Transcript. As they are equally applicable in this latitude, where our vocalists are striving for the ridiculous "wiggle". We give them insertion.

> 'Do enlighten me, —is it from weakness or choice,
>   Comes this villainous tremolo habit of singing, —
> This new "wiggle" —as somebody terms it—of voice,
>   Which these lyrical songsters are constantly bringing?
>
> 'If I go to the opera, —big, burly throats
>   Of the amorous tenors and chivalrous basses,
> That appear as if formed for sustainment of notes,
>   And the even prolongment of all vocal graces. —
>
> 'Their heroics declaim in a quivering way,
>   That all vocal propriety clearly outrages,
> And in shaky cadenzas their passions convey,
>   To remind one of ague in all its bad stages.
>
> 'And obese prima-donnas—whose figures suggest
>   An addiction to lager, if not a style largo,
> With their arias wavy with vocal unrest,
>   On legitimate pleasure lay hopeless embargo.
>
> 'Cavatinas are corkscrewed, and recitatif
>   Is a weak undulation of vocal delivery,
> Nor does sonorous unison bring its relief,
>   But is tipsy in tone, and in climaxes quivery.

'If at church I attend—where some petted quartette
   of their florid accomplishment give exhibition,
In the place of devotional method—I get
   The same tremolo, only in cheapened edition.

'I had thought that the concert-room nuisance had reached
   Its extent in the ignorant chatter and giggle, —
But let ballet be sung or bravura be screeched,
   There's a trial yet worse – the inveterate "wiggle".

'The great organ is played, —I am there, —for at length
   Is the fortunate time to hear harmonies semblant
To the instrument's massiveness, finish and strength;
   The performer commences—and out comes the "tremblant"

'It would seem that all vocalisation, before
   It were fit to the auditor's ear to be taking,
Must, like physic, observing medicinal law,
   Undergo the anterior process of shaking.

' "Wiggle" on, then, ye singers, both lyric and local, —
   Fashion tolerates, so I submit without blinking;
But, as strange as it seems, such performance as vocal
   Are, in popular phrase, "no great shakes", to my thinking'
[Jan. 23, 1864: CT]

'SIR—During the past musical season a tendency to indulge in the "vibrato" singing on the part of many vocalists who have occupied prominent positions has been only too frequent, and, so far as I have seen, the press has passed by this terrible failing without the censure it assuredly deserves.

'In the case of the quartett of vocalists brought here by Verdi to sing in his Requiem, and who presented so many admirable qualities in their singing, the public press seemed deaf and blind to the fatal fault in which I have referred. The soprano [Madame Teresa Stoltz] was quite incapable of sustaining with a steady tone A above the staff, and I heard, during one of the Requiem performances, a lady near me, remark, "what a beautiful shake the vocalist had", when composer and singer were guiltless of any intention to introduce a shake.

'Now, all true and well educated vocalists know that a shaking or trembling voice is not a desirable thing to cultivate, but the very reverse, and that it is also a sure indication of insufficient or false training, or of taxing the vocal organs beyond their natural capabilities. It is, of course, sometimes the result of failing powers from old age, and frequently in such cases we can admire the skill of the artist who, triumphing over his physical failings, causes me to regard chiefly his ripened judgment and mental superiority; but when youth begins to imitate the *palsies* of old age it is time for those who stand by to raise a warning voice. Yours, etc., W.H.C.

'Our correspondent W. H. C. is entitled to speak with authority, and his warning against the constant indulgences of the *vibrato* should engage, not only the serious attention of vocalists themselves, but the careful consideration of the musical profession and public. A couple of years ago we ourselves attacked the evil, and now that there is no sign of the diminution of the disease, it is high time again to comment on it, and protest against the pernicious practice. Like many current vices, it might have had its origin in what—for the nonce—we may term a virtue. It is probable that a singer, carried away by intense feeling at some specially dramatic situation, may have first employed the *vibrato*, to intensify the effect of the music. And this was only in accordance with the dictates of nature, for the voice invariably trembles with deep passionate feeling. Used in this unaffected and natural way, the *vibrato* is charming, and unquestionably heightens the effect of the situation thus treated. But we may have too much even of the best things, and the misuse of this grace, and the exaggeration into which it has grown, have now assumed alarming proportions. That which gave a thrilling intensity to certain notes in particular passages, has developed into a lachrymose trembling on every note sung; and now the abuse of a useful feature has created in unsophisticated minds a strong objection to its employment at all. This indeed is not to be wondered at, for the vice is spreading so widely, and rapidly becoming so fashionable, that, unless checked, we shall soon have our musicians imitating "the palsies of old age", as W. H. C. puts it, instead of interpreting their art with robust strength. Let it be clearly understood that a trembling voice is a blemish, not a beauty; and that the unpleasant feature is not a thing to be desired, but a defect to be regretted. Its constant use denotes not only bad taste, but bad training, or else a worn out voice. Hitherto this detestable style has been exclusively confined to foreign singers—chiefly French—but there are signs of its adoption by some of our young English singers. There is no need to mention names, but concert goers of the present season must have heard more than one aspirant for the palsied *rôle*. These young vocalists would soon abandon the practice could they but appreciate the sorry exhibition that they make of themselves; they should reflect that this vocal asthma eliminates all healthy vigor from music, and only supplies in its place, a feeble enervating effect that quickly palls on the ear, and soon excites weariness and disgust.

'But the evil takes a wider range than even our correspondent points out; it has extended very considerably into the instrumental world of music. Solo players on the violin have not been permitted its exclusive use, but all the members of the stringed family freely employ it. The various kinds of wind instruments are following suit; from the gentle flute to the brazen ophicleide, all seem afflicted with the senseless wobble. The street cornet player is great in the tremolo; as to the precise kind of taste which causes its employment here, we care not to enquire. Even the majestic organ has become addicted to the vice; mechanical tremulants, and registers of the "Unda Maris" and "Voix celeste" qualities find favor among the admirers of this nuisance. Of course the harmonium has coarsely imitated the feature; and very distressing it is to hear some choice ditty wobbling its shaky length along on the sixteen foot stop to which the tremolo is attached. The evil has thus become so general, that, unless a change takes place,

the uninstructed public will fancy the whole body of musicians to be suffering from a sort of St. Vitus's dance.'
[4 Sep. 1875: Letter from William H Cummings to the Musical Standard, plus ensuing diatribe, reproduced in *Dwight's*, Vol. XXXV, 'The "Vibrato", alias "Tremolo", alias "Wobble".']

'The pure female voice is fast disappearing from the opera, the concert, the performing church choirs, and all other places of pretentious singing. We mean not the voice of the pure female, but the pure voice of a female. It is fast degenerating into that shaking palsy, which is sometimes called the tremolo sometimes the vibrato, but which is more correctly described by the vernacular term wabbling. Singers accepted as *prima donne* in opera practice this wabbling till they cease to have a single correct note. Such shallow tricks and meretricious ornaments are always more quickly limited than any correct manner, because this affords an easy way to sing like an opera singer. Fond mammas think their girls are quite up to *prime donne* when they get this shaking palsy. The soprano of a performing quartet, set up before the congregation as in the concert or minstrel hall, and reducing this affair, which is satirically called worship, to a performance, "executes"—that is the apt word—solos in this shaking palsy, whose high aim is to degrade the godlike human voice to the mechanical twitter of a canary bird. The probability is that the generation which shall be born from this time on shall never hear the pure female voice, nor know what it is, save in some unsophisticated mother's lullaby, or in very primitive congregations on the frontier. The Italian opera, which should be an elevator of the tastes of the people, corrupts it, and the progress which we boast so much is to the acceptance of this shaking palsy as high art. Nor is it of women alone. The same wabble has grown greatly among men singers in the opera during the last twenty years, and thus all singing is getting shattered. A high taste for music is not diffused among any people outside of Italy. There may be a few in every large city in the circuit of the opera who are competent to judge, and who have distinct ideas, but the number is much less than is commonly fancied, as any one can find by observing the audiences. The greater number find a sort of dull interest in the spectacle, the dramatic action, the general crash of voices and orchestra, the sight of a much advertised *prima donna*, without any distinct notion of anything, save that it is the fashion to go.

'This condition of the people does not encourage the highest attainments in the singer's art, but it gives a chance to captivate in an easier way by false ornamentation. So corrupted has the public taste become by this that it tolerates and even applauds such a wabbler as * * * * who in a whole opera never strikes a correct note, scattering herself all round the note, like a charge of bird shot. She has no distinct note, only a blurr. She can make runs by semi-tones or quarter-tones as well as by whole tones; nobody can tell which they are, for they have no single tones. In florid music she makes no articulation of notes; it is simply a mixing up of all—a muddle. Add to this her strokes of tremendous force in the prolonged high notes, on which her voice becomes a scream, and a manner of drawing out some particularly favoured low notes into a prolonged howl, like somebody's last strain in "Baby Thine", and the total is about the worst that has yet been set before opera-goers as a standard for cultivation in music. But this singer goes down the public throttle, and most of those that rank lower are cultivating the shaking palsy more or less. We suppose that the time is coming when if a singer shall attempt to sing in opera, or on the concert of church stage, in a true or pure voice, it will be as much out of character as if a circus performer should ride seated in a saddle instead of standing up and turning somersaults through hoops. Probably we shall have to submit to this universal corruption, but it shall not be without a protest. And we have to remark that if the Cincinnati College of Music shall assist in this degradation of the human voice, lightning ought to strike it, or the earth open and swallow it, or some equally mild but effectual corrective ought to be applied to this sacrilege.

'Your Beethovens, your Cherubinis, your Meyerbeers, your Halévys, aye, even your Verdi's— but, before all, your Wagners— are answerable for this. How often must we say that the "tremolo" is not voluntary, but involuntary, the result of bad early training, or of the screaming and dwelling upon high notes, to the detriment of the middle and lower registers. No one does it purposely, and no one, either vocalist or auditor, thinks it—as poor Molique used to say—"quite beautiful".' [27 Dec. 1879: MW, *A MILD WABBLE ABOUT WABBLING', from 'Cincinnati Wabbler'*]

'I hear of discontent about the Opera troupe. There is, so it seems, a liberal display of vibrato or tremulo. I was much disgusted with this abominable disease of the voice even in London at the Italian Opera, but feel pleased if people in Adelaide do not approve of a constant wave-line. If this mild musical delirium tremens takes universal hold we may depart in architecture too from the straight, sober line, and see all pillars and lamp-posts in zigzag, and get seasick—as these vibrato-singers make us earsick. Hoping that the subject will draw more and more sympathy, and other correspondents keep it alive—I am, &c., CHRISTIAN REIMERS, Edinburgh, February 5, 1883.' [8 Feb. 1883: *South Australian Register*]

'The *vibrato* or *tremolo* was unknown when Rossini produced his opera in 1823, and he has consequently afforded no provision for its exercise. His music requires to be sung steadily, accurately, and firmly, as by those trained in the true Italian school, and not in the undesirable method arising from the grafting of German musical requirements upon the classic Italian stock, to its designed extinction. The day will come when old Italian operas must be laid aside for this cause. The traditional method of performing them will be lost, and their modes of expression become dead. "Semiramide", which is in itself a survival of thirty-six operas on the same subject or bearing the same title, will in time have to yield to a less melodious successor, if it is written in accordance with modern lyrical needs. For all its faults, it is doubtful whether such a change would be advantageous.' [7 Jul. 1887: MP, Review of *Semiramide*]

'SIR, — The vibrato or tremulo is universally condemned, yet, strange to relate, nine vocalists out of every ten persist in its use and abuse, much to the annoyance—I might say, the disgust—of those who assemble to listen to them. We have had several very pronounced specimens of these "wobblers" as the Americans term them,—at our concerts recently (young lady vocalists especially), many of whom possess excellent voices, and appear to enjoy robust health, yet, from sheer affectation, they shake and tremble in a pitiable manner, as though they were shivering with cold and were suffering from an attack of ague. Our musical committees, before making engagements with vocalists, in the future, should stipulate that they abstain from the use and abuse of this senseless appendage. yours etc., A PROVINCIAL CRITIC.' [28 Feb. 1896: MusS, Correspondence, 'The Vibrato or Tremulo', p.122]

The following report on an article by **William James Henderson** is not so much a diatribe as one of the first historically informed pieces of musicology.[36] It's also largely consistent with my own findings.

'The use of the vibrato was introduced into singing by Rubini says W. J. Henderson, writing of the vibrato and tremolo in the New York Sun. So far as any records can show, he continues, the vibrato was not a characteristic of the singing of what is called the golden age of song.

'The skill of singers in the delivery of florid music of the most difficult kind was developed early in the seventeenth century and before its close there was a coloratura as brilliant as that of the following period, the golden age. / In the delivery of cantilena the singers of the golden age ([Gaetano Mairorano] Caffarelli, [Carlo Broschi] Farinelli, Faustina [Bordoni], Tesi [Vittoria Tesi Tramontini] and their contemporaries), were probably greater than their predecessors, and this was no doubt due in some measure to the superiority of the composers who wrote for them and who forced upon their attention the potency of pure sustained phrases. In other words, there was a higher vocal art in the early eighteenth century than in the late seventeenth, but no greater florid technic.

'In reading accounts of the manner in which Caffarelli, Farinelli and their contemporaries sang we meet with praise for their wonderful breath control, their sustained phrasing, messa di voce, their purity of tone, their accuracy of intonation, their skill in the delivery of ornament and their ability to pour pathos into the air; but we nowhere find any record of any such trick as the vibrato. On the contrary steadiness of tone seems to have been a sine qua non among these singers.

'[Giovanni Battista] Rubini introduced the vibrato as a dramatic effect. He sang it in places where a human being's voice would be likely to quiver with emotion. The effect was admirable, and would still be so if employed as he then employed it. But alas! Rubini fell himself a victim to his own innovation. He cannot be said to have contracted the habit. No, it was even worse than that, for Rubini began to use the vibrato thru all his singing at just the time when it became necessary to do something to distract public attention from the deterioration of his voice.

'It is hardly necessary to go into a history of the subsequent development of the vibrato. It is sufficient to remind observers of singing that it speedily came to be a fixed feature of vocal delivery. The result was that its original purpose was completely obscured, and it became a mannerism of song, devoid of artistic reason or even sensuous beauty.

'Ferri, a singer who flourished in the '50s, went to the extreme in his employment of the quivering tone, for he developed a tremolo which he employed intentionally on every note. Just as many silly ideas were advanced in favor of the tremolo as had already been advanced

---

36 Readers who think I'm exaggerating Henderson's importance are referred to his *Early History of Singing*.

for the vibrato. / The truth is that neither the vibrato nor its reductio ad absurdum the tremolo need be absolutely excluded from the domain of artistic singing, but each should be employed for a specific expressional purpose, and for that only. [25 Jan. 1910: *Lewiston Evening Journal*, William James Henderson, 'Uses and Abuses of Vibrato and Tremolo', quoted from the *New York Sun*]

One of the last diatribes came from William Cooper in 1929, by which time tremolo singing was firmly established: 'Nearly twenty years ago I had the temerity to draw attention, at a meeting of a literary and debating society, to the rapidly increasing vogue of the use of the tremolo in singing in all its various forms, which ranged from the comparatively harmless and sometimes not altogether unpleasant rapid ripple to the powerful pump, invariably succeeded by the gigantic gasp. The substance of my remarks appeared in the columns of the "Auckland Star". Since that time the tremolo in singing appears to have travelled all over the civilised world, with the most disastrous results, in opera, concert and church. When a vocalist, in a moment of weakness, vanity or insanity, takes to the tremolo it very speedily takes hold of him and its continual use becomes a complete obsession. No matter what the theme of the song he is about to render may be, no matter what may be the nature of the music to which the song has been set, the awful tremolo is applied to it; and kept to it from beginning to end. I remember some years ago a singer selecting as the unhappy subject of his vocal talent the 23rd Psalm. That Psalm, as everyone knows who has read it, is an exquisite little production characterised throughout its length by perfect confidence, calm content, serene satisfaction, quiet courage and grateful thankfulness for benefits received. It is unnecessary to dwell on the details of the singer's performance; it is sufficient to say that it was an outrage; and I could not help thinking that had the sweet singer of Israel been able to rise from the dead and confront the vocalist he would have slain him there and then with as little compunction as he slew the mighty Goliath. A multitude of other instances could be quoted. It is satisfactory to notice that there are some of our vocalists, both male and female, who have not yet bowed the knee to the tremolo Baal, and apparently do not intend to do so.' [17 July 1929: AuckS, 'That Awful Tremolo']

The coming of BBC broadcasting generated many complaints about vibrato: 'Whether broadcasting has a good or ill effect on the concert world, it cannot fail, writes a correspondent, to have a beneficial influence upon our singers and their teachers. That wonderful hyper-sensitive little instrument the microphone is telling us many things which we did not know, or, if we did, to which we turned a deaf ear. One point which it is making emphatically clear is that many present-day singers lack clear enunciation. Words which would be more or less intelligible in a concert hall, where the eye assists the ear, become a meaningless jumble to the wireless listener. Even more important is its revelation of the terrible failing which it shows so many singers to possess, and not only the mediocre singer, but the better-known and highly-rated vocalist. This is the tremolo, vibrato, or shake, whichever one chooses to call it. / Caused by either lack of breath control, relaxed throat, over-strain, nervousness, or sheer carelessness, this evil has been so long rampant that we have become inured to it. In its milder form, it is not, perhaps, very perceptible in a large hall. But, nevertheless, a singer who allows his or her voice to shake is never dead in tune. There is always a deviation from the correct pitch of the note, sometimes sharp, more often a little flat. / Voices having this weakness are it is quite evident of no use for broadcasting. Whether the transmitting intensifies the tremor and makes it more pronounced, or whether it is because the singer is in a comparatively small room, and all the sound waves are scrupulously gathered up by the microphone, none being permitted to escape or disperse, and so the listener hears far more of the vibration of the voice than he would in a concert hall, has yet to be discovered. But the fact remains that only a pure, steady, musical tone, with clear enunciation, is suitable for broadcasting.' [12 Jan. 1926: *Western Morning News*, 'Wireless Tests for Singers, Why Some Vocalists Fail to Please']

Editors even allowed vibratoists to be mocked by gratuitous *ad hominem* jibes. For example, two New York Times critics were unsparing of the unfortunate Émil Cossira:

'The tenor was M. Cossira, a gentleman who disported himself as a Romeo of 200 pounds avoirdupois and possessed a small tremulant voice like the patter of rain on a tin roof. In the expressive language of the American boys, he made me tired. The rest of the singers are absolutely not worth mentioning. They would be considered bad in comic opera in New-York. They all possessed small wooden voices and displayed the French vibrato in all its iniquity. I never heard worse singing, not even in the American Opera Company.' [30 Jul. 1889: NYT]

'There is, or has been, trouble in the French opera company at New-Orleans, owing to a disagreement between Mme. Martini, soprano, and Mme. Cossira, wife of the tenor. Cossira received some flowers intended for Mme. Martini. She delicately called his attention to the fact, and he delivered them to their rightful owner, with a courteous apology for his mistake. But the incident annoyed Mme. Cossira. So one night when the tenor was handed some flowers intended for Mme. Martini, Mme Cossira carried them to the soprano, and, saying "You took the others, now take these!" threw them at her. Such are the gentle amenities of life among the song birds. It may be mentioned that Mr. Cossira is a large, fat tenor with a small, lean voice. The little voice and the large body wobble in unison with an obese French tremolo when the tenor is at work. The writer had the misfortune to see and hear this gelatinous shaker in Gounod's 'Romeo et Juliette' at the Paris Grand Opera. Physically he was the greatest Romeo we ever saw. Otherwise he wasn't.' [28 Dec. 1890: NYT, 'Trouble in the French opera company at New-Orleans']

What were are the arguments of the pro-vibrato school? I searched for notices and articles defending vibrato singing, but these were not forthcoming until around 1870. Indeed, contemporary reviewers sometimes noted the complete absence of any sort of counsel for the defence. However, I did find a rare accommodating comment from the *Graphic* on the tenor [Ernesto] Nicolini, Patti's husband, who was criticised for his vibrato on about 90 occasions, as follows:

'Signor Nicolini has rare advantages, both of person and talent. His appearance and bearing are more than commonly agreeable, and he is not without admirable qualities, both as actor and singer. True, the modern French *vibrato* is a drawback to English ears; but we are getting accustomed to it, and the fault is less noticed than ever before.' [20 Apr. 1872: *Graphic*]

This is not so much a defence of vibrato, as a reluctant concession to real-life developments.

The evolving views of **Francesco Lamperti**, an important Milan-based vocal coach, are significant. In his treatise, translated by J.C. Griffith and published in 1877, Lamperti says:

> 'In conclusion, I would put the pupil on his guard once more against the trembling of the voice, a defect which in the beginning of this century was sufficient to exclude any singer from the stage. I would not have him however confound this with the oscillation produced by the expression of an impassioned sentiment.' [1877: Lamperti, *A Treatise on the Art of Singing*]

However, in the updated 1887 edition of Lamperti's book, translated by Walter Jekyll, the last sentence has been changed to:

> 'I should remark that tremulousness must not be confounded with oscillation, which is a good effect produced by a strong, vibrating, sonorous voice.' [1887: Lamperti, *The Art of Singing according to ancient tradition and personal experience*]

This is a major change of emphasis. Lamperti has clearly dissented from García's directive, that tremolo may only be deployed selectively to express powerful emotions, by stating that it is a natural effect and implying that it should be used continuously. Other contributors supported Lamperti:

> An anonymous writer supported this interpretation by a Question and Answer type article: 'In Italy my master was Lamperti, who deservedly has the reputation of being the greatest teacher in Europe. Among his pupils who have gained fame are Albani and Campanini. Lamperti teaches the old Italian system ... When I was in Milan over 300 Americans were there studying music.' In reply to the following question: 'What have you to say of the tremolo so often noticed in singers?' the writer says 'That comes from the explosive use of the breath. It is a defect, but the vibrato, often confounded with the tremolo, is a natural effect. The natural mode of breathing is the only one by which the larynx is left wholly unconstrained—the sine qua non of the good singer.' [1886: BDG, 'About the Old Italian System of Tone Production: Many Hints to singers and Teachers']

> Lamperti was also supported by an ex-pupil: 'A pupil of Lamperti, Madame Bonner imparts his methods with marked success, and under her tuition the best is made of the voice, the principles laid down being of that unartificial kind which teaches the student to make the best use of the favourable points in the voice without forcing and to improve the bad. No tremolo was heard, only the natural vibration, or "oscillation" as Lamperti used to term it, brought about by proper production and use of the resonance cavities.' [7 Jul. 1906: MP]

There is little question that tremolo/vibrato levels were becoming more noticeable, that is, oscillating more widely, as the end of the century drew near. A *Times* reviewer commented on a performance by Victor Maurel in *Rigoletto*:

> 'Some years ago the French baritone [Victor Maurel in Rigoletto at the Royal Italian Opera] was considered to be one of the worst victims of the *vibrato* on the stage; this is so no longer, not on account of any remarkable improvement in his method, but for the reason that the

epidemic has worked such fearful ravages of late years as to make him appear, by comparison, to sing almost steadily.' [18 Nov. 1890: T]

Definitions were changing rapidly. I've already noted that, in the first half of the century, any sort of vocal unsteadiness, whether oscillation or bleating, was nearly always described as 'tremulousness'. It was followed shortly after by 'tremolo' and then, from around 1835, 'vibrato'. All three terms are synonymous through most of the century. But in the last two decades, commentators start to discriminate between oscillation levels. If narrow, it was called 'vibrato' and the singer was sometimes praised. If wider, it was dubbed 'tremolo' and the singer censured. Worst of all, very wide oscillation was described as 'wobbling' (UK), or 'wabbling' (US), and condemned as unacceptable.

One of the first distinctions between acceptable and unacceptable degrees of vibrato was made in a review of Ilma de Murska by the Pall Mall Gazette, in 1865:

> 'She perpetually strains it, and straining it makes it gritty, and to overcome this, she has recourse to the bane of modern singers, the horrible vibrato, which is synonymous really with an uncultivated and half-settled voice. Upon this *vibrato* much confusion exists in the public mind. There are two kinds of *vibrato*, which are not only legitimate, when genuine, but in the highest degree beautiful. One is the result of dramatic emotion, as of a voice broken by sobs, and upon this we need say nothing. The other is the fine, transparent, liquid thrill, the rapid and almost imperceptible pulsation of a note, when it is so true and the voice so perfect that the musical vibrations are allowed perfectly free play. Whenever this is the case, the particular note approaches to theoretical perfection, and clutches the feeling of the hearer at once, just as a perfectly lovely flower at once enthrals the eye.' [29 May 1865: PMG]

The following review, published in *Longman's Magazine*[37] 'hit the spot' and was widely published elsewhere. The author accepts vibrato, not only because it was a *fait accompli*, but because 'ordinary vibration' is 'essential to every well-produced note' and it also (supposedly) allows the singer to obtain much greater power. But, he reaffirms his disapproval of the more extreme tremolo.

> 'Many singers, especially young singers, fall into the habit of using the "tremolo" or "vibrato". The former is, as the word implies, a trembling of the voice, and may be dismissed as simply vulgar and offensive. The "vibrato" stands on a different footing. It is impossible to pass a sweeping condemnation upon it, seeing that it is adopted by nearly the whole Italian school—that school to which we are accustomed to look for the proper production of the voice. Where it does not arise from an unsteadiness due to straining the open tones in large theatres and music halls, it would appear upon analysis to be an exaggeration of the ordinary vibration, which is essential to every well-produced note. It enables the singer to obtain much greater power, a desideratum in opera singing and in the large concert halls, and, if kept within bounds, is not open to objection. But some singers use it to such an exaggerated extent that

---

37   Not available online in full text form at the time of writing. Besides *Murray's Magazine*, it appeared in the *Non Conformist Musical Journal* (1890) in the UK. US sources include the *New York Times* (March 4, 1888), *Lima Daily Democratic Times*, Ohio (April 25, 1888), and the *Daily Huronite*, South Dakota, (May 1, 1888).

it is sometimes difficult to tell on what note the singer intends to dwell. The voice is swayed backwards and forwards instead of resting on the note, and this exaggeration produces a most unpleasant sensation on a sensitive. There is one of our leading sopranos at the present day who will make a nervous person with a sensitive ear fidget on his chair from the irritation her singing causes; and yet her singing is always spoken of with enthusiasm by the entire press. On the whole, I may say that, happily, our English singers have declined to follow the Italian School into this exaggerated style, but it is not altogether unnecessary to warn the beginner against it.' [Feb. 1888: *Murray's Magazine*]

There are review comments from the last couple of decades of the nineteenth century implying that **some** vibrato was just about acceptable or even desirable, certainly in opera if not in concert singing. Here are some typical review extracts:

'Signor Rawner is a robust tenor of the school now popular in Italy. He has a powerful voice, which he uses unsparingly [singing *Il Trovatore* at Covent Garden]; and although not free from the vibrato, the defect is not so pronounced as to become unpleasant.' [26 May 1890: DN]

'His voice, Mr. William Ludwig might have been steadier with an advantage; an amount of tremolo which is scarcely noticed on the stage at the present day is most obtrusive in the concert-room.' [2 Nov. 1891: T, at Crystal Palace Concert]

'The vibrato is used effectively [by Mme. Emma Eames during recital at Chickering Hall] and not indiscriminately.' [24 Nov. 1893: BDG]

'[Denis] O'Sullivan was an ideal Shamus O'Brien ... In Concert he is afflicted with a vibrato that borders on a tremolo, but in opera this defect is scarcely apparent, and otherwise his singing leaves nothing to be desired.' [27 Apr. 1897: *San Francisco Call*]

'He [William Keith] needs to guard against his tendency to indulge in the tremolo, to the extent of almost wabbling on some of his notes.' [28 Apr. 1896: *San Francisco Call*]

'Mr. [Charles] Hedmondt's Tannhaüser was a most powerful and impressive performance ... in place of the sentimental lyrical lilt which seems to be the ideal of so many he brought out a voice vibrating in every note with strenuous masculine passion. This is just what is wanted for a Tannhaüser. We heard his slight tremolo criticised, but it cannot be said that it spoilt or even noticeably detracted from his performance.' [6 Mar. 1900: *Sheffield & Rotherham Independent*]

'Signor [Giuseppe] Kaschmann was the barytone of the "Lucia" performance [at the Met on 24 Oct. 1883]. He had a handsome face and figure, a good bearing, and disclosed familiarity with the stage, and considerable talent as an actor, but he was afflicted with that distressful vocal defect which singers of his school often call vibrato in order to affect to find a virtue in it. There is, indeed, artistic merit in a true vibrato which lends vitality to a voice, but when it degenerates into a tremolo, or wabble, it is a vice of the most unpardonable kind.' [1883: Krehbiel, p. 96, reflecting the author's views when his book was published in 1908]

The general disapproval of any kind of unsteadiness in singing continued towards the end of the century and beyond. I've already quoted from the 'Vocalists and Wobblers' article [p. 265] The author goes on to mention other singers supposedly free from the tremolo. There is a problem with this list, which I will come to shortly.

As we've seen, some reviewers distinguished between acceptable and unacceptable degrees of vocal wavering. However, for others, 'vibrato' remained just as much a term of abuse as 'tremolo'. Singers in particular found euphemisms to replace the word. From around 1910, reviewers started to describe modest levels of vibrato as 'the thrill':

> 'But "vibrato" comes from "vibrare", which differs essentially from "tremolo", "tremoloare". "Vibrato" means resonant, sonorous. A voice may be said to vibrate with emotion. Therefore it means a certain colouring of the voice induced by the artist's feeling, and is very far removed from a shaky, trembling voice. It is said of Rubini (1795–1854) that no one seems ever to have equalled him in emotional vocal expression, and the adjective "vibrato" was first applied to his singing. So please remember that vibrato is the "thrill" in the voice, and tremolo its unsteadiness.' [18 Nov. 1911: *Dominion*]

Certainly by 1905, perhaps earlier, another new term defining the permissible level of wavering was introduced: 'resonance'. It's still in use, mainly as a technical term used by singers and vocal coaches. Here are two quotes using this new word.

> 'The coming of [Nellie] Melba, it is to be hoped, will have a lasting impression upon the musical circles of Cedar Rapids. The young vocalists who heard her last night can now appreciate the difference between resonance and that "tremolo stop" effect that so many are acquiring, to the irreparable injury of their voices and the disappointment of their friends.' [19 Jan. 1905: *Cedar Rapids Evening Gazette*]

> 'Sir, —Referring to the notice of a vocal recital your always interesting and careful critic will forgive my pointing out that he for once sinned in making "tremolo" and "vibrato" synonyms. The best Italian and French schools of singing thoroughly and emphatically deprecate the "tremolo" as a proof of diaphragm instability, or other fault of vocal production, and hold the "vibrato" to be the true ringing resonance of the well-trained voice, heard in every good singer from Melba and Caruso downwards. Murri Moncrieff, 3 Gordon-mansion, W.C.' [27 Jan. 1906: *Daily Mail*, Letter to the Editor]

The second part of the last sentence in the Daily Mail quote was by now the received wisdom, and it remains so today, over a century later.

Sarah Potter, after citing my observation about singers finding euphemisms to replace the word vibrato, noted that 'This has in fact continued in the ambiguous discussion of 'sweetening' or 'warming' vocal sound, which modern singers often interpret as being a direction to use (additional or different) vibrato effects.' [2014: Sarah Potter, p. 72]

This is an appropriate place to ask the question: What did composers think about tremolo/vibrato? It seems that, more often than not, they disliked it:

Gioachino Rossini [1792–1868]. '"Then he [Rossini] sighed, "ahi noi! Perduto il bel canto della patria!" [Alas for us!—our homeland's bel canto is lost!] / Then he added: "At present, with our so-called singers, bel canto is produced with a convulsive thrusting of the lips, from which there emerges, particularly with tenor-baritones, a tremolo that closely resembles the buzzing produced in my ears by the way the floor shakes at the approach of my brewer's chariot; whereas tenors and prime donne allow themselves—the former, vociferations, the latter, garglings [Gargouillardes], and these have in relation to real vocalizations and roulades nothing but the consonance of the rhymes".' [1858: Michotte, p. 106]

'Rossini detested the modern vice of French singing, the vibrato. While living at Passey, a young French baritone went with a letter of recommendation to the great composer, who received him cordially and asked him what he would sing. The vocalist pulled out a sheet of music. It was a baritone air from *Semiramide*, but the singer, partly through timidity, so exaggerated the vibrato that Rossini turned round and said merrily, "Pray, Monsieur, stop a moment. If you continue to shake like that you will certainly fall to pieces before you reach the last bar".' [1858: *Era Almanack,* Jan. 1879]

Camille Saint-Saens [1835–1921]. 'The Execution of Classical Works, Notably Those of the Older Masters, By Camille Saint-Saens, Translated by Herman Klein for "The Musical Times", being the text of a lecture delivered on June 1, 1915, at the San Francisco Exhibition. THE ABUSE OF THE TREMOLO. Another blot on modern execution is the tremolo (chevrotement) indulged in by singers and instrumentalists. In the case of singers this trembling is often the result of fatigue of the voice—when it is involuntary and merely to be regretted. / With violinists and violoncellists it is not the same thing. It is a fashion born of the desire to make an effect at all costs, and of the depraved taste of the public for impassioned playing. Now art does not depend on passion alone. In our epoch, wherein art, thanks to its admirable working out, has conquered every domain, music should be capable of expressing everything, from the most perfect calm to the most violent passion. / When one is strongly moved the voice alters; in moving situations the singer should let his voice vibrate. Formerly German singers used to sing everything full voice without any variation in the sound, whatever the situation might be; they might have been so many clarinets. / Now it is nothing but vibration. I once heard the quintet from the "Meistersinger" sung in Paris. It was frightful, and the piece was incomprehensible. Happily all singers do not suffer from this defect, but it has got hold of all the violinists and violoncellists. Franchomme, the violoncellist, friend and colleague of Chopin, did not play in this way, neither did Sarasate, Sivori, or Joachim.' [20 Oct. 1915: *Brisbane Courier*]

Sir Frederic Hymen Cowen [1852–1935]. 'Some years ago the eminent English composer, Cowen, withdrew his opera *Signa* from the stage at Genoa because he found it could not be properly interpreted. In his judgment "singing has so greatly deteriorated in Italy that, in the 'land of song', it soon bids fair to be a lost art. Whether it is true that the old race of Italian teachers is extinct, or that the $2.50 a lesson of the fair Americans has demoralized them, or that the pernicious tremolo is actually cultivated by Italian masters as a vocal grace, it is certain that we now get our best vocal recruits from the United States, France, Poland, or almost anywhere else than Italy ... In the supply of new oratorio and other concert singers," he adds, "Great Britain and America have long enjoyed something very like a monopoly"—a fact worth remembering.' [1910: Finck, p. 92] It is apparent from Cowen's autobiography that his disappointment in Genoa must have occurred in the autumn of 1892, although there is no mention of the tremolo problem, only that the vocalists 'were not such as would be at all likely to insure the success of my work.' [1913: Cowen, *My Art and My Friends*, p. 250]

Charles Villiers Stanford [1852–1924]. 'Dr. Stanford, returned to London from a visit to Italy, rises up as a fresh witness to the spread of "the malignant disease" of the vibrato in the land of song. The very street boys, he says "are now afflicted with this vocal delirium tremens". Describing the performance of Verdi's Falstaff in Milan, this capable critic declares that the part of Mrs. Ford was entrusted to a singer "whose vibrato was so persistent that at times it was difficult to tell within three tones the note which she intended to sing", while an unaccompanied quartette of rapid staccato is said to have been "so quavered and shaken that it was a matter of sheer impossibility to follow either the harmonies or even the single notes". Dr. Stanford, lamenting the growth of this evil habit, very justly remarks: "Not only is cantabile singing destroyed by it, not only is the finest melody corrupted by it, but the vibrato itself, a power by which, when used in its proper place, an overpowering effect can be produced, is reduced to a position of that contempt which familiarity proverbially produces. If singing is polluted in Italy, the world will be infected by the stream".' [5 May 1893: *Table Talk*, Melbourne]

Giacomo Puccini [1858–1924]. 'The composer of "Manon Lescaut" has been continuing some of his early experiences to a representative of the "Daily Chronicle". Asked as to the use of the tremolo, he said that no Italian liked it. "They loved the bel canto, the sweet smooth singing voice. The tremolo was partly due to the fact that modern singers came out too soon, which is perhaps another way of saying that they are not sufficiently trained".' [16 Nov. 1904: *Falkirk Herald*]

Vaughan Williams [1872–1958]. 'Dr. Vaughan Williams [at the Halifax Musical Festival] was very severe upon the vibrato habit, which he said was due to lack of breath control. It was true it could be heard in the voices of singers of fame, but the fact was they went travelling up and down the country and took so many engagements that they were tired out, and could not help their vibrato. So the only way was to make a virtue of necessity. But he implored young singers not to imitate it.' [25 Nov. 1922: YPLI] I can add to this a couple of recollections from my own experience, dating from my first exposure to practical music making in 1951, when I sang choral bass in rehearsals and a performance of Bach's *Matthew Passion* directed by Vaughan Williams in the Dorking Halls as part of the Leith Hill Musical Festival. First, he would sometimes direct the choir in chosen chorales sung a cappella in the Martineau Hall; as I recall, the singers in the choir, all untrained amateurs, produced a beautifully clear and smooth sound, with no vibrato audible. Second, my mother, who sang soprano at the festival for many years, told me that ageing sopranos had to be careful, as vibrato perpetrators would be asked to retire.

As I shall show, the composers Dr **Varley Roberts** [1841-1920] and Sir **Richard Terry** [1865-1938] were both strongly opposed to vibrato singing.

However, **Giuseppe Verdi** [1813–1901] was probably an exception, certainly later in his career, when he directed the UK premiere of his *Requiem* at London's Royal Albert Hall in 1875. Several reviews of this event make clear that all four of the soloists, Teresa Stoltz (soprano), Maria Waldmann (contralto), Signor Medini (tenor) and Signor Masini (bass) had been brought over by Verdi for the occasion. Both ladies had also sang in the Milan premiere of the work on 22 May 1874. Here are some review comments:

> 'A better quartett of soloists than those who have sung in the Requiem it will be hard indeed to find. Vocally they are individually fine, and in each case the singing bespeaks the conscientious artists; but the greatest charm is the manner in which the ensemble is managed, and the perfect accord that prevails in the concerted singing. Madame Stoltz and Madame Wildman are both blessed with glorious vocal organs, and it is to be hoped that the fallacious method of instruction which has left evidences of the baneful vibrato in either case will be abandoned for a worthier and purer school. The ladies are both young, and have an exceptionally brilliant future before them. Signor Masimi sings with taste, but he, too, is somewhat tremulous at times, notwithstanding which his sweet-toned tenor voice asserts its charm. Signor Medini is already known to opera-goers, he having "débuted", as the Americans say, at Her Majesty's Opera not very long since. His voice is a pure bass, round and full in tone, and with a smoothness of quality seldom united to an organ of such sonority.' [23 May 1875: ST]

> 'The tenor, Signor Masini, possesses scarcely power enough for so large a building, and was at times almost overpowered by the other performers. He possesses a pleasant voice, though the high notes—a remark which to a less extent may apply to all the singers—are marred by the constant use of the vibrato …' [12 Jun. 1875: *Baltimore Bulletin*]

> 'Mddle. Teresina Singer, despite the severe trial of following Madame [Teresa] Stoltz in Aïda, has met the approval of the Parisians at the Italian opera-house. Her chief defect was that of her predecessor, the predominance of the tremolo.' [25 Nov. 1876: Ath]

I've already quoted the letter from **William H. Cummings** on Page 243 above, where he reports the comment of a lady in the audience on Teresa Stoltz's voice 'what a beautiful shake the vocalist had', which makes clear that she sported a wide pitch vibrato.

My point is that all four soloists had been personally selected by Verdi himself, suggesting that he had no problem with vibrato singing.

After reviewing composers' views, I'll go up a level and consider the opinions of William Ewart Gladstone, one of Britain's best prime ministers. Gladstone discussed his views over a dinner with Mr. Chauncey M. Depew, a distinguished US railway magnate, a friend and supporter of Gladstone, as published shortly after Gladstone's death in the Dundee Evening Telegraph of 30 May 1898, and in the Nottingham Journal a day later. They were related by Depew to a journalist from the London Daily News, as quoted below. While the date of the dinner was not disclosed, I believe this was in July

1889, when Depew visited London. This date is consistent with [1] the growing fame of the de Reszke brothers after 1887 and [2] the home rule struggle being 'at its height', given that the first Irish Home Rule Bill was in 1886 and the second in 1893:

> ' 'At the time when the Home Rule struggle was at its height I dined one evening with him at Lord Rosebery's' ... MR. GLADSTONE AND THE OPERA / 'The same year', Mr Depew continued, 'I was one evening at the opera in a box with Mr Gladstone. He listened intently to the performance, and during the *entr'acte*, he gave me a history of musical progress during his lifetime. 'For sixty years', he said, 'I have been a lover of the opera', and he went on to relate the whole story of opera during that time. He mentioned all the great composers contemporary with himself and their principal works, giving the weak points and distinctive marks of one man's music against those of another, balancing the strength of the one against the claims of a rival, differentiating between the exact shades of distinction in two men of the same school. Then he went on to the singers, and compared the singers of yesterday, the Marios and the Grisis, with the Pattis, the Albanis, and the De Reszkes of to-day. Had anyone who did not know him heard him talk he would have said, 'Here is some old musical critic who for half a century has devoted his life to nothing but musical studies'. After he had finished his review, Mr Gladstone said, 'For 30 years opera was to me a constant source of enjoyment, but for the last 30 years I have been unable to listen to it with any real pleasure. The conductors of Covent Garden Theatre raised the musical pitch, and this led to the introduction of the tremolo. Where the pitch was raised many singers could not take their top notes without the tremolo, and since the tremolo has come in opera has been spoiled for me'.' [30 May 1898: *Dundee Evening Telegraph*]

If my dates approximate to the truth, Gladstone would have enjoyed the opera from 1829 to 1859, but his visits between 1859 and 1889 would have been spoiled by tremolo. In response to a Facebook discussion, **Graham O'Reilly** kindly supplied some information[38] on pitches, suggesting that pitch at Covent Garden could well have increased around 1859. **Henry Chorley** complained about high pitch levels in 1845 (as noted on p. 137 above) and in 1868. The singer Sims Reeves supported Chorley, writing: 'Not only foreigners accustomed to foreign orchestras will be indebted to you for thus protesting against, as you most truly remark, the human voice, the most delicate of all instruments, being sacrificed to the false brilliancy attained by perpetually forcing up the pitch, but English artists generally. And as you truly remark, 'the pitch in this country is a half-tone higher than that of most

---

38   'The report for the pitch commission in France in 1859 gives 3 pitches for London, supplied by John Broadwood and all used for different pianos. The lowest is 434, said to have been used by the Philharmonic Society 25 or 30 years earlier (i.e. c.1830). It is described by Broadwood as "the best for the voice", and still used for pianos made for accompanying vocal concerts. The second (452.5) is most widely used, because it is more or less (sic) the same as that used by instrumentalists (e.g. "harmoniums and flutes"). The 3rd (455+) is the pitch used now (i.e. 1858/9) by the Philharmonic Society. If the Philharmonic Society's raise in pitch echoes that of Covent Garden, it accords more or less with Gladstone's commentary and posits a big change between 1830 and 1860, perhaps led largely by instrumental practices. It's worth remembering that the commission's main task was not only to set some kind of standard but also (and perhaps mainly) to stop pitch constantly rising (the figures given show a rise from 423 to 448 at the Paris Opéra between 1810 and 1858).' [1860: *Histoire du Conservatoire impérial de musique et de déclamation*]

foreign orchestras and a whole tone higher than it was in the time of Gluck'.' Sims Reeves felt so strongly about the issue that he vowed to sing no further for the Sacred Harmonic society while 'the pitch of the orchestra was maintained at its present height'.

4.6 Non-Vibrato Singing in the Nineteenth Century

It is apparent from Illus. 47 that 1,400 reviews praising non-vibrato singing were published in the second half of the nineteenth century. Of course, just because a critic reports that Mario has no vibrato, that in itself does not constitute incontestable proof that he sang with a totally straight voice. However, the evidence suggests that straight, non-vibrato singing was a reality, even later in the century. I focus first on two celebrated female singers, Clara Novello and Melitta Otto Alvsleben.

The following notices on Clara Novello leave little doubt that she sang in straight voice.

> '"On mighty pens", was sung by Miss C. Novello [singing at the Yorkshire Musical Festival] with that purity of tone and chasteness of style, which have so frequently called forth our eulogiums.' [11 Sep. 1835: HP]

> Her voice was cited on p. 88 as 'soft as the tones of musical glasses'.

> The following quotation is included in Clara Novello's *Reminiscences*: 'Schumann, in his "Music and Musicians", essays and criticisms [1854], says, "Clara Novello was the most interesting of these (artists). She came to us from her friendly London circle, heralded as an artist of the first rank, and this weighed with us in Leipzig. For years I have heard nothing that has pleased me more than this voice, predominating over all other tones, yet breathing tender euphony, every tone as sharply defined as the tones of a keyed instrument; besides the noble performance, the simplicity, yet art, which seemed to desire prominence for the composer and his work only. She was most in her element with Handel, amid whose works she has grown up and become great ... Miss Clara Novello is not a Malibran, and not a Sontag, but she possesses her own highly original individuality, of which no one can deprive her.' [11 Nov. 1837: Clara Novello, *Reminiscences*, p. 66]

> 'It will be seen in the following pages that, when Grisis and Persianis were still to the fore, Rossini was anxious that the young English singer should be secured to take the leading part in the "Stabat Mater" in Italy. With her clear resonant voice, ranging from C below the stave to D in alt, the florid music of the modern Italian school was well within her compass ... Afterwards Rossini used to rehearse us, the quartet especially, "Quando corpus", which soon went as smoothly as an accordion, so that I would say to Rossini, "If you rehearse us because you enjoy hearing it, all right, but don't say it can be improved!".' [1 Oct. 1848: Clara Novello, *Reminiscences*, p. 134]

> 'I travelled with her in England, Ireland and Scotland during her farewell tour in 1860. Daily contact with her gave me a high opinion of her knowledge and intelligence, and above all, of her good heart ... Her voice, was clear, resonant, and beautiful, absolutely free from vibrato. She had been well-trained, and had inherited the best traditions from the past. Her method of

singing was admirable, particularly in the management of the breath; hence the correctness of her phrasing. As an example, take the opening of Handel's "I know that my Redeemer liveth". She sang the words in one long continuous breath, and thereby preserved the sense. Nowadays it is quite common to divide the phrase into three portions.' From Letter by **Dr. William Cummings**. [20 Oct. 1860: Clara Novello, *Reminiscences*, p. 23]

Melita Otto Alvsleben, after débuting in 1860, was hired as a lyric and coloratura soprano at the Dresden Court Theater. The reviews that have come down to us date from 1873 and 1874, when she visited London, and in 1879 when she went to the US. Once again, it is clear that she sang in straight voice, possibly one of the last female divas to do so:

I've already quoted [p. 171] the *Musical Standard's* comment to the effect that her voice was reminiscent of the 'bell-like quality' of Clara Novello's voice.

'Mozart's aria, "Non mi der, bell' idol mio", by Madame Alvsleben, was sung very sweetly, and with a pure, clear tone, devoid of the objectionable tremolo in which many foreign artists like to indulge.' [17 Mar. 1873: LM]

'Madame Otto-Alvsleben led the double terzetto of soloists with all the decision and artistic self-reliance that we remember to have admired in her some four years ago in Dresden. Her voice is strong and agreeable in quality, although a certain flutiness of timbre, a want of the fine, mordant, reedy quality that we notice in most of the great soprani, makes her singing lose in absolute distinctness of outline what it gains in perhaps rather insipid sweetness.' [26 Jul. 1873: *Atlantic Monthly*]

A *Manchester Guardian* review also rated Melita Otto-Alvsleben highly, when she performed in Rossini's Stabat Mater at Mr. C. Halle's Grand Concert: 'The purity of her tone is delightfully in harmony with the luscious sequences and symmetrical form of Rossini's later arias. Singing more absolutely perfect in tune we think we have never heard. We are not certain, however, whether, in these days of the *vibrato,* so much used and abused as to be almost universal, this very steady purity of tone does not give to her singing a certain coldness to ears depraved by listening to singers who indulge in the vicious practice which is so prevalent. Whether or not, we hope that we shall still be able to count upon her as representing a school of singing where purity of tone and truthfulness of intonation were of, at least, equal importance with vocal facility, and far above mere meretricious trickery of whatever kind.' [7 Nov. 1874: MG]

The slightly critical undertone of the last two reviews suggests that Otto-Alvsleben's sound, absent the 'fine, mordant, reedy quality', was out of line with contemporary expectations.

I've already quoted reviews on 11 singers who were clearly tremolo-free:

- Every note of Angelica Catalani's voice was 'as firm as the tone of a trumpet' [p. 46].
- Ronzi de Begnis imitated the oboe exactly 'by rather closing her mouth' [p. 144].
- Josephine Fodor-Mainvielle's voice 'exceeds the purest tones of a first rate flute' [p. 140].

- Nicola Ivanoff compared favourably to Rubini in one respect because he 'has the advantage in steadiness of tone, and continuity of sound' [p. 186].

- Gilbert Duprez 'is totally free from that tremulousness which throws a sameness—a certain languor over all the performances' of Rubini' [p. 185].

- Miss Charlotte Birch's voice possessed 'that glassy tone' [p. 87] which strongly reminded the reviewer of Eliza Salmon's voice.

- Laure Cinti-Damoreau's voice sounded 'like drops of water upon a musical glass' [p. 148].

- Giovanni Matteo Mario was reported a 'pure and perfect tenor, every note of which … strikes the ear with the clearness and precision of the finest-toned bell' [p. 190].

- Joseph Maas's voice was always in tune, with no exaggeration or forcing, and consequently free from 'tremolo' [p. 197].

- Antonio Giuglini sang with 'the firmness and smoothness of a clarinet' [p. 208].

Some 18 other celebrated singers were also probably tremolo-free:

'He [Napoleone Moriani] carefully avoids … that too common trick with Italian artistes of all grades of voice, the use of the tremolo, or voce vibrato.' [30 Jun. 1844: Obs]

'In the duett "A quel suono" her clear and joyous tones told with great effect; but it was in the quartett "A te o cara" that she [Anaida Castellan] most clearly brought to memory the extreme finish of execution of Persiani. Her sustained alto notes here were so pure, and free from wavering—so searching and telling, that a burst of admiration, too premature, prevented the whole of the music being heard.' [7 Sep. 1846: *Saunders's News-Letter*]

The Times critic praised the bass Antonio Superchi in *La Favorita* at Her Majesty's Theatre, as follows: 'It is impossible for a singer to be more free than Superchi from this defect of his predecessor' [Luciano Fornasari, who was widely faulted for his tremulousness]. 'His notes are as firm as possible, and his flow of song is in the highest degree smooth and even.' [17 Feb. 1847: T]

'The tremulous style of singing so observable in some of the popular favorites of the day, I judge to be of modern origin. Effective as this is in producing the rich, cantabile expression of the violin, it's too frequent abuse by vocalists would lead us to cherish the firm, un-Italianized, sustained tone which comes from the throat of a [Jenny] Lind.' [Dec. 1851: *Dwight's*]

'Scarcely the slightest symptom of tremulousness was apparent in her sonorous voice, which rang like the sound of a silver trumpet, sweet, clear, and penetrating … Mademoiselle [Johanna] Wagner's voice, as we have already said, unites all the excellences of the soprano and contralto. Her upper notes are wonderfully true and pure; and if the middle ones are less rounded than we could wish, the lower ones are perfect. Nothing, in a word, can be finer than the quality of the organ.' [21 Jun. 1856: SatR]

'The last-named artist [Pietro Neri-Baraldi] has a song introduced for him, and his singing is very grateful to those who do not care for the eternal vibrato of Tamberlik, who is nevertheless a great artist.' [10 Jul. 1858: MusG]

'Herr [Theodore] Wachtel's vocal resources are, moreover, quite exceptional, for he sings up to C sharp in alt with wonderful force and resonance of tone, and no tremulousness whatever.' [9 Jun. 1862: MP]

'The roundness and the steadiness of her sustained notes [Thérèse Tietjens] are in themselves a treat, and contrast strikingly with the tremulousness of most singers. On what principle singers deliver their notes in waves instead of straight lines it is hard to say. A saw is more penetrating on account of the zigzag edge, but it is doubtful whether high chest-notes are, as a rule.' [6 Feb. 1869: *Sphinx*]

'Mdlle. [Marie] Marimon, for example, has a high soprano voice of singular purity, and of that "sympathetic quality"—to use an accepted phrase—which makes it resemble the voice of Mdlle. Nilsson. The range of her organ is extensive, and, from the highest note to the lowest, it travels with remarkable freedom and precision. There is a noteworthy absence of the vibrato—a defect which mars so many naturally fine voices—though, when necessary, Mdlle. Marimon can make the vibrato do excellent service. Moreover, she sings perfectly in tune, and delivers the most daring and original bravura passages with surprising ease.' [5 May 1871: DT]

'Signor [Giuseppe] Fancelli's high notes are extremely brilliant and resonant, and he sings without that eternal tremolo which is the bane of nearly all tenor singers just now. It is a system which not only hinders greater effects than it produces, but in the course of time it destroys the quality of tone, and makes the singer's intonation uncertain and false.' [15 May 1871: Era]

'The tenor is also a new-comer, brought from England for this occasion, Mr. [William Hayman] Cummings. He is a slightly-built gentleman, about five feet ten inches high, has light hair, a receding forehead, a light gentlemanly-looking (but not *distingue*) mustache, and stands quietly while singing. His voice is a tenor of good volume, and admirable quality—like a silver trumpet. The intonation is to be relied on, and his delivery of the tone pleasant. The words are delivered as well as possible, both in recitative and the airs. I doubt whether Mr. Cummings be a great singer, yet he is a better oratorio tenor than I have heard. He is entirely innocent of tremolo and absurd affectation.' [15 May 1871: CT]

'In fact, in seeing Madlle. Zaré Thalberg, we beheld the ideal Zerlina of Mozart ... [she] was careful to make no undue effort for the sake of effect, contenting herself rather with singing in an easy, unaffected manner, with a nice discrimination between the ostentation of simplicity and that of self-reliance. Madlle. Thalberg possesses a pure soprano voice, round and velvety as to tone, and of equal timbre throughout the entire register. From such faults as the tremolo or vibrato the singer is perfectly free, and indeed, her entire performance may be epitomised as being natural, artless, and captivating.' [18 Apr. 1875: ST]

'Her voice [Ethelka Gerster] is a pure soprano, not rich or powerful in the lower and middle registers, but bright and penetrating in the upper portion of its compass, which extends to F in alt. Her voice has been well cultivated, and she sings florid music excellently; she is also able to sustain holding notes without the slightest suspicion of a tremolo.' [26 Jun. 1877: *Theatre*]

'… possesses a legitimate tenor voice, of fair compass and agreeable quality, which he knows how to employ without resorting to the so-styled "tremolo", often criticized as an abuse of taste, but really nothing more than a defect of method. From this M. [William] Candidus is entirely free–a fact upon which alone he may be congratulated.' [20 May 1879: T]

'A purer method never came beneath our notice; there is no vibrato, no trick of manner or blemish of education to detract from the effect of her singing [Amalie Joachim], which forcibly reminds one of Titiens [Thérèse Tietjens] in her best days.' [14 Apr. 1878: ST]

Eleonora Robinson's voice was approved on her début as 'full and rich, of almost contralto timbre in the middle register, and of smooth quality throughout; the singer has no difficulty in reaching the higher notes, and the execution is excellent. There is no suspicion of *tremolo* in the production, the tone being as round and even as an organ diapason.' [12 Jun. 1880: Ex]

The tenor Wladyslaw Mierzwinski was welcomed on his début: 'He won success in the first act by some brilliant vocal efforts which fairly excited the audience to an unusual pitch of demonstrative applause. There is no question as to his voice. It is brilliant, clear, and he can use it without resorting to any tricks. There is no vibrato in it, his tone being as steady as a mechanical instrument.' [19 Oct. 1882: NYT]

The high notes of Mr. Heinrich Gudehus 'were as clear and true as those of an instrument.' [11 Dec. 1890: Brook]

4.7   The Other Side of the Story

I've noted that only about 7% of notices approved of vibrato, generally when used selectively to express intense feelings. Further, continuous vibrato was occasionally praised where the oscillation was a slight shimmering. Such singers were also described as possessing 'natural vibrato' or as having 'tears in the voice'. A present-day singer whose voice comes closest to this quality is Jeni Melia. Jeni specialises in lute songs and folk ballads. You can find her album *The Last of Old England* on Spotify. I classified at Section 1.4 'tears in voice' sound as the type BC voice.

Marietta Alboni is a historical candidate for the type BC voice:

> I quoted Henry Chorley's inspired remarks on Marietta Alboni's 'tremulous quality which reminds fanciful speculators of the quiver in the air of the calm, blazing, summer's noon.' [p. 134]

> Alboni's voice was praised as 'melting' and 'tremulous', using language which is consistent with Chorley's description: ' "Ah! non credea", and "Ah! non giunge" from the *Sonnambula* … The introductory Andante was delivered with a melting, tremulous, and yet chaste pathos,

in which there was no sentimental weakness, but a sustained purity of style, and a complete realization of that tearful quality of natural tone which we have heard ascribed to her.' [25 Dec. 1852: MW, 'Alboni in America']

By contrast, seven further notices either fault Alboni's vibrato, or commend her for its absence:

I've noted the Examiner's criticism of her brain-damaging *vibrazione di voce*. [p. 167]

Her execution has already been noted as 'exact and true to time as though performed by a piece of mechanism' with the intonation as 'clear and ringing as a series of chimes'. [p. 167]

She was recorded as employing 'an artificial *tremolo*…throughout.' [p. 167]

'It is, however, the unhappiness of the initiated to be enabled to discover shortcomings; and to these it was evident that Alboni's voice and style were both susceptible of amelioration. In the former, for instance, they remarked an occasional tremulousness, which might have proceeded from physical weakness, or over anxiety, whilst, with respect to the latter, it was found that she had not as yet thoroughly mastered the difficult art of uniting and blending the various registers of her voice so as to produce but one quality of tone throughout.' [14 Jul. 1851: MP]

'Any voice superior in quality to it [Madame Giulia Amadei[39]], betwixt F and F, we do not recollect;—since that octave has all Mdlle. Alboni's luscious sweetness without her tremulousness,[40] and is twice as powerful as hers.' [24 Jan. 1854: Ath]

'The clear rich tones of Madame **Alboni** are given with no less power, facility of execution, and purity of style than they were many years ago. Her steadiness of enunciation is an additional qualification, and contrasts favourably, in our opinion, with the *tremolo* characteristic which is so often associated with high cultivation.' [9 May 1861: *Bradford Observer*]

As noted [p. 167], her voice at 60+ was 'unimpaired' with 'none of that detestable tremolo'.

Alboni's vibrato must have been very delicate or narrow to have generated critiques ranging from brain damaging *vibrazione di voce* to a laudable absence of the detestable tremolo, suggesting that critics c.1850 were severe on even the slightest suspicion of unsteadiness. Note that, while Chorley praised Alboni and one other tremoloist, Angiolina Bosio, his *Recollections* convey clear disapproval of six further tremoloists, namely, Henriette Méric Lalande, Giovanni Battista Rubini, Luciano Fornasari, Enrico Tamberlik, Anna De La Grange and Maria Spezia. Perhaps, for Chorley, it was a matter of degree—a barely detectable shimmering would have been acceptable, but not a perceptible wavering.

Another candidate for the 'tears in voice' sound was Christine Nilsson. One reviewer distinguished her 'delicate yet passionate thrill' from the offensive Italian tremulo: 'The absolute purity of her voice,

---

39   However, Giulia Amadei herself was taken to task on four occasions for her tremolo, which was in one case characterised as continuous.

40   The reviewer is likely to have been Henry Chorley himself, on this occasion expressing slight disapproval of Alboni's tremulousness rather than praise for its shimmering quality.

a purity so unfaltering and pervading that it blends with every impression, and rounds and deepens and enforces every emotion; and with this its exquisite vibration, the delicate yet passionate thrill— as far removed from the hardness of the German school, on the one hand, as from the offensive tremulo of the ultra Italian on the other.' [24 Oct. 1871: EPNY]

Italo Campanini was another 'tears in voice' singer, certainly when in cantabile mode: 'According to the judgement of the most eminent critics in London, Signor Campanini's voice is singularly sweet, pure and equal, his high B flat being of the most exquisite tone … As regards expression, Signor Campanini has intensity where it is required, but in all cases avoids "tearing a passion to tatters", as the melancholy Prince of Denmark observes. His command of the *cantabile* is perfect, and his phrasing an exemplification of the true principles of vocal art. It is not a "still, small (sweet) voice", but an organ of power, sonority and weight. The *mezza voce* is delicious, and the *voix larmoyante* expressive beyond conception. There is an unspeakable sweetness and charm spread around the singer when he utters passages of sorrow and tenderness. It is said of him, as once was remarked of Rubini, "he has tears in his voice".' [19 Aug. 1873: NYHT]

A critic for the Irish Times reviewed Thekla Friedländer favourably, as she sang 'with a curious vibration, not at all disagreeable, which no one who knows anything about voice production will be tempted to confound with what is called the vibrato or tremolo (words constantly used by the way in the most absurdly incorrect fashion). The peculiarity is caused by intensity of feeling and dramatic expression, and is neither an organic defect or a vicious mannerism.' [29 Mar. 1879: *Irish Times*]

The fact remains that many vibratoists continued to sing their way, against strong opposition. I've been unable to find accounts from commentators, whether singers or not, justifying the trend towards vibrato singing, apart from praises by various commentators for 'the thrill', already noted. If they could speak, they might say something like: 'I am a free, creative artist. When I sing and act, the vibrato helps me to convey my intense feelings. My way is the future. Vibrato and the new romantic music go together. Hostile anti-vibrato notices are just symptoms of conservative resistance to change.' A few critics conceded that vibrato might have helped singers like Rubini and Tamberlik achieve dramatic truth, possibly at the expense of vocal beauty. Also, some disapproving reviewers admitted that audiences often applauded vibrato. For example, Rosina Carandini's singing was described: 'The voice is perfectly under command, and is used, as a rule, with remarkably good taste. There seems to be a tendency to indulge in a tremulousness of tone, when much feeling is desired to be expressed, which is very easily, by indulgence, made a blemish on pure expression, but which, it must be admitted, is often very popular with mixed audiences. We do not believe that Miss Carandini needs any such aid to even popular effectiveness; and it would be regrettable if the tendency should be encouraged.' [24 Aug. 1867: *Otago Daily Times*]

I discussed on Page 78 Mozart's observation that 'the human voice trembles naturally'. Could Mozart have had in mind the melting and tremulous voice of singers like Alboni?

4.8 Two Case Studies

Singer	DoB	Recording	Vibrato Notices	Non-Vibrato Notices
Giovanni Matteo Mario	1810		5 (selective)	12
Clara Novello	1818	-	3 (selective)	2
Jenny Lind	1820	-	6 (selective)	5
Antonio Giuglini	1827	-	1 (selective)	5
Therese Tietjens	1831	-	0	2
Giuseppe Fancelli	1833	-	0	6
Sir Charles Santley	1834	1913	4 (+3 selective)	7
Zelia Trebelli	1838	-	1 (selective)	3
Christine Nilsson	1843	-	3	6
Adelina Patti	1843	1905	14 (+7 selective)	27
Italo Campanini	1845	-	1 (+1 selective)	13
Dame Emma Albani	1847	1903	82	9
Edouard de Reszké	1850	1903	1 (nearly free!)	3
Jean de Reszké	1853	1901	4	10
Marie Basta-Tavary	1856	-	3	0
Lillian Nordica	1857	1907/11	4	7
Zélie De Lussan	1861	1903	10	3
Margaret MacIntyre	1865		25	5

Illus. 50: Notices and Recordings of Alleged Non-Tremolo Singers

I mentioned that there is a problem with the list of supposedly non-tremolo singers in the Wobblers article I quoted from earlier.

The table at Illus. 50 lists all the singers mentioned, in date-of-birth order.[41] I've included the number of reviewers' notices criticising these singers' vibrato, or praising the lack of it, plus recording dates (shown in red) in some cases. The problem is that many of these singers, certainly those in the bottom half of the list, attracted some unfavourable notices for their vibrato. The claims of the article's author appear to be inconsistent with some reviews and with the available recordings, all of which display some vibrato. There might be three reasons for this: (1) By 1890, when the article was written, most singers were emitting at least a narrow vibrato, which I have shown was quite acceptable to many, perhaps even the author of this article, although not the wider tremolo; (2) Between 11 and 21 years elapsed from 1890 until the recordings were made, during which time the singers probably adjusted their vibrato levels to match the wider oscillations customary in the first decade of the twentieth century; and (3) The recorded vibrato might in a few cases be age related.

I'll look at two important examples from the list, both famous divas:

Adelina Patti. At the start of her career, Patti received the only really hostile reviews in her whole life, mainly from Henry Chorley of *The Athenaeum* and the *Musical Examiner* [Klein, *The Reign of Patti*, 1920]. He objected to her fatigued voice and vibrato. And, right at the end of her career, a noticeable vibrato is evident from her 1905 and 1906 recordings. But I have also identified reviews praising her vibrato-free voice. I've tried to find more data to throw light on the question, with only limited

---
41   A further non-vibrato singer mentioned in the article was Pietro Mongini. He has been omitted from the table as there were no notices commenting on his vocal timbre, or, of course, recordings.

success. A particular problem with Patti arises from the fact that she was not merely a vocal Queen, but the Empress of Song worshipped worldwide. Honest criticism of Patti highlighting faults as well as virtues was rare, because critics were expected to abase themselves dutifully in her presence, lavishing only the most fulsome raptures and sycophantic hyperbole. However, I found a few reviews suggesting that Patti's voice featured vibrato to a considerable extent, if not constantly.

> '… there were symptoms of nervousness about her—very natural and excusable certainly—that were not apparent at Tuesday's miscellaneous concert. This circumstance will explain some little defects in an otherwise superb performance, and especially the tremulousness which marked her voice throughout, and a slight uncertainty of time in the runs.' [29 Aug. 1861: BDP]

> I've already noted the 'reedy quality' of Patti's voice [p. 200], as well as the 'slight tremolo noticeable' [p. 200].

> 'We have been so often disgusted by the abuse of the vibrato that we sometimes forget how effectively it may be used as an occasional ornament. Madame Patti illustrates this by frequent, but never tedious employment, and she has never permitted it so to affect the perfect control of her voice as to deprive her of the power of sustaining sounds with a steadiness and purity such as we too seldom listen to.' [5 Oct. 1883: MG]

Dame Emma Albani was almost as famous as Patti, with a huge audience of devoted fans in four continents. Her case is of particular interest, as she was criticised 80 times for excessive vibrato between 1873 and 1906. Albani's reviews through most of her 41-year career are displayed on a time line at Illus. 51. This shows that favourable and unfavourable notices are evenly distributed throughout her career, suggesting that her vocal timbre and style may not have changed much. Such critical extremes tell us more about the varying preferences of reviewers than differences in her performance style. As the chart makes clear, there were many more negative than favourable notices on her vibrato singing. Here are some notices containing negative comments on her tremolo or vibrato:

> I've noted the critique on her tremolo sounding like 'a succession of shakes' [p. 201].

> 'When a few performances have familiarised Mdlle. Albani with the part her Margherita will rank amongst the best of her many admirable assumptions. Only one piece of advice we would offer—to beware of that obnoxious tremolo which we hope it is a mistake to fancy she has lately exhibited an inclination to adopt.' [4 May 1875: Std]

> Her 'Angels ever bright and fair' was taken to task, because 'not one of the sweet long-drawn notes was held steadily for two seconds'. [p. 202].

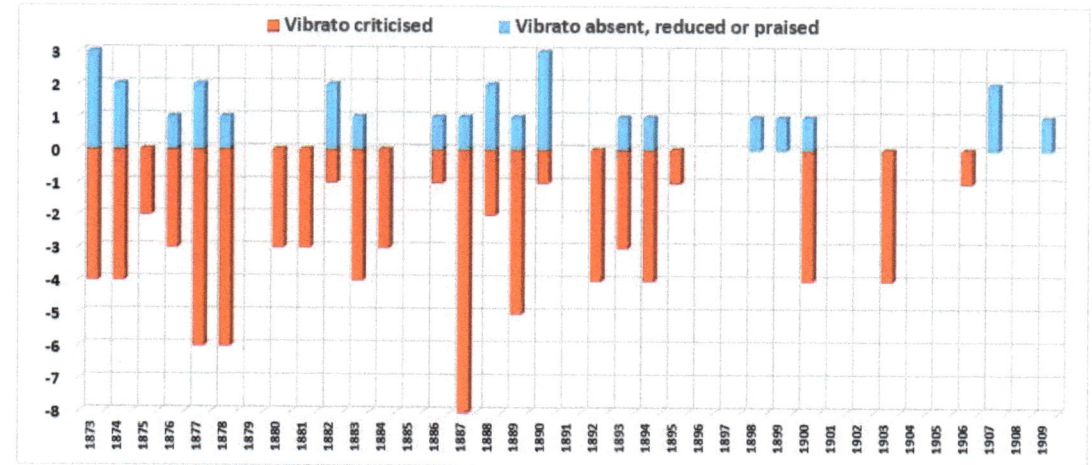

Illus. 51: Reviews of Albani's Vibrato or the Lessening of it

'... not altogether free from the excessive tremolo and the holding of high notes which are her besetting sins.' [9 Dec. 1887: T]

'Her fine voice was in excellent condition, and she sang with more than usual pathos and expression. On two occasions, however, she condescended to introduce the commonplace and mechanical device of the artificial tremolo and on both occasions the effect of her otherwise delightful singing was much injured. The tremolo was so obviously artificial that the listener found himself suddenly awakened from the dramatic illusion previously created by Madame Albani's spontaneous and natural pathos, and the perfunctory voice-trembling—bearing some likeness to an imperfect shake—could not for a moment be mistaken for the involuntary tremor of genuine emotion. Madame Albani on so many other occasions has proved herself able legitimately to command and enchain the sympathies of her audience, that her employment of a stale device, unworthy of so admirable an artist, was much to be regretted.' [17 May 1881: Globe]

'... indulged rather freely in an obnoxious vibrato.' [22 Dec. 1892: LM]

I've quoted [p. 202] a review tabulating a long list of her faults, including vibrato.

Here are four positive reviews.

'Albani has almost completely emancipated herself from the unpleasant tremolo which disfigured her singing at the commencement of the season, and now produces pathetic effects by legitimate means.' [18 May 1873: Obs]

I've quoted [p. 202] a review conceding that she used vibrato but explaining that it was 'a beautiful embellishment, used sparingly and at the proper time'.

'We were never among the flatterers of the Canadian songstress, and when necessary we tempered abundant praise with words of warning in reference to the defects which until recently militated against her success. She has evidently studied hard in a good school; her execution of scale passages is wonderfully improved, her shake is now excellent, and the unpleasing tremolo has almost entirely disappeared. No artist has ever reached perfection, but Mdlle. Albani has approached it more nearly than most of her chief rivals.' [5 May 1877: ISDN]

One of her last reviews [p. 203] admits that she 'does not altogether discard the tremolo either, this being noticeable from time to time in sustained notes'.

But it so happens we have a recording of Albani's 'Angels Ever Bright and Fair'. This and other of her recordings have been put into the public domain. At this point, I invite the reader to play this song from Spotify or YouTube. You have to wonder, what were the critics fussing about? Is her vibrato really persistent? Excessive? Unpleasant? Obnoxious? They were certainly severe on what would be viewed today as minimal (and not continuous) vibrato, just as they were even more so for Marietta Alboni, as we've seen. You understand why contemporary reviewers were also concerned with her too frequent portamentos (in the modern, sliding, sense) and tempo dragging. But the voice is beautiful, with a magnetic quality which comes across. Another important feature of Albani's voice was that she sang in a neutral or high larynx position.

David Badagnani commented about this recording on Facebook: 'Albani: gorgeous, and completely unlike any opera singer of the modern day. The control she had! The vibrato is very subdued and does not detract from the music. And the subtle sliding tones remind me of a skilled player of the theremin (an instrument developed in the 1920s when such refined singing was still practiced). If she was criticized 80 times for using too much vibrato when in this recording she's using almost none, that does seem to be very good proof that just a century ago straight-tone singing really was the standard.'

Albani's vibrato, in terms of width and frequency, is not dissimilar to that of her namesake, Dame Emma Kirkby, who was born exactly 102 years later. Kirkby looks the part as a Wagnerian heroine. If she had been born 100 years earlier, her beautiful voice and professional musicianship would have earned huge fees at the Met, where she would have starred with Jean and Édouard de Reszke in Wagner opera. But the critics might have taken her to task for her minimal vibrato, which has often been assumed (incorrectly) to be zero. She (Kirkby) had no vibrato at all at one time—I can attest that her singing at Clifford Bartlett's wedding, soon after she started out, was absolutely vibrato-free. Her original voice would certainly have been a big hit in the eighteenth century and first half of the nineteenth.

4.9   Recordings show widening vocal vibrato from 1905

My starting point is the earliest vocal recordings, most of which were made around 1905. I have made a Spotify/YouTube playlist [see Illus. 52] containing some of these. All were available in February 2019. Male singers are shaded blue and female singers pink.

Taking females first, it will be apparent that two vocalists [Ellen Beech Yaw and Helen Trix] use virtually no pitch vibrato. In all other cases, vocalists typically use a fast but narrow vibrato, generally less than a semitone wide from peak to trough, but with considerable variation from the relatively wide vibratos of Lilli Lehmann and Clara Butt to the fast trillo exhibited by Irene Abendroth, who had virtually no detectable pitch waver.

Turning to the men, the oldest artist recorded was Charles Santley, who was a remarkable 79 when he recorded *Simon the Cellarer*. Not surprisingly, his voice exhibited some vibrato. But when I looked up my review database, it appears that Santley's vibrato was a lifelong possession, given that he was rebuked for his tremulousness at the age of 24, as noted at p. 207. Victor Capoul was censured 33 times for tremolo. For example: 'M. Capoul is a representative French tenor, and not only introduces the tremolo in pathetic situations of strong dramatic interest—such as occur once or twice in an opera—but is perpetually trembling. As it is absurd to suppose that this kind of emotional display can be appropriate on all occasions, and as its repeated presentation must produce either a painful or an absurd effect, we coincide with those who condemn the introduction of the artificial tremolo.' [28 Apr. 1877: ISDN]

Artist	DoB	on[1]	Title
Charles Santley	1834	SY	Simon the Cellarer (rec 1913!)
Victor Capoul	1839	SY	Au rossignol #
Adelina Patti	1843	SY	Che soave zeffiretto
Emma Albani	1847	SY	Ombra mai fu
Lilli Lehmann	1848	SY	Heil'ge Quelle
Robert Watkin-Mills	1849	SY	Is His Word Not Like a Fire
Andrew Black	1859	SY	O ruddier than the cherry
Ellen Beech Yaw	1869	SY	C'est l'histoire amoureuse
Irene Abendroth	1871	SY	Act 1: Bel raggio
Clara Butt	1872	SY	Ombra mai fu
Friedrich Brodersen	1873	SY	Schwanengesang, D. 957, No. 4
Enrico Caruso	1873	SY	Una furtiva lagrima [Donizetti]
Ada Crossley	1874	SY	Caro mio ben
Billy Murray	1877	SY	Dixie Dan
Julia Culp	1880	SY	Du bist die Ruh
Helen Trix	1886	SY	I've Told His Missus All about Him

[1]Source: S=Spotify, Y=YouTube   #Accompanied by Jean de Reszke

Illus. 52: 'Vibrato-Lite Early 20th-Century Voice' Playlist

My subjective assessment of the singers listed in Illus. 52 is that they generally exhibit voice type BC, apart from Ellen Beech Yaw and Helen Trix (as noted), plus three male singers without any detectable vibrato (Robert Watkin-Mills, Andrew Black and Billy Murray).

Before moving on from Illus. 52, I will focus briefly on the trill, still described then as the 'shake'. This was still something of a party piece exhibited by most divas at the dawn of the recording era. Properly performed trills in this playlist can be heard from Emma Albani and Irene Abendroth. However, Adelina Patti and Ellen Beech Yaw also displayed perfect trills in pieces not listed here. Listen to the succession of impeccable trills from Yaw in her rendition of the *Skylark*.[42] I have to observe that trills are rarely performed well by modern opera or classical singers.

---

42 Her recording of Skylark [1913] can be heard on both YouTube and Spotify.

Looking more generally at the 1900 to 1924 period, it can be seen from Illus. 47 that the volume of protests diminished with only 347 complaints in the lustrum from 1920-24 compared to 1,302 in the peak period from 1890 to 1894. However, there was no let-up in the hostile tone of the reviews, with singers regularly admonished in ferocious anti-tremolo diatribes. It sometimes seems as if, once it was clear that vibrato singing was well entrenched, protests against it became even more vehement. Nor were these limited to opera and concert singing. A heartfelt rant by the spokesman for the adjudicators at an Eisteddfod, Dr. **Varley Roberts**, was widely reported in the provincial press. He claimed that 'twenty-two out of the twenty-seven in one particular competition [Welsh National Eisteddfod at Liverpool] were defiled…by this abominable tremolo'. Interestingly, his proportion of 'defiled' vibratoists is close to Sims Reeves's estimate quoted earlier.

> 'Dr. Varley Roberts, who was the spokesman of the judges, again delivered himself of a fierce diatribe against the tremolo, which he described as a failing in Welsh singing. Waxing more and more vehement, he with pardonable tautology cried that the vibrato must be utterly, entirely, and completely obliterated. He did not care what Wales said, or what the musical critics said, he abominated the tremolo. While Dr. Varley Roberts was thus indignantly eloquent, his own voice became tremulous. "Physician, heal thyself." What sane musical critic would defend the constant vibrato?' [22 Sep. 1900: *Liverpool Mercury*]

Hostile comments by eisteddfod and musical competition adjudicators continued. These events were popular and well attended, with the Brisbane Eisteddfod in April 1913 supposedly attracting an audience of between eight and nine thousand. Dr. Varley Roberts was followed by other judges, often repeating themselves, as shown at Illus. 53:

Competition	Adjudicator	Typical Comment and Date
Bendigo	Professor Peterson	Professor Peterson's remarks should mitigate the practice in Bendigo, but it is a very difficult matter to totally dispense with a vibrato when once the habit is obtained. [8 Jun. 1901: *Bendigo Advertiser*]
Rhyl Eisteddfod	Dr. William Cummings	made some rather disparaging remarks about the quality of Welsh tenor singing, with special reference to the foolishness of overdoing the tremolo business. [8 Sep. 1904: MG]
Otago Competitions	Mr Orchard	It [a little vibrato] was telling sometimes, but unfortunately singers were sometimes so fond of vibrato that they used it anywhere instead of using it as a means of expression for certain passages. [2 Nov. 1904: *Otago Witness*]
Blackpool Festival	Dr. McNaught	Sir,--Referring to the paragraph in Wednesday's 'Post', giving an extract from Dr. McNaught's adjudication notes on the last Blackpool Festival, I am glad to see that he is at last almost violently humorous in his onslaught on the 'vibrator cheap veneer'. [10 Feb. 1905: *Lancashire Evening Post*]

Competition	Adjudicator	Typical Comment and Date
Feis Ceoil	Mr Ivor Atkins	He would like to impress on all their singers that they could not get the perfect sense of any chord if they wobbled in their notes with this wretched tremolo, which, while it was to be condemned in solo singers, was absolutely unendurable in ensemble music. He looked for some explanation of this defect, which is so common, and he believed that the vocalists modelled their singing on singers of great repute when they sing in quartets. [19 May 1906: *Irish Times*]
Austral Festival	Mr. H. J. King	Like another ton of bricks he came down on the use of the tremolo. With great care he explained how it was done, and how destructive of all good singing—and of all good voices—it was. To their credit be it said, however, most of the singers were entirely free of the obnoxious habit. The only case in which he would allow it to be used, said Mr. King, was in French music—for the tremolo was taught in French schools. Nevertheless, 'there is nothing more destructive to the vocal chords than the tremolo'. [21 Nov. 1906: *Brisbane Courier*]
Bala Eisteddfod	Mr. Harry Evans	said that Welsh tenors were degeneration, and were becoming an absolute nuisance at many eisteddfodan. First of all they had a few years ago the tenor who shouted himself red in the face. Then they had the high-collared tenor, with a finicking tone in the back of his head, but nowadays the tenor was a sort of bleat. A good bleat could be admired as sheepish, but bad bleating was extremely bad. The vibrato voice, general throughout the country, was spoiling the voices of Wales. They wanted more voices of the type of Eos Morlais, who sang naturally. Nowadays tenors produced their songs in a tremendously foggy voice, and he recommended them to dispense with the vibrato, and sing clearly and straightforwardly…The vibrato style of singing is becoming a musical disease in Wales, and the sooner we rid ourselves of it and stamp it out the better. [6 Jul. 1907: *Australian Star*]
Mount Barker Literary and Musical Competition Society	Mr Sanders	Vibrato or tremolo should be strictly avoided. It was quite hard enough to sing correctly in three- or four-part harmony without any wobbling going on. Vibrato gave a pretty grace in solos when judiciously introduced, but on the whole the less it was used the better would it be for the singer. The greatest artists seldom used it. Vibrato was extremely dangerous in a duet and absolutely fatal in a trio or quartet. [27 Mar. 1908: *Mount Barker Courier*]
Bristol Eisteddfod	Mr. Dan Price	Voices which were good by themselves were not always good in duets. Tremolo would do sometimes in solo singing, but it would not do in a duet. [14 May 1908: *Western Daily Press*]
Eaglehawk A.N.A. Competitions	Mr. W. Hautrie West	Faulty breathing and the tremolo were again in evidence and in making his criticisms on these defects he desired to say that he hoped the competitors would take them in the spirit in which they were made. [22 Jul. 1908: *Bendigo Advertiser*]
Austral Competitions	Herr Hugo Alpen	The chief fault he had noticed was the undue use of the tremolo, and that spoiled the best singing. The indulgence of the vibrato should be avoided. [15 May 1909: *Bendigo Advertiser*]

Competition	Adjudicator	Typical Comment and Date
Ballarat competitions	Mr. C. N. Baeyertz	Mr. Baeyertz finds much of his time as adjudicator taken up in undoing the work of so-called 'professors'. The tremolo, or 'wobbling', and the vibrato have been by this time almost universally condemned. Though each may be excusable at times for purposes of impressiveness in solo singing, they are abominable in part singing; and, when indulged in by a singer with a loud and aggressive voice, they are calculated to throw a whole chorus out of tune. The tremolo was once even taught and practised, but is now happily devoted to the limbo of hideousness and discord, to be emulated only by the maddening efforts of a Chinese band at its worst. Old-fashioned persons do it still, for it is a habit which, once acquired, can rarely be thrown off. [10 Jan. 1911: *Kalgoorlie Miner*]
Musical and Elocutionary Competitions at Shepparton	Mr. Graham W Weir	'Those philippics of yours against the tremolo. Did it disagree with your digestion?' / 'Um—It might have. But I was very sorry having had to speak so much in condemnation of the tremolo. It is a vicious mode; it is destructive to the voice and painful to the ear. No thorough master would ever encourage such production. Unfortunately, it is practised by a prominent institution in Melbourne.' [14 Oct. 1910: *Coburg Leader*]
Lytham Musical Festival	Dr. McNaught	Dr. McNaught severely criticised the introduction of vibrato by several of the competitors. The only excuse for it was to cover up a bad voice, but in a good voice it deteriorated the vocalisation. He did not believe that one in an audience would say they like it, and he certainly did not. [16 Jun. 1911: MCLGA]
Launceston Competitions	Mr Carl Sauer	Mr [W. C.] Stiebel was too indistinct, and was also a little quick. The necessary vibrato and intensity of feeling were missing. [17 Apr. 1912: *Daily Telegraph*, Launceston]
The Competitions	Professor Ives	He holds very strongly that the user of the tremolo is committing musical suicide. If indulged in, it became a habit, and developed from a mere waver into absolute untunefulness. It was sometimes hard to tell whether a singer was singing C or C sharp. The vibrato was one of the singer's devices for expressing deep feeling, but it should be kept for special occasions, or the user would lose control of his voice, and use it on every occasion. There were various causes of it. The first, and most frequent, was affectation; another cause was physical weakness, which prevented the singer sustaining a long note; and a third cause was a bad system of breathing. The aim of a singer should be to produce a pure steady tone. His experience had convinced him that the user of the vibrato could not be given more than a couple of years of musical life. [24 May 1912: *Press*]

Descent from Default Straight Voice to Permanent Vibrato

Competition	Adjudicator	Typical Comment and Date
Grand National Eisteddfod, Ballarat	Mr Gray	Mr. Davies' letter, consisting of twenty-nine pages of closely-written matter, would take up too much space to print in full…dealing more particularly with the vocal portion of the recent Grand National Eisteddfod, held in Ballarat, should prove interesting to all the musical public residing on the fields:- … Solo Work: I think many of our girls and boys would stand well up. It was difficult to decide, for the judge (Gray), imported, condemned all the best voices; he 'harped' all the time on that 'obnoxious habit, vibrato', if a lady or gent was nervous (and the majority of competitors were very)—the 'vibrato' was their doom. It was so strong with him that decisions seemed to be wrong—result, a 'strike' took place with a great many lady soloists, no less than 38 refusing to compete in other items, under him. Something must have got to the ears of the executive, for later on Mr. Felix Gade, of Melbourne, was seen judging solo work. [30 Jan. 1913: *Kalgoorlie Miner*]
Halifax Musical Festival	Dr. Vaughan Williams	The winner was Mrs. S. Robinson, of Northampton, who gained 62 for the piece and full marks (10) for the sight-singing test. Concerning her performance, Dr. Vaughan-Williams said it was correct and firm; rather too quick; tone wanted improvement and the vibrato must be got rid of, and the singer must try and make her vowels broad—by which he meant alive. [23 May 1913: *Leamington Spa Courier*]
Mrs Sunderland competition	Dr. Brewer	He was so much struck by the general excessive use of the vibrato effect that he described all the forty-three competitors in the soprano solo competition as 'forty-three vibratos'. There is little exaggeration in the description, but most people of any musical taste will agree very heartily with the intention of Dr. BREWER'S criticism. There is no doubt at all that the vibrato effect has become a general mannerism. Singers deliberately cultivate it as if it were a virtue, a natural quality which all voices should always have. The truth is, of course, that the vibrato is a special effect to be used for special purposes of expression. [17 Feb. 1914: *Huddersfield Daily Examiner*]
Exeter Eisteddfod	Dr. Ferris Tozer	He had had to turn down two excellent singers because of what he said one or two sessions ago concerning his dislike for tremolo singing. He might be old-fashioned on the matter, but he very much objected to it, and had come to the conclusion that it was not real music. (Applause.) [23 Jan. 1920: *Exeter and Plymouth Gazette*]
Manawatu Competitions	Mr Robert Parker	There was no steadiness in the work of young singers. The voices trembled, which was bad. Perhaps it was merely nervousness, or it may have been faulty breathing, or even affectation which was responsible for it. However, the tremolo effect was distinctly wrong, except in the case of a finished vocalist. Some amateurs used it to express pathos, but they made a great mistake in so doing. 'Avoid the tremolo like a poison'. [28 Jul. 1922: *Manawatu Standard*]

Competition	Adjudicator	Typical Comment and Date
Blackpool Musical Festival	Sir Richard Terry	It was distressing to find that nearly every competitor in the solo class had acquired vibrato, the curse of modern vocalism. Nobody needed to sing vibrato, and anybody who did sing it had either been taught to do so or had copied some bad singer. / Vibrato always had been and would always be a vocal vice, and it was astonishing to hear competitor after competitor troubled with it. One never heard great singers wobble; no great singer wanted to wobble. [14 Oct. 1924: *Yorkshire Evening Post*]

Illus. 53: Views of Singing Competition Adjudicators

As in earlier times, critics only rarely gave their reasons for disliking tremolo/vibrato. Quite simply, it was something they hated. It therefore sufficed to describe vibrato offensiveness variously as: abominable, aggressive, annoying, appalling, beastly, deplorable, destructive, detestable, disagreeable, disconcerting, diseased, distressing, dread, evil, excruciating, execrable, fatal, hateful, hideous, monotonous, nasty, nauseating, noxious, objectionable, outrageous, painful, pernicious, repulsive, tiresome, troublesome, trying, ugly, uncomfortable, unpleasant, vicious, virulent, vitiated, vulgar or wearing. Where reasons were given, the usual objection was that tremolo damages tuning. In addition, critics sometimes noted that it interfered with enunciation, was unsuitable for some operatic characters (for example, by projecting feebleness or uncertainty, when strength was required) or complained that an effect which was constantly switched on couldn't possibly be expressive.

Up until the end of the nineteenth century and well beyond, singers continued to lead public taste, whether or not they had institutional authority. The generally anti-vibrato views of singers and influential critics were often quoted, although the emphasis varied according to the country of origin. English speaking countries were uniformly hostile to tremolo and vibrato. Here are some typical comments by singers and qualified critics in the UK and Australasia:

George Bernard Shaw, an influential reviewer who had been vocally trained, wrote 36 negative reviews on tremolo singing between 1877 and 1894. However, it should be mentioned that GBS changed his mind in old age, when he wrote, shortly before his death: 'Let us hear no more of a golden age of *bel canto*. We sing much better than our grandfathers.' But he did concede elsewhere in the article 'Where we fall short is in *roulades*, shakes, and *gruppettos*, which many of our singers simply cannot sing at all.' [11 Nov. 1950: *Everybody's Magazine*]

The Musical Times pronounced 'we were surprised to hear an unsteadiness of tone [by singer Amy Frodsham] tolerated in an institution [Royal College of Music] where the vibrato is expressly forbidden by the rules.' [1 May 1899: MusT]

I've already noted [p. 235] retired singer Sims Reeves's comments to the effect that five out of six modern singers were afflicted with the wobble.

'A conversation ensued on singing in general. "I hate the eternal vibrato", declared Madame [Nellie] Melba, emphatically, "I like pure singing, and—" / "Sir John Forrest", announced a voice at the door, and the genial Minister for Defence entered without further ceremony. / "Come and be interviewed, Sir John", exclaimed Madame Melba, gaily, evidently relieved to be excused from further cross-examination, with the temperature at 105, and our reporter withdrew.' [17 Jan. 1903: *Western Mail*, Perth]

Adelina Patti, as quoted in an interview: 'The tremolo, one of the most objectionable and unbearable of vocal faults, is but a phase of this forcing, and comes of the spreading of vocal chords through straining.' [2 Jan. 1904: *Evening Post*, New Zealand]

'But to return to Dr. [William Hayman] Cummings, who began singing at St. Paul's Cathedral as a chorister 68 years ago, and who is to-day universally regarded as an eminent authority on voice production. He [principal, Guildhall School of Music, 1896-1910, in a talk on 'Vocal Culture'] administered a crushing rebuke to those who indulge in what is known as the "tremolo". It is, as the Doctor said, a reprehensible habit. Apart from the fact that it mars the beauty of many fine voices, it is, I agree, "a most distressing fault to the auditors, who frequently listen in doubt as to the precise pitch of the note the singer is endeavouring to produce". I have quoted this opinion of an erstwhile great singer as a warning to young men and women who may be tempted to follow the example of modern artists in this respect.' [4 Jan. 1907: *Derby Daily Telegraph*]

'If a musician of olden days, a stranger to the performances of the vocalists of our time, were told that the majority of modern singers, of set purpose, used their voices in such a way as to make them sound harsh, unpleasant and continuously out of tune, he would probably reply that there must be an epidemic of *dementia* abroad in the vocal world. And his observation would be entirely just. The vice of vocal *vibrato* and *tremolo* is amazingly prevalent. And while it is not altogether a novel phenomenon, it appears to have a vitality and staying power similar to that of influenza or the plague.' **J Alfred Johnstone** [Start of tirade 'The Vice of vibrato, and the Torture of Tremolo' quoted in *Musical Standard* and published in *Essentials of piano playing and other musical studies*] [5 Nov. 1910: *Musical Standard*]

Similar views were echoed by critics on North American singers:

'It is a luscious mezzo-soprano of ample range,—rich in its lower tones, exquisitely musical in its medium ones (especially when not urged to its greatest power), and clear, without special brilliancy, in the upper register. Not a grand and commanding voice like Parepa's [Euphrosine Parepa-Rosa], and not that artiste's magnificent breadth and nobility of style, but a delicious, alluring, beautiful,—such a voice as one could easily guess might have sung to Rossini in his dreams, and, emphatically, not such a voice as could be trusted in the echoing spaces of a great hall. / At the very first, it was demonstrated that the singer [Mrs Charles Moulton] was not only blessed by nature, but splendidly schooled by art. The organ is American; the training the best Italian. Of the vulgar tremolo, there was none.' [28 Oct. 1871: Spring]

'… apart from a tendency to the tremolo [by Miss Lillian Russell], from which American artists are usually free.' [10 Sep. 1894: DN]

'How rare is it to hear an Italian or French singer who does not use the tremolo to an extent that makes it ridiculous or unpleasant. I dislike the word "tremolo" as applied to this vocal vice, because in instrumental music it simply means a rapid repetition of a note or notes. Our musical terminology is sadly wanting in definiteness in many respects. The result of experience makes one think that after all the best representative English and American singers cannot be excelled anywhere for purity of style, clearness of enunciation of the words, and beauty of voice.' [10 Dec. 1898: *Toronto Globe*]

Composer and singing teacher **Frederick W Root** wrote: 'This execrable tremolo must not be confounded with the rich vibratory quality of some of the finest voices, which resembles the vibrato of a skilled violinist or 'cellist, and which is as different from the affected tremolo as the flush of youth is different from the tawdry adornment of rouge.' [10 Jun. 1900: Spring]

Richard Aldrich, Music Reviewer for the New York Times, replied to a correspondent complaining about vibrato: 'This correspondent's view of the "wobbling methods" of some singers is entirely correct, and the distress they cause him are shared by all who know and admire good singing. But his memory must have failed him if he cannot recall any animadversions by the musical critics of the New York press upon what is almost universally condemned as one of the most vicious improprieties in vocal method. The columns of this paper have constantly borne witness to the disapproval in which the tremolo in singing is held by every listener of discrimination, and they will continue to do so.' [15 Mar. 1903: NYT]

William James Henderson, US music critic and author, was quoted: 'It is probably quite hopeless to make a plea for the abolition of the cheap and vulgar vibrato in the delivery of these old airs. It is indeed painful to hear "Caro mio ben" sung with a French opera vibrato, which robs it of half its noble simplicity.' [6 May 1906: *Sun*, New York]

"Mr. **Edison** in his search for voices for his phonograph has made trial records of more than three thousand singers in nearly every city in Europe and almost an equal number of trials in America. He finds that as a rule the European voice is afflicted with a very disagreeable tremolo, variable timbre and poor interpretation—whereas the American voice is far more frequently free of tremolo, has a fairly even timbre and as to interpretation the Americans surpass the European singers." [14 Nov. 1914: *Muscatine Journal*]

The next question I address is this. To what extent did tremolo/ vibrato get wider during the first few decades of the twentieth century [Illus. 54]? The basis for selecting examples was threefold: (1) Were they included, as famous singers, in the series *Record of Singing*?[43] (2) Was there at least one review commenting on their vibrato, either on its presence or absence? And (3) Did the best part of their career fall during the inter-war period?

Illus. 54 highlights female singers in pink, and male singers in blue. As well as the dates of birth and début, I've included the years in which reviews appeared criticising their tremolo/vibrato [Vib Bad], the years in which their vibrato was praised, chiefly for artistic value or limited use [Vib Good], and

---

43   The *Record of Singing* is a compilation of classical-music singing from the first half of the twentieth century, issued by EMI on a series of 47 LPs between 1977 and 1989. Volume 1 covered 1899 to 1919, Volume 2 1914 to 1925 and Volume 3 1926 to 1939.

the years in which reviews commended their absence of vibrato [Vib None]. Reviews for any years later than 1939 were excluded.

Singer	Born	Début	Vib Bad	Vib Good	Vib None
Joseph Hislop	1884	1914		1931	1920
Francesco Merli	1887	1916	1926 [X2], 1928		
Lotte Lehmann	1888	1914	1931		1934
Elisabeth Schumann	1888	1909			1933
Mariano Stabile	1888	1909	1927, 1930		
Maggie Teyte	1888	1907	1910, 1912, 1914, 1918, 1927		1912
Charles Hackett	1889	1919	1928		1924 [X3]
Tito Schipa	1889	1910		1937 [X2]	1928
Margaret B. Sheridan	1889	1918	1928 [X2]		
Beniamino Gigli	1890	1914	1926	1939	1928
Dino Borgioli	1891	1914		1928	1924 [X2], 1929
Richard Tauber	1891	1912	1933	1937	
Marian Anderson	1892	1919	1930, 1932		
Florence Austral	1892	1922	1928		1922, 1928, 1935
Ezio Pinza	1892	1914	1929, 1934		
Toti Dal Monte	1893	1916	1931		1925
William Heddle-Nash	1894	1924	1926, 1934, 1937		
Elisabeth Rethberg	1894	1915	1935, 1939	1928	
Isobel Baillie	1895	1921	1930		1931
Conchita Supervia	1895	1910	1933, 1934, 1935 [X2], 1939	1931, 1935	1931
Georges Thill	1897	1924			1928
Lily Pons	1898	1928	1931		
John Brownlee	1900	1926	1929		1932 [X2]
Gina Cigna	1900	1923	1933, 1937		1937
Dusolina Giannini	1902	1923	1924, 1929 [X2], 1934, 1936, 1937	1929	1928, 1939 [X5]
Joseph Schmidt	1904	1924	1932 [X2]		
Maria Cebotari	1910	1929	1936 [X2]		

Illus. 54: Famous Singers during the Interwar Period

I then listened on Spotify or YouTube to a selection of tracks recorded for each vocalist listed in Illus. 54. My clear impression is that, singers generally used a type A vibrato, i.e. about a tone wide from peak to trough. I did find a few singers (**Elisabeth Schumann**, **Isobel Baillie**, **Toti Dal Monte** and **Beniamino Gigli**) who sometimes produced a type B sound in a few songs. Although vocalists were often described as having zero tremolo or vibrato, in no case did the Spotify check confirm such assessments. This compares with the type B or C voices of the singers listed at the start of this section.

I conclude that vocal vibrato in recordings made between 1918 and 1939 had widened noticeably compared to those made the first recordings of 1905. I stress that these conclusions are subjective and need to be confirmed scientifically, as suggested in the final section of this book [p. 357]. In the meantime, I invite readers to make their own comparisons. However, these findings have been supported by both **Will Crutchfield** and **Robert Philip**. Crutchfield wrote: 'It is certain that the degree of vibrato present in an artist's everyday singing is largely a matter of (subconscious) cultivation during training, and that during the history of Western artistic singing the steady trend has been towards the cultivation of stronger, wider and slower vibrato.' [W. Crutchfield writing in *Performance Practice after 1600*, p. 295] Philip concluded: 'What is clear from recordings is that many singers of the early years of the century used a shallower vibrato than singers later in the century.' [R. Philip, *op. cit*, p. 477]

4.10 Vocal Science Influential—against underground resistance

I believe that, from around 1925, the vocal establishment was affected by what might be described as a sea change in attitudes to vocality. The main factor was the new recording industry in conjunction with vocal science, which was emerging as important in assessing the quality of singers, initially in the person of **Thomas Edison**, who invented the phonograph amongst other things. It does seem that, in spite of his comments quoted on page 276 above, he was more favourably disposed towards tremolo than straight vocal sound:

> 'There is not a sign of a tremolo, which is remarkable, for the tremolo is the natural voice. The critics usually think a tremolo is an affectation, the result of poor teaching. I have proved that it is not an affectation. It is natural to sing with a tremolo and it takes a good deal of practice to get rid of it.' [3 Aug. 1913: Thomas Edison, quoted in the *Plain Dealer*]

> 'Mr Edison demonstrated to an interviewer, by means of a record, what he described as "The finest voice in the world". / It was a voice of superlative purity and wonderful compass, with no sign of a tremolo and no break between the registers, but, on the other hand, it was utterly mechanical and expressionless.' [3 Oct. 1913: *Poverty Bay Herald*]

> 'It is now possible to put the voice "under the microscope". The invention is Mr. Thomas A. Edison's and it is stated that most of the great singers are sending records of their voices every two years for Mr. Edison to discover signs of deterioration, if any. It is on the overtones that the richness of a voice depends, and in one famous tenor's record he has noted as many as nine overtones. When a voice spoils the overtones wear off. A tremolo, the inventor has proved, is the natural voice, and it is not an affectation, or the result of poor teaching, as some critics think.' [20 Nov. 1919: *Lake County Press*]

The academic work of **Carl E Seashore** and his colleagues at the University of Iowa was even more important. Indeed, Seashore might be viewed as the founding father of vocal science in music, given that this function continues to help singers in most universities and musical academies optimise their talents, albeit generally with the aim of excelling as standard operatic artists, rather than from the standpoint of historically informed performance.

> 'Canned music is not new; but canned thrills, extracted from canned music and preserved as an aid in the study of human emotion may follow from recent work done by Dr. C. E. Seashore, head of the department of psychology at the Iowa State university. It has been found, for example, that the appealing vibrant quality in a singing voice, known to musicians as "the vibrato", is a combined pulsation of pitch and intensity averaging about six oscillations a second. It can therefore be expressed in terms of three variable quantities, pitch or frequency of the sound wave, intensity or loudness, and time. Within these three factors all possible variations of emotionable [sic] expression possible to the vibrato may be found.' [27 Oct. 1923:

San Francisco Chronicle]

'One of the most characteristic evidences of the tender emotion effectively expressed in singing is the vibrato. There is no end of confusion among musicians as to what the vibrato is, its desirability, how it may be acquired or eliminated, what it really means, and the factors that control it. It is, however, universally admitted that the vibrato represents an attempt to express emotion musically. / With all these factors under control, the personal characteristics of great singers and the laws for the expression of different kinds of emotion through the vibrato can be studied, and the relation of a feigned emotion or a genuine emotion, according as the music was or was not actually expressed emotionally, can be investigated. A tender emotion, says Dr. Seashore, is a condition of nervous instability, and the vibrato shown on the photographed voice records can be correlated with recognized principles of nervous discharge, and the relation of artistic expression in music to this instability shown. By J. Herbert Duckworth.' [13 Dec. 1925: *Miami Herald*]

'From sound photographs, says Popular Science Monthly, Dr. Seashore and others are studying the factors that make singing beautiful and appealing. For example, they have discovered that the quivering vibrato is an important means of portraying emotion in music and speech.' [17 May 1927: Spring]

A report in *The Times* was interesting. Besides commenting on Dr. Seashore's findings, their critic took them further with experimental slowing down[44] of gramophone records:

'Is vibrato desirable? The general answer of the lay public and musicians alike is No to a singer and Yes to a violinist; certainly, most teachers try to eliminate it from the voice and to inculcate one on the violin. If pressed to give a reason for this anomalous aesthetic verdict the listener would probably say that he finds a great deal too much of it in singing and not enough to notice consciously as a separate element in violin playing. That this answer is substantially correct is confirmed by scientific inquiry in the psychological laboratory. But a great deal more emerges from the experiments which the University of Iowa has conducted over a number of years and whose findings have now been published in two volumes. The second and more recent one issued this year will give the musician all the information he is likely to want. The earlier (1932) volume of collected papers consists of the technical findings in thesis form on which the more generally useful abridgement is based. The editor is Dr. Carl Seashore, whose famous "tests" of musicality have never established them–selves here but whose eminence and acumen in a field of study very little cultivated by English universities are unquestioned.

'The chief instrument of investigation is a camera that photographs tones and shows in graphical form on squared paper just exactly what the singer or player did. For photographic purposes gramophone records have an advantage over single performances *viva voce* not only because they can be controlled and repeated but because through them the world's greatest

---

44 The reader should know that similar results can be achieved with YouTube recordings, but without suffering an octave drop in pitch. If you select Settings, and then speed, you can slow the speed as recorded down to a quarter, half or three quarters of performance speed, easily enabling one to estimate the extent of vibrato oscillation.

artists can be dissected painlessly to the victim and profitably to us who are curious about the expression of personality in art. The reader may verify for himself by a comparatively crude experiment on his own gramophone the first conclusion of the Iowa psychologists—namely, that vibrato is present in all singing. For the purpose of writing this short summary the writer put four records on his own machine, two of male voices ([Rudolph] Bockelmann and [Enrico] Caruso) and two of female voices ([Sigrid] Onegin and [Frida] Leider). After playing portions of each at the right speed the turntable was slowed down as slow as it would go—so much as to effect a drop in pitch of nearly an octave. One did not need to slow down Caruso to hear his vibrato; Bockelmann when retarded yielded a suspicion of vibrato to the naked ear even on short, unsustained notes; but Onegin, whose singing is usually prized for its "straight" quality, proved Seashore's statement—a perceptible wobble of something like half a tone, unnoticeable at speed, was revealed by a slow-motion record; Leider showed a vibrato whose extent was often a good deal wider than a semi-tone, thus confirming common experience and the Iowa investigations that operatic singers have a bigger and more conspicuous vibrato than any other type of musician, as was exemplified by the startling contrast of the sustained notes of the horn in the orchestral opening of Wagner's "Träume", in which not a tremor was to be discovered.

'A semi-tone appears to be the optimum extent of the vibrato in singing, and the fluctuation travels on each side of mean pitch. In the best violin playing it is only about half of this extent. But the optimum rate seems to be almost the same for both; 6.5 oscillations a second for singers and seven for violinists. Anything much slower comes into the category that is usually called "tremolo" and sounds bad—though Dr. Seashore pleads for the abolition of the word "tremolo" altogether, except just possibly to denote fluctuations of intensity such as are produced by the mechanism of interference in the tremulant stop of the organ.'
[29 Aug. 1936: T, 'Vibrato a Scientific Enquiry']

Seashore's research produced, for the first time, quantitative information on the speed and width of vibrato, as well as an explicit view that it is desirable, as the following confirms: 'But that is not to say that this vibrato, even when it is perceptible, is unpleasant. Usually it is not perceptible as long as the voice does not vary from true pitch. These researches assure us, more than 0.5 tone and six times per second—the vibrato within that range being a sort of tone color, and not even the delicately organised apparatus of the ear registering the tone as something that is not quite pure. The upshot of the matter, therefore, and the Iowa researches have been so minute as to establish firmly the conclusions arrived at—is that the natural vibrato, by no means the same thing as the distressful tremolo, is part and parcel of even the most highly cultivated vocal tone. Only—singers must still beware lest they confuse vibrato with tremolo.' [10 Oct. 1936: *Age*, Melbourne]

In contrast to the angry anti-vibrato diatribes which occurred through much of the previous century, it is clear that Seashore himself approved of vibrato. Here is his definition on 'The Nature of the Vibrato': 'A good vibrato is a pulsation of pitch, usually accompanied with synchronous pulsations of loudness and timbre, of such extent and rate as to give a pleasing flexibility, tenderness, and richness to the tone.' [1938: *Seashore*]

Two conclusions about Seashore's work are immediately apparent. First, Seashore and his Iowa colleagues viewed the vibrato's 'emotionable characteristics' as desirable in a voice. Second, the vibrato was viewed by them as most pleasant if its width averages about a semitone, i.e. 100 cents, equating to a Type B vibrato as defined in Section 1.

From the 1930s onwards, most critics, singers and musicians generally accepted that vibrato was a legitimate part of musical expression. However, there were dissenting voices, which I can only characterise as an underground resistance movement. In particular, some sources continued to censure tremolo and vibrato singing, especially the five newspapers identified in Illus. 55, one from the US, two from the UK and two from Australia. A total 235 reviews assessed vocal tremolo unfavourably [red bars = bad]. Some 20 reviews praised the artist for diminution of tremolo [yellow bars = less]. 13 reviews approved of tremolo, typically when used selectively or expressively [blue bars = good]. 18 reviews claimed that the vocalist used no tremolo at all [green bars = none].

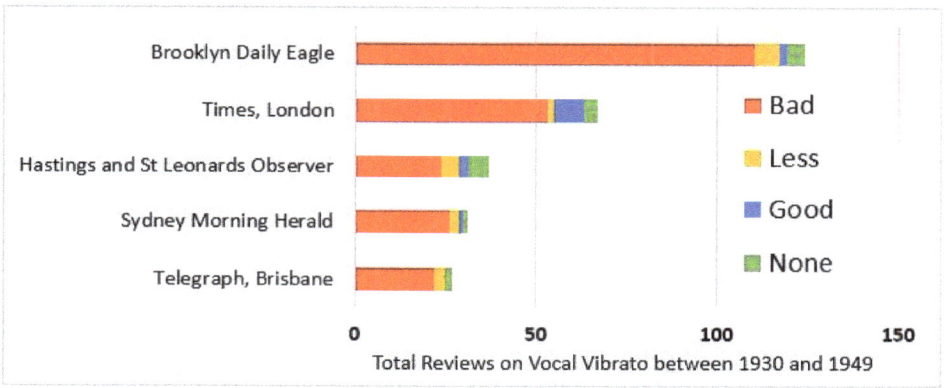

Illus. 55: Sources Frequently Reviewing Tremolo and Vibrato Singing

I'll take the Brooklyn Daily Eagle first, which generally printed bylines. Several reviewers were used until 1937, quite often **B. H. Haggin**. From 1938 to 1946, **Miles Kastendieck** was the chief reviewer. In 1948 and 1949, **Paul Affelder** was usually named. Typical reviews follow:

> 'At this moment I feel very much as I would if I were watching a great work of art being wantonly destroyed. With the arrival of Kirsten Flagstad we were privileged to hear one of the most glorious voices of the century. Its extraordinary freshness was due to the fact that it had not been severely taxed—that Mme. Flagstad was singing Bruennhilde for the first time in her career; and I expressed my fear of what a few years of Wagner would do to it. The results were apparent sooner than I had anticipated: In Friday's "Tannhaeuser" Mme. Flagstad began with a marked tremolo and gave other signs of fatigue. B. H. HAGGIN.' [19 Mar. 1935: Brook] The reader can listen to Flagstad's type A voice in 'Dich, teure halle, grüss' ich wieder' from *Tannhaüser*, on Spotify.
>
> '[Stella Roman] sang vibrato much of the time, a method which finds little favor with Metropolitan audiences. While she could float an appealing pianissimo top, she drove many of her upper notes hard. MILES KASTENDIECK.' [2 Jan. 1941: Brook] Her massive vibrato in

'Miserere' from *Il Trovatore*, ranging from a minor to a major third wide,[45] equating to a type AA voice, can be heard on Spotify or YouTube.

'[Miss Eleanor Steber] was inclined to force her tone throughout, making for insensitivity, and a constant, annoying tremolo caused her to be always a trifle sharp in pitch. Paul Affelder.' [15 Apr. 1949: Brook] Spotify reveals her huge vibrato in 'Un Bel di Vedremo', *Madame Butterfly*.

The London *Times* featured the highest proportion of 'good' reviews on vibrato, with the reviewer condemning non-vibrant voices and approving Seashore's findings several times. While the reviewer finds fault with the vibratoing London Singers, he's generous with Adele Leigh's supposed non vibrato.

'If the microphone can destroy wobbling singers, or rather persuade them to seek some more suitable occupation, every one would have cause to bless it. But if it distorts the vibrant qualities of good voices, confounding them with the wobblers, then it is destroying singing … But that point of view may be destructive to music, if it gives judgment in favour of the non-vibrant, "white" toned voices.' [8 Apr. 1933: T]

'Vibrato has been photographed and found to be satisfactory if it consists of fairly even variations of frequency of 6 or 7 cycles a second. Such a vibrato may not be heard as such, but gives life and warmth to the tone.' [25 May 1945: T]

'This capable consort of six madrigal singers [Margaret Ritchie and Elsie Morison, sopranos, Richard Lewis and William Herbert, tenors, Bruce Boyce, baritone, in Monteverdi's *Vespers*] has developed a certain amount of vibrato which has ulterior consequences detrimental to blend, intonation, and articulation.' [12 Jun. 1947: T] You can hear on Spotify wobbling from the sopranos in 'Pulchra es' and the tenors in 'Duo Seraphim'.

'Miss Adele Leigh's Cherubino was enchanting, and her singing the more persuasive for its boyish purity and absence of vibrato.' [13 Jun. 1949: T] While the reviewer was generous here, she uses a fair amount of vibrato in her contribution to *Dido and Aeneas*.

Here are some reviews from the Australian papers mentioned:

'It was pleasing to hear a master in opera [John Brownlee] sing with gestures that were no more than suggestive and with entire freedom from the explosive and vibrato qualities which are traditionally associated with that sort of music…the German group compiled from Richard Strauss and Schumann—"Zueignung", "Ich Grolle Nicht", and "Du Bist Wie Eine Blume".' [3 Oct. 1932: *Telegraph, Brisbane*] But Spotify reveals Brownlee's considerable vibrato in Mozart.

It is difficult to understand a review of a Gaston Micheletti recording to the effect that 'his voice possesses a good top register and is entirely without tremolo' [5 Aug. 1933: SMH], given that all recordings of him display some tremolo.[46]

---

45   This subjective estimate can be verified by playing the track on YouTube at a quarter of the recorded speed.
46   If the reader will play his 'la fleur que tu m'avais jetée' on YouTube at quarter speed, he will discover a vibrato of about a semitone wide, i.e. Type B.

'She [Conchita Supervia] sings "Si Tu M'Ami" of Pergolesi, and "Occhiatti Amati" (Falconeri) with an excessive vibrato which takes, especially from the Pergolesi, the sustained legato quality which is one of the fundamentals necessary for its success.' [14 Feb. 1935: *Telegraph, Brisbane*] While neither song is on Spotify, elsewhere she reveals a very fast, noticeable vibrato.

'And for all the intentness of Miss [Joan] Hammond's manner—which is consistently high-minded and absorbed—she could not give us the note of lonely lamentation which is crystallised in the phrases of Purcell's "When I am Laid". / The slightest hint of the tremolo of the theatre will not suit this great air, with its "period" symbolism of grief, broken-pillar and all.' [15 Aug. 1946: SMH] You can hear her Type A vibrato in this piece, about a whole tone wide,[47] in Disc 2 of *Glorious Divas of Yesteryear*.

Clive Brown summed up the situation well when he wrote that, whereas 'During the period from 1750 to about 1900 the various types of vibrato then in use were regarded almost exclusively as ornamental', by contrast 'Universal acceptance of continuous vibrato in singing and on other instruments followed even later. At least until the 1930s there were still many influential performers and teachers who remained unreconciled to this new attitude towards vibrato, continuing to believe that its too-frequent use impaired rather than improved tone quality, that it deprived performance of an important level expressiveness, and that it was inimical to purity of intonation and ensemble.' [1999: Clive Brown, *Classical & Romantic Performing Practice 1750–1900*, p. 521] Brown then illustrated this statement by quoting **Sir Henry Wood**'s comments in his *The Gentle Art of Singing* (1927), as follows:

'There has been a good deal written and said lately about the vocal tremolo which is out of place, but it is no new fault. I think I have explained fairly clearly why it exists, and how it can be cured. If it is not taken in hand at the very first singing lesson, it grows rapidly into a habit, and becomes so firmly established that it is most difficult to eradicate and is always liable to crop up from time to time. A tremolo often reaches the audience as out-of-tuneness, and any teacher who has tried to teach the octave duet for soprano and mezzo soprano, Agnus Dei in Verdi's *Requiem*, to singers of whom one has a decided tremolo and the other a true even, still tone, will understand why. It is impossible to get the octaves to sound in tune. The voice with the tremolo never blends in with the still tones of the other. The sharpness and flatness of the tremolo become clear.' [1927: Wood, Vol. IV, p. 87]

Percy Alfred Scholes presented his forthright views on tremolo and vibrato even later, in his masterpiece *The Oxford Companion to Music*, which was published in 1938. By this date, he was clearly out of step with colleagues and singers on the subject:

'To say that the effects [of tremolo and vibrato] are in the twentieth century tremendously overdone by a large number of vocalists is to speak mildly. They both have their place for purposes of emotional expression, corresponding to the unsteadiness that comes into the speaking voice of all of us in moments when we are exceptionally moved; but many vocalists

---

47   Again, this can be verified by playing the YouTube version at quarter speed.

so habitually use the effect that it becomes clear either (*a*) that they imagine it adds a beauty to the music as such, or (*b*) that there is a lack of control of the diaphragm or the tightening of certain muscles in the throat ... As confirming explanation (*b*) it may be added that very many singers addicted to the fault are, on inquiry, found to be unaware of it, so that it certainly does not result from their volition.

'There is a very good psychological case for the abandonment of the practice of incessant tremolo or vibrato. One of the strongest bonds between a musical artist and his audience is the audience's unconscious recognition of the artist's confidence in himself. Now tremolo and vibrato (being associated with timidity and indeed often a symptom of actual "stage fright") weaken this feeling; the audience does not analyse its experiences but that is what occurs. A clear, strong, melodic line brings into existence an impression of artistic purpose and quiet power, a wavering line one of doubt and insecurity. The "suggestion" of the two is widely different.

'The public at large detests the effect of tremolo and vibrato, as the numerous letters received by music critics and radio authorities testify. But many singers seem to be unaware of the feeling of the public, and adopt a convention that is accepted by inferior teachers and by many of their colleagues of the platform and stage ...' [1938: Scholes]

4.11 Conclusions—Implications for Historically Informed Practice

I think these depend on when the music was first performed. Music in the baroque and early classical periods, plus the vocal compositions of early romantic composers including Schubert, Beethoven, Rossini, Bellini, Mendelssohn, Donizetti and probably Auber and Meyerbeer, should normally be sung in default straight tone, sometimes with expressive but intermittent vibrato, if singers are to reflect typical vocal production at the time this music was composed, plus (in Rossini's case) his own clearly expressed opinions. Verdi's early operas are historically correct either with modest vibrato, as used by Tamberlik, or without, as sung by Mario. While critics often deplored the use of vibrato in Wagner's music, the fact remains that Wagnerian tenors' vibrato ranged from zero (Italo Campanini), to minimal (Jean de Reszké) and quite wide (Hedmondt). Despite the evident disagreements, diversity prevailed in practice, suggesting that any of these approaches can be viewed as 'historically informed' for music composed after about 1850.

The purpose of the charts at Annexes A & B is to list most celebrated nineteenth-century singers, indicating whether they were straight toners or tremoloists. Some 185 female singers are included at Annex A and 125 male singers at Annex B. It will be seen that, in a few cases, a singer's category changes during his or her career. This typically occurs when a singer débuts as a straight toner but at some point starts to emit tremolo or vibrato.

Close inspection of female singers' dates will reveal that some débuted only a few years after they were born, explained by a fashion for welcoming children on the concert platform. The youngest was Louisa Vinning, aged 4 or 5, known as the 'Infant Sappho', who sang for Queen Victoria. She was reviewed thus: 'Miss Vinning, the precocious musical child [4 years old!], whose gracious reception by her Majesty we announced a day or two back, gave a petite concert in the theatre of the Polytechnic

Institution on Wednesday evening, which was attended by a numerous and even fashionable company, who had evidently been drawn together by the novelty of the circumstance, and a natural curiosity to see and hear what had so much interested the Queen ... We have stated, and we again observe, that the remarkable musical qualities possessed by this little girl are, purity of intonation and precision of time.' [7 Sep. 1840: T]

Other child singers included Rebecca Isaacs (aged 6), Eliza Poole (7), Mary Anne Paton (8), Adelaide Phillipps (9) and Jenny Lind (10). All enjoyed long and successful careers subsequently on stage and/or concert platform.

4.12 Annex A. Lists of Female Tremoloists and Straight Toners

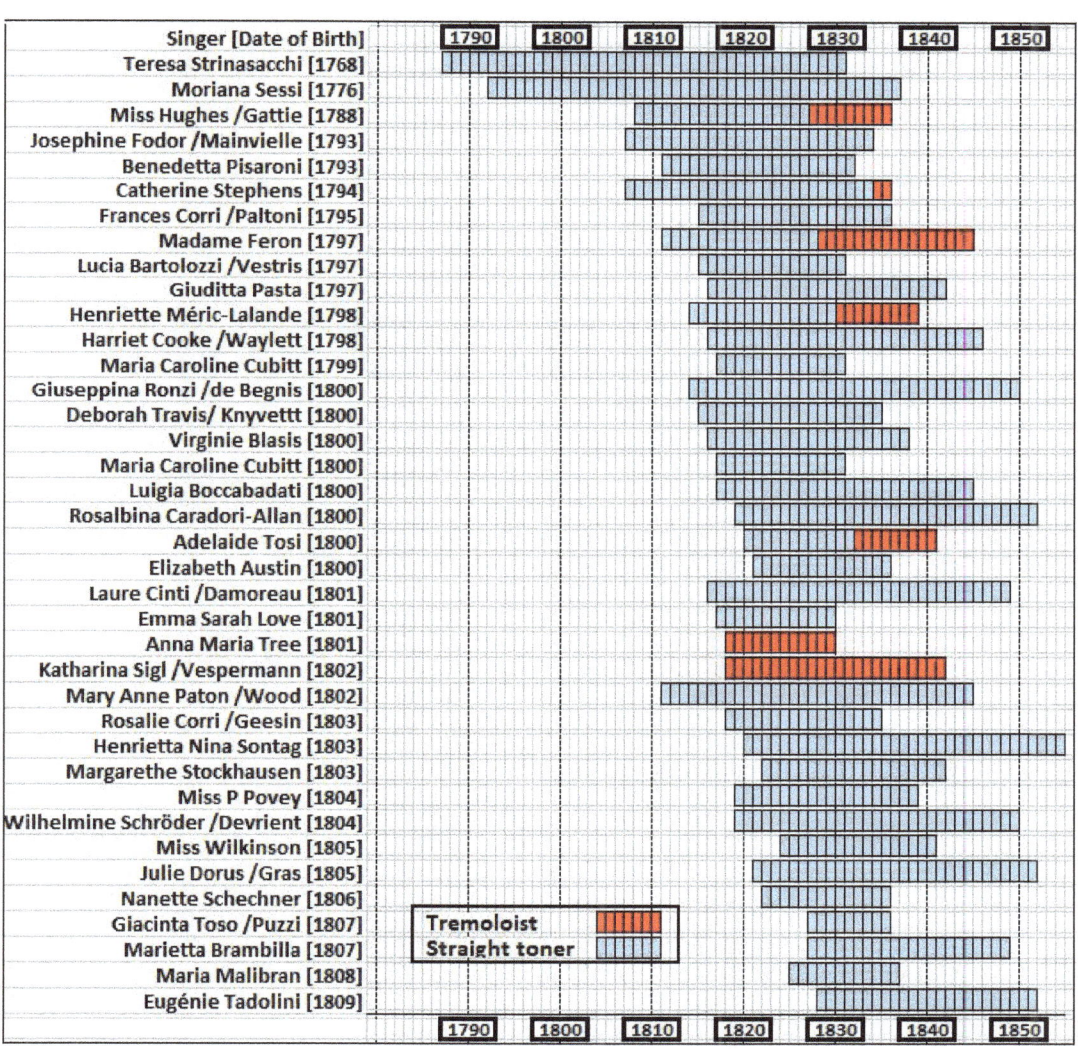

Illus. 56: Female Tremoloists and Straight Toners up to around 1850

Descent from Default Straight Voice to Permanent Vibrato

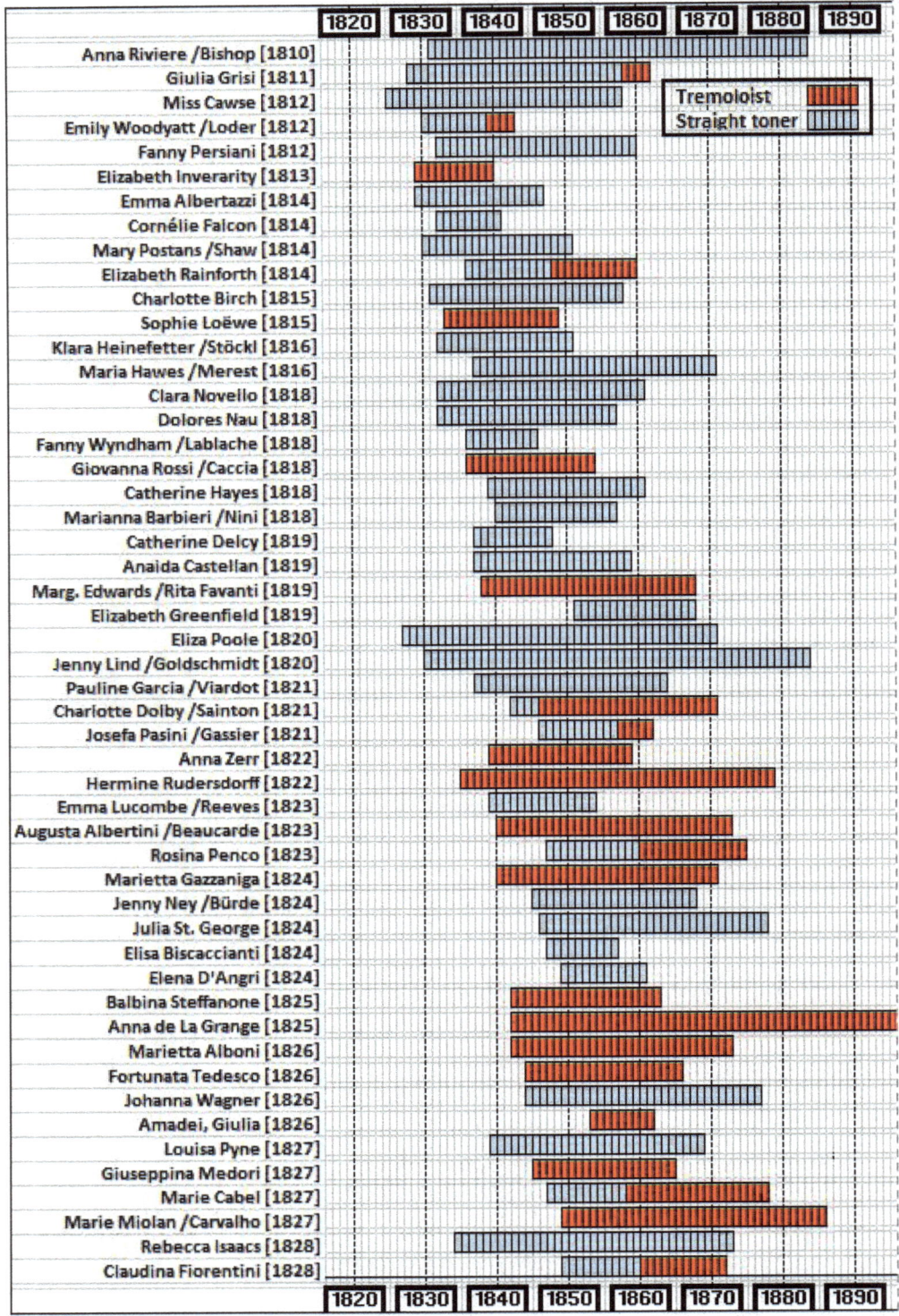

Illus. 57: Female Tremoloists and Straight Singers: c. 1820 to c. 1890

Descent from Default Straight Voice to Permanent Vibrato

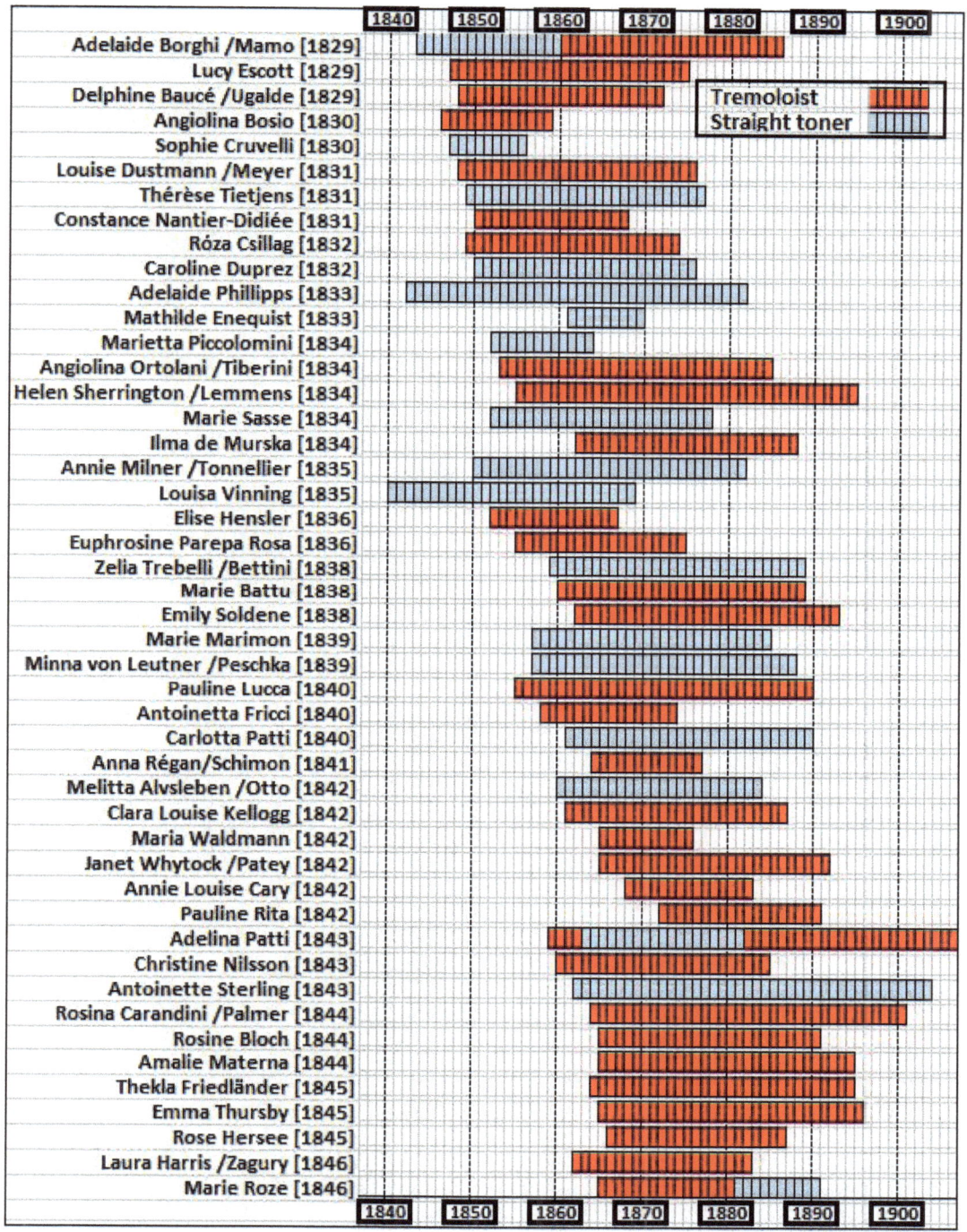

Illus. 58: Female Tremoloists and Straight Singers: c. 1850 to c. 1900

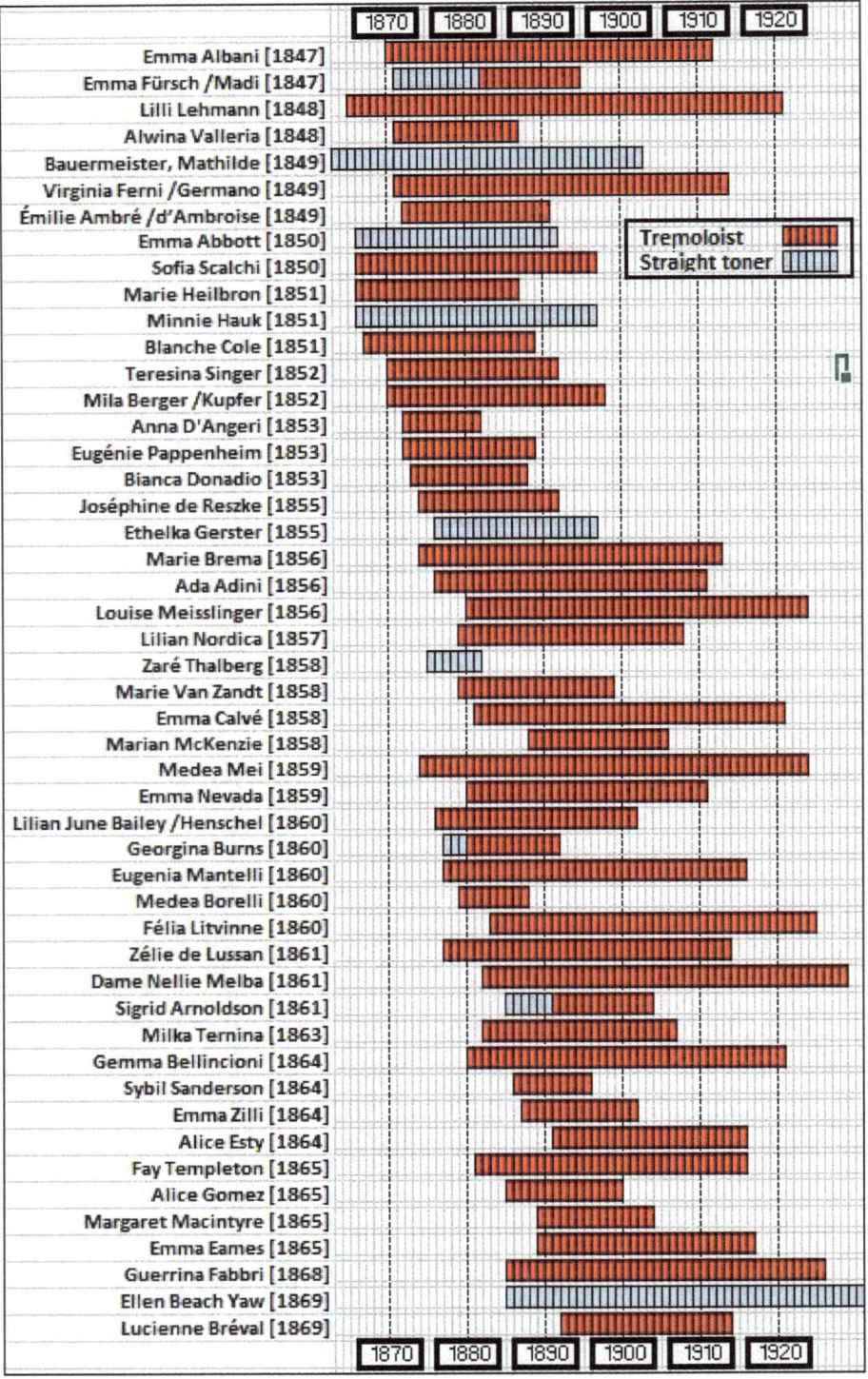

Illus. 59: Female Tremoloists and Straight Singers; c. 1870 to c. 1925

4.13 Annex B. Lists of Male Tremoloists and Straight Toners

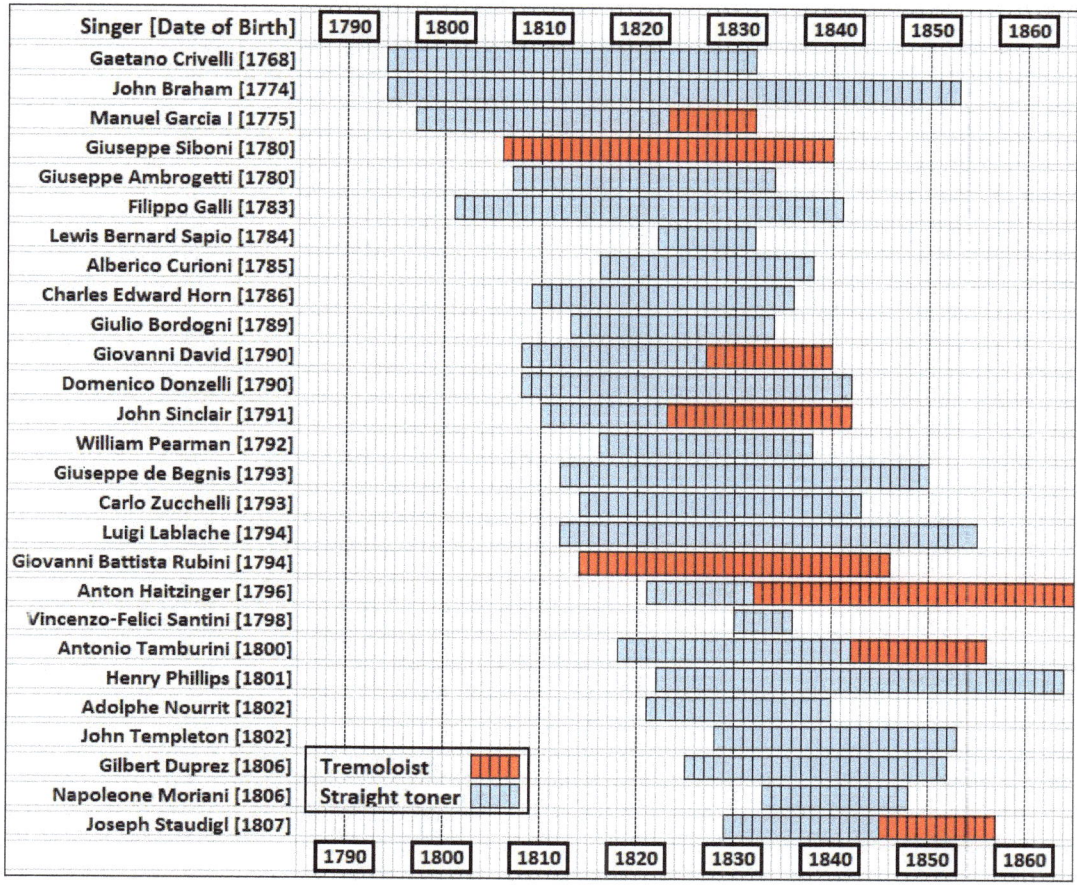

Illus. 60: Male Tremoloists and Straight Singers up to around 1850

Descent from Default Straight Voice to Permanent Vibrato

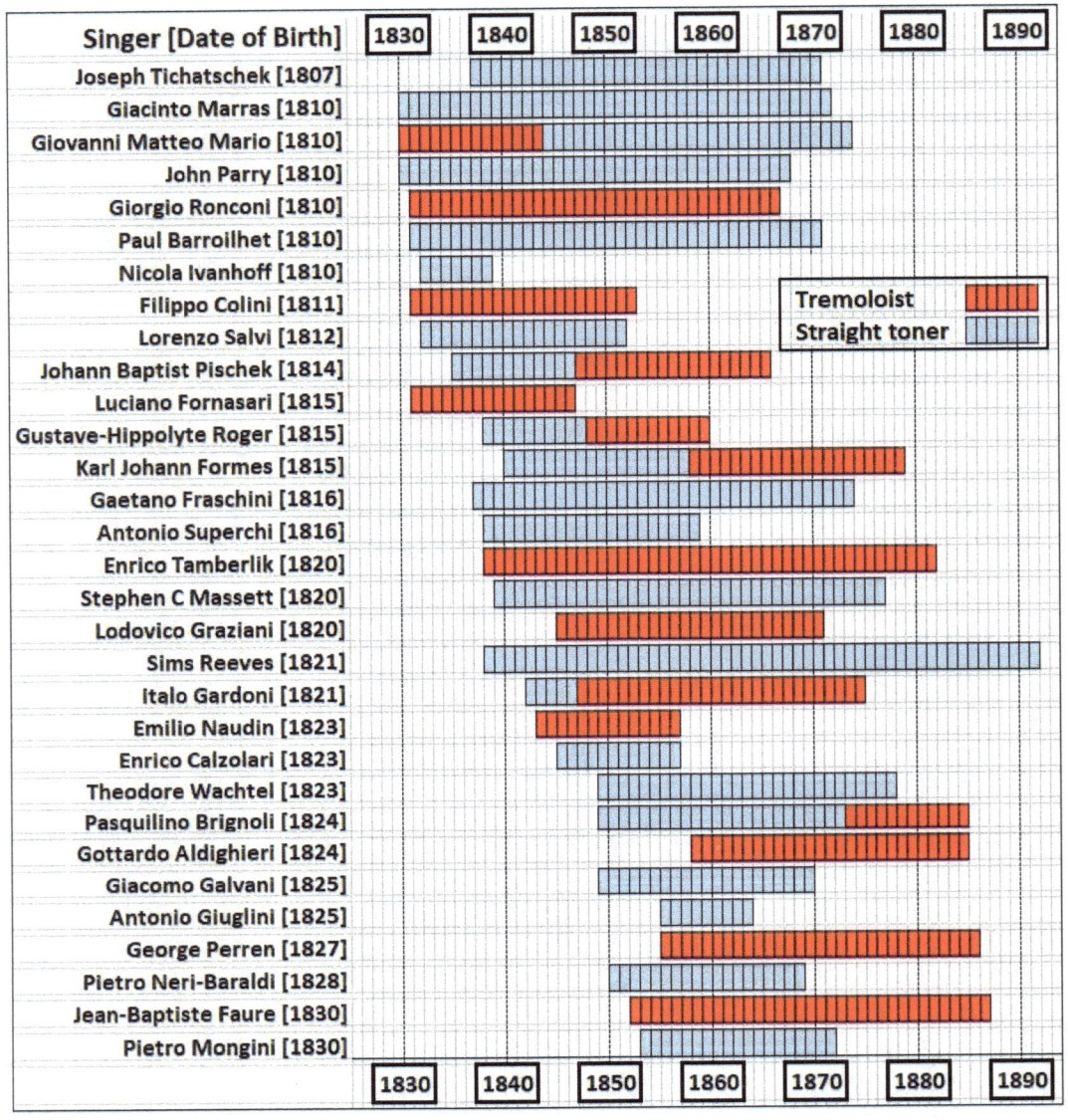

Illus. 61: Male Tremoloists and Straight Singers: c. 1830 to c. 1890

Descent from Default Straight Voice to Permanent Vibrato

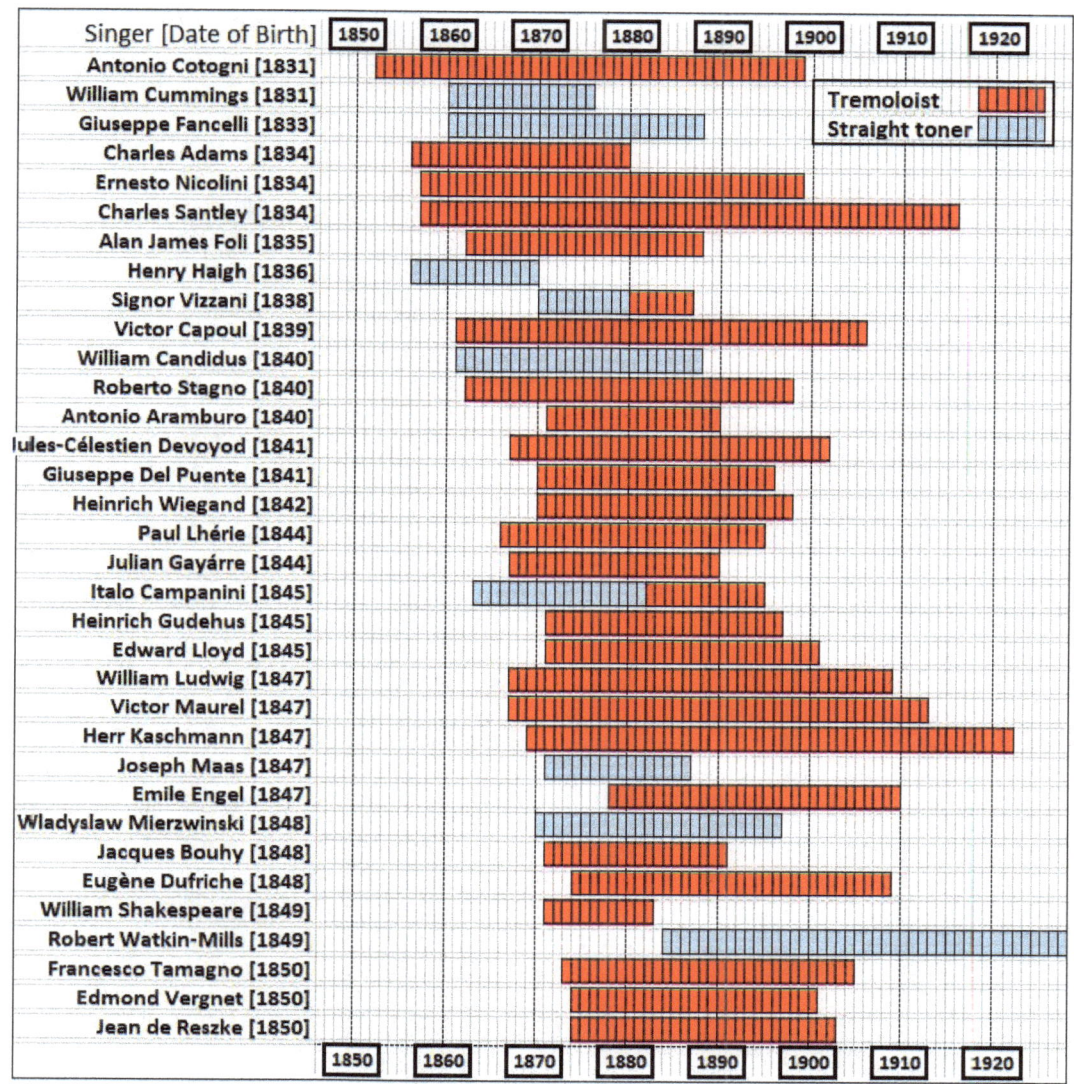

Illus. 62: Male Tremoloists and Straight Singers: c. 1855 to c. 1915

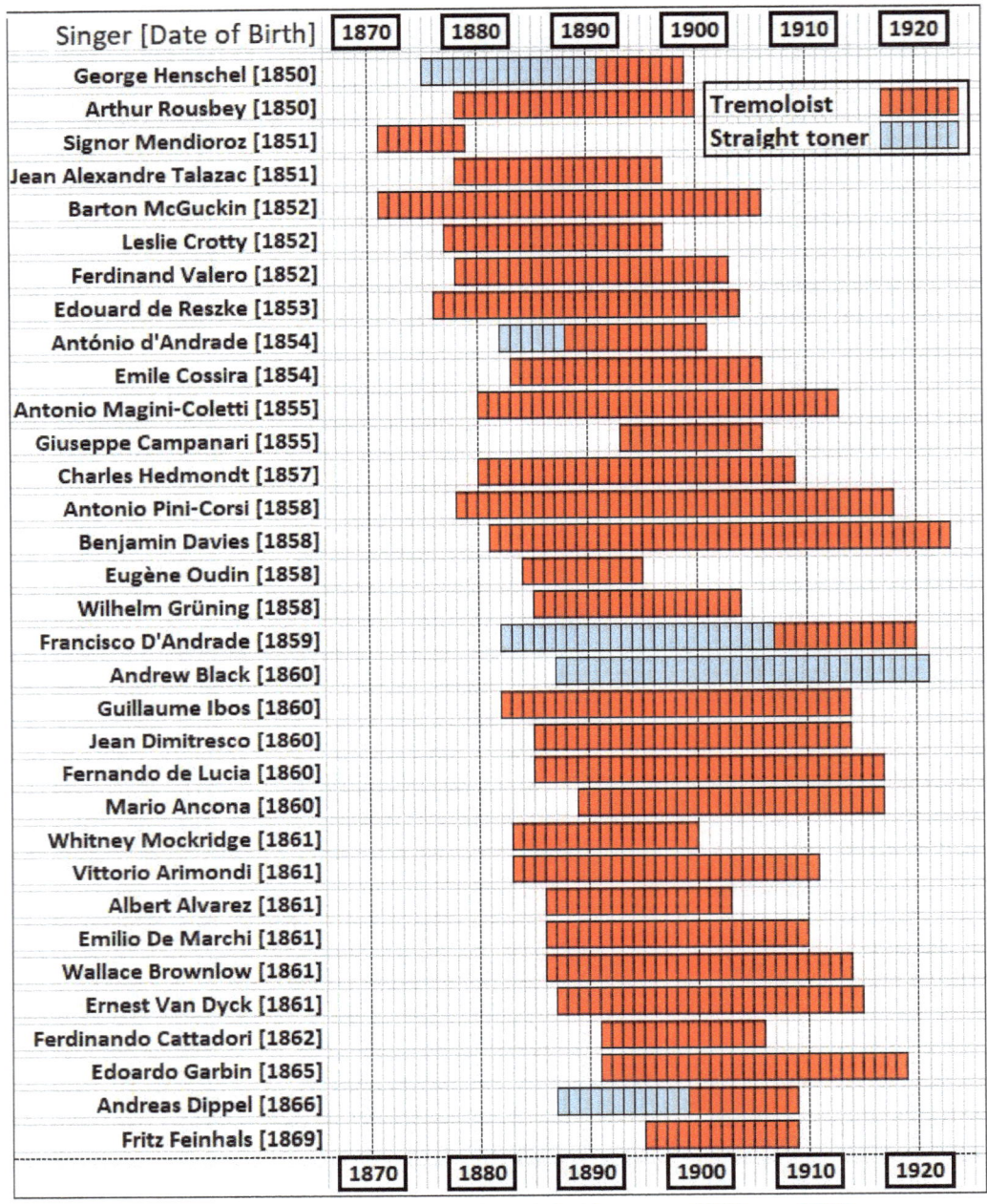

Illus. 63: Male Tremoloists and Straight Singers: c. 1875 to c. 1920

5 Descent from Dual Register Emission to Constant Chest Voice

As I've shown in Section 2, singers of both sexes, besides the castrati, exploited their falsetto extensions through the long eighteenth century. In fact, it was unusual around 1800 not to utilise a falsetto register. In this Section, I will show how male and female singing evolved between 1830 and 1900, with males exhibiting a delicate falsetto extension being eventually displaced by *tenore di forza*, and female nightingales rivalled by dramatic sopranos.

5.1 A Top Down View of Male Falsetto

I start by summarising some 1880 reviews where the critics have indicated, either explicitly or implicitly, whether they like or dislike falsetto. The results are shown in Illus. 64. Two conclusions can be drawn from this data. First, the heat went out of this topic in the second half of the nineteenth century, with fewer critics expressing a view one way or the other. This trend contrasts with the negative views on vocal vibrato which peaked at the end of the nineteenth century. Second, while reviews up to 1870 were generally favourable to vocal falsetto, they were mostly hostile after that date.

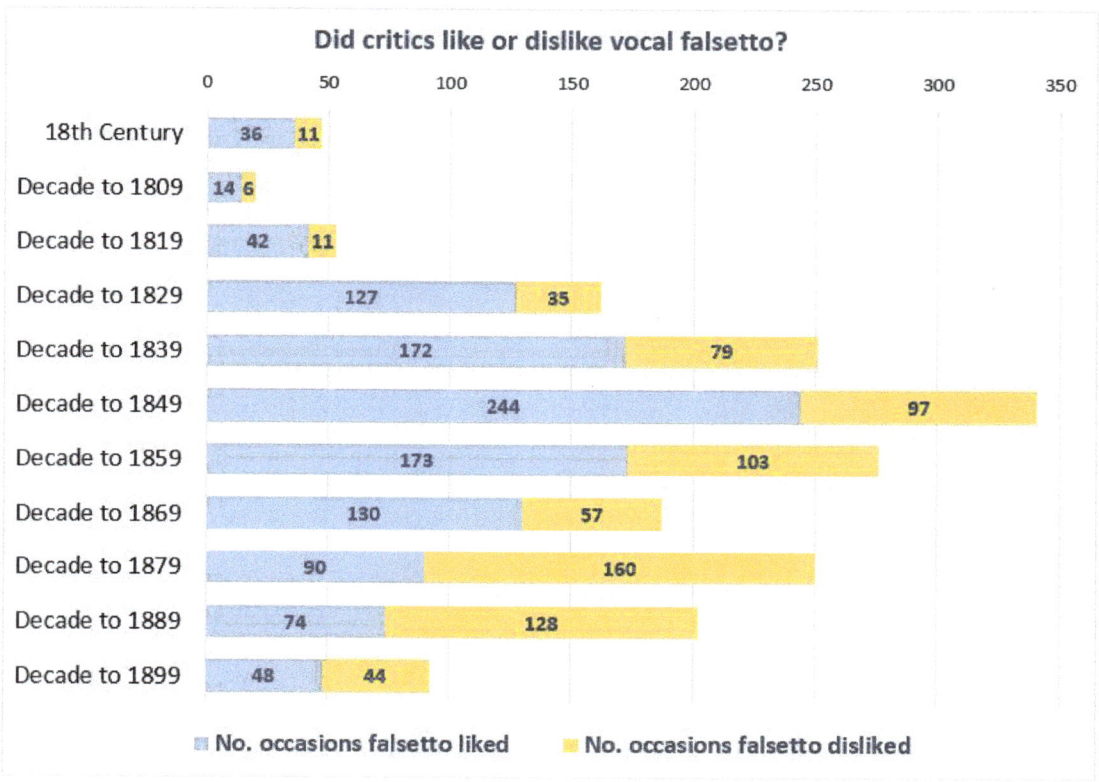

Illus. 64: Critics' Views on Vocal Falsetto

5.2 Reviews Endorsing Male Falsetto

Several writers through the middle part of the nineteenth century accepted the orthodox views of Tosi, Mancini, Quantz, Burney and other long-eighteenth-century authorities to the effect that male singers needed to adopt a well-joined falsetto extension:

Gilbert Duprez in 1837, as recalled by Rossini in 1858: 'Well then Maître, tell me sincerely, does my C please you?' Rossini: 'Very sincerely, what pleases me most about your C is that it is over, and that I am no longer in danger of hearing it. I don't like unnatural effects. It strikes my Italian ear as having a strident timbre, like a capon squawking as its throat is slit. You are a very great artist, a true new creator of the role of Arnold. Why in the devil abase your talent by using that humbug?' [1859: Michotte, p. 98] Rossini in 1858: 'Duprez was the first one to think of chafing the Parisians' ears by disgorging in Guillaume Tell that chest-tone C of which I had never dreamed. [Adolphe] Nourrit had been satisfied with a head-tone C, which was what was required.' [1858: Michotte, p. 97]

'In singing the scala filata, namely, that scale which is composed of long notes, great care should be taken to combine these qualities in singing those notes where two registers meet. In order to produce this connection, it is advisable not to carry the chest voice to its highest pitch, but rather to make use of the falsetto instead. This is called uniting the registers. As the notes on which this union is effected are generally very weak, they should, in order to render them as equal as possible with the others, be particularly exercised, by dwelling on them, and modulating the voice by beginning Pianissimo, and proceeding gradually to forte, then diminishing to Pianissimo again. This is termed equalising the voice.' [1837: Maria Anfossi, *Trattato*, p. 11]

'Most advantages have their corresponding evils, and something of the kind may be remarked with reference to the "new school" of tenor singing. This new school, while it avoids extraneous embellishment, introduces the falsetto as little as possible, and using the chest-voice to a great extent, avoids all unmanly sweetness. The "old school", however, with all its meretriciousness, has this advantage, that it allows the artist to husband his voice, and by not requiring that constant forcing of the chest, affords greater repose to the organ. Hence a singer of the old school would last till he was old himself: whereas in the artists of the new it is impossible not to observe how, even at an early age, the voice becomes worn, or, as the French call it, usée.' [13 Jul. 1844: Ex]

'The blending the falsetto and the natural voice, so as they become completely assimilated, gliding, as it were, imperceptibly the one into the other, is the great perfection of vocal art.' [1845: Anon, *Musical Guide for Singing and the Piano-Forte*, p. 20]

'But, as there may be too much of any good thing, so may these virtues be carried to excess, and so they are, in this new process of manufacturing the new school of tenors, of whom [Gaetano] Fraschini is said to be the last now expected from Italy. The perpetual strain on the voice of [Napoleone] Moriani, [Gilbert] Duprez, and even of [Lorenzo] Salvi, to produce the high notes without using the falsetto, gives a sense of pain to almost all hearers; and this feeling is present still more vividly during the singing of [Gaetano] Fraschini, as the effort is greater, though so also is the effect in the more impassioned scenes, for his shrill pipe is heard above the whole orchestra and chorus, as distinctly as the rolling of bass Lablache; and yet every note is propelled from the chest only. As in the case of Duprez and Moriani, his voice already gives evidence of decay.' [24 Mar. 1847: CE]

'The cultivation of falsetto and its possible extension downward as far as the chest register is as essential as the soprano's head voice for a tenor who wishes to preserve his voice and not blow it out at the top, who wishes to have piano at his command, and who wishes to rejoice in the requisite coloratura and lightness as well as elegance and refinement. The familiar "but", namely, that falsetto is too conspicuously different in color from the chest tone, and too weak, simply reflects what happens when the falsetto has not been sufficiently, steadily and carefully cultivated, and joined to the chest register almost imperceptibly by the introduction of mixed tones.' [1852: Wieck, *Piano and Song*, p. 78]

'I should caution the pupils against straining their voices—encouraging them, however, to sing the high tones by using the falsetto, a certain amount of cultivation in that register being good for all, although only used in fine singing, by a certain kind of voice.' [Dec. 1865: G. F. Root, *The Coronet*]

'Yet the great Italian masters used to train tenors with a full and strong falsetto, which united with the chest voice imperceptibly, and continued upward easily and purely. Now the tenors go as high as the chest voice can be painfully urged, and consider it something great if they get up to the A. In old times good singers used to preserve their voices to old age. We had here such trained tenors when the English Glees were sung.' [May 1868: Emma Seiler, writing in the *American Journal of Science and Arts*]

5.3 Reviews Criticising Male Falsetto

But dissenting voices appeared from 1830, with male falsetto often deplored as offensive, disagreeable, unfortunate and distressing. While authors gave no musical reasons for their distaste, they typically objected to unmanly, effeminate, emasculate and girlish falsetto singing. By contrast, forcible performers were making the running from this time onwards.

'We liked the execution of the whole of it, saving a solitary mount into his falsetto towards the close [by singer Mr Millar]. The overuse of the falsetto is the abomination of tenor singing, and yet no one will set the example of avoiding it. It is supposed to show compass. If this be a merit, John Reeve distances all the singers of the day.' [21 Aug. 1831: *Atlas*]

In his *Music of Nature* **William Gardiner** defined what he meant by *voci di petto* tones, concluding that they 'are the most passionate we utter; they express our inmost feelings, and are termed the language of the heart, as it is from the region of the heart that they spring ... The tones of the voce de testa are of a very opposite kind to that deep and inward feeling of the lower voice. Its high and piercing cry is rather the language of imposture than sincerity*.' [*Footnote: 'On hearing a criminal whipt in a public market-place, I was persuaded the cry was not that of pain or anguish; and upon enquiry, I learnt from the jailor that the culprit was so little hurt, that he said he would undergo the punishment again for half-a-crown. In the voices of men the voce de testa is sometimes termed a falsetto, or feigned voice, the tone of which is similar to the constrained effect of over-blowing an organ pipe, or a flute. This fictitious voice is now abandoned by composers of the present day, as being devoid of strength and expression.]' [4 Jun. 1832: Gardiner, *Music of Nature*]

'This gentleman [Mr. Hawkins] has talent, but the unfortunate quality of his voice will always keep this talent below the poetry of his art. "O, it offends me to the soul", to see a huge man with fierce-looking whiskers and breadth of shoulders for a drayman, tuning up almost to "childish treble", in a hard, catarrhal voce di testa, attended with a few notes of a phthisical voce di petto. Those notes by which a female contr'alto would express the deepest energy of passion, are powerless and contemptible in a male voice. But these hybrid gentlemen say that their voice is not a "contr'alto", but a "counter tenor", which is different. This is not true. Contr'alto, haute contre, high counter, and counter tenor, mean precisely the same thing, and form the same diapason of voice, which, to be effective, can be used only by women, or boys.' [5 Nov. 1834: LBA]

'It is to be regretted that a singer, with such beautiful tones in the middle of his voice should be so fond of piping up to the heights of an unmanly falsetto. [Nicola] Ivanhoff, who cannot be described imberbis Apollo [beardless Apollo], should consider that it is out of all keeping for a gentleman with such gallant mustachios, and, moreover, "bearded like a pard", to be uttering such girlish squeaks. If the lawful province of the ladies be thus invaded, we may expect to see basses in tuckers bent upon a just retaliation.' [12 Jun. 1836: *Atlas*]

Lowell Mason obviously disapproved of falsetto singing: 'The Barytone voice sings fewer of the low tones with fulness than the base. In the high tones, on the contrary, it passes beyond the base, and indeed often sings E and F with the natural voice. It has usually a tolerably strong falset, and with it can ascend to A and even higher; yet these tones always continue to be forced and disagreeable.' [1836: Mason, *Manual of the Boston Academy of Music*]

Chorley suggested that falsetto was a French peculiarity: 'A gallery of French tenor singers would not be the least edifying chamber in the Pantheon of Art. Few traces would be there found, it is true, of the well-toned and well-cultivated voices, which distinguished the great men of the Italian opera. That they sung through their noses, is as certain as that the Parisian opera songstresses terrified Dr. Burney and Horace Walpole by their energetic screaming. Many of them, too, were afflicted with that diseased tendency towards a falsetto, which, in our own country, has run the inordinate length of pushing innocent, portly, middle-aged gentlemen into warbling (more oddly to the eye than agreeably to the ear) the sublimest songs of Handel's "Messiah".' [Chorley, *Recollections*, Vol. 1, p. 234] But Chorley was inconsistent in approving of Nourrit's falsetto: 'But though his banishment to Italy was self-inflicted, his ambition was not dead. Possibly, in his less gloomy moments, he believed that his day was not yet over; that he had still energy to recompose himself anew; that he would, in short, have a chest voice in place of his own nasal and brilliant falsetto di testa, and learn that honeyed and long-drawn cantabile which his countrymen were beginning to prize as an indispensable treasure.' [26 Aug. 1841: Chorley, *Music and Manners*, Vol. 1, p. 74]

Domenico Crevelli wrote on the tenor voice: 'Great care should be taken not to force the higher sounds. They should be sustained firmly though lightly, and without making use of falsetto, a quality of voice dissonant and unpleasant, and which ought never to exist in a well-cultivated voice.' [1842: Crevelli, *Art of Singing*]

'[Giovanni Matteo] Mario has, therefore, adopted the style enforced at the Academie de Musique. This consists in avoiding as much as possible every species of trickery of execution, singing fairly from the chest, without abuse of the artificial voce di testa, and with great parsimony in fioriture, always to be treated as secondary and subservient to feeling and expression, and to the written intentions of the composer. [Luciano] Fornasari and other of our new favourites prove that this opinion has been lately adopted in Italy, which disputes with France the glory of the reform. Our English singers, on the contrary, appear to seek to imitate Rubini.' [22 May 1843: MP]

'It is rather remarkable that within a very limited space of time we have had a great number of those rarae aves—pure tenor singers. We mean singers who produce the higher notes by the compass of their natural voice, without eking out the scale by a falsetto. [Giovanni Battista] Rubini is the precise instance of what we do not mean: and it is worthy of note, that while the falsetto is retiring from our lyrical drama, the florid style, of which Rubini is so great a master, is retiring also. [Gilbert] Duprez gave the first impulse to pure tenor singing; he has been followed by [Lorenzo] Salvi; and a third great man of the class appeared on Thursday night, in the person of Signor [Napoleone] Moriani.' [29 Jun. 1844: Ex]

'He [M. Arnaud] impressed the audience very favorably, although we can never find an excuse for the use of falsetto—that singing through the key-hole of the chest, as it were, which is no proper human sound, and ought to be tolerated nowhere.' [17 Jun. 1845: *New York Daily Tribune*]

'The love of popularity seems to gain upon [Giovanni Matteo] Mario, and leads him [Italo Gardoni] into some excesses in the employment of his falsetto, which are at variance with his general manly and feeling style. We cannot wish the employment of the falsetto—the superannuated frippery of such tenors as the once famous [Giovanni] David, revived to any extent. A note or two beyond the compass of the chest may be endured, and is often judiciously introduced by Gardoni; but when the passages extend into the higher range of the treble staff an unnatural effect results, and the ideas of sex become confused. As for David, what between his roulades in the treble, his effeminate face and excessive painting, we could never make up our mind whether he were man or woman. The natural voice of Mario is eminent for its masculine tone and character, and we deprecate any sacrifice of these good qualities for purposes of temporary applause.' [26 Jun. 1847: *Atlas*]

'The falsetto tone is produced entirely by a wrong action, and ought never to be used in singing. From this explanation, it follows as a necessary consequence, that if the falsetto is made use of, the voice must be weakened and perhaps ultimately lost altogether.' [1861: Cazalet, *The Art of Singing*, pp. 33–4]

'It is singular that the use of this mode of utterance or production, the very name of which, falsetto, is a reproach, and the result of which is a quality of sound which if not exactly effeminate, is certainly epiceane.' [26 Oct. 1864: MG, from a paper on church music by John Hullah]

'It is remarkable how blinded some people have become by custom and prejudice, to the absurdity of men singing in a false voice the part intended for women or boys ... It is simply inconceivable that any one knowing natural voices, soprano, contralto, tenor, bass, at all could listen for the first time to the poor, artificial, squeaky, disagreeable, effeminate tones of the best of men altos, without laughing outright.' [1 Jan. 1870: Alfred Stone, MusS]

The Pall Mall Gazette's music reviewer was unremittingly hostile to falsetto singing, as he showed in this review of Cox's *Musical Recollections*: 'But there can be no doubt as to the author of these volumes being in error when, speaking of the falsetto voice, he tells us that "both Rubini and Mario used this resource with the utmost advantage." "With as little disadvantage as possible," he should have said. If there could be any sort of advantage in using the artificial instead of the natural voice, composers would have written for it; which, we need scarcely say, they have not done.' [18 Dec. 1872: PMG]

5.4 Male Singers Using or Avoiding Falsetto

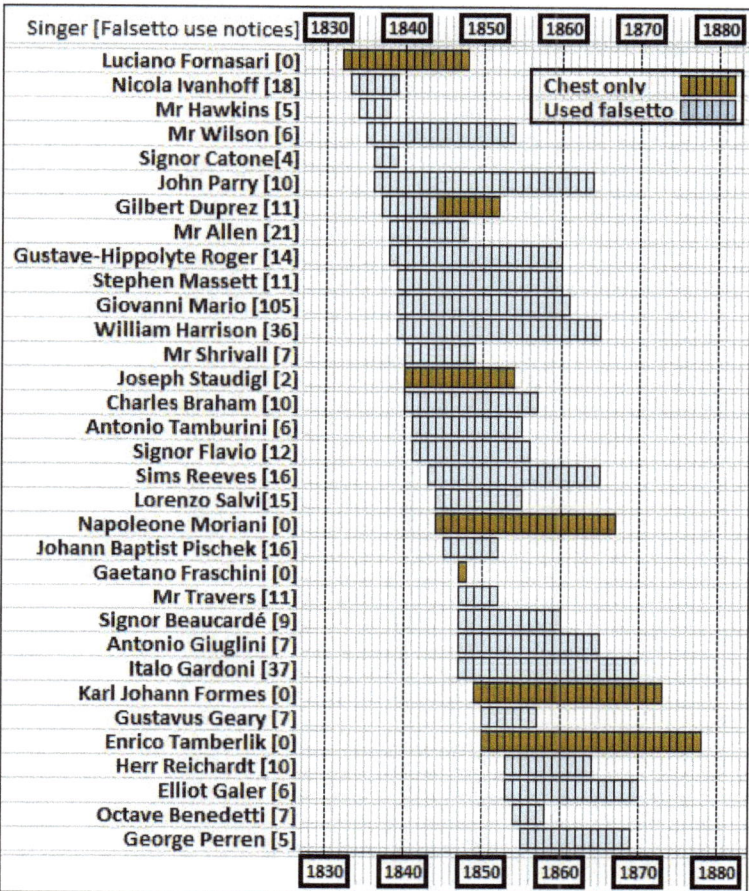

Illus. 65: Male Singers with and without Falsetto 1830 to 1870

The next question I address is this. Which singers seemingly used falsetto, and which didn't? The chart at Illus. 65 above shows male singers in both categories active from 1830 to around 1870, together with the number of reviews suggesting that they used falsetto. Selected reviews for some popular artists are included below. I've supplied compasses for both registers, in a few cases where data are available.

Luciano Fornasari and Napoleone Moriani. 'The concerted music suffered much from Signors Moriani and Fornasari; the first bawled incessantly, the second was never in tune, and when left alone, was more growling and tremulous than ever. His "day of grace" is passing, we suspect, with the subscribers. We shall be glad, for the sake of all parties, to believe that the point to which "the forcing system" has been carried, is already beginning to work its downfall. Rumours have been for some time gathering, of a potent opposition in projection for next season—and could Persiani, or Tadolini, Viardot, Rubini, Ivanhoff, Tamburini, and a basso be brought together—our epithet would be well merited.' [5 Jul. 1845: Ath]

Nicola Ivanhoff. His pure falsetto was praised, as reported on p. 187, and his clear well joined voce di testa was likewise approved [p. 187].

Gilbert Duprez. As quoted at p. 185 above, Duprez had a beautiful falsetto, reaching e. [30 Jan. 1840: MW]

Giovanni Matteo Mario. 'His falsetto is exquisite as ever, sweet in tone, and joined on to the chest-notes without anything like break or interruption.' [T, 21 Apr. 1847] 'Mario's voice has not its former charm; it is a bigger and burlier kind of tone, which he now alternates with his extensive falsetto; but the beautiful and compact tenor notes which distinguished him in former times are never heard.' [20 May 1848: *Atlas*] 'This song, the melody of which is unaffectedly beautiful, was the gem of the opera, and the exquisite falsetto of the voice was as pure and liquid as the notes of the flute which accompanied it.' [22 Jul. 1849: Era] 'Mario has a voice of marvellous purity, and in some of his favorite sentimental airs is certainly transcendant, but his upper tones are weak, and he has to be so sparing of his powers that he cannot be great through a whole evening. His falsetto on D, E, and F, is wonderfully resonant, and it is difficult to believe for the time being that you are not listening to a genuine soprano. To display these tones, he of course has to introduce notes foreign to his part. When he comes down from his falsetto, we know not which to admire most: the neatness with which he unites his head and chest registers, or the consummate art by which, in doing this, he conceals the weakness of his upper chest tones … [from The Traveller]' [12 Aug. 1854: *Dwight's*] 'Would you consider a voice having the compass of two octaves, ending with the first F in the treble, a good tenor voice!—We should call this a baritone voice; whether "good" or not would depend upon its quality. We are not admirers of the falsetto voice, but its culture is certainly desirable. The first A of the treble is, we think, the highest chest tone Mario can take with any appearance of ease.' [28 Sep. 1854: MusR]

Sims Reeves. 'His voice is a tenor fashioned on the new and admirable school of [Lorenzo] Salvi and [Giovanni Matteo] Mario:—the falsetto is discarded, in a great measure, if not altogether … The chest register of Mr. Reeve's voice is of greater compass than that of any contemporary singer we are acquainted with—always, of course, excepting [John] Braham; and he has the secret of managing its upper range, without trespassing on the head notes, so as to lend to it the effect of a falsetto, to a degree we never heard surpassed on the English stage.' [26 Oct. 1844: MCLGA] I've noted at p. 192 the flute-like tone of Sims Reeves's falsetto, as well as the 'extraordinary purity' of his voice through his whole compass. [15 Dec. 1847: CE]

Lorenzo Salvi. 'The first quality that strikes is the extraordinary elevation of his register … The phrases he executed in his falsetto were delicious.' [26 Apr. 1844: MP] 'His voce di testa, or falsetto, he only employs in extension of his natural voice when the music occasionally requires two or three notes beyond the reach of the voce di petto; for, if we do not deceive ourselves, he is too sensible a musician to have frequent recourse to an artifice which is distasteful to the real connoisseur, though it may bring the plaudits of an undistinguishing multitude.' [4 May 1844: Ex] 'His voice is flutelike, smooth, and flexible, without any traits of that hardness which is the characteristic of some of his most celebrated contemporaries. Cultivated to the extremest degree, it enables him to deliver the passionate music of his country with the most exquisite finish, to colour it with the most refined feeling, and to produce an effect upon the sympathies beyond which no advance could possibly be made. Under these circumstances of polished executancy and impassioned method his performance was throughout admirable. His duet with Lucia, in the first act, was an exquisite piece of vocalisation, imbued with a certain tone of effeminacy, which, however, was far from inappropriate or displeasing … Seldom has it been our lot to hear the renowned "Fra poco" sung so beautifully as it was by him last night. Pregnant with sadness and emotion, it penetrated to the very quick; and the tones of his voice, tremulous with the sobbing agony of a broken heart—his miserable sighs as life is oozing away—and his unexaggerated paroxysms of death, produced a climax singularly touching and impressive.' [14 Apr. 1847: Std]

Gaetano Fraschini. 'Signor Fraschini, though originally gifted with greater vocal power [than Signor Gardoni], was less fortunate.—Fourteen years ago, we were little used to the coarse and stentorian bawling which the Italian tenors have of late affected. The newcomer, naturally anxious to recommend himself by the arts which had delighted his own people, seemed to become more and more violent in proportion as the "sensation" failed to be excited. But he "piled up the agony", forte on forte in vain. That so much noise should be received so coolly was somewhat whimsical—bitter disappointment though it must have been to one misled by home raptures.—Alas! I already look back to Signor Fraschini as a moderate, if not a temperate, Italian tenor, when compared with many who have since made the ears of right-minded persons suffer.' [Dec. 1846, Chorley, *Reminiscences*, Vol. 1, p. 297]

Italo Gardoni. 'According to the fashion of the modern vocal school, he sings with great simplicity, indulges in few embellishments, and trusts to the effect of beautiful tone and expressive delivery. He makes hardly any use of the falsetto, for which, indeed, he has little occasion, his full chest voice reaching without effort to A, or B flat.' [18 Feb. 1847: DN] 'The compass of his voice is so ample that he rarely is obliged to ascend to the falsetto; but when he does so the transit is remarkably easy, and his notes equally sweet and perfect as those within the natural register of his voice.' [21 Feb. 1847: ST] '… and his falsetto (which he has the good taste not to use very frequently) wants a great deal of cultivation, for though we do not approve of its too frequent use, yet in executing Rossini's music, and in the florid style, its use is indispensable.' [4 Dec. 1847: MCLGA]

Gustavus Geary. 'This highly-gifted vocalist will not, we are sure, feel annoyed when we remind him that the "falsetto" is only un resort vocale, and that it is hardly excusable to have recourse to the "neck voice"—as the Germans call it—when nature has bestowed a pectoral organ of such power and improveable sweetness.' [5 Oct. 1850: *Freeman's*] 'His voice is a fine robust tenor, with a falsetto of great compass.' [12 Oct. 1854: *Bradford Observer*]

Herr Reichardt. 'This was followed by the air of Donizetti from Don Sebastian, "In terra solo", which was sung very tastefully by Herr Reichardt, who was new to a Brighton audience, on whom he made a favourable impression, especially in the softer parts of his voice. He has a good falsetto; but his forte notes fall somewhat harsh and grating upon the ear, and are rendered more so than necessary, by a straining after effect. He has, what we rarely find in a leading tenor, a good shake; and his cadences are given with judgment, skill, and sweetness.' [15 Nov. 1855: BG]

Elliot Galer. 'Mr Elliott Galer is a singer of the Sims Reeves school; and his voice is not unlike the popular English tenor in many points. His style is pure and chaste; but in some scenes he is too inanimate, and, although he appears, by occasional bursts, to possess great power of voice, he fails at times to exercise it in those parts which would be rendered more effective by a little more energy. He has an excellent chest voice from F to A in alt, and his falsetto is extensive and good.' [22 Mar. 1855: BG]

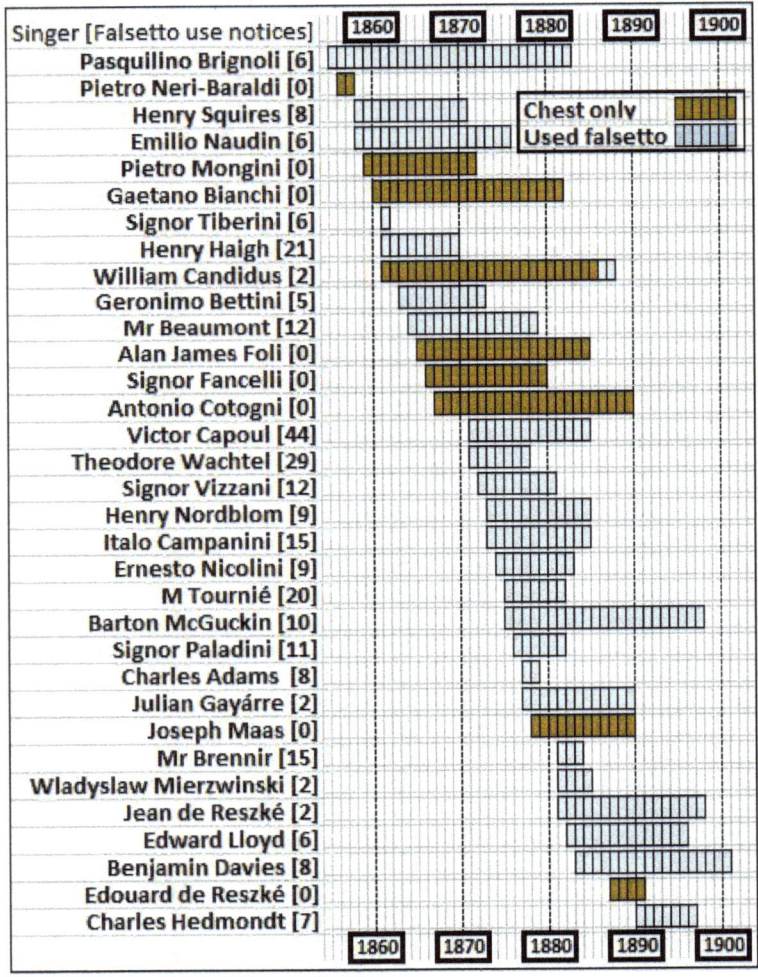

Illus. 66: Male Singers with and without Falsetto 1860 to 1900

The chart at Illus. 66 includes singers flourishing from around 1860 to 1900. Reviews of some of the main singers are appended below:

Pasquilino Brignoli. 'It cannot be disguised that the voice of Brignoli is failing; and his best efforts are comparatively feeble when compared with those of former days. We miss the delicate merging of the tenor into the falsetto, which once used to delight Brignoli's admirers, and now find that the transitions are often abrupt.' [25 Jun. 1864: *Buffalo Courier*] '[Richard Grant White's] estimate of the tenor [Brignoli] in *The Century Magazine* for June, 1882, is scarcely flattering either to the singer or the public that liked him … Says Mr. White: "Her admiration [Isabella McCullough, an American soprano] of Brignoli was not greatly to the credit of her taste. He had one of those tenor voices that seem like the bleating of a sheep made musical … But there never was a tenor of any note in New York whose singing was so utterly without character or significance and who was so deficient in histrionic ability. His high and long continued favor is one of those puzzling popular freaks not uncommon in dramatic annals".' [Jun. 1882: Krehbiel, *Sections of Opera*] 'The qualities of Brignoli's voice were such as rarely are heard upon the stage to-day. The falsetto, which has been a species of bugbear, has been banished, and tenor singers have been educated to carry what is known as the medium voice way above register and thus obliterate the beautiful head or falsetto voice. The mistake of doing this is very apparent when the high notes, instead of being pure and brilliant, are rough and full of breath. The mellow B flat and C in Brignoli's voice were precisely the character of those on which **Sims Reeves** prides himself to day and which made for him a reputation years ago. No singer now before the public boasts a more perfect register than Brignoli possessed, and even in advanced age the voice remained smooth, true and clear.' [9 Nov. 1884: Obituary in *Buffalo Courier*]

Emilio Naudin. 'He uses the falsetto freely—a resource by no means grateful. In Signor Naudin's case it is used with skill and effect; but he appears to be quite capable of dispensing with it. Sometimes he makes it the shadow or echo of his own voice, and then, perhaps, it is admirable. But on the whole it is not a good feature—at best there seems a striving through it which deprives it of purity and suggests effort and the finger of time.' [7 Oct. 1875: *Freeman's Journal*] 'This gentleman, born in Italy of French parents, is the incarnation of the bad taste which distinguishes the present Italian school of vocalism. He knows no mode of expression except the screaming forte preceding or immediately following the softest piano, giving one phrase forte and the next piano in almost uninterrupted successions, and, of course, not paying the slightest regard to the words. This habit is the more to be deplored, as Signor Naudin's voice is by no means a disagreeable one in the upper notes.' [16 Aug. 1862: MW]

Pietro Mongini. '"Non merta piu consiglio", where the entire scale is taken, from A to B in alt, was given entirely from the chest, with a gradual development of power, from piano to the loudest intensity, that we have not heard surpassed by any singer.' [1 Jul. 1860: Era] 'The chief demand on the singer's powers is the scena in the last act, "Corriam" ("Suivez moi"), in which Arnold calls on his followers to aid him in the rescue of Tell. Here there is no escape from the use of the high chest notes in the ascending scale passage mounting to C—falsetto will not serve against the weight of the accompanying orchestra and hence some singers who have managed to go through the previous scenes after a fashion, have broken down here. Signor

Mongini's powers, however, sustain him through all this strain, unparalleled, perhaps in the whole range of operatic tenor parts.' [3 Apr. 1871: DN] 'He made use of the falsetto in some of the passages, but the experiment was the reverse of successful.' [29 Jan. 1881: *Press*, NZ]

Henry Haigh. 'Mr Haigh commenced with the serenade, "Lonely I wander" ("Deserto salla terra") which he sang with much sweetness of expression. It would not be right to draw invidious comparisons, but we have not heard a tenor among our English singers that has pleased us more. Of course Mr Sims Reeves, our great English tenor, will be referred to. Mr Sims Reeves may have had more experience and acquired a well-earned fame, but we doubt whether Mr Haigh will suffer at all by comparison with him. He has some powerful chest notes, and a really exquisite falsetto, which he occasionally introduces with judgment and skill.' [31 May 1860: BG]

William Candidus. 'delivered the numerous high notes—in chest voice—with pure intonation and abundant power, and without the smallest indication of throatiness or tremolo.' [27 Jun. 1897: *Globe*]

Italo Campanini. 'His voice is wonderfully sweet, far sweeter and more touching than ever [Pasquilino] Brignoli's was,—and yet is possessed of great power and compass. He is a true artist, does not overwork his voice, or indulge in any show-passages, and is cautious about too many holds in the very highest notes. If he has a fault, it is the occasional use of the falsetto, and a tendency to rather too much pianissimo singing, to which he is tempted by the extraordinary softness and sweetness of his voice.' [28 Jul. 1872: CT] 'So artfully does he accomplish his changes of register that it is next to impossible to tell where he joins his chest tones to those of his head, and the falsetto in which he usually sings the mezzo voce passages is very pleasing.' [27 Oct. 1878: BrookN]

Julian Gayárre. 'He never uses the detestable falsetto.' [10 Apr. 1877: PMG] 'Signor Gayarre possesses all the elements that go to make a remarkable, if not an absolutely great, singer. He has a sonorous voice of genuine tenor *timbre*, with beautiful chest notes up to A and B flat, and the transition from the chest-voice to the falsetto—one of the greatest difficulties of vocal art—is accomplished with remarkable ease. In addition to this he commands a fine *mezza voce*, and his enunciation of the words is, especially for a singer of the Italian school, remarkably distinct. But the tenor has the faults of the virtues, or rather he knows his strong points so well that, by exaggeration, he converts them into weaknesses. For instance: a melody, especially an Italian cantilena, is like a gold thread of all but equal strength and circumference throughout; by continuous changes of chest and falsetto notes, and by the abrupt introduction of the subdued tone of voice, technically called *mezza voce*, Signor Gayarre produces a column of tone changing in volume from the thickness of the Atlantic cable to the tenderest gossamer. The necessary result is want of continuity and harmony.' [21 Apr. 1877: MW]

Victor Capoul. 'His voice is light, and sweet and true, with an unobtrusiveness in its ordinary habit which distinguishes him from coarser, more "robustious" tenors. Its power is feebly felt at first, but it grows upon you, and the man grows upon you as the passion and the plot develops. Then to see the intensity of his feeling struggling for expression with his small and slender frame, you think for a time of the gesticulative and grotesque type of Frenchman; but you soon find that the passion is genuine, you feel its dignity, and that you are in the presence of a superior artist, both dramatically and vocally. What if he does use the falsetto sometimes? Shall he not follow his music, the best way he can, where it transcends his range?' [18 Nov. 1871: *Dwight's*]

Theodore Wachtel. 'The World says of the debut: "The new tenor, if we can call an artist who is fifty-two years old new was cordially received ... Coming to us with the one great superiority of compass extolled to the skies, it was with some disappointment that we found him unequal to Le Franc. It is hardly necessary to say that a lavish use of the falsetto voice is somewhat antique, and we failed to hear the much boasted-of chest C during the evening".' [21 Sep. 1871: CT] 'The aria in which he drew the sword and ran up to the high C (with an ease and brilliancy quite unlike those piratical falsettos who commit murder on the high C) drew down deafening applause.' [31 Oct. 1871: EPNY]

Joseph Maas. 'Mr. Maas sings in really "finished" style. His phrasing and his intonation are faultless; he never condescends to the use of a tremolo; and the extended compass of his voice enables him to dispense with falsetto, and to produce bell-like tones in exceptionally high notes.' [13 Feb. 1879: *Globe*]

Wladyslaw Mierzwinski. 'He substitutes a manly tone and expression for [Italo] Campanini's sweet sentimentality, and sings his tones honestly, instead of resorting to the falsetto every third bar, as Campanini did last year to save his voice and conceal its defects.' [19 Oct. 1882: EPNY] 'He resorted to the falsetto, which, though delicately and admirably managed, is considered in this country a fault in a tenor.' [26 Oct. 1882: *New York Herald*]

Jean de Reszké. 'It is strange that a vocalist and a man of taste like Mr. Jean de Reszke should in "Salve Dimora" have recourse even for one single note to the always detestable falsetto. This is sinning for the sake of sinning, since the high chest notes of this artist are excellent, and help to stamp him as what he unquestionably is—the manliest of tenors.' [14 Jun. 1887: *Star*]

Benjamin Davies. 'Took the high note near the close in a distressing falsetto; the audience broke into the loudest applause of the evening and made the singer repeat the number, falsetto squeak and all.' [10 May 1894: BrookN]

5.5   The Reign of Forcible Tenors

I've already quoted reviews of Gilbert Duprez, Luciano Fornasari, Gaetano Fraschini, and Emilio Naudin, showing that all these sang as forcible tenors, using falsetto rarely if at all. Descriptions of other forcible singers or *tenore di forza* follow. Note that forcible singing is quite often accompanied by vibrato emission.

'Signor [Luigi] Lablache however is not heard to the best advantage in a concert-room; he is essentially a dramatic singer, and though a very fine and correct one, he appears to be in trammels when not in action. And then the portentous exorbitance of his voice, and which he cannot restrain within due bounds for three bars successively, without its bursting forth with the explosions of a volcano, render his exhibitions in the penfold of a concert-room amusing. In the duet with Mrs Wood, his magnificence descended to her level—at times: as for poor little Mr Bennett, he could have eaten him with a pin and a corn of salt.' [9 Mar. 1831: *Tatler* No. 160, p. 639]

'[Anton Haitzinger] is a tenor of considerable compass upwards, of sufficient power, and of good quality when he does not force it; but the latter is a fault certainly imputable to him: he falls into the error of many singers,—that of supposing bawling to be an indicator of passion, and his voice thereby becomes often tremulous.' [31 Apr. 1832: Har]

'Signor Conti, who enjoyed a great continental reputation as a "tenore di forza", and had been long a popular favourite at Madrid, was announced as the other tenor for "the lead".' [11 Mar. 1843: Lumley, p. 59]

'His voice [Mr. Travers] is a pure tenor, distinguished in more musical Italy by the appellation of tenore robusto. A vocalist of this character is of rare occurrence. Donzelli, our musical readers will remember, was a splendid example. More recently Duprez, the great French tenor, who sang on these boards two seasons ago, was nearly of the same class. Duprez, however, did not essay that style of singing until long after his organ had been completely developed; hence his constant attempts to produce great and sustained effect strained his voice, and rendered it necessary for him frequently to resort to the falsetto—a shift which the tenore di forza, or robusto, is never put to.' [5 Feb. 1847: MA]

'[Geronimo Bettini] was considered, as a tenore di forza, to have a certain merit; but deficient both in sweetness of voice and smoothness of style, he was never a favourite with the public.' [15 Jun. 1852: Lumley, p. 342]

'His reputation has been chiefly acquired in Verdi's operas; and to this may be attributed the fact of what must originally have been a fine and powerful voice, having already deteriorated in quality. Fulness of tone and sonority, however, are still, in a great degree, its characteristics, and make up for what, at a first hearing, appears to be a limited register. In his style of singing Signor Negrini betrays an adhesion to that school which, most successful in the boisterous music of Verdi, is most at fault where real vocal expression and legitimate execution are demanded. He has a habit of vociferating on all the higher notes, which is very monotonous ... He has no flexibility, and he is unable to sing piano.' [11 Aug. 1852: *Dwight's*]

'Sig. [Gottardo] Aldighieri has all the faults of the Italians of the present day—faults which Signora Piccolomini and Sig. Giuglini have not, or, at least, only in a very limited degree—without their good qualities. His singing is screeching, such as, unfortunately, our German singers imitate; besides this, too, he cannot divest himself of the insupportable tremolo. That this excess of strength of tone, falsely squeezed out, however, does not, or, at least, must not belong to the good singers of Italy, was proved by Signor Giuglini in the next scene, where he sang the reluctant composition so beautifully, that we really forgot it while listening to him.' [12 Dec. 1857: MW, quote from L. Rellstab]

'[Signor Steffani] has a voice of good ring and volume, quite musical and sweet when moderately employed, but of a splitting quality, when forced to fortissimo in high notes; it is as if the tone clove the air, like a touch resisting medium, with wedges. He reminds you somewhat of [Octave] Benedetti, though without his magnetic, intellectual force. He sings well, but with far less smoothness, sweetness and finish than [Pasquilino] Brignoli.' [28 May 1859: *Dwight's*]

'He [Signor Ferri] is a singer of whom much might be made, for his voice is melodious, deep toned, sympathetic, and his judgment is often very sound. All is spoilt at present by a habit of tremulous roaring, which Signor Ferri carries to a greater excess than we ever remember to have heard in any other singer. Occasionally it approached burlesque more nearly than a singer need desire who has still his way to make with the public.' [22 Oct. 1861: *Liverpool Daily Post*]

' "He split the ears of the groundlings", and obtained the applause of the gallery by his roaring, but he [Theodore Wachtel] never for an instant touched the true connoisseur, nor won his esteem or confidence. Happily, his presence at Covent Garden was of short duration; but even that was longer than was desirable.' [1 Jul. 1862: Cox, Vol. 2]

'He [Lodovico Graziani] sometimes forced his voice into a passionate vibrato not wholly pleasing.' [2 Apr. 1870: Ex]

'[Antonio Aramburo] is a tenore robusto of considerable vocal power, but his voice lacks steadiness, and his performance wants finish … The very marked vibrato in his voice when he begins to strain it greatly mars the effect of his singing.' [6 Dec. 1873: BDP]

'Signor Cabero [as Manrico] belongs to the class of tenori robusti whose claims to that title are enforced with undeniable, and perhaps for that reason, not always agreeable, force. Everything about Signor Cabero is, indeed, emphatically robust—voice, and gesture, and appearance.' [5 May 1877: Ex]

'Of the familiar Mephistopheles of Signor [A J] Foli it would be superfluous to speak in any detail. It is as forcible and picturesque, if not quite so fantastic as ever.' [7 Dec. 1886: BDP]

'Signor [Francesco] Tamagno is essentially a declamatory singer. In tenderer moments, the tremolo and other vocal defects of the Continental school, it is true, are apparent; but, when under the sway of passion, Signor Tamagno is superlatively grand, and no one who heard his delivery on Friday night of certain passages in the great jealousy duet in the second act is likely readily to forget the effect caused by a voice more powerful even than that of [Enrico] Tamberlik or [Pietro] Mongini, two singers now deceased, but who have hitherto been considered the most forcible tenors of our generation.' [13 Jul. 1889: *Graphic*]

'David Bispham has aptly described Tamagno "another type of great voice which came to its own by its own methods. No master could teach him much of voice culture. Vanuccini said he 'bleated like a goat', and told him so"…In the following citations from my notices of his New York appearances (1894) his faults are perhaps more than sufficiently accentuated: "Signor Tamagno's voice is not of agreeable quality, but it has a certain dramatic forcefulness which might have been turned to good account had it not been directed into vulgar channels and exaggerations by the applause of the injudicious. As long as he can secure more violent applause by standing at the footlights and hurling his notes at the audience than by remaining in the frame of the picture and addressing his song to the dramatic personage it is intended for, he will doubtless continue to do so, whatever the judicious minority may say. This world is ruled by majorities".' [1894: Finck, *Success in Music and How it is Won*, pp. 206/7]

'[Signor Rawner] has a hard, metallic voice, a faulty production, and some rather telling high notes, which are brought out with obvious effort. His style is declamatory enough, but it is never pleasant; he seemed far more at home in shouting "Di quella pira" than in phrasing "ah si ben mio". Altogether we did not like Signor Rawner, despite his high C, which he duly exhibited last night, and even despite his reputed high D, which he did not exhibit.' [25 May 1890: ST] 'Signor Rawner is a robust tenor of the school now popular in Italy. He has a powerful voice, which he uses unsparingly; and although not free from the vibrato, the defect is not so pronounced as to become unpleasant. Signor Rawner is credited with the possession of a high D.' [26 May 1890: DN]

'The Italian tenor's shrill screaming voice [Francesco Tamagno] and fierce temper were tremendously effective here and there.' [21 Jul. 1894: Shaw, Vol. 2, p. 280]

'To make up for general deficiency in tone he gave way to terrific detonations on the high notes, which reminded one forcibly of the habits of the firth-rate Italian opera at Pisa or Milan … M. [Eugène] Dufriche has got rid of a good deal of his terrific tremolo.' [9 Nov. 1898: CT]

5.6   Female Falsetto

The best female singers all cultivated a falsetto extension. This remained the case through much of the nineteenth century, given that sopranos and altos, as well as tenors and bases, still felt the need to 'scale the altitudes', just as their predecessors did in the long eighteenth century. I've already referred to Chorley's witty article [at p. 137] on this topic, citing the voices of Mrs Alfred Shaw, Madame Emma Albertazzi, Madame Meerti Blaes, and Madame Frederic Lablache. Here are further examples:

'[Signora Cecconi's], however, is a pure contralto, and, to sing the music [Meyerbeer's *Il Crociato in Egitto*], she is perpetually obliged either to fly into a most intolerable falsetto, or suddenly to fall down an octave, and thus entirely to ruin the effect of the passage.' [30 Jun. 1827: *Oriental Herald*]

'Madame Pasta, who is the most remarkable example within our recollection [of using different registers], could take G above the staff either in her breast or her head voice. Thus when she wanted force she employed the one, when she desired facility—the other. Being able to descend very low in the scale by means of her head voice, she could thus transfer the sweetness, softness, and ductility which appertain to the falsetto, to most of the middle notes of the staff, and vary the passion at pleasure.' [1828: QMMR, Vol 10, p. 324]

'… but the quality of her tone [Benedetta Rosmunda Pisaroni] is extremely disagreeable to us. We never before heard a female voice possessing a falsetto, nor do we wish to hear another.' [1 Mar. 1829: *Atlas*]

'Miss M. Williams' voice is remarkable for its compass (an extraordinary feature in a contralto), and we now suggest that this may be accounted for by the circumstance of equalization, as regards both power and quality, of the voci di petto e di testa, or to use plainer terms, of the natural and falsetto. In this particularly it is dissimilar to Miss [Maria B] Hawes' voice, the inequality of whose conjoined powers is so perceptible.' [12 Dec. 1846: MCLGA]

'Indeed she [Elizabeth Greenfield] appears to possess two distinct voices—one, of a falsetto character, in which she sings ballad music with simplicity and plaintive sweetness: the other (which may be called her natural, as opposed to her acquired voice), is low and uniform, yet melodious. Her transition of the uses of the one to the other is so sudden and complete that it takes the stranger to it completely by surprise.' [26 Nov. 1853: *Leeds Intelligencer*]

'Mdlle. [Marietta] Alboni has improved in skill and variety as a songstress since last year; but whether her resolution to emancipate herself from the limitations of her natural occupation will ultimately redound to her benefit or not may already be questioned. Loss of power in the lower tones, loss of certainty in the upper ones, rarely fail to attend the metamorphosis of a contralto into a soprano; while the former voice, even if as impressive and extensive as Mdlle. Angri's, never possesses that brightness—that mordant quality indispensable to her who is to dominate in the rich and powerful concerted music of modern Opera.' [26 May 1849: Ath]
'A contralto may be a prima donna, but not "assoluta"; and who, knowing anything about the musical theatres of Europe, can be unaware that the soprano not only takes precedence of others, but pockets by far the largest salary? … The full rich quality of her lower tones may possibly have suffered a little from her constant performance in operas composed for soprano; but their purity remains untouched, while the range of characters has been materially extended. Alboni's method is the old and true Italian method, of which no one possesses the secret so thoroughly. She never strains or forces, and therefore can never damage, her voice. She never sings Verdi, and thus has no inducement to rant.' [22 May 1856: *Dwight's*]

'At present, Madame [Jenny Lind] Goldschmidt, Madame [Anna] de la Grange, Miss Louisa Pyne, Madame [Marie] Cabel, Madame [Marie Caroline] Miolan-Carvalho, Madame [Caroline] Van den Heuvel Duprez, Mademoiselle [Adelina] Patti, and many others—all command the altissimo register, —and this, too, at a time when a dramatic force and declamation are expected in combination with execution, never thought of by most of the bird-like warblers of the old school.' [1862: Chorley, *Recollections*, Vil. 2, p. 149]

'She [Madame Helen Lemmens-Sherrington] is in the possession of a soprano of rare quality and immense compass. Her countenance is earnest and pleasing in its expression, and she may be accounted one of the most perfectly endowed soprano singers of the age. The lower portion of her register is firm, rich, and round, and whilst always powerful, even in the deepest notes, sweetness of tone is ever in the ascendant. The middle portion of her voice is broad, ringing, and silvery, and full of dramatic force and vigour, and above it springs a falsetto of exceeding flexibility. It is sometimes so elastic and delicate as to resemble the highest notes that can be produced on the violin, and occasionally it gushes out with a thrilling vibration.' [16 Dec. 1865: YG]

'But Miss [Rose Alice] Ettinger has a sort of shadow voice, a feminine falsetto, the lightest whisper of which reaches the remotest corner of the hall, and the range of which appears to have no limit. It is with this dainty, tricky, bird-like voice that she surprises and charms her audience.' [13 Dec. 1900: Scot]

It's also clear that several female singers with ranges in excess of 2½ octaves must have deployed a falsetto, as shown in Illus. 67 below.

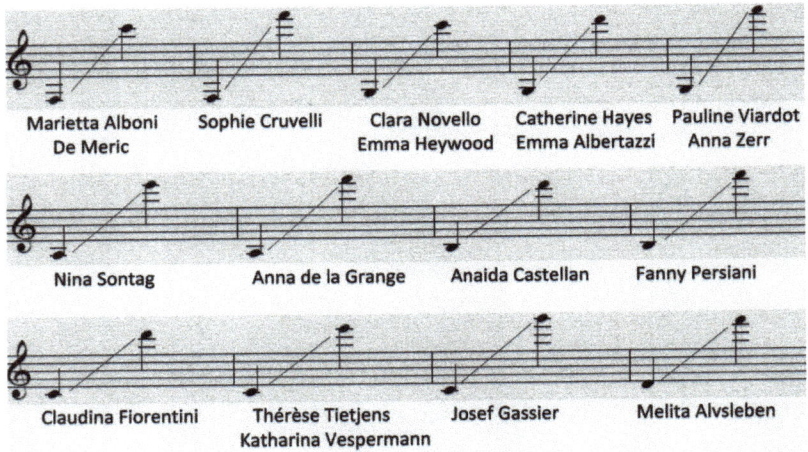

Illus. 67: Female Singers with Falsetto Extensions

5.7   Emergence of Dramatic and Forcible Sopranos

Dramatic sopranos were the female counterparts of *tenore di forza*. The Pall Mall Gazette's critic took a particular interest in distinguishing between dramatic and light sopranos through the 1870s:

'Her figure [Mdlle Ethelka Gerster], her calibre of voice—greater than that of most artists who confine themselves to "light soprano" parts—and her capabilities as an actress will probably incline her before many years to undertake what are called "dramatic" parts.' [15 May 1767: PMG]

' "La Sonnambula", too, is one of the most charming of the many charming operas written more especially for the exhibition of the prima donna. Composed for Mdme. [Giuditta] Pasta, before the distinction between "light soprano" and "dramatic soprano" existed, it has at last fallen entirely into the "light soprano" domain. Every "light soprano" of the requisite endowments is sure sooner or later, to be heard as Amina; and when such a vocalist and such an actress as Mdlle. Ilma de Murska undertakes the part, we may be sure that it will receive the fullest justice at her hands.' [13 May 1870: PMG]

'Prima-donna parts having been naturally divided into parts for the soprano and parts for the mezzo-soprano—and soprano parts having been, less naturally, divided into parts for the light soprano and parts for the dramatic soprano—the next distinction will, we fancy, be a subdivision of light soprano parts into parts for the brilliant light soprano and parts for the sentimental light soprano. Rosina, for instance, is eminently a part for what we propose to call the brilliant light soprano; while Lucia is, above all, a part for the sentimental light soprano. Mdlle. [Christine] Nilsson is a sentimental light soprano of the highest degree of development.' [13 May 1870: PMG]

'Although our two Italian theatres have in their well-stocked collections many works in common ("Lucia", "Dinorah", "Faust", "The Marriage of Figaro", "Don Giovanni", for instance), grand opera is more especially cultivated at Covent Garden, where, in addition to certain scenic advantages, the company includes two sopranos of the "dramatic" type, Mdlle. Titiens [Thérèse Tietjens] and Mdlle. [Pauline] Lucca, whose equivalents are not to be found at Drury Lane. The modern distinction between light sopranos and dramatic sopranos will probably not last for ever. It was a distinction Rossini did not know of when he composed the ten operas which contain each a part for Mdlle. [Isabella Angela] Colbran.' [5 Jul. 1870: PMG]

'Meyerbeer, while setting himself against a good many operatic conventions, introduced into his operas certain conventions of his own. Thus in all his works for the French Académie a "light soprano" and a "dramatic soprano" figure together and in contrast, as a matter of course; the former corresponding more or less closely to the fair heroine, the latter to the dark heroine of Sir Walter Scott's novels … Her true soprano voice [Mdlle. Carlotta Grossi as Marguerite de Valois] is of the clearest, purest quality, and sufficiently high to enable her to sing the music of the Queen of Night without transposition.' [27 Jun. 1872: PMG]

'The great success of the evening was, of course, obtained by Mdlle. Titiens [Thérèse Tietjens], whose Lucrezia, always incomparable, now stands altogether alone. It is a remarkable thing, to which the attention not of critics and musicians but of physiologists might be called, that for half a dozen successful light sopranos and sopranos with medium voices (accompanied in most cases by medium dramatic power) not one successful soprano of the [Giuditta] Pasta and [Giulia] Grisi type makes her appearance.' [16 Apr. 1873: PMG]

'Among the new singers at the Royal Italian Opera may almost be counted Mdme. [Maria] Vilda, who until the present season had not been heard for some years in London. Mdme Vilda reappeared as Norma, the part in which she was first introduced to the English public, and she has more than renewed the favourable opinion she created.' [Reviewer goes on to discuss Vilda's position as continuing in the tradition of Grisi's and Tietjens's 'dramatic sopranos'.] 'She has a magnificent voice; but singing alone goes for less in the part of Valentine than in that of Norma, which itself, to be fully represented, should be played by a vocalist who is also a great tragic actress. Apart from its fine tone, Mdme. Vilda possesses a voice so even, so equally developed, and so entirely at her command that the very certainty of her execution is alone a source for satisfaction.' [17 Jun. 1874: PMG]

'Mdlle. Titiens's [Thérèse Tietjens] departure from England at the end of the present season for a long tour in the United States will leave vacant on our operatic stage a place which cannot be filled. We will not enter into a discussion as to the merits of "light sopranos" and "dramatic sopranos", which might easily take the form of the discussion between the comic author and the serious author in "Le Diable Boiteux". The best authors can be serious or comic according to the requirements of their subject; and the perfect prima donna ought, perhaps, to excel equally in "light" and in "dramatic" parts. As a matter of fact, however, considerable volume of voice and remarkable "agility" of execution are rarely found together; and all the soprano voices which of late years have excited the enthusiasm of the English, of the Russians, and of the Americans have been of "light" quality.' [8 Jun. 1875: PMG]

'It can be seen from Miss [Minnie] Hauk's actual performance that she is particularly well fitted for what are called "dramatic" parts; by which, in operatic phraseology, is meant parts demanding from the impersonator much animation and force … Those who remember Miss Hauk's beautiful but somewhat slender voice of ten years ago will be surprised to find how fully and richly it has developed.' [4 May 1878: PMG]

'In Meyerbeer's operas the contrast between "light soprano" and "dramatic soprano" is so marked that this composer may well pass for the inventor of the distinction, which during the Rossini period and in the days of [Giuditta] Pasta and of [Maria] Malibran] seems to have been unknown. The part of Alice in "Robert le Diable" is not, it is true, a very "robust" one; nor can the part of the Princess Isabella in this same work be considered particularly "light". Indeed, the music given to Isabella is quite as expressive and almost as little adorned with scale passages and fioriture as that of Alice herself. In "Les Huguenots", however, the music of Valentine and that of Marguerite de Valois are quite in opposite styles, as are equally those of Bertha and of Fidès in "Le Prophète", those of Inez and of Selika in "L'Africaine", and the latest Marguerite de Valois who has been heard at the Royal Italian Opera may be looked upon as a perfect type of the "light soprano". Mdlle. Schou, the artist in question, has a singularly pure voice of extensive range and—what makes this range more remarkable than it otherwise would be—of the same quality throughout. Thus there is not even in her very highest notes the least trace of forcing. She sings delightfully in tune, and executes the most difficult passages with the certainty of a Joachim executing them on the violin.' [28 May 1879: PMG]

'Not only the acting but also the singing of Mdme. [Adelina] Patti has this season taken new developments. She depends less than formerly on her high staccato effects; and though the brilliancy of her upper notes has not, generally speaking, been impaired, it is no longer in high soprano parts that she is heard to the greatest advantage. On the other hand, her middle and lower notes have gained in volume and in sonorousness; and she is more qualified than she ever was before to sustain what are called "dramatic" parts.' [23 Jun. 1879: PMG]

There are references throughout the century, often viciously hostile, to forcible female singing, which was sometimes accompanied by tremolo:

I've already quoted Edgcumbe's comment [p. 143] to the effect that, while Giuditta Pasta was too loud in a room, all blemishes disappeared in the theatre.

'No audience is more critical than this one [Leipzig], or apt to hiss with extremer violence if ladies or gentlemen on the stage expose themselves by attempting too much. I was sorry to find that Mademoiselle Marschner, from Cassel, in playing Rossini's Tancred, incurred this ungallant sibilation; but if screaming renders such conduct justifiable, I will not undertake to defend her. It is always unfortunate for a singer when the audience, at the conclusion of a song, instead of being struck with admiration, burst out into loud laughter, the more vulgar part mimicking and hissing; and though incapable of joining in this, I could not hear some staccato passages which were like the fast quacking of a frightened, overdriven duck, without feeling extremely flushed and uncomfortable.' [1 Aug. 1827: Holmes]

'Madame Lalande [Henriette Méric-Lalande] has a voice of the highest compass, but necessarily sings her parts in precisely the same key as other singers of her class. It is not therefore the thin elevation of her voice, but its shrill tone,—its hysterical volume,—that is faulty, and offends, as that power always must offend which imparts sharpness for sweetness, and tremor for equality.' [7 Aug. 1830: *Dramatic Magazine*]

'If Miss [Anne] Romer ever did sing, which we will not dispute, she certainly does not now, her voice by being constantly forced, is rendered harsh, not one sound of it vibrates, it is hard and unpleasant at all times; she appears to possess a feeling for music but throws all expression into an everlasting tremolo; a little reflection we should have thought would have proved to her that the most beautiful part of the voice itself is a fully sustained sound; but setting this aside, we would ask her if she herself wished to express a sentiment, let us suppose a tender one, I love, for instance, would the effect of this be heightened by thus uttering it—I lo—tremolo—ve? Just let her imagine a repetition of this and what would be the effect. We can only say if the sentiment referred to us, we should wish her and it at the——, but we will not offend ears polite.' [25 Jun. 1845: MP]

'Throughout the part of Lucrezia Borgia, in which she [Erminia Frezzolini] made her appearance, she wrought her effects with these tones forcibly produced,—wearing out our enthusiasm by too prodigal a display of her own ... in the concerted music she was ineffective, save where an a or b in alt permitted her to scream. Madame Frezzolini is possibly the most attractive and finished specimen extant of the songstress dear to and destroyed by Verdi; and the present plight of her voice, its former even beauty considered, may wisely be taken to heart by all cantatrice who find the new school, so called, easy and seductive.' [25 May 1850: Ath]

'We must confess, we have not heard for a long time an Italian singer who gave as little evidence of any training whatever. Not only that there is no connection between the registers of her voice, that each of them has a different color, but this difference will be found even between most of the single tones of these registers. Her voice represents a multiplication of rainbows. Besides this, the lady [Marietta Gazzaniga] can not sustain a single tone without shaking and trembling. Madame de Lagrange has a similar defect; but this most accomplished artist came to it after having vanquished almost all the difficulties of her art, while Madame Gazzaniga has not yet conquered one … She did not sing the part, but howled, screamed, and sobbed it.' [2 May 1857: MusR]

'Every note was disfigured by a sort of tough vibration, which entirely neutralized every other such good quality as its owner may have originally possessed… If Mademoiselle Spezzia [Spezia] may be commemorated as a fair specimen of the forcible prima donna of modern Italy…Mademoiselle [Angiolina] Ortolani [-Tiberini] was in some degree a comparative specimen of what now passes in the South for light or florid singing … but her voice was shrill and wiry, qualities which are more easily pardoned (who can explain why?) in French than in Italian voices.' [Dec. 1857: Chorley, *Recollections*, Vol. 2, p. 280]

'She [Ida Gillies] will do well to avoid forcing her voice on the high notes, some of which are more powerful than pleasant.' [4 Feb. 1866: ST]

'So far as Mdlle. [Mathilde] Sessi's vocalisation is concerned, we have heard nothing from her that is calculated to induce us to change the opinion we formed of the quality of her voice on the night of her début—that it is unsympathetic, thin in quality, and not always quite true in intonation; whilst the constant use of the tremolo, and a tendency to force it especially in the higher register, which degenerates into nothing less than a scream, renders it painfully unpleasant to be listened to for any length of time.' [23 Apr. 1870: *Bell's Weekly Messenger*]

'If there was anything amiss in this [terzetto "Lift thine eyes" from Elijah] it was that Madame [Janet Monach] Patey sang too loud. Beautiful as her voice is, there are times when one may hear too much of it.' [18 Nov. 1871: *Dwight's*]

'When she [Madame Lorenzini Gianoli] sings with her full power—and especially when she attacks high notes—she screams rather than sings, and her voice in florid passages is thin and wiry.' [27 Oct. 1880: *Globe*]

'[Miss Eugenie Bonner] has rather a robust contralto voice with a strong vibrato, and in all points is more forcible than finished.' [8 Sep. 1889: *Daily Inter Ocean*]

'[Miss Sybil Sanderson] already has acquired something of a wiggle—polite term for vibrato—yet the natural quality of the organ, once upon a time, must have been very pleasant. It is a phenomenally high voice, and her higher and highest notes are easily produced and sound musical. But this has been gained at a sacrifice of medium and lower tones, which, while they do not lack power, are unvital. Yet Miss Sanderson's mezzo voce is quite charming. The defects in her method and her uneven scale are apparent when the dramatic situation becomes urgent, how she forces the tone and its character is sacrificed.' [29 Sep. 1889: *Pittsburgh Dispatch*]

'The attack was forced nearly all the time [Fraulein Lola Beeth], the placing of the tones in the lower register was very faulty, and there was an excessive vibrato.' [3 Dec. 1895: NYT]

5.8   Decline in Sweetness and purity

I discussed in section 2 the four components of the *portamento di voce*, viz.: sweetness, purity, clearness and appeal to the heart. I promised some data, which is presented below.

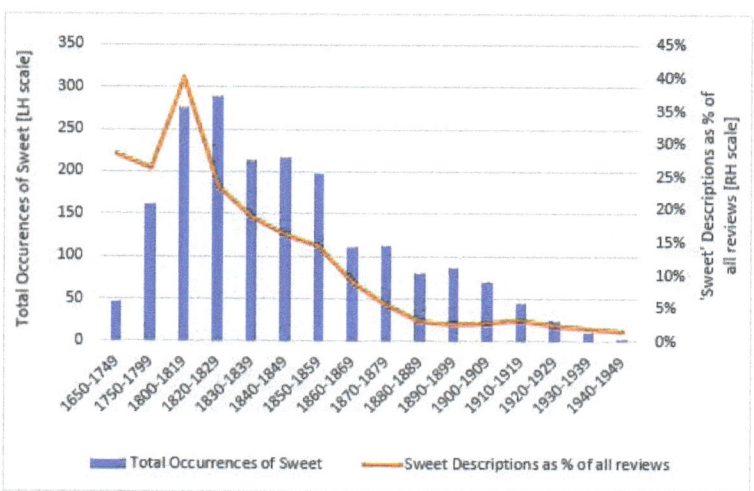

Illus. 68: Singers' voices described as 'sweet' less often from early 19th century onwards

It will be apparent from the furious diatribes cited above that the reduction in descriptions of nineteenth-century singing as 'sweet' and 'pure' is accounted for by the increased prevalence of 'unsweet' and 'unpure' characteristics, especially (1) screeching or bellowing in chest voice, in place of sweet, beautiful falsetto, and (2) continuous tremolo, instead of default straight voice. These trends are associated with the entry of dramatic sopranos on the musical scene around 1870, joining the *tenore di forza*, who had been rampant since the 1840s. The chart at Illus. 68 shows the decline in descriptions of singing as sweet through the nineteenth century. A similar trend in the decline of 'pure' descriptions is apparent from the chart at Illus. 69.

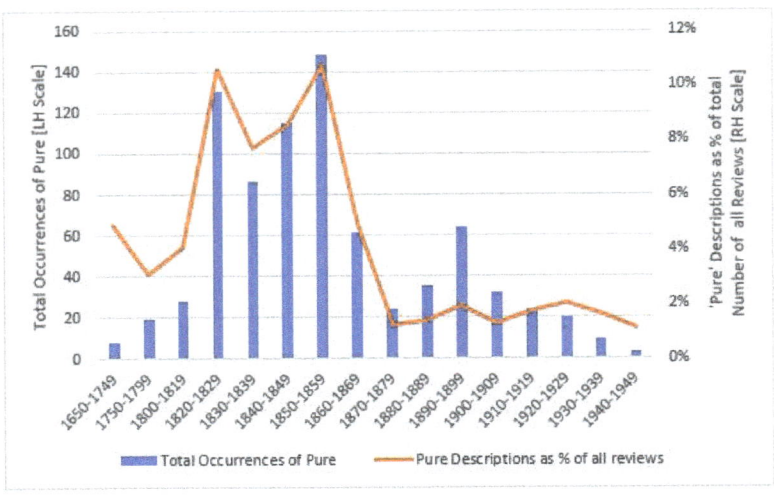

Illus. 69: Singers' voices described as 'pure' less often from 1870

5.9 Main Conclusions on Vocal Registration and Volume

It is something of a surprise to find that most male singers, besides their female counterparts, were able up to the end of the nineteenth century, at least on occasion, to deliver some notes in falsetto, as my charts at Illus. 65 and 66 show. **George Newton** summed up the situation well: 'But all singers and their mentors were struggling with the problem [from around 1850] of developing larger voices to meet the demands of the operatic music now being written, voices that would still have flexibility and agility, but, above all, voices that would still be beautiful. There was one part of the old technique that could not be adjusted to meeting the new demands; it could only be abandoned. That was the blending of the falsetto into the rest of the voice, which had been one of the most important parts of *bel canto* technique. Falsetto could still be retained for special effects, but in dramatic singing proper it had no place.' [1984: George Newton, *Sonority in Singing*, p. 101]

But, while reviewers were generally well disposed towards falsetto singing up to around 1870, critical attitudes after that date tended to be more hostile. Also, the volume of comments on falsetto declined during the last three decades of the century, suggesting that most male vocalists sang almost entirely in their chest voice.

It is apparent that, from around 1840 onwards, the performance climate began to favour loud singing, with stars such as Gilbert Duprez sporting high Cs from the chest. Other *tenore di forza* included Luciano Fornasari, Gaetano Fraschini, and Emilio Naudin.

The trend away from nightingales to dramatic sopranos began rather later, in 1870. Several commentators made the point that there was no distinction between light and dramatic sopranos in earlier years when Rossini was launching his operas. While many references to dramatic sopranos, or sopranos with forced voices, were hostile, Thérèse Tietjens was often cited as an example of a good dramatic soprano, and reviewed favourably.

In my view, it is clear that *portamento di voce*, the fundamental prerequisite of singing through the long eighteenth century, reduced in importance as the nineteenth century progressed. This conclusion is supported by the diminishing frequency of the descriptions 'sweet' and 'pure' applied to singers' voices.

The developments discussed above continued in the twentieth century. **Will Crutchfield** concluded: 'Since all these developments [emphasis on chest notes, emergence of high baritones and dramatic mezzo-sopranos, arrival of the "voix sombre", increased use of vibrato] have been continued, and in some cases steeply exaggerated, in the twentieth century, it is worth pointing out that the priority given to sheer volume, sustained high notes, vowel modification and the like—as well as the neglect of florid technique—was still notably less at the turn of the century (as observed through phonograph recordings) than in, say, 1930 or 1950.' [Crutchfield, writing in Brown, Mayer and Sadie, *Performance Practice: Music after 1600*, p. 429]

The almost universal prevalence of stentorian level vocal volume in today's opera (and sometimes) concert productions is a matter of common observation. **George Newton** commented: 'There is one characteristic of today's operatic singing that seems to know no national boundaries: no matter how large the voice, the possessor of it seems impelled to continue driving it to make it larger. Very few singers, male or female, international star or local aspirant, are immune from this "disease". The result, in most individuals, is an increase in the vibrato, especially a pitch vibrato, which increases from year to year as he or she tries to keep up with everyone else. Even worse is the loss of tonal beauty which comes from pressing and not allowing the tone to float. By now the audience is so conditioned to hearing this effort-ful sound that any singer who does not appear to be "giving his all" is dismissed as not having an operatic voice. The unusually large voice has become the expected norm, and those whose voices are of ordinary size are simply not engaged to sing opera.'[1984: G. Newton, p. 130]

It is also clear that, given almost ubiquitous[48] forte or fortissimo vocal production levels, especially on high notes, falsetto still has no place in the 21st-century skill-set of tenors, baritones and bases, although specialist falsettists continue to have an important function in playing castrato roles in early opera. Other classical singers have yet to rediscover the value of a falsetto register in early music, as many pop singers have done in recent decades.

---

48 Certainly by operatic and oratorio soloists, although there are exceptions, e.g. in lieder and some sacred music.

Descent from Dual Register Emission to Constant Chest Voice

6 Descent from Natural Voice to Made Voice

As I've noted in Section 2, the best singers during the long eighteenth century were praised for their natural voices, typically described as 'clear'. Synonymous with 'clear' were: 'silvery' 'limpid', 'good portamento'. By contrast, singers were censured if they modified their natural tone by low larynx emission, known today as laryngeal development.

6.1   Analysis

As Illus. 70 shows, low larynx vocalism continued to be viewed as a fault through the rest of the nineteenth century and the first few decades of the twentieth. Such singing was described as 'throaty' in the great majority of cases. A rich variety of other pejorative terms were applied such as: 'guttural', 'fatty', 'thick', 'smothered', 'plummy' 'cloudy', 'oily', 'foggy', 'veiled', 'quaggy', 'woolly', 'fleecy hosiery', 'squeezed', 'constricted' 'pinched', 'muffled', 'sombre', 'hollow', 'compressed', 'choked', 'oaken' and 'tonsillitic'. Throaty singers were told that their throats contained 'a marmalade lozenge' or 'batter pudding'. They were described as 'necktie singers', with voices strangled by a 'neckcloth' or 'shut up in the larynx/trachea', singing through 'a bale of cloth', and advised to 'get the voice further forward'. 79% out of a total 738 reviews fell into this category. Low larynx singing was praised only in very few cases, mostly in the 1920s.

By contrast, 152 reviews [21%] either praised singers with voices described as clear, silvery, pure, or high in head, or awarded desirable negatives such as avoidance of throatiness. A few singers with voices described as 'whiteness' or 'frontale' were criticised.

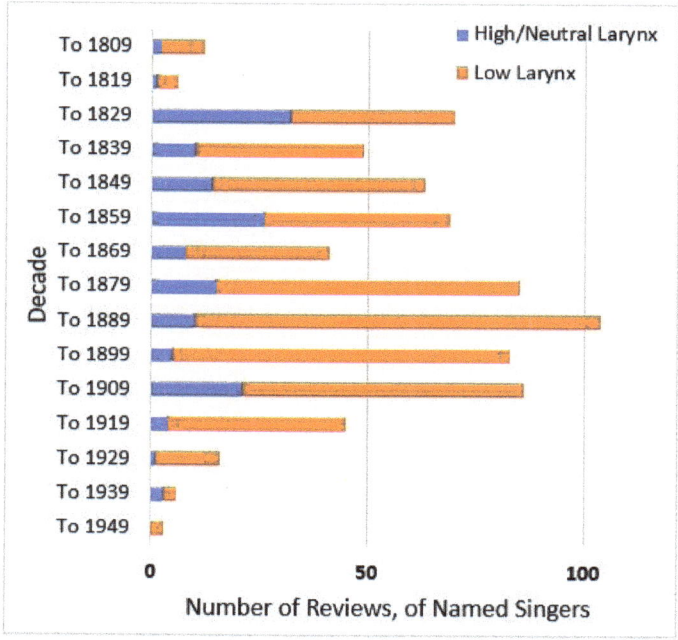

Illus. 70: Reviews Criticised as Low Larynx or Praised as High/Neutral Larynx

The critical profile viewed historically was not dissimilar to that for tremolo/vibrato [see Illus. 46 and 47], with adverse reviews of guttural singing peaking between 1870 and 1909. Unfavourable reviews quite often cited both tremolo and throatiness as faults. Illus. 70 also shows that, during the three decades from 1920 to 1949, both positive and negative comments on vocal timbre reduced sharply. As I've noted elsewhere, continuous vibrato and laryngeal development are viewed today as fundamental to good classical singing, with low larynx production perceived as a vital constituent of the 'singer's formant' . For example, **Jean Callaghan** summarised [2014]: 'The Ekholm et al. study clarified the attributes of good voice quality appropriate for Western classical singing. Such voice quality needs a balance of vibrato rate and extent, a low rate of amplitude vibrato, and a vibrato present throughout each note. It needs good vowel definition and the warmth of tone conferred by a lowered larynx, balanced by the "ring" of the singer's formant with its spectral location within the appropriate bandwidth for the voice classification.' [2014: Callaghan, *Singing and Science*]

6.2   New Thinking from Manuel García

From Part 1 of Garcia's treatise: 'Des deux timbres principaux: le timbre clair, le timbre sombre.' 'The leading qualities of the voice are two: the clear or open, and the sombre or closed.' [1840: Manuel García, *Ecole de García*, trans Albert García, 1924, p. 3]

García goes on to explain the physical mechanism involved:

> 'On conçoit donc qu'il y aura autant de nuances dans les timbres que de variétés dans la combinaison de ces conditions mécaniques. / Pour bien comprendre les mouvements du pharynx, il faut se figurer un tuyau profond et extensible qui commence au larynx, se courbe à l'arcade palatine et se termine à l'ouverture de la bouche. Ce tuyau peut se raccourcir, et alors il ne décrit qu'une courbe légère: ou bien il peut s'allonger, et alors il se brise à angle droit. Dans le premier cas, le larynx remonte vers le voile du palais, et celui-ci s'abaisse vers le larynx; dans le second cas, c'est-à-dire quand le tuyau s'allonge, le larynx descend et le voile du palais remonte. / La forme courte et faiblement arrondie produit le timbre clair, la forme allongée et fortement courbée produit le timbre sombre.'

> 'Hence the varieties of *timbre* will correspond to the multitudinous mechanical changes of which the vocal tube is susceptible. We shall understand these movements if we consider the vocal tube as a deep and highly elastic pipe, beginning below at the larynx, forming a curve at the arch of the palate, and ending above at the mouth;—a tube, which, when at its shortest dimensions, forms only a slight curve, and at its longest, nearly a right angle; the larynx in the first case, rising towards the soft palate, and the latter, dropping to meet it; whereas, in the second case, the larynx drops and the soft palate rises; thus making the distance between them greater. The short and gently-curved shape produces the clear timbre, while the sombre is caused by the lengthened and strongly-curved form.' [García, *op. cit.*, p. 4]

In Part 2, García explains at considerable length exactly how the two opposing timbres should be used to express the 'emotion of the soul from which they spring'. After giving a number of examples, he summarises: 'From our preceding observations, many important results may be deduced:—first.

Sounds that have no brilliancy serve to express poignant sentiments, such as tenderness, timidity, fear, confusion, terror, &c. Those, on the other hand, which possess their full brilliancy, best express sentiments exciting to the energy of the organs; such as animation, joy, anger, rage, pride, &c.—2ndly. The two opposing *timbres* pursue an exactly similar course to that of the passions. They start from an intermediate point, where the expression of the softer sentiments is placed, and thence move in an opposite direction. The *timbres* attain their greatest exaggeration, when the passions themselves reach their utmost limits. Lively or terrible passions, that burst out with violence, require open *timbres*; while serious sentiments, whether elevated or concentrated, demand covered *timbres*.' [García, *op. cit.*, p. 68]

Thus, Garcia's key innovation was to insist that, depending on the emotion to be imparted, **both** the clear/open timbre and the sombre/closed timbre need to be exploited, in contrast to the preceding era when low larynx production was effectively forbidden in all circumstances.

6.3 Additional Pedagogy on 19th- and 20th-Century Low Larynx Singing

As I've already reported in Section 2.13, low larynx singing was expressly condemned by treatise writers during the long eighteenth century, i.e. up to 1830. In spite of García's innovations, these attitudes persisted up to as late as the 1920s, when the vocal scientists, as exemplified by Mrs Bretz in 1927, came out in favour of low larynx production.

Thomas Busby's *Dictionary of three thousand terms* advised: 'In the early stages of vocal practice, the pupil should rid the voice of all pectoral, guttural, or nasal qualities ... let it issue unaccompanied by any wheezing, gurgling, or reedy sound.' [Dec. 1840: Busby, *Dictionary*]

George F. Root wrote: 'I am satisfied for example that the clear tone rather than the sombre or mixed should be commonly used, even in the highest chest tones of men's voices. With us, the sombre voice, has, it seems to me, prevailed too much.' [5 Nov. 1859: *Dwight's*]

William Newton wrote in his *Anglo-Italian Elements of Singing*: 'Guttural or throaty sounds are caused by allowing the tongue to rise at its root while producing the sound. This defect may be overcome by vocalizing upon the slender vowels, which ring the tongue forward in the mouth, thus facilitating the correct emission of the voice, which should at the same time be suddenly brought from the chest, through the mouth. The slender e, as in me, and a, as in fate, are the vowels to vocalize upon. / Nasal sounds are very intolerable; and the defect is so bad, that M. Tosi, a celebrated authority on singing, of the Old Italian school, pronounces it "past all remedy when once grown into a habit".' [Dec. 1861: W. Newton, p. 18]

Charlotte Sainton-Dolby advised in her *A Complete Course of Practical Instruction in the Art of Singing*: 'ON THE FORMATION OF THE VOICE...the most important study of all, especially for beginners, is that of the medium or mixed voice ... Unless a pupil be closely watched there is danger of subsiding into a throaty or a nasal production of these tones, either habit being most difficult to correct when once formed.' [Dec. 1872: Sainton-Dolby, p. 4]

John D'Esté [Mus. Doc., M.A., Sidney Sussex College, Cambridge] pejoratively dismissed low larynx production: 'Gutteral or Throat Voice. This is of the quality of voice found in the parrot, or of persons who have an excrescence in their throat. This quality of tone, so offensive to a delicate ear, is caused by improperly contracting, or narrowing the tonsils, as in the action of swallowing, and consequently, contracting the lips of the glottis. The throat voice is sometimes (but rarely) caused by organic defects, but it proceeds much oftener from bad habits, and art can do much, either to prevent or eradicate it.' [1872: D'Esté, *Vocalists' Vade Mecum*, p. 14]

However, Garcia received support from **Sabrina Dow**, who amplified Garcia's position: 'In the cultivation of the voice, two artistic timbres are recognized as possible and necessary to the highest purposes of singing. The clear or ordinary voice, called by the French and the Italians la voix blanche and voce bianca, or white voice, and its opposite, the richly-colored, sombre voice, the voce coperta—covered voice, of the Italians. The beauty of singing depends upon a judicious use of both these timbres, with their intermediate shades, according to the sentiment of the song. The first is the natural quality of most voices, the last is only occasionally a gift of nature. These resources may however be united in the cultivated singer. The same musical phrase, without change of time or pitch or power, may express joy or sadness by this artistic varying of timbre. / The clear timbre is suited to joyous, heroic or tender situations; the sombre expresses the profoundest feelings of our nature; the artist employs it in tragic scenes. The clear voice is the most far-reaching, the sombre is the most voluminous. In the clear timbre, the singer executes all light fioriture, while the dramatic sostenuto requires the sombre tones. The clear timbre is the one for habitual use; the sombre, from the greater expense of strength in its production, should not be used habitually, but as a resource of high expression. The power of using the sombre voice first leaves us with the coming on of years.' [1883: Dow, *Artistic Singing*, p. 33]

Edwin Holland, in an article 'Method of Voice Production' noted: 'For example, it is a matter of common knowledge that, although the English voice, by reason of the language, is naturally of a guttural tendency, this defect has been so far overcome, that we seldom now hear in our English operas, and good concerts, those throaty tones which were once so unpleasantly common.' [17 Mar. 1884: ISDN]

Mr C. E. Rowley said in a lecture: 'Bad habits are acquired of using the voice; instead of a free natural emission of vocal sounds we have a hollow or guttural or "throaty" effect, and as this habit goes on for years, when the singing master is called in he finds that his work lies in telling his pupil what not to do, rather than what to do. Then, in all probability when he has broken through this formidable barrier of bad habits, and when he is hoping to make a singer and an artiste of his pupil, the amateur, content with a miserable mediocrity, gives up, and, of course, sinks back into his old habits again to a greater or lesser extent.' [16 Jun. 1893: MT]

Sims Reeves was quoted thus: 'On the subject of "placing the voice" he says: "The voice must not be felt in the throat, for it is then throaty; nor in the nose, for it is then nasal; nor in the cheeks, for it is then woolly; but it should be felt right above the front teeth, with a strong vibratory sensation across the bridge of the nose. When the singer feels this vibration the voice has been properly placed".' [20 Dec. 1899: MP]

'Mr. **Paul le Vallon** [adjudicator] had to judge 38 dramatic contraltos, the majority of whom he found "throaty".' [12 Oct. 1911: MCLGA]

Lecturer **Charles Tree** said: '… and the throaty tenor also came in for scathing criticism. He emphasised the importance of the natural tone of the voice being adopted in singing as against the too frequent habit of "forcing" the voice.' [28 Feb. 1923: *Taunton Courier*]

' "They [female voices] were all pleasing to listen to, and, generally speaking, they were free from vice, and the singing was very pleasant indeed; but one of the tendencies was that of throatiness"— adjudicator **Dr Whittaker**.' [8 May 1925: *Ballymena Observer*]

Mrs Bretz was the first to praise low larynx singing: 'The three fundamentals of beautiful singing are, then: pure vowel form, correct breathing, and, lastly, depth of tone. This means low larynx and open throat—pharynx resonance—the maximum of acoustic space. Tone produced in observance of these fundamental principles will have depth, fullness and brilliance.' [23 Apr. 1927: BrookN]

6.4 Reviews of Clear [Non throaty] Singing from 1830

Reviews of clear, non-throaty singing are given below, prefaced by a few already reported:

- Dwight's praise for Luigi Lablache's 'purely natural voice … did not seem to include one made note'. [p. 180]

- The comparison of Clara Novello's voice to a Virginian mint julep. [p. 160]

- Nina Sontag's predominantly clear voice, matched by Jenny Lind's preference for the sombre voice. [p. 163]

- The description [p. 169] of Thérèse Tietjens's suggests a 'pure soprano of exquisite quality, in its tone clear and liquid as a silver bell', and 'an openness of sound'.

- William Candidus sang 'without the smallest indication of throatiness'. [p. 304]

'The Signorina [Miss Hughes, at The Park Theatre, in Rossini's *Cinderella*] could pass higher and lower, and thrill you with more extraordinary and triumphant exhibitions of science and power; but for that inherent quality of tone which composes *sweetness*—for the silvery softness in which the ear can detect nothing but a consciousness of pleasure; a clearness like that which delights the eye upon a sleeping stream in summer, when there is not a ripple to break its motionless beauty, or stir the images in its transparent depths—this faculty is the gift of nature, and is possessed by Mrs. [Elizabeth] Austin above any singer we ever heard. Upon this she depends, with a quiet trust in its influence. Its spell is every where through her music. It sinks down into the smallest breath—the lowest tone—and, with a strange distinctness, through the clash of the chorus you hear it running along as you see the line of a silver river, winding through woods and fields, from your stand on the mountain top. In addition to this, Mrs. Austin discovers a curious facility of execution, as if music escaped from her involuntarily as fragrance from a flower. Miss Hughes excelled her in *points*. She burst out sometimes like a star from behind a cloud, and added surprise to our admiration. Mrs. Austin never goes behind the cloud. She floats through the whole part with no apparent effort. In the two duets, "Mildly beaming—brightly gleaming", and "Let thine eyes", this distinction forcibly struck us, and Mrs. Austin's style is here the more finished, easy, natural, and soothingly sweet.' [25 Sep. 1831: *New York Mirror*]

'Mme [Fanny] Persiani's voice is one of the most extensive we know of in the register of the real soprano. It includes eighteen notes, which exceeds the usual limits of the soprano voice; add to this incomparable suppleness and flexibility. It is one of those obedient voices which adapt themselves not only to the execution of the greatest difficulties, but also to the boldest caprices of vocalisation. Let it not, however, be thought that she is indebted to nature for all those qualities; labour claims a large share in them. It is study that has taught her to rinforzare and smorzare, or strengthen and diminish the voice, by bringing it out full, broad, and free from all nasal and guttural influence, to manage the breath, and prolong it beyond its ordinary duration; it is study also that has taught her to execute with so much felicity and precision those chromatic gamuts, ascending and descending, which astonish and delight her audience.' [21 Jul. 1840: MP]

'As a singer, he [Charles Braham] reminded us a good deal of his father [John Braham]. He inherits a great deal of his magnificent tenor voice; which flows freely from his chest in a rich and beautiful volume. It is free, too, from any vicious formation—neither nasal (to which his father's had some tendency) nor throaty; and his falsetto is well joined to his chest-notes.' [21 Oct. 1848: *Spectator*]

'And what best and surest proof, the voice of Jenny Lind, not large, not strong, not imposing, at the bottom even inadequate, hoarse, or at least veiled, and nevertheless effective on peoples and individuals everywhere. I have spoken of this in greater detail before, and I repeat now only that such a forward-lying, easily produced tone, of no innately imposing quality, carries in the largest halls and theaters, while the apparently much stronger and fuller throat-voice, no matter how forced—or because so forced—remains unsatisfactory and ineffective, and in piano makes a childish impression. Exactly the same is true of pianos if the tone remains stuck in its own resonance, and flows inward (throat-tone) rather than outward (sonorous tone).' [Dec. 1853: Wieck, p. 175]

'Miss Lascelles, who is evidently a thorough lover of her art, possessing an excellent contralto voice, free from the common defect of being forced to a throaty quality, sang in a most finished manner that pearl of contralto songs "He was despised".' [22 Feb. 1861: DubDE]

'It [voice of Theodore Wachtel] is clear, too, of that throaty tone which habitually spoils our pleasure in the tenors of this country, and which call on us "to forgive and forget" even in the case of men so renowned as Herren Wild, Haitzinger, Tichatschek, and (the other day) [Aloys] Ander.' [8 Jun. 1861: *Dwight's*]

'Germont was, of course, undertaken as usual by Signor [Lodovico] Graziani, who appears to be the baritone par excellence for Verdi's music. His voice, always round as a bell, rich, powerful, and free from any taint of throatiness, seems this year to be, if possible improved.' [17 Apr. 1866: *Bristol Times and Mirror*]

'She [Euphrosine Parepa Rosa] assuredly possesses 99 out of the 100 requisites that Italians say a singer should have—in other words, she has a fine voice, on a really large scale, the quality of the lower notes rich, and not in the least throaty while that the lady's upward range is most exceptional was last night made abundantly evident by her soaring to D above the stave, a note quite out of the reach of most soprano voices.' [24 Apr. 1866: DubDE]

'In addition to a pleasing appearance, Miss [Annie] Beauclerk is possessed of a voice of much natural sweetness … has her voice well under control, and happily sings without any inclination to the harsh "throatiness" somewhat peculiar to opera bouffe singers.' [20 Jul. 1873: *Era*]

'With the exception of Herr Stockhausen, we scarcely know of a German singer whose voice is entirely free from the admixture of guttural sounds.' [23 May 1874: Ex]

'I am glad to say that one defect in his singing [Italo Campanini] has in great measure disappeared—the throaty quality of his voice.' [2 Jun. 1874: GH]

'He [Signor Carpi] has the better kind of Italian vocalisation, inasmuch as he sings with ease and grace, refraining from forcing his voice, and has a truly fine organ of great compass and rich quality, entirely free from that throatiness which is the too common fault of modern tenors.' [1 Nov. 1874: *Era*]

'Her enunciation is distinct and clear; she [Miss Louise Rollwagen] attacks a note with precision and firmness, instead of sliding up to it with feebleness and fear; she opens the mouth, and produces a full, round, pure tone from the throat, instead of half shutting the mouth and contracting the muscles of the throat, so that the choked and imprisoned sound comes wandering and clattering against the teeth ere it reaches the open air.' [14 Feb. 1877: *Cincinnati Commercial Tribune*]

'We may remark, moreover, that the judgment pronounced at Birmingham on the occasion of the first performance of the Elijah by no less sterling a critic than Mendelssohn himself as to the superiority of an English chorus has never yet been falsified. It would have been simply impossible, even in Germany, to collect such a steady mass of voices as that which has assembled this week at the Crystal Palace, and the total absence of tremolo, nasal twang, and throatiness, rendered the intonation of this army of singers clear, crisp, and equable.' [30 Jun. 1877: *Berrow's Worcester Journal*]

'Miss Helen D'Alton has about as little of the "harsh and throaty" about her as any cultured ear could desire.' [9 Mar. 1880: *Sunderland Daily Echo and Shipping Gazette*]

'Madame [Nina] Sontag, when she came to this country, had only her voix blanche remaining, which, though wonderful in its suppleness and beauty, was only a portion of the power she once possessed. That superb artist, Madame Lagrange [Anna de La Grange], when in America, employed a beautiful, clear timbre, except in tragic scenes, like the Miserere in Il Trovatore, when she gave occasional phrases of intense feeling in sombre tones with thrillIng effect. Exaggeration of either of these timbres must be avoided. The clear voice intensified becomes sharp and disagreeable, while an exaggerated sombre timbre is heard in a blurred articulation and a monotony of vocal color.' [Dec. 1883: Sabrina H. Dow, p. 36]

'His upper notes [Mr. Orlando Harley] are singularly sweet and there is an entire absence of throatiness in the lower register. Possessing these gifts, which judicious training has improved, he sings without unduly straining his voice, and yet fills the auditorium.' [15 Nov. 1888: *Bath Chronicle and Weekly Gazette*]

'Every word falls distinctly from her lips [Miss Carpenter], without any of that mushy throat tone or nanny goat tremolo, which provincial audiences seem to think high art. Pure tone, artistic finish and musicianly art, never sacrificing time to sentiment and drawl.' [17 Feb. 1889: *Dallas Morning News*]

'As a vocalist, M. [Jean] de Reszke was pre-eminent; his fine voice, free from tremolo and throatiness; rich and powerful, but sympathetic and sweet when necessary, invested all that he sang with powerful interest.' [22 Jun. 1889: ISDN]

6.5   Reviews of Throaty Singing in the Century from 1830

Here are some reviews of the most important singers who performed over the next 100 years. Recordings are available for some of the later ones, including Francesco Tamagno, David Bispham, Lucienne Bréval, Albert Alvarez, Louise Kirkby-Lunn, Plunkett Green, Luisa Tetrazzini, John McCormack, George Formby and Tudor Davies. While the reviews are nearly all pejorative, with very few exceptions, the large number of throaty singers involved (42 men and 21 women), could nevertheless point to a nineteenth-century trend.

'The principal characters were sustained by [Carlo] Zucchelli, and Madame Meric Lalande. The former has got so fat that his voice is almost smothered.' [2 Nov. 1830: *Dramatic Magazine*, p. 351]

'Her style [Julie Dorus Gras] and method are essentially French. Like most singers of that school, her voice is throaty, and devoid of the sweetness of the Italians. Although she sings with evident ease, she has a method of forcing up the notes, which is not to be greatly commended.' [19 Feb. 1848: MW]

'... though manly, and seconded by a correct ear and taste, [Henry Phillips's voice] is too much in his throat, seeming to be invested with fat. We miss genius in him, and the power of touching the feelings.' [11 Nov. 1830: *Tatler* No. 60, p. 239]

I've quoted the criticism of Mary Anne Paton, as Mrs Wood] for her guttural tone [p. 132].

'[Anton Haitzinger] was a meritorious musician, with an ungainly presence and a disagreeable throaty voice—an actor whose strenuousness in representing the hunger of the imprisoned captive in the dungeon trenched closely on burlesque.' [Dec. 1832: Chorley, *Recollections*, Vol.

1, p. 58]

'The two [Sontag and Lind] had learned to sing—Madame [Wilhelmine] Schröeder Devrient not. —Her tones were delivered without any care, save to give them due force. Her execution was bad and heavy. There was an air of strain and spasm throughout her performances—of that struggle for victory which never conquers.' [Dec. 1832: Chorley, *Recollections*, Vol. 1, p. 55]

'This new candidate for British patronage [W P de Chavonnes Vrugt, principal tenor to the King of Holland] has a strong voice, of considerable compass, and of a quality which we should deem good, were it not somewhat guttural.' [19 May 1834: *Musical Library Monthly Supplement*]

'Mr STRETTON is a bass, formed after the approved models of the modern Italian opera. He has the facility of vocalization and flexibility of PORTO or [Vincenzo-Felici] SANTINI, with that *fat* quality of tone which was their chief defect.' [20 Dec. 1835: *Atlas*]

'The guttural tenor voice of [Adolphe] Nourrit, I confess, renders his enunciation more offensive to my ears than that of Levasseur's, the bass singer.' [26 Jan. 1838: LG]

I've reported on the plummy middle and lower voices of Giovanni Matteo Mario [p. 188].

Sims Reeves was urged on debut to dispose of his throatiness, reminiscent of John Templeton [p. 192].

'From A to E (la to mi), it [voice of Signor Naudin] is even unpleasantly throaty.' [26 Jun. 1841: *Spirit of the Times*, New York]

'The thick voice of Mrs Grattan is unfavourable to her performance of Orsini, but she gets through the song "Il Segreto per esser felici" with tolerable credit.' [6 Jan. 1844: Ex]

'Naturally there is a thickness in the organ [of Gilbert Duprez], and it is not till he has done something that shows us how he can manage that organ, that he gives cause for admiration.' [10 Mar. 1844: *Lloyd's Weekly*]

'The tone, too, of the voice [Madame Anaida Castellan], though not disagreeable, was, somehow, squeezed in its production.' [Dec. 1845: Chorley, *Recollections*, Vol. 1, p. 257]

'It seems (voice of [Signor Gaetano] Fraschini, the much-talked of tenor) throaty rather than mellow—forcible on single notes, but not in amplitude or volume to compare with [Domenico] Donzelli's voice, or, in its better days, [Napoleone] Moriani's—and guttural and inexpressive when measured with the organ of [Gilbert] Duprez.' [23 Feb. 1847: Ath]

'In this most exquisite and astonishing voice there are a few notes which do not possess the richness and vibration of the remainder. These take place in the middle register, on the sol, la, si, which forms the break between the chest-voice, which is of unparalleled beauty, and that vulgarly called, head-voice. When the singer [Marietta Alboni] does not take sufficient care, these notes assume a throaty character, and seem somewhat strangled.' [23 Oct. 1847: MW]

'Madame [Pauline] Viardot, to whom we come at last, possesses another family peculiarity which we do not remember to have seen dwelt upon in print. Her voice is Spanish, having that touch of bitter orange (some will understand the phantasy) analogous to that characteristic beauty, partly sullen, partly piquant, which distinguishes the women of Murillo from those of Titian:—a rich, guttural tone, entirely distinct from the timbre of Italy or those of Germany, France, or England.' [Dec. 1848: *Bentley's Miscellany*]

'[Enrico Calzolari] lacks purity of tone, is nasal and throaty, and he occasionally rather slides to a note than falls direct upon it.' [25 Aug. 1849: MT]

'[The voice of Angiolina Bosio] is powerful, of a good ringing quality, and although throaty, betraying its Gallic education, is very agreeable.' [16 Apr. 1853: MW]

'It [Madame Giuseppina Medori's voice] is a magnificent soprano, large, thick, powerful, and brilliant. In quality it hardly possesses the roundness, richness, or voluptuous sympathy of the Italian soprano organ. It is a little in the throat, more especially in the middle register, and does not proceed pure and clear from the chest, like [Marietta] Alboni's, [Giulia] Grisi's, [Pauline] Viardot's, or most of the best Italians.' [25 Jun. 1853: *Dwight's*]

'Mdlle. [Jenny] Ney's voice was harsh and guttural, and her method of the coarsest …' [19 Apr. 1855: Cox, p. 279]

'Her execution [Miss Adelaide Phillipps], in ornate passages, is superior, but not faultless. There was always a certain thickness in her articulation, which she has not quite got rid of,—an affair of organization, it is likely,—and which causes a little indistinctness in her rapid running passages.' [10 Nov. 1855: *Dwight's*]

'His voice [Mr. Henry Squires as Manrico in Il Trovatore] is very "throaty", and thus lacks that pleasant roundness which a good chest voice always possesses. We fancy that by a little more care Mr. Squires could cure this defect; if so, it would be a great improvement.' [7 Nov. 1857: *Hull Advertiser*]

'She [Madame Vestvali] is extremely tall, of commanding appearance, and even more masculine in looks and bearing than Mdlle. Johanna Wagner, with whom, by the way, she has many things in common. Her voice is deep, full-toned, powerful, and in timbre singularly sonorous. She possesses nothing of the Italian fluidity and clearness, but sings more after the manner of your English artists, whose voices seem to be, as it were, confined to the throat. Madame Vestvali is too prone to display her low notes, which, being greatly guttural, are by no means greatly agreeable … Madame Vestvali is not a finished singer, like Alboni or [Carolina] Guarducci; she is rough and rugged, like Mdlle. Johanna Wagner, and resembles her more than any one I have seen.' [17 Sep. 1859: MW]

'In the earlier airs allotted to Mrs Bodda [née Louisa Pyne] we could not reconcile ourselves, notwithstanding her highly-finished execution, to the want of clearness in her voice. Either there was indisposition, or there was inability to rise and fall with ease,—a sort of huskiness that robbed her notes of mellowed sweetness.' [2 Jan. 1869: Ex]

I quoted a report [p. 234] on Jean-Baptiste Faure's throaty French-academical style of barking or gargling.

'Mr. [Henry] Nordblom, who ought to sing well, having a voice of some fair character, does not, but shows a want of interest in his work and a forced and throaty production which, with a want of accuracy of intonation, will never tend to make his singing acceptable. It was a surprising thing to find his name occupying a place in a programme of a Crystal Palace concert.' [21 Nov. 1870: MP]

'Her voice [Madame Hermine Rudersdorff] is thick, deep in her throat, uses the tremolo liberally, and is worked by main force, after the German method.' [2 Jul. 1872: CincDG]

'His vocal style is of the robust kind, and he [Antonio Aramburo] depends very largely for effect upon the intensity thrown into a few phrases of his music, without paying proper heed to the equality of style which is so essential in tenor singing. His voice is somewhat throaty and wanting in purity of tone, and therefore he failed to create anything like a lasting impression upon the large and discriminating audience.' [12 Nov. 1873: *Liverpool Mercury*]

'Despite abundance of good critical advice, kindly administered, Signor [Italo] Campanini persists in producing his high notes—or, indeed, we may say, the entire upper half of his compass—in a "throaty" manner. This defect, which is rare among Italians, is the result of bad teaching. A good teacher always watches the manner in which his pupil employs his vocal organs; and when he finds the pupil begin to sing "throatily", he knows that the tongue is out of its proper place, and compels the pupil to keep it at the bottom of the mouth. Tenor singers are especially liable to fall into this defect, from their anxiety to produce powerful high notes. They effect this by diminishing the cavity of the mouth; and any one who looks at Signor Campanini, while singing loud high notes, will observe that his tongue is elevated almost to the roof of his mouth. Habits of this kind are difficult to cure.' [30 May 1874: ISDN]

'It was probably owing to the state of the weather—especially unfavourable to vocalists—that the first few phrases she [Adelina Patti] had to sing, were somewhat marred by the throaty character of the production of the lower notes and the thin, shrill quality of the upper register, signs which might be mistaken for wear in the voice.' [22 May 1876: MP]

'Although he [Fred C. Packard] had an encore for his solo of "Eily Mavourneen", he did not render it full justice, a certain throatiness marring the complete enjoyment of the solo.' [8 Aug. 1877: HP]

'Mr. [Joseph] Maas must, however, guard against a tendency to throatiness and forcing; then he will do well, in any province of his art.' [29 Aug. 1879: Std]

'I am sorry to see that M. [Victor] Capoul, most throaty and lackadaisical of tenors, is to return to Covent Garden.' [8 Mar. 1879: ISDN]

'Her voice [Mdlle Teresina Singer], truly grand, and of the kind that carries away an audience, is not evenly good—a tendency to tremolo, together with, at times, a certain hollowness of tone, half spoils, but cannot erase from the memory the superb effects she produces.' [8 Feb. 1880: *Era*]

'Signor [Wladyslaw] Mierzwinski's mezzo voce, on the other hand, is not good, and altogether the production of his voice is not as equal and as free from throatiness as might be desired.' [28 Apr. 1881: T]

'Her vocalisation [Miss Lilian La Rue] was even less satisfactory than her acting, her intonation being often defective, her "throaty" production of tone injuring the effect of a voice which, though light, is naturally of agreeable quality.' [27 Jan. 1882: *Globe*]

'[Mlle Paolina Rossini] gave a characteristic assumption of Selika, singing it in her own intense and impulsive style, with excessive harshness and throatiness at times and with extreme use of the tremolo, but with stirring moments of brilliancy and force and with sustained feeling.' [27 Feb. 1883: BDA]

'The new tenor [Roberto Stagno] has high C in his voice—a ringing, trumpet-toned C—and this note is likely to be the be-all and end-all of his work as Manrico. It makes all that precedes the "Di quella pira" merely a prelude, and all that follows only a postlude … The voice that came from behind the scenes was decidedly throaty. The tones seemed squeezed out and there was such dissimilarity between the high and low notes that the memory of poor "Orator Puff" with "two tones in his voice" was involuntarily revived.' [27 Oct. 1883: *New York Daily Tribune*]

'We have heard Mr William Davies sing in much better voice than on this occasion, the top G's in Sullivan's "I will arise", being painfully throaty.' [15 Nov. 1884: *North Wales Chronicle*]

'Mr. [William] Candidus was declamatory and emphatic, though his emission was more than usually throaty.' [6 Feb. 1886: *New York Herald*]

'Mr. [Whitney] Mockridge's best endeavors are invariably spoiled by the disagreeably throaty manner in which he produces his tones. In Germany such singers are appropriately known as "necktie tenors".' [20 Mar. 1886: *New York Herald*]

'In spite of his [Barton McGuckin's] somewhat throaty quality of voice, and a disposition to sing sharp at times, is an excellent and serviceable tenor.' [7 May 1887: *London and Provincial Entr'acte*]

'In the last act his delivery [by Signor Julian Gayarré] of the beautiful air "Spirto gentil" was full of the most intense expression; which, however, was marred by a certain throatiness which, if it is as disagreeable to the singer as it is to the audience, must cause him a certain degree of pain.' [25 May 1887: *St. James's Gazette*]

'Miss Bertha Hochheimer sang the Queen's music tolerably well; but the "throaty" quality of her voice is against her.' [13 Nov. 1888: Scot]

'Mr. Max Eugene, though his vocalisation was too much affected by throatiness and "wobbling" to be pleasant, was an adequate Eric.' [24 Apr. 1890: YP]

'[Mr E C Hedmondt] was a very acceptable tenor, making a good impression generally, but sometimes singing harshly. He was a little throaty also, but sang his high notes well.' [1 Nov. 1890: *Trenton Evening Times*]

'[William Ibos] is far from a perfect tenor, his voice, although pleasing, being unequal and guttural.' [21 Jan. 1893: *Era*]

'Mr. Bantock Pierpoint was an efficient, if rather throaty, Forester.' [5 Oct. 1893: YP]

'But, even then, and while thrilling American audiences with this remarkable feat [high Cs], there were always those in the theatres where he sang who could not help noticing how rough and throaty were his lower tones [Francesco Tamagno], and it was noticed, also, that an annoying vibrato showed itself all too frequently.' [15 Mar. 1896: *Boston Herald*]

'Mr. Ben Davies … His rendering of the immortal recitative, "Deeper and deeper still", was beyond doubt the artistic feature of the evening. The skilful use of the sombre register at the opening lines, the slow pained "Oh, let me whisper it"; the effective sustaining of the note at the word "must", the frenzied "That lash me to madness"; the awesomeness at "Horrid thought, my only daughter", and the thrice despairing "It must be so", were so many points of exalted singing which held the listeners spellbound.' [25 Nov. 1896: *Sheffield & Rotherham Independent*]

'He [David Bispham] received the heartiest applause of the evening for his performance of "Why do the Nations", yet we found this rather throaty and less artistic in phrasing than "The Trumpet shall sound", which Mr. Bispham sang magnificently.' [21 Dec. 1896: BDA]

'She [Miss Lucienne Bréval] uses too much French vibrato and she scoops at too many of her tones. Furthermore, she employs the French method of tone emission, which favors an undue straining of the muscles of the throat and leads to a pinched quality of tone.' [17 Feb. 1901: NYT]

'[Albert Alvarez's] voice is uneven and "throaty", and possesses a constant tremolo which is anything but musical, and then his method is positively bad.' [9 Feb. 1902: NYT]

'Mme [Louise] Kirkby-Lunn, whose conception of the style demanded by the music is fine, and whose voice is delightful in volume and quality, though it is difficult to reconcile one's self to her throaty production of tone.' [7 Jan. 1906: Spring]

'While this young tenor [Mr. Plunket Greene] is doubtless capable of much feeling and dramatic fervour, his singing is somewhat marred by a "tight" and throaty production. ' [18 Nov. 1907: Std]

'These all were sung with a pinched glottis [by Madame Luisa Tetrazzini], with a color so pallid and a tremolo so pronounced that they often were not a bad imitation of the wailing of a cross infant.' [16 Jan. 1908: CT]

'… for although Mr. John McCormack has not yet got rid of an occasional "throatiness", he sings now with an increasing sense of freedom and ease.' [23 May 1913: PMG]

'Miss Marie Dainton ... provides a turn that is the last word in impersonation. Cultured in all her numbers, she gives an impression of the throaty-voiced [George] Formby, with all his original eccentricities.' [23 Jun. 1914: *Dundee Courier*]

'Tudor Davies had his moments as Julian, though the microphone seems to exaggerate the throaty tones of his voice, which appears to have lost some of the quality of earlier days.' [7 Dec. 1929: *Graphic*]

'Her intonation is good [Miss Isabel Leslie], and one could, nearly always, hear her words, but on certain notes the voice seemed a little too far back, giving a closed kind of tone, which at times, had a tendency to destroy the clarity of her enunciation.' [12 Dec. 1931: *Folkestone, Hythe, Sandgate & Cheriton Herald*]

6.6   Conclusions on Clear versus Throaty Singing

As noted in section 2.13, singers trained during the long eighteenth century, especially Italians, were renowned for their clear, silvery voices, with high/neutral larynx emission and excellent *portamento di voce*. This is confirmed both by vocal reviews and treatises, with García being the first to suggest that the *voix sombrée* had its role in emotional expression. And, as I've shown, throaty singing gained ground through the nineteenth century. Today, some low larynx formation is an essential component of the 'singer's formant'. But it's quite clear that singers wanting to re-discover a historically informed *portamento di voce* in early music need to develop a neutral/high larynx sound.

7 Recovery of Historically Informed Singing

7.1   A Theory on the Historical Development of Vocal Sound

I have shown in this book that the desired vocal tone, as taught by the treatise writers, practiced in the opera house or concert room, and praised by connoisseurs of singing, remained broadly unchanged over the period from around 1650 to at least 1830. My theory, admittedly simplistic, is that classical vocal sound in Western civilisation has been characterised by long stable periods, interrupted by shorter spans of instability. I've shown these periods at Illus. 71, roughly aligned against a time scale.

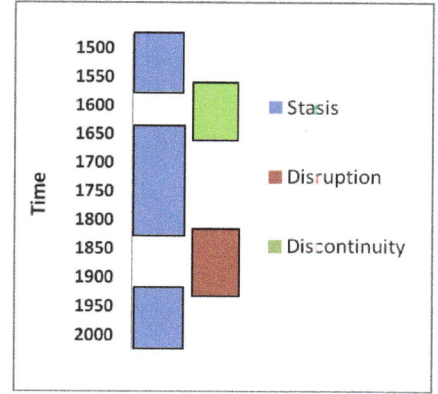

Illus. 71: Classical Vocal Sound Trends

I'll only touch on the first period of instability around 1600, which arguably was akin to a discontinuity, as I think vocal sound in the sixteenth and seventeenth centuries was broadly similar. But the differences in vocal tone between the long-eighteenth-century hegemony and our current vocal tradition, which had solidified into dogma by the third decade of the twentieth, were fundamental and disruptive, as proved by the historical record after 1800, rich with reviews of vocal sound. I have 17,000+ references to named singers supporting my conclusions on the transformations in the nineteenth century and the first half of the twentieth.

7.2   Differences between Long 18th and 20th C Traditions

Vocal Sound Feature	Long 18th Century	Now, since 1920
Voice type	Natural Voice	Made Voice
Best voices praised as	Sweet, pure, clear	Vibrant, exciting
Ideal Vocal Tone	Portamento di voce	Singer's Formant
Timbre	Either rich or thin	Always rich, never thin
Laryngeal Development	Forbidden	Integral to Singer's Formant
Enunciation	Good, quite often	Generally poor
Falsetto Register	Commonly used	Very rare
Vibrato	Occasional expressive use OK. But Straight Tone was the norm	Continuous and up to a major third wide
Messa di voce	Essential and quite frequent	Rarely used
Trill (performance of)	While always difficult, was well delivered by the best performers	Typically either omitted or performed badly
Volume	Natural Variation	Often forte or fortissimo
High Notes	Soft	"Urla Francese"

Illus. 72: Classical Vocal Sound: Traditions compared

Just consider for a moment the key attributes of the long-eighteenth-century vocal soundscape compared to the conventional operatic sound now in force [Illus. 72]. It can't have escaped your attention that they are diametrically opposed, in every respect. What reviewers expected, throughout the eighteenth century, and much of the nineteenth, was sweet, pure, clear and affecting vocal sound, **without** continuous vibrato, shrieking or low larynx delivery, but **with** a falsetto extension. The key question I now address is: Can such 'sweet, pure, clear and affecting' singing be found today, not only in classical music, but in other genres including pop, jazz and folk singing? Following some conclusions, I finish this section with a few suggestions on what we should do now.

First, here is a short review of my last trip to the opera, when I saw Garsington Opera's production of Rossini's *Maometto Secondo*, in July of 2013. The singers were trained in the traditional way, with singer's formant, plummy low larynx development, and a huge pitch vibrato oscillating up to a minor third wide. And LOUD. Indeed, I was blown away, with ears ringing, deafened by the stentorian screeching or bellowing at an almost constant fortissimo by the vocalists, with high notes which were actually painful; and, upset by the desecration of Rossini's beautiful music. I've indicated that Quantz, Rousseau, Wolfgang Mozart, Kelly, Edgcumbe, Burney, Castil-Blaze, Bacon and Rossini would have reacted much as I did to the 'Urla Francese' on offer. But looking round the applauding audience, as Burney did in Paris, I concede that they seemed to enjoy the opera. If asked, I think most would describe the singing as 'vibrant' and 'exciting'. It certainly represented the current vocal tradition. But, I conclude by urging, now that we are well into the 21st century, let's dispense with dogma and embrace TRUTH and BEAUTY instead! Also, judging from the Facebook feedback reported below, there must be many people like me who never attend Handel's vocal works or Rossini operas because they can't bear the singing.

I pleaded towards the end of my contribution to NEMA's 2009 conference with the University of York: 'Some Period Voices by 2015, please'. And, I've been looking for them over the last five years. So, where did I go?

7.3   Sources of Contemporary Historically Informed Singing

I explored four main sources, as follows:

1. **Early Music Review and Blogs.** *Early Music Review* is no longer printed, but still comes out online. **Andrew Benson-Wilson** and **Brian Robins** sometimes review singers from an HIP viewpoint. These have put me on to a few singers of interest.

2. **Newspapers.** Unfortunately, reviewers usually ignore HIP issues. But I look each week at 'On Record' published in the *Sunday Times*, mainly for the latest pop, rock and jazz CDs featuring vocalists. The problem with 'On Record' is that, while the reviews are always succinct and even witty, you are never told anything about the singers' voices. The reader is expected to climb through an impenetrable jungle of genre labels, such as the meaningless term 'Indie'. I understand what rock and jazz singing is, even jazz-rock, but I struggle with 'slacker-rock', 'rococo indie-rock', 'prog-rock', 'alt-rock', 'garage-rock', 'soft-rock', 'funk-rock', 'space-rock' or the mysterious 'math-rock'. Longer articles examine in depth the singer's personality,

sexuality, healthality and orientality, but never vocality!

3. **Facebook**. I often take part in discussions hosted by the Facebook's *Historical Performance Research* group. I've posted extracts from my playlists there and had good suggestions from 'Facebook friends' on singers and songs to include.

4. **Spotify**. This is helpful as I can invariably find singers' recordings streamed here. I've also found YouTube useful. Unless otherwise shown, tracks from my playlists are available on Spotify (S) and Youtube (Y).

I've created five Spotify playlists containing recordings by selected singers:

- Vibrato-Free Classical Singing [Illus. 73/74]
- Vibrato-Free Female Pop [Illus. 75/76]
- Vibrato-Free Male Pop [Illus. 77]
- Vibrato-Free Folk [Illus. 78]
- Vibrato-Free Ensemble Singing [Illus. 79/80]

7.4 'Vibrato-Free Classical Singing' Playlist

The singers in this list at Illus. 73 and 74 took a lot of finding. Straight singing of classical music is still so rare as to be virtually non existent, mainly because vocal dogma (the tyranny of the status quo) enforces constant vibrato, low larynx production and (counter tenors apart) falsetto avoidance. When natural, straight singing occurs, this may have resulted from the benign influence of directors or instrumental partners. Male singers are shaded blue, female singers pink and mixed duettists green. All were available on Spotify as at December 2018, with one exception. Most were on YouTube.

Vocalist, Group	on[1]	Composer	Title
Marc Mauillon, Pierre Hamon	S	G. de Machaut	Dame vostre doulz viaire
Sigrid Lee, Ars Italica	SY	G. Dufay	J'ayme bien celui
Raitis Grigalis, Ensemble Leones	SY	H. Ghizeghem	De tous bien plaine
Maria Skiba, Instrumenta Musica	SY	A. Scandello	Schein uns du liebe Sonne
Owain Phyfe, with vilhuela	SY	T. Arbeau	Belle qui tiens ma vie
Paulin Bündgen, Ensemble Céladon	SY	W. Byrd	Ye sacred muses, race of Jove
Filipe Faria & Sérgio Peixoto	S[2]	M. Machado	Dos estrellas le siguen
Jeni Melia, C Goodwin	SY	J. Dowland	Time stands still
Dominique Visse, Fretwork	S	J. Dowland	Sorrow Come
Sting, with Edin Karamazov	SY	J. Dowland	Weep you no more
Deborah York, Coll. Vocale Gent	S	Franz Tunder	Wend' ab deinen Zorn
Stephan MacLeod, Ricercar Consort	S	Franz Tunder	Da mihi Domine
Susanne Lebloch, Coll. Mus. Plagense	SY	Franz Tunder	Wachet auf, ruft uns die Stimme
Pal Benko, Affetti Musicali	SY	A. Steffani	Lagrime dolorose
Marc Mauillon	S	M. Lambert	Beth. Plorans ploravit in nocte
Roger Drabble, boy soprano	SY	H. Purcell	When I am laid in earth
Elisabeth Popien, Cantus Köln	SY	N. Bruhns	Ich hab Gottlob

[1]Source: S=Spotify, Y=YouTube   [2]Source: Available from Soundcloud, but not YouTube

Illus. 73: Vibrato-Free Classical Singing Playlist, Part 1

Most items are from sacred pieces. The musical mood is often weighed down by anguished chromaticism appropriate for expressing sadness, sorrow, penitence, regret, or laments related to death. Even the single operatic piece by Mozart at the end of Illus. 74, translated as 'I have lost it, woe is me!' fits into this category. But my brother Tom Bethell, while musical, is unlikely to enjoy most items in the list, as he is afflicted with a type of musical colour blindness, as he is constitutionally unable to enjoy music in the minor key.

Vocalist, Group or Director	on[1]	Composer	Title
Miriam Feuersinger, Cap C. Basel	SY	C. Graupner	Aria: Angst und Jammer
Miriam Feuersinger, Cap C. Basel	SY	C. Graupner	Chorale: Ach Gott und Herr
Jennie Cassidy, ad hoc group	Y	J. S. Bach	Sheep may safely graze
Gerlinde Sämann, after organ solo[3]	SY	J. S. Bach	Jesu, meine Freude
Carolyn Sampson, Suzuki	SY	J. S. Bach	Agnus Dei
Margot Oitzinger, J. S. Bach Stiftung	S	J. S. Bach	Recit: Ach Golgatha
Paul Elliott, Hogwood	SY	G. F. Handel	Behold the Lamb of God
Susanne Rydén, + Niklas Eklund	SY	G. F. Handel	Eternal Source of light divine
Magali Léger, RosaSolis	S	G. F. Handel	Qui tollis peccata mundi
Lezhneva & Jaroussky, Diego Fasolis	SY	G. Pergolesi	Stabat mater dolorosa
Natalya Kirillova, Currentzis	SY	W. A. Mozart	L'ho perduta, me meschina!

[1]Source: S=Spotify, Y=YouTube
[3]Gerlinde Sämann heard 3:10 minutes from start on YouTube, and 2:08 minutes in on Spotify

Illus. 74: Vibrato-Free Classical Singing Playlist, Part 2

Singling out individual items is difficult. But here goes. First, listen to the pure, clear, sweet, soft singing (some in falsetto) of **Filipe Faria** and **Sérgio Peixoto** of the group **Sete Lágrimas** in the beautiful piece 'Dos Estrellas Le Siguen' from the Album *En Tus Brazos una Noce*. Composer Manuel Machado (Lisbon, c. 1590–Madrid 1646) was new to me.

Three Dowland recordings by **Jeni Melia**, **Sting** and **Dominique Visse** are included. **Jeni Melia** has a really beautiful voice. I suggested earlier that she exhibits in some pieces the slightest possible vibrato, barely detectable. I characterised her singing as an example of 'Tears in Voice' singing, which might be an example of the 'natural vibrato' mentioned by Wolfgang Mozart. Early music types do get a bit sniffy about **Sting**'s Dowland, noting that he sometimes abbreviates long notes. But to my mind, this is artistic, as he matches the swift decay of lute sound. People also say his voice is worn. But this is not surprising after 2+ decades of rock band gigging, and some quality remains. Also, **Peter Holman** reviewed his singing well: 'Sting has a light, slightly husky tenor voice, sings in tune, and knows how to use the words to put over a song; for this reason, his performance of 'In darkness let me dwell' is outstanding. There are some pop-derived vocal mannerisms, and a mid-Atlantic accent, though I found them no more irritating than the more familiar mannerisms of modern concert singers. Sting has an untrained voice, and this is a positive advantage, since he does not have the plummy, covered quality that is still unfortunately the default, even among many early music specialists. Dowland lived long before modern vocal training developed, and his songs, with generally short phrases and modest ranges, are ideally suited to sensitive singers with untrained voices, as the late **Robert Spencer** used to demonstrate so eloquently.' [Dec. 2006: EMP] I chose **Dominique Visse**'s version of *Sorrow Come* for the discussion programme *Throwing a Wobbly* on Radio 3, which I took part in.[49] He sings this piece without vibrato but with excellent *messa di voce* as advised by Caccini. Falsettists were rare birds at the time, but **Thomas Coryat** approved of one in 1611 when he wrote 'Of the singers there were three or foure so excellent that I think few or none in Christendome do excell them, especially one, who had such a peerelesse and (as I may in a maner say) such a supernaturall voice for such a privilege for the sweetnesse of his voice, as sweetnesse, that I think there was never a better singer in all the world, insomuch that he did not onely give the most pleasant contentment that could be imagined, to all the hearers, but also did as it were astonish and amaze them. I alwaies thought that he was an Eunuch, which if he had beene, it had taken away some part of my admiration, because they do most commonly sing passing wel; but he was not, therefore it was much the more admirable. Againe it was the more worthy of admiration, because he was a middle-aged man, as about forty yeares old.' [1611: Thomas Coryat, *Coryat's Crudities*, p. 390] Dominique caps this description, as he must have been about 60 when he recorded this piece.

The singing of **Marc Mauillon** in Michel Lambert's *lecons de tenebres* was commended by my Facebook friend **Christopher Price Pontifex**. **David Badagnani** replied: 'Thank you for the recommendation—the music and singer are excellent. He does allow his note endings to dissolve into a very modest, nearly infinitesimal vibrato on most un-ornamented long tones, a habit which I have noticed being used by many other mostly non-vibrato singers, and which leaves me unable to add their videos to my playlist, just for the sake of adhering to the definition.' [16 Apr. 1018: *Facebook*[50]]

I have two Graupner pieces sung by **Miriam Feuersinger** with Capricornus Consort Basel, which won the Deutschen Schallplattenkritik prize for this recording. Voice, strings, oboe and basso continuo achieve good, expressive dynamic balance. Her *Angst und Jammer* is beautiful, smooth, mostly straight singing. I've included the second chorale piece *Ach Gott und Herr* largely because it's unusual in being in a major key. Feuersinger may have been inspired by the excellent oboist (**Xenia Löffler**); the Mozarts, father and son, would have liked her pure tone. Both performers apply selective but subtle *messa di voce*.

I arranged for **Jennie Cassidy** to sing *Sheep May Safely Graze*, in preparation for NEMA's 2009 conference.[51] She sings without vibrato. Most singers perform this piece with continuous vibrato, conflicting against the smooth recorder playing.

Paul Elliott deployed a pure, clear, non-vibrato sound in his Messiah singing, in the version conducted by **Christopher Hogwood**, without the typical tenor's plumminess.

Susanne Rydén, in her *Ode for the Birthday of Queen Anne*, lays aside her conventional operatic voice to some extent, certainly on most of her higher notes, thereby matching Nicklas Eklund's historically

---

49   *Throwing a Wobbly*, Radio 3 broadcast, 21st September 2017. Unfortunately, this cannot currently be streamed.

50   This and subsequent Facebook references were public posts on the 'Historical Performance Research' Group.

51   Besides Jennie, Michael Piraner and myself were on recorders, with Louise Jameson [cello] and Masumi Yamamoto [harpsichord continuo]. Available from Youtube: https://www.youtube.com/watch?v=odjp47Xc2V0

informed trumpet (albeit not 'holeless'), although she can't quite match his perfect trills. You can get some idea from this track what Farinelli's famous contest with a trumpeter would have sounded like.

Magali Léger normally uses lots of vibrato in her staple late-nineteenth-century operetta. But her singing of Handel's 'Qui Tollis Peccata mundi' is very different and almost perfect, apart from the occasional 'shriekette'. Was she advised by the excellent **RosaSolis**?

Turning to Pergolesi's famous *Stabat Mater*, Julia Lezhneva and Philippe Jaroussky have at times replaced their conventional operatic production by pure, clear sound, certainly in the suspension-laden pieces I 'Stabat mater dolorosa' and XII 'Quando corpus morietur'. Unfortunately, they relapse into their habitual vibrato style in allegro movements such as II 'Cujus animam gementem' and IV 'Quae moerebat et dolebat'. A YouTube version includes a running commentary from **Diego Fasolis**, which specifically mentions vibrato reduction. It is apparent from Spotify that Fasolis's account is very popular, with *Stabat Mater dolorosa* receiving over 1 million views, very high for a baroque piece.

I have a note on the singing of Natalya Kirillova, with *MusicAeterna*, directed by **Teodor Currentzis**. Currentzis made a splash six years ago, announcing that he was undertaking a "long march" to Perm, in Siberia, to (exhaustively) rehearse and record Mozart's operas. He would look anew at everything, reduce the vocal volume and cut down, if not cut out, vibrato. I invested in his CD set of *Le Nozze di Figaro*, with lavishly produced book containing the libretto in four languages. Currentzis certainly discovered Kirillova's voice, mostly vibrato free. But I felt that the overall results were otherwise disappointing, with tenors, baritones and basses displaying conventional loud, plummy and vibratoey voices, undifferentiated from conventional operatic sound. **Christopher Price Pontifex** commented: 'His Figaro was more successful in HIP reduced vibrato terms than his subsequent Mozart opera recordings have been. It was also more successful in drama terms. There is some kind of mania that grips even HIP singers when they come to sing Mozart, which causes them to drop the whole reduced vibrato they employ for pre-1750s music and whack on the heaviest vibrato they can manage.' [19 Aug. 2017: *Facebook*]

The list is something of a misnomer in one respect, as some singers emit a little vibrato. My Facebook friend **David Badagnani** has created his own YouTube playlist of 'Early music singers who sing without vibrato', using criteria more stringent than mine. To see his list and play the items, paste the following into the address line of your browser, or, select it from my website:

https://www.youtube.com/playlist?list=PLm8mLM41EccDP_yIh_ZWuLrrqomoPD0rF

7.5 'Vibrato-Free Female Pop' Playlist

At least two contributors at NEMA's 2009 Singing conference observed that many of today's pop, rock and jazz singers (which I will bracket under the single term 'pop') exhibit vocal qualities similar to those employed by singers in the long eighteenth century, with both male and female singers often displaying a natural, straight voice, without low larynx emission, and often supplemented by a falsetto extension. Thus, **Leila Heil** presented on 'What Singers of Early Music can Learn from Listening to Vocal Jazz', and **Robert Toft**, speaking on 'Bel Canto: the Unbroken Tradition', suggested that bel canto has not died away but re-emerged in some pop-music singing today.

Female pop vocal timbre covers a wide tonal spectrum, from thin to rich. Early nineteenth-century critics made similar distinctions. Thus, Richard Mackenzie Bacon commented on the soft, thin, infantine, but penetrating voices of Maria Caradori-Allan and Giuseppina de Begnis, which he compared to louder, rich voices like Angelica Catalani's and Pasta's. Their counterparts can be found today in the mostly soft, sweet, 'cutie pie' singing of Kathryn Williams, Mary Timony, Aurora Aksnes and Lenka Kripac, contrasted against rich voiced, passionate tragediennes at the other end of the spectrum, such as Eva Cassidy, Charlene Soraia, Christina Perri and Sarah McLachlan.

My list [13 names at Illus. 75, and 36 at Illus. 76] might seem overlong. But there were still huge barriers to including singers in my list, given that for every vocalist included, at least twenty have been excluded. Curiously, this is almost never due to the singing, as you hardly ever hear a pop, rock or jazz singer delivering the operatic vocal style; exceptions to this (where vocalists have been taught to sing 'properly' by vocal coaches) are rare.

Artist	DoB	Song [Album}
Blossom Dearie	1924	Manhattan [Once upon a Summertime]
Astrud Gilberto	1940	Agua De Beber
Brenda Lee	1944	I Wonder
Sade	1959	By Your Side [Lovers Rock]
Eva Cassidy	1963	Fields of Gold
Diana Krall	1964	Night and Day [Turn up the Quiet]
Sarah McLachlan	1968	Angel [Surfacing]
Mary Timony	1970	The Owl's Escape, The Golden Dove
Alison Krauss	1971	A Living Prayer
Dido	1971	White Flag [Life for Rent]
Shelly Fraley	1971	All That I Wanted [Hush]
Kathryn Williams	1974	Mirrorball [Old Low Light]
Emiliana Torrini	1977	Sunny Road [Fisherman's Woman]

Timbre code: Rich: "Passionara", Thin: "Cutie Pie", Black: between the two
A few DoB dates estimated. All tracks on both Spotify and YouTube

Illus. 75: Vibrato-Free Female Pop Playlist, Part 1

There are three main reasons for exclusion from the list:

- First, some singers, keen to find favour with their public, differentiate themselves by seeking originality in their songs, but only finding pretentious, faux-creative, avant-garde rubbish. I call this as the **Arty Farty** tendency, or **AF** for short. I can't resist quoting **Rod Liddle** here, now Britain's wittiest male journalist since the death of A. A. Gill. Describing Mike Oldfield's *Tubular Bells* as 'tortuous, flatulent, pompous drivel', Liddle noted: 'This was a time when rock music was busy dressing itself up in adult clothes and pretending to be important and clever, instead of fun and exhilarating. Dark Side of the Moon was bad enough and then along came Oldfield with his gobbet of vapid prog, more wallpaper music for well-to-do thirty somethings who wished to be observed listening to "serious" music but couldn't quite manage even Philip Glass.' [20 May 2018: ST] *Tubular Bells* is the Arty Farty piece par excellence.

- Second, the listener sometimes encounters the **Studio Interference** (**SI**) problem. There is a tendency for producers and studio managers to be less than satisfied with simply recording a song, but to engage in extensive studio adjustments attempting to 'add value', e.g. by including backing singers, overdubbing and autotuning the result. Increasingly, recorded songs are not so much sung by the vocalist but 'made' in the studio. However, I concede that a singer's innate qualities can shine through **SI**, as happened in Kelly Sweet's *Dream On*. Kelly's voice is basically straight-tone, with frequent ornamental vibrato. Her singing also features wide dynamic contrasts, with expressive *messa di voce*, for example from 2:50 to 3:00 in the Spotify track.

Artist	DoB	Song [Album]
Imogen Heap	1977	Hide and Seek [Speak for Yourself]
Lenka Kripac	1978	Everything's Okay [Two]
Norah Jones	1979	Don't Know Why [Come Away from Me]
Butterfly Boucher	1979	A Bitter Song [Scary Fragile]
Sarah (Rumer) Joyce	1979	On My Way Home [Seasons of My Soul]
Regina Spektor	1980	Black and White [Remember Us to Life]
Jenny Owen Youngs	1981	Here is a Heart [Transmitter Failure]
Rosi Golan	1981	Flicker [Lead Balloon]
Nellie McKay	1982	David [Get Away from Me]
Priscilla Ahn	1984	Wallflower
Katie Melua	1984	Tiger in the Night [Le Coeur Des Hommes]
Julia Holter	1984	He's Running Through My Eyes
Skylar Grey	1986	Love the Way You Lie
Christina Perri	1986	Human [Head or Heart]
Lights [Poxleitner-Bokan]	1987	River [Acoustic]
Amy Stroup	1987	Just You [The Other Side of Love]
Kelly Sweet	1988	Dream On [We are One]
Charlene Soraia	1988	Wherever You Will Go
Holly Drummond	1988	Fade [Diving In]
Kacey Musgraves	1988	Follow Your Arrow [Same Trailer Different Park]
Cécile McLorin Salvant	1989	Monday [For One to Love]
Lucy Schwartz	1989	Gone Away [Help me! Help me!]
Taylor Swift	1989	Mean [Speak Now]
Hailey Tuck	1990	Alcohol [Junk]
Lola Kirke	1990	Not Used
Katie Costello	1991	Lost & Far From Home [The City in Me]
Gabrielle Aplin	1992	Waking Up Slow-Piano
Mariah McManus	1992	Unarmed
Selena Gomez	1992	Bad Liar
Charli XCX	1992	Boys (Acoustic)
Nina Nesbitt	1994	The Best You Had
Sarah Close	1995	Perfect After All
Lauren Acquilina	1995	King [Fools]
Freya Ridings	1995	Lost Without You
Aurora [Aksnes]	1996	Little Boy in The Grass [Running with the Wolves]
Maisie Peters	2000	Place We Were Made

Timbre code: Rich: "Passionara", Thin: "Cutie Pie", Black: between the two

A few DoB dates estimated. All tracks on both Spotify and YouTube

Illus. 76: Vibrato-Free Female Pop Playlist, Part 2

- Third, otherwise artistic vocalists singing good songs have been discarded because the inartistic, aggressive, unvarying, fortissimo crashing of the rhythm section subdues the voice into inaudibility. I characterise this tendency as **Bang Crash Wallop** (or **BCW**). For example, Aurora Aksnes was forced to struggle against aggressive BCW. I'm sure that many readers, accustomed to subtle rhythmic/harmonic underpinning of baroque music by the softer tones of bass viol plus lute or harpsichord, will agree that triple fortissimo BCW is unacceptable. Unfortunately, BCW is so common as to be almost the rule. For example, out of 23 pieces reviewed over two weeks in 'On Record' (24 June and 1st July 2018), I rejected two AF items and discarded twenty marred by BCW. Only a single piece by Freya Ridings met my criteria. Although the list is dubbed 'vibrato-free', readers will hear some expressive vibrato. Eva Cassidy in *Fields of Gold* and Sarah McLachlan in *Angel* communicate passions strongly. Delicate vibrato certainly has a place in their skill sets. But other singers have largely dispensed with it without losing expressiveness. Thus, Christina Perri in *Human*, Charlene Soraia in *Wherever you will* and Alison Krauss in *A Living Prayer*, all achieve wide dynamic variation, albeit with excess BCW in forte sections of Perri's song.

What you won't hear in this list, or for that matter any of the lists in this section, is operatic style shrieking or bellowing. Listen to Katie Costello, Selena Gomez, Nina Nesbitt, Sarah Joyce or Regina Spektor. What you get from them is sweet, clear, pure and affecting vocalism, with really soft high notes, as high as G''' in Nesbitt's case.

I have a few notes on some other singers. While some of Mary Timony's pieces verge on AF territory, her *Owl's Escape*, with daring simultaneous major and minor thirds at section closes (hard to tune), makes the cut. Some pieces are both melodically inventive and well sung, including Lenka Kripac's *Everything's OK*, Jennie Own Youngs's *Here is a Heart*, Nellie McKay's *David*, Skylar Grey's *Love the Way You Lie*, Amy Stroup's *Just You* (I recommend the Spotify version, as she's rather flat in one of her YouTube videos) and Charlene Soraia's *Wherever You Will Go*. Mariah McManus reminds me of a quality described in Josephine Fodor-Mainvielle's voice [see 3.5.1 above] as 'her hard, firm style of execution, something like the dragging of the painter's pencil'. Classically trained Katie Melua is an interesting artist. In some pieces, as in *Tiger in the Night*, she starts long notes slightly flat, gradually reaching up to pitch. Is this attractive or, as they would have put it in 1800, an 'affectation'? I can't make up my mind.

7.6 'Vibrato-Free Male Pop' Playlist

This list is much shorter, with only 24 tracks, as shown in Illus. 77, available from Spotify or YouTube. About half the singers use some falsetto, just as their predecessors around 1800 did. It's obviously viewed as a useful skill by pop singers, unlike their classical counterparts.

The list would have to be curtailed by 50%, if all singers afflicted with serious BCW were removed. These items are shown in red, enabling discerning listeners to avoid them if desired. As it is, I have excluded Liam Gallagher's *For What It's Worth* and Michel Bublé's *It's a Beautiful Day* altogether. Both items, while well sung, are ruined by triple forte drum bashing. Having said that, there is a point in very light BCW, given that jazz and rock music does require a firm underlying rhythm helping singers and instrumentalists to place their syncopated back beats accurately. **Sting** illustrated how to do this by light clicks on the beat in *Shape of My Heart*. I sometimes wonder if there are commonalities between the rock/pop rhythm section and the baroque basso continuo. Is there anything in this idea? A basso continuo group will comprise a cello or bass viol, plus lute or harpsichord, supporting the harmonic content of a baroque piece. In similar fashion, a double bass or electric guitar, plus guitars and/or piano, provides both harmonic and rhythmic support for pop. The only element in rock/pop not present in the basso continuo group is the output from the rhythm section. So, there could be some similarities. The key difference lies in relative volume levels. While a basso continuo section is balanced with the rest of the ensemble, a rhythm section is much, much louder than all other voices and instruments combined, often to an extent which, in my view, can't be justified from any standpoint.

Other picks, also sung expressively without vibrato, are: *April Come She Will* from **Simon & Garfunkel** (their music was good, by any standard), **Brad Paisley** & **Alison Krauss** in the tragic love story *Whiskey Lullaby*, which, I hear from **David Badagnani**, is sung in 'high lonesome' style, and **Robin Warren-Adamson** of Wise Children in *Keep Quiet* (again, good music, with Warren-Adamson completing his song in excellent falsetto).

Singer	DoB[1]	Title [Album] BCW infected items in red
Mel Tormé	1925	Lullaby Of Birdland [Songs of New York][f]
Don & Phil Everly	1937	Wake Up Little Susie
John Lennon [The Beatles]	1940	Cry Baby Cry[f]
Simon & Garfunkel	1941	April Come She Will [Sounds of Silence]
Sting	1951	Shape Of My Heart [Ten Summoner's Tales]
Randy Travis	1959	Let Me Try [High Lonesome]
Gary Cherone [Extreme]	1961	More than Words[f]
Billy Yates	1963	Famous For Bein' Your Fool [Bill's Barber Shop]
Ben Folds	1966	The Luckiest [Rockin' The Suburbs]
Train [Patrick Monahan]	1970	Hey, Soul Sister[f]
Gary Barlow	1971	Said It All [The Circus][f]
Brad Paisley [+Alison Krauss]	1972	Whiskey Lullaby [Mud on the Tires]
Gavin Mikhail	1975	I Will Wait [And You Let Her Go...]
Chris Martin [Coldplay]	1977	Fix You, [X & Y][f]
Adam Levine [Maroon 5]	1979	She Will Be Loved [Songs about Jane][f]
Jamie Cullum	1979	High and Dry [Pointless Nostalgic][f]
Jannis Makrigiannis	1984	Hollow Talk [This is for the White in Your Eyes]
Robin Warren-Anderson	1985	Keep Quiet [Absence & Reunion][f]
Austin Plaine	1985	Never Come Back Again
Tyler Ward	1988	Dynamite, acoustic[f]
Phillip Phillips	1990	So Easy [The World from the Side of the Moon][f]
Niall Horan	1993	This Town
Zayn Malik	1993	Let Me [Icarus Falls][f]
Tamino	1997	Habibi[f]

[1] DoB estimated in a few cases   [f] evidence of falsetto

Illus. 77: Vibrato-Free Male Pop Playlist

7.7 'Vibrato-Free Folk' Playlist

Twenty folk songs, accessible from Spotify or YouTube, are listed at Illus. 78. Male singers are shaded in blue, females in pink, and male/ female duets in green.

Lester Flatt has the lowest bass voice I've heard, down to a solid D below the bass stave.

Martin Carthy is a personal old favourite. There is a little unobtrusive vibrato. I was always moved when I used to hear him as a young artist singing *Scarborough Fair* live 55 years ago in *The Troubadour*, a basement club in London's Earls Court.

Note Texas Gladden's portamento [slide], in both ascending and descending situations.

David Badagnani wrote on Hazel Dickens: 'American country and bluegrass, with roots in Appalachian folk singing (religious singing and secular ballads) was traditionally non-vibrato. I think Hazel Dickens (b. 1925) from West Virginia is the best example. Her tone is flat as a board but at the same time robust and vibrant (something some vibratists insist isn't possible).' [12 Aug. 2017: *Facebook*]

Soprano Sierra Hull recorded *The Hard Way* when only 16, at an age when many female vocalists in the long eighteenth century débuted. She sports an unusually high falsetto here, with her pure voice reaching a high c#.

I was initially put off by excessive BCW in Lucy Ward's piece, but was won over by the guitar cross-rhythms.

Vocalist	Recorded	Title [Album]
Davis Sisters	1953	I Forgot More Than You'll Ever Know
Estil C & Orna Ball	1959	Jennie Jenkins [Sounds of the South]
Lester Flatt	1962	The Ballad of Jed Clampett
Martin Carthy	1965	Scarborough Fair
Texas Gladden	1978	The Bad Girl [Virginia Traditions]
Albion Band	1979	Poor Old Horse [Rise Up Like the Sun]
Ricky Skaggs	1980	Bury Me Beneath The Weeping Willow
Osborne Brothers	1982	Rocky Top
Hazel Dickens	1990	The Rebel Girl [Don't Mourn-Organize!]
Simon Friend	1991	Another Man's Cause [Levelling the Land]
Rhonda Vincent	2006	All American Bluegrass Girl
Laura Veirs, Colin Meloy	2007	Soldier's Joy [Tumble Bee]
Sierra Hull	2008	The Hard Way [Secrets]
Olivia Chaney	2011	False Bride [The Longest River]
Emily Portman	2012	Sunken Bells [Hatchling]
Rachel & Betty Unthanks	2012	A Great Northern River [Songs from Shipyards]
Lucy Ward	2012	Maids When You're Young [Adelphi Has to Fly]
Sarah Jarosz	2014	Build Me Up From Bones
Jon Whitley, Jay LaBouchardiere	2016	Weave Her a Garland [Releasing the Leaves]
Danielle Svonavec	2016	Lord Ronald

Illus. 78: Vibrato-Free Folk Playlist

7.8 'Vibrato-Free Ensemble Singing' Playlist

The first half of the playlist [Illus. 79] is allocated to some of the best music by medieval, renaissance and early baroque composers, recorded by a variety of ensembles, often in recent years, and generally without vibrato.

The **Hilliard Ensemble** offer the listener a model of sweet, pure and well balanced ensemble singing. Cristóbal de Morales's piece was sung by **David James**, **John Potter**, **Rogers Covey-Crump** and **Gordon Jones**.

The Monteverdi piece was posted on Facebook by **David Badagnani**. I commented: 'I've listened to this lovely music several times, following it on a score. This is Monteverdi in prima pratica mode … They sound like a well balanced, beautifully tuned organ, following in one respect Herman Finck's prescription in 1556: 'The treble should be sung with a delicate and sonorous tone, the bass, however, with a harder and heavier tone; the middle voices should move with uniformity and try to match themselves to the outer parts sweetly and harmoniously' … Finck then states that a constant dynamic level should be maintained throughout a composition 'so that there is no discrepancy in sound between the beginning and the end: the tone should not be too soft or too loud, but rather like a properly built organ, the ensemble should remain unaltered and constant'. [1556: F. E. Kirby, *Hermann Finck on Methods of Performance*] Of course, the music being Monteverdi's, the dynamic is not constant but expressively steered from MP to MF. No vibrato of course, apart from a brief tremor from the second soprano at bar 47, 2:21 from the start.'

Group	On*	Composer	Title
Triphonia	S	Anon	Ich was ein chint so wolgetan
VivaBiancaLuna Biffi	SY	Guillaume de Machaut	Puisqu'en oubli suis de vous
Ars Italica	SY	Anon	Ave mater o Maria
Hespèrion XXI	SY	Guillaume Dufay	Veni sancte spiritus
Organum	SY	De Févin, Divitis	Sanctus
Stimmwerck	SY	Heinrich Isaac	Innsbruck, ich muss dich lassen
Musica Antiqua of London	SY	Anon, after Josquin	Lamentatio super morte Josquin
Musica Antiqua of London	SY	Claudin de Sermisy	Dont vient cela
Blue Heron	SY	John Taverner	Dum transisset sabbatum (II)
Hilliard Ensemble	SY	Cristóbal de Morales	Parce mihi, Domine
Ensemble Doulce Mémoire	SY	Eustache du Caurroy	Susanne un jour
Profeti Della Quinta	SY	Orlando di Lasso	Psalmi Davidis poenitentiales
Voces8	SY	Michael Praetorius	Es ist ein Ros entsprungen
Vox Luminis	SY	Thomas Weelkes	Death hath deprived me
Voces8	Y	Claudio Monteverdi	Adoramus Te, Christe
Ad hoc group	SY	Heinrich Schütz	Das Blut Jesu Christi, SWV 298
Lautten Compagney	SY	Samuel Scheidt	Nun komm der Heiden Heiland
Matthew Curtis	SY	Giacomo Carissimi	Plorate filii Israel [Jephthah]
Profeti Della Quinta	SY	Carlo G. Manuscript	Veni dilecte mi

*S=Spotify, Y=YouTube

Illus. 79: Vibrato-Free Ensemble Singing, Part 1

The second half of the playlist [Illus. 80] starts with three unusual vocal versions of baroque instrumental pieces from the Comedian Harmonists [*Die Goldene Ara Deutsche Vocalensembles*, recorded 1928-38], Asperger Beeblebrox and the Swingle Singers.

Six pieces of Sacred Harp and shape-note music follow. These are typically psalms composed in four widely-separated parts with their signature open fifths. The tune is generally in the tenor. The singing is forthright and vibrato free, although not 'beautifully pure' in the Anglican cathedral sense.

While I confess that the chromatic harmonies featured in the three barbershop pieces make me feel a bit seasick, the one-to-a-part ensembles are notable for good balance and accurate tuning. As I've noted below, there is an opportunity for a good barbershop group to 'crossover' by performing some eighteenth century glees, albeit in a strongly contrasted harmonic idiom.

Then there are some modern songs and duets, including Nina And Frederik sporting their faux-West Indian style.

The list is concluded by three non Western items sung by the Gundecha Brothers (Indian classical music), the South African Black Umfolosi and the Corsican Tenores Supramonte Orgosolo, posted by Paul Poletti in *Facebook's* 'Historical Performance Research' Group. The Corsican group sound like a cross between a regal and a reed organ.

Group	On*	Composer	Title
Comedian Harmonists	SY	Luigi Boccherini	Menuett
Asperger Beeblebrox	SY	Johann Pachelbel	Canon in D [a capella]
Swingle Singers	SY	J S Bach	Suite No. 3 in D Major
Tudor Choir	SY	William Billings	Emanuel
His Majestie's Clerkes	SY	William Billings	Jordan
Northern Harmony	SY	Anon	Newbury
Anonymous 4	SY	American Angels	New Britain (Amazing Grace)
The Tudor Choir	SY	Shapenote Album	Montgomery
Word of Mouth Chorus	SY	Anon, Rivers of Delight	Weeping Mary
Four Teens	S	75 Years of Barbershop	Tie Me to Your Apron Strings
Bluegrass Student Union	SY	75 Years of Barbershop	Midnight Rose
Four Freshmen	SY	4 Freshmen & 5 Trombones	Angel Eyes
Vienna Teng	SY	Vienna Teng	Hymn of Acxiom
Betty Carter, Ray Charles	SY	Baby It's Cold Outside	Christmas with Sinatra & Friends
Diana Krall, M. Bublé	SY	Gilbert O'Sullivan	Alone Again (Naturally)
Nina And Frederik	SY	Nina And Frederik	Mango Vendor
The Flying Pickets	SY	.	Only You
The Jamies	SY	.	Summertime, Summertime
Brian Wilson, P Hollens	SY		Our Special Love
Gundecha Brothers	SY	Anon, Ancestral Voices	Raga Charukeshi-Dhrupad
Black Umfolosi	SY	Anon	Shosholoza
Tenores Supramonte Orgosolo	SY	Anon	Desizos e Ammentos

*S=Spotify, Y=YouTube

Illus. 80: Vibrato-Free Ensemble Singing, Part 2

7.9   My Conclusions

Over some 65 years of adult life, thanks to the post-WWII early instrument revival, I've enjoyed inspirational, historically informed performances on strings, double reeds, windcaps, lute, recorder, cornetto, brass, organ, and baroque keyboards, sometimes taking part myself. Unfortunately, as I've noted in the introduction, classical singing has been marooned in a time warp, gripped by a century-old orthodoxy. This is not meant derogatorily. **John Potter** and **Neil Sorrell** noted in their excellent *A History of Singing* [2012: p. 215] that 'the ossified conservatoire system is designed to maintain the status quo. It produces far more singers than the profession can absorb, which creates a vicious circle of competition with more and more singers chasing fewer opportunities to sing a very small amount of music'.

Topic [page in source]	Gioacchino Rossini's Views, as related by Edmond Michotte
The importance of **sound early teaching**, and his teaching methods outlined. [p. 110/111]	Rossini taught singing at the Bologna Liceo and was thoroughly familiar with teaching methods: "Ah, yes, in those days the formation of the voice, the instrument, was an ungrateful labor. / It began with work exclusively on the pure and simple emission of sound. Homogeneity of timbre, equalization of the registers—that was the basis of the apprenticeship upon which all later study was based. That practical instruction filled up at least three years of exercises."
High Cs and C-Sharps from the chest as excruciating shouts. [p. 96/7]	We chatted on ... precisely about Tamberlik's performances at the Théâtre-Italien. "On that subject, Heugel," Rossini said. "I read in your *Ménéstrel* [sic] that at the performance of *Otello* the day before yesterday, after the explosion of the famous C-sharp, the audience seemed *transported ... transported*, I suppose, by that excruciating shout, to an operating session in the maternity hospital. Oh, the ninnies!"
Falsetto required, not high Cs from the chest [p. 97/8]	"Duprez was the first one to think of chafing the Parisians' ears by disgorging in *Guillaume Tell* that chest-tone C of which I had never dreamed. Nourrit had been satisfied with a head-tone C, which was what was required ..." [Duprez:] 'Well, then, Maître, tell me sincerely, does my C please you?' [Rossini's reply:] 'Very sincerely, what pleases me most about your C is that it is over, and that I am no longer in danger of hearing it. I don't like unnatural effects. It strikes my Italian ear as having a strident timbre, like a capon sqawking as its throat is slit.'
Tremolo from 'our so-called singers' strongly disapproved [p. 106]	"At present, with our so-called singers, *bel canto* is produced with a convulsive thrusting of the lips, from which there emerges, particularly with tenor-baritones, a tremolo that closely resembles the buzzing produced in my ears by the way the floor shakes at the approach of my brewer's chariot; whereas tenors and prime donne allow themselves—the former, vociferations, the latter, garglings [*gargouillades*], and these have in relation to REAL *vocalizations* and *roulades* nothing but the consonance of the rhymes."
Low larynx emission is dangerous [p. 115/6]	"A student showing any tendency to roll his r's, to lisp, to quaver, or to spice his emission with a dash of the guttural would have been singled out as a dangerous being liable to banishment if he remained impervious to correction ... To a person who sang a cavatina for him in an obstinately guttural manner: "There's a cavatina", he said, "that seems to be coming out of a cave. You must know that caves are said to produce good mushrooms? frankly, I'd have preferred a plate of that sort".'

Illus. 81: Vocal Sound Problems emerging in 1858, as Perceived by Rossini

Some of us thought that **Greta Haenen**'s *Das Vibrato in der Music des Barock*, published 30 years ago, would prompt a revival of vibrato-light singing. It didn't. In my case, nearing the end of life's journey, I'm imbued with an intense longing (probably shared with many readers) to hear Bach's cantatas, Handel's operas/oratorios and Rossini's music sung in line with the historical record before I pop my clogs. But I remain thwarted. We are often told that we don't know what Handel and J. S. Bach thought about singers in their time. But, the views of their contemporaries Pierfrancesco Tosi and Johann Quantz have been recorded and can help us achieve historically informed singing today. Additionally, Rossini has given us his cogent views, spiced with wit, which I've outlined at Illus. 81 [1858: Michotte]. Rossini certainly deplored the malign vocal trends emerging in his time. As composer, singer and singing teacher himself, he clearly knew what he was talking about. Unfortunately, the vocal attributes disliked by Rossini, including high notes sung from the chest instead of in falsetto (shaded blue), tremolo (shaded pink) and low larynx production (shaded green) are fundamental to 21st-century classical vocal technique.

So, was my expressed wish for some period voices by 2015 achieved? I have to say the answer to this is no, given that institutions and singers trained in the traditional modern opera-house style are continuing to exert their stranglehold on vocal sound and style, regardless of when the music was composed. After seeing my occasional comments on shrieking and bellowing indulged in by today's classical singers, two Facebook friends urged me to name names. If I were to do this honestly, I would have to write things like: 'I hear that young soprano Y— Z— is beginning to make a name for herself as a specialist early music singer. I cannot understand why, given that she displays a permanent wide vibrato, a dark throaty timbre and, especially, ear-splitting fortissimo screeching on most high notes, all of which were viewed as faults in the long eighteenth century. In her frequent staccato passages, she reminds me of a Mdlle Marshner whose voice in 1827 was likened to 'the fast quacking of a frightened, overdriven duck'.' But I won't name names, for three reasons. First, I don't wish to offend opera and concert goers who actually *enjoy* the modern opera house vocal sound. Second, today's singers can't be blamed for singing how they've been taught. Third, I don't want to be on the receiving end of solicitors' letters threatening to sue Peacock Press and myself for defamation. If anyone is to be faulted, it is the institutions, which for the most part have failed to adopt the teaching of Tosi and Mancini, et. al. That is why I've focused in this section on singers who are trying to do it right. Fortunately, I am not a lone voice. Many musicians think as I do. Here are just some examples, mainly from my *Facebook* friends who have posted their views, sometimes vibrato related, in the 'Historical Performance Research' group:

> **Mike Bayliss** 'One questions here not the physiology but the concept of vibrato – as **Robert** [**Rawson**] says, who defines what is 'normal'? Normal for whom? [Rawson had asked 'On what basis is 5–8 cycles per second a "normal rate"?'] Certainly not for those singing/ playing music of the period I normally engage with, from the 17th & eighteenth centuries, where vibrato is a coloration used sparingly for effect, not something that is permanently switched on.' [19 Jan. 2016]

> **Tim Braithwaite** 'What I do agree with you [Richard Bethell] on is that the modern operatic

tone, and approach to vibrato, is very different to historical ideals. I think the general description of horizontal mouth shapes and higher larynxes suggests a tone much more similar to pop or musical theatre singing which almost always has the result of reducing vibrato width/noticeability. I'd love to hear more modern hip singers combine this approach with ideals of rhetorical delivery and falsetto high notes, as well as the various unwritten practices (such as tremolo, accenti/port de voix etc.) applied as judiciously as we find in historical examples.' [12 May 2018]

Klaus Miehling 'At least we know that vibrato was an ornament and not used thoroughly [continuously]. (The only exceptions are Italian and German sources from early baroque, but they obviously mean only a very slight fluctuation.)' [15 Dec. 2015]

Jeremy Montagu 'Surely the key is that until very recent times vibrato, tremolo, et al, were ornaments, not constants, on instruments as well as voices.' [27 Jan. 2016]

John Moraitis 'Well, 17th and 18th century musicians regarded vibrato at best as an ornament that should be applied in specific places, and at worst as a bad habit.' [31 Jan. 2016]

Ian Pittaway 'The point with vibrato, I'd have said, is this: that it is an ornament, not a thick sauce to be spread over everything, a condiment, not the whole flavour. What I often find is the case in the "vibrato wars" is that it is either/or: you use vibrato or you don't. But there is a rich historical resource of commentary on adding flavour/ornamentation to the voice. Perhaps I'm reading all the wrong things, but I can barely remember this even being mentioned in the same breath as vibrato in a discussion, as if vibrato or the lack of it is the only issue in singing early music.' [19 Aug. 2017]

Paul Poletti 'I think there are two causes for the use of vibrato in the Western primarily-operatic tradition: (1) it makes the sound bigger and fuller by replacing a tone with a tonal blur, i.e. a cluster of frequencies rather than a frequency; (2) since vibrato destroys the ability to objectively verify accurate tuning (i.e. since there is no one pitch, one cannot speak of correct pitch), it masks the ugliness of equal-tempered thirds and sixths.' [29 Jan. 1816]

Christopher Price Pontifex 'All too often the debate about historically informed singing is limited to vibrato, the most obvious shortcoming of the many in the modern, historically inapt style that is applied indiscriminately (and lauded by critics and the indiscriminate alike) to every kind of music from Monteverdi to (especially) Mozart and later. But the debate is about much more, as many of us who have participated in it have tried to explain. Let's talk about vocal or tonal weight, if that's the right word to describe the modern sempre fortissimo, over-muscled voice production too often heard in period instrument baroque opera productions these days. · [6 Mar. 2017]

Robert Rawson 'And now that I've read the whole article*, I still regard continuous, persistent vibrato as an abomination … especially the "persistent" sort. A vibrato that ticks long constantly, however light, is incompatible with good tuning. It has NO place in polyphony or "close harmony" and is frankly unimpressive in solo singing or playing. And most of my favorite singers are NOT guilty of that continuous light vibrato described by the author as "natural".' [*Article in *The Strad*[52] by **Beverley Jerold** suggesting that a light vibrato was the order of the day for eighteenth-century musicians] [11 Mar. 2016]

Brian Robins 'For some [*Facebook* contributors] the all-important criterion [in good early music singing] is the lack of vibrato (there is actually no such thing as a total lack of vibrato). For others—such as myself—it is correct training in the techniques of the period according to such authorities as Tosi. The vast majority of "early music singers" cannot execute a trill correctly and few employ the messa di voce, both considered absolutely essential facets of a singer's armoury during the Baroque. So searching for a useful answer to your question is always going to be like finding the chimera. What I think can be fairly said is that given the inadequacy of most specialist early music training we are still some way from finding all but a very few early music singers who are likely to fulfil all the criteria, whomsoever they sing with.' [12 Jan 2019]

Alexander Skeaping 'The outrageous wobble of most singers today makes so much vocal performance into an offensive, unpleasant & outrageous caricature of good taste.' [28 Jan. 1816] 'I have for many years been frustrated by the universal domination of vibrato, often with such a wide pitch-oscillation as quite to obscure the intended pitch of the note, with which almost all classically-trained singers manage to ruin my enjoyment of the song they are singing.' [12 Aug. 1817]

Martin Spaink 'Apart from Indian classical music I have delved into the earliest medieval repertoires. Using no vibrato at all, but all the other means at my disposal, like maximizing resonance, I never had any problem singing alone in big cathedrals. I never wanted to have voice lessons from western conservatory trained singers in those days, as I am totally allergic to vibrato. A specific type of controlled vibrato in the right context can be very nice indeed, but in all other cases, I'm out asap before I start frothing at the mouth.' [30 Jan. 2016]

Timothy Tikker 'Vibrato used to be considered an ornament, not a constant. This is made explicit in singing methods e.g. Tosi from the early 18th century.' [29 Sep. 2017] **George Kennaway *Group admin.*** 'No shit. There's a huge body of research that nailed this one years ago.' [29 Sep. 2017] **Timothy Tikker** 'George Kennaway, yep, uh huh, right, sho' 'nuff. And when will all this knowledge finally have an effect on how music is performed today?!' [29 Sep. 2017]

One point made several times was the huge, and widening, gulf between instrumental playing (invariably historically informed these days) and singing. For example:

David Badagnani 'Regarding the proper style for solo/operatic/art song singing from the 18th century onwards, Mr. Bethell has collected by now I believe several thousand text excerpts from that time period (from concert reviews, treatises, method books, etc., many being extremely detailed), and if one reads them they'll find the aesthetic preferences were fairly unanimous against what we generally hear from "early music" singers today—at the same time their instrumentalist counterparts are playing beautifully and with the correct sound and

---

52   'Did early string players use continuous vibrato?', *The Strad*, 20 February 2015.

style.' [22 Sep. 2018]

Roger Evans 'Glorious [commenting on Miriam Feuersinger's singing of Graupner's *Ach Gott Und Herr* with excellent oboe playing by Xenia Löffler]. Almost any other style of singing would be jarring after the oboe. Similarly, I find intolerable the many recordings of, for example, the Choir of King's College Cambridge singing oratorios with the stark discontinuity of conventional professional soloists. The meaningless contrast between two types of singing is as pointless as that between Baroque instruments and our ordinary conservatory-trained singers.' [18 Sep. 2018]

David Hansell 'Very few (any?) singers have more than one way of singing and I doubt that conservatoires (outside their Early Music depts) ever float the notion that different periods/composers might need to be sung in different ways. What really gets me is the sense that, stylistically, we are often offered two simultaneous performing worlds—one from the orchestra and another from the singers. It's a bit depressing, really.' [17 Sep. 2018]

Graham O'Reilly 'The point is that some of us feel quite strongly that after many years of progress in the HIP movement we're now going backwards as far as singing is concerned. At the same time instrumental practice continues to advance and the sounds some baroque bands make now are as far from Mantovani's 1001 strings and the plodding insistence of much mid 20th century orchestral baroque playing as can be. So the disconnect between intelligent playing and "anything-goes" singing gets bigger by the minute. I understand the economic imperatives that make good singers try to be "jacks-of-all-trades". Opera is still where the big money is. But to go from there to somehow try to pretend that this disconnect is either unimportant or somehow "harrying performers" is, in my view, dishonest.' [26 Apr. 2019]

Colin St Martin 'I think if contractors and music directors had the expectation/desire for the singers they hire to have knowledge of HIP and experience with it, there would be less cognitive dissonance between period instrumentalists and many vocal soloists. A quick survey of period ensembles' recordings of 20 and 30 years ago shows how the stylistic divide has become wider and not narrower. Just listen to the rerecorded operas of established period groups which quickly reveal that the updated versions often have vocal soloists unconcerned or just ignorant of HIP. Now, the more informed among them are often relegated to minor parts and the title roles go to those more suited to the Met or La Scala. I suppose it's just for name recognition (selling tickets and recordings) but that is a marketing success and not an artistic one. The result is that the performance is more about "the voice" than the music which becomes hijacked by the soloist's inflexibility and/or ignorance.' [30 Dec 2018]

Sarah Potter made similar points: 'Presenting what are essentially modern singers alongside historically-informed accompaniments often results in performances that exhibit contrasting approaches to musical style and expression. This dichotomy does not reflect a deliberate disengagement from historical vocal practices by modern singers, but rather that professional, commercial, and public expectations of stylish singing in period repertoire have yet to reflect the attributes and requirements of singing that is genuinely informed by knowledge of historical practices.' [2014: Sarah Potter,

Changing Vocal Style, p. 3]

John Potter wrote likewise: 'Some aspects of early music singing have seemed anachronistic, such as… the strange coupling of highly researched instrumental playing with academically under-nourished singers.' [2000: John Potter, *Cambridge Companion*, p. 3]

But it would be wrong to give the impression that I've won unanimous support for my position from all my Facebook [FB] friends, as my comments have triggered as many objections as supporting posts, albeit typically from the standpoint of personal likes and dislikes, and very seldom from differing interpretations of historical sources. Oliver Webber, a respected and well-informed contributor to FB debates, as well as a distinguished and historically informed professional violinist, sometimes takes issue with my generalisations. Here is an example:

> A key question was posted by **Max Hummus** on 31 Dec. 2017: 'Is there a point at which a rigid adherence to historical performance research could/should be set aside in favour of the performance itself?'
>
> **Joe Bolger** responded on 9 Jan. 2018: 'I think perhaps the way in which the original question was worded is not so much about how people perform but the rhetorical style many HIP researchers have used in print to defend their positions. Now, my experience pretty much exclusively pertains to singing, but I have encountered quite a lot of literature from 1965 to the present day which makes unfounded assumptions about the attitudes and aptitudes of "modern singers". Frequently, both the criticism of these (often imaginary) singers and the specific ways of singing researchers think they should be adopting are expressed in very "rigid" terms. Plenty of examples upon request …' He then appended an example of a comment I included in my contribution to the University of York 2009 singing conference proceedings: '… today's 'one size fits all' operatic voice is, more often than not, hated by early music fans. I believe that there is extensive, inarticulate, subterranean discontent with this tremendous debasement of classical singing by the professionals.'
>
> **Oliver Webber** replied as follows: 'Ah. Richard is notorious. He has done absolutely tremendous archival work, especially on the subject of vocal vibrato, collecting and categorising reviews and other comments over centuries. This has the potential to offer great insights—including (if I may be so bold) a rethinking of what the ideal qualities of a voice might be, and a questioning (always healthy) of some trends in modern singing teaching. But—and it's a very big but—he has an unfortunate tendency to write in a very insulting and generalising way, which I can assure you is rejected by most of us working in the field.'

I replied to Oliver conceding his point and admitting I was 'guilty as charged'. I've tried to learn my lesson in writing this book. The reader can find many generalisations; but I'm hoping Oliver will agree that these are supported by data, arguments and such rhetoric as I can command. Nor will he find critical comments on living singers which might be viewed as insulting. Before moving on from discussions, the reader should be aware that several interesting discussion threads on Facebook's 'Historic Performance Research' Group can be downloaded from NEMA's website (included in the

Primary and Secondary Sources). I believe that public social media discussions will in time form part of the historic record.

Some vocal reform was achieved in the 60s and 70s, with Dame Emma Kirkby and others reviving more historically informed vocal sound. Largely thanks to them, good work is being done today by a few individual artists and ensembles, especially in medieval and renaissance repertoire, as examples at Illus. 73, 74 and 79 above show. Unfortunately, most solo singing in baroque and classical music, especially opera and oratorio, remains historically uninspired. Why is this? One factor was the training of early music directors, nearly all of whom have an instrumental background, often with some research involvement. These have contributed significantly to instrumental performance practice, although they may not have been sufficiently confident to instruct singers how to go about their business. As a result, we have many excellent period instrumentalists, but hardly any period voices. **Michael Morrow**, who directed **Musica Reservata** with John Beckett, certainly tried to wean his singers off vibrato. I performed in the group and sometimes helped Michael by copying parts before rehearsals. We discussed vocal vibrato several times during our late night sessions. He felt that it clashed with instrumental sound and interfered with intonation, but admitted that he couldn't win most singers round to his viewpoint. His concerns were reciprocated. I have it on good authority that his vocalists often complained in the pub after gigs about Michael's attitude.

Classical solo singing has changed little since the 1930s. Take Rossini's operas. His music, often delicate apart from some tub-thumping choruses, requires sweet, beautiful singing, not bellowing and screeching. Unfortunately, tenors always project top As, Bs and Cs forcibly from the chest, not in delicate falsetto, as they did in 1820, and some pop singers do now. Massive vibratos oscillate up to a major third from peak to trough. Both faults were expressly condemned by Rossini himself, as I've shown. Consequently, Rossini's operas are never performed, only vandalised. This isn't good enough. We must reform.

I don't suggest that good singing is just a matter of dispensing with historically uninspired practices. On the contrary, it is about touching the heart, or, hooking up composer's, singer's and listener's emotions on the same wavelength (**Judy Tarling**'s brilliant work *The Weapons of Rhetoric* (2004) discusses the 'mirror neurons' idea).[53] For this, the singer needs good taste (an unfashionable concept, but I declare that there **is** such a thing!), rhetorical and creative skills, appropriate technique, and, above all, to **feel** the music. As for delivery, Shakespeare's Hamlet offers the best guide. Singers should, like actors, 'use all gently; for in the very torrent, tempest, and … whirlwind of passion, you must acquire and beget a temperance that may give it smoothness'. **Pierfrancesco Tosi** [1747: Tosi, trans. Galliard] was of like mind. Noting 'how great a Master is the Heart' [p. 157], he urges on singers 'noble simplicity' [p. 150] in the aim to 'preserve music in its chastity' [p. 98]. He praises Luigino's 'soft

---

53   'The chain of experience in any performance is in three parts: the composer, the performer and the listener. Quintilian describes these as the nature of the subject, the nature of those engaged in the discussion (which would include the audience) and the nature of the speaker.' [Tarling, op. cit, p. 71] 'Most writers view the imagination of the performer as the principal source of this power, drawing on his own experience to reproduce the emotion required. It is now commonly reported that 'mirror neurons' facilitate the communication of emotion to sympathetic listeners, supporting Quintilian's instinctively felt process. [Tarling, op. cit. p. 72]

and amorous style' [p. 103] and Santa Stella Lotti's 'penetrating Sweetness of Voice, which gained the Hearts of all her Hearers' [p. 104]. He writes: 'Ask all the Musicians in general, what their Thoughts are of the *Pathetick*, they all agree in the same Opinion, (a thing that seldom happens) and answer, that the *Pathetick* is what most delicious to the Ear, what most sweetly affects the Soule, and is the strongest Basis of Harmony.' [p. 107] I've quoted many reviews in this book showing that some eighteenth- and nineteenth-century vocalists appealed to the heart as Tosi expected.

Timothy Tikker's final question hits the nail on the head. But he will, like me, remain disappointed until the pedagogical pennies have dropped and at least some vocalists learn to sing in a historically informed way. It seems to me that the best chance of vocal reform is to get on with some initiatives to make things happen. Here are seven ideas.

7.10   Amateur Handel Singing Competition

Handel took risks in introducing Giulia Frasi, a non sight-reading amateur, to his London audience. We need an individual or institution to endow an annual Frasi prize. I'll be happy to do this when I win the lottery. I'll also sit on the judges' panel! The winners will qualify to receive professional training and eventually be in demand to sing solos in Purcell, Handel's oratorios, and the easier classical repertoire. It might be claimed that a Handel Singing Competition already exists. Unfortunately, this is for professionals, and it is quite clear from the results that most of the singers appear to have ignored historically informed practices, given that they usually perpetuate continuous vibrato, low larynx emission and high notes delivered forte, all of which would have been unacceptable to all reviewers from Tosi to Rossini.

7.11   Professional Vocal Training

Amateurs won't suffice for Baroque opera or Rossini, where professional training is required to master difficult skills, including languages, improvisation, falsetto production (plus linking with chest voice) and the delivery of rapid passages and trills. A few universities/academies, in the UK, North America, mainland Europe and elsewhere, need to launch early music vocal courses, perhaps as a second study, backed by research, each covering different periods and styles.

This view is supported by singer/musicologists such as Richard Wistreich: 'The techniques described by Tosi and Mancini reflect a long tradition of voice training, passed on from one generation to the next in the master-apprentice system of professional voice training; there is no reason why it should not still form the basis of singing teaching today.' [2000: Richard Wistreich, 'Reconstructing pre-Romantic singing technique' in John Potter (ed.), *Cambridge Companion,* p. 184]

We will know that institutions running such courses are on track when their graduates sing Handel and Rossini stylishly *without* continuous vibrato, low larynx production, or shrieking on high notes, but with clear diction, a proper trill, an excellent *messa di voce*, a good falsetto extension, and blending beautifully with instruments. Teaching will be guided by authoritative research. This will involve a departure from the traditional modern opera-house style. We would have to take on board **Greta Haenen**'s findings on vibrato, currently ignored by most vocalists (but not instrumentalists), and other musicologists' work.

However, there may be problems and (potentially) conflicts associated with this approach. Some ten years ago, when a NEMA deputation visited a London institution with the aim of jointly launching a conference on singing, it became clear that the professor responsible for vocal studies wasn't interested in the historic record and NEMA's proposal was turned down. Fortunately, we found in **John Potter** (University of York) a like-minded conference director, who was certainly interested in the historic record as well as singing. At the time of writing, NEMA is trying to arrange further conferences on singing, possibly in London. I therefore looked at the teaching staff in the three major London colleges (Royal College of Music, Royal Academy of Music and Guildhall School of Music and Drama) to see who might be available. Certainly, all three institutions are prominent standard bearers for the early music movement, employing a total of 96 named professors/tutors, of whom 28 specialised in historic woodwind, 26 in early music strings (both fretted and unfretted), 15 in historic brass, 12 in harpsichord and other early keyboard, 7 in plucked strings (including harp) and 6 in general historical/research instruction. But the 'vocal studies department' appeared in all cases to exist mainly for the purpose of training singers to sing opera in the accepted modern style, given that I could only find[54] two named individuals identifiable as early music singing specialists, viz. Dame **Emma Kirkby** (visiting professor at the Guildhall) and **Richard Wistreich** (Director of Research, RCM). This suggests that vocal studies departments currently lag behind other departments in being open to historical research. Hopefully, this problem will lessen over time.

Such courses should be twinned with initiatives to identify (and start to train) talented vocalists at secondary school level. Classical singers should make an early start, just as most pop singers do now. There would be scholarship funding for secondary-school students with beautiful natural voices, bearing in mind that the best eighteenth- and early nineteenth-century singers (especially women) often débuted in their mid-teens. There must be hundreds of potential Cuzzonis, Bordonis, Cibbers, Frasis, Billingtons and Clara Novellos out there, just waiting to be discovered. What treats in store! Plus a huge amount of work for singers graduating from these institutions, given that the complete oeuvre of Purcell, Handel, Bach, Mozart and Rossini would have to be re-recorded.

Obviously, secondary school involvement must be carefully managed. I recall an occasion when **Peter Holman**, as director of Ars Nova, recruited 3 secondary school students to sing in a concert of late sixteenth century music, given in a West London church. The programme included two seven part motets by Giaches de Wert, each featuring three soprano parts. During a planning meeting, a group of us agreed how dreadful these pieces would sound with modern 'one size fits all' trained sopranos. So, Peter decided to seek suitable 17 year olds from a nearby grammar school. He successfully persuaded the school to make three 6th formers available. Their beautiful voices made an excellent contribution to the concert. The only problem was that all three girls fell in love with our young, good-looking and charismatic viol playing tenor, **Robert Oliver**. Fortunately, Robert behaved impeccably, displaying tact and diplomacy in handling the situation.

---

54 When I last checked, in November 2018.

7.12 Unfinished Research Business

I've come across some gaps in my work. Two in particular need plugging soon:

First, we need full publication of Dr **Charles Burney**'s letters. Burney's writings are an essential source of first hand reports on singers through the late baroque and early classical periods. Volume 1, well edited by **Alvaro Ribeiro**, covered the period 1751-1784 and was published in 1991. Four further volumes have been announced as forthcoming. Volume 2 (1785-1793) is being edited by **Lorna Clark**. Volumes 3 (1794-1801) and 4 (1802-1807) are being edited by **Stewart Cooke**. **Peter Sabor** is editor of Volume 5 (1808-1814).[55] But no publication dates have been announced. One must conclude that the work is only progressing, if at all, at sub-glacial pace. How can it be expedited?

Second, the journals of **John Waldie** need to be fully transcribed and analysed. Waldie compiled extensive journals from 1799 to 1864—his last journal entry was on 28 October of that year. He reviewed most of the singers he heard, not only in his home stamping ground of Newcastle, but during frequent trips to London, other parts of the UK, France, Germany and Italy. Moreover, as an accomplished tenor, he was eminently well qualified for this work, given that he was intimate with Angelica Catalani and John Braham (two of the best professional singers at the time) and frequently sang with them at private parties. Waldie took his task very seriously, describing it as his 'profession'. His journals from 1799 to 1832 have been transcribed and edited by **Frederick Burwick**, from which I have extracted 160 reviews, mostly of named singers, some of them quoted in this book. Frederick also wrote a useful introduction.[56] While the California Digital Library has helpfully made the completed transcriptions available, Burwick was unfortunately unable to complete his transcription of the journals compiled after 1832. This is a pity, given the potential for recovering Waldie's reviews over a period (1833 to 1864) when huge changes in vocal sound and style took place. There is surely a PhD available for a scholar who (i) completes the transcription of the diaries held in the UCLA's central collection of rare books and manuscripts, (ii) undertakes a detailed analysis of the results and (iii) comments on their significance for a full understanding of vocal practices in much of civilised Europe over the whole 66-year period documented by Waldie.

7.13 Encouraging Informed Critical Attitudes

I've argued the case for vocal reform. But, how much support am I likely to get, both from institutions and the national/specialist press?

I'll take the institutions first. Expecting support for HIP singing from this quarter is probably optimistic, certainly initially, given that institutions are currently devoted to training singers to excel in the traditional modern opera-house style. Hopefully, this will slowly change as the institutions gravitate towards HIP objectives for vocal as well as instrumental studies.

---

[55]   The Letters of Dr Charles Burney (1751-1814) at https://www.mcgill.ca/burneycentre/publications/current-projects

[56]   The Journal of John Waldie Theatre Commentaries 1798-1830: Introduction:- https://escholarship.org/uc/item/07t1w8fv

The best magazine around today for early music concert and CD reviews is the *Early Music Review* [EMR][57]. EMR reviewers sometimes censure singers' recordings for historically uninformed practices, e.g. continuous vibrato,[58] using similar language to their counterparts in the 1890s. There are also independent reviewers, for example **Andrew Benson-Wilson** and **Brian Robins**, who review concerts and CDs from an HIP perspective. Likewise, several reviewers for *Gramophone* magazine are clearly aware of, and educated in, the historical record of vocalism.

Turning to the national press, I sense that reviewers have little interest in hearing historically informed singing of early music, certainly judging from the papers and periodicals I read (*Daily Telegraph*, *Sunday Times* and *Spectator*). Here's an example. **Ivan Hewett** [1 Nov. 2018: DT] wrote in an article headed 'Why "early music" has had its day' that 'Early music is beginning to feel distinctly dated' offering four reasons why: [1] early music had 'lost its novelty', [2] the boost from the displacement of LPs by CDs has long since dissipated, [3] early music has lost its intellectual authority, as its protagonists can no longer claim 'authenticity' for their work, and [4] 'authenticity' has been watered down to 'a knowledge of style, leavened with personal interpretation', dissolving the boundaries between early music and the rest of classical music. I noticed that there was no mention of singing in the article. My letter in response [6 Nov 2018: DT] noted: 'Ivan Hewett claims that the early music movement is 'job done'. But one huge problem remains: historically ill-informed classical singing, for example the use of continuous vibrato a minor third wide. This has been the elephant in the music room—or the mammoth in the opera house—for a century now.' A correspondent (Victoria Edge) questioned 'how one can become historically well-informed on this topic as I cannot find any recordings of the human voice earlier than 1860'. My reply [8 Nov. 2018: DT] mentioned that my book 'will show that vocalists sang in straight tone during the long 18th century, relieved by much *messa di voce* but only occasional expressive vibrato'. While most of a long subsequent discussion[59] in Facebook's 'Historical Performance Research' group focused on vibrato, several correspondents protested that early music is certainly not 'job done'. During the Facebook discussion, **Brian Robins** observed: 'Mainstream critics as a whole are ignorant when it comes to HIP. Most of them would think Tosi referred to some kind of fetish. But the central problem is that the majority rejoice in their ignorance. I speak to them at festivals etc. and they are simply not interested in HIP. One very well-known critic told me he was delighted that early music performance had become more integrated with the mainstream because it meant getting away from singers with 'pure' voices and incorporating singers with nice juicy vibrato and rich tone into its ranks. And the truth of that having happened over the past 15 years is clear for all to hear.' [29 Jan 2019]

---

57 Although this magazine, containing reviews of books, music and CDs, is no longer printed, it is available online.

58 For example, in the August 2010 issue Andrew Benson-Wilson criticised a singer for 'a huge vibrato' and gave faint praise (on two occasions) for good work when singers 'rein in' their vibrato. Selene Mills censured two wobbly sopranos with 'far too much' vibrato. Brian Robins noted that a vocal quartet uses 'oceans' of vibrato.

59 Readers can find the whole discussion as Thread V46 in *Vibrato Discussions Threads V36 to* V47, available from NEMA's website

7.14 Unrealized Performance Research Opportunities

I've already noted [p. 36] Burney's reported comment by Metastasio on soprano Cecilia Davies's duets with her glass-harmonica-playing sister Mary to the effect that it was 'sometimes impossible to distinguish one from the other'. Glass harmonicas are, once more, being manufactured and played. There is an obvious opportunity here to simulate the performances of Cecilia and Mary Davies.

Another simulation opportunity arises from Charles Burney's comments on the singing of Francesca Le Brun, previously known as Danzi, suggesting that when she sang together with her oboist husband in thirds or sixths, it was impossible to discover who was uppermost [see p. 42 above]. Alternatively, Mary Paton's singing with flute might be re-created as it sounded in 1830, when the reviewer noted [see p. 77 above] that 'When the flute and her voice went together, you sometimes hardly knew which was which'.

Finally, there is an opportunity to simulate the organ flute-stop sound of castrato Signor Jeronimo, as described by D'Ancillon in 1705 [p. 21]. The erstwhile vocal science department[60] at the University of York did some good work bringing the castrato sound to life, and could be the best choice to simulate Jeronimo's sound.

If you listen to the early-twentieth-century singing playlist at Illus. 52 above and compare with today's traditional modern opera-house style singing, it is apparent that pitch vibrato has got much wider over the last 100 years, begging the question: 'How much wider has it got?' This project might be tackled by a vocal science department, or perhaps by an unaffiliated individual who knows the best software for the job. After asking on Facebook what software would be best, I did follow up some suggestions, but concluded that this is work for a specialist.

It has been suggested that low larynx production is the best way for singers to make themselves heard in large spaces. But, has this theory been tested? I quoted on page 108 above Richard Bacon's views on this subject, from which it is clear that he wouldn't agree with the theory, albeit it is probably 'received wisdom' today. He observed that the thin, soft, 'high larynx' voices of Eliza Salmon and Maria Caradori were heard more easily in the large spaces, respectively of Covent Garden and York Minster, than other female singers with louder voices. As I've noted on Page 107, he also emphasised that vocal tone, when forced, is neither so audible or so agreeable as vocal sound which is 'more easily produced', citing the distinction made between noise and tone by Ernst Chladni (the father of acoustics). Other comments by Bacon are of interest: 'In conversation with a friend of very acute parts, great learning, and fine taste (but no musician), he threw out a conjecture, that tone, like light, may be composed of parts divisible as the rays, though no musicometer similar in effect to the prism has yet been discovered. To the absence of some of these rays of sound he imagined differences in tone might be owing. The idea is fanciful, and to me new—therefore I repeat it; but we apprehend organic or mechanical circumstances are quite sufficient to account for all the different powers and qualities of tone enjoyed by singers.' [Sep. 1820: QMMR, p. 256] He added: 'But there was in the vast space of the Minster, and in the sacred performances, a power which operated (however strange it

---

60 Now known as the Department of Electronic Engineering.

may seem) to equalize the principal singers far more than might have been suspected … It is indeed, we are experimentally assured, one of the most striking properties of pure and finished tone to make its way through space, and we conceive this to be founded in nature—in the doctrine of vibrations itself.' [26 Sep. 1823: QMMR, p. 520] I think there could well be an opportunity for vocal science to leave the studio and launch experiments to test whether soft, thin, high larynx voices can be heard more easily in large spaces than loud, forced, thick, modern operatic-style voices.

7.15 Pop to Classical Crossover Opportunities

I've already discussed Sting's work on Dowland, where he broke new ground. But I'm not aware of a single pop or folk singer who has followed his lead, even though many of them are good musicians, often singing to their own guitar or piano accompaniment. While Rossini is a step too far for such singers, much of Handel's work is within their grasp.

To illustrate, I'll discuss one of Handel's most beautiful songs, 'As steals the morn', from *L'Allegro, il Penseroso ed il Moderato*. Handel took a lot of trouble over this piece, elaborately scored for soprano and tenor, with oboes and bassoons (often interchanging material with the voices), four-part strings and continuo. Listen to a performance by any supposedly historically informed modern group. You will hear strings, oboe and bassoon played beautifully,[61] but with both singers wobbling their parts. Added to this problem, singers usually fail to deliver *messa di voce* in appropriate places, for example the long B flat on 're and melts' (bars 20-22) and again on 're-storing' (bars 51-52). In some recordings, the soprano shrieks on higher notes, something condemned by Tosi. Also, while oboe and bassoon manage perfect cadential trills, these are usually omitted by the singers.

Classical sopranos who could, if they wanted, deliver the right sound include Miriam Feuersinger, Gerlinde Sämann, Magali Léger or Natalya Kirillova. Possible tenors include Filipe Faria & Sérgio Peixoto (both of *Sete Lágrimas*), Marc Mauillon or Sting himself. But I still despair whether this piece will ever be sung properly by classical singers.

We need to look at pop singers with beautiful voices who could, with help, make excellent Handel singers. Of course, much depends on whether they actually wish to sing Handel. Most of my 49 female pop vocalists could do it if only they wanted to. Voices I like are: Sarah Joyce, Regina Spektor, Jenny Owen Youngs, Julia Holter and Skylar Grey. Good younger singers (under 30 at the time of writing) include Katie Costello, Charli XCX, Nina Nesbitt, Sarah Close and Aurora. Male pop singers eligible for Handel, equipped both with straight tone and a falsetto register, include Chris Martin, Adam Levine, Jamie Cullum, Robin Warren-Adamson, Tyler Ward, Phillip Phillips and Tamino. Promising female folk singers include Sierra Hull, Lucy Ward and Sarah Jarosz, with either John Whitley or Jay LaBouchardiere of *Ninebarrow* as tenor choices.

Turning to ensemble pieces, I'd like an accomplished barbershop group to 'cross over' by performing some eighteenth- and early nineteenth-century glees in the way extravagantly praised by a *Hull Packet* reviewer, quoted in full on p. 63: 'It is impossible to describe the rich effect of the combined

---

61 While this piece is seemingly scored for string orchestra, with doubled oboes and basoons, it is often performed as a chamber piece, with string quartet plus single oboe and bassoon.

voices, as they broke upon the ear, in this first glee. The fine harmony of the composition, aided by the full and perfect union of the according tones, and the delicacy with which the lights and shades of the melody were touched by the whole party, as if by one voice or instrument, produced a tout ensemble, truly magical.'

In concluding their *History of Singing*, **John Potter** and **Neil Sorrell** commented: 'During the second half of the twentieth century, the breakdown of commercial and academic categories of singing (and the emancipation of almost any genre) legitimised almost any variety of singing as being of potential value. The twentieth century gave Western music the distinction between 'classical' and 'popular'; the twenty-first is replacing that absurd polarity with a plurality of singings.' [p. 294] Let's hope that this 'plurality of singings' is extended to operatic and classical concert performances.

7.16   Campaign for Real Singing

There are societies for every instrument under the sun, but I don't think one exists for Historically Informed Singing. Such a group is needed to deliver Timothy Tikker's and my vision. It might be called Campaign for Real Singing, after the successful CAMRA (Campaign for Real Ale) pressure group. I've set up domain names for CAMREALS.COM and CAMREALS.CO.UK. I don't have the energy or capability to lead such a group, but could help. Would anyone happy to get such a group going, or contribute to the enterprise, please email me on richardbethell@btinternet.com?

Full Text Databases: Service Providers and Sources

Australian Newspaper [Trove]: http://newspapers.nla.gov.au/
Boston Globe Archives: https://www.bostonglobe.com/1970/01/12/serp/LRzdrFYs8Li3rVYB2kghyL/story.html
British Newspaper Archive: https://www.britishnewspaperarchive.co.uk/search
Brooklyn Newsstand
    Brooklyn Daily Eagle Online (1841-1950): https://bklyn.newspapers.com/#
California Digital Newspaper Collection: https://cdnc.ucr.edu/cgi-bin/cdnc
Chicago Tribune: https://chicagotribune.newspapers.com/#
Colorado Historic Newspapers Collection: https://www.coloradohistoricnewspapers.org/
Cornell University Library
    Making of America Collection: http://digital.library.cornell.edu/m/moa/
Digital Library of Georgia:
    https://www.galileo.usg.edu/scholar/databases/dlg1/?Welcome
Fulton History Collection: http://fultonhistory.com/
Google, Various Platforms including:
    Google Advanced Book Search: https://books.google.co.uk/advanced_book_search
    With Internet Archive (American Libraries & other sources): http://www.archive.org/details/americana,
        including *Dwight's Journal of Music*
Gale, Cengage Learning: http://www.cengage.co.uk/
    British Newspapers 1800 – 1900: http://newspapers.bl.uk/blcs [at British Library]
    Daily Telegraph: https://www.gale.com/uk/c/the-telegraph-historical-archive
    Illustrated London News: https://www.gale.com/uk/c/illustrated-london-news-historical-archive
    19th-Century US Newspapers: https://www.gale.com/uk/c/19th-century-us-newspapers
Genealogy Bank: https://www.genealogybank.com/explore/newspapers/all
Guardian and Observer Digital Archive: http://archive.guardian.co.uk
Hathi Trust Digital Library: https://www.hathitrust.org/
Internet Archive: https://archive.org/
Library of Congress Chronicling America: http://chroniclingamerica.loc.gov/. https://chroniclingamerica.loc.gov/lccn/sn83030214/1896-12-13/ed-1/seq-34/
Manitoba Life and Times:
    https://digitalcollections.lib.umanitoba.ca/islandora/object/uofm%3Amanitobia_newspapers
New York Times: http://query.nytimes.com/search/query
Newspaper Archive: http://www.newspaperarchive.com/
Papers Past, National Library of New Zealand: https://paperspast.natlib.govt.nz/
ProQuest LLC [through institution]:
    Periodicals Archive Online: http://britishperiodicals.chadwyck.co.uk/info/about.do
    ProQuest historical newspapers, including Boston Daily Globe, Chicago Daily Tribune, Hartford Daily Courant, Irish Times, Manchester Guardian and Observer, New York Times, Times of India, Washington Post:
        http://www.proquest.com/en-US/catalogs/databases/detail/pq-hist-news.shtml
Quincy Public Library: http://archive.quincylibrary.org/Olive/APA/QPL/default.aspx#panel=search
Scotsman Publications Ltd, The *The Scotsman*: http://archive.scotsman.com/
***The Times* Digital Archive:** http://archive.timesonline.co.uk/tol/archive/
World Vital Records: https://www.myheritage.com/

Primary and Secondary Sources

For Newspapers, Magazines and other periodicals, see pp. 371-4

Adolphus, John, *Memoirs of John Bannister, Comedian*, 2 vols, 1839

Agricola, Johann Friedrich, *Introduction to the Art of singing*, 1757 (including translation of, and commentary on, Tosi's treatise, q.v.); trans. and ed. Julianne C. Baird, 1995

Anfossi, Maria, *Trattato Teorico Pratico sull'arte del canto*, 1840

Anon., *A.B.C. Dario Musico* [biographical Notices of the Musicians, Composers and Singers of the Period], 1780

Anon., *Musical Guide for Singing and the Piano-Forte*, 1845

Arnold, *Complete Psalmodist*, 1753, 1761, 1779

Aprile, Giuseppe, *The Modern Italian Method of Singing*, 1795; includes 'Necessary Rules For Students and Dilettanti of Vocal Music'

Bacon, Richard Mackenzie, *The Quarterly Musical Magazine and Review* (QMMR), 1818–28; available online at https://catalog.hathitrust.org/Record/012155933

Bacon, Richard Mackenzie, *Elements of Vocal Science*, 1824, [serialized in QMMR]

Barbier, Patrick, *The World of the Castrati: The History of an Extraordinary Operatic Phenomenon*, 1989

Barbier, Patrick, *Opera in Paris 1800–1850: A Lively History*, 1995

Bayly, Anselm, *Practical Treatise on Singing and Playing*, 1771

Bayly, Anselm, *The Alliance of Musick, Poetry and Oratory*, 1789

Bernard, John, *Retrospections of the Stage*, Vol. II, 1784

Bernhard, Christoph, *Writings*, 1650

Bethell, Richard, *Vocal Vibrato in Early Music*, 2010; available at www.york.ac.uk/music/conferences/nema/bethell/

Bethell, Richard, *NEMA Survey Report*, October 2009; available at www.tvemf.org/NEMA/NEMA survey report.pdf

Bethell, Richard, ed., Facebook transcripts from NEMA website:
www.earlymusic.info/Scholarly Rigour and or Artistic Inspiration.pdf
www.earlymusic.info/Vibrato Discussions, Part 1 Threads V1 to V19.pdf
www.earlymusic.info/Vocal Discussions, Part 2 Threads V20 to V35.pdf
www.earlymusic.info/Vocal Discussions, Part 3 Threads V36 to V47.pdf
www.earlymusic.info/Vocal Discussions, Part 4 Threads V48 to V60.pdf

Billings, William, *Singing Master's Assistant*, 1778

Billington, Thomas, *Te Deum, etc., with Instructions to the Performers*, 1784

Borghese, Antonio D. R., *A New and General system of Music*, 1790

Bowen, Frederic Hymen, *My Art and My Friends*, 1913

Brough, Robert Barnabas, *The Welcome Guest*, 1860

Brown, Clive, *Classical & Romantic Performing Practice 1750–1900*, 1999

Brown, Howard Mayer and Sadie, Stanley (eds.), *Performance Practice: Music after 1600*, 1989, *see* Crutchfield, Will *and* Philip, Robert

Brown, John, 'Letters upon the Poetry and Music of the Italian Opera' in *The Analytical Review*, July 1789

Burgh, Allatson, *Anecdotes of Music*, 1814

Burke, Edmund, *On the Sublime and Beautiful*, 1756

Burney, Charles, *Memoirs of Dr. Charles Burney 1726–1769*, ed. from autograph fragments by Slava Klima, Garry Bowers, and Kerry S. Grant, 1988

Burney, Charles, *The Present State of Music in France and Italy*, 1771

Burney, Charles, *The Present State of Music in Germany, the Netherlands and United Provinces*, 2 vols, 1773

Burney, Charles, *An Account of the Musical Performances in Westminster Abbey and the Pantheon, in Commemoration of Handel* (includes 'Sketch of the life of Handel'), 1785

Burney, Charles, *The Letters of Dr Charles Burney*, Vol. 1: 1751–1784, ed. Alvaro Ribeiro, SJ, 1991

Burney, Charles, *A General History of Music*, 4 vols, 1789

Burney, Charles, *Memoirs of the Life and Writings of the Abate Metastasio*, 3 Vols, 1796

Burney, Charles, *Rees's Cyclopædia,* articles on music, 1814

Burney, Fanny, *Journals and Letters*, selected by Peter Sabor and Lars E. Troide, 2001

Burney, Sarah Harriet, *The Letters of Sarah Harriet Burney*, ed. Lorna J. Clark, 1997

Burney, Susan, *see* Olleson, Philip

Burrows, Donald and Dunhill, Rosemary, *Music and Theatre in Handel's world: The Papers of James Harris 1732–1780*, 2002

Burton, Anthony, series ed., *A Performer's Guide to Music of the Baroque Period*, 2002

Burton, Anthony, series ed., *A Performer's Guide to Music of the Classical Period*, 2002

Burton, Anthony, series ed., *A Performer's Guide to Music of the Romantic Period*, 2002

Busby, Thomas, *Complete Dictionary of Music*, 1811

Busby, Thomas, *Concert Room and Orchestra Anecdotes*, 3 vols, 1825

Busby, Thomas, *Dictionary of three thousand terms*, 1840

Butt, John, *Music Education and the Art of Performance in the German Baroque*, 1994

Butt, John, *Playing with History*, 2002

Callaghan, Jean, *Singing & Science, Body, Brain & Voice*, 2014

Cazalet, William Wahab, *The Art of Singing*, 1861

Charlton, David, *Opera in the Age of Rousseau: Music, Confrontation, Realism*, 2012

Cheetham, Andrew J; Knowles, Joseph; and Wainwright, Jonathan P., *Reappraising the Seicento: Composition, Dissemination, Assimilation*, 2014

Chorley, Henry F., *Music and manners in France and Germany*, 1841–1844

Chorley, Henry F., *Thirty Years' Musical Recollections*. 2 vols, 1862

Cibber, Colley, *An apology for the life of Mr. Colley Cibber written by himself*, 1740

Clayton, Ellen Creathorne, *Queens of Song*, 1865

Cobb, Buell E., *The Sacred Harp: A Tradition and its Music*, 1978, 1989

Cone, John Frederick, *Adelina Patti, Queen of Hearts*, 1981

Cooke, Thomas, *Singing Exemplified*, 1828

Corfe, Joseph, *A Treatise on Singing*, 1799

Corri, Domenico, *Singer's Preceptor. or Corri's Treatise on Vocal Music*, 1810

Coryat, Thomas, *Coryat's Crudities: Hastily gobled up in Five Moneth's Travells in France, Savoy, Italy, Rhetia commonly called the Grisons country, Helvetia alias Switzerland, some parts of high Germany, and the*

Netherlands, 1611

Cowden, Robert H., *Classical singers of the Opera and Recital Stages: A Bibliography of Biographical Materials*, 1994

Cowen, Frederick Hymen, *My Art and My Friends*, 1913

Cowgill, Rachel and Poriss, Hilary, *The Arts of the Prima Donna in the Long Nineteenth Century*, 2012

Cox, John Edmund, *Musical Recollections of the Last Half Century*, 2 vols, 1872

Crivelli, Domenico Francesco, *Instructions and Progressive Exercises in the Art of Singing, with Scales, Solfeggios, Variations, Etc.* 1841

Crosse, John, *Account of the Grand Musical Festival ...* , 1825

Crutchfield, Will, 'Voices' (Section 15, in the section 'The Classical Era') in Brown, Howard Mayer and Sadie, Stanley (eds.), *Performance Practice: Music after 1600*, 1989

Crutchfield, Will, 'Voices' (Section 21, in the section 'The 19th Century') in Brown, Howard Mayer and Sadie, Stanley (eds.), *Performance Practice: Music after 1600*, 1989

Cumberland's British Theatre, with Remarks, Biographical and Critical, Vol. VIII, 1826

d'Ancillon, Charles, *Eunuchism Display'd*, 1705

Daniel, George, *Cumberland's British Theatre: with remarks, biographical and critical*, 1875

Dart, Thurston, *The Interpretation of Music.* 1954

de Crui, Duchess, *Letters from the Duchess de Crui and others: on subjects moral and entertaining*, 1777

Delany, Mary, Mrs *see* Pendarves

D'Esté, John, *Vocalists' Vade Mecum; or, Pocket Companion: Practical Hints on Singing, and the Cultivation of the Voice*, 1872

Deutsch, Otto Erich, *Mozart, A Documentary Biography*, 1966

Dibdin, Charles, *Professional Life of Mr Dibdin, Written by Himself*, 1803

Dibdin, Charles, *Musical Mentor*, 1805

Dibdin, Thomas, *Biography of the English Stage*, 1827

Dictionary of Musicians, 1827, *see* Sainsbury, John S. and Choron, Alexandre

Dolmetsch, Arnold, *The Interpretation of the Music of the XVII & XVIII Centuries*, 1916

Donington, Robert, *The Interpretation of Early Music*, 1963, 1974, 1977

Donington, Robert, *Baroque Music. Style and Performance: A Handbook*, 1982

Dow, Sabrina H., *Artistic Singing*, 1883

Duffin, Dr. Ross W., *Baroque Ensemble Tuning Introduction: Translation of Tosi's passage on tuning*, 2018

Eastes, afterwards D'Esté, John, *see* D'Esté

Ebers, John, *Seven Years of the King's Theatre*, 1828

Edwards, Henry Sutherland, *History of the Opera from its Origin in Italy to the present Time With Anecdotes of the Most Celebrated Composers and Vocalists of Europe*, 1862

Edgcumbe, Richard, second Earl of Mount Edgcumbe, *Musical Reminiscences, containing an Account of the Italian Opera in England, from 1773*, 1834

Edwards, Henry Sutherland, *History of the Opera*, 1906

Elliott, Martha, *Singing in Style: A Guide to Vocal Performance Practices*, 2006

Encyclopædia Britannica, third edition, 1797

Evelyn, John, *Diary*, ed. E. S. De Beer, 2006

Ewen, David, *Encyclopedia of the Opera*, 1963

Fenner, Theodore, *Opera in London: Views of the Press 1785–1830*, 1994

Ferrari, Giacomo Gotifredo, *Concise Treatise on Italian Singing*, 1818

Finck, Henry Theophilus, *Success in Music and How it is Won*, 1910

Fiske, Roger, *English Theatre Music in the Eighteenth Century*, 1973

Gable, Frederick Kent, 'Some Observations Concerning Baroque and Modern Vibrato', *Performance Practice Review*, Vol. 5, No. 1, 1992; available at https://scholarship.claremont.edu/cgi/viewcontent.cgi?article=1105&context=ppr

Gänzl, Kurt, *Victorian Vocalists*, 2018

García, Manuel Patricio Rodríguez, *Ecole de García: traité complet de l'art du chant par Manuel García fils*, 1840, 1847; trans. and ed. Albert Garcia as *Garcia's Treatise on the Art of Singing: A compendious method of Instruction with examples and exercises for the Cultivation of the Voice*, 1924

Gardiner, William, *Music of Nature*, 1832

Gardiner, William, *Music and Friends; or, Pleasant recollections of A Dilettante*, 3 vols, 1838

Gardiner, William, *Sights in Italy, with some Account of the Present State of Music and the Sister Arts in that country*, 1847

Genest, John, *Some Account of the English Stage*, 10 vols, 1832

Gilliland, Thomas, *Dramatic Mirror, containing the History of the Stage, from the earliest period to the present one, Vol. II*, 1808

Gislason, Donald Garth, *Castil-Blaze, De L'opéra en France and the Feuilletons of the Journal Des Débats: 1820–1832* (PhD thesis, University of British Columbia), 1992

Gunn, John, *Art of Flute Playing*, 1793

Haenen, Greta, *Das Vibrato in der Musik des Barock*, 1988

Haslewood, Joseph, *The Secret History of the Green-Room*, 2 vols, 1795

Hawkins, John, *History of the Science and Practice of Music*, 1776

Hawkins, William, *Miscellanies in prose and verse: Containing candid and impartial observations on the principal performers belonging to the two Theatres-Royal*, 1775

Haydn, Joseph, *Collected Correspondence, London Notebooks*, 1804

Hayes, Catherine, Miss, *Memoir*, by 'A Contributor to the Dublin University Magazine', 1852

Haynes, Bruce, *The End of Early Music: A Period Performer's History of Music for the Twenty-First Century*, 2007

Hazlitt, William, *A View of the English Stage, or, a series of dramatic criticisms*, 1818

Henderson, William James, *The Art of the Singer*, 1906

Henderson, William James, *Early History of Singing*, 1921

Heriot, Angus, *The Castrati in Opera*, 1960

Hervey, Charles, *Theatres of Paris*, 1847

Hewlett, Henry Gay, *Henry Fothergill Chorley; Autobiography, Memoir, and Letters*, 1897

Highfill, Philip H., Burnim, Kalman A., and Langhans, Edward A., *A Biographical Dictionary of Actors, Actresses, Musicians, Dancers, Managers, and Other Stage Personnel in London, 1660–1800*, 1975

Hiller, Johann Adam, *Treatise on Vocal Performance and Ornamentation*, 1780; trans. and ed. Suzanne J. Beicken, 2001

Hogarth, George, *Memoirs of the Opera in Italy, France, Germany and England*, 1851

Holcroft, Thomas, *Convivial Songster*, 1782

Holmes, Edward, *Ramble among the Musicians of Germany*, 1828

Hone, William, *Every-day Book*, Vol. 2, 1802

Hooper, Lucy H., *Souvenirs of Song*, 1871

Howard, Patricia, *The Modern Castrato. Gaetano Guadagni and the Coming of a New Operatic Age*, 2018

Hunt, Leigh, *Critical Essays on the Performers of the London Theatres*, 1804

Hunt, Leigh, *London Journal*, 1835

Jackson, Roland, *Performance Practice. A dictionary-guide for musicians*, 2005

Jackson, William, *Observations on the present state of Music in London*, 1791

Jerold, Beverly, 'Did early string players use continuous vibrato?', *The Strad*, 20 Feb. 2015

Jerold, Beverly, 'Distinguishing Between Artificial and Natural Vibrato in Premodern Music', *Music Performance Issues: 1600–1900*, 2016, Section 16; first published in *Journal of Singing* 63/2 (Nov./Dec. 2006)

Jocelin, Simeon and Doolittle, Amos, *Chorister's Companion*, 1782

Johnstone, J. Alfred, Article 'The Vice of Vibrato, and the Torture of Tremolo' included in *Essentials in piano playing and other musical studies*, 1910

Jones, George, *Anecdotal reminiscences of distinguished literary and political characters*, 1830

Jousse, Jean, *Vocal Primer*, 1815

Kelly, Michael, *Reminiscences of Michael Kelly*, 1826

Kimball, Jacob, *Rural harmony*, 1793

Kirby, F. E., 'Hermann Finck on Methods of Performance' in *Music & Letters*, July 1961

Klein, Hermann, *Thirty Years of Musical Life in London*, 1903

Klein, Hermann, *The Reign of Patti*, 1920

Krehbiel, Henry Edward, *Sections of Opera: Being Historical and Critical Observations and Records concerning the Lyric drama in New York from its Earliest Days down to the Present Time*, 1908

Lampe, John Frederick, *Art of Musick*, 1740

Lamperti, Francesco, *A Treatise on the Art of Singing*, 1877

Lamperti, Francesco, *The Art of Singing according to ancient tradition and personal experience*, 1887

Lanza, Gesualdo, *Elements of Singing*, 1813

Lassabathie, Théodore, *Histoire du Conservatoire impérial de musique et de déclamation*, 1860

Leiser, Clara, *Jean De Reszke and the Great Days of Opera*, 1934

Lumley, Benjamin, *Reminiscences of the Opera*, 1864

Lysons, Daniel and Amott, John, *Origin and progress of the meeting of the Three Choirs of Gloucester, Worcester & Hereford*, 1895

MacClintock, Carol, *Readings in the History of Music in Performance*, 1982

MacDonald, Cheryl, *Emma Albani. Victorian Diva*, 1984

Mackinlay, Malcolm Sterling, *Garcia the centenarian and his times, being a memoir of Manuel Garcia's life and labours for the advancement of music and science*, 1908

Macy, Laura (ed.), *The Grove Book of Opera Singers*, 2008

Mancini, Giambattista, *Practical Reflections on Figured Singing*, 1774 and 1777; trans. and ed. Edward V. Foreman, 1967 and 1996

Marsh, John, *The John Marsh Journals, 1752-1828*, 2 vols, ed. Brian Robins, 2011, 2013

Mason, Lowell, *Manual of the Boston Academy of Music, for Instruction in the Elements of Vocal Music, on the System of Pestalozzi*, 1836

Mason, Lowell, *Musical Letters from Abroad*, 1854

Mathews, W. S. B., *A Hundred Years of Music in America*, 1889

Mendelssohn, Felix, *A Life in Letters*, ed. Rudolf Elvers, trans. Craig Tomlinson, 1986

Michotte, Edmond, *An Evening at Rossini's in Beau-Sejour, 1858*, trans. Herbert Weinstock, 1968

Monson, William John, *Journal*, 1817

Montgomery, David, *The Vibrato Thing*, 2003; available online at. https://douglasniedt.com/TechTipVibratoPart3TheVibratoThingByDavidMontgomery.pdf

Moore, Thomas, *Memoirs, Journal and Correspondence*, 8 vols, 1853–6

Mozart, Leopold, *Violinschule*, 1756

Mozart, *Letters of Mozart and his Family*, ed. and trans. Emily Anderson, 1966

Musical Guide for Singing and the Piano-Forte, [Anon.], 1845

Nares, Dr. James, *A Treatise on Singing*, 1778

Nathan, Isaac, *Musurgia Vocalis*, 1836

Nathan, Isaac, *Theory and Practice of Singing*, 1846

Nettl, Paul, *Forgotten Musicians*, 1951; contains translation of Quantz, Johann Joachim, *Life as Sketched by Himself*

Neumann, Frederick, *Ornamentation in Baroque and Post-Baroque Music: with Special Emphasis on J. S. Bach*, 1978

Neumann, Frederick, *Performance Practices of the Seventeenth and Eighteenth Centuries*, 1993

Newton, George, *Sonority in Singing: A Historical Essay*, 1984

Newton, William, *Anglo-Italian Elements of Singing*, 1861

North, Roger, *Roger North on Music, Transcribed from his Essays of c. 1695–1728*, ed. John Wilson, 1959

North, Roger, *The Musical Grammarian*, 1728, reprinted 1990 and 2006

North, Roger, *Notes of Me*, ed. Peter Millard, 2000

Novello, Clara, *Reminiscences*, ed. Valeria Gigliucci, 1910

Novello, Vincent, *A Mozart Pilgrimage*, 1829

Olleson, Philip, *The Journals and Letters of Susan Burney: Music and Society in Late Eighteenth-Century England*, 2012

Oxberry, William, *Oxberry's Dramatic Biography and Histrionic Anecdotes*, 1827

Parke, William Thomas, *Musical Memoir*, 2 vols, 1830

Parker, John R., *A Musical Biography: or Sketches of the Lives and Writings of Eminent Musical Characters, Collated and Compiled by John R Parker*, 1825

Parrott, Andrew, *Composers' Intentions? Lost Traditions of Musical Performance*, 2015

Pearce, Charles E, *Sims Reeves. Fifty Years of Music in England,* 1924

Pendarves, Mary, Mrs, née Granville, *The Autobiography and Correspondence of Mary Granville, Mrs Delany*, ed. A. Llanover, 1861–2; Vol. 1 (1729)

Penny Cyclopædia, 1843

Pepys, Samuel, *Diary*, 1661–1669; ed. R. Latham and W. Matthews, 1970–1983

Percy, Sholto and Percy, Reuben, *Percy Anecdotes of Music*, Vol. 17, 1822

Philip, Robert, '1900–1940' (Section 22 in the section 'The 20th Century') in Brown, Howard Mayer and Sadie, Stanley (eds.), *Performance Practice: Music after 1600*, 1989

Phillips, Henry, *Musical and Personal Recollections*, 1864

Planché, J. R., *Recollections and Reflections*, Vol. 1, 1826

Pleasants, Henry, *The Great Singers*, 1966

Potter, John, *Vocal Authority: Singing Style and Ideology*, 1998

Potter, John (ed.), *The Cambridge Companion to Singing*, 2000

Potter, John, *Tenor: History of a Voice*, 2009

Potter, John and Sorrell, Neil, *A History of Singing*, 2012

Potter, Sarah, *Changing Vocal Style and Technique in Britain during the Long Nineteenth Century* (Ph.D. thesis, University of Leeds), 2014

Quantz, Johann Joachim, *Life*, see Nettl, Paul

Quantz, Johann Joachim, *Versuch einer Anweisung die Flöte traversiere zu spielen*, 1752; trans. by Edward D. Reilly as *On Playing the Flute*, 1966

Raguenet, François, *A Comparison between the French and Italian Musick and opera's*, 1709

Rauzzini, Venanzio, *Set of Twelve Solfeggi*, 1820

Ravens, Simon, *The Supernatural Voice: A history of high male singing*, 2014

Reggio, Pietro, *The Art of Singing or A Treatise, wherein is shown how to sing well any song whatsoever*, 1677

Riva, Giuseppe, *Advice to the Composers and Performers of Vocal Musick*, 1727

Roberts, Francis, *Some Famous Singers of the 19th Century*, 1914

Root, George. Frederick, *The Coronet: A Collection of Music for Singing Schools, Musical Conventions and Choirs; consisting of a Course for Elementary Instruction and Training*. 1865

Rousseau, *Lettre sur la Musique Francaise*, 1753

Sadie, Stanley and Fortune, Nigel, *New Grove Dictionary of Music and Musicians*, 1980

Sadie, Stanley and Macy, Laura, *The Grove Book of Operas*, second ed. 2009

Sainsbury, John S. and Choron, Alexandre, *Dictionary of Musicians*, 1827

Sainton-Dolby, Charlotte, *A Complete Course of Practical Instruction in the Art of Singing*, 1872

Santley, Sir Charles, *Student and singer: the reminiscences of Charles Santley*, 1892

Scholes, Percy A., *The Oxford Companion to Music*, 1938

Seashore, Carl E., *Psychology of Music*, 1938

Shaw, [George] Bernard, *Shaw's Music*, 3 vols, 1981

Simond, Louis, *A Tour in Italy and Sicily*, 1828

Smyth, Charles John, *Six Letters on Singing*, 1810

Spohr, Louis, *Grand Violin School*, 1833

Spohr, Louis, *The Musical Journeys of Louis Spohr*, trans. and ed. Henry Pleasants, 1961

Stark, James, *Bel Canto*, 1999

Stendhal, *Life of Rossini*, 1824, trans. Richard N. Coe, 1985

Stevenson A., of Montreal, *The Vocal Preceptor*, 1811

Stewart, Martyn, 'Honey Bee', in *The Sound of Critters: Bird and Animal Sounds Across the Planet*, previously available online at http://soundofcritters.com/1306

Strunk, Oliver, *Source Readings in Music History*, 1950

Tans'ur, William, 'The Musical Alphabet', Section 11 in *A New Musical Grammar*, 1746

Tans'ur, William, *The Elements of Musick Display'd*, 1766

Tarling, Judy, *The Weapons of Rhetoric, a guide for musicians and audiences*, 2004

Tenducci, Giusto, *Instruction of Mr. Tenducci to his scholars*, 1785

Tetrazzini, Luisa, *How to Sing*, 1923

Toft, Robert, *Heart to Heart. Expressive Singing in England 1780–1830*, 2000

Toft, Robert, *Bel Canto: A Performer's Guide*, 2013

Toft, Robert, *With Passionate Voice*, 2014

Tosi, Pierfrancesco, *Opinioni de' cantori antichi e moderni o sieno osservazioni sopra il canto figurato*, 1723; trans. [1] by Johann Ernst Galliard as *Observations on the Florid Song; or, Sentiments on the Ancient and Modern Singers*, 1743, reprinted 1968;

trans. [2] by Edward Foreman as *Opinions of Singers Ancient, and Modern, or Observations on Figured Singing*, 1986

Von Raumer, Frederick, *England in 1835, being a series of letters written to friends in Germany, during a residence in London and excursions into the provinces*, trans. Sarah Austin and H. E. Lloyd, 1836

Von Weber, Max Maria, *Carl Maria von Weber: the Life of an Artist*, trans. J. Palgrave Simpson, 1865

Waldie, John, *The Journal of John Waldie, Theatre Commentaries* 1799–1830, transcribed by Frederick Burwick, accessible at http://escholarship.org/uc/uclalib_dsc_waldie/

[NB 1833–1864 not yet transcribed]

Waldron F G, *Candid and Impartial Observations*, 1795

Walpole, Horace, *Private Correspondence of Horace Walpole, Earl of Orford. Now first collected*, 1820

Welsh, Thomas, *Vocal Instructor*, 1825

Whalley, Thomas Sedgewick, *Journals and Correspondence*, 1786

Wieck, Friedrich, *Piano and Song (Didactic and Polemical)*, 1852; trans., ed. and annotated by Henry Pleasants, 1988

Wistreich, Richard, 'Reconstructing pre-Romantic singing technique', in John Potter (ed.), *The Cambridge Companion to Singing*, 2000

Wood, Sir Henry, *The Gentle Art of Singing*, 1927

York, University of, Conference Proceedings, *Singing music from 1500 to 1900*: www.york.ac.uk/music/conferences/nema/

List of Newspapers and Periodicals, with abbreviations if applicable

The titles listed were published in Great Britain or Ireland, if not otherwise stated, or unless the location is indicated by the title.

Academy	
Age, Melbourne	
Albion and The Star	
Allgemeine Musikalische Zeitung, Leipzig	
American and Commercial Daily Advertiser, Baltimore	
American Journal of Science and Arts	
Anglo American Times	
Ann Arbor News, Michigan	
Argus, Melbourne	
Aris's Birmingham Gazette	
Athenaeum	Ath
Atlantic Monthly, Boston	
Atlas	
Auckland Star	AuckS
Australian Star	
Australasian	
Ballymena Observer	
Baltimore Bulletin	
Bath Chronicle and Weekly Gazette	
Bath Gazette	
Belfast Telegraph	
Belle Assemblée, La	LBA
Bell's Life in London and Sporting Chronicle	
Bell's Life in Sydney	
Bell's Weekly Messenger	
Bendigo Advertiser, Victoria	
Bentley's Miscellany	
Berrow's Worcester Journal	
Birmingham Daily Post	BDP
Blackwood's Edinburgh Magazine	
Boston Daily Advertiser	BDA
Boston Daily Globe	BDG
Boston Evening Transcript	
Boston Herald	
Boston Journal	
Boston Musical Gazette	
Bradford Observer	

Brighton Gazette	BG
Brighton Gleaner	
Brighton Guardian	
Brisbane Courier	
Bristol Times and Mirror	
British Mercury	
Brooklyn Daily Eagle	Brook
Brooklyn Newsstand	BrookN
Brother Jonathan, New York	
Buffalo Courier, New York	
Bury & Norwich Post	
Caledonian Mercury	CM
Cambridge Chronicle and Journal	
Camperdown Chronicle, Victoria	
Carlisle Journal	
Cedar Rapids Evening Gazette, Iowa	
Century, New York	
Cheltenham Chronicle	
Cheltenham Looker-On	
Chicago Tribune	CT
Cincinnati Commercial Tribune	
Cincinnati Daily Enquirer	
Cincinnati Daily Gazette	CincDG
Coburg Leader	
Connoisseur	
Cork Examiner	CE
Courier, Louisville, Kentucky	
Court Gazette	
Court Journal	
Court and Lady's Magazine	
Cumberland Pacquet	
Daily Atlas, Boston	
Daily Inter Ocean, Chicago	
Daily Mail, London	
Daily News, London	DN
Daily Telegraph	DT
Daily Telegraph, Launceston	

List of Newspapers and Periodicals, with abbreviations if applicable

Dallas Morning News		Harper's	
Derby Daily Telegraph		Herald, Melbourne	
Derby Mercury		Hereford Times	
Deseret Evening News, Utah		Herts Guardian, Agricultural Journal, and General Advertiser	
Dominion, New Zealand			
Drama, or Theatrical Pocket Magazine		Huddersfield Daily Examiner	
		Hull Advertiser	
Dramatic Magazine		Hull Packet	HP
Dublin Daily Express	DubDE	Illustrated London News	
Dublin Evening Mail		Illustrated Review	
Dundee Courier		Illustrated Sport	
Dundee Evening Telegraph		Illustrated Sporting and Dramatic News	ISDN
Dwight's Journal of Music, Boston			
Early Music Performer	EMP	Illustrated Times	
Early Music Review	EMR	Independent Democrat, Ohio	
Edinburgh Annual Register		Ipswich Journal	
Edinburgh Evening Courant	EEC	Irish Times	
Era		Kadina and Wallaroo Times, South Australia	
Era Almanack		Kalgoorlie Miner, Western Australia	
European Magazine	EM	Knickerbocker	
Euterpeiad	Eut	Knight's Quarterly Magazine	
Evening Journal, Adelaide		La Belle Assemblée	LBA
Evening Mail, London		Lake County Press, Indianapolis	
Evening News, Lincoln		Lancashire Evening Post	
Evening Post, Auckland		Lancaster Gazette	
Evening Post, New York	EPNY	Lancet	
Evening Star, New Zealand		Leader	
Everybody's Magazine		Leamington Spa Courier	
Examiner, Launceston		Leeds Intelligencer	
Examiner, London	Ex	Leeds Mercury	LM
Exeter and Plymouth Gazette		Leeds Times	
Falkirk Herald		Leicester Journal	
Fife Herald		Lewiston Evening Journal, Maine	
Figaro in London		Limerick Reporter, Ireland	
Folkestone, Hythe, Sandgate & Cheriton Herald		Literary Gazette	LG
Freeman's Journal, Dublin		Liverpool Daily Post	
Gentleman's Magazine		Liverpool Mercury	
Glasgow Herald	GH	Lloyd's Weekly	
Globe		London Courier	
Gloucester Journal		London and Provincial Entr'acte	
Gramophone		London Magazine	LMag
Graphic		London Review	LR
Hampshire Advertiser		Los Angeles Herald	
Harmonicon	Har	Mackay Mercury, Queensland	

List of Newspapers and Periodicals, with abbreviations if applicable

Magazine of Music		Northern Argus, Rockhampton	
Manawatu Standard, New Zealand		Northern Whig	
Manchester Courier and Lancashire General Advertiser	MCLGA	Norwich Mercury	
		Nottingham Evening Post	
Manchester Evening News		Observer	
Manchester Guardian	MG	Orchestra	
Manchester Times	MT	Oriental Herald	
Mercury, Hobart		Otago Daily Times	
Miami Herald		Otago Witness, New Zealand	
Mirror Monthly Magazine		Oxford Chronicle	
Monthly Mirror	MM	Pall Mall Gazette	PMG
Monthly Review		Pateley Bridge & Nidderdale Herald	
Morning Advertiser, London	MA	Philadelphia Chronicle	
Morning Chronicle, London	MC	Philadelphia Inquirer	
Morning Post, London	MP	Pilot, Dublin	
Mount Barker Courier, South Australia		Pittsburgh Dispatch	
Murray's Magazine		Plain Dealer, Ohio	
Muscatine Journal, Iowa		Poverty Bay Herald	
Musical Courier		Press, New Zealand	
Musical Gazette	MusG	Preston Herald	
Musical Herald	MusH	Prompter	
Musical Library Monthly Supplement		Punch, Melbourne	
		Quarterly Musical Magazine and Review	QMMR
Musical Review	MusR		
Musical Standard	MusS	Reader	
Musical Times	MusT	Reynolds's Newspaper	
Musical World	MW	Royal Cornwall Gazette	
National Magazine		Royal Devonport Telegraph, and Plymouth Chronicle	
New Bon Ton Magazine		St James's Gazette	
New Monthly Magazine	NMM	Sacramento Daily Record, California	
New Times, London		San Francisco Call	
New World, New York		San Francisco Chronicle	
New York Daily Tribune		Saturday Review	SatR
New York Herald		Saunders's News-Letter	
New York Herald Tribune	NYHT	Scots Magazine	
New York Mirror		Scotsman	Scot
New York Review		Sheffield & Rotherham Independent	
New York Sun		South Australian Register	
New York Times	NYT	Southern Reporter and Cork Commercial Courier	
New Zealand Herald			
Norfolk Chronicle		Southland Times, New Zealand	
North Otago Times, New Zealand		Spectator	
North Wales Chronicle		Sphinx	
Northampton Mercury		Spirit of the Times, New York	

Springfield Republican	Spring	*Times-Picayune*, New Orleans	
Staffordshire Advertiser		*Times,* Richmond, Virginia	
Standard, London	Std	*Theatre*	
Star		*Theatrical Inquisitor*	TI
The Strad		*Tomahawk*	
Sydney Mail		*Toronto Globe*	
Sydney Monitor		*Trenton Evening Times*, New Jersey	
Sydney Morning Herald	SMH	*Weekly Herald*	
Sun, New York		*Weekly Standard and Express*	
Sunday Times, London	ST	*West Australian*, Perth	
Sunday Times, Sydney		*Western Daily Press*	
Sunderland Daily Echo and Shipping Gazette		*Western Mail*, Perth	
		Western Morning News	
Table Talk, Melbourne		*Worcester Palladium*	
Tasmanian		*Yorkshire Evening Post*	
Tatler		*Yorkshire Gazette*	YG
Taunton Courier		*Yorkshire Post*	YP
Telegraph, Brisbane		*Yorkshire Post & Leeds Intelligencer*	YPLI
Times, London	T		

Subject Index

Achieving historically informed singing
    Complete John Waldie transcription, 355
    Complete publication of Burney's letters, 355
    Encourage informed critical attitudes, 4, 355
    Encourage pop to classical crossover, 4, 358
    Enhance professional vocal training, 4, 353
    Find performance research outcomes, 4, 357
    Help promising secondary school vocalists, 354
    Launch amateur Handel vocal contest, 4, 353
    Launch Campaign for real Singing, 4, 359

Chaste Singing, 29, 35, 40, 44, 47, 50, 58, 85, 91, 126, 140, 141, 145, 146, 147, 150, 157, 159, 164, 166, 174, 187, 222, 258

Conclusions, essential for early music singing
    Good *portamento di voce* vital, 10, 12, 16, 17, 21, 71, 115, 332
    High notes soft not loud, 11, 105
    Larynx high or neutral, 11, 102, 115, 117, 332
    Messa di voce vital, 11, 97
    Registral exploitation, males & females, 11, 101
    Shake correctly performed, 11, 93, 95
    Straight tone by default, 11, 84, 90, 284, 333
    Vibrato, expressive not constant, 81, 90, 211

Early Music Directors/Groups
    Capricornus Consort Basel, 337
    Currentzis, Teodor, MusicAeterna, 336, 338
    Fasolis, Diego, 338, 352
    Hogwood, Christopher, 336, 337
    Holman, Dr. Peter, Ars Nova, Parley of Instruments, 1, 336, 354
    Michael Morrow & John Beckett, Musica Reservata, 1, 92, 352
    Rosa Solis, 336, 338
    Sete Lágrimas, 358

Facebook Contributors, 335
    Abadie, Lisandro, 68
    Badagnani, David, 268, 337, 338, 342, 343, 344, 349
    Bayliss, Mike, 347
    Benson-Wilson, Andrew, 334, 356
    Bolger, Joe, 351
    Braithwaite, Tim, 17, 347
    Clapton, Nicholas, 81
    Evans, Roger, 350
    Hansell, David, 350
    Hummus, Max, 351
    Kennaway, George, 349
    Miehling, Klaus, 348
    Montagu, Jeremy, 348
    Moraitis, John, 348
    O'Reilly, Graham, 17, 350
    Pittaway, Ian, 348
    Poletti, Paul, 345, 348
    Pontifex, Christopher Price, 337, 333, 348
    Rawson, Robert, 347, 348
    Robins, Brian, 334, 349, 356
    Skeaping, Alexander, 349
    Spaink, Martin, 349
    St Martin, Colin, 350
    Tikker, Timothy, 349, 353
    Webber, Oliver, 351

Falsetto, Use or Avoidance
    21st C, 335, 338, 341
    Long 18th C, 11, 31, 71, 103, 105, 110, 113, 293, 332
    Long 19th C, 293, 294, 295, 299, 302, 305, 308, 310, 317, 333, 334

Gladstone, William Ewart
    Pitch forced up, causing vibrato, 257

Heart Appeal, Castrati
    Caffarelli, Gaetano Mairorano, 26
    Conti, Gioachino Gizziello, 26
    Crescentini, Girolamo, 30
    Farinelli, Carlo Broschi, 25
    Millico, Giuseppe, 28
    Orsini, Gaetano, 23
    Pacchierotti, Gasparo, 28
    Rubinelli, Giovanni, 29

Heart Appeal, Men
    Bartleman, James, 58, 234, 241

Braham, John, 173
Curioni, Alberico, 174
Harrison, Samuel, 55
Nourrit, Adolphe, 183
Phillips, Henry, 183
Tramezzani, Diomiro, 59
Vaughan, Thomas, 61

Heart Appeal, Women
Agujari, Lucrezia, 37
Alboni, Marietta, 222
Banti, Brigida Georgi, 41
Billington, Elizabeth, 44
Bland, Maria Theresa, 44
Camporese, Violante, 48
Caradori-Allan, Maria, 145
Carew, Miss, 51
Catalani, Angelica, 47
Cibber, Susannah Maria, 34
Cinti-Damoreau, Laure, 148
Colbran, Angela Isabella, 48
Crouch, Anna Maria, 43
Cuzzoni, Francesca, 33
Dolby, Charlotte, 165
Fodor-Mainvielle, Josephine, 140
Gabrielli, Caterina, 35, 42
Grassini, Josephina, 45
Hayes, Catherine, 156
Lind, Jenny, 163
Linley, Elizabeth, 41
Lotti, Stella, 32
Mara, Gertrud Elizabeth, 40
Novello, Clara, 159
Oldmixon, Amelie, 44
Pasta, Giuditta, 144
Paton, Mary Anne, then Mrs Wood, 148
Pisaroni, Benedetta Rosmunda, 140
Poole, Eliza, 152, 153, 164
Postans, Mary, 155
Pyne, Louisa, 168
Salmon, Eliza, 49
Sontag, Henrietta Nina, 149
Stephens, Catherine, 141, 142
Tennant, Miss, then Mrs Vaughan, 50
Travis, Deborah then Mrs Knyvett, 146
Weber, Aloysia, 80

Historically Informed Practice
Early Signs, 135, 247, 357

Instrumental Models for Singers
Besozzi, Carlo, Oboe, 80, 86
Cartwright, Violin, 88
Christian, Johann, Oboe, 80
Eklund, Nicklas, Trumpet, 336, 338
Jarnovich, Violin, 88
Jeronimo, Organ Flute Stop, 21, 76, 357
Lebrun, Ludwig August, Oboe, 42
Lindley, Robert, Cello, 58
Löffler, Xenia, Oboe, 337, 350
Ramm, Friedrich, Oboe, 80
Vieuxtemps, Henri, Violin, 88

Instruments, similar to voices
Æolian harp, 16, 74, 86, 87, 125, 187
Bassoon, 16, 86, 172
Bell, 16, 21, 27, 31, 65, 77, 80, 84, 91, 149, 155, 158, 161, 163, 165, 169, 171, 189, 190, 193, 195, 197, 198, 203, 224, 235, 259, 260, 305, 323, 324
Bugle or trumpet, 16, 40, 46
Clarinet, 77, 163, 171, 208, 260
Flageolet, 16, 43, 44, 77, 139, 145
Flute, 43, 51, 56, 77, 95, 103, 106, 140, 147, 148, 151, 159, 161, 163, 164, 166, 171, 179, 189, 192, 200, 201, 259, 300, 357
Glass Harmonica, 16, 31, 36, 46, 49, 55, 65, 86, 87, 88, 106, 141, 144, 148, 162
Oboe, 42, 77, 141, 144, 148, 176, 200, 259, 350
Organ, 21, 37, 46, 63, 76, 91, 167, 205, 262, 344, 345, 357
Trumpet, 77, 149, 160, 161, 163, 174, 260, 261, 330, 338

Large Spaces, Vocal Audibility, 4, 10, 21, 88, 105, 108, 109, 144, 275, 357
Caradori-Allan, Maria, 108
Knyvett, William, 61
Novello, Clara, 160
Salmon, Eliza, 107

Tietjens, Theresa, 171

Luscious Singing
    Foody Comparisons, 15, 134, 166, 188, 189, 195, 263, 275, 297

National Singing Methods, 18C Long
    English, 94, 121, 208
    French, 3, 9, 69, 78, 113, 115, 126, 131, 208
    German, 208
    Italian, 9, 10, 16, 19, 113, 115, 121, 126, 175, 208

Opera House Style, Traditional Modern, 2, 269, 333, 347, 348, 353, 357, 358

Pitch, mid 19th C
    Raised pitch levels, 4, 137, 257

Recitative
    Should be spoken not sung, 38, 55, 75, 76, 127, 130, 131, 168, 182
    Should be sung not spoken, 155, 163, 170

Recordings, Streaming Sources
    Soundcloud, 335
    Spotify and YouTube, 335

Rock and Baroque Rhythm Sections, 342

Singers1, 18C Long, Castrati
    Annibali, Domenico, 22, 24, 117
    Aprile, Giuseppe, 27, 72, 80, 97
    Astolfi, 22
    Bernacchi, Antonio, 24
    Berselli, Matteo, 104, 117, 124
    Buzzoleni, Giovanni, 70
    Caffarelli, Gaetano Mairorano, 21, 22, 25, 247
    Carestini, Giovanni, 21, 22, 24, 26, 81, 91, 104, 234
    Conti, Gioachino Gizziello, 22, 26, 99, 104
    Crescentini, Girolamo, 21, 22, 27, 30, 99, 124, 166
    Farinelli, Carlo Broschi, 21, 22, 24, 25, 26, 30, 91, 93, 97, 98, 104, 124, 247, 338
    Ferri, Baldassare, 10, 22, 91
    Guadagni, Gaetano, 21, 27, 35, 124, 125
    Jeronimo, 21, 22, 76, 91, 357
    Luigino, Signor, 70, 352
    Manzuoli, Giovanni, 21, 22, 26
    Marchesi, Luigi, 22, 27, 30, 91, 95, 97, 118, 124
    Matteuccio, Matteo, 22, 23
    Millico, Giuseppe, 27, 28
    Nicolini, Nicolo Grimaldi, 21, 22, 23, 26, 98
    Orsini, Gaetano, 21, 22, 23, 91, 97
    Pacchierotti, Gasparo, 15, 27, 28, 42, 91, 94, 97, 99, 104, 179
    Pasi, Antonio, 22, 24
    Pasqualini, 21, 22
    Patroni, Mariano, 22
    Pauluccio, 21, 22
    Pistocchi, Francesco Antonio, 24, 69
    Rauzzini, Venanzio, 19, 21, 27, 29, 35, 55, 97, 124
    Roncaglia, Francesco, 27, 29, 97, 104
    Rubinelli, Giovanni, 27, 29, 42, 97, 104, 127
    Senesino, Francesco Barnardi, 22, 23, 24, 25, 26, 28, 91, 97, 124, 126, 127
    Siface, Giovanni Grossi, 22, 23, 70, 98
    Tarquini, 22
    Tenducci, Ferdinando, 27, 28, 51
    Terri, 22
    Velluti, Giovanni Battista, 27, 30, 64, 104

Singers1, 18C Long, Ensemble, 62
    Bohemian Brothers, 64, 66, 86, 87
    Hungarian Singers, 64
    Les Trois Troubadours, 64
    Singers of the Alps, 64
    Sistine Chapel choir, 87
    Spray family, 118
    Tyrolese Minstrels, 64

Singers1, 18C Long, Men
    Adamberger, Johann Valentin, 81
    Ambrogetti, Giuseppe, 129
    Angrisani, Carlo, 52, 57, 124
    Ansani, Giovanni, 28, 52
    Bannister, Charles, 51, 52, 56
    Bartleman, James, 16, 52, 55, 58, 62, 63, 83, 91, 104, 124, 135, 182
    Beard, John, 51, 56, 127
    Beaumavielle, François, 75
    Begrez, Pierre Ignace, 52, 62
    Bellamy, Richard, 63, 64, 124

Benson, Mr, 214
Braham, John, 173
Crivelli, Domenico Francesco Maria, 177
David, Giacomo, 28
Dibdin, Charles, 127
Dignum, Charles, 52, 56, 118
Doyle, Mr, 119
Duruset, John B, 120
Fischer, Johann Ignaz, 52, 53, 104
Geni, Signor, 213
Goss, John Jeremiah, 52, 58
Harrison, Samuel, 52, 54, 58, 61, 62, 63, 86, 91, 97, 99, 111, 124
Hill, James, 213
Incledon, Charles Benjamin, 2, 52, 55, 77, 97, 102, 104, 112, 124, 128, 177, 179, 213
Isaacs, Mr J, 119
Johnstone, John Henry, 52, 54
Knox, Mr, 105
Knyvett, William, 52, 55, 59, 61, 63, 91, 95
Lacy, Mr, 124
Lainée, M, 114
Matthews, Mr, 120
Meissner, Joseph, 78, 234
Miarteni, Signor, 20, 213, 234
Miartini, Signor, 20
Millar, Mr, 295
Miller, Mr, 119
Naldi, Giuseppe, 57, 128
Norris, Mr, 118
Nozzari, Andrea, 108, 175
Pearman, William, 77, 86, 87, 120, 178, 179, 289
Pellegrini, Felice, 52, 58
Placci, Signor, 57
Plumer, Mr, 120, 132
Ponchard, M, 119
Porto, Mathieu, 52, 60, 64, 327
Raaff, Anton, 108
Remorini, Ranieri, 52, 57, 58, 62, 124, 132
Sale, Mr, 124
Skelton, Mr, 63
Smith, J, 111, 119, 213

Stansbury, Mr, 120
Thévenard, Gabriel Vincent, 75, 118
Tramezzani, Diomiro, 20, 52, 59
Vaughan, Thomas, 52, 61, 63, 91, 97, 103, 124
Viganoni, Giuseppe, 52, 53, 59, 174

Singers1, 18C Long, Women
Agujari, Lucrezia, 2, 31, 37, 39, 80, 95, 97, 103, 125, 204
Albert, Madame, 114
Allegranti, Maddalena, 39, 41, 43, 125
Amicis, Anna de, 31, 38, 42, 80
Antier, Marie, 113
Arne, Cecilia, Mrs, Née Young, 127, 357
Astrua, Giovanna, 39
Austin, Elizabeth, 285, 323
Bacon, Jane, 103, 106
Banti, Brigida Georgi, 39, 41, 43, 53, 97, 106, 125, 144
Bellchambers, Mrs, 128
Bellochi, Georgia, 39, 48, 129
Bertinotti, Teresa, 18, 39, 45, 128
Billington, Elizabeth, 39, 43, 44, 45, 46, 47, 63, 76, 97, 99, 103, 106, 127, 131, 144, 172, 213
Blacket, Mrs, 214, 229
Bland, Dorothea, then Miss Francis, then Mrs Jordan, 128
Bland, Maria Theresa, 39, 44, 97, 125, 128, 130, 131
Bonini, Signora, 215, 216
Bordoni, Faustina, 31, 33, 39, 70, 97, 99, 127, 234, 247
Boschi, Francesca Vanini, 32
Branchia, Madame, 114
Buggins, Miriam Hammersley, 112
Byrne, Miss, 214
Camporese, Violante, 48, 97, 106, 107, 112, 119, 125, 147
Canonici, Madame, 129
Carew, Miss, 39, 51, 76, 77, 91, 95, 97, 106, 132
Catalani, Angelica, 2, 18, 20, 39, 45, 46, 47,

77, 83, 86, 88, 89, 91, 97, 99, 103, 106, 123, 125, 128, 140, 148, 154, 158, 217, 229, 234, 339, 355
Catley, Anne, 31, 38
Cecconi, Signora, 308
Childe, Mrs, 87
Cibber, Susannah Maria, 27, 31, 34, 125, 126
Colbran, Angela Isabella, 18, 39, 48, 97, 99, 106, 108, 129, 131, 311
Cornega, Madame, 120
Crouch, Anna Maria, 39, 43, 50, 131
Cuzzoni, Francesca, 31, 32, 39, 70, 91, 97, 99, 125
Davies, Cecilia, 31, 35, 36, 86, 92, 95, 97
De Lihu, Demoiselles, 229
Frasi, Giulia, 31, 35, 97, 127, 353
Gabrielli, Caterina, 31, 35, 42, 80, 99
Galli, Catherine, 68
Grassini, Josephina, 14, 39, 44, 111, 118, 125
Greene, Miss, 128, 214
Hallande, Miss, 120
Hoffer, Josepha, 103
Holman, Mrs, 214
Kaiser, Mlle, 80
Kelly, Miss, 129
Kemble, Miss, 128
Knyvett, Deborah, née Travis, 18, 63
Lacey, Bianchi, Mrs, 129
Le Brun, Francesca, 39, 42, 77, 103, 125, 357
Lemaure, Catherine-Nicole, 113
Linley, Elizabeth, 11, 35, 39, 40, 91, 97, 127
Lotti, Stella, 31, 32, 97, 353
Mara, Gertrud Elizabeth, 2, 39, 40, 41, 44, 46, 83, 97, 103, 106, 124, 125, 127
Mel, Marie, 31, 34
Minutolo, Matilde, 42
Mombelli, Ester, 39, 50
Mountain, Rosemond, Née Wilkinson, 131
Oldmixon, Amelie, née George, 39, 44, 77, 97, 103, 104, 106, 127
Pélissier, Marie, 113
Poole, Maria, 18, 39, 45, 87, 118, 131, 213
Saint-Huberti, Antoinette, 114
Salmon, Eliza, 12, 18, 39, 49, 86, 87, 91, 95, 97, 106, 107, 111, 117, 122, 125, 132, 141, 150, 214, 357
Schutz, Madame, 216
Sessi, Madame, 111
Sestini, Giovanna, later Joanna Stocqueler, 234
Storace, Nancy, 50, 127
Strada, Anna Maria, 26
Tofts, Catherine, 31, 32
Tramontini, Vittoria Tesi, 31, 34, 91, 247
Vaughan, Mrs née Tennant, 39, 50
Weber, Aloysia, 39, 42, 80
Weichsell, Frederica, 77
Wilson, Miss, 132

Singers2, 19C, Men
Adams, Charles, 291, 302
Aldighieri, Gottardo, 290, 306
Allen, Mr, 299
Ambrogetti, Giuseppe, 60, 229, 289
Amodio, Signor, 231
Ander, Aloys, 324
Aramburo, Antonio, 291, 307, 329
Arimondi, Vittorio, 292
Arnaud, M, 297
Atkins, Mr, 130
Barroilhet, Paul, 290
Beaucardé, Signor, 299
Beaumont, Mr, 302
Benedetti, Octave, 108, 299, 307
Bettini, Geronimo, 302, 306
Bianchi, Gaetano, 302
Bland, Mr C, 130
Bodda, Franks, 230
Bordogni, Giulio, 289
Bottero, Signor, 232
Bouhy, Jacques, 291
Braham, Charles, 324
Braham, John, 16, 46, 47, 54, 59, 61, 77, 83, 84, 87, 95, 97, 99, 102, 104, 111, 123, 124, 128, 129, 131, 136, 171, 175, 193, 218, 234, 289, 299, 300, 324, 355
Brennir, Mr, 302

Brignoli, Pasquilino, 196, 290, 302, 303, 304, 307
Broadhurst, Mr, 130
Cabero, Signor, 307
Calzolari, Enrico, 290, 328
Campanini, Italo, 76, 196, 250, 264, 265, 284, 291, 302, 304, 305, 325, 329
Candidus, William, 262, 291, 302, 304, 323, 330
Carpi, Signor, 190, 325
Caruso, Enrico, 269, 280
Catone, Signor, 299
Chavonnes Vrugt, Willem Pasques de, 327
Colini, Filippo, 226, 290
Conti, Signor, 306
Cossira, Émile, 249
Cotogni, Antonio, 226, 232, 291, 302
Crivelli, Gaetano, 129, 174, 176, 289
Crotty, Leslie, 292
Cummings, William H, 259, 261, 275, 291
Curioni, Alberico, 62, 174, 289
David, Giovanni, 97, 175, 176, 289, 297
Davies, William, 330
de Begnis, Giuseppe, 91, 179, 289
de Reszké, Jean, 198, 265, 268, 284, 291, 302, 305, 326
Del Puente, Giuseppe, 291
Dérivis, Nicolas-Prosper, 58, 115
Devoyod, Jules Célestien, 291
Dobler, M, 120
Donizelli, Domenico, 77, 99, 125, 130, 176, 178, 181, 185, 189, 190, 193, 217, 241, 289, 306, 327
Dufriche, Eugène, 291, 308
Duprez, Gilbert, 185, 186, 191, 260, 289, 294, 295, 297, 299, 300, 305, 306, 316, 327
Engel, Emile, 237, 291
Eugene, Max, 330
Fancelli, Giuseppe, 261, 265, 291, 302
Faure, Jean-Baptiste, 225, 228, 234, 290, 329
Ferri, Signor, 231, 247, 307
Flavio, Signor, 299
Foli, Alan James, 226, 291, 302, 307
Formes, Karl Johann, 170, 225, 290, 299
Fornasari, Luciano, 219, 260, 263, 290, 297, 299, 305, 316
Fraschini, Gaetano, 290, 294, 295, 299, 301, 305, 316, 327
Galer, Elliott, 299, 302
Galli, Filippo, 58, 118, 289
Galvani, Giacomo, 290
Gambetti, Signor, 233
Garcia 1, Manuel, 120, 173, 174, 176, 289
Gardoni, Italo, 193, 200, 225, 230, 290, 297, 299, 301
Gayárre, Julian, 135, 233, 291, 302, 304, 330
Geary, Gustavus, 299, 301
Giuglini, Antonio, 169, 194, 195, 197, 208, 222, 260, 265, 290, 299, 306
Graziani, Lodovico, 226, 290, 307, 324
Gudehus, Heinrich, 262, 291
Gustave-Hippolyte, Roger, 225, 290, 299
Haigh, Henry, 291, 302, 304
Haitzinger, Anton, 187, 289, 306, 324, 326
Harley, Orlando, 326
Harrison, William, 192, 299
Hawkins, Mr, 296, 299
Hedmondt, Charles, 252, 284, 302, 331
Henschel, George, 292
Horn, Charles Edward, 97, 119, 175, 289
Ivanhoff, Nicola, 186, 290, 296, 299, 300
Kaschmann, Giuseppe, 252, 291
Keith, William, 252
Lablache, Luigi, 58, 125, 179, 180, 289, 295, 305, 323
Levasseur, M, 327
Lhérie, Paul, 291
Lloyd, Edward, 291, 302
Lorrain, Signor, 237, 238
Ludwig, William, 252, 291
Maas, Joseph, 197, 260, 291, 302, 305, 329
Mario, Giovanni, 154, 186, 188, 189, 190, 192, 193, 195, 196, 218, 220, 222, 240, 241, 258, 260, 265, 284, 290, 297, 298, 299, 300, 327
Marras, Giacinto, 290

Masini, Signor, 224, 256
Massett, Stephen C, 290, 299
Maurel, Victor, 226, 250, 291
McGuckin, Barton, 292, 302, 330
Medini, Signor, 224, 256
Mendioroz, Signor, 234, 292
Mierzwinski, Wladyslaw, 262, 291, 302, 305, 330
Mockridge, Whitney, 292, 330
Mongini, Pietro, 265, 290, 302, 303, 307
Moriani, Napoleone, 192, 260, 289, 294, 295, 297, 299, 327
Naudin, Emilio, 225, 290, 302, 303, 305, 316, 327
Negrini, Signor, 306
Neri-Baraldi, Pietro, 200, 261, 290, 302
Nicolini, Ernesto, 226, 228, 233, 249, 291, 302
Nordblom, Henry, 302, 329
Nourrit, Adolphe, 183, 185, 289, 294, 296, 327
Packard, Fred C, 329
Paladini, Signor, 302
Pantaleoni, Signor, 219
Parry, John, 290, 299
Perren, George, 225, 290, 299
Petit, M, 226, 228, 232
Phillips, Henry, 107, 131, 182, 289, 326
Pierpoint, Bantock, 331
Pischek, Johann Baptist, 189, 290, 299
Rawner, Signor, 252, 308
Reeve, John, 295
Reeves, Sims, 94, 135, 190, 192, 193, 194, 197, 228, 235, 236, 242, 257, 270, 274, 290, 299, 300, 302, 303, 304, 322, 327
Reichardt, Herr, 170, 299, 301
Ronconi, Giorgio, 223, 290
Rousbey, Arthur, 292
Rubini, Giovanni Battista, 97, 181, 184, 185, 186, 187, 188, 189, 190, 191, 216, 218, 219, 237, 247, 253, 260, 263, 264, 289, 297, 298, 299
Salvi, Lorenzo, 192, 240, 294, 297, 299, 300

Santini, Vincenzo-Felice, 289, 327
Sapio, Lewis Bernard Sapio, 61, 62, 77, 94, 97, 117, 123, 124, 129, 174, 289
Shakespeare, William, 226, 291
Shrivall, Mr, 299
Siboni, Giuseppe, 59, 118, 213, 289
Sinclair, John, 91, 95, 97, 111, 124, 129, 178, 214, 289
Squires, Henry, 302, 328
Stagno, Robert, 226, 291, 330
Staudigl, Joseph, 225, 289, 299
Steffani, Signor, 307
Stockhausen, Herr, 325
Stretton, Mr, 327
Suane, Signor, 135
Superchi, Antonio, 260, 290
Sylva, Signor, 234
Talazac, Jean Alexandre, 292
Tamberlik, Enrico, 190, 191, 192, 195, 219, 230, 241, 261, 263, 264, 284, 290, 299, 307
Tamburini, Antonio, 219, 289, 299
Templeton, John, 184, 192, 218, 289, 327
Thorne, Mr, 215
Tiberini, Signor, 302
Tichatschek, Joseph, 222, 290, 324
Tournié, M, 228, 302
Travers, Mr, 306
Valero, Ferdinand, 292
Villani, Signor, 232
Vizzani, Signor, 291, 302
Wachtel, Theodore, 261, 290, 302, 305, 307, 324
Werth, M, 121
Wiegand, Heinrich, 291
Wild, Herren, 324
Wilson, Mr, 299
Zucchelli, Carlo, 94, 289, 326

Singers2, 19C, Women
Abbott, Emma, 288
Adini, Ada, 288
Albert, Madame, 228
Albertazzi, Emma, 136, 137, 286, 308, 310

Alboni, Marietta, 18, 134, 161, 162, 166, 167, 222, 223, 231, 240, 262, 263, 264, 268, 286, 309, 327, 328
Alvsleben, Melitta, 171, 258, 259, 287, 310
Amadei, Giulia, 263, 286
Ambré, Emilie, 238
Arnoldson, Sigrid, 288
Ayton, Fanny, 130
Barbieri, Marianna, 286
Basta-Tavary, Marie, 265
Battu, Marie, 226, 231, 287
Bauer, Jenny, 232
Bauermeister, Mathilde, 288
Beaucarde, Augusta née Albertini, 286
Beauclerk, Annie, 325
Birch, Charlotte, 76, 85, 87, 97
Biscaccianti, Elisa, 286
Bishop, Anna, 152, 153, 162, 232, 286
Blaes, Meerti, 136, 308
Blasis, Virginie, 77, 97, 106, 109, 125, 146
Bloch, Rosine, 287
Boccabadati, Luigia, 285
Bonheur, Stella, 228
Borelli, Medea, 288
Borghese, Signora, 230, 240
Borghi-Mamo, Adelaide, 222, 287
Bosio, Angiolina, 200, 222, 224, 263, 287, 328
Brambilla, Marietta, 285
Brema, Marie, 288
Bürde-Ney, Jenny, 286
Burns, Georgina, 198, 288
Cabel, Marie, 227, 286, 309
Caradori-Allan, Maria, 18, 76, 97, 99, 106, 108, 109, 117, 126, 130, 145, 147, 285, 339, 357
Carandini, Rosina, 264, 287
Carey, Annie Louise, 287
Carpenter, Miss, 326
Cary, Anne Louise, 224
Castellan, Anaida, 260, 286, 310, 327
Cawse, Miss, 120, 130, 286
Centroni, Signora, 130
Cinti-Damoreau, Laure, 18, 77, 86, 88, 97, 106, 109, 115, 125, 129, 147, 260, 285
Cole, Blanche, 228, 288
Colson, Miss, 231
Cooke, Harriet, 285
Cordner, Mrs, 224
Corri, Frances, 63, 285
Corri, Rosalie, 63, 111, 130, 285
Cruvelli, Sophie, 169, 287, 310
Csillag, Róza, 222, 287
Cubitt, Maria Caroline, 131, 285
D'Alton, Helen, 325
D'Ambroise, Emilie née Ambré, 288
D'Angeri, Anna, 224, 288
D'Angri, Elena, 286
de Begnis, Giuseppina Ronzi, 20, 77, 103, 106, 109, 122, 126, 129, 144, 147, 152, 259, 339
De Fonblanque, Miss, 233
de la Grange, Anna, 220, 221, 263, 286, 309, 310, 314, 325
De Lussan, Zélie, 265, 288
de Murska, Ilma, 223, 251, 287, 311
De Reszke, Joséphine, 288
Delcy, Catherine, 286
Dolby, Charlotte, 165, 183, 286
Donadio, Bianca, 288
Doria, Madame, 221
Dorus Gras, July, 285, 326
Dustmann-Meyer, Louise, 287
Enequist, Mathilde, 170, 287
Escott, Lucy, 221, 287
Ettinger, Rose Alice, 310
Falcon, Cornélie, 286
Favanti, Rita née Edwards, 286
Ferni-Germano, Virginia, 288
Feron, Elizabeth, 111, 216, 285
Fiorentini, Claudina, 286, 310
Fodor-Mainvielle, Josephine, 18, 48, 63, 76, 106, 112, 115, 125, 139, 144, 285, 341
Frezzolini, Erminia, 313
Fricci, Antoinetta, 223, 287
Friedländer, Thekla, 264, 287
Gassier, Josefa, 231

Gazzaniga, Marietta, 286, 314
Gerster, Ethelka, 138, 262, 288, 310
Gianoli, Lorenzini, Madame, 314
Gillies, Ida, 223, 228, 314
Gordosa, Fanny, Née Botibol, 241
Graddon, Miss, 130
Grattan, Mrs, 327
Greenfield, Elizabeth, 286, 309
Grisi, Giulia, 18, 136, 152, 153, 154, 162, 167, 171, 229, 240, 241, 258, 286, 311, 328
Grossi, Carlotta, 226, 228, 311
Guarducci, Carolina, 328
Guidotti, Emilia, 239
Hauk, Minnie, 288, 312
Hawes, Maria, 286, 309
Hayes, Catherine, 18, 107, 156, 158, 164, 224, 286, 310
Heilbron, Marie, 233, 288
Henschel, Lilian June née Bailey, 239, 288
Hensler, Elise, 221, 287
Hersee, Rose, 232, 287
Heygendorf, Madlle, 109, 111
Hochheimer, Bertha, 330
Hughes, Miss, 112, 132, 285, 323
Inverarity, Elizabeth, 120, 132, 286
Isaacs, Rebecca, 285, 286
Joachim, Amalie, 262
Kellogg, Clara Louise, 138, 197, 223, 287
Knyvett, Deborah, née Travis, 2, 63, 97, 108, 111, 119, 125, 129, 145
Krauss, Gabrielle, 230
Kupfer-Berger, Mila, 288
L'Allemand, Pauline, 236
La Rue, Lilian, 330
Lablache, Demeric, 226, 231
Lascelles, Miss, 324
Lemaire, Madame, 231
Lemmens-Sherrington, Helen, 287, 309
Liebhart, Mdlle, 232
Lind, Jenny, 18, 86, 109, 154, 156, 158, 161, 162, 163, 167, 168, 193, 199, 200, 240, 260, 265, 285, 286, 309, 323, 324, 327
Litvinne, Félia, 288

Loëwe, Sophie, 286
Love, Emma Sarah, 122, 285
Lucca, Pauline, 223, 287, 311
MacIntyre, Margaret, 265
Malibran, Maria, 18, 77, 85, 88, 97, 107, 109, 136, 143, 150, 152, 153, 155, 161, 180, 183, 217, 224, 241, 258, 285, 312
Mantelli, Eugenia, 288
Marimon, Marie, 261, 287
Marschner, Mademoiselle, 313
Materna, Amalie, 287
May, Alice, 233
Medori, Giuseppina, 221, 230, 286, 328
Meisslinger, Louise, 288
Méric-Lalande, Henriette, 216, 217, 227, 263, 285, 313, 326
Meyer, Sophie, 287
Miolan/Carvalho, Marie, 168, 222, 241, 286, 309
Morandi, Signora, 48
Moulton, Mrs Charles, 275
Nantier-Didiée, Constance, 222, 287
Natali-Testa, Mdlle, 233
Nau, Dolores, 286
Ney /Bürde, Jenny, 169, 170, 328
Nilsson, Christine, 138, 224, 261, 263, 265, 287, 311
Nordica, Lillian, 265, 288
Norton, Miss, 232
Nott, Cicely, 230
Novello, Clara, 18, 86, 88, 107, 135, 158, 159, 160, 171, 183, 230, 233, 258, 265, 286, 310, 323
Orgeni, Aglaja, 135
Ortolani-Tiberini, Angiolina, 222, 287, 314
Panorma, Madame, 229
Pappenheim, Eugénie, 288
Parepa Rosa, Euphrosine, 88, 222, 275, 287, 325
Pasini/Gassier, Josefa, 200, 223, 231, 286, 310
Pasta, Giuditta, 83, 86, 97, 103, 106, 108, 122, 125, 130, 140, 143, 144, 150, 151,

153, 169, 229, 285, 310, 311, 312, 313, 339
Patey-Whytock, Janet, 223, 287, 314
Paton, Mary Ann, 18, 77, 85, 95, 97, 106, 125, 132, 143, 148, 229, 285, 326, 357
Patti, Carlotta, 287
Penco, Rosina, 222, 286
Persiani, Fanny, 136, 152, 156, 258, 260, 286, 299, 310, 324
Peschka, Minna née Von Leutner, 287
Phillipps, Adelaide, 285, 287, 328
Piccolomini, Marietta, 200, 287, 306
Pisaroni, Benedetta Rosmunda, 18, 49, 97, 99, 125, 131, 140, 285, 309
Poole, Eliza, 163, 164, 285, 286
Postans, Mary, 18, 136, 154, 156, 183, 286, 308
Povey, Miss, 86, 87, 106, 285
Pyne, Louisa, 167, 169, 286, 309, 328
Rainforth, Elizabeth, 286
Reboux, Madlle, 228
Redeker, Louise, 234
Reeves, Emma née Lucombe, 286
Rita, Pauline, 224, 287
Robinson, Eleonora, 262
Rollwagen, Louise, 325
Romer, Anne, 313
Rossi, Giovanna, 286
Rossini, Paolina, 330
Roze, Marie, 224, 287
Rudersdorff, Hermine, 223, 225, 231, 241, 286, 329
Russell, Lillian, 275
Sala, Adelaida, 111
Sanderson, Sybil, 288, 314
Sasse, Marie, 287
Scalchi, Sofia, 224, 288
Schechner, Nanette, 125, 285
Schimon-Regan, Anna, 223, 235, 287
Schou, Mdlle, 312
Schröder /Devrient, Wilhelmine, 170, 285, 327
Sessi, Mathilde, 314

Sessi, Moriana, 285
Shirreff, Miss, 99
Sigl-Vespermann, Katharina, 216, 217, 285, 310
Singer, Teresina, 256, 288, 329
Sofia, Fraulein, 230
Soldene, Emily, 287
Sontag, Henrietta Nina, 18, 77, 95, 97, 99, 107, 109, 125, 131, 136, 149, 151, 152, 159, 161, 163, 168, 199, 240, 241, 258, 285, 310, 323, 325, 327
Spezia-Aldighieri, Maria, 220, 221, 222, 263, 314
St. George, Julia, 286
Steffanone, Balbina, 221, 286
Stephens, Catherine, 18, 50, 51, 86, 91, 97, 106, 108, 111, 122, 125, 128, 141, 144, 215, 285
Sterling, Antoinette, 287
Stockhausen, Margaretha, 106, 149, 187, 285
Stöckl-Heinefetter, Klara, 170, 286
Stoltz, Teresa, 224, 243, 256
Strinasacchi, Teresa, 285
Sunderland, Mrs, 229, 230
Tadolini, Eugénie, 285, 299
Tedesco, Fortunata, 230, 286
Thalberg, Zaré, 261, 288
Thomas, Effie, 238
Thursby, Emma, 287
Tietjens, Thérèse, 135, 165, 169, 170, 171, 222, 261, 262, 265, 287, 310, 311, 312, 316, 323
Tonnellier, Annie née Milner, 287
Tosi, Adelaide, 229, 285
Toso-Puzzi, Giacinta, 285
Trebelli/Bettini, Zelia, 265, 287
Tree, Anna Maria, 214, 215, 285
Truffi, Teresa, 221
Tuczek-Herrenberg, Leopoldine, 230
Ugalde-Baucé, Delphine, 227, 287
Valleria, Alwina, 224, 288
Van den heuvel Duprez, Caroline, 287, 309
Van Zandt, Marie, 138, 288

Vestris, Lucia Elizabeth, 94, 97, 106, 125, 131, 142, 285
Vestvali, Madame, 328
Viardot, Pauline, 222, 286, 299, 310, 327, 328
Vilda, Maria, 135, 311
Vinning, Louisa, 284, 287
Wagner, Johanna, 260, 286, 328
Waldmann, Maria, 224, 256, 287
Wilkinson, Mrs, 106, 108, 122, 285
Williams, Miss M, 309
Williams, Misses, 229
Wippern, Harriers, 227
Woodyatt, Emily, 286
Wright, Mrs John B, 239
Wyndham, Fanny, 76, 99, 136, 286, 308
Zagury, Laura née Harris, 287
Zerr, Anna, 221, 286, 310
Zilli, Emma, 288

Singers3, Early Recorded, Men
Alvarez, Albert, 292, 326, 331
Ancona, Mario, 292
Bispham, David, 198, 307, 326, 331
Black, Andrew, 209, 269, 292
Bockelmann, Rudolph, 280
Bonci, Allesandro, 239
Borgioli, Dino, 277
Boyce, Bruce, 282
Brownlee, John, 277, 282
Brownlow, Wallace, 292
Capoul, Victor, 207, 208, 228, 269, 291, 302, 304, 329
Caruso, Enrico, 253, 280
Cattadori, Ferdinando, 292
d'Andrade, António, 292
Davies, Benjamin, 302, 305, 331
Davies, Tudor, 326, 332
de Lucia, Fernando, 292
De Marchi, Emilio, 292
de Reszké, Édouard, 265, 268, 292, 302
Dimitresco, Jean, 292
Dippel, Andreas, 292
Feinhals, Fritz, 292
Formby, George, 326, 332
Garbin, Edoardo, 292
Gigli, Beniamino, 277
Greene, Plunket, 326, 331
Hackett, Charles, 277
Heddle-Nash, William, 277
Herbert, William, 282
Hislop, Joseph, 277
Ibos, William, 292, 331
Lewis, Richard, 282
McCormack, John, 326, 331
Merli, Francesco, 277
Micheletti, Gaston, 282
Murray, Billy, 269
O'Sullivan, Dennis, 252
Pinza, Ezio, 277
Plançon, Pol, 198
Santley, Charles, 58, 194, 207, 225, 226, 241, 265, 269, 291
Scaramberg, Émile, 239
Schipa, Tito, 277
Schmidt, Joseph, 277
Stabile, Mariano, 277
Tamagno, Francesco, 291, 307, 308, 326, 331
Tauber, Richard, 277
Thill, Georges, 277
Van Dyck, Ernest, 292
Vergnet, Edmond, 291
Watkin-Mills, Robert, 208, 269, 291

Singers3, Early Recorded, Women
Abendroth, Irene, 268, 269
Albani, Emma, 190, 201, 250, 265, 266, 268, 269, 288
Alda, Frances, 239
Anderson, Marian, 277
Austral, Florence, 277
Baillie, Isobel, 277
Beeth, Lola, 315
Bellincioni, Gemma, 288
Bonner, Eugenie, 250, 314
Bréval, Lucienne, 288, 326, 331
Butt, Clara, 268, 269
Calvé, Emma, 237, 288
Cebotari, Maria, 277

Cigna, Gina, 277
Crossley, Ada, 205, 208, 269
Culp, Julia, 269
Dainton, Marie, 332
Dal Monte, Toti, 277
Dolores, Antonia, 208
Eames, Emma, 198, 237, 252, 288
Steber, E, 282
Esty, Alice, 288
Fabbri, Guerrina, 288
Flagstad, Kirsten, 281
Frodsham, Amy, 274
Fürsch-Madi, Emma, 288
Giannini, Dusolina, 277
Gomez, Alice, 237, 288
Hammond, Joan, 283
Hunt, Gertrude, 239
Jouve, Jean, 237
Kirkby-Lunn, Louise, 326, 331
Lehmann, Lilli, 268, 269, 277, 288
Leider, Frida, 280
Leigh, Adele, 282
Leslie, Isabel, 332
Macintyre, Margaret, 237, 288
Marchesi, Blanche, 204
Mazzi, Nini, 239
McKenzie, Marian, 288
Mei, Medea, 288
Melba, Nellie, 203, 204, 208, 237, 253, 274, 288
Morison, Elsie, 282
Nevada, Emma, 288
Onegin, Sigrid, 280
Patti, Adelina, 136, 138, 168, 199, 200, 201, 203, 205, 225, 231, 237, 265, 266, 269, 275, 287, 309, 312, 329
Pons, Lily, 277
Rethberg, Elisabeth, 277
Ritchie, Margaret, 282
Roman, Stella, 281
Schumann, Elisabeth, 277
Sheridan, Margaret B, 277
Supervia, Conchita, 277, 283

Templeton, Fay, 288
Ternina, Milka, 237, 288
Tetrazzini, Luisa, 326, 331
Teyte, Maggie, 277
Torbari, Carmen, 240
Trix, Helen, 268, 269
Yaw, Ellen Beach, 204, 268, 269, 288

Singers4, Contemp, Ensemble Classical
Ad Hoc group in Schütz, 344
Anonymous 4, 345
Ars Italica, 344
Asperger Beeblebrox, 345
Blue Heron, 344
Comedian Harmonists, 345
Curtis, Matthew, 344
Ensemble Doulce Mémoire, 344
Hespèrion XXI, 344
Hilliard Ensemble, 344
His Majestie's Clerkes, 345
Lautten Compagney, 344
Musica Antiqua of London, 344
Northern Harmony, 345
Organum, 344
Profeti Della Quinta, 344
Stimmwerck, 344
Swingle Singers, 345
Triphonia, 344
Tudor Choir, 345
VivaBiancaLuna Biffi, 344
Voces 8, 344
Vox Luminis, 344
Word of Mouth Chorus, 345

Singers4, Contemp, Men Classical
Benko, Pal, 335
Bündgen, Paulin, 335
Covey-Crump, Rogers, 344
Drabble, Roger, 335
Elliott, Paul, 337
Faria, Filipe, 335, 336, 358
Grigalis, Raitis, 335
James, David, 344
Jaroussky, Philippe, 336, 338
Jones, Gordon, 344

MacLeod, Stephan, 335
Mauillon, Marc, 335, 337, 358
Oliver, Robert, 354
Peixoto, Sérgio, 335, 336, 358
Phyfe, Owain, 335
Potter, John, 344
Spencer, Robert, 336
Sting, 335, 336, 358
Visse, Dominique, 335, 336
Wistreich, Richard, 354

Singers4, Contemp, Women Classical
Cassidy, Jennie, 336, 337
Chen, Peyee, 5, 7, 8, 12
Feuersinger, Miriam, 336, 337, 350, 358
Kirillova, Natalya, 336, 338, 358
Kirkby, Dame Emma, 6, 8, 268, 352, 354
Lebloch, Susanne, 335
Lee, Sigrid, 335
Léger, Magali, 336, 338, 358
Lezhneva, Julia, 336, 338
Melia, Jeni, 262, 335, 336
Oitzinger, Margot, 336
Popien, Elisabeth, 335
Ryden, Susanne, 336, 337
Sämann, Gerlinde, 336, 358
Sampson, Carolyn, 336
Skiba, Maria, 335
York, Deborah, 335

Singers5, Pop, Ensemble
Bluegrass Student Union, 345
Four Freshmen, 345
Four Teens, 345
Nina and Frederik, 345
The Flying Pickets, 345
The Jamies, 345
Vienna Teng & Ensemble, 345
Wilson, Brian & Hollens, Peter, 345

Singers5, Pop, Men
Barlow, Gary, 342
Bublé, Michel, 341, 345
Charles, Ray, 345
Cherone (Extreme), Gary, 342
Cullum, Jamie, 342, 358

Everly, Don & Everly, Phil, 342
Folds, Ben, 342
Gallagher, Liam, 341
Horan, Niall, 342
Lennon, John, 342
Levine (Maroon 5), Adam, 342, 358
Makrigiannis, Jannis, 342
Malik, Zayn, 342
Martin, Chris, 342, 358
Mikhail, Gavin, 342
Monahan (Train), Patrick, 342
Paisley, Brad, 342
Phillips, Phillip, 342, 358
Plaine, Austin, 342
Simon, Paul & Garfunkel, Art, 342
Sting, 342
Tamino, 342, 358
Tormé, Mel, 342
Travis, Randy, 342
Ward, Tyler, 342, 358
Warren-Adamson (Wise Children), Robin, 342, 358
Yates, Billy, 342

Singers5, Pop, Women
Acquilina, Lauren, 340
Ahn, Priscilla, 340
Aksnes, Aurora, 339, 340, 341, 358
Aplin, Gabrielle, 340
Boucher, Butterfly, 340
Carter, Betty, 345
Cassidy, Eva, 339, 341
Close, Sarah, 340, 358
Costello, Katie, 340, 341, 358
Dearie, Blossom, 339
Dido, 339
Drummond, Holly, 340
Fraley, Shelly, 339
Gilberto, Astrud, 339
Golan, Rosi, 340
Gomez, Selena, 340, 341
Grey, Skylar, 340, 341, 358
Heap, Imogen, 340
Holter, Julia, 340, 358

Jones, Norah, 340
Joyce, Sarah (Rumer), 340, 341, 358
Kirke, Lola, 340
Krall, Diana, 339, 345
Krauss, Alison, 339, 341, 342
Kripac, Lenka, 339, 340, 341
Lee, Brenda, 339
Lights, [Poxleitner-Bokan], 340
McKay, Nellie, 340, 341
McLachlan, Sarah, 339, 341
McManus, Mariah, 340, 341
Melua, Katie, 340, 341
Musgraves, Kacey, 340
Nesbitt, Nina, 340, 341, 358
Perri, Christina, 339, 340, 341
Peters, Maisie, 340
Ridings, Freya, 340, 341
Sade, 339
Salvant, Cécile McLorin, 340
Schwartz, Lucy, 340
Soraia, Charlene, 339, 340, 341
Spektor, Regina, 340, 341, 358
Stroup, Amy, 340, 341
Sweet, Kelly, 340
Swift, Taylor, 340
Timony, Mary, 339, 341
Torrini, Emiliana, 339
Tuck, Hailey, 340
Williams, Kathryn, 339
XCX, Charli, 340, 358
Youngs, Jenny Owen, 340, 341, 358

Singers6, Folk, Ensemble
Black Umfolosi, 345
Gundecha Brothers, 345
Tenores Supramonte Orgosolo, 345

Singers6, Folk, Men
Albion Band, 343
Ball, Estil C, 343
Carthy, Martin, 343
Flatt, Lester, 343
Friend, Simon, 343
LaBouchardiere, Jay, 343, 358
Meloy, Colin, 343
Osborne Brothers, 343
Skaggs, Ricky, 343
Whitley, Jon, 343, 358

Singers6, Folk, Women
Ball, Orna, 343
Chaney, Olivia, 343
Davis Sisters, 343
Dickens, Hazel, 343
Gladden, Texas, 343
Hull, Siera, 343, 358
Jarosz, Sarah, 343, 358
Portman, Emily, 343
Svonavec, Danielle, 343
Unthanks, Rachel & Betty, 343
Veirs, Laura, 343
Vincent, Rhonda, 343
Ward, Lucy, 343, 358

Soprano sfogato, 152, 162, 189

Strong Vocal Work Ethic
Blasis, Virginie, 147

tenore di forza, 105, 112, 186, 190, 198, 208, 227, 293, 295, 299, 301, 303, 305, 306, 307, 308, 315, 316

Timbre, High or Low Larynx
Historically Informed, for Early Music, 4, 5, 11, 16, 115, 117, 118, 121, 124, 333
In Long 19th C, 320, 321, 323, 326, 332
Modern Conventional Practice, 320, 332, 333

Treatise Authors, 18C Long
1650, Bernhard, Christoph, 68, 97
1677, Reggio, Pietro, 109
1695, Bontempi, Giovanni, 22
1695, North, Roger, 68, 84, 93
1717, Riva. Giuseppe, 71
1723, Burney, Charles, 12, 17, 25, 71, 77, 89, 90
1723, Gardiner, William, 20
1723, Tosi, Pierfrancesco, 3, 9, 10, 12, 17, 18, 21, 68, 69, 71, 81, 82, 90, 91, 92, 97, 101, 110, 115, 131, 294, 321, 347, 352, 353, 358
1740, Lampe, Johann Friedriche, 84
1746, Tans'ur, William, 89

1752, Galliard, John Ernest, 71
1752, Quantz, Johann, 9, 10, 71, 72, 82, 90, 115, 294
1752, Riva, Giuseppe, 71
1753, Arnold, John, 89
1756, Burke, Edmund, 105
1756, Mozart, Leopold, 79
1757, Agricola, Johann Friedrich, 9, 10, 81
1771, Bayly, Anselm, 7, 9, 10, 75, 82, 86, 91, 98, 101, 116
1774, Mancini, Giambattista, 9, 10, 12, 18, 21, 23, 24, 25, 32, 34, 70, 75, 82, 98, 102, 110, 116, 126, 294, 347, 353
1778, Agricola, Johann Friedrich, 71
1778, Billings, William, 90
1778, Nares, James, 71, 72, 116
1780, Hiller, Johann Adam, 9, 10, 71, 82
1782, Doolittle, Amos, 90
1782, Holcroft, Thomas, 116
1782, Jocelin, Simeon, 90
1784, Billington, Thomas, 19, 90
1785, Aprile, Giuseppe, 9, 10
1785, Tenducci, Giusto, 9, 10
1789, Brown, John, 10
1789, Burney, Charles, 72
1790, Borghese, Antonio, 19
1791, Jackson, William, 110
1793, Kimball, Jacob, 89
1795, Burney, Charles, 72
1797, Aprile, Giuseppe, 71, 72, 111
1797, Encyclopædia Britannica, 87
1799, Corfe, Joseph, 71, 72
1805, Dibdin, Charles, 41, 93, 116
1810, Corri, Domenico, 9, 10, 18, 19
1810, Smyth, Charles, 19, 71, 72, 73, 102, 116
1811, Stevenson, A, 89
1813, Lanza, Gesualdo, 76, 117
1815, Jousse, Jean, 9, 10, 18, 19, 71, 73, 84, 102, 117
1818, Anfossi, Maria, 71
1818, Bacon, Richard Mackenzie, 9, 10, 15, 17, 18, 19, 21, 71, 74, 90, 98, 105, 126, 357
1818, Ferrari, Giacomo, 110
1818, Nathan, Isaac, 18, 20, 71
1818, Porpora, Nicola, 19
1820, Rauzzini, Venanzio, 20
1828, Cooke, Thomas, 20, 71, 74
1834, Edgcumbe, Richard, 94
1836, Nathan, Isaac, 9, 74, 76, 84, 99, 101
1837, Anfossi, Maria, 74, 294
1840, Garcia, Manuel, 9, 71, 74, 124, 237, 250, 320, 321
1841, Crivelli, Domenico Francescc, 110

Treatise Authors, 19C
Anon, Musical Guide, 294
Busby, Thomas, 321
Cazalet, 298
Crevelli, 297
Cummings, William H, 245, 270, 275
D'Esté, John D, 233, 321
Dow, Sabrina, 322, 326
Encyclopædia Britannica, 205
Garcia, Albert, 320
Holland, Edwin, 322
Lamperti, Francesco, 202, 250
Mason, Manual, 296
Newton, William, 321
Root, George F, 321
Rowley, C E, 322
Sainton-Dolby, Charlotte, 321
Wieck, Friedrich, 109, 295, 324

Treatise Authors, 20C
Bretz, Mrs, 323
Henderson, William James, 247, 248, 276
le Vallon, Paul, 323
Root, Frederick W, 276, 295
Tree, Charles, 323
Whittaker, Dr, 323

Treatise Authors, Modern
Barbier, Patrick, 30
Brown, Clive, 93, 283
Burwick, Frederick, 355
Callaghan, Jean, 320
Clark, Lorna, 355

Cooke, Stewart, 355
Crutchfield, Will, 93, 277, 317
Donald Burrows & Rosemary Dunhill, 25, 26
Donington, Robert, 66, 67, 93
Elliott, Martha, 3
Fenner, Theodore, 3, 29, 53, 214
Gable, Frederick, 4, 93
Ganzl, Kurt, 3
Gislason, Donald Garth, 115
Haenen, Greta, 68, 92, 93, 347, 353
Heil, Leila, 338
Heriot, Angus, 26, 30
Howard, Patricia, 28
Jerold, Beverly, 67, 79, 349
Montgomery, David, 66, 67
Morrow, Michael, 1, 92, 352
Neumann, Frederick, 66, 67, 79, 81, 93
Newton, George, 67, 316, 317
Olleson, Philip, 28
Philip, Robert, 93, 277, 278
Pleasants, Henry, 22, 30, 149, 176
Potter, John, 5, 12, 93, 144, 346, 351, 354, 359
Potter, Sarah, 88, 215, 253, 350
Ribeiro, Alvaro, 355
Sabor, Peter, 355
Scholes, Percy Alfred, 283
Sorrell, Neil, 346, 359
Stark, James, 69, 79
Tarling, Judy, 352
Toft, Robert, 76, 92, 218, 338
Wistreich, Richard, 93, 353
Wood, Sir Henry, 283

Vibrato
Choral Avoidance of, 255, 325
Continuous, 5, 67, 92, 93, 220, 236, 262, 333
Definitions of, 218, 250, 251
Measurements of, 5, 6, 7, 278, 280, 281
Ornamental or Expressive, 7, 67, 68, 70, 74, 79, 81, 85, 92, 262, 283

Vibrato, Composers' Views on
Cowen, Frederic Hymen, 254
Puccini, Giacomo, 255

Roberts, Varley, 256, 270
Rossini, Gioachino, 254
Saint-Saens, Camille, 254
Stanford, Charles Villiers, 255
Terry, Richard, 256, 274
Verdi, Giuseppe, 256
Williams, Vaughan, 1, 255, 273

Vocal Intensity Pulsations, 79, 81

Vocal Science
Chladni, Ernst, 107, 357
Edison, Thomas, 278
HIP, Opportunities for, 357, 358
Seashore, Carl E, 278, 279, 280, 281

Vocal Sound, Historical Development, 333
Hegemonic Tendencies, 333
Long 18C Hegemony, 333
Modern Orthodoxy from 1920, 333, 334

Vocal Sound, Pop Singing, Some Objections, 339
Arty Farty [AF], 339
Bang Crash Wallop [BCW], 341
Studio Interference [SI], 339

Vocal Sound1, Types
Definitions, General, 218
Preferences Survey, 5, 7
Type A, 5, 6, 277, 281, 283
Type AA, 5, 282
Type B, 5, 6, 277, 281, 282
Type BC, 6, 262
Type C, 5, 7

Vocal Sound2, Desired Outcomes, 18C Long, 10
Bocca Ridente, 18, 19, 20, 74, 117, 164, 176
Brilliant, 16, 33, 40, 43, 50, 54, 60, 103, 152, 161, 170, 201
Clear articulation, 11, 40, 45, 48, 49, 117, 126, 127, 128, 129, 130, 131, 140, 146, 147, 148, 155, 164, 183, 205, 229, 333
Clear High Larynx, 16, 17, 21, 116, 117, 118, 122, 177, 321
Even emission, 11, 19, 23, 24, 25, 27, 30, 32, 42, 44, 48, 50, 55, 58, 62, 72, 73, 74, 94, 98, 105, 118, 126, 127, 141, 151, 153, 155, 156, 157, 160, 161, 164, 165, 168, 169,

171, 181, 186, 191, 196, 199, 200, 204, 206, 210, 219, 260, 261, 262, 264, 294, 312

Extended Register, 10, 11, 21, 25, 27, 28, 37, 38, 44, 52, 53, 54, 56, 71, 101, 102, 103, 104, 105, 110, 137, 172, 174, 175, 176, 177, 184, 294, 295, 333

Flexibility, 11

Heart Appeal, 11, 146

High notes soft, 11, 33, 37, 42, 71, 72, 90, 109, 110, 178

Larynx High or Neutral, 116

Messa di Voce, 11, 22, 23, 28, 33, 49, 68, 72, 73, 74, 80, 84, 86, 87, 97, 98, 99, 100, 140, 158, 176, 193, 204, 294, 324, 333, 337, 340, 358

Natural, 16, 111, 121, 319, 323

Portamento di Voce, 10, 11, 12, 16, 17, 21, 24, 25, 30, 32, 34, 39, 49, 71, 72, 115, 153, 159, 333

Pure, 15, 16, 17, 22, 24, 27, 30, 34, 40, 42, 45, 47, 49, 55, 58, 60, 61, 68, 71, 73, 74, 80, 87, 90, 91, 92, 117, 122, 124, 125, 130, 137, 140, 141, 142, 145, 146, 148, 149, 150, 152, 153, 155, 156, 157, 160, 161, 162, 163, 164, 165, 168, 169, 170, 171, 177, 178, 179, 186, 192, 193, 196, 197, 199, 201, 203, 224, 245, 246, 312

Registers well joined, 10, 172, 174, 175, 177, 183, 184

Silvery, 16, 21, 28, 30, 32, 34, 43, 49, 61, 99, 117, 128, 140, 142, 144, 145, 147, 149, 155, 158, 159, 165, 168, 169, 171, 174, 187, 190, 195, 202, 260, 261, 310, 323

Straight Toning, 34, 37, 42, 50, 51, 55, 61, 68, 69, 71, 72, 73, 74

Sweetest, 15, 17, 20, 23, 26, 28, 32, 35, 38, 41, 43, 44, 47, 50, 54, 63, 122, 130, 142, 145, 148, 149, 150, 151, 162, 164, 165, 169, 171, 173, 174, 178, 183, 184, 185, 187, 188, 195, 196, 206, 259, 264, 337

Timbre Rich, 16, 25, 28, 41, 42, 45, 48, 50, 54, 55, 57, 58, 59, 60, 61, 63, 64, 65, 87, 103, 106, 122, 123, 124, 125, 134, 140, 141, 143, 145, 147, 149, 151, 153, 156, 160, 161, 164, 167, 174, 177, 178, 180, 190, 194, 195, 197, 200, 205, 209, 215, 219

Timbre Thin, 16, 40, 41, 49, 104, 108, 117, 124, 125, 126, 144, 156, 174, 200, 215, 216, 223, 226, 227, 235, 241, 339, 357

Tremolo, Expressive, 47, 70, 74, 81, 82, 83, 84, 85, 86, 148, 229

Trill or Shake, 11, 22, 23, 25, 28, 32, 33, 35, 36, 41, 42, 45, 49, 50, 54, 61, 71, 72, 74, 80, 86, 94, 95, 140, 146, 154, 157, 158, 161, 162, 163, 172, 176, 181, 199, 203

Vocal Volume, 21, 23, 26, 29, 30, 34, 37, 38, 42, 43, 46, 49, 105, 106, 107, 108, 140, 144

Vocal Sound2, Desired Outcomes, Modern
Loud Singing, 317
Low Larynx Emission, 320, 323
Singer's Formant, 320
Vibrato, Continuous, 66, 67, 320

Vocal Sound2, Unwanted Outcomes, 18C Long
Forcing, 10, 21, 25, 74, 78, 107, 110, 112, 113, 114, 115, 171, 174, 188
Poor Enunciation, 49, 131, 132
Registers badly joined, 54, 56, 179
Shrieking on High Notes, 10, 109, 111, 112, 113, 114, 115, 334, 347, 353
Space too large, 108, 109, 145, 146, 147, 150
Throaty Low Larynx Emission, 10, 11, 16, 30, 115, 117, 118, 119, 120, 121, 174, 336
Tremolo, 10, 11, 50, 68, 69, 71, 72, 73, 74, 75, 77, 78, 85, 86, 141, 167, 169, 176, 181, 185, 188, 191, 198, 200, 201, 202, 204, 333

Vocal Tone
Fundamental to 'affect', 3, 11
Importance of, 3, 10, 17

Vocalist Reviewers, Books
A.B.C. Dario Musico, 13, 118
Adolphus, John, 52
Bernard, John, 45, 56
Brough, Robert Barnabas, 165

Burgh, Allatson, 41, 128
Burney, Charles, 10, 12, 13, 15, 17, 21, 26, 27, 28, 29, 30, 33, 34, 35, 36, 38, 39, 40, 41, 42, 51, 52, 53, 68, 75, 77, 78, 86, 91, 92, 95, 103, 104, 113, 114, 118, 125, 127, 294, 296, 334, 355, 357
Burney, Fanny, 13, 28, 38, 95
Burney, Susan, 13, 28
Castil-Blaze, François-Henri-Joseph, 115, 334
Chorley, 125, 135, 136, 154, 156, 162, 166, 178, 180, 194, 219, 227, 230, 262, 263, 296, 297, 301, 309, 314, 326, 327
Cibber, Colley, 12, 23, 32
Coryat, Thomas, 337
Cowen, 255
Cox, John, 14, 31, 58, 97, 130, 135, 140, 177, 180, 181, 186, 195, 227, 298, 307, 328
Crosse, John, 14, 49, 60, 61, 146
Cumberland's British Theatre, 142
d'Ancillon, Charles, 12, 21
Dibdin, Charles, 41
Dictionary of Musicians, 58, 130, 179
Ebers, John, 147
Edgcumbe, Richard, 11, 13, 14, 29, 30, 40, 41, 42, 43, 47, 48, 53, 59, 71, 76, 89, 94, 108, 114, 115, 118, 120, 126, 128, 144, 153, 176, 179, 186, 213, 235, 313, 334
Edinburgh Annual Register, 128, 131
Edwards, Henry Sutherland, 175
Evelyn, John, 12, 23
Finck, 308
Gardiner, William, 13, 14, 45, 46, 50, 55, 58, 61, 63, 71, 83, 95, 106, 118, 119, 131, 142, 144, 296
Genest, John, 52, 128
Gilliland, Thomas, 128
Handel, George Frideric, 34
Haslewood, Joseph, 13, 43, 44, 57, 118
Hawkins, John, 12, 127
Hawkins, William, 38
Haydn, Joseph, 128
Hazlitt, William, 125, 140
Hervey, 186

Hiller, Johann Adam, 24, 27, 81, 91, 99
Hogarth, George, 113, 334
Holmes, 313
Holmes, Edward, 131
Hooper, Lucy H, 207
Hunt, Leigh, 95, 136, 183
Johnstone, J Alfred, 275
Kelly, Michael, 13, 44, 82, 114, 334
Klein, 170, 194, 198
Klein, Hermann, 135
Krehbiel, 252, 303
Lamperti, 250
Lumley, 195, 306
Lysons, Daniel, 68
Makinlay, 237
Marsh, John, 43, 47, 109, 172
Mendelssohn, Felix, 143
Metastasio, Pietro, 25, 36, 108
Moore, Thomas, 114
Mozart family, 13, 27, 37, 38, 39, 42, 53, 68, 79, 80, 81, 92, 103, 114, 204, 264, 334, 337
Nathan, Isaac, 99
Novello, Clara, 14, 135, 158, 159, 258
Novello, Vincent, 121
Oxberry, William, 14, 54, 120
Parke, William Thomas, 13, 14, 29, 41, 63, 94, 104, 215
Parker, John R, 44
Pearce, Charles E, 95, 258
Penny Cyclopædia, 151, 155, 159, 183
Pepys, Samuel, 12, 23, 86
Phillips, Henry, 60, 97, 150, 159
Pierpont, Mrs, 38
Quantz, Yohann, 12, 23, 24, 25, 32, 33, 34, 91, 104, 113, 117, 127, 334, 347
Raguenet, François, 126
Rossini, Gioachino [ed Michotte], 31, 105, 191, 246, 254, 284, 294, 334, 346, 347, 352, 353
Santley, Sir Charles, 194
Shaw, 135, 192, 198, 202, 274, 308
Simond, Louis, 87

Smyth, Charles John, 14, 127
Spohr, 84, 108
Stendhal, 48, 50, 58, 143
Tosi, Pierfrancesco, 12, 23, 32, 69
Von Raumer, Frederick, 108, 150, 187
Waldron, F G, 43, 57

Vocalist Reviewers, Magazines
Academy, 224
American Journal of Science and Arts, 295
Athenaeum, 14, 76, 85, 94, 134, 135, 136, 137, 147, 151, 159, 169, 170, 184, 185, 188, 189, 200, 222, 227, 256, 263, 265, 299, 309, 313, 327
Atlantic Monthly, 149
Bacon, Richard Mackenzie, 9, 55, 83, 94, 108, 117, 118, 140, 148, 151, 334, 339
Bentley's Miscellany, 328
Blackwood's Edinburgh Magazine, 214
Connoisseur, 165
Court and Lady's Magazine, 188
Drama, 173
Dramatic Magazine, 313, 326
Dwight's, 107, 135, 137, 149, 160, 163, 168, 170, 180, 199, 200, 216, 220, 221, 222, 225, 230, 231, 241, 245, 260, 300, 305, 306, 307, 309, 314, 321, 324, 328
Early Music Performer, 336
Early Music Review, 334, 356
European Magazine, 13, 14, 50, 56, 62, 127, 128, 132, 175
Euterpeiad, 182, 214
Everybody's Magazine, 274
Examiner, 14, 20, 45, 46, 48, 51, 56, 59, 60, 61, 64, 77, 86, 87, 95, 97, 106, 111, 112, 119, 120, 128, 129, 130, 131, 135, 136, 140, 141, 143, 145, 148, 151, 153, 154, 161, 164, 167, 169, 171, 173, 174, 175, 176, 178, 182, 183, 186, 200, 213, 215, 216, 223, 225, 226, 227, 241, 242, 262, 294, 297, 300, 307, 325, 327, 328
Gentleman's Magazine, 55
Gramophone, 356
Harmonicon, 14, 20, 53, 109, 118, 125, 127, 128, 129, 130, 132, 140, 144, 147, 149, 150, 173, 177, 180, 182, 219, 306
Harper's, 165
Illustrated Review, 224
Knickerbocker, 168
Knight's Quarterly Magazine, 215
Knights Quarterly Magazine, 89
La Belle Assemblee, 14, 120, 187, 217, 296
Lady's Magazine, 97
Lancet, 214
Leader, 220
Literary Gazette, 14, 99, 129, 130, 132, 140, 159, 178, 191, 221, 327
London Magazine, 14, 54, 130, 214, 216
London Saturday Journal, 89
Macmillan's Magazine, 170
Magazine of Music, 194
Mirror Monthly Magazine, 164
Monthly Mirror, 13, 14, 46, 119, 128, 175
Monthly Review, 217
Murray's Magazine, 252
Musical Gazette, 220, 222, 261
Musical Herald, 198, 239
Musical Library Monthly Supplement, 327
Musical Review, 219, 300, 314
Musical Standard, 171, 247, 298
Musical Times, 134, 254, 274
Musical World, 45, 54, 57, 88, 135, 137, 150, 154, 155, 158, 159, 162, 165, 166, 171, 172, 181, 185, 188, 189, 190, 191, 193, 198, 223, 229, 230, 235, 238, 246, 263, 300, 303, 304, 307, 326, 327, 328
National Magazine, 200
New Monthly Magazine, 14, 49, 54, 56, 58, 59, 62, 77, 117, 129, 141, 145, 147, 172, 174, 177, 215, 216
Non Conformist Musical Journal, 251
Prompter, 131
Punch, Melbourne, 207
QMMR, 14, 16, 17, 49, 50, 51, 54, 57, 59, 60, 61, 62, 95, 97, 103, 105, 106, 107, 111, 115, 119, 120, 121, 122, 124, 126, 129, 130, 140, 141, 142, 143, 144, 146, 173,

174, 175, 176, 179, 182, 216, 309
Reader, 223
Scots Magazine, 120
Spectator, 195, 324, 356
Sphinx, 261
Table Talk, Examiner, Launceston, 240
Table Talk, Melbourne, 240, 255
Tatler, 62, 77, 95, 176, 183, 306, 326
Theatre, 202, 262
Theatrical Inquisitor, 14, 44, 45, 48, 51, 57, 97, 105, 112, 119, 129, 173, 175, 213
Tomahawk, 131
Tomahawk, Musical World, 13
Waldie, John, 14, 44, 46, 48, 50, 53, 55, 107, 114, 119, 120, 126, 129, 135, 174, 175, 176, 181, 184, 215, 355

Vocalist Reviewers, Newspapers

Age, Melbourne, 280
Albion and The Star, 186
American and Commercial Daily Advertiser, Baltimore, 175
Anglo American Times, 226
Ann Arbor News, 204
Argus, Melbourne, 205
Aris's Birmingham Gazette, 168, 195
Atlantic Monthly, 259
Atlas, 138, 154, 182, 188, 190, 230, 295, 296, 298, 300, 309, 327
Auckland Star, 210, 233, 239, 248
Australasian, 239
Australian Star, 271
Ballymena Observer, 323
Baltimore Bulletin, 256
Bath Chronicle and Weekly Gazette, 326
Bath Gazette, 178
Belfast Telegraph, 209
Bell's Life in London and Sporting Chronicle, 228
Bell's Life in Sydney, 107, 158, 223
Bell's New Weekly Messenger, 164
Bell's Weekly Messenger, 314
Bendigo Advertiser, 270, 271
Berrow's Worcester Journal, 167, 325
Birmingham Daily Post, 171, 197, 203, 207, 209, 266, 307
Boston Daily Advertiser, 330, 331
Boston Daily Globe, 192, 233, 238, 250, 252
Boston Evening Transcript, 230
Boston Herald, 331
Boston Journal, 237
Boston Musical Gazette, 145
Bradford Observer, 263, 301
Brighton Gazette, 169, 183, 184, 200, 221, 223, 230, 231, 232, 302, 304
Brighton Gleaner, 145
Brighton Guardian, 223
Brisbane Courier, 254, 271
Bristol Times and Mirror, 206, 325
British Mercury, 127
Brooklyn Daily Eagle, 137, 138, 223, 232, 236, 262, 281, 282
Brooklyn Newsstand, 304, 305, 323
Brother Jonathan, 148
Buffalo Courier, 303
Bury & Norwich Post, 87, 170
Bury and Norwich Post, 120
Caledonian Mercury, 14, 88, 129, 146, 178, 184, 187, 218, 231
Cambridge Chronicle and Journal, 167
Camperdown Chronicle, Victoria, 210
Carlisle Journal, 190
Cedar Rapids Evening Gazette, 253
Century, 240
Cheltenham Chronicle, 229
Cheltenham Looker-On, 225
Chicago Tribune, 196, 201, 203, 242, 261, 304, 305, 308, 331
Cincinnati Commercial Tribune, 325
Cincinnati Daily Enquirer, 233
Cincinnati Daily Gazette, 88, 224, 329
Coberg Leader, 272
Cork Examiner, 192, 193, 295
Courier, 181
Court Gazette, 188
Court Journal, 187
Cumberland Pacquet, 146

Daily Atlas, Boston, 179, 184, 192, 193
Daily Huronite, 251
Daily Inter Ocean, 314
Daily Mail, 253
Daily News, London, 138, 163, 202, 221, 238, 252, 275, 301, 304, 308
Daily Telegraph, 138, 225, 232, 233, 239, 261, 356
Daily Telegraph, Launceston, 272
Dallas Morning News, 326
Derby Daily telegraph, 197, 275
Derby Mercury, 14, 55, 111, 229
Deseret Evening News, 239
Dominion, 253
Dublin Daily Express, 201, 231, 232, 238, 324, 325
Dublin Evening Mail, 148
Dundee Courier, 195, 332
Dundee Evening Telegraph, 239, 256, 257
Edinburgh Evening Courant, 121, 132, 223
Era, 137, 138, 145, 156, 165, 166, 167, 168, 169, 189, 192, 196, 206, 228, 254, 261, 300, 303, 325, 330, 331
Evening Journal, Adelaide, 204
Evening Mail, London, 61, 62, 120
Evening News, Lincoln, 239
Evening Post New York, 179, 196, 239, 264, 305
Evening Post, Auckland, 208, 275
Evening Star, 222, 233
Examiner, Launceston, 204
Exeter and Plymouth Gazette, 64, 273
Falkirk Herald, 255
Fife Herald, 168
Figaro in London, 180
Folkestone, Hythe, Sandgate & Cheriton Herald, 332
Freeman's Journal, 65, 66, 83, 138, 143, 156, 157, 158, 166, 237, 301, 303
Glasgow Herald, 167, 197, 207, 209, 224, 325
Globe, 138, 149, 207, 208, 267, 304, 305, 314, 330
Gloucester Journal, 161

Graphic, 138, 228, 237, 249, 307, 332
Hampshire Advertiser, 229
Herald, Melbourne, 204
Hereford Times, 165
Herts Guardian, Agricultural Journal, and General Advertiser, 66
Huddersfield Daily Examiner, 273
Hull Advertiser, 328
Hull Packet, 14, 63, 107, 145, 146, 150, 159, 183, 258, 329
Illustrated London News, 138, 153
Illustrated Sport, 205
Illustrated Sporting and Dramatic News, 138, 197, 208, 234, 268, 269, 322, 326, 329
Illustrated Times, 228
Independent Democrat, 224
Ipswich Journal, 43
Irish Times, 202, 264, 271
Kadina and Wallaroo Times, 240
Kalgoorlie Miner, 272, 273
Lake County Press, 278
Lancashire Evening Post, 270
Lancaster Gazette, 64
Leamington Spa Courier, 240, 273
Leeds Intelligencer, 309
Leeds Mercury, 58, 134, 171, 209, 259, 267
Leeds Times, 165, 221
Leicester Journal, 168
Lewiston Evening Journal, 248
Liddle, Rod, 339
Lima Daily Democratic Times, 251
Limerick Reporter, 168
Liverpool Daily Post, 222, 307
Liverpool Mercury, 270, 329
Lloyd's Weekly, 164, 224, 327
London and Provincial Entr'acte, 330
London Courier, 62, 186, 187
London Review, 200, 226
Los Angeles Herald, 239
Mackay Mercury, 228
Manawatu Standard, 273
Manchester Courier and Lancashire General Advertiser, 156, 206, 223, 225, 229, 272,

300, 301, 309, 323
Manchester Evening News, 234
Manchester Guardian, 134, 192, 193, 201, 221, 224, 226, 232, 259, 266, 270, 298
Manchester Times, 106, 134, 145, 157, 168, 322, 328
Miami Herald, 279
Morning advertiser, 228
Morning Advertiser, 215
Morning Advertiser, London, 14, 138, 148, 155, 196, 306
Morning Chronicle, London, 14, 46, 56, 61, 85, 94, 95, 118, 125, 128, 130, 131, 138, 147, 150, 154, 161, 165, 177, 184, 187, 195, 219
Morning Post, 14, 44, 60, 61, 62, 87, 112, 125, 134, 138, 144, 146, 150, 152, 153, 155, 160, 161, 162, 165, 172, 174, 177, 179, 185, 187, 188, 189, 190, 193, 199, 214, 217, 219, 222, 223, 226, 228, 232, 233, 234, 246, 250, 261, 263, 297, 300, 313, 322, 324, 329
Mount Barker Courier, 271
Muscatine Journal, 276
Musical Courier, 198
New Times, London, 179, 229
New World, 148
New York Daily Tribune, 163, 297, 330
New York Herald, 305, 330
New York Herald Tribune, 138, 153, 226, 232, 264
New York Mirror, 164, 324
New York Times, 138, 167, 220, 249, 251, 262, 276, 315, 331
New Zealand Herald, 203
New-York Review, 58
Norfolk Chronicle, 163
North Otago Times, 205
North Wales Chronicle, 208, 330
Northampton Mercury, 50
Northern Argus, 203
Northern Whig, 158, 165, 230
Nottingham Evening Post, 206

Nottingham Journal, 256
Nottinghamshire Guardian, 197
Observer, 201, 228, 234, 238, 260, 267
Oriental Herald, 308
Otago Daily Times, 264
Otago Witness, 270
Oxford Chronicle, 170
Pall Mall Gazette, 138, 201, 208, 234, 239, 251, 298, 304, 310, 311, 312, 332
Pateley Bridge & Nidderdale Herald, 205
Philadelphia Chronicle, 179
Pilot, Dublin, 65
Pittsburgh Dispatch, 197, 314
Plain Dealer, 278
Poverty Bay Herald, 278
Press, NZ, 272, 304
Preston Herald, 228
Reynold's Newspaper, 203
Royal Cornwall Gazette, 50, 237
Royal Devonport Telegraph, and Plymouth Chronicle, 163
Sacramento Daily Record, 201
San Francisco Call, 252
San Francisco Chronicle, 278
Saturday Review, 138, 169, 191, 195, 196, 228, 231, 260
Saunders's News-Letter, 195, 260
Scotsman, 130, 226, 231, 310, 330
Sheffield & Rotherham Independent, 238, 252, 331
South Australian Register, 206, 246
Southern Reporter and Cork Commercial Courier, 38
Southland Times, 208
Spirit of the Times, New York, 327
Sporting Times, 228
Springfield Republican, 206, 275, 276, 279, 331
St. James's Gazette, 330
Staffordshire Advertiser, 230
Standard of London, 134, 138, 155, 161, 168, 169, 195, 198, 219, 224, 226, 266, 301, 329, 331

Star, 305
Sun, New York, 276
Sunday Times, London, 14, 31, 134, 138, 168, 194, 198, 199, 225, 256, 261, 262, 301, 308, 314, 339, 356
Sunday Times, Sydney, 204
Sunderland Daily Echo and Shipping Gazette, 325
Sydney Mail, 205, 206, 224
Sydney Monitor, 65, 87
Sydney Morning Herald, 202, 240, 282, 283
Tasmanian, 206
Taunton Courier, 323
Telegraph, Brisbane, 282, 283
Times, London, 14, 44, 45, 57, 106, 127, 130, 137, 138, 139, 152, 191, 207, 213, 217, 220, 238, 251, 252, 260, 262, 267, 280, 282, 285, 300, 330
Times-Picayune, 221
Toronto Globe, 276
Trenton Evening Times, 331
Weekly Herald, 149
Weekly Standard and Express, 235
West Australian, Perth, 239
Western Daily Press, 271
Western Mail, Perth, 275
Western Morning News, 249
Worcester Palladium, 197
Yorkshire Evening Post, 274
Yorkshire Gazette, 47, 85, 148, 310
Yorkshire Post, 197, 202, 255, 330, 331
Voce Vibrata, 188, 189, 218

www.ingramcontent.com/pod-product-compliance
Lightning Source LLC
Chambersburg PA
CBHW061752290426
44108CB00029B/2969